Grounds Maintenance Handbook

OTHER McGRAW-HILL HANDBOOKS OF INTEREST

Azad · Industrial Wastewater Management Handbook
Baumeister and Marks · Standard Handbook for Mechanical Engineers
Brater and King · Handbook of Hydraulics
Callender · Time-Saver Standards for Architectural Design Data
Chow · Handbook of Applied Hydrology
Crocker and King · Piping Handbook
Croft, Carr, and Watt · American Electricians' Handbook
Davis and Sorensen · Handbook of Applied Hydraulics
DeChiara and Callender · Time-Saver Standards for Building Types
Fink and Carroll · Standard Handbook for Electrical Engineers
Harris and Crede · Shock and Vibration Handbook
Hicks · Standard Handbook of Engineering Calculations
Karassik, Krutzsch, Fraser, and Messina · Pump Handbook
LaLonde and Janes · Concrete Engineering Handbook
Maynard · Handbook of Business Administration
Merritt · Building Construction Handbook
Merritt · Standard Handbook for Civil Engineers
O'Brien · Scheduling Handbook
Perry · Engineering Manual
Rothbart · Mechanical Design and Systems Handbook
Smeaton · Switchgear and Control Handbook
Stubbs · Handbook of Heavy Construction
Tuma · Engineering Mathematics Handbook
Tuma · Handbook of Physical Calculations
Tuma · Technology Mathematics Handbook
Urquhart · Civil Engineering Handbook
Watt and Summers · NFPA Handbook of the National Electrical Code
Woods · Highway Engineering Handbook

HERBERT S. CONOVER

GROUNDS MAINTENANCE HANDBOOK

THIRD EDITION

McGRAW-HILL BOOK COMPANY

New York St. Louis San Francisco Auckland Bogotá Düsseldorf
Johannesburg London Madrid Mexico Montreal
New Delhi Panama Paris São Paulo Singapore
Sydney Tokyo Toronto

Library of Congress Cataloging in Publication Data

Conover, Herbert S.
Grounds maintenance handbook.

Includes index.
1. Grounds maintenance. I. Title
SB476.C6 1977 635.9 76–18901
ISBN 0–07–012412–4

First published in 1953 by Tennessee Valley Authority.

1 2 3 4 5 6 7 8 9 0 KPKP 7 8 6 5 4 3 2 1 0 9 8 7

The editors for this book were Harold B. Crawford and Virginia Fechtmann, the designer was Elliot Epstein, and the production supervisor was Frank P. Bellantoni. It was set in Bodoni Book by The Kingsport Press.

It was printed and bound by The Kingsport Press.

CONTENTS

PREFACE

The maintenance of public, industrial, and institutional grounds has steadily increased in importance since the publication of the second edition of the "Grounds Maintenance Handbook." Today public interest and awareness is aroused by the interrelation of the natural environment and the wise use or abuse of our natural resources. This interest has restimulated environmental planning of facilities by both government and industry, as well as the proper maintenance of all facilities.

Careless, inadequate maintenance invites misuse and destruction of property in public grounds and a loss of morale and efficiency of employees in industrial plants. Careless use of chemicals for insect and disease control perpetuates the degradation of the environment. Good maintenance means timely repairs and cleanup, wise use of chemicals, constant inspection, and a never-ending endeavor to maintain clean, neat, and orderly grounds in order to minimize misuse, vandalism, and environmental abuse.

The Tennessee Valley Authority long ago recognized this need for clean and orderly grounds maintenance as a necessary adjunct to inviting the public to their reservations. In experiencing maintenance problems on its reservations, TVA discovered the need for some standardization of accepted maintenance practices. As a result, looseleaf memoranda and pamphlets, each treating some phase of grounds maintenance, were issued from time to time to the field men responsible for such maintenance. As the information grew in volume, it became apparent that a handbook based solely on grounds maintenance would be a useful document. In such a manner the "Grounds Maintenance Handbook" originated. TVA first produced a few copies for its own use within the organization. Other agencies responsible for grounds maintenance became aware of the book, and after a large number of requests for copies were received, TVA decided to publish the handbook on a limited-distribution basis.

The first edition published by TVA was based solely on the particular grounds maintenance problems of TVA reservations. The second edition was broadened, improved, and brought up to date. This third edition has again been expanded to recognize the many innovations which have been made in materials, methods, and equipment and in particular the environmental causes and effects over the last 16 years.

As stated in the second edition, it is still obvious that the subject of grounds maintenance is so large that it cannot be treated completely in one volume. I have tried to treat some of the most important phases of grounds maintenance and to provide a guide to the know-how needed to perform such tasks. The book is written primarily for use by those responsible for the maintenance of large acreages such as public parks on the national, state, county, and metropolitan scale, large industrial and institutional grounds, semipublic lands such as Boy Scout and YMCA camps, large estates, country clubs, and similar areas.

Material for the book has come from my own experience in TVA, from many well-known technical works of other authors on individual topics, from manufacturing firms and research personnel, and from engineers and architects. In addition, the experience gained as Chief of the Site Planning Staff of Chas. T. Main, Inc. since 1963 has contributed greatly to the revised book. To all of these I am sincerely grateful for their cooperation and interest in the development of the handbook. The Tennessee Valley Authority has also graciously permitted me to use the material from the original and second editions as I see fit, for which I express my thanks. Thanks are also due to the individuals and organizations who have permitted me to use quotations or reproductions of previously published material. I would also like to express my appreciation to Daniel S. Conover, who worked so diligently to prepare the many drawings and sketches found in the handbook.

I hope that this revised volume will contribute in some manner to the better maintenance of grounds, improved budget requirements, the betterment of the environment, and the greater enjoyment of public lands by the public.

H. S. Conover

PLANNING, SCHEDULING, AND PUBLIC RELATIONS

More leisure time, expanding population, increased ownership and use of automobiles, improved highways—all work to get more and more people out of doors. Leisure has been variously defined as the "first principle of all action" (Aristotle), "the main content of a free life," and "the opportunity for disinterested activity." The public heads for state and national parks, seashore and mountain resorts, hunting and fishing preserves, ski slopes, and historical sites, subjecting such recreational areas to the hardest use they have ever suffered, yet expecting to find everything clean, convenient, and attractive when they arrive. The public can afford to be fussy: if all is not well, they can drive on to a spot where the grass is greener. Leisure activity may not be socially useful and paid for, but like virtue, and unlike labor, it is its own chief reward. The quality of its leisure activity sets the tone of any society.

Not only the pleasure-bent public but also economy-minded industry is moving out into the countryside. Highways are lined with the lawns of handsome new buildings which might be mistaken for schools were it not for the neat signboards identifying them as factories, offices, or laboratories. Owners and employees both take pride in carefully landscaped grounds, which advertise the firm to passing motorists. For such companies good maintenance has become a necessity. The schools and hospitals they resemble are becoming even more conscious of the need for good maintenance, since they often make practical use of their attractive grounds.

Unfortunately, the cost of maintenance has increased along with its importance, and those responsible must exercise their ingenuity to stretch available dollars as far as possible. This means utilizing mechanized equipment, chemicals, and all sorts of laborsaving devices. For those responsible for public rather than company grounds it also means formulating policies and standards that will demonstrate to the holder of the purse strings the need for adequate budgets.

For grounds which merely form a setting for a building or a group of

Fig. 1.1 A man-made beach on a power reservoir: Robert Moses State Park, Massena, N.Y. (*Power Authority of the State of New York.*)

buildings, the maintenance problems may be fairly simple, although probably not so simple as a layman or a member of the board of directors might picture them. For grounds intended for recreational use, however, the problem becomes more complex. Besides lawns, flowers, and ornamental shrubbery there are wide scenic drives, overlooks, meadows, and forests, and such facilities as visitor reception buildings, picnic

Fig. 1.2 The use of flowering shrubs enhances any vista: overlook area, Robert Moses Power Plant. (*Power Authority of the State of New York.*)

areas, playgrounds, boat harbors, swimming pools, beaches, access roads, and parking areas, with attendant traffic problems. Many large tracts require special planning for drainage and waste disposal because of watershed complications. Most reception buildings contain public rest rooms and information displays; some have restaurants or refreshment stands as well (Figs. 1.1 and 1.2).

Machine technology, which has made free time possible in large quantities, also has done much to confound its use. With work robbed of its deeper satisfactions, there arose a great need and desire for participative use of leisure time. Recreation is a broad term, but it is often defined as the activity in which one participates of his own free choice and on his own time. In Tom Sawyer's terms, work is what you are obliged to do; play is what you are not obliged to do.

RECREATION DEMAND

Studies and research indicate that the demand for recreation is related to the amount of free time available and the affluence of the society. In the United States, leisure business has become big business. Shorter hours, earlier retirements, longer vacations, and longer weekends have all wrought dramatic changes in our way of life. At the end of the 1950s about 10 per cent of all incomes, 50 billion dollars, was available for luxury spending. By the middle 1960s, that amount had more than doubled. By 1980 a further increase may be expected, its size depending upon the state of the economy and population growth. The increased number of households, new technology, high levels of education, new spending patterns—all are elements of the driving force which seems certain to bring tremendous expansion of American prosperity.

HOW TO PLAN

A compilation of adequate information on the land area under consideration is required before proper planning for development can be undertaken. Many factors must be considered, some of the most important of which are discussed briefly in the following paragraphs.

Ecology involves the patterns of relationships between organisms and their environment. The word itself is derived from the Greek oikos, which means house; in modern scientific terms this means nature's house, or environment.

Hydrology is the study of water, its location, quantity, and quality. Groundwater and surface waters are both important in any area studied. As rain falls, a portion percolates through the ground and becomes groundwater. A large percentage of the surface water evaporates, some transpires from plants to the atmosphere, and the balance runs off into streams and lakes and then to sea.

The study of *topography* involves the compilation of data, contour maps, property lines, and legal descriptions that will be used for development purposes.

Complete information should be available on the *geology* and *soils* of the area (Fig. 1.3), particularly for sections that will be under intensive development. This information will make it possible to avoid such mistakes as placing roads and structures on unstable soils or making heavy or excessive cuts; it also indicates the location of rock which might cause excessive construction expense and high maintenance costs.

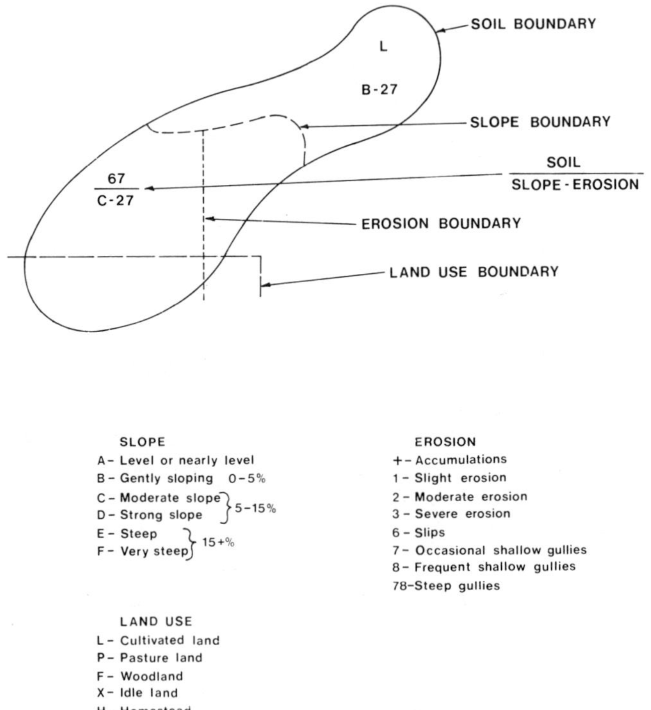

SLOPE
A- Level or nearly level
B- Gently sloping 0-5%
C- Moderate slope } 5-15%
D- Strong slope
E- Steep } 15+%
F- Very steep

EROSION
+- Accumulations
1- Slight erosion
2- Moderate erosion
3- Severe erosion
6- Slips
7- Occasional shallow gullies
8- Frequent shallow gullies
78-Steep gullies

LAND USE
L- Cultivated land
P- Pasture land
F- Woodland
X- Idle land
H- Homestead

Fig. 1.3 Typical map legend for soils and their characteristics. (*USDA Soil Conservation Service.*)

A thorough analysis should be made of the existing *transportation* patterns, including auto, bus, and airplane access (Fig. 1.4). Projected transportation expansion should be investigated with various public agencies and given careful consideration. The travel corridors (whether federal, state, county, or park roads) should be studied to determine their capacity (Fig. 1.5).

A study of *population centers* to be served by the proposed development is most important and should show projections of potential population growth (Fig. 1.6). The information can supply age group-

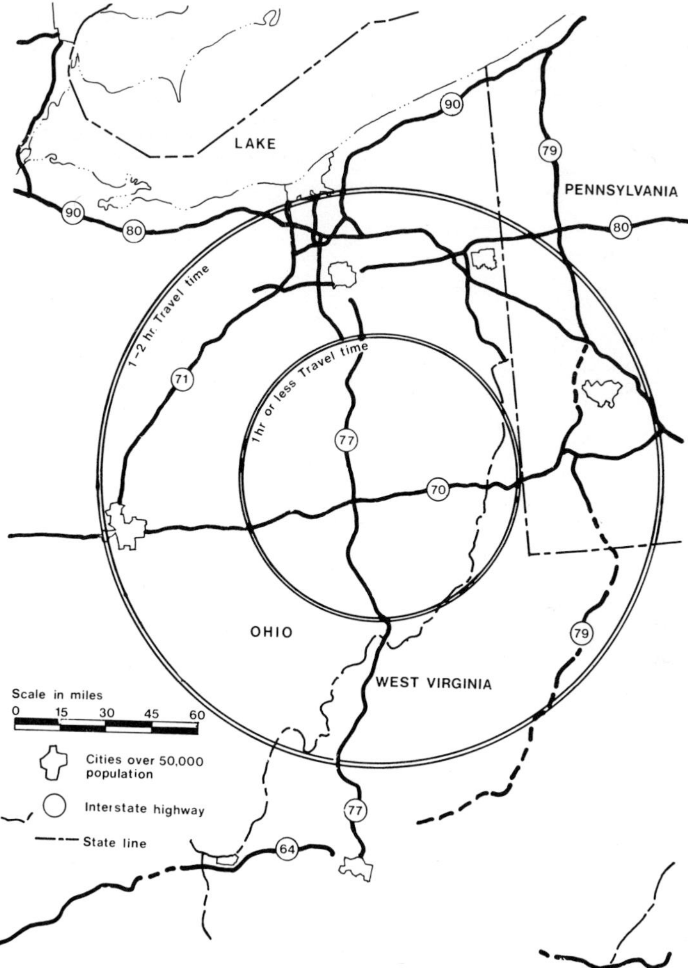

Fig. 1.4 Travel time to land development. (*Chas. T. Main, Inc.*)

ings as well as *socioeconomic data*. This statistical information is available through many sources and must be developed for each project.

The study of *climate* (Fig. 1.7) is an important part of planning, since it will be influential in determining the type of facilities to be built. Climate will determine whether the facilities can be used on a seasonal or year-round basis. Factors like temperature, precipitation, wind currents, etc., must be carefully compiled and analyzed.

The occurrence, type, and size of *vegetative cover* are pertinent to the type and quality of the area. Of course, it varies in different parts of the country; e.g., the desert areas of the southwest will differ considerably from the forest areas of the southeast. The vegetative cover can channel

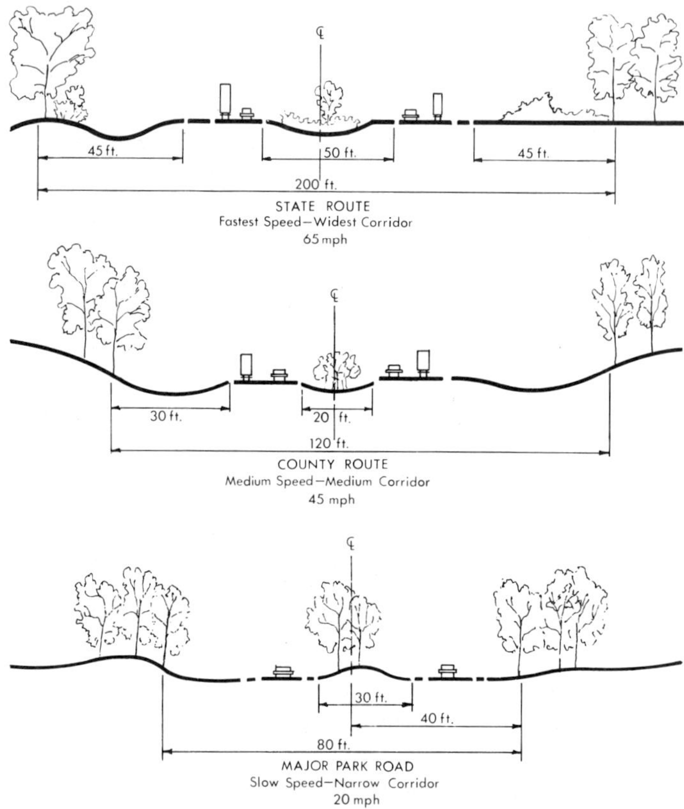

Fig. 1.5 Specifications for travel corridors to development. (*Chas. T. Main, Inc.*)

cool breezes, reduce unwanted environmental noises, prevent erosion, protect wildlife, and provide shade and windbreaks.

Fish and *wildlife* contribute to the setting in which outdoor recreation takes place and enhance the recreation experience and environment. Hunting and fishing depend directly on the quality and quantity of game and fish.

Physiography is the single science most useful in describing the landscape character of any area under study and is most important in determining to what uses various sections of the area can be put as well as providing a description of its scenic features.

An investigation into the *historical* and *archeological* background of a particular site and its surrounding area will often produce information that may influence the design of a project. Historical points can be featured or possibly used as development and operational themes.

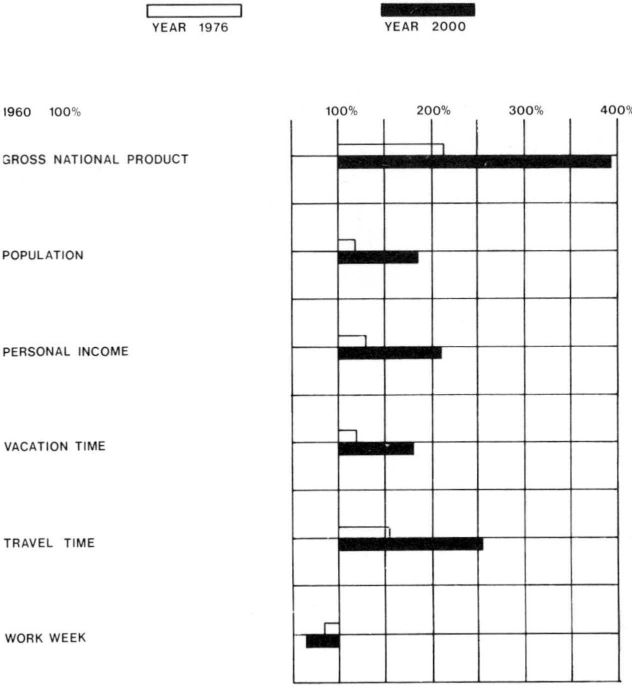

Fig. 1.6 Nationwide projection of estimated changes in population, income, work, leisure, and travel time. (*Chas. T. Main, Inc.*)

ENVIRONMENTAL ASPECTS

Man responds to his environment, and the most successful of all planned facilities will reflect careful analysis and study of the various environmental aspects of the site. Planning will call for a careful review of the entire site because the value of the land development will depend on the best use of such factors as water orientation, slopes, views, and types of vegetation.

The potential user has as one of his objectives escape from the city humdrum. Therefore, aesthetics plays a key role in the land-development process, calling for careful selection of a site, both to ensure favorable features and their survival when permanent facilities are built.

The site planning and design must harmonize with the environment rather than despoil it.

Zoning of land use is becoming more widespread, and many counties and state agencies are establishing zoning standards. It is of utmost importance to check the standards and requirements of various governmental agencies, particularly because of the great interest in environmental control shown by all levels of government. The general public is also becoming increasingly interested in the management of the environment.

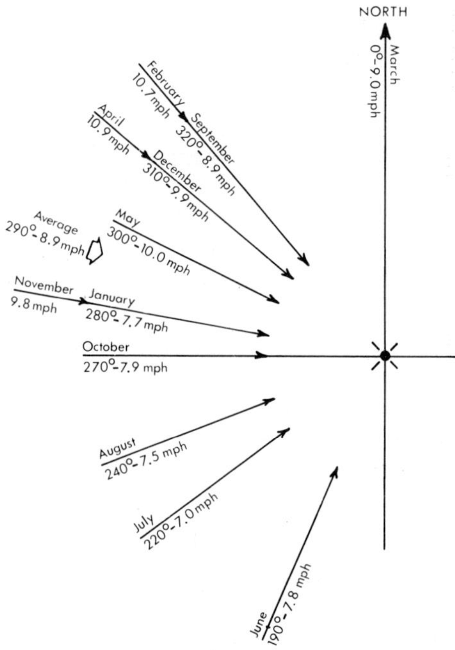

Fig. 1.7 Study of wind direction and velocity. (*Chas. T. Main, Inc.*)

In the development of all land, public health factors are playing a larger role, e.g., provision for proper sanitary facilities and potable water is often regulated by state agencies. In any long-term investment, these factors must be carefully considered and special skills and technical knowledge provided to ensure proper systems.

In many cases, contemplated developments can provide an additional tax base for the community. This factor alone, however, should not be the sole consideration in securing permission for land development. Public and political agencies are giving increasing consideration to other factors (noise, traffic problems, policing, and the influence on the environment) that a major development may engender. In other words, a well-designed, long-range proposal that has been thoroughly exposed to public view is the one that will receive the best response.

Installation of underground utilities is becoming an accepted practice. The potential user expects this type of approach to land development. Added cost, if any, will be reflected in higher land values and a stabilization of the investment. The potential user wants to have a usable environment, as close to nature as possible, but one that still provides most of the modern conveniences.

In any type of land development, safety hazards, insurance, and liability are important factors of the operating features. They must be given careful consideration during the design process so the layouts, materials, and equipment will minimize the chances of injuries and damage claims.

Maintenance and operation are two of the highest-priority factors to be considered in designing and planning. It can only be anticipated that labor and material costs will continue to increase, but careful planning will help to keep expenditures down. An example of this is selection of low-maintenance construction materials even though they may be more expensive initially. Another example is planning the facility so that supervisory and maintenance personnel can be kept to a minimum. This may call for concentrating certain types of facilities, possibly giving consideration to a year-round development to attract and maintain competent employees.

AGE OF PROTEST

Make haste slowly: this is no longer the age of slipshod planning. The public, political agencies, and conservation groups are very sensitive, some very militant, on the matter of the environment, which in all its forms has become a national issue. The public is becoming better informed and is active in the promotion of laws and regulations governing the use of land. Examples are the Federal Interstate Sales Act, under the jurisdiction of the U.S. Department of Housing and Urban Development, which became effective Apr. 1, 1970. The law requires that a detailed property report (topography, soil, drainage) be supplied before the sale of land in subdivisions of 50 lots or more when a significant number are sold interstate. Another example is the National Environmental Policy Act, enacted into law in 1971, which establishes a national policy to:

(1) fulfill the responsibilities of each generation as trustees of the environment for succeeding generations;
(2) assure for all Americans safe, healthful, productive, and esthetically and culturally pleasing surroundings;
(3) attain the widest range of beneficial uses of the environment without degration, risk to health or safety, or other undesirable and unintended consequences;
(4) preserve important historic, cultural, and natural aspects of our national heritage, and maintain, wherever possible, an environment which supports diversity and variety of individual choice;
(5) achieve a balance between population and resource use which will permit high standards of living and a wide sharing of life's amenities;
(6) enhance the quality of renewable resources and approach the maximum attainable recycling of depletable resources.

In order to achieve this policy as established by the federal government every recommendation or report on proposals for new projects which significantly affect the quality of the human environment must contain a detailed statement covering the following:

(1) the environmental impact of the proposed action,
(2) any adverse environmental effects which cannot be avoided should the proposal be implemented,
(3) alternatives to the proposed action,
(4) the relationship between local short term uses of man's environment and the maintenance and enhancement of long-term productivity, and
(5) any irreversible and irretrievable commitments of resources which would be involved in the proposed action should it be implemented.

Since the enactment of the environmental act the states have been rapidly following suit. In many instances the states are enacting far more stringent laws pertaining to the environment and are setting up ways to enforce the laws.

COMMONSENSE DEVELOPMENT

Good land planning will produce good long-term economic returns and calls for a commonsense approach. This requires complete information on the land itself. Vegetative cover, depth and quality of soil, drainage and climate, sanitary requirements, and availability of reliable potable water are some of the physical features that should be considered. In addition, proper recognition should be given to the environment including provision for open space.

Picnic Complex

Figure 1.8 shows a diagrammatic plan of a picnic complex, planned as indicated below and in Table 1.1.

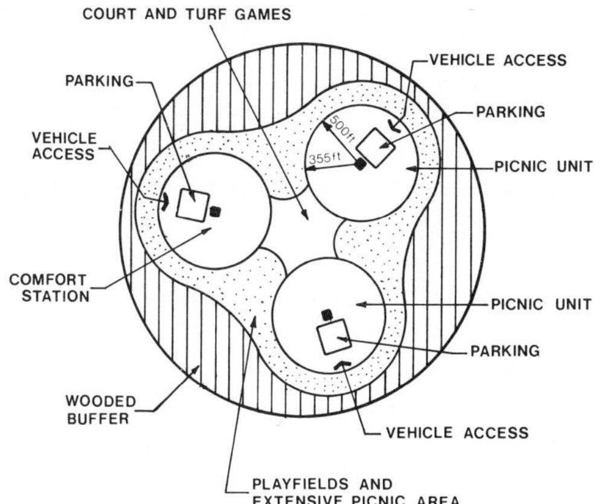

Fig. 1.8 Diagrammatic self-contained picnic complex. (*Chas. T. Main, Inc.*)

TABLE 1.1
Space Calculations for Picnic Complex

Population size	Requirements	Acres
3.5 people per car	Picnicking:	
1 car per picnic site	10 sites per acre, 3	
90 cars per parking lot	units at 10 acres	
315 people per picnic unit	each (with parking)	30
3 units to justify court and turf	Active reacreation center	5.7
games area	Buffer areas (wooded for	
Total = 945 people	wildlife conservation)	27
	Playfields and "extensive"	
	picnicking	27
	Total	89.7

CONCEPT

Picnicking is enhanced by the proximity of other types of recreation facilities; i.e., most persons seek a multifaceted recreation day. Therefore the area is an active recreation center with paved and turf games, recreation apparatus, and spray-wade pool. It is capable of furnishing recreation activities instantly for 200 people and supporting a picnicking population 5 times larger. Toilet facilities are provided at each picnic unit and at the recreation center.

ORIENTATION

This complex is planned for family picnicking. No sites are more than 350 ft from the parking area.

USERS

The complex is planned for families, i.e., normally 3.5 people per site.

Swimming Pool Complex

Figure 1.9 shows a diagrammatic plan of a swimming pool complex, planned as indicated below and in Table 1.2. Figure 1.10 shows an aerial plan of such a complex.

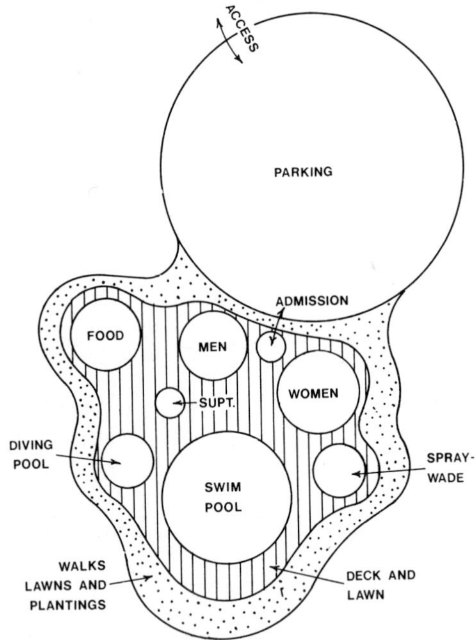

Fig. 1.9 Diagrammatic swimming-pool complex. (*Chas. T. Main, Inc.*)

CONCEPT

Water recreation is popular with all age groups, particularly the young. Water quality that meets public health department standards is more easily maintained in swimming pools. Quality water recreation for large groups can be achieved by combining generous water-deck-lawn space ratios with strict enforcement of designed capacity of the facility.

ORIENTATION

This complex is planned for all age groups, with special design considerations for the young and older groups. The population size is as follows:

Persons in the water in various pools, 500
Persons in pool enclosure on lawns and decks and in shelters, 1500

TABLE 1.2
Space Calculations for Swimming Pool Complex

Area requirements	Ft^2	Acres
Buildings:		
Entry shelter and admissions	1,300	
Men's change, locker, toilet	2,400	
Women's change, locker, toilet	2,500	
Pool administration	1,300	
Pool equipment	2,000	
Concession and shelter	2,300	
Sun and rain shelters	5,000	
Total	16,800	0.44
Pool surfaces	14,000	0.3
Decks (not less that twice pool surfaces)	28,000	0.6
Lawns (not less than 3 times water surfaces)	42,000	0.96
Site development outside pool enclosure	212,800	5.0
Parking with planting, per car	600	8.2
Total		15.5

FACILITIES

Buildings Included are buildings for pool administration, superintendent's office, male and female lifeguard accommodations, first aid and storage, entry shelter and admissions office, men's and women's locker, shower, toilet, storage facilities, concession building and shelter, sun and rain shelters, decks, and areas for lounging.

Pools Diving, spray-wade, and general swimming pools are provided, with protective fences and ornamental planting. Outside the pool enclosure are observation areas.

Parking Space for 600 cars is provided.

Fig. 1.10 Aerial plan view of a swimming-pool complex, Mine Kill State Park. (*Power Authority of the State of New York.*)

CONSERVATION FOR CONSERVATIONISTS

Land development does not necessarily imply land destruction. Careful technical study and use of land forms can produce good development and still satisfy conservation requirements. As an example, the cluster approach to land development can be practiced. This is based on the theory that facilities and developments be clustered or concentrated in groups and the open-space conservation areas retained.

MAINTENANCE AND DESIGN

Unless maintenance problems are carefully considered in the design of all these structures and grounds, those responsible for their upkeep will have difficulty both in planning for maintenance and in doing the actual work. Maintenance budgets are notoriously inadequate, and poor design can only make them more so. If possible, a competent maintenance engineer should be retained as an advisory member of every design staff to check maintenance provisions. Otherwise, arrangements should be made for the plans to be reviewed by field personnel, who should give them close scrutiny. This constructive criticism should help to iron out many maintenance problems before construction begins.

It is the landscape architect, however, who is responsible for creating the design. He should be interested in all the ground components of the park and make careful studies to determine the kinds of planting—trees, shrubbery, turf—that best suit each specific use.

In addition to the maintenance of plantings and special facilities, there are erosion control, the control of insect pests and plant diseases, equipment maintenance, and the never-ending problem of budgeting available funds. Each of these topics should be the subject of lengthy study, and each is fully treated in the later chapters of this volume. But in planning for maintenance it is first necessary to formulate (1) objectives, (2) standards, and (3) a maintenance plan.

MAINTENANCE OBJECTIVES

The general objectives of maintenance are to ensure the clean and orderly appearance of grounds, structures, and facilities and to protect the health, safety, and convenience of the people using them.

Specific objectives, however, must be formulated to suit each situation. Type and intensity of use vary widely; some areas require thorough and frequent cleaning, weeding, seeding, fertilizing, spraying, or repair, while others less frequently used or partially left in their natural state can be maintained on a much less exacting schedule. Good judgment must be used in setting up both objectives and standards.

MAINTENANCE STANDARDS

For the purpose of establishing maintenance standards, most lands requiring maintenance can be classified into two major areas:

> *Area 1* includes all grounds surrounding the major and auxiliary structures considered a part of the operating unit and those areas in parks and other public lands defined or developed specifically for use by the general public, including picnic areas, observation points, entrance triangles from highways, and major access roads to the general developed area.
>
> *Area 2* includes all meadow, pasture, farm, and forest lands within public grounds property lines and all other areas not covered under area 1.

Standards for these two areas have been set as follows by the Tennessee Valley Authority, and may be adapted or modified as required.

For Area 1

1. Roads and parking areas shall be maintained in good structural and smooth riding condition, free from all grass, weeds, and other debris. Access roads within public domains shall be maintained according to the standards of state or municipal parkways (Figs. 1.11 and 1.12).
2. Grass areas shall be maintained as lawns.
3. Shrub beds and specimen trees shall be maintained according to the methods described later. Naturalistic plantings shall receive only such maintenance as needed to ensure their continued growth, free of disease and clear of all dead and fallen material.
4. Picnic-area maintenance shall conform to exceptionally high standards. Trash and garbage removal shall be as frequent as necessary to keep the grounds in a clean and sanitary condition. Repairs to equipment and grounds are to be undertaken as required for the use of the area.
5. Footpaths shall be maintained in good and safe condition, free from grass, weeds, and other debris.
6. All other specific items of maintenance, such as signs, riprap, structures, guardrails, etc., are to be maintained

Fig. 1.11 An example of construction devastation. (*Power Authority of the State of New York.*)

Fig. 1.12 An area similar to that in Fig. 1.11 after completion of parking areas, roadways, and landscaping. Note clean lines and adequate maintenance. (*Power Authority of the State of New York.*)

in accordance with the objective of ensuring clean, orderly, and attractive grounds. Structural repairs, paintings, etc., are to be done as field conditions dictate, so that all structures and facilities are maintained in good structural condition and present the appearance of being well kept.

For Area 2

1. Prevent and control fires.
2. Prevent and control erosion.
3. Other maintenance of mature forest lands shall be confined to the control and removal of dead, down, and diseased timber and such timber harvesting as may be carried out under the best forestry practices. Improve and expand seedling plantings where required.
4. Meadows shall be mowed whenever grass is 6 to 12 in. high, depending upon the locality, and shall be fertilized and improved as necessary.

5. Pasturelands shall be limited to areas specifically designated for that purpose by the proper authorities.
6. General farming may be permitted in areas specifically designated for that purpose by the proper authorities.

Maintenance of leased or licensed areas on public parks or lands has always been a problem. A good rule to follow in the administration and maintenance of such areas is to limit the responsibility of any lessee or licensee to the maintenance of the structures and grounds essential to the efficient operation of the concession, not including areas for the general use of the public, such as picnic areas, public comfort stations, etc., except where such facilities are leased to another public agency or where special conditions make such inclusion practicable, and where a good standard of maintenance can be assured and enforced. If local conditions and requirements are such that public use areas are included, adequate safeguards to the public should be written into contracts and enforced in their administration, to ensure that maintenance by the concessionaire shall be equal to other maintenance standards in the public domain.

THE MAINTENANCE PLAN

After maintenance objectives and standards have been formulated and a study has been made of maintenance problems, the program can be put into effect by means of a written maintenance plan. Such a plan will also promote more efficient preparation of budgets.

Organization of the Plan

The plan should be readily understood by the men in the field. It should present the maintenance standards in some detail and also recommend improvements to unfinished areas. Other pertinent data which a field supervisor may find useful may also be included.

The maintenance problems usually can be divided into three major segments: intensive-use areas, scenic areas, and natural areas. These segments provide a convenient organization for the plan.

Intensive-use areas are those which contain the major structures and are the focal points for all visitors. Such areas must necessarily be maintained on a very high level, and the plan should therefore describe a pattern of maintenance similar to that followed in large city parks, where large expanses of lawn predominate.

Scenic areas include any point from which a view can be seen. In many cases the park is developed around these views, and parking overlooks become a natural adjunct. Maintenance of such areas is often difficult because many of them are on rugged terrain, but nevertheless these scenic spots must be kept open for the full enjoyment of the public.

Natural areas are those which have been left undisturbed. These areas form the immediate foreground from all overlook points and complete the transition from man-made structures to undisturbed native landscape. Wherever man-made areas have encroached, it may be necessary to do certain cleanup work, such as removing dead, down, and diseased timber and thinning underbrush.

Form of the Plan

Physically, the maintenance plan is an instruction sheet divided into a graphic and a written section, both designed for easy reading and interpretation.

The graphic section shows each area in a different shade or tone, so that those responsible for the maintenance program can tell at a glance where any particular type of maintenance begins and ends. The written section describes in detail the type of maintenance prescribed for each of the shaded areas.

These printed instructions describe methods of maintenance for lawns, meadows, trees and shrubs, structures, roads and parking areas, picnic grounds, and general policing. Soil and grass improvement recommendations, fertilizer and seed quantities, and general notes on the care of lawns, trees, and shrubs, methods of pruning, and other general information on maintenance policies should also be included.

Such a document provides the basic data for all planning and scheduling and the preparation of budgets. The cost of maintenance for each section of the plan can be easily estimated, so that any proposed changes in budgets or allotments can be intelligently interpreted.

MAINTENANCE AND PUBLIC RELATIONS

Putting the plan into practice, however, involves one of the most difficult problems of all. This is the human problem, which is concerned with the public, park employees, and friendly relations between the two.

It is a peculiar characteristic of the American citizen that he feels it beneath him to clean up his own debris on public lands, and he somehow justifies his actions by pointing to what others are doing. It never occurs to him to set an example for others to follow. His behavior does not improve the dispositions of surly, discourteous employees, and such employees tend to drive the citizen to defy correction. Thus are master litterbugs created.

PUBLIC RELATIONS

For any proposed development, land planning calls for bringing together public agencies, including township agencies, school boards, conservation authorities, as well as various state agencies, early in the planning process. Early consultation will expose local ordinances and regulations and will produce a better rapport with the local groups.

Many developments result in the concentration of so-called seasonal or "sunshine" residents, who require public services but are not residents of the community. Without proper communication early in the development stage, constant friction and disenchantment are bound to arise. Careful study and consideration should be given to the various requirements while investigating and developing the concept of the proposed land development. More and more communities are reviewing the advantages and disadvantages of large developments. They will no doubt require better developments and higher standards as far as zoning, utility requirements, and other similar items are concerned. Complete knowledge and understanding of the standards and good communication with the community before a development is undertaken will help to forestall the pitfalls of delayed projects and public misunderstanding.

Encouraging Public Neatness

How can the public's careless habits be corrected or counteracted?

1. Provide exemplary housekeeping. Do not let garbage pails overflow or allow picnic tables to remain littered so that each group must clean up after the one before.
2. Do not let litter accumulate over the grounds until it becomes a major task to clean it up. Daily policing will be more economical (Fig. 1.13).
3. Keep grass mowed, weeds cut, shrub beds and walks neatly edged, so that the grounds look cared for, not abandoned.
4. Try to teach the public to be considerate of others. This is where a courteous employee may be able to make real progress against vandals and litterbugs. An employee who sees an infraction of the rules or an act of just plain

thoughtlessness should try to show the offender, firmly but tactfully, how such behavior hurts others as well as the offender himself. Nine times out of ten an appeal to the pocketbook brings quick results; the employee can then explain how negligence increases the cost of maintenance, which must be borne by the taxpayers, and might also point out that by littering or damaging the place chosen

Fig. 1.13 A well-designed picnic area, well equipped and well maintained. (*Power Authority of the State of New York.*)

for recreation the citizen is endangering his own future holiday pleasure.

5. Have neat and appropriate signs (Figs. 1.14 to 1.16). Signs that are too big overpower everything in the vicinity, and signs that are poorly maintained obviously do not practice what they preach. There is nothing so damaging to public morale as a sagging, peeling sign with a notice like "This is your park. Help us keep it clean." This is the sign of a tired, run-down park, and the public will treat it accordingly.

Fig. 1.14 Visitors' building at dam, showing data marker. Good design, clean and attractive surroundings, and durable and easily read signs are essential to the success of any public area. (*Tennessee Valley Authority.*)

6. Sponsor talks by personnel in civic clubs, schools, churches, and the like. Provide films of good and proper use of parks. Laws and rigid enforcement are not the answer to carelessness and vandalism; education and example offer much better chances of success.

Fig. 1.15 Typical park sign. (*Power Authority of the State of New York.*)

Fig. 1.16 Typical park sign. (*Power Authority of the State of New York.*)

Employees and Public Relations

Unlike the public, employees can be selected, at least to the extent that the employment market will permit. They should be chosen not only for their ability to perform the task assigned, but also for neatness, interest, personality, and knowledge of the area in which they are working. It is difficult to find persons with all the necessary attributes, especially when higher-paid jobs are competing for the same people. It therefore behooves the park superintendent or supervisor to assign work on the basis of the capability of the employee and the degree to which he or she will be in contact with the public. In addition, it is a wise supervisor who takes the time to train people into these jobs and to explain not only the immediate job to be done but also the overall operations of the park or grounds.

The laborer, who does all the menial tasks from mixing concrete to collecting garbage, cannot be expected to answer detailed questions on the park operation, but he can be trained to refer the questioner to the proper source for his information. He should be trained to be courteous, to help the public in every way, and to be as neat and clean as his work permits him to be. A good way of counteracting any tendency to sloppiness is to provide regulation work uniforms for all field employees, and special coveralls to be used for really greasy or dirty work.

The second class of employees includes the skilled laborers. These are the power-mower operators, tractor operators, skilled mechanics, gardeners, and their supervisors or foremen. These people should be able to answer questions concerning maintenance practices and to identify trees and shrubs. The standard of personal appearance should be even higher for these employees than for laborers. Uniforms and coveralls should be furnished them, and they should be personally neat and cleanly dressed to the extent that their work will permit.

In the third classification are the park attendants or custodians. These are the employees who meet and talk with the public most frequently: the guards, swimming-pool attendants, concessionaires, restaurant or refreshment stand employees, guides, and administrative personnel. These people should be well trained in all phases of park or grounds operations. They must be intelligent and tactful as well as neat and courteous. They must be able to say no without antagonizing visitors and to dispense information in a way that can be easily understood and appreciated.

All public park employees should be reminded that parks and recreational areas are nearly all tax-supported and that people using them consider themselves part owners. Employees should also consider themselves part owners, and should treat visitors as equals rather than as enemies or necessary nuisances.

It is obvious, then, that skillful supervision of both employees and the public, like planning and scheduling, is an important means of reducing maintenance problems and winning financial support for the maintenance program. Details of specific maintenance practices will be treated in the chapters that follow.

THE GROWING AND MAINTENANCE OF TURF

The seeding and care of grass areas are an important feature of well-developed public grounds. It is important that (1) the soil be prepared properly, following correct fertilization and liming procedures; (2) suitable grasses or grass mixtures be selected; and (3) good maintenance practices be followed after planting.

SOIL PREPARATION

The properties desired in any soil to be seeded to grass include good drainage, good soil texture with sufficient depth for good root development, abundant organic matter, and high fertility. However, many soils, even soils from excavations, can be made to produce good grass if the necessary steps are taken to secure the physical properties mentioned above.

Drainage

It is difficult to establish a good turf without good drainage. It is essential that the water drain rapidly through the soil in order to have a good root system and strong top growth. Under conditions where the soil will not drain properly and the soil remains soggy and wet after heavy rains, it is essential that a system of underground drains be built.

Soil Texture

Sandy soils are generally too light in texture to hold water and fertilizer materials. As a result, grass cannot do its best for lack of water and plant nourishment. A very sandy soil can be improved by working organic material into it. Such materials may consist of 1 to 2 in. of heavier soils or a combination of heavier soil and organic matter. The heavier soils should be thoroughly worked into the top 6 in. of the sandy soil.

Clay soils are generally classed as heavy soils. If a soil becomes slippery and sticky when wet and shrinks and cracks open when it dries, the grass cannot survive. A heavy clay soil does not provide enough air in the soil for good root growth. People walking on it pack a clay soil even tighter. To improve a clay soil, work in organic matter. Sand in a clay soil will not improve it but is likely to pack it harder than before.

Addition of Organic Matter

Organic matter may come from several sources. The one that is the most handy and the cheapest will probably be the one selected. The quantity of organic matter to use varies, but basically for each 1000 ft^2 of area, use three bales of peat moss, from 2 to 3 yd^3 of manure, or 3 to 4 yd^3 of well-rotted sawdust or compost. On large areas, it may be advisable to use cover crops and green-manure crops to help build up the soil. All these soil conditioners should be thoroughly worked into the top 6 in. of soil. Chemical soil conditioners like Krilium must be used with great care but can be beneficial. They are costly, however, and not economical on a large scale.

Analysis and Cultivation

After the soil has been conditioned properly, the following steps should be taken before seeding:

1. Make a soil analysis.
2. Cultivate the soil thoroughly, using a heavy disc. This will loosen the soil and work the organic matter into it.
3. Remove all debris and stones turned up because of the heavy discing.
4. Disc or cultipack the area smooth (or rake by hand if the area is small) before application of lime and fertilizers.

Chapter 4 describes mechanical equipment that can be used for cultivation.

LIMING AND FERTILIZATION

To produce the best turf, it is important to provide the necessary food materials in the soil. Such materials are lime, nitrogen, phosphate, and potash. Lime is used to make the three basic chemicals more readily available to the grass and to break down other chemicals already present in the soil in trace amounts.

Liming

A slightly acid soil (with pH of 6.0 to 6.5)* is more desirable for grasses and legumes than soils more acid or alkaline. Many grass areas are commonly overlimed, to the detriment of old established lawns as well as newly seeded areas. For this reason an acidity test should always be made before lime is used.

The presence of moss and certain other plants on a lawn is no true indication of an acid soil. Moss may be an indication of improper soil reaction, but it also may indicate low fertility, particularly a nitrogen deficiency. A soil test is the most reliable guide to determining soil acidity. If no equipment is available to make soil acidity tests, it is easy to have the soil tested by the local county agricultural agent or university. Once the soil reaction has been corrected, lime need not be applied more than once every 5 to 6 years.

TABLE 2.1
Quantities of Limestone for Specific Soil Reactions

pH	pH desired	Lb per 1,000 sq ft	Tons per acre
6.0	6.5	0–46	0–1
5.5	6.5	46–92	1–2
5.0	6.5	92–138	2–3

* A list of pH values is given in Appendix Table A.1.

Lime should be applied either 2 or 3 months before the application of fertilizer or before the last discing mentioned under Soil Preparation. Most soils will not require over 2 tons of ground limestone per acre, and often less is required. Table 2.1 shows the amount of limestone needed for various soil reactions on the basis of 1000 ft^2 and an acre.

If slaked (hydrated) lime is used, apply only two-thirds as much as of ground limestone, since slaked lime is more alkaline than unslaked.

Where excessive liming has been practiced, sulfur is the best material to use to lower the soil reaction from high pH values to the best point suited for turf growth. The amounts needed for reduction of soil reaction of 1 pH unit are about 25 lb per 1000 ft^2, or ½ ton/acre.

In the pH scale, a value of 7.0 indicates a neutral soil, neither acid nor alkaline. Values less than 7.0 (as pH 6.5) indicate acidity (the smaller the number, the more acid, or "sour," the soil) and pH values more than 7.0 (as pH 7.5) indicate alkalinity (the larger the number, the more alkaline, or "sweet," the soil).

Fertilization

The chemical substances most commonly lacking in soils for grass are nitrogen, phosphorus, potash, and calcium. Soil analysis will indicate the approximate amounts needed. The average subsoil from excavations requires, on the acre basis, approximately 60 lb of nitrogen, 240 lb of phosphorus, and 100 lb of potash. This is equivalent to a ton of 3-10-5 fertilizer per acre, or 45 lb per 1000 ft^2. A ton of 3-9-6, 4-12-4, or 5-10-5 is close enough to the above formula.

Fertilizers higher in nitrogen content are available, such as 10-10-10 or 12-12-12. These number designations always are interpreted as follows: the first number indicates the percentage (units) of nitrogen, the second the number of units of phosphate, and the third the number of units of potash. Proportionately smaller amounts of fertilizer will be needed if the higher-analysis (higher-nitrogen-content) fertilizers are used.

There are also various high concentrations of chemical fertilizers which are soluble in water and can therefore be sprayed directly on the grass without injuring or browning it. Such soluble chemicals are very high in the basic nutrients—nitrogen, phosphate, and potash—and contain a few of the trace food elements such as calcium, iron, boron, etc. These soluble fertilizers come in various analyses such as 17-26-19 or 20-20-20 and must be dissolved in water before they can be used. The advantages of using a water-soluble fertilizer are safety at any time of the growing season and compatibility with insecticides and herbicides. Results have been astonishing wherever water-soluble fertilizers can be used economically. It is not yet economically practical to apply all fertilizers as a water spray to very large turf areas, but this type of application can be useful on small lawns, greens, etc.

When complete fertilizers are not necessary, nitrogen can be applied in various forms such as nitrate of soda (20 per cent N), ammonium nitrate (33 per cent N), or uramon (42 per cent N). The amount of nitrogen applied will vary with the type; e.g., a given amount of ammonium nitrate will produce twice as much nitrogen as the same quantity of nitrate of soda. Phosphorus is available as 20 per cent superphosphate or as triple superphosphate (45 per cent P_2O_5). Potassium is available as potassium chloride (muriate of potash) (50 to 60 per cent K).

Manure and compost are often used as physical conditioners of the soil, but weed seeds will in all probability be introduced. They can be eliminated by sterilizing or pretreating the manure with methyl bromide compounds. One ton of manure is equivalent to about 100 lb of 10-5-10 fertilizer.

Sawdust is an excellent soil conditioner and is being used more and more for this purpose. Well-rotted sawdust is preferred to fresh. If it is necessary to use fresh sawdust, an additional 200 lb of ammonium nitrate is required per acre, or 4 lb per 1000 ft^2. This additional nitrate is needed to replace the nitrogen in the soil used up in breaking down, or decomposing, the fresh sawdust.

In order to maintain a green color through the winter, and especially to give the turf extra vigor for combating weeds, applications of nitrogen fertilizers are desirable. One autumn application of 150 to 200 lb of sodium nitrate or its equivalent per acre (4 to 5 per 1000 ft^2) is sufficient without producing a mowing problem in the spring. These fall applications should be made in mid-October to November when the grass is dry, to prevent burning. A high-analysis nitrogen fertilizer which will not burn when applied is Uramite (42 per cent N), which gives excellent results. Earlier applications will necessitate additional mowing, and later applications will not produce the desired response. Good results in the South have been obtained by applying smaller amounts of nitrogen more frequently during the winter months. Amounts may vary, but usually 50 lb/acre will be adequate.

The quantity of fertilizer to apply at any one time varies greatly with the soil and the job to be done. The best and most practical method is to follow the soil analysis, but lacking that it is possible to apply the phosphate and potash in quantities that will last for several years. This is not possible with nitrogen fertilizer, since it is made available rapidly and any surplus not used by the plants will only leach away. On soils which are of poor quality, such as cherty soils, yellow clay soils, or glacial till subsoils, it is best to apply as much fertilizer as the soils will take, 1 to 2 tons/acre in many instances.

SELECTION OF GRASSES

It is important to select the proper grass or combination of grasses to attain good results. Today the successful turf is not a combination of four or five different grasses but a concentration of one or at most two predominant grasses. The introduction of new and better strains of the common lawn grasses in time will probably revolutionize the entire concept of turf building and maintenance.

The Bent Grasses

The genus *Agrostis* includes all the grasses commonly known as bent and the species known as redtop. These grasses, including redtop, have a more or less creeping habit of growth and are low to moderately tall annuals or, more usually, perennials. They are adapted to regions I(a), I(b), and the more northerly portions of IV (see Fig. 2.1).

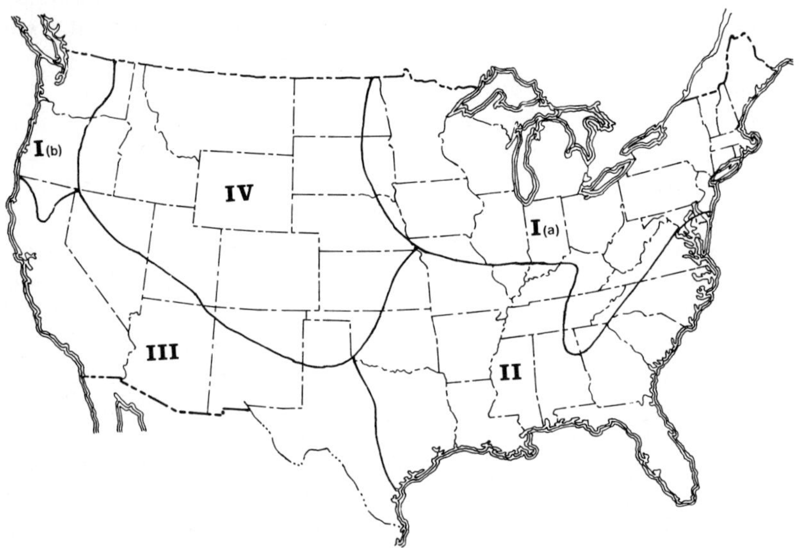

Fig. 2.1 General regions of grass adaptation. (*USDA*.)

REDTOP

Redtop is a perennial with a creeping habit that makes a coarse, loose turf. The leaves are about $^1/_4$ in. wide, stems are slender, and the panicle is loose, pyramidal, and usually reddish. It grows from Canada to the Gulf of Mexico and from New York to California. Redtop is used in pasture mixtures under humid conditions, as a soil binder, and as a winter lawn and golf-green grass in the Southeast. Its main value, its quick and vigorous growth, helps form a compact turf that protects the soil until the slower-growing grasses become established. Redtop will grow under a variety of conditions. It is one of the best wetland grasses but will also resist drought, and it will grow on soils too high in lime content for most other grasses. Because the seeds are small, best results are obtained from planting on a compact, well-prepared seedbed. Usually, it is broadcast 8 to 15 lb to the acre when seeded alone or 2 to 6 lb in a mixture. Fall is the best time for seeding. Redtop will persist for several years, depending upon the fertility of the soil.

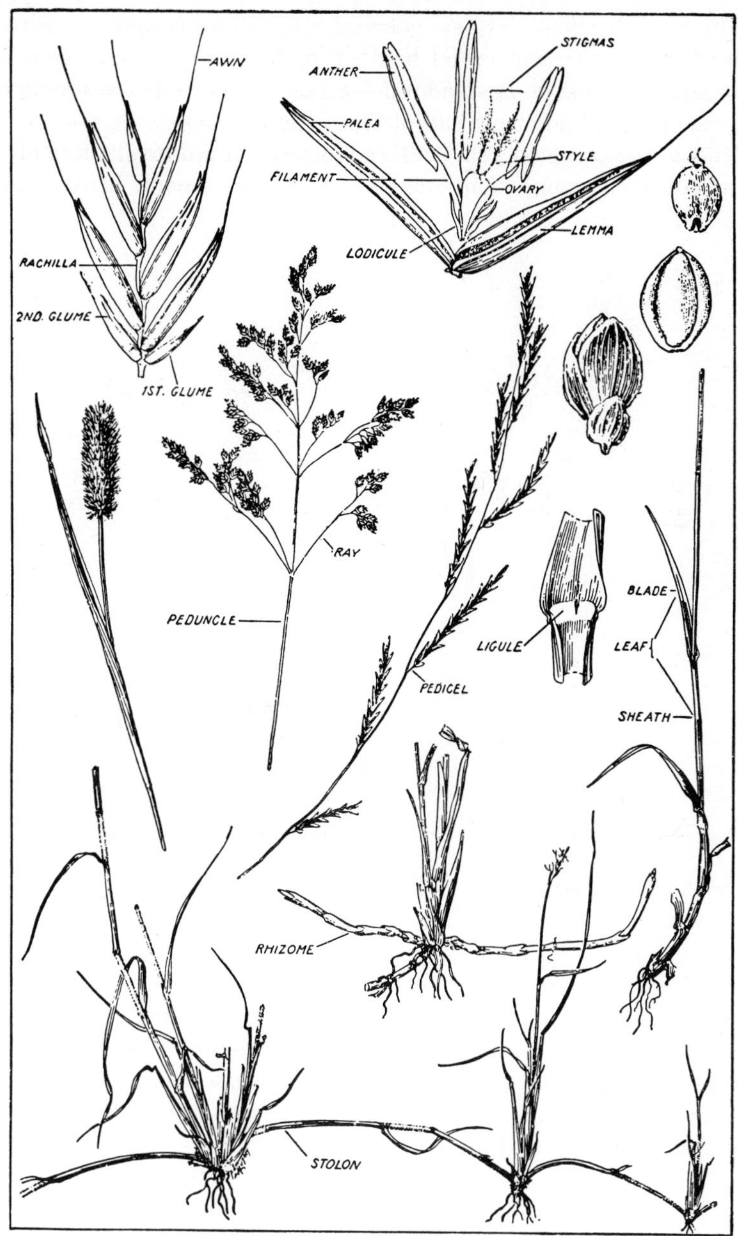

Fig. 2.2 The structure of grasses. (*USDA*.)

Three of the bent grasses, colonial bent (*Agrostis tenuis*), creeping bent (*A. palustris*), and velvet bent (*A. canina*), have been found well adapted for putting greens and in mixtures with other grasses for lawns, over much of the northern half of the United States.

Most of the creeping bent grasses must be started by planting pieces of the stolons or runners, although a few, notably seaside bent or velvet

Fig. 2.3 Colonial bent grass (*left*); **creeping bent grass** (*right*). (*USDA.*)

bent grasses, can be started from seed now commercially available. All the colonial bents have given good results in lawn mixtures, although they are affected by large brown patch, a fungus disease. Seeds of the bent grasses run about 8 million to the pound.

The Bluegrasses (*Poa*)

The bluegrasses are generally distinguished by small, awnless spikelets, lemmas with a heavy midnerve like the keel of a boat, glumes one- to three-nerved, and flat or folded leaf blades, with boat-shaped tips. They are useful for pasturage, hay, and lawn. Generally, they should be planted in the fall when there is more moisture and temperature conditions are better than in summer. Where bluegrass is used for lawns, nitrogen is required to promote vigorous growth and to maintain a desirable dark green color. For best growth, phosphorus, potassium, and nitrogen are all essential. Lime is not essential unless the soil is deficient in calcium. Bluegrasses are adapted to regions I(a), IV, and I(b) and the more northerly portions of II and III.

KENTUCKY BLUEGRASS (*Poa pratensis*)

Kentucky bluegrass, grown principally for lawns and turf, may also be used for pasture grass. It grows 18 to 24 in. tall and under very favorable conditions may reach 36 in. It is a long-lived perennial, spreading by underground rhizomes. During periods of hot, dry weather in summer it remains dormant and will turn brown unless ample water is applied. However, it will stay green all winter in most localities if properly managed and fertilized. Common Kentucky bluegrass is the old standby for lawn grass. Although it is a very satisfactory grass in most localities, it has not been very successful south of upper Tennessee, since it is dormant during the summer months and is easily crowded out by other grasses or weeds. It has two inherent weaknesses: susceptibility to leaf spot in spring, and an aversion to close mowing. Bluegrass does best in full sun in the North, in partial shade in the South, and on soils of high fertility and slight acidity (pH of 6.0 to 6.5). It is slow to germinate, taking about 1 week under ideal conditions and 2 to 3 weeks under more adverse conditions. For this reason, it is advisable to seed in late summer and early fall (Aug. 1 to Oct. 15). Close mowing (less than 2 in.) is very harmful to a good closed bluegrass sod.

MERION BLUEGRASS

Merion, an improved type of Kentucky bluegrass, is a development of the Merion Country Club at Philadelphia. In appearance, Merion bluegrass is very similar to the Kentucky strain. The Merion strain will outperform common bluegrass and can be classed as a superior grass on the following counts:

1. It will thrive under mowing as low as ½ in.
2. It is highly resistant (but not immune) to leaf spot disease.
3. It has a much higher drought tolerance than common bluegrass.

A turf of Merion bluegrass will consistently have less crabgrass than the common bluegrass, particularly at the low cut essential to golf turf. Merion bluegrass is not thinned by disease to the same degree as common bluegrass and therefore will tend to eliminate crabgrass by competition.

Other factors work to the disadvantage of Merion bluegrass:

1. The seed of Merion bluegrass is slow to germinate, and therefore it is difficult to establish a turf in a short time.
2. Merion bluegrass responds well to generous fertilization and will suffer from neglect.

Fig. 2.4 Bermuda grass (*left*); **Kentucky bluegrass** (*center*); **Canada bluegrass** (*right*). (*USDA.*)

3. Merion bluegrass will suffer if it is watered too much and may even fail if watered constantly at night.
4. Seeding Merion bluegrass into old established turf is a slow process, because of the slow-starting seedlings. A fresh, weed-free seedbed is the surest way to establish a good Merion turf. It is also best to seed Merion alone at the rate of $\frac{1}{2}$ to 1 lb of seed per 1000 ft^2.

CANADA BLUEGRASS (*Poa compressa*)

Canada bluegrass resembles Kentucky bluegrass but varies in its blue-green foliage, distinctly flat culms, and short and much contracted panicles. It spreads by underground rootstocks. It grows well in rather poor, dry soils. For lawns, golf links, and similar purposes, it can be used to good advantage under conditions too dry or otherwise unfavorable to Kentucky bluegrass.

FYLKING KENTUCKY BLUEGRASS

Development of a new strain of bluegrass called Fylking Kentucky bluegrass has brought a new dimension to fine turf in North America. Fylking is exceptionally fine-textured and responsive to low mowing. It will withstand a cutting height of less than 1 in., compared with traditional bluegrasses, which are mowed at $1\frac{1}{2}$ in. or higher.

Fylking leaf blades are gently arched, which, combined with a short sheath and abundant tillering, results in a fine-textured lawn. It has an extremely aggressive rhizome root system. Its dense growth and closely woven roots strangle weeds.

Fylking may be seeded alone or in combination with other grasses, e.g., other bluegrasses, fine fescues, or colonial bent grass. When seeded alone, 2 or 3 lb to 1000 ft^2 is ample. When temperatures are 85 to 95°F, germination occurs within 8 days. Below 85°F it takes 12 to 16 days.

Fylking is highly resistant to disease such as leaf spot, stem rust, leaf rust, and stripe smut.

Bermuda Grass (*Cynodon dactylon*)

Bermuda grass is a long-lived perennial with a spreading habit of growth. It propagates by runners, underground rootstocks, and seed. The runners vary from a few inches to 3 to 4 ft in length and under favorable conditions may grow 15 to 20 ft in a season. The rootstocks, which may become stolons or runners on hard soils, are thick and white. The erect, flowering branches are usually 6 to 12 in. high, depending on the fertility and moisture of the soil. The leaves are short, flat, bluish-green, and 1 to 4 in. long. At the base of each leaf is a fringe of white hairs; the leaf sheath is compressed and slightly hairy. The flowers are in slender spikes, three to six in a cluster, and similar in appearance to those of crabgrass.

Bermuda grass will grow well on almost any soil that is fertile and not too wet but grows better on heavy soils. Because the seeds are small and light, a well-prepared seedbed is desirable. Spring seedings, 5 to 7 lb/acre, are usually ample. The seed should be covered by use of a cultipacker or a light harrow.

The most common method of planting stolons is to plow furrows 4 to 6 ft apart, drop the stolons 2 to 3 ft apart in the furrow, and cover by plowing or with the foot. If the stolons are not watered when planted, they should be planted deep enough to prevent their drying out. Rolling or cultipacking the soil after planting is desirable. Apply a well-balanced fertilizer just ahead of the planting. A 4-12-4 fertilizer at the rate of 500 lb/acre should be enough. An application of 100 to 200 lb/acre of ammonium nitrate or nitrate of soda in midsummer will help in rapid establishment of a good Bermuda sod.

Bermuda grass is a common lawn grass throughout the South, but it is generally not considered a good grass to use except for specific purposes such as erosion control, slope treatment, playgrounds, golf courses, and athletic fields. There are several things in favor of Bermuda such as hardiness, drought resistance, and its adaptability to a wide range of soils and soil reactions. Since Bermuda is not hardy as a seedling and does not stay green in winter, it should be seeded between May 1 and July 1 or sprigged between May 1 and Aug. 1. Bermuda is best used in full sun, and it will do well in droughty places, on steep banks, and where heavy traffic is expected. For best results, under normal fertilization programs, it should not be clipped closer than 1½ in.

Several strains of Bermuda grass are much superior to the common Bermuda; e.g., the U-3 Bermuda grass, the Tifton 57 (Tiflawn), the Tifton 127 (Tiffine), and the Tifton 328 have all proved useful for various activities. They are adapted to regions II and III.

U-3 BERMUDA GRASS

U-3 is a fine-bladed strain of Bermuda which was selected in Savannah, Ga. It is cold-tolerant to the extent that it has survived the winters in the vicinity of Washington, D.C., for many years. It has been grown at State College, Pa., since 1940 without suffering winter injury and has been used successfully at Norfolk, Neb., Cleveland, Ohio, and in the St. Louis district.

This grass will find its greatest use in the so-called crabgrass belt, which is defined, roughly, as a triangle having its points at Richmond, Va., Philadelphia, Pa., and St. Louis, Mo. U-3 Bermuda grass may do well in other areas where crabgrass is a serious pest and where the cool-season grasses (bent, blue, and fescue) suffer during midsummer. This grass is adapted to regions II and III, and southern parts of I(a) and IV.

The best uses for U-3 Bermuda grass are for golf tees in open sun, fairways, athletic fields, playgrounds, park areas, and sunny lawns. Use on lawn areas is probably the least important of these. U-3 Bermuda grass is a fast-growing grass, and it produces a wear-resistant turf that will heal rapidly and withstand close mowing, even to putting-green height (3/16- to ¼-in.). It is one of the few grasses that will thrive during hot, dry weather with little or no irrigation. It is highly disease-resistant during hot, muggy weather. It can be mowed without injury to the grass as close as the mower can be set. When this grass is properly fertilized and mowed, practically no weed can encroach. It makes its best growth during the late spring, summer, and early fall, when turf is used most.

The chief disadvantages of Bermuda grasses, particularly U-3, are as follows:

1. They have poor winter color. U-3, however, retains green color longer than most strains. When frost occurs, Bermuda grass becomes dormant and takes on a light straw color, although the playing quality of golf courses is not affected. The color can be masked by seeding a cool-season grass into the Bermuda. Results indicate that Kentucky bluegrass and highland bent may provide color for the cool season and may not require reseeding each year. These grasses should be planted in the fall.
2. U-3 Bermuda grass is not a shade-tolerant grass. It makes its best growth in the open sun. Neither will it tolerate neglect. It must be mowed and fertilized regularly for best results.
3. Seed is not available for U-3, and it is necessary to plant this grass vegetatively. It can be planted any time after the last frost in the spring and throughout the summer until mid-August.

The U-3 grass may be planted by spot sodding with 2-in. square blocks of sod, by strip sodding with 1-in. strips of sod, or by sprigging. Spot sods or strip sods placed at 1-ft intervals will form a solid turf in 6 weeks or less. If sprigs are planted at 8-in. intervals, similar results will be obtained. Sods or sprigs may be planted farther apart if material is scarce or if rapid coverage is not essential. The newly planted area should be kept moist until the grass is well established. These planting methods apply whether U-3 Bermuda grass is started on a prepared seedbed or introduced into established turf. Spreading will be less rapid in turf than on a clean seedbed.

To maintain U-3 properly, feed it heavily and mow it frequently. Bermuda grass should be fertilized each year at the rate of approximately 50 lb of a 10-6-4 fertilizer to 1000 ft^2. This should be applied in three equal treatments, one in early spring, one in early summer, and one in early fall.

U-3 Bermuda grass thrives under a mowing height of $\frac{1}{2}$ to $\frac{3}{4}$ in. This has been found to be a desirable height for many turf uses. One mowing a week is the minimum requirement. Two or three mowings a week will pay dividends in a well-groomed appearance.

U-3 Bermuda grass is very resistant to chemicals. Where crabgrass threatens a newly planted area, sodium arsenite or any other proved crabgrass killer may be used with safety at rates which will kill softer, weaker grasses.

TIFTON 57, 127, AND 328 BERMUDA GRASSES

These strains were developed and produced in a breeding program by G. W. Burton at Georgia Coastal Plain Experiment Station, Tifton, Ga. The differences between the three strains are in the color, texture, and rapidity of growth. The Tifton 57 and 328 strains are dark-green color. The 328 strain is a finer-bladed grass than the 57 strain, with slightly better color and much faster growth. The 127 strain of Bermuda grass is a very fine-bladed light-green grass which grows densely. All three strains produce a very tough turf which will stand considerable wear. The following comparisons can be made between these three strains of Bermuda grass and the common variety:

1. The newer strains spread faster and become established more rapidly after sprigging.
2. They make a denser turf, which means fewer weeds.
3. They tolerate more punishment and wear, which makes them better for athletic-field use.
4. They stay green longer because of greater resistance to frost and disease.
5. They are injured less by winter ryegrass and recover faster when ryegrass goes out in the spring.
6. They require less fertilizer under normal conditions, but given ample fertilizer, they will make an excellent response.
7. They are shorter and look better than common Bermuda with infrequent mowing. For the development of high-quality turf, however, they should be mowed regularly.
8. The Tifton strains, like the common Bermuda, will not do well in shade and should not be planted in shady areas. They can be grown under very light shade if mowed less frequently and cut higher.
9. They are very drought-resistant and will do well on dry soils if properly fertilized.

ESTABLISHMENT OF HYBRID BERMUDAS

Since the hybrid Bermudas produce few viable seeds, they must be propagated by planting sprigs. In planting sprigs, the following recommendations should be followed:

1. Prepare the soil as for planting seed or a garden. It is important to begin with a well-prepared and cultivated seedbed.

2. Apply lime if the soil test indicates that lime is needed.
3. Spread 30 to 40 lb of a complete fertilizer, such as an 8-8-8, per 1000 ft^2 and work both lime and fertilizer into the soil thoroughly. At this time, be sure to establish the final grade, working out all pockets and finally harrowing or cultipacking it smooth.
4. Secure fresh sprigs of the hybrid Bermuda you wish to plant and when there is ample moisture in the ground, begin planting the sprigs as soon as possible after they have been received. Do not let the sprigs wilt or dry out. If they must be stored, keep them in a shady place, well covered and damp.
5. One of the best planting methods is to drop the sprig on the ground and push the basal end into the soil with a stick with a rounded end until only the tip leaves are left protruding. Then remove the stick and firm the soil around the sprig by stepping on it.
6. Another method is to plow furrows approximately 2 in. deep with a cultivator and drop the sprigs into the furrow so that only the tips of the leaves are showing. Rake the soil back into the furrow and firm by stepping on the sprig.
7. Whatever planting method is used, the entire area to be sprigged should be rolled with a corrugated roller weighing about 300 lb.
8. Water the sprigs immediately after planting to ensure maximum stands. Watering should be a good soaking and not just a light sprinkling.
9. For rapid coverage, plant the sprigs on 12-in. centers. One bushel of sprigs, containing about 2000 to 4000 sprigs, should plant 2000 to 4000 ft^2 on 12-in. centers.
10. Control weeds by hand weeding or mowing until the grass has covered the soil. To hasten its growth, it is best to mow the grass often, and as short as possible. The trick is to force growth in the early stages into the roots and to keep it out of the tops as much as possible. This method will develop a good tough and thick sod in the shortest possible time.

MAINTENANCE OF HYBRID BERMUDAS

In March each year apply approximately 10 lb of complete fertilizer (such as an 8-8-8) per 1000 ft^2. Follow at intervals of 4 to 6 weeks with applications of 3 lb of ammonium nitrate, 6 lb of nitrate of soda, or 15 lb of cottonseed meal or Milorganite per 1000 ft^2, until the grass has reached the desired thickness and color. Apply the fertilizer evenly with a fertilizer spreader and apply only when the grass is dry. If the fertilizer is applied properly, little or no burning should result. To avoid burning, water the plants immediately after applying the fertilizer to wash all traces off the leaves. During the summer months, mow at $\frac{1}{2}$ to $\frac{3}{4}$ in. at weekly intervals to develop the best turf. In the spring and fall less frequent mowing will be adequate. Do not remove clippings unless they are heavy enough to smother the grass.

Carpet Grass (*Axonopus affinis*)

This perennial creeping grass makes a dense sod. It is distinguished by its compressed, two-edged, creeping stems, which root at each joint, and by its blunt leaf tips. The slender flower stems grow 1 ft high (rarely 2 ft) if the soil is fertile. It is especially adapted to sandy or sandy-loam soils, particularly where the moisture is near the surface most of the year. It is adapted to regions II and III.

Carpet grass is most valuable for permanent pastures but also is valuable for firebreaks in forests, lawns and turf, roadsides, and open areas in pine forests.

Carpet grass is usually sown 5 to 10 lb/acre. It can be sown on a well-prepared seedbed or broadcast on burned-over open areas in timber

Fig. 2.5 Carpet grass (*left*); centipede grass (*right*). (*USDA*.)

land. Seeding is best done in spring, early summer, or even in midsummer. One pound contains approximately 1,350,000 seeds, and a bushel weighs 18 to 36 lb.

Centipede Grass (*Eremochloa ophiuroides*)

This low-growing perennial spreads by stolons and is perhaps the best all-around lawn grass that can be grown in the deep South. Its appearance is somewhat between carpet grass and Bermuda grass, with shorter nodes than Bermuda. It makes a dense mat of creeping stems and leaves. Like all other grass, centipede grass has its desirable and undesirable features. It is adapted to region III and southern portions of region II (south of Tennessee).

Some of the desirable features of centipede grass are as follows:

1. It makes a dense, weed-free sod.
2. It grows on poor soils.
3. It requires very little fertilization.
4. It requires less mowing than carpet or Bermuda grass.
5. It tolerates more shade than Bermuda grass but less than St. Augustine grass.
6. It is more resistant to disease and insect attack than most grasses.

Some of the undesirable features of centipede grass are the following:

1. Like carpet and Bermuda grass, it turns brown with the first freeze and usually stays brown until spring.
2. It makes such a dense sod that it is rather difficult to start over seeded ryegrass.
3. It is not suitable for planting on farm lands, where it soon spreads and rapidly crowds out the other grasses. When centipede grass has replaced the other grass, the pasture will be ruined; cattle can make little gain and often lose weight. Nutritionally, it is about the poorest of all the grasses.

ESTABLISHING A NEW CENTIPEDE LAWN

Prepare the lawn area as for any other seedbed. Apply a complete fertilizer (such as 4-12-4 or 5-10-5) at a rate of 10 to 15 lb per 1000 ft^2. Harrow or rake the fertilizer into the soil.

To establish a centipede lawn from seed, follow these steps:

1. Broadcast 2 oz of good seed uniformly over each 1000 ft^2 of lawn. It is a good plan to mix the seed thoroughly with 1 gal of dry sand to facilitate uniform distribution.
2. Rake the seed lightly into the soil. Use the back of the rake for best results.
3. Water the newly planted seed thoroughly and keep the soil moist until the grass is well established. Centipede seedlings have little drought resistance and will die if not watered during dry periods.
4. Mow often to reduce weed competition.
5. About 2 months after planting, topdress with 2 to 4 lb of nitrate of soda or 5 to 10 lb of Milorganite per 1000 ft^2 of area. Apply fertilizer only when the grass is dry and wash in to prevent burning.

To establish a centipede lawn from sprigs:

1. Plant fresh, live sprigs in furrows 2 to 3 in. deep and spaced 10 to 18 in. apart. Place the sprigs about 6 in.

Fig. 2.6 Dallis grass (*left*); **meadow fescue** (*right*). (*USDA*.)

apart in the furrows and cover immediately to prevent drying. Leave 1 in. or more of the plant showing above the surface.

2. To produce a more rapid growth and coverage, plant the sprigs closer together, water well, and topdress with a nitrogen fertilizer. Spring-planted sprigs spread as much as 8 to 10 ft in a season.
3. Approximately 15 to 20 lb of stolons will set 1000 ft^2 of area at the spacing given above.

ESTABLISHING CENTIPEDE GRASS ON AN OLD LAWN

Centipede grass can be established on an old lawn without plowing the soil if the area is level and properly graded. Seed directly on top or dig each sprig into the soil. Plenty of water must be used to keep the seedlings or sprigs from drying out and dying. Use very little fertilizer if there is Bermuda grass in the old lawn because fertilizer favors the Bermuda at the expense of the centipede grass.

Dallis Grass (*Paspalum dilatatum*)

This upright growing, bunching grass requires a moist but not wet soil; growth is best where organic matter is abundant. It requires a higher fertility than carpet grass. Since it seldom forms a dense sod, it is an excellent grass to mix with legumes and other grass. Seeded alone, it often fails to make a perfect stand.

Fescues (*Festuca*)

Fescues are adapted to regions I(a) and I(b) and northerly portions of region IV.

There seem to be few differences between the several named red fescues on the market—Illahee, Trinity, Oregon creeping red, Penn State Chewings, Olds, and Pennlawn. They are all strains of creeping red fescue and have the same general requirements for management. These grasses are drought-resistant, sun- and shade-tolerant, and adaptable to a wide range of soil types, soil reactions, and fertility levels. They respond to high fertility and pH levels of 6.0 to 6.5. They are sod formers and do not require so frequent mowing as bluegrass and Bermuda grass. A combination of a creeping red fescue and Kentucky bluegrass in equal quantities will usually produce an excellent lawn in the cooler or more temperate climates.

These strains of creeping red fescues have definite advantages over the more common varieties. For one thing, because the seed is usually awnless, it can be thoroughly mixed with other seeds and will flow quite freely in seed equipment. These new strains are definitely creepers by underground roots and stems, and they do not grow in clumps, as Chewings fescue has a tendency to do as it gets older. They are not tough like creeping red fescue, can be mowed shorter, and seem to have a much fresher, darker green color than the other fescues.

Fig. 2.7 Sheep fescue (*left*); **red fescue** (*right*). (*USDA.*)

MEADOW FESCUE (*Festuca elatior*)

This is a hardy perennial which flourishes in deep, rich soils; when well established, it will grow to 15 to 30 in. The leaves are bright green and rather juicy. The leaf sheaths are smooth and reddish-purple at the base, and the young leaves are rolled inward in the bud. The blade is glossy on the under surface. When the panicles are open, they resemble those of

Kentucky bluegrass, although they are much larger and coarser. Flowering is in June and July.

Meadow fescue does not propagate itself by rootstocks or form a dense sod. The seed weighs 22 to 27 lb to the bushel and has 225,000 seeds/lb. Seed at the rate of 25 or 30 lb/acre.

SHEEP FESCUE (*Festuca ovina*)

This is a bunchgrass that forms dense tufts with numerous rather sharp, bluish-gray leaves. It succeeds better than most grasses on sandy or gravelly soils; its greatest use is for making a durable turf on sandy soils. Seeds weigh 10 to 15 lb/bushel. Seed at the rate of 25 to 30 lb/acre.

THE TALL FESCUES

There are two tall fescues, Alta and Kentucky 31, which seem to be preferred. Both are relatively coarse-bladed, deep-rooted, drought-tolerant grasses with good wear resistance and a high tolerance to chemicals. The fescues will tolerate low fertility but will respond to good fertilization programs. The tall fescues, especially the Kentucky 31, will tend to be bunchy unless seeded heavily. When thickly seeded they will produce a good tough sod that will withstand the encroachment of weeds and even of Bermuda grass. Recommended rates of seeding if seeded alone are from 2 to 5 lb of seed to 1000 ft^2 of area.

Ryegrasses (*Lolium*)

Italian ryegrass (*Lolium multiflorum*) is usually an annual and is generally distinguished from perennial ryegrass by the awned lemma and stem characters and by the arrangement of the leaf in the bud. Awns are present on seed of Italian ryegrass and usually absent on perennial. The culm or stem of Italian is cylindrical, but that of perennial ryegrass is slightly flattened. The leaves of Italian are rolled in the bud, but in the perennial the leaves are folded in the bud. Italian is yellowish-green at the base, and perennial is commonly reddish. Italian ryegrass is generally used in mixtures or seeded alone for quick green effects. Its use in lawn work is extremely doubtful, and it should be used only where a quick grass cover is essential. It is a difficult grass to mow and is a heavy feeder, taking away essential mineral elements from the permanent grasses. It is often used on Bermuda sod, but this involves reseeding every fall and many mowings, especially in the spring. Bermuda grass tends to run out under it, but this can be prevented by topdressing with a nitrogen fertilizer in late June or early July, after the ryegrass has mostly disappeared. It is adapted to all regions.

PERENNIAL RYEGRASS (*Lolium perenne*)

Perennial ryegrass is used principally for permanent pasture seedings. It starts growth early in the spring and affords grazing while the more permanent or longer-lived grasses are becoming established. It is not considered desirable for lawns because the toughness of its leaves makes mowing difficult and it will not give a good turf in the summer months.

Fig. 2.8 Italian ryegrass (*left*); **perennial ryegrass** (right). (*USDA*.)

Ryegrass can be seeded in the fall or early spring. Seed may be broadcast by hand or seeder and covered with a smoothing harrow or rake, or it may be sown with a grain or seed drill. The seed should be covered with approximately ½ in. of soil. When it is seeded alone, the rate should be 20 to 25 lb/acre. When it is seeded with small grain or legumes for annual pasture, 8 to 10 lb/acre is ample. On established lawns for winter green or when ryegrass is seeded alone in spring or fall for temporary lawn, 3 to 4 lb per 1000 ft^2 is commonly used. It is adapted to all regions.

MANHATTAN PERENNIAL RYEGRASS

Manhattan ryegrass is adaptable to either sandy or heavy clay soils. It does not maintain a dense sod in extremely wet soils or in heavy shade. It thrives in the cool, moist areas of the east coast, northward from Virginia. On the west coast it will grow from mid-California northward to British Columbia. It is also adapted to the Midwest from the Mason-Dixon line north into Canada.

It requires moderate fertilization with a balanced fertilizer, selected and applied to provide 2 to 5 lb of actual nitrogen per year. It should be seeded at the rate of 4 lb per 1000 ft^2 and will germinate in 5 days.

Its foliage is uniform, dense, and dark green. It fills in rapidly with an erect growth habit. The leaf blades are finer than Kentucky bluegrass. It is winter-hardy and will withstand heavy traffic.

Manhattan ryegrass is tolerant to snow mold and pythium blight. It is susceptible to leaf spot, red thread, and leaf rust. Timely applications of 1 lb nitrate of soda per 1000 ft^2 reduce or eliminate this threat.

Orchard Grass (*Dactylis glomerata*)

This is a long-lived perennial grass, distinctly of the bunch type, with folded leaf blades and compressed sheaths. It does not produce stolons or underground rhizomes and therefore never forms a dense sod. It does best on rich soil but also succeeds on light soil of medium fertility

Fig. 2.9 Orchard grass (*left*); **St. Augustine grass** (*right*). (*USDA.*)

and on moist, heavy land. It does well in shade and is good in orchards, woodland pastures, and other similar areas. It is cold-resistant and continues growth until the first severe frosts. Orchard grass is adapted to all regions.

St. Augustine Grass (*Stenotaphrum secundatum*)

This is an extensively creeping, rather coarse, glabrous perennial that produces stolons with long internodes and branches that are short, rather leafy, and flat. The sheaths are flat and folded, and both terminal and auxiliary blades are short (4 to 6 in. long).

St. Augustine grass thrives in shaded areas and is especially adapted for lawns. It is naturally a seashore plant and withstands salt spray. Because it has no seed available, rooted runners must be used to start a new planting. These are planted in rows or disced into the soil during moist periods and subsequently packed. It should be well watered and

Fig. 2.10 **Timothy** (*left*); **soybean** (*right*). (*USDA.*)

fertilized with nitrogen at the rate of 5 lb per 1000 ft^2, an essential requirement for vigorous growth.

This grass is subject to damage by brown patch fungus and chinch bugs. The fungus can be controlled by stimulating growth with nitrogen fertilizer or by using calomel and corrosive sublimate. Chinch bugs can be controlled by blowing tobacco dust down between the stems of the grass or by spraying with nicotine sulfate, using 1 part nicotine sulfate to 500 parts water. St. Augustine grass is adapted to regions II and III.

Timothy (*Phleum pratense*)

This grass has stems, or culms, 20 to 40 in. tall. They emerge from a swollen or bulblike base and form large clumps. Timothy differs from most other grasses in that one or two of the lower internodes is swollen into an ovoid body which is referred to as a *bulb* or *corm* although it is really only a thick internode. These corms form in early summer and die the next year when seed matures. The leaves are elongate; the panicle is cylindrical and commonly 2 to 4 in. long. Timothy grows best on clay loams, although it will also grow on light-textured, sandy soils. Fall seedings are best when the grass is planted alone or with winter wheat. Less seed is required for fall than spring seeding; usually fall seeding requires 3 to 4 lb/acre and spring seeding requires 10 lb/acre. To maintain better soil productivity, timothy is commonly sown with clover, medium red, mammoth, or alsike.

The Zoysia Grasses

There are three common species of zoysia and two hybrid zoysias in the United States: Manila grass (*Zoysia matrella*), Japanese lawn grass (*Z. japonica*), Mascarene grass (*Z. tenuifolia*), and the hybrids Emerald and Meyer zoysias. The zoysias are adapted to regions II and III, and southern portions of I(a) and IV.

MANILA GRASS (*Zoysia matrella*)

This grass was introduced into the United States many years ago from Korea. It is a low, sod-forming grass native to tropical and eastern Asia, where it is found growing abundantly on the sandy shores and river banks. Importations of both roots and seed have been distributed widely throughout the United States, but it has not been used extensively because it is slow in becoming established and lacks seed. In regions where Bermuda grass can be grown it is usually preferred to Manila grass.

Manila grass appears especially valuable for lawns, playgrounds, athletic fields, and other places where a thick turf is desired and speed of establishment is not a factor. It is also useful on road shoulders and embankments, since it requires little or no mowing; the entire season's growth is seldom over 4 to 6 in. Despite the saving in maintenance this represents, lack of seed and slowness in establishment militate against the use of Manila grass for such purposes.

Since Manila grass is sensitive to frost, it appears to be most promising in regions having a warm to mild temperate climate (regions II and III). In its northern limits, it turns brown with the first heavy frost in the

Fig. 2.11 Manila grass. (*USDA*.)

fall and does not renew growth until after the last heavy frost in the spring. This brown or straw color makes Manila grass less desirable than Kentucky bluegrass or other lawn grasses that maintain a partial green color during the winter months and are adapted to the central and northern latitudes. In the latitude of Washington, D.C., Manila grass will remain green from mid-April to late October, while farther south, as in Alabama, it remains green for 9 to 10 months of the year. While it has survived as far north as Rhode Island, when covered with a light mulch, its northern limit is approximately 40 degrees latitude.

Manila grass will withstand partial shade and still maintain a good sod if properly managed and fertilized. It is not adapted to dense shade but is one of the best grasses in the South for shady lawns.

Because this grass sets little or no seed and the seed is difficult to harvest, it is necessary to establish it by vegetative planting. The matted, wiry root system forms a dense sod mass, which can be cut up into small plugs about 2 in. square or divided into plant fragments commonly referred to as *sprigs*. Solid sodding is not recommended since supplies are limited and costs prohibitive.

Whether done with sprigs or with small sod plugs, planting should be made in rows about 1 ft apart and set a similar distance apart in the rows. This grass is slow to spread, and if quicker cover is desired, thicker planting will ensure earlier establishment. On slopes and terraces it is advisable to plant solid rows across the slope to prevent washing and to ensure earlier establishment. In vegetative planting, it is important that the sprigs or sod plugs be firmly set and that the tip ends of the plants extend above the soil surface, since the plants are killed if covered completely.

One square yard of thick sod is sufficient to sprig-plant 750 to 1000 ft^2 with rows 8 to 10 in. apart and the sprigs 3 in. apart in the rows. With wider spacing (planting in rows 12 in. apart and 12 in. in the row), 1 yd^2 of sod will set 3000 to 4000 ft^2. Using 2-in. sod plugs, spaced 1 ft apart, 1 yd^2 of sod will plant 324 ft^2. It is impractical to use wider spacing with a sod that is so slow to establish.

CARE OF SOD BEFORE PLANTING

The dense mass of sod, even after the dirt has been removed, can be transported for some distance without injury. The sod for transplanting should be kept moist and in a shady place until planted. The sod is usually transported in blocks 1 ft square. Upon receipt of the sod (it usually comes in blocks 1 ft square), wet down an area and lay the sod out as though solid-sodding an area. Soak the sod thoroughly at once, and then keep it moist until it is planted.

Use the same methods of soil preparation as for preparing a seedbed for lawn or garden. Be sure the soil is free of all stones and other debris.

Since the grass is for permanent planting, fertilizers should be worked into the soil before the planting is started. Phosphorus and potash should be applied at the rate of 25 to 30 lb per 1000 ft^2, and just before planting a complete fertilizer should be applied at the rate of 15 to 20 lb per 1000 ft^2. Do not allow sod or sprigs to come into direct contact with heavy applications of nitrogen fertilizers. If the soil is low in organic matter, well-rotted manure, peat moss, or other available organic matter materials should be worked into the seedbed. Manila grass, while not too exacting in its soil requirements, does respond to proper soil and fertilizer treatments. Lime is not essential unless the soil is extremely poor and highly acid.

TIME OF PLANTING

Since this grass is sensitive to cold, it is best established as soon in the spring as the soil is warm. In the extreme South plantings may be made in late summer or early fall. If adequate amounts of water can be given for planting and for subsequent maintenance, Manila grass may be planted all summer long.

CARE OF PLANTING

The soil should be rolled after planting, to ensure an even turf. It is essential that the soil be kept moist, and it should be watered if rains do not occur to hasten growth. Weeds should be removed by cultivation or hand weeding. It is necessary to encourage as rapid growth and spread as possible since Manila grass is slow to establish itself. If sod plugs 2 in. square are used in place of sprig planting, a temporary seeding may be made of such grasses or legumes as redtop, ryegrass, lespedeza, or even Kentucky bluegrass. These seedings should not be heavy, as competition will reduce the rate of spread of the Manila grass. Grass seedings are not recommended if the Manila grass has been sprig-planted, as these will not stand so much competition as the sod plugs. After establishment, the usual methods of lawn care and management should be followed.

One of the principal weaknesses of Manila grass is its slow growth. When sprigs or 2-in. plugs are spaced 12 in. apart, it usually requires 2 years to obtain a good cover and lawn; under the same conditions, Bermuda grass will have a good cover in 2 months.

Manila grass is not seriously injured by insects or diseases common to other turf and lawn grasses, although brown patch, a fungus disease, has been found on it.

RELATED SPECIES

Zoysia japonica, Japanese lawn grass, has a broad coarse leaf similar to redtop. While it does not grow so tall as redtop, it makes a very dense cover. It is extremely hardy and persistent when once established. It is tough, harsh, and unpalatable to cattle and can be established only from runners or plugs.

MEYER ZOYSIA

Meyer zoysia was the first improved strain of zoysia to be recognized and named. It is a coarser grass than Manila grass, slow-growing compared with Bermuda but faster than Manila grass. Meyer zoysia loses its green color in late fall after the first or second killing frost. It holds its green color a little longer than Manila grass, however, and regains it a little earlier in spring. It must be planted vegetatively by plugs or sprigs. The method is the same as for Manila grass.

Meyer zoysia has the following advantages:

1. It resists crabgrass and other summer weeds, although dormant zoysia turf may be entered by such winter weeds as chickweed, speedwell, henbit, clovers, ground ivy, and broadleaf weeds. They can be controlled with 2,4-D and potassium cyanate.
2. It thrives during the heat of summer.
3. It grows on almost any kind of soil.
4. It is very drought-tolerant.
5. Turf insects apparently do not affect it.
6. It requires less mowing than most turf grasses and can be mowed at heights from ½ to 4 in. without loss of vigor and beauty.
7. It develops a firm, resilient cushion of turf and has a strong resistance to wear.
8. Its color is a dark green similar to Kentucky bluegrass.

EMERALD ZOYSIA*

This improved hybrid lawn grass, a cross between Japanese lawn grass and mascarene grass, was introduced by Ian Forbes at the Plant Industry Station, Beltsville, Md., in 1949. This hybrid combines to varying degrees the greater winter hardiness, nonfluffy growth habit, and faster rate of spread of its *japonica* parent with the finer leaves, denser turf, greater frost tolerance, and darker green color of its *tenuifolia* parent. It exhibits hybrid vigor in rate of spread at both Tifton and Beltsville and in the browning and density ratings at Tifton. All these characteristics are desirable in a turf grass. The zone of adaptation of emerald zoysia is not fully known. At present, it is not recommended for planting farther north than a line from Washington, D.C. west to St. Louis, Mo. Emerald zoysia received its name because of its beautiful, dark green color. Since it is the product of a wide cross, it must be propagated vegetatively to preserve its superior characteristics. Planting methods are the same as specified for the other zoysias.

Legumes

Alyce clover (*Alysicarpus vaginalis*) is a summer annual, but when left as a cover crop or green manure, it will volunteer for several years. In thin stands, it tends to spread and be moderately branched; in thick

* The following information is from an abstract from the cooperative investigations at Beltsville, Md., and Tifton, Ga., of the Field Crops Research Branch, Agricultural Research Section, USDA; the University of Georgia Coastal Plain Experiment Station, Tifton, Ga.; and the United States Golf Association Green Section.

stands, it tends to be ascending with very few branches. It grows to a height of about 3 ft on moderately fertile soil. The stems are coarse but fairly leafy. The leaves are unifoliate, broadly oval, and borne the entire length of the stems on short leafstalks. The seed weighs about 60 lb/bushel and is borne in jointed pods; 275,000 seeds are counted to the pound. Alyce clover is used principally for hay and soil improvement and also for pasture. It does not like wet land and grows poorly on soils of low fertility. It should be seeded about the first of May at the rate of 15 to 20 lb/acre.

SOYBEANS (*Glycine max*)

The soybean (Fig. 2.10), an annual summer legume, is an erect, branching plant, resembling in its early growth the ordinary field or navy bean. The pods, stems, and leaves are covered with fine brown or gray hairs. The leaves vary widely in shape, size, color, and degree of persistence. They usually fall before the pods mature. The flowers, either white or purple, are small and inconspicuous and are borne in the axil of the leaf. They are self-fertile. The pod usually contains two or three and occasionally four seeds. The seeds are varicolored—green, brown, black, straw-yellow, or greenish-yellow. Soybeans will succeed on nearly all types of soil, but best results are obtained on mellow, fertile loams or sandy loams. Inoculation of the seed (treatment with nitrogen-fixing bacteria) is essential for the best results when it is grown for the first time. Soybeans are sown from early spring, after the soil has become warm, until midsummer. For soil-improvement purposes, sow $1\frac{1}{2}$ to 2 bushels of seed to the acre.

LESPEDEZA

Three species of Lespedeza are most commonly used: *Lespedeza striata*, common lespedeza (Fig. 2.12); *L. stipulacea*, Korean lespedeza; *L. cuneata*, sericea lespedeza. In all species, the leaves are trifoliate but vary in shape from linear to ovate. The lavender flowers are inconspicuous in the three species listed. The common and Korean species are annuals, and the sericea is a perennial. Korean and common lespedezas are especially useful on acid soils of low fertility and for soil-improving purposes on poor soils. Usually they reseed themselves for several years if not harvested for seed. Sericea is used for cover crops on poor soils and is excellent for preventing soil erosion on road slopes. Seedings are always made in early spring, either broadcast or in close hills, using 20 to 25 lb of seed per acre. Fertilizers, especially phosphates, are essential.

SWEET CLOVER (***Melilotus***)

The sweet clovers are upright plants. The leaflets are linear oval, and the flowers are yellow or white. There are three species of clover of agricultural importance: white (*Melilotus alba*), yellow (*M. officinalis*), and sour clover (*M. indica*). The white and yellow species are principally

Fig. 2.12 Common lespedeza. (*USDA.*)

biennial; sour clover is a winter annual. Sweet clover will make good growth in regions where the effective rainfall is 17 in. or more if the soil reaction is neutral or if limestone and other minerals are applied. After a stand is established, sweet clover is more tolerant of summer drought than other legumes. Sweet clover is valuable for hay crops and grazing and for maintaining soil productivity.

The True Clovers (*Trifolium genus*)

The clovers are perennial or annual, and in general thrive in a cool, moist climate on soils where there is an available supply of phosphorus, potassium, and calcium. There are wide differences in growth habit, flowering, and reproduction. Red clover, alsike clover, and crimson clover form crowns; zigzag and kura clovers produce underground rootstocks. White and strawberry clovers spread by creeping stems that

Fig. 2.13 White sweet clover (*left*); **red clover** (*center*); **hairy vetch** (*right*). (*USDA.*)

root at the nodes. Subclover is decumbent, with stems lying on the soil, and Hungarian clover produces stiff, woody stems. The flowers of all species are borne on heads, the number of flowers varying from as low as 5 in subclover, to as many as 200 per head in red and white clovers. The number of seeds per pod varies from one to eight, depending upon the species.

There are eight species of clover that are of agricultural importance:

Red clover (*Trifolium pratense*) is an upright perennial and is composed of two forms, medium red (or double) cut and mammoth (or single) cut.

White clover (*T. repens*), a decumbent perennial, is composed of three general types, large, intermediate, and small. Ladino represents the large type, Louisiana white and New Zealand the intermediate, and English wild white and New York wild white the small type. Common white clover, often called white Dutch clover, is of the intermediate or small type, or a mixture of the two. It is one of the most important pasture plants and is also used extensively in lawns.

Crimson clover (*T. incarnatum*), an upright winter annual, is used for hay, pasture, and soil improvement.

Alsike clover (*T. hybridum*) is an upright perennial, suitable for wet soils and used for hay and pasture.

Small hop clover (*T. procumbens*), a winter annual, is tolerant of unfavorable soils and climatic conditions.

Strawberry clover (*T. fragiferum*) is a perennial, adapted to low-lying, wet soils and tolerant of soil salinity.

Persian clover (*T. resupinatum*) is a winter annual, best suited to the heavy, low-lying soils of the south. It is valuable for pasture and hay.

Subclover (*T. subterraneum*), used mainly for grazing, is decumbent. It is a winter annual adapted to the Pacific Northwest.

Vetch (*Vicia*)

The vetches are weak-stemmed or semivining plants. The leaves are semivining, terminating in tendrils. The flowers are light to dark lavender, with few or many in a raceme. The pods are linear, never inflated, and burst open readily when ripe.

Hairy vetch has about 18,000 seeds per pound, and common vetch has about 8000 seeds per pound. Nearly all species weigh 60 lb/bushel. Vetches require a cool climate for the best development. In regions with mild winters, they are planted in the fall; in regions with cold winters, however, they must be planted in the spring. Hairy vetch is the most winter-hardy and is best adapted on sandy or sandy-loam soils.

CROWN VETCH (*Coronilla varia*)

Crown vetch is an ideal plant for many purposes—soil improvement, weed control, erosion control, and general conservation. It is a legume and a strong, deep-rooted perennial. It grows on a wide variety of soils and seems to thrive under conditions of moderate acidity and alkalinity. It is capable of weathering droughts and hard winters. During June and July it is a mass of pinkish-white flowers. Crown vetch may be seeded or planted as crowns. It is a slow starter, taking approximately 2 to 3 years to become established. As a result it is best to seed it in combination with other grasses, such as alta fescue, the perennial ryegrasses, or both. Within a few years all other grasses and weeds will have been eliminated. Since crown vetch should never be mowed or it will disappear, it is economically attractive from a maintenance standpoint. Its uniform height and dense growing habit are always pleasing wherever planted. It is ideal for steep road slopes.

Lawn Mixtures

The common lawn mixtures usually found in the commercial seed houses are not recommended for establishing good lawns. Many of these mixtures contain lawn grasses which are not adapted to the region or which are added to cheapen the product, e.g., redtop, timothy, and Italian and perennial ryegrasses. In general, these have a much more vigorous early growth, particularly the ryegrasses, than the adapted grasses, and thus offer a mowing problem soon after seeding and before the grasses are established. If not mowed regularly, they will smother and shade out the desired grasses and make reseeding necessary. Filler species are not necessary for the establishment of good turf if proper lawn fertilization is followed.

If a lawn mixture is desired, equal parts of Kentucky bluegrass and creeping red fescue strains are recommended. To improve this mixture, add a small quantity of the Merion bluegrass strain. Any of the three grasses will nearly always make a much more desirable lawn or turf if seeded alone and properly cared for, however. White Dutch clover may also be added, if desired, and is most compatible with bluegrass. After the desired lawn grass has been established, the white clover can be killed by spraying it with 2,4-D. However, white clover usually disappears in well-drained situations.

Combination Turf

Two types of grass are often planted together in the hope of producing a lawn with the best qualities of each. One such combination, Meyer zoysia and Merion bluegrass, is designed to provide a relatively weed-free, disease-resistant turf which will remain green all the year round.

Meyer zoysia is a warm-season grass which makes its maximum growth during the hot summer months, while Merion bluegrass grows during the cool spring and fall. The Merion bluegrass is green during the winter when the Meyer zoysia has lost its color.

Both grasses are drought-tolerant and resistant to diseases and insects. Compared with Kentucky bluegrass, Merion bluegrass is more resistant to helminthosporium leaf spot and has a better appearance. It resists drought better than common bluegrass.

Under good management, Meyer zoysia will withstand wear and resist weeds, but because it cannot be reproduced from seed, vegetative material must be used for planting and the grass is slow to spread.

The combination of Meyer zoysia and Merion bluegrass is best adapted to the triangular area defined by Philadelphia, St. Louis, and Norfolk. Climatic conditions limit the growth of Meyer zoysia north of this area and of Merion bluegrass south of it.

ESTABLISHMENT OF COMBINATION TURF

In a new lawn, the Meyer zoysia should be established before the Merion bluegrass. A well-prepared, weed-free seedbed is desirable; 2-in. plugs of Meyer zoysia planted 1 ft apart will produce a solid turf in approximately 2 years. Sprigs of Meyer zoysia planted in solid rows, 1 ft between rows, will produce a solid turf in 2 to 3 years. Planting of Meyer zoysia should be done between May 1 and Aug. 1.

The Merion bluegrass may be overseeded into the lawn the first fall following spring or summer planting of the Meyer zoysia sprigs or plugs. Merion bluegrass should be seeded at a rate of 2 lb per 1000 ft^2. Care should be taken to distribute the seed evenly over the entire area.

If it is desirable to plant into an existing turf, the Meyer zoysia may be plugged as described above, without the seedbed preparation. Merion bluegrass may then be seeded into the existing turf during any subsequent fall.

During the first year of establishment of Meyer zoysia, light applications of fertilizer should be made every month from April to October (the active growing season). After the combination turf has been established, it should be fertilized spring and fall with 30 lb of 5-10-5 or similar fertilizer per 1000 ft^2. In addition, for good maintenance it would be desirable to apply 25 lb of an organic fertilizer per 1000 ft^2 during the summer.

Unless the soil is extremely acid, 75 lb of ground limestone per 1000 ft^2 applied every 3 years will maintain a desirable reaction.

Meyer zoysia should be watered at 3- to 4-day intervals until established. When Merion bluegrass is being overseeded, the area should be kept moist until the seed has germinated and become established. Established combination turf should be watered very infrequently, but sufficient water should be applied each time to wet the soil to a depth of 6 in. Frequent shallow watering should be avoided.

Combination turf should be mowed at a height of approximately ½ in. during the spring and fall and 1 in. during the summer.

Dates and Rates of Seeding

The best seeding results in regions II and I(a) are obtained in the mild period beginning in the fall, when night temperatures are ideal (38 to 60°F), (Table 2.2). Day temperatures of 75 to 80°F are optimum, but warmer days will not harm germination if night temperatures are low.

TABLE 2.2
Rates and Times of Seeding

Grass	Lb of seed per 1,000 sq ft	Fall seeding	Spring seeding
Kentucky bluegrass	2–3 (not over 5)	Aug. 1 – Oct. 1	Feb. 15 – March 15
Creeping red fescue	3–5	Aug. 1 – Oct. 1	Feb. 15 – March 15
Chewings fescue	3–5	Aug. 1 – Oct. 1	Feb. 15 – March 15
Colonial bentgrass	2–4	Aug. 1 – Oct. 1	Feb. 15 – March 15
Creeping bentgrass	1–2	Aug. 1 – Oct. 1	Feb. 15 – March 15
Orchardgrass	1–2	Aug. 1 – Oct. 1	Feb. 15 – March 15
Redtop mixture *	2–4	Aug. 1 – Oct. 1	Feb. 15 – March 15
Alta fescue	1–2	Aug. 1 – Oct. 1	Feb. 15 – March 15
Kentucky 31	1–2	Aug. 1 – Oct. 1	Feb. 15 – March 15
Bermuda (hulled seed)	2	———	May 1 – July 1
Ryegrass	1–2	Aug. 1 – Nov. 15	May 1 – July 1

* Spring seeding can be extended to June 15 in many Northern states. Along the Canadian border successful seedings have been done all summer long.

These mild temperatures should prevail over a period of from 3 weeks to 3 months of Midsouth winters before the May heat. Winter injury is less harmful to good cover than May and June temperatures are to young seedlings. Seedings made in August and September enjoy the longest periods of correct conditions. It is important that seedings not be made later than mid-October, since early cold snaps in late November and December may cause the seedlings to be heaved out of the ground. This condition will apply only to temperate climates and not to northern climates. In regions II and III and southern portions of IV, late seedings, after Mar. 15, invariably run into dry weather in May and June, making excessive watering necessary. In regions I(a) and I(b) and northern parts of IV seedings may be extended as late as June 15 and under good weather conditions could be extended through the summer. February and March seedings afford the desired temperatures, but usually there is not enough time for the seedlings to obtain a sufficient depth of root or dense enough cover to meet the drying atmosphere, high temperatures, and poor distribution of rainfall in May and June. Sometimes not even watering will prevent failure.

In seeding with Bermuda, the problem is entirely different. This species requires high temperatures, is normally drought-resistant, and will respond to watering and mulching.

In sowing grass seed either by hand or by machine, the seed should be divided into two equal parts. The second half should be distributed at right angles to the first sowing. Lightly rake or cultipack in order to cover the seed no deeper than ¼ in. and then mulch.

HYDRO SEEDER

An improvement over the above method is the hydro seeder. This equipment is principally a tank mounted on a truck, in which is mixed a slurry consisting of 1000 gal water mixed with 1 ton fertilizer and from 200 to 300 lb seed. The slurry is kept in motion by an agitator. This mixture will cover approximately 2 acres. Connected to the tank truck, but as a separate unit, are the pumping unit and nozzle tower. The tower permits a 360° swing and a 90° vertical travel, and the pump will force the slurry a distance of 100 ft. For fast, economical seeding and fertilizing of slopes, ditches, shoulders, and large open areas, this method is unsurpassed. If it is combined with use of the mulch spreader, the entire operation of liming, fertilizing, seeding, mulching, and anchoring the mulch can be done in two operations.

Mulching and Rolling

Failures of new seedings are minimized if a good small-grain straw is applied over the seeding. This mulching provides protection from low and high temperatures and slows evaporation. It should be applied at the rate of 2 tons/acre, or about one bale per 1000 ft^2, to give a ¼-in. cover. For the best results the seeded area should be rolled after the mulch has been applied. On large areas, a cultipacker may be used both to roll and to press the straw into the ground. Mulch on steep banks should be held in place with brush or chicken wire. A newly seeded area should be thoroughly watered daily until the grass is well established. Mulch should not be removed but allowed to rot in place. If large numbers of leaves fall on the newly seeded area they must be removed if the grass is to survive, but only a bamboo or flexible steel rake should be used and as much of the straw as possible should be left.

Since mulching of newly seeded areas has become an absolute must in most regions, more economical means of spreading the mulch have had to be found. One such means is the mulch spreader,* a machine equipped with a chute into which bales of hay or straw are fed. The straw is forced into a hopper, where it is beaten apart and blown by a powerful fan into a discharge tube. The straw emerging from the end of the discharge tube is distributed evenly over the ground, with a minimum of bunching. To hold the mulch in place on the ground, asphalt can be applied by means of three jets at the end of the discharge tube, which are connected to a drum of asphalt mounted on the side of the machine. The operator can control the amount of asphalt discharged by means of a lever on the discharge tube. As the straw is being discharged, just enough asphalt adheres to it to make the straw form a mat on the ground. Approximately 100 gal of asphalt per acre is required to do an effective holding job on mulch spread at the rate of 2 tons/acre. Normally the mulch can be blown to a distance of 50 to 75 ft effectively.

The practical application of the above method of tacking mulch simultaneously with the spreading operation has not proved successful. This method has inherent dangers of drifting molecules of the asphalt damaging passing automobiles, neighboring houses, etc. The system has been modified in some instances by separating the operations into two parts: (1) spreading the mulch and (2) tacking it down with asphalt. This permits a more concentrated and accurate spray, thereby minimizing the drift. An improvement on the straw-asphalt mulching process has been developed as follows.

WOOD-CELLULOSE FIBER MULCH

There are several wood-cellulose fiber mulches on the market today (Fig. 2.14). The principal advantage of using a wood-cellulose fiber mulch is its ease of application, its aesthetic qualities, savings in labor and time, and economical use of equipment. In general its use is about 80 per cent successful; the remaining 20 per cent poor results can be attributed to a combination of such factors as very light soils, sandy soils, drought, and excessively low or high fertility and liming rates.

The basic process in applying a wood-cellulose fiber mulch consists of adding the fiber to a slurry of seed, fertilizer, and water, which is then sprayed hydraulically to the seedbed. A typical slurry mixture contains 333 lb of wood-cellulose fiber, regular seed, and fertilizer specifications for ⅓ acre and the water to fill a 1200-gal tank of a hydro-

* The mulch spreader can be adapted to other uses, such as spreading lime, seed, fertilizer, sand, and topsoil. Any combination of seed, fertilizer, and lime can be blown onto the area to be seeded at an even rate by feeding through the jets from the tank of water, fertilizer, and seed. The water shows the operator where he has applied the mixture. From 35 to 150 lb of mixed seed and fertilizer can be applied per minute.

seeder. Fertilizers used are generally the regular commercial mixes or as specified as a result of soil tests. The wood-cellulose fiber is usually dyed green for visual metering of the application, which assures a more even distribution of fertilizer and grass seed. Full specifications for the use and application of the fiber mulch are available from the manufacturer.

Fig. 2.14 Conwed Hydro mulch. (*Conwed Corporation.*)

ADDITIONAL MULCHING MATERIALS

Other mulch materials have proved successful under special conditions. Mulch materials made from jute, aspen fibers, fiber glass, etc., are useful for erosion control for ski slopes or any steep slope exposed to heavy water or strong winds.

These mulches are made in the form of a netting, which is unrolled over a prepared seedbed and anchored to the ground securely with staples. This mulch material can be applied either before or after seeding and is equally successful if used in conjunction with ground-cover plantings. The preferred method is to apply the blanket after the area has been properly prepared, fertilized, and seeded or planted. In ditches the blankets should be applied in the direction of the flow of water and on slopes applied either horizontally or vertically to the slopes.

MAINTENANCE PRACTICES

Renovation becomes necessary when the turf is thin or weedy or the desired species of grass was not used in the beginning. Such areas can be brought back by following these suggestions:

1. Take soil samples for analysis 4 to 5 months in advance of the seeding date.
2. Destroy all weed growth. To accomplish this, it is best to mow closely and remove the clippings. The use of strong chemicals such as sodium arsenite to kill weeds is justified in a renovation program provided its effect on the soil is known and proper precautions are taken to safeguard other materials.
3. Apply lime as recommended by the analysis, preferably during the winter.
4. Late in February or early March or during moist periods in early fall or late summer, use an aerifying machine. These machines cut regularly and closely spaced holes in the ground and deposit the cylindrical plugs on the surface, where they may be left. Aerifying with a machine is practical only on large areas. For small lawns, a common spading fork or heavy spiked roller may be used. Use the fork by thrusting it into the sod and moving it back and forth. The forking should be done in rows the width of the fork. Aerifying sod permits water, fertilizer, and oxygen to reach the roots, where they will do the most good.
5. Apply the fertilizers recommended by the soil analysis. A nitrogen application should be made whether or not it is recommended by the soil analysis. Sodium nitrate or its equivalent can be applied at the rate of 140 to 200 lb/acre, or about 4 to 5 lb per 1000 ft.^{2}
6. Roll and water.

Shade Problems

It is usually impossible to obtain a good stand of grass under dense shade conditions. Magnolias, maples, and oaks, in particular, present conditions under which grass will not thrive unless some remedial measures are taken. Removing the lower branches up to 12 to 15 ft will increase the light intensity enough to satisfy the needs of shade-loving grasses. Selective thinning of the upper branches will also help. Grasses are very heavy feeders on nitrogen, and they respond in proportion to the amounts available in the soil. Where roots are close to the surface and the soil cover is thin and very deficient in nitrogen, a new soil should be applied to a depth of 6 in. After the new soil is fertilized, shade-adapted grasses can be sown.

GROUND COVERS FOR SHADE

Whenever it has been determined that grass will not grow under a particular shade condition, the following ground covers may be used:

1. English ivy (***Hedera helix***) may require some pruning to prevent excessive growth and matting. Baltic ivy is a lower-growing form and may be better suited than the commoner English form.
2. Common periwinkle (***Vinca minor***) is a hardy trailing evergreen plant with blue flowers and dark-green foliage.
3. Wintercreeper (***Euonymus fortunei***) is an evergreen plant and thrives in dense shade.
4. Canby pachistima (***Pachistima canbyi***) is a small-leafed evergreen with red berries which makes a matted mass about 6 to 8 in. high.
5. Japanese spurge (***Pachysandra terminalis***) is best adapted to soils of high organic content and dense shade conditions.

Care and Maintenance of Grass

The following suggestions for efficient watering of grass areas should be followed in order to maintain a green turf:

1. All watering should be done in the afternoon or at night. This enables the soil to absorb a maximum amount of water with a minimum of evaporation.
2. During drought periods, the only way to maintain a desirable greenness is to give the lawn a thorough soaking once or twice a week. Light daily sprinkling does more harm than good. As a general rule, it requires from 500 to 750 gal of water for every 1000 ft^2 of grass area to give an equivalent of $^3/_4$ to $1^1/_4$ in. of rain. This will moisten the soil to a depth of 3 to 5 in.

IRRIGATION

Many localities experience cycles of lower rainfall, especially during the summer months when sufficient water is essential to the proper development of turf, trees, and shrubs. Where an adequate supply of water is available from ponds or rivers, an irrigation system can be installed which will compensate for a lack of rainfall and more than pay for itself in better turf or in the preservation of newly planted trees or shrubs.

There are two general types of irrigation systems, surface and overhead. The surface irrigation system is usually associated with the flooding of land from irrigation ditches and the overhead system with the use of various types of sprinklers.

For parks, industrial property, or other lands maintained exclusively for public use, the sprinkler type of irrigation system is practical. Sprinkler irrigation may be as simple as a hose with one sprinkler attachment or a perforated hose or pipe, or it may be an engineered system of underground pipes with automatic pop-up sprinkler heads at regular intervals or a portable system using aluminum pipe on the surface of the ground with sprinkler heads spaced to provide adequate coverage. The portable system has become the most popular, principally because of its flexibility, ease of handling and moving, and a lower capital cost for installation. One man can lay and install 800 ft of aluminum pipe, connect the sprinkler heads, and begin watering within 30 minutes. Sprinkler heads are spaced every 20 ft and, depending upon the type of nozzle used and the pressure available, each sprinkler will cover an area from 60 to 100 ft in diameter. A system of this size will irrigate 1 to 2 acres at one setting and supply the equivalent of approximately 1 in. of rainfall in 3 hours' time.

More elaborate and costly systems can be installed which will provide pinpoint control in confined areas. These systems are usually installed underground with the sprinkler heads spaced to give complete coverage to one specific area. They are controlled from one valve. Such systems are ideal for turf areas in parking lots, road or highway islands, shrub beds, etc., where it is necessary to cover the grass or planted areas and to avoid pavements, cars, or buildings. Although the initial cost of installation is high, such systems usually save enough in cost of labor and water to pay for themselves. Labor is saved because there is no need to move individual sprinklers and hundreds of feet of hose from one location to another. Water is saved because sprinkler heads can be obtained to cover full circles, half circles, or quarter circles, and a properly designed system would therefore cover only the actual areas to be watered. Thousands of gallons of water can be wasted in a short time on unplanted areas like pavements and parking lots.

A variation of this same underground, automatic system—one much easier and less expensive to install—has been developed by several of the major rubber companies. This system utilizes the same principle of underground installations and flush sprinkler heads as the more elaborate systems but uses rubber which has been treated to withstand underground conditions. The system is installed just under the sod, making it a simple procedure to lift established sod, open a trench no deeper than 6 in., lay the hose in the trench, backfill, and tamp the sod into place over the finished system. A layout like this is ideal for confined areas between curbs, parking area islands and sections close to buildings, sidewalks, or paths where a controlled flow of water is desired.

TOPDRESSING

Every lawn or turf, to be successful, should be topdressed once a year. Topdressing helps to keep the grass level, helps prevent compaction,

TABLE 2.3
Volume of Topdressing Material Required for Applications to Various Depths*

Depth of topdressing required, in.	Approximate volume of material needed for:									
	1000 ft²		3000 ft²		5000 ft²		7000 ft²		10,000 ft²	
	ft³	yd³	ft³	yd³	ft³	yd³	ft³	yd³	ft³	yd³
1/8	10.4	0.4	31.2	1.2	52.0	1.9	72.8	2.7	104.0	3.9
1/4	20.8	0.8	62.4	2.3	104.0	3.9	145.6	5.4	208.0	7.7
3/8	31.2	1.2	93.6	3.5	156.0	5.8	218.4	8.1	312.0	11.6
1/2	41.7	1.5	125.1	4.6	208.5	7.7	291.9	10.8	417.0	15.4
5/8	52.1	1.9	156.3	5.8	260.5	9.6	364.7	13.5	521.0	19.3
3/4	62.5	2.3	187.5	6.9	312.5	11.6	437.5	16.2	625.0	23.1

* From H. Burton Musser, "Turf Management," rev. ed. Copyright McGraw-Hill Book Company, 1962. Used by permission.

and promotes good root growth. Topdressing material may be a very loose, pliable topsoil, sand, or a well-shredded compost of organic materials. Before it is used, all topdressing material should be treated with chemicals to kill insects, diseases, and weeds. See Table 2.3.

MOWING

One of the major reasons for failures in turf is close clipping. It is important that the mower be set not closer than 1½ in., and preferably 2 in. This is the minimum height which supplies enough leaf surface to build the plant foods needed for vigorous root development. Lower clipping will starve the roots, and the turf will thin out, giving poor cover and allowing room for invasion of low-growing weedy species. Such turf is shallow and weak-rooted and is baked by hot daytime temperatures. The only grasses which can withstand close clipping are the bent grasses, the Bermudas, and the zoysias. They require a constant good moisture condition and heavy and continuous fertilization.

Rake the leaves or chop them up with a leaf grinder in the fall to prevent matting and consequent smothering of evergreen turf grasses.

AERIFYING GRASS AREAS

Aerification of turf and grass lands has been standard practice in England for many years. Here in the United States, interest in the aerification principle has increased rapidly in the last few decades. Today it is generally accepted practice for golf course and playfield maintenance.

The principle of aerification is to loosen and aerate the soil under the turf without disturbing the turf surface. Aerification is necessary because rainfall, artificial watering, and traffic by people and maintenance equipment all tend to compact the soil. When the soil is compacted, water, air, and plant foods cannot penetrate and grass becomes shallow-rooted. The resulting shallow-rooted turf will not stand up during hot, dry weather. Frequent watering, which becomes necessary under such conditions, increases the disease and weed problem.

The frequency of aerification will vary with the type of soil, the turf-grass area, and the amount of use or traffic to which the area is exposed. On golf course greens thorough aerification is done in spring and fall. The ¼-in. spoon is now available and should be used during the hot summer months, when slight opening of soil on greens will permit freer movement of cooling air and of water. On athletic fields, and other hard-use areas, aerification once a month is recommended by many of the turf-grass authorities. When aerification is done during hot, dry weather, immediate and thorough watering is recommended.

Soil compaction is not the only condition improved by aerifying. Established turf will form a thatch of dry roots and stems at the surface, preventing water, air, and fertilizer from penetrating into the soil. Aerification will break through this thatch so that air, water, and fertilizer can get into the soil. In time, regular aerification will help to break down thatch and cause it to decay more rapidly. Vertical mowing, combined with aerification, will improve the surface and the soil. With the introduction of the Verti-cut mower by West Point Products Corporation, the combination of Verti-cutting and aerifying has become standard procedure on most golf courses.

Aerifying can also be used successfully for preparing a seedbed in existing turf. The soil brought to the surface forms a light topdressing to cover the seed. When the surface soil and dry plant material are broken through, seed will come in contact with the soil and germinate. Where grass is sprigged, the stolons can be planted into the aerifier holes. The aerifier loosens soil by actual removal of soil cores. It is equipped with hollow spoons that are curved at a 15° angle so they enter and leave the soil without tearing the turf. Two types of spoons are used on the aerifier, open and thatch spoons. The open spoon scoops out a core of soil and brings it to the surface, leaving a loose-walled cavity in which roots can expand freely. The thatch spoon is used where it is necessary to cut through a thick layer of surface material. Since only the tip of the spoon is closed, the problem of clogging is minimized. Spoon sizes range from 1/4 to 1 in., and all spoons are interchangeable on the various aerifier units. For golf course greens, 1/2-in. open or 1/2-in. thatch spoons are used for regular aerification as outlined above, but the 1/4- and 3/4-in. thatch spoons are recommended for fairways. Where a thatch condition exists or fairway grasses are shallow-rooted, aerifiers should be equipped with the 3/4-in. thatch spoon. For lawns, athletic fields, and other comparable areas, the 1- or 3/4-in. spoon is used.

Proper aerification of grass will reduce maintenance cost. Watering can be cut in half, and less fertilizer and seed is wasted due to runoff; in addition, the turf will be stronger and better able to stand hard usage, disease, and drought. In the simplest terms, aerification will do four things:

1. Make the soil porous and the turf springy
2. Allow air, moisture, and fertilizer to get to the roots
3. Increase growth rapidly, particularly when fertilizer is applied while cavities are still open
4. Prepare a good seedbed without destroying existing turf

USE OF GRASS BARRIERS

One method of ensuring neat and even edges to shrub beds, around specimen trees, and along walks, driveways, and roads is to install a steel barrier. This barrier helps avoid several maintenance problems:

1. It prevents damaging trees with mowing equipment.
2. It keeps grass from encroaching upon paths and roadways.
3. It maintains an even, smooth edge to grass areas.
4. It retains mulch.

5. It keeps Bermuda and zoysia grasses from encroaching on shrub or floral beds.
6. It reduces hand trimming to a minimum.

These barriers, or curbs, can be made in the maintenance shop from scrap metal, or they can be purchased ready-made. The metal used should be approximately 12-gage galvanized steel, flexible enough so

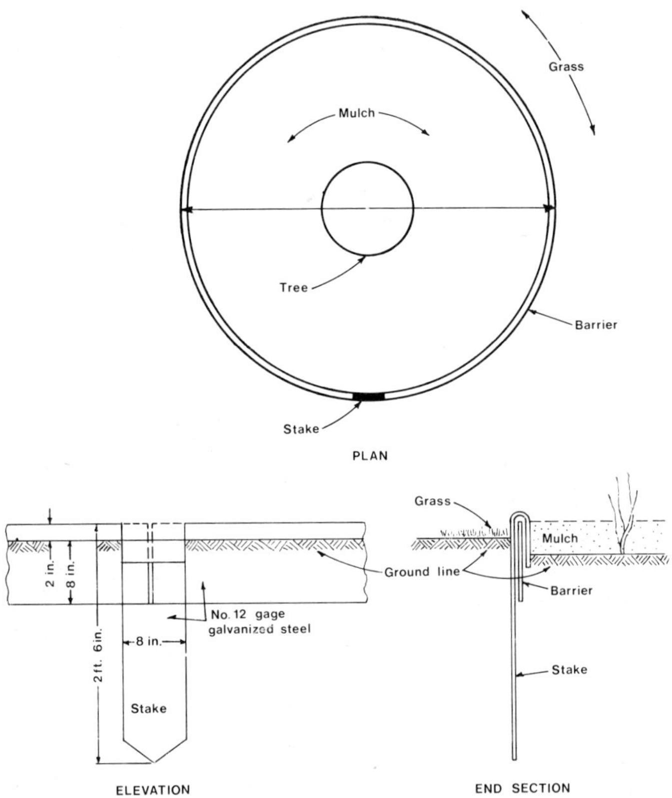

Fig. 2.15 Grass barrier for specimen trees.

that it can be curved. The curbs should be cut to a minimum width of 10 in. and driven into the ground 8 in.; in hard or rocky ground it may be necessary to dig a trench. A good way to set the proper curve or alignment around a shrub bed is to place a flexible hose on the ground in the line desired, mark the ground with a pick, and begin placing the curb. Along roads or parking areas a heavier metal should be used, approximately ¼-in. thick. The grass line is always to be flush with the top of the curb. This will prevent a tire from being cut if it should strike the curb. See Fig. 2.15.

Control of Pests and Diseases

Several turf pests and diseases are harmful to grass in varying degrees.

Leaf Spot A fungus disease known as leaf spot may appear where there is excess moisture. The spots begin as tiny brown specks scattered over the blades, and as they enlarge, they may extend right across the leaf, the center becoming straw-colored. The bordering area varies in color from dark brown to black. The best way to combat the disease is to follow cultural practices that will encourage a strong growth of grass. Higher clipping is also advisable.

Brown Patch The fungus disease known as brown patch causes much grass to turn brown during the summer months. Attacks of brown patch usually come during periods of hot, humid weather, when grass is in a weakened condition. A peculiarity of this disease is that the attack is usually in definite patches which are roughly circular in outline. Part of the grass within the circle usually escapes injury. The disease is worse in turf that is overfertilized; or where the soil is very acid. It can be controlled by applications of mercurical fungicides. Commercial fungicides include such brand names as Calo-clor, Semesan, Nu-Green, and Curex. A mixture of two parts calomel and one part corrosive sublimate can also be used. This should be applied at the rate of 2 or 3 oz per 1000 ft^2, as a spray or mixed with soil.

Dollar Spot Another fungus disease is dollar spot. The most noticeable characteristic is the size of the injured spots, usually limited to a diameter of 2 in. The affected turf presents a moth-eaten appearance, and the leaves are more bleached than after an attack of brown patch. Control measures are the same as for brown patch.

Mildew At times a stand of grass suddenly appears to have been dusted with flour. This is caused by powdery mildew, which resembles the mold that grows on old shoes left in damp places. If the mildew is wiped off the surface, it will usually be found that the grass blade is green and uninjured. Fortunately, mildew causes little real injury and soon disappears.

Damping-off When seedling turf is spotted with dead patches varying in diameter from 1 in. to several inches, it is likely that damping-off has occurred. Sometimes this fungus disease kills the sprouts before they emerge from the ground, making it appear that the seed failed to germinate. At other times the disease comes after the grass is well started. The young grass turns black at first and then withers and turns brown. Damping-off is often responsible for a spotted growth of young grass where parts of the lawn have a good stand and other patches show no grass at all. The growth of damping-off is favored by an ample supply of water near the surface of the ground and an oversupply of fertilizer. After an attack, there is nothing to do but let the fungus spend itself and then repair the damage by reseeding.

Bluegrass Leaf Spot During periods of wet weather, leaf spot may attack bluegrass. The grass blades show purple spots that enlarge and turn straw-colored with purple borders. A spot may girdle the leaf, kill the tip and destroy the entire blade. In severe attacks the bluegrass turf becomes thin and weak and therefore open to invasion by summer weeds. High mowing and adequate fertilization decrease the damage from leaf spot. Merion bluegrass is less susceptible to injury by leaf spot than the Kentucky bluegrass.

Melting Out In the spring, and until hot weather arrives, bluegrass, fescues, and bents may be attacked by melting out. The diseased areas are smoky blue in color at first, later become yellow, and finally turn brown when the grass plants are killed. The injured areas are irregular, without any particular pattern.

Curvularia This fungus produces a disease sometimes called fading out because of its indefinite symptoms. The disease appears in the hot summer months, following the leaf spot and melting-out seasons. At first the lawn appears to be drying out, even when there is no lack of moisture. The turf turns pale green, then yellow, and may eventually die. The affected areas are without definite outline, and frequently bright green islands of healthy grass remain in the injured areas.

Leaf spot, melting out, and curvularia can be controlled by phenyl mercury compounds in liquid or dry form. Another treatment is cyclohexamide, an antibiotic sold under the trade name of Actidone. Grasses can be protected partially or completely from turf diseases if the grass blades are covered with one of these materials, either before the disease starts or in its very early stages.

Turf Pests

Mushrooms Both edible and inedible mushrooms often develop in turf, due to an excess of decaying organic matter. Regular mowing will give all the control needed, since they do no harm.

White Grubs There are two kinds of white grubs that attack turf. The most common is the larva of the green June beetle, easily distinguished by the fact that it crawls on its back. Other white grubs, usually smaller and shaped more like the letter U, are the larvae of the May beetle. These grubs eat the roots of grass and the sod, sometimes cutting roots so completely that heavily infested sod can be rolled back.

The larvae of the green June beetle damage the sod by boring holes in the ground and mounding the earth adjacent to each hole. They live upon decaying organic matter, and their damage is done while searching for food. They can be controlled by applying 5 lb of 10% gamma benzene hexachloride per acre, using fertilizer as a carrier. For example, if 50 lb of fertilizer per acre is desired, add 5 lb of insecticide to the fertilizer and spread. For small areas, use 2 oz of 10% gamma benzene hexachloride per 1000 ft^2 mixed with 20 oz of fertilizer.

The May beetle grub can be controlled by applying 25 lb of 40% chlordane* per acre. This application will give control for 5 or more years. It should be applied as evenly as possible and then washed into the sod. It will also control the green June beetle grub. For small areas, use ½ lb of chlordane solution (emulsion) or dust with 5% chlordane.

OTHER INSECTS

The Japanese beetle, sod webworm, cutworm, and chinch bug are other insects that injure grass in various parts of the country. They feed on the stem and leaves of the grass and not on the roots, as grubs do. Of these pests, only the chinch bugs are truly injurious. They cause yellowing or browning of the grass, usually in patches that gradually enlarge.

Chinch bugs are worst in thick turf and particularly in bent grasses. To find the tiny bugs, examine the turf closely at ground level. Some are red, but others are dark; they are about ⅛ in. long. Flood a small area with water and you will see the bugs struggling to the surface. To control chinch bugs use as specified in Table 2.4. A single chemicals application at the grub-proofing dosage is effective for at least 5 years.

Ants and earthworms are not actually damaging to turf, but the mounds they form can spoil the appearance of a good turf.

Japanese Beetle Control

GRUB-PROOFING METHODS

Grub-proofing may be done by using granulated insecticides in a fertilizer spreader, by wet spraying with a compressed air or a power sprayer, by hose-on sprayers, or by dusting.

* New restrictions have been placed on the use of "chlordane" and other insecticides by the EPA. Check the local health authorities for the latest information; see also Chapter 6.

TABLE 2.4

Lawn Pests and Insecticides to Use in Controlling Them[a]

Insecticide and formulation	Dosage of formulation per 1000 ft²						
	Grubs and ants[b]	Sod webworms, wireworms, cicada killer wasp, and wild bees[c]	Chinch bugs and false chinch bugs[d]	Armyworms, cutworms, and mole crickets[e]	Earwigs, fiery skipper, and lucerne moth[f]	Chiggers, fleas, and ticks	Leafhoppers, leaf bug, and mites[g]
Granules:							
Carbaryl, 10%		2 lb	2 lb				
Chlordane, 5%	5 lb	2½ lb		2½ lb	2 lb		
Diazinon, 10%		2 lb	2 lb				
Ethion, 5%			5 lb				
Sprays:							
Wettable powders:							
Carbaryl, 50%		8 oz	8 oz	8 oz	12 oz	8 oz	8 oz
Chlordane, 40%	10 oz	5 oz		5 oz	4 oz	2 oz	2 oz
Diazinon, 50%		4 oz	6 oz	4 oz		1¼ oz	1¼ oz
Ethion, 25%			12 oz				
Emulsifiable concentrates:							
Chlordane, 75% (8 lb/gal)	4 fl oz	2 fl oz		2 fl oz	1½ fl oz	½ fl oz	1 fl oz
Diazinon, 4 lb/gal		4 fl oz	6 fl oz	4 fl oz		1¼ fl oz	1¼ fl oz
Ethion, 4 lb/gal			8 fl oz				
Malathion, 5 lb/gal						5 fl oz	1 fl oz
Nemacide, 8 lb/gal			12 fl oz				

[a] Reprinted from Lawn Insects: How to Control Them, *USDA Home Gard. Bull.* 53, rev. September 1971, by permission of the USDA.

[b] In hot, dry areas, lower dosages may be necessary to prevent burning the grass; consult your state agricultural experiment station. If only a few ant nests are present, treat them individually. Wash the insecticide into the nests or drench the mounds with it. Special treatment is required to control fire and harvester ants; consult your state agricultural experiment station for latest recommendations.

[c] To control sod webworms, apply the insecticide in late afternoon or evening and delay watering until the following morning. To control wireworms, the cicada killer wasp, and wild bees, apply chlordane. To eliminate a nest of the wasp, pour or spray the insecticide into the nest after dark and seal the entrance with dirt.

[d] A preventive spray program to control chinch bugs in the South requires treatment about every 6 weeks.

[e] To control cutworms, apply the insecticide in late afternoon.

[f] A ready-mixed bait is also effective against earwigs. Follow the directions on the container. Apply the bait in the evening. To control the fiery skipper and lucerne moth, apply chlordane.

[g] To control leafhoppers, apply carbaryl or Malathion. To control the leaf bug and mites, apply Malathion. To control the eriophyid mite, apply diazinon.

Granulated Insecticides To use granulated insecticides in a fertilizer spreader, adjust the spreader by weighing the amount run out over a known area of ground. Put in a weighed amount of granulated insecticide, spread over 100 ft^2, and weigh what is left in the spreader. The difference between the two weighings multiplied by 10 gives the rate per 1000 $ft.^2$ Most common fertilizer spreaders will require an aperture less than one-fourth open.

Wet Spraying Grub-proofing can also be done by wet spraying. This is the most satisfactory way to control chinch bugs, sod webworms, cutworms, and ants. Mix the insecticide thoroughly with 20 gal of water per 1000 ft^2 and spray the turf thoroughly and evenly.

Dusting This is a poor way of grub-proofing the turf but a very good way to treat smaller spots damaged by chinch bugs, sod webworms, cutworms, or ants. Dust the area thoroughly with a 5% chlordane dust. For occasional anthills, place a teaspoon of 5% chlordane dust in and around each hill.

For large areas, large power sprayer equipment should be used. It is safe to use insecticides recommended for turf-insect control with fertilizers or with 2,4-D weed killers. For dry application it is a good idea to mix fertilizers with the insecticides. Do not use hydrated lime with insecticides; use ground limestone instead.

Precautions Do not allow children or pets to walk or play on recently treated grass; water in all treatments with a hose or regular sprinkler system.

Moles To control moles, first roll down or otherwise flatten the tunnels and for the next day or so determine which of the tunnels are open again. This indicates where the animals are working. Then in the newly opened tunnel apply a poison bait every few feet. A teaspoon of flaked naphthalene or two or three moth balls may also be used. Control can be expected only gradually.

Japanese Beetle Grub Control

Lawns, golf courses, and ungrazed grassy areas can be protected from injury by the Japanese beetle grub for 8 to 9 years by topdressing once with chlordane. Apply it at 2 oz active ingredient per 1000 ft^2, or $5\frac{1}{2}$ lb/acre. Water thoroughly after application. Allow to dry before people or pets are allowed on the turf.

Emulsifiable concentrates or wettable powders mixed with water may be substituted for the dry application. On large grassy areas, e.g., golf courses, these formulations can be applied as a coarse spray by means of a boom attached to a sprayer or with a hose and nozzle at the rate of 25 gal per 1000 ft^2 or 1000 gal/acre.

Chlordane may be applied any time the ground is not frozen.

Grubs of the Japanese beetle can be controlled by applying a dust containing spores of the milky disease. However, the disease may require several years to spread and reduce beetle populations appreciably. In general the spore dust should not be applied to soil that has been treated with an insecticide. Although the insecticide does not harm the disease spores, it reduces the grub population and thereby greatly

TABLE 2.5
Guide for Mixing Sprays for Fruits, Vegetables, and Ornamentals*

Common formulation (purchased product)	Amount of insecticide to mix with: 1 gal water	10 gal water
Carbaryl,†		
50% wettable powder	1½ tbsp	3 oz
Malathion,		
57% emulsifiable concentrate	1 tsp	1½ fl oz
Methoxychlor:		
50% wettable powder	3 tbsp	5 oz
25% emulsifiable concentrate	6 tsp	9 fl oz

* Do not exceed 1 qt of spray per 50 ft of row or 1 qt per 125 ft^2 for vegetables and berries; do not exceed 15 to 20 gal per tree for fruit trees.

† Use of carbaryl may also provide treatment for aphids and mites.

lowers the chances of establishment and spread of the disease. Spore-dust powder can be purchased. Apply it when the ground is not frozen. Follow directions on the label. See Table 2.6 for other chemical control of turf diseases.

PASTURES

Many public grounds have open grass areas which are suitable for development as pastures. Generally speaking, a program of land and grass improvement should be established along the following lines:

1. Remove trees and brush except those needed for shade. Put land in good shape for mowing and keep sprouts cut back to starve out root system.

2. Leave shade trees on high and poorer areas.
3. Provide watering places and plan them so that livestock cannot crowd around and be a source of disease. Do not have shade trees around watering places.
4. On poor soils and old croplands, plant a crop of winter legumes before seeding to pasture.

TABLE 2.6
Turf Control Chemicals

Disease	Chemical treatment
Brown patch	Dyrene turf fungicide, Calo-clor, Semesan, Nu-Green
Dollar spot	Dyrene turf fungicide, Calo-clor, Semesan, Nu-Green
Leaf spot	Dyrene turf fungicide, Calo-clor, Semesan, Nu-Green
Melting out	Dyrene turf fungicide, Calo-clor, Semesan, Nu-Green
Snow mold	Dyrene turf fungicide, Calo-clor, Semesan, Nu-Green
Copper spot	Dyrene turf fungicide, Calo-clor, Semesan, Nu-Green
Cottony blight	Dexon turf and soil fungicide
Chewing insects:	
Webworms	Baygon, Dylox
Chinch bugs	Dasanit, chlordane
Cutworms	Dasanit, chlordane
Army worms	Dasanit, chlordane
Ants	Dasanit, chlordane
Japanese beetle	Dasanit, chlordane
Asiatic beetle	Dasanit, chlordane
Oriental beetle	Dasanit, chlordane
May and June beetles	Dasanit, chlordane
Nematodes	Dasanit

5. Land preparation: break land several weeks before time to seed. Harrow and disc to form a good firm seed-bed. For August and September seeding, break in June or early July and fallow until seeding time. For spring seeding, break land in November and December.
6. Fertilization and liming: take a soil analysis to determine the kind and amount of fertilizer to use. Also determine the reading of the soil and add lime accordingly.
7. Disc fertilizer and lime into a soil a week or 10 days before time to seed.
8. Selecting the right grasses to grow is important. Choose

the grasses best adapted to your locality. Consult the local extension service or the county agent's office.

9. For rates of seeding for most commonly used pasture grasses see Table 2.7.

TABLE 2.7
Rates of Seeding for Most Commonly Used Pasture Grasses

Grass	Lb per acre in mixtures	Lb per acre alone
Ladino	3 – 5	—
Kentucky bluegrass	5 – 10	14
Orchard grass	10	25
Kentucky 31	10 – 15	25
Alta fescue	10 – 15	25
Louisiana white clover	1 – 2	—

10. Time to seed: Fall seeding should be made after the first good rain in August and not later than Sept. 15. Spring should be made between Mar. 1 and Apr. 1, weather permitting.
11. How to seed: freshen the seedbed with a section harrow or weeder. Divide the seed into equal parts and cross-sow to get even distribution.
12. Covering: cover seeds about ¼ in. on heavier soils and about ½ in. on sandy soils. A corrugated roller with seeder attachment will do the job in one operation.
13. Mow at least twice annually, to control weeds and sprouts.

Management of Pastures

1. Do not graze newly seeded pastures until plants are well established and will not be pulled up by grazing animals.
2. Do not overgraze. Manage grazing so the pasture is never grazed closer than 3 in. Seven acres of pasture per head for a 5-month grazing period is generally considered desirable.
3. To eradicate weeds, mow two or three times a year before seeds form. Keep top growth cut back to starve out root systems. Sprouts must be kept cut during the growing season. Some sprouts may be controlled by chemicals or burning.
4. Bermuda pasture: disc or plow it every year or two and fertilize. If Bermuda sod is not plowed or disced, it tends

to get sod-bound and unproductive. Annual lespedeza may also be sown in the fall for some winter pasture.

5. Do not undergraze. Undergrazing will tend to lower pasture quality because it allows less desirable plants to mature and seed.
6. Winter pastures may be established on old pastures, wherever desired, by the following methods:
   a. Make soil test and fertilize accordingly. Lightly disc after fertilization.
   b. Seed 25 lb crimson clover and 25 lb Italian ryegrass per acre. Make seeding in September or early October.
   c. Begin grazing when plants are 3 in. high.

REHABILITATION OF BORROW AREAS

Major construction often requires that large areas of land be used for borrow-pit and storage-yard purposes. Unfortunately, these areas cannot always be hidden from roads or public places. Two methods of soil improvement have been developed which are rather similar, but one requires a longer time. For lasting results, method 2 is preferable.

Method 1

1. Regrade the area to eliminate all erosion ditches. Provide adequate drainage, terrace (if the slope is steep), and shape the borrow into a smooth rolling terrain devoid of all sharp cuts and frills.
2. Break up subsoil as deeply as possible.
3. Mulch at least 6 in. deep with hay or sawdust. Use straw or hay mulch at rate of 10 tons/acre. If fresh sawdust is used, add 250 lb ammonium nitrate per acre.
4. Disc with a heavy disc, cutting mulch material into the soil and breaking up heavy clods. Remove all large rocks.
5. Make an acidity test and add lime as indicated if the pH reading is less than 6.5.
6. About 1 week or 10 days before seeding, make another soil test and fertilize as indicated.
7. Disc thoroughly in order to work the fertilizer and lime into the soil. Continue discing until a smooth seedbed is formed, free of all heavy clods and rocks.
8. All the above work should be done during early summer or early enough to permit the land to lie fallow before seeding time (Aug. 15 to Oct. 1).

TABLE 2.8
Characteristics, Seeding Rates, and Propagation of Turf Grasses

Common and scientific name	Cultivars	Major uses	Region	Purity, %	Germination, %	Seed per pound	Longevity*	Seeding rate for meadows and pastures, lb/acre	Seeding rate for lawns, lb/1000 ft²	Best seeding time	Type of material	Vegetative propagation		
												Method of planting	Quantity for 1000 ft²	Best planting time
Bermuda grass (*Cynodon dactylon*)	Ormond, Santa Ana, Tifdwarf, Tifway, Tifgreen, common	Fine lawns and golf greens; common seeded for general cover	II, III	97	85	1,787,000	1	6–8	1–2	Spring	Sprigs	In rows by hand or machine; sprigs 6 in. apart in 12-in. rows	5–10 ft² nursery sod	Warm humid spring, summer, and fall
Bent. colonial (*A. tenuis*)	Exeter, Highland, Holfior	Low-mowed turf especially in humid locations, irrigated golf fairways	I(a), I(b). IV	95	90	8,723,000	3	—	1–2	Fall, spring	Stolons	Broadcast on prepared seedbed	80–100 ft² nursery sod	Early fall
Creeping (*A. palustris*)	Penncross, Cohansey, Congressional, Toronto	Highly kept luxury turf, especially golf greens	I(a), I(b), IV	95	90	7,800,000	3	—	1–2	Fall, spring				
Velvet (*A. canina*)	None	—	I(a), I(b), IV	95	90	10,800,000	3	—	1–2	Fall, spring				

Bluegrass, Canada (*Poa compressa*)	None	Used in areas unfavorable to Kentucky bluegrass	I(a), I(b), IV	80	80	2,495,000	2	15–25	2–3	Fall, spring				
Kentucky (*P. pratensis*)	Arboretum, Arista, Baron, Fylking, Merion, Nugget, Pennstar, Prato, Sydsport	Lawns and athletic fields; best on good soils and moderately tended	I(a), I(b), IV	85	80	2,177,000	2	15–25	3–5	Fall, spring			
Carpet grass (*Axonopus affinis*)	None	Pastures and firebreaks	II, III	92	90	1,222,000	3	5–12		Spring, early summer			
Centipede grass (*Eremochloa ophiuroides*)	Oklawn	Minimum-care lawns	III, southern II	43	70	408,000	1	15–25	2–3	Spring	Sprigs	In rows by hand or machine	5–10 ft² of nursery sod	Spring, summer, fall
Dallis grass (*Paspalum dilatum*)	None	Used as a mix with legumes and other grass	All	70	70	220,000	1	8–20	–	Spring			
Fescue, Chewings (*Festuca rubra commutata*)	None	Lawn mixtures	I(a), I(b), northern IV	97	80	615,000	2	15–40	2–3	Fall, spring			
Creeping red (*F. rubra*)	Illhahee, Golfrood, Jamestown, Pennlawn, Ruby, Ranier, Highlight	In bluegrass mixtures, especially adapted to infertile, light soils and shade	I(a), I(b), northern IV	97	80	615,000	2	15–40	2–3	Fall, spring			

TABLE 2.8 (Continued)

Common and scientific name	Cultivars	Major uses	Region	Purity, %	Germination, %	Seed per pound	Longevity*	Seeding rate for meadows and pastures, lb/acre	Seeding rate for lawns, lb/1000 ft²	Best seeding time	Type of material	Vegetative propagation: Method of planting	Vegetative propagation: Quantity for 1000 ft²	Vegetative propagation: Best planting time
Meadow (*F. elatior*)	None	Pastures	I(a), I(b), northern IV	97	90	230,000	2	10–25	—	Fall, spring				
Sheep (*F. ovina*)	None	Makes a durable turf on sandy soils	I(a), I(b), northern IV	96	85	680,000	2	15–25	—	Fall, spring				
Tall (Kentucky 31 and Alta) (*F. arundinacea*)	None	Deep-rooted, drought-resistant grass	I(a), I(b), northern IV	95	90	500,000	2	15–25	3–5	Fall, spring				
Manila grass (*Zoysia matrella*)	None	Lawns, athletic fields	II, III, and southern I(a) and IV	97	50	681,000	2	—	Vegetative	Spring, summer	2-in. sod blocks, sprigs	Sod, blocks set 12-in. on center; sprigs 6–12 in. apart in 12-in. rows or broadcast on prepared seedbed	Sod, block 30 ft²; sprigs, 3–6 ft² of nursery sod	Early summer
Mascarene grass (*Z. tenuifolia*)	None	Lawns, golf fairways	II, III, and southern I(a) and IV	—	—	—	—	—	Vegetative	Spring, summer	Blocks, sprigs	Sod, blocks set 12-in. on center; sprigs 6–12 in. apart in 12-in. rows or broadcast on prepared seedbed	Sod, block 30 ft²; sprigs, 3–6 ft² of nursery sod	Early summer

Japanese lawn grass (*Z. japanica*)	Meyer, Emerald	Lawns, athletic fields, golf greens	II, III, and southern I(a) and IV	—	24	1,300,000	2	—	Vegetative	Spring, summer	Blocks, sprigs	Sod, blocks set 12-in. on center; sprigs 6–12 in. apart in 12-in. rows or broadcast on prepared seedbed	Sod, block 30 ft²; sprigs, 3–6 ft² of nursery sod	Early summer
Orchard grass (*Dactylis glomerata*)	None	Pastures, orchards	All	85	85	654,000	1	6–15	—	Spring, early fall				
Red top (*Agrostis alba*)	None	Pasture, mixtures in humid conditions	All	92	90	4,990,000	1	5–10	1–2	Fall, spring				
Ryegrass, Italian (*Lolium multiflorum*)	None	Quick cover	All	98	90	227,000	2	25–35	3–5	Fall, spring				
Perennial (*L. perenne*)	Combi, Manhattan, NK-100, Pelo	Quick cover, special maritime locations, and athletic fields where winter not too severe	All	98	90	227,000	2	25–35	3–5	Fall, spring				

TABLE 2.8 (Continued)

Common and scientific name	Cultivars	Major uses	Region	Purity, %	Germination, %	Seed per pound	Longevity*	Seeding rate for meadows and pastures, lb/acre	Seeding rate for lawns, lb/1000 ft²	Best seeding time	Type of material	Vegetative propagation: Method of planting	Vegetative propagation: Quantity for 1000 ft²	Vegetative propagation: Best planting time
St. Augustine Grass (*Stenotaphrum secundatum*)	Bitter Blue, Floratine	Lawns of deep South and Gulf area, shade-tolerant	II, III	–	–	–	–	–	Vegetative	–	2-in. sod blocks, sprigs	Sod blocks set 12 in. on center sprigs, 6–12 in. apart in 12-in. rows or broadcast on prepared seedbed	Sod block 30 sq. ft²; sprigs 3–6 ft² of nursery sod	Early summer
Timothy (*Phleum pratense*)	None	Pasture	All	99	90	1,230,000	2	6–12	–	Fall, spring				

Legumes

Common and scientific name				Purity, %	Viable seed, %		Seed per pound	Weight per bushel, lb	Longevity*	Seeding rate, lb: Per acre for meadows and pasture	Seeding rate, lb: Per 1000 ft² for lawn	Best seeding time				
Alyce clover (*Alysicarpus vaginalis*)				98	85		300,000	60	3	10–12		Fall, spring				

Clover, alsike (*Trifolium hybridum*)				97	90†		700,000	60	3	6–8		Fall, spring				
Crimson (*T. incarnatum*)				98	85		140,000	60	2	15–20		Fall (early)				
Red (*T. praetense*)				98	90†		275,000	60	3	8–12		Fall, spring				
White Dutch (*T. repens*)				96	90†		800,000	60	3	2–4	$\frac{1}{4}$–$\frac{1}{2}$	Fall, spring				
Lespedeza, common (*Lespedeza strata*), Kobe variety				97	90		190,000‡	25‡	1	10–15‡		Spring				
Tennessee no. 76 variety				96	90		310,000‡	25‡	1	8–10‡		Spring				
Bicolor (*L. bicolor*)				98	80†		82,000	60	2	1–2		Spring				
Korean (*L. stipulacea*)				97	90		225,000‡	60	2	10–15		Spring				
Sericea (*L. cuneata*)				98	90†		250,000	60	2	10–15		Spring				

* 1 = comparatively short-lived seed; 2 = intermediate; 3 = long-lived seed.
† Medium per cent of hard seed.
‡ Unhulled.
§ Planted in rows 3 to 4 ft apart.

9. Use a corrugated roller with seed attachment for best seeding results on large areas.
10. Recommended seed mixtures:

Fall seeding
4 lb Ladino clover or Louisiana white clover
10 lb Orchard grass
15 lb Alta or Kentucky 31 fescue

Spring seeding
20 lb Korean lespedeza
4 lb Ladino clover or Louisiana white clover
15 lb Alta or Kentucky 31 fescue

11. Cultipack after seeding and mulch with straw at the rate of 2 tons/acre.

TABLE 2.9
Grass-Seed Data*

Name	Number of grains in 1 lb pure seed	Good germination, %	Weight per English bushel, lb	Weight of 10,000,000 grains; size as in col. 1, lb
Awnless brome grass	137,000	75–90	13–14	72.99
Kentucky bluegrass	2,400,000	80–90	14–32	4.17
Perennial ryegrass	336,800	95–98	18–30	29.7
Italian ryegrass	285,300	95–98	12–24	35.1
Meadow fescue	318,200	75–95	12–30	31.42
Redtop	6,030,000	90–95	12–40	1.65
Alsike clover	707,000	95–98	60–64	14.14
White clover	740,000	95–98	60–64	13.51

* By permission of Intertec Publishing Corp.

Method 2

Steps 1 to 6 as for method 1.

7. Disc thoroughly in order to work the fertilizer and lime into the soil. Continue discing until a smooth seedbed is formed, free of all heavy clods and rocks. Cultipack before and after seeding.
8. Use a corrugated roller with seed attachment for best seeding results on large areas.
9. Recommended seed mixture:

25 lb Crimson clover per acre
20 lb Italian ryegrass per acre

10. Permit this planting to grow until May, when the crop is to be plowed under while still green.
11. Make a new soil test and fertilize as indicated.
12. Disc fertilizer into the soil and continue discing land into a smooth seedbed.
13. Sow 90 to 100 lb of inoculated soybeans per acre.
14. After the soybeans have matured but are still green, plow under. Make a soil analysis to determine the amount and quality of fertilizer and lime to be added.
15. Work the fertilizer into the soil by discing into a smooth seedbed.
16. After the soil has been thoroughly worked and is ready (Aug. 15 to Oct. 1) seed, using a corrugated roller with seed attachment for best results.
17. Recommended seed mixture (quantities per acre):

    2 lb Louisiana white clover
    8 lb Kentucky bluegrass
    12 lb Alta or Kentucky 31 fescue

18. Mulch with straw at rate of 2 tons/acre.

WEED CONTROL

The control of weeds in turf is receiving more attention than it once did. The use of chemicals has advanced rapidly, and research into new chemicals continues. The best method of weed control is to combine good management practices with chemical control.

Management practices that favor the desired grasses and tend to reduce weeds are cheaper and easier than chemical treatment and should be done before or in connection with chemical use.

The following practices will help to reduce weeds:

1. Fertilize regularly and adequately to keep the turf going and to shade out any new weed plants.
2. Mow at the correct height to keep a dense turf, which will shade out young weed plants.
3. Avoid keeping the soil continuously so wet that weed and crabgrass germination is favored.
4. Avoid damaging or aerating turf at times when weeds are germinating freely.

The best control treatment for general weed infestation on large areas is an overall treatment with a selective chemical that will kill the weeds and leave the grasses in good condition.

Controlling Broadleaf Weeds

The best material to kill broadleaf weeds without damaging the grass is 2,4-D. Usually one application will eliminate dandelions, plantains, and many other larger weeds. Such weeds as chickweed and other mat-forming weeds may require two or more applications at intervals of about 1 month. Clover may be somewhat damaged by 2,4-D, especially after spring treatments, but it usually recovers rather rapidly.

In most instances 2,4-D works slowly. It works best in warm weather, when a reaction can usually be seen within 24 hours. Within that time the weeds are not generally killed, but the stems and leaves curl and become crisp. In about 3 or 4 weeks after treatment the weeds dry up. On new turf it is good practice to wait until the grass is at least 1 in. high before treating the weeds with 2,4-D. Bent grass may be damaged slightly by 2,4-D applications, but the bluegrasses and fescues are generally unharmed.

The broadleaf weeds usually killed by a single or double application of 2,4-D are as follows:

- Black medic
- Broad-leaved plantain
- Buckhorn or narrow-leaved plantain
- Cinquefoil
- Dandelion
- Field sorrel or sheep sorrel
- Gosmore
- Ground ivy
- Hawkweed or paint brush
- Heal-all
- Moneywort
- Purslane
- Water pennywort
- Winter cress or yellow rocket
- Yarrow

A summer annual that thrives on turf that is thin and on compacted soil is knotweed. It is very hard to kill in the summer, but when it is in the seedling stage, in April and May, it can be killed easily with a single 2,4-D treatment.

Other weeds that are hard to kill are wild garlic and onion. They should be treated very early in the spring, and the treatment should be repeated a year later; two treatments are needed to kill both the plants of the current season and those that will grow in the autumn from hard budlets already in the soil.

Common and mouse-ear chickweed cannot be controlled with a single 2,4-D treatment. Usually it requires three treatments at 2-week intervals, beginning early in the spring. Potassium cyanate may also give control.

The greatest weed pest, and the one on which most control effort is expended, is an annual grass known as crabgrass. The seeds of crabgrass germinate in the late spring, and the plants grow rapidly, often crowding out the more desirable grasses. The seed is set in the early fall, and any control program must be based on these facts. Cornell

Extension Bulletin 922 lists seven steps to follow in preventing an infestation of crabgrass in new turf or to improve an old turf:

1. Plant your new lawns in early fall; prepare the soil properly and select the right kind of seed for the situation. Crabgrass seed is rarely an impurity in even the cheapest and poorest seed mixture. The plants come from the seed already present in the soil.
2. Fertilize the established lawn in early fall. If you fertilize in the spring, use an inorganic fertilizer before the lawn starts to grow and at about one-half the rate normally used in the fall. Late spring fertilization gives the permanent grasses 5 or 6 months of good growing conditions before competition from the crabgrass begins again.
3. Cut the grass at least $1\frac{1}{4}$ in. high. A large leaf area enables the permanent grasses to make strong growth. Crabgrass cannot tolerate shade, and many crabgrass seedlings die.
4. If the established turf has crabgrass troubles, check the sod for grub injury. Beetles damage lawns most seriously in late spring, just when crabgrass is ready to fill in the bare spots. If the lawn is infested with grubs, you cannot hope for lasting crabgrass control until the soil is grub-proofed.
5. If possible, prevent crabgrass from seeding. This is more easily said than done. Raking the seed stalks so that they can be mowed, collected, and discarded is a tiresome and time-consuming job, but it will reduce the next year's seed supply. Several attachments designed to fit on the front of the lawn mower will pull the seed stalks up where they can be cut. These devices merely eliminate hand raking.
6. Hand weed crabgrass when the plants are small. Such weeding is sometimes practical on small areas of particular importance. If the plants are large, pull them out with a dandelion rake just before fall reseeding. The dandelion rake has a head of sheet metal, with triangular teeth that hook under the crowns of the plants.
7. Water the lawn well or not at all.

SOIL TREATMENT FOR KILLING CRABGRASS SEED

Methods for killing crabgrass or other weed seeds in the soil are still in the experimental stage. Calcium cyanamid has been used successfully for this purpose, however, This fertilizer material should be mixed into the new seedbed thoroughly in mid-August at the rate of 50 lb to 1000 ft^2.

Before planting the grass seed, allow 3 weeks for the weed-killing action to take place and for the excess chemicals to disappear. It is important to apply the calcium cyanamid when the soil is fairly moist. Do not plant the new grass until after there have been several good rains or irrigations.

CHEMICAL CONTROL OF CRAB GRASS*

There are three types of selective crabgrass chemicals on the market, potassium cyanate, phenyl mercuric acetate, and methyl arsenate.

Potassium Cyanate This is foliar burning material which is not toxic to the user. It kills by burning the existing crabgrass leaves. If new shoots appear on older plants after the first treatment, a second treatment must be given. It is a chemical which can be used repeatedly to remove crabgrass and chickweed without damage to permanent grasses. Apply the potassium cyanate compound in late summer, near the end of July and in August, for best results. Potassium cyanate has been formulated into organic fertilizers. In this way adequate fall fertilizer is added as the weekly doses of potassium cyanate burn out the crabgrass. The temporary browning of desired turf, the need for repeat treatments, and the possibility of reinfestation are limitations of this chemical.

Phenyl Mercuric Acetate This compound does its best work early in the season, in June and early July, when the crabgrass plants are small. It can be obtained in solution or as a dry spreader. This material is poisonous, and the user must be very cautious in handling it. With repeated applications it has been used successfully to kill young crabgrass, reduce disease attacks, and inhibit reinfestations. Phenyl Mercuric Acetate mixed with other fungicides, particularly Tersan, has been successful on putting greens. The two are mixed in solution so that each is applied at three-fourths the usual rate and treatments are begun in late spring as dollar spot or crabgrass begin to grow.

Methyl Arsenate This compound was developed in 1955. From all indications it appears to offer definite selectivity and good cleanup of weedy grasses and crabgrass. It may be particularly desirable for removing weeds infesting spring plantings or emergency plantings made under adverse conditions. For golf course use, methyl arsenate may be used for smooth and hairy crabgrass control on tees, aprons, and

* Information on chemical control of crabgrass was obtained from a report by W. H. Daniel, Turfgrass Specialist, Purdue University.

approaches. It has been used without damage on several selections of bentgrass under putting conditions in cool weather and may be used with caution on putting greens, with treatments repeated until the weedy plant is dead. It is manufactured as Sodar, Weedone L-850, Artox, Dimet, and Crab-E-Rad.

See Chap. 6 for other chemical control methods of crabgrass.

PLANTING AND CARE OF TREES AND SHRUBS

Adequate preparation of the soil before planting trees and shrubs reduces future maintenance problems. Ample depths of topsoil should be provided for shrubbery groups, and holes should be excavated and refilled for specimen trees. Generally the depth of topsoil required varies with the species of plant, but a good rule to follow is to provide a minimum of 12 in. for most deciduous shrubs, 18 in. for evergreen shrubs, and 24 in. for broadleaf evergreen shrubs. Topsoil for individual trees will vary with the size of the tree and the size of the ball.

Competition for food, water, and sunlight sometimes prevents satisfactory growth of cultivated plants. If the competition is from weeds, the remedy is usually mulching and tillage. Weed control requires much more attention in new plantings than in old ones because in the top growth of newly set plants there is less foliage to discourage weeds. In new plantings, too, the soil has been recently turned and disturbed, and buried weed seeds have come to the surface; in older plantings, weeds generally come from other sources. Complete weed eradication each season for a few years, whether in new or old plantings, greatly reduces the amount of weed growth the following years.

CHOICE OF MATERIALS

A general description, together with growth habits, pruning requirements, and pests and diseases, is given in Appendix Tables A.5, A.6, and A.7, respectively, for shrubs, evergreen trees, and deciduous trees.

WEED CONTROL WITH CHEMICALS

Chemical control of weeds has improved rapidly in the past few years. Most chemicals, however, are not adapted for use in and around shrubbery. One material which is safe to use in shrub beds for the control of weeds is known as Crag Herbicide-1. This material eliminates annual broadleaf and grass weeds by killing the seeds before they germinate. Weeds such as pigweeds, purslane, chickweed, and carpet-weed, and grasses such as crabgrass and foxtail are controlled for 3 to 6 weeks. Late summer applications help prevent fall and winter weeds such as chickweed.

This chemical is inactive until it reaches moist soil, where soil bacteria make it work. It will not harm plants if drift adheres to the leaves during spraying operations. Hard, crusted soil should be worked so that this material can penetrate. Also, if the soil is dry, the area should be thoroughly watered. Grown weeds will not be killed by this type of herbicide.

Table 3.1 shows application rates for Crag Herbicide-1 for various soil types. Use at least 30 gal of water per acre of ground actually

TABLE 3.1
Application Rates for Herbicide-1

Soil types	Lb per acre of actual area sprayed
Light	2
Medium	3
Heavy	4

treated. For small areas, use 5 level tablespoons per 1000 ft^2 of ground sprayed in 10 gal of water. A good reason for using a material which will kill weeds before they germinate is that the labor formerly needed for hand weeding can now be used for more useful work, and its use saves time and money.

Later culture should not be neglected, but in humid climates plantings will be found to require very little care if the work has been well done the first 3 years. Plants collected from natural sources are likely to require special attention for a longer time than well-grown nursery plants if both are handled with the same care.

CULTIVATION

The soil around trees and shrubs is cultivated to control and eliminate weeds, but this work does not seem to have any other value in stimulating plant growth. With small and newly planted trees and shrubs, cultivation may be the most convenient way to ensure a good start, especially for the first 2 or 3 years. Once the plantings are established, continued tillage is seldom warranted on large public grounds, particularly in remote portions or along highways.

Cultivated areas are spaded each year, thus bringing to the surface new, mellow soil not occupied by growing roots. Such deep working (to the same depth each year) is usually done in the spring; as the season progresses, cultivation should be gradually shallower. Such culture destroys the feeding roots that formed in the cultivated area the previous year but does not disturb the carrier roots from which they came. If cultivation is omitted for a few years, however, these feeding roots grow into carrier roots with feeding roots mainly at their ends, so that if deep working of the soil is begun again, many of the main roots will be destroyed. If cultivation must be resumed after such an interval, extra care is necessary not to prune the roots too severely. The injurious effects may be partially offset by a correspondingly severe pruning of the top at the same time.

When the need for deep cultivation makes it necessary to root-prune a plant severely, the best method is to divide the operation into two or three parts, spading to the desired depth part way around the plant one year and farther the next. Each section, as root-pruned, should be kept cultivated to the desired depth.

MULCHES

After plantings of trees and shrubs are thoroughly established, a mulch similar to a woodland ground cover is more satisfactory for weed control than cultivation, especially if the plants on the edges of the group have their lower branches close to the ground so that leaves that drop remain and decay. Leaves in sufficient quantity will develop a mulch worth more to the plants than constant clean cultivation. The combination of mulch and shade from the plants will keep down most weed growth; occasionally a few may need pulling. Such a mulch will provide as good a moisture-retaining cover to the soil as the best of culture, and the decaying leaves will supply fertility. It is often desirable to supplement leaves that drop from any tree or shrubbery group with other leaves or other mulching materials. Wood-chipping machines made it possible to transform brush and small trees accumulated from cleanup operations into an excellent mulch material for all kinds of trees and shrubs.

Newly planted trees and shrubs are commonly cultivated for 2 or 3 years after planting, but frequently it is desirable from the start to control weed growth with mulch rather than by cultivation.

The most widely used materials for mulching are straw, strawy manure, cut cornstalks, leaves, litter, peat moss, wood chips, and cottonseed hulls. Sawdust, if well rotted, makes an excellent mulch for practically all types of planting. Mulching is essential for azaleas, rhododendron, mountain laurel, and other plants of the same family, and it is desirable for nearly all evergreens, both broadleaf and coniferous, as well as for deciduous plants. These mulches are best maintained continuously from year to year, the leaf drop of each year being permitted to remain under the plants with material added to help maintain a sufficiently deep cover on the soil. Deciduous trees and shrubs should have at least 2 to 4 in. of mulch material; evergreens and broadleaf evergreens do well with a mulch kept 4 to 6 in. deep.

WATERING

There are great differences in the needs of various plants for water and their tolerance of drought conditions, although all plants require large quantities in their life processes.

Watering is normally done with a hose, and often it is applied too rapidly to be efficient. Water should be applied so slowly that it does not run off and should be continued long enough to penetrate at least 5 to 6 in. into the soil. The ideal way is to supply a small amount per minute continuously for several hours. Whenever practicable, the ground should be covered with a mulch to keep artificially applied water from evaporating.

Clay soils should not require rewatering for at least a week, possibly three; gravelly soils may need watering twice a week. Water repeatedly applied in limited quantities penetrating only 2 or 3 in. may be injurious, since such watering will stimulate root growth toward the surface where a few days' drying will kill them. Less frequent but heavier watering stimulates deeper root growth, where the moisture is likely to fluctuate less. Watering plants in groups, whether trees or shrubs, old plantations or new, is usually easier than watering single specimens, especially newly planted ones.

To make sure that the water penetrates deeply about newly planted specimens, the earth should be ridged about them to form a basin that will prevent the water from running off before it has an opportunity to soak into the soil. By refilling such a basin several times, water can be supplied to the maximum depth of root growth.

Trees growing in lawn areas are especially likely to suffer from lack of water. Where this occurs, both trees and turf reflect the need, the turf showing it first and recovering first. Here again, infrequent drenchings rather than frequent surface waterings give best results.

In areas where long periods of dry weather occur, efficient watering can be done by placing drain tile vertically in the soil. The top should be even with the lawn level or slightly below it, so that there is no chance of the lawn mower's striking the top of the tile (see Fig. 3.1). The lower end should be 1 or 2 ft in the ground, depending on the character of the soil and the depth of the tree roots. Tiles 3 or 4 in. in diameter are usually used, although those 2 and 5 in. in diameter are sometimes preferred. No large roots should be cut in digging the holes for the tiles;

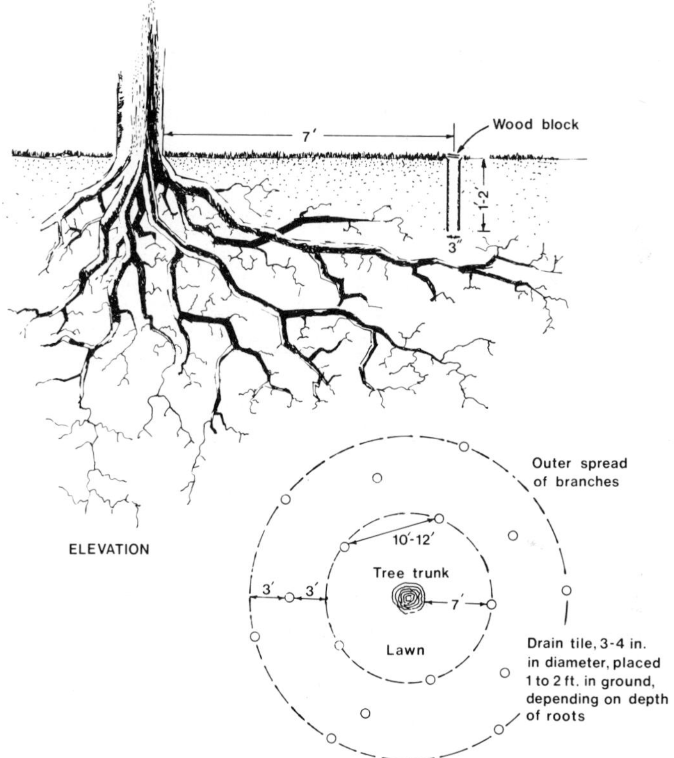

Fig. 3.1 Method of watering large trees in lawns during extended dry weather.

if necessary the location of the holes may be shifted a little to avoid roots. If the bell end of the tile is placed upward, it will form a cup which can be closed with a block of wood when not in use. This block will prevent the hole from being filled with leaves and debris, and prevent people and animals from stepping into it. Filling the tile with coarse gravel or stone will serve the same purpose. Tiles should be placed 10 to 12 ft apart, beginning about 7 ft from the trunk of the tree and extending to the end of the branches for flat- or round-headed trees, and $1\frac{1}{2}$ to 2 times the spread of the branches for upright ones.

Water should be run in a slow stream directly into the tiles, one at a time, until all have been filled, and the process repeated until the soil halfway between the holes is thoroughly saturated.

The amount and frequency of watering must be determined by local conditions. A soil with a loose gravelly or sandy subsoil will require more frequent light waterings than one with a heavier subsoil. There is no advantage in putting water below the level where roots are growing. A stiff clay subsoil is nearly always the limit of root extension.

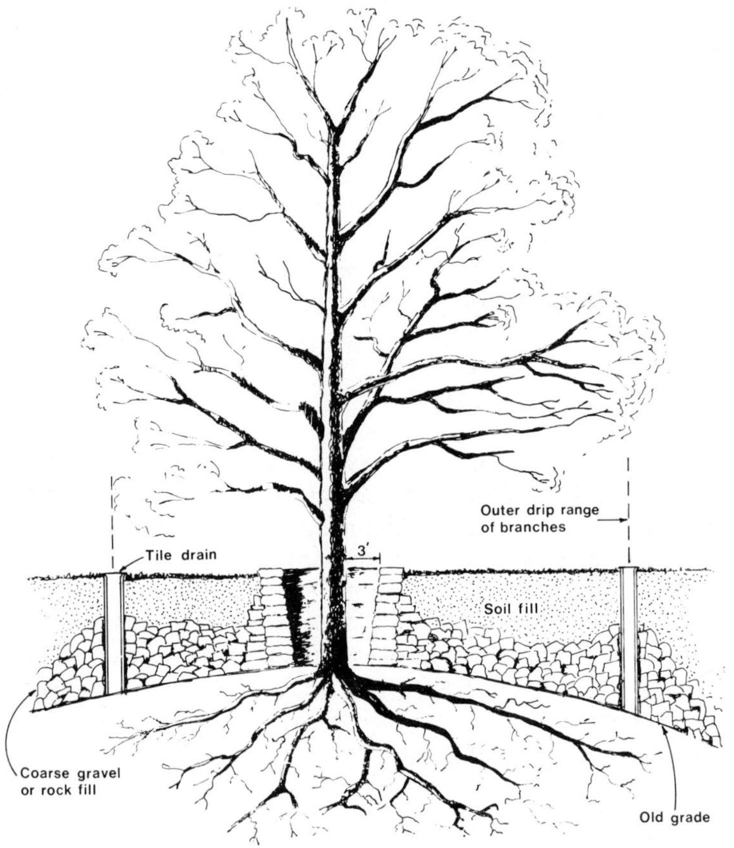

Fig. 3.2 Method of watering large trees in lawns during extended dry weather.

FERTILIZATION

Fertilizers should be so applied that growth is steady throughout a long season but is finished before freezing weather comes. Unripened wood is more likely to be injured by cold than well-ripened wood, and even old wood may be killed by the advent of freezing weather before growth has stopped.

Organic Matter

Organic matter is an important part of the soil and is more likely to be deficient than any of the other constituents necessary for plant growth. An abundance of such material will facilitate drainage, increase water-holding capacity, improve clay soils, and make sandy soils more retentive of moisture.

Heavy mulching, combined with the action of earthworms and burrowing insects, is the nearest approach to introducing organic matter into the soil after plantings have been established. Fresh manure is suitable for many plants, including the most vigorous deciduous trees and shrubs, such as oaks, maples, lilacs, and crepe myrtles. Cow manure produces the least heat of any of the more common manures and is especially valuable for roses, lilacs, and plants that do not respond to heating manures or to an abundance of quickly available nitrogen. It produces its results more uniformly over a longer period.

Horse manure probably produces the most heat of the readily available manures; it should not be used about evergreens until it is composted. Sheep, chicken, and rabbit manures are all rich in nitrogen and should be used in moderation, as they may cause extra stimulation and produce soft growth or growth too late in the season. Compost is also good for deciduous shrubs, and it is the only manure that should be used about coniferous evergreens, including pines, spruces, junipers and arborvitae, and broadleaf evergreens such as evergreen magnolias, camellias, hollies, and rhododendrons. With most of these it should be used only as a mulch and should not be worked into the soil.

Some other organic materials that can be purchased are prepared stockyard sheep and cattle manures, tankage, dried blood, fish scraps, sewage sludge, cottonseed meal, soybean meal, ground bone and steamed bone, and many brands of peat moss and humus. The degree and duration of nuisance should of course be considered in planning use of any natural fertilizer. Applications can be scheduled to avoid subjecting the public unnecessarily to unpleasant odors.

Preparation of Composts

Composts are mixtures of manure and other organic matter which have become sufficiently rotted to break up readily and thus be easily worked into the soil. They are made by piling manure and litter together and keeping the mound moist to prevent too rapid fermentation. The mound should be spaded over at intervals of 6 to 8 weeks during the summer, so that all parts decompose equally. Sods are often added to the pile in layers to add to its bulk and to produce a more friable compost.

A compost pile is made by placing in alternate layers manure, sod, and loam, repeating this process until the pile is as high as can be conveniently handled, usually from 3 to 5 ft. The top layer of the pile should be of soil, to catch any ammonia that might otherwise escape. The layers are thoroughly tamped and each one slightly dipped toward the middle, so that all the water will soak into the pile instead of running off. Add water whenever necessary to stimulate decomposition during hot and dry weather. It is not necessary to carry the composting so far when it is used as a top dressing as when it is worked into the soil. The addition of sulfate of ammonia and lime, superphosphates, and potash salts will benefit the compost and speed up decomposition. Leaves and garden trash and even household garbage can be successfully composted the same way. Diseased plants should not be composted.

To decompose 2000 lb of refuse in a pile 10 by 10 by 6 ft requires one of the following:

60 lb of sulphate of ammonia at rate of 5 lb per 6-in. lift
60 lb of lime at rate of $4\frac{1}{6}$ lb per 6-in. lift
30 lb of superphosphate at rate of $2\frac{1}{2}$ lb per 6-in. lift
25 lb of potash at rate of 2 lb per 6-in. lift

Smaller quantities of refuse and a smaller pile will require proportionately less of the above chemicals. Other chemicals such as calcium cyanamid and commercial mixtures are especially prepared to do the job of decomposition in a shorter time. Manufacturers' instructions should be followed implicitly.

Prepared Fertilizers

Most of our soils require the addition of complete plant foods to produce good growth. Fertilizers containing nitrogen, phosphate, and potash are usually sufficient, although it is advisable to take periodic soil tests to determine the amount and kind of fertilizers to use (see Table 3.2).

For all trees and shrubs, fertilizer should be applied as close as possible to the feeder roots but away from the trunk to avoid injury to the plant. On small trees, fertilizer should be applied in a circle approximately $1\frac{1}{2}$ ft beyond the spread of the overhead branches and thoroughly worked into the soil to a depth of about 10 in.

After fertilizer is applied, the ground should be watered thoroughly, to soak the fertilizer into the ground. Well established and older trees, particularly those in picnic or other public-use areas, should also be fertilized regularly; however, the fertilizer must penetrate deeper into the soil than for small trees in order to reach the proper roots. This can be accomplished by drilling or digging a staggered arrangement of holes along the outer drip range of the overhead branches, depositing the proper amount of fertilizer, backfilling with soil and/or mulch, and watering if necessary. The holes should be approximately 1½ to 2 ft deep.

Fertilizer should normally be supplied to trees or shrubbery in late winter or early spring, up to June 1 at the latest; however, fall applications are also valuable. Applications during the hot summer months are likely to be harmful to the plant unless the material is used in smaller amounts and thoroughly dissolved by artificial watering. A high-nitrogen fertilizer (Uramite) can be applied safely at any time without danger of burning the plant (Table 3.3).

TABLE 3.2
Safe Quantities of Fertilizers

	Lb per acre	Sq ft covered by 1–2 lb
Phosphate potash ash	200–400	200
Triple superphosphate	200	200
Nitrate of soda	50	800
Sulfate of ammonia	50	800
Superphosphate (16%)	500	80
Sheep manure	4000	10
Dried cattle manure	4000	10
Cottonseed meal	2000	20
Bone meal	2000	20
Soybean meal	2000	20
Dried blood, tankage, and fish scraps	1000	40

Table 3.4 shows formulas for compounding 1 ton of fertilizer from materials of known composition. In using this table, look in the first column for the percentage content of the material used and in the first horizontal row for the percentage wanted; the figure at the point where the two lines intersect will represent the amount of the material to use in making 1 ton of the mixture wanted. For example, if a mixture containing 4 per cent nitrogen, 12 per cent phosphoric acid, and 4 per cent potash is wanted, the following materials are to be used: 16 per cent nitrate of soda, 20 per cent superphosphate, and 50 per cent muriate of potash. Proceed thus: as the nitrate contains 16 per cent, find 16 in the first column and follow across to column headed 4; the number

500 at the intersection is the weight in pounds of 16 per cent nitrate of soda required. In like manner for phosphoric acid, follow row 20 to column 12, and 1200 is the weight of 20 per cent superphosphate required. For potash, follow row 50 to column 4, and 160 is the weight in pounds of 50 per cent muriate of potash required. We have thus

TABLE 3.3
Composition of Fertilizer Materials

Materials Supplying:	N (Nitrogen)	P (Phos.)	K (Potassium)	Availability
	Per cent			
Nitrogen				
Ammonium nitrate	30	0	0	Quick
Calcium cyanamide	22	0	0	Medium
Cal-Nitro	16–20.5	0	0	Quick
Cottonseed meal	6.5–7.5	1.5–2	2–3	Slow
Concentrated tankage	11–12.5	1–2	0	Medium
Dried blood, high grade	12–16	0	0	Medium
Dried blood, low grade	10–11	3–5	0	Medium
Dried fish scrap	7–10	6–8	0	Slow
Leuna saltpeter	26	0	0	Quick
Nitrate of soda	16	0	0	Quick
Sulfate of ammonia	20	0	0	Quick
Tankage	5–6	11–14	0	Slow
Uramon	42	0	0	Quick
Phosphoric Acid				
Basic slag	0	13–18	0	Quick
Calcium metaphosphate	0	60–64	0	Quick
Fused rock phosphate	0	28–30	0	Quick
Ground bone (raw)	2.5–4	20–25	0	Very slow
Potassium metaphosphate	0	60	30	Quick
Raw rock phosphate	0	26–35	0	Very slow
Steamed bone meal	1–2.5	22–30	0	Medium
Superphosphate	0	16–20	0	Quick
Triple superphosphate	0	40–50	0	Quick
Potash				
Kainite	0	0	12–20	Quick
Muriate of potash	0	0	50–62.5	Quick
Potassium nitrate	13	0	46	Quick
Sulfate of potash	0	0	48–52	Quick
Sulfate of potash Mg	0	0	25	Quick
Tobacco stems	2–4	.5–1.5	4.9–9	Medium
Wood ashes	0	1–2	2–8	Medium

nitrate of soda, 500 lb, 20 per cent superphosphate, 1200 lb, and 50 per cent muriate of potash, 160 lb, making a total of 1860 lb. By adding 140 lb of limestone or sand (filler) we have 2000 lb of 4-12-4 fertilizer.

TIME TO PLANT

The time to plant varies with the section of the country. In the South the best time to do most planting is in the fall, from Nov. 1 to Jan. 1.

TABLE 3.4
Formulas for Compounding 1 Ton of Fertilizer from Materials of Known Composition

Percentage of material used	Desired percentage of chemical in final mixture														
	1	2	3	4	5	6	7	8	9	10	11	12	14	16	20
	Amount of material needed (lb)														
2	1000	2000													
3	667	1334	2000												
4	500	1000	1500	2000											
5	400	600	1200	1600	2000										
6	333	667	1000	1333	1667	2000									
7	286	572	858	1144	1430	1716	2000								
8	250	500	750	1000	1250	1500	1750	2000							
9	222	444	667	889	1111	1334	1556	1778	2000						
10	200	400	600	800	1000	1200	1400	1600	1800	2000					
11	182	364	546	728	910	1092	1274	1456	1638	1820	2000				
12	166	333	500	667	833	1000	1167	1334	1500	1666	1833	2000			
13	154	308	462	616	769	924	1077	1232	1384	1538	1692	1845			
14	143	286	430	570	715	860	1000	1143	1286	1430	1570	1715	2000		
15	133	267	400	533	667	800	933	1067	1200	1333	1467	1600	1867		
16	125	250	376	500	625	750	875	1000	1125	1250	1375	1500	1750	2000	
17	118	235	353	470	588	706	824	940	1059	1176	1294	1410	1647	1882	
18	111	222	333	444	556	667	778	889	1000	1111	1222	1333	1556	1778	
19	105	210	316	421	526	631	737	842	947	1053	1158	1263	1474	1684	
20	100	200	300	400	500	600	700	800	900	1000	1100	1200	1400	1600	2000
21	95	190	285	381	476	571	667	762	857	952	1047	1142	1333	1524	1905
22	91	182	273	364	455	546	636	727	818	909	1000	1091	1273	1455	1818
23	87	174	261	348	435	522	609	696	783	870	957	1044	1217	1391	1739
24	83	166	249	332	422	500	583	666	749	835	917	1000	1167	1333	1667
25	80	160	240	320	400	480	560	640	720	800	880	960	1120	1280	1600
47	43	86	127	170	212	253	298	340	383	425	468	511	596	681	851
48	42	84	125	168	208	250	294	336	375	417	458	500	583	667	833
50	40	80	120	160	200	240	280	320	360	400	440	480	560	640	800

TABLE 3.5
Quantities of Chemicals to Use for Composting

Straw or other refuse, tons	Dimensions of pile 6 ft high, ft	Quantity for pile				Quantity for 6-in. layers			
		Sulfate of ammonia, lb	Lime, lb	Super-phosphate, lb	Potash, lb	Sulfate of ammonia, lb	Lime, lb	Super-phosphate, lb	Potash, lb
First formula:									
1	10 × 10	60	60	30	25	5	$4\frac{1}{6}$	$2\frac{1}{2}$	2
$\frac{1}{2}$	7 × 7	30	25	15	$12\frac{1}{2}$	$2\frac{1}{2}$	2	$1\frac{1}{4}$	1
$\frac{1}{6}$	4 × 4	10	$8\frac{1}{2}$	5	$4\frac{1}{6}$	$\frac{5}{6}$	$\frac{2}{3}$	$\frac{5}{12}$	$\frac{1}{3}$
Second formula:									
1	10 × 10	80	60	30	—	$6\frac{2}{3}$	5	—	$2\frac{1}{2}$
$\frac{1}{2}$	7 × 7	40	30	15	—	$3\frac{1}{3}$	$2\frac{1}{2}$	—	$1\frac{1}{4}$
$\frac{1}{6}$	4 × 4	$13\frac{1}{3}$	10	5	—	$1\frac{1}{9}$	$\frac{5}{6}$	—	$\frac{1}{2}$

Broadleaf evergreens are best transplanted in the spring. In the North, planting has been done successfully in both fall and spring. Planting with a ball of earth can be done all summer if the leaves and stem are treated with a plastic spray. The essential point to remember is to provide the plant with adequate amounts of water after planting so that the root system can survive without drying out.

SOIL ACIDITY

Besides differing in fertility and water-holding capacity, soils differ in acidity. Some are neutral, some acid, and still others are alkaline. The

TABLE 3.6
Use of Powdered Sulfur to Maintain Soil Acidity*

Condition of soil	pH	Powdered sulfur per 100 ft², lb
Medium acid	5.5–6.0	2
Slightly acid	6.0–7.0	4
Slightly alkaline	7.0–7.5	7
Strongly alkaline	7.5–8.0	Unsuitable

* Compiled by Owen B. Schmidt, Superintendent, F. D. Moore & Sons, Landscape Contractors and Nurserymen, and reproduced here by his permission.

acidity of soil can be changed for the benefit of plants requiring it. Lime is the standard material for making acid soils alkaline. Hydrated lime, finely ground limestone, and wood ashes are used in quantities less than sufficient to neutralize soil acidity. Where soil tests indicate that 8 tons or more of lime per acre would be required to neutralize the soil, often only 1 ton or even ½ ton/acre (or 1 lb to 20 or 40 ft^2) is used and seems to produce satisfactory results.

To make soil more acid in as short a time as possible, as required for rhododendrons, azaleas, and laurel, it is possible to use aluminum sulfate at a rate up to 1 lb for 20 ft^2. It is not advisable to use this treatment over an extended time. For most acid-soil plants, however, it is better to provide acidity with a mulch. In order to produce the desired effect the mulch must remain about the plants and rot; acidity is not produced until the material is partially decayed, about the second year. Soil acidity can also be maintained by addition of powdered sulfur, as shown in Table 3.6.

PRUNING

Prune trees at the time of planting to ensure a well-developed framework and to reduce top growth to compensate for roots lost in moving. Do not cut back vigorous trees that were thoroughly thinned out at the time of planting. Cutting back the branches removes a year or more of growth and gives trees a formal shape until the condition is outgrown.

Prune new trees before setting them in the hole, to save time and trouble. The chance to use hand tools, which cut closer than the pole pruners needed for trees in an upright position, is one of the advantages. Start at the top of the tree and work down; remove closely parallel branches, crossing and broken limbs, and superfluous growth at the base of the main branches.

Cutting Branches When removing a branch, make the cut flush with the branch. Any remaining stub may decay and permanently injure the tree, since the healing callus cannot close over it. For the same reason, cut close to a bud when cutting back a branch, so as not to leave a stub. All pruning wounds over 1 in. in diameter should be painted with a tree-wound compound to retard checking and decay of the exposed wood.

Cutting Leaders When pruning, do not cut back central leaders (main stalks or trunks). When the terminal bud is removed, the one nearest the cut becomes the terminal bud and on trees with opposite buds each bud produces a shoot that competes with the other, resulting in a structurally weak double-leader tree. Cutting back the leader always flattens the top and stunts the tree.

Pruning Existing Trees

Large trees should be pruned only by experienced climbers. Each should be equipped with 125 ft of ½-in. rope having a bowline knot in one end. The climber passes the bowline through a stout crotch and around his thighs, using the loose end, or tail, of the bowline to tie a taut-line hitch in the rope leading to the ground (see Fig. 3.19). The climber is free to work with both hands and can swing back to the trunk without injury if a limb should snap. A ground man should always work with a climber to tie needed tools to the rope and to keep it free of brush. When pruning is done on street trees, the ground man must keep the climber's rope out of the road, where it might cause a serious accident.

Pruning large trees from extension ladders is hazardous. Satisfactory work cannot be done because pole saws and pole runners must be used instead of hand tools. New and more satisfactory methods have been devised using hydraulic lift platforms (Fig. 4.18) from which the treeman can prune high off the ground with perfect safety. These platforms are equipped with pneumatic power tools for easier pruning.

PROCEDURE

Prune large trees by working from the top down. Prune each large branch individually. Remove crossing limbs, broken branches, and

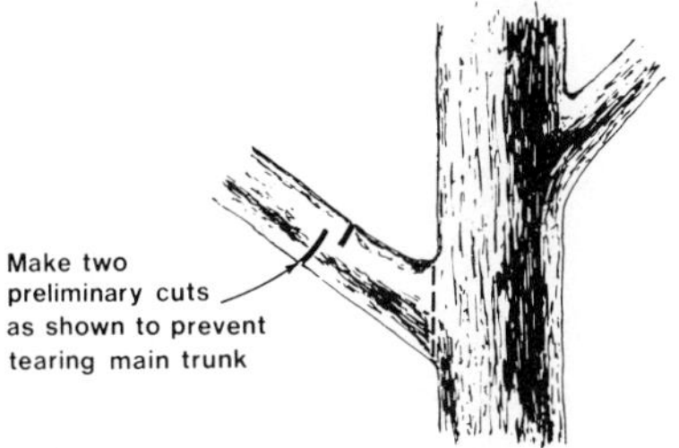

Method of removing large limb. Final cut is made along dotted line to allow tree to heal over wound.

Correct and incorrect method of removing branch stubs.

Fig. 3.3 Removal of limbs and stubs.

superfluous growth next to the tree to admit sunlight and air circulation; this helps to control insects and diseases. Paint all pruning cuts with a good tree-wound compound immediately.

To remove large, dead, or broken branches, make three saw cuts to prevent ripping the bark of the tree trunk (Fig. 3.3). Start the first cut on the underside of the limb about 1 ft from the trunk and saw through one-third of the branch. Start the second cut on top of the branch, about 3 in. behind the bottom cut, sawing until the branch splits off at the parallel point of the two cuts. Saw off the stub flush with the trunk to allow the wound to heal and paint with tree-wound compound.

Bark Tracings

Treat bark abrasions on tree trunks promptly to permit rapid healing of the wound and to prevent decay. See Figs. 3.4 and 3.5.

TOOLS AND MATERIAL

A sharp curved-blade pruning knife and a ½-in. paintbrush are needed. If the bark is thick, a sharp wood chisel and light mallet are used to cut it. Small quantities of shellac and tree-wound paint are also required.

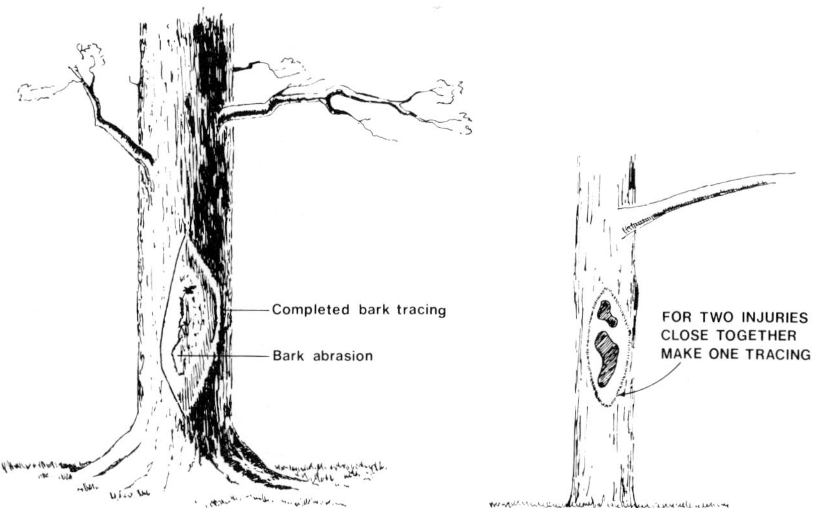

Fig. 3.4 Bark tracing of abrasion on trunk of tree.

Fig. 3.5 Bark tracing.

PROCEDURE

Determine the extent of injury and carefully remove all loose bark. Start the bark tracing in sound bark above the injury and work a knife or chisel down on a slight curve to one side of it, removing all sprung bark. Hold the chisel at a slight angle away from the injury, with beveled edge toward the sound bark. Shellac the exposed edge of bark as tracing progresses to prevent drying. Continue tracing downward until distances above and below the center of the injury are equal, and then repeat the procedure on the opposite side of the injury. Apply a second coat of shellac to the exposed bark edge and paint the exposed wood with a tree-wound compound.

The top and bottom points of the tracing must be established on the centerline of the injury to permit uniform healing. The healing callus does not develop on the lower side of a bark tracing made on an angle.

When two small injuries are close together (Fig. 3.5), make one bark tracing, because the thin strip of bark between two abrasions dries out and tracing must be repeated.

Pruning Shrubs

When transplanting deciduous shrubs, remove part of the woody growth in order to compensate for partial loss of the root system. Shrubs pruned when planted recover and regain natural shape more quickly than unpruned plants. In general, prune away about one-third of the top growth. Shrubs produce new growth near the base of the plant while trees grow from the ends of the branches. Tree trunks do not grow upward; a nail driven 3 ft above the ground always remains at that height. Vigorous, established shrubs do not have to be pruned unless they have outgrown their location to block sunlight from buildings or interfere with walks.

NEW SHRUBS

Prune all newly planted deciduous shrubs according to their natural habit of growth. Do not shear them uniformly, because varieties are usually chosen for their contrasting growth habits. Shearing produces a formal shape, destroys the plant's identity, and is monotonous and unsightly. Cut heavy canes at a greater height from the ground than smaller canes.

ESTABLISHED SHRUBS

Prune old, oversized shrubs by cutting the heavy canes back to the ground so that new shoots grow from the base of the plant. Unsightly shrubs can be reclaimed by this method. When a shrub consists entirely of old, heavy canes, remove only half of the canes the first year to avoid the undesirable brushlike effect of a mass of stiff stalks.

Prune such shrubs as forsythia immediately after flowering to prevent the following year's bloom from being destroyed. Prune fruiting types before and after they bloom in early spring or in the fall. Shrubs pruned severely in the late fall have a dehorned appearance all winter.

HEDGES

There is a right and wrong method of trimming a formal hedge. The usual tendency is to prune the sides, gradually sloping inward until the top is considerably broader than the base. Such pruning will cut off all sunlight from the lower branches, thereby causing the plant to become thin at the base with a heavy leaf crown supported by a few open stems. See Fig. 3.6.

The proper method of pruning is to keep the top narrower than the base, with the sides sloping outward. This method takes advantage of full sunlight from top to bottom, thereby maintaining the whole hedge compact and dense.

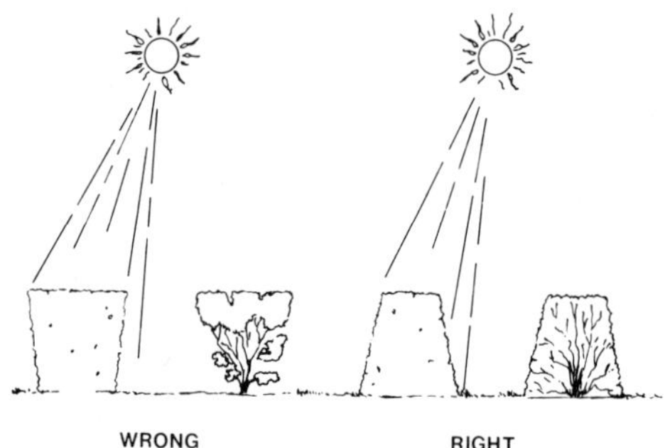

Fig. 3.6 Right and wrong methods of hedge pruning.

Following are suggestions for pruning the most common shrubs. The number following the common name of the plant refers to its botanical name found in the master list in Table 3.41.

Abelia (1) Remove old flower heads and thin the plant out occasionally. The shrub needs no regular pruning.

Azalea see Rhododendron.

Barberry (25–29) Most of the common species do not require regular pruning. It may be necessary to remove deadwood in old stock.

Bayberry (175) No formal pruning necessary.

Beautyberry (35–36) These shrubs should be thinned out when necessary, retaining as much young wood as possible through shortening the points or tips.

Boxwood (33–34) No regular pruning is necessary. Hedge effects may be cut during the summer.

Buckthorn (219–220) No special pruning required.

Cotoneaster (68–76) No special pruning required.

Daphne (81) No special pruning required.

Deutzia (82–85) Should be thinned out well once in 3 years by removing as much of the old wood as possible. The best time for pruning is in early summer, after flowering period is over.

Dogwood (52–63) Can be successfully grown without specific pruning. Overgrown plants can be cut back severely without injury, and the many kinds grown for the colored bark can be cut to the ground in the spring.

Eleagnus (87–89) Does not require regular pruning except to curb straggling habits of growth by shortening the longest shoots during the summer. Green-leaved shoots that often appear among the variegated varieties should be removed as soon as they are observed.

Euonymus (90–99) Most of the species need no pruning. The evergreen burning bush (*Euonymus japonica*) requires a little shaping when grown as a shrub, but treated as a hedge it should be clipped once or twice during the summer. The wintercreeper (*E. radicans*), grown normally as ground cover under trees or as a border for shrub beds, should be trimmed or cut over either in spring or summer.

Forsythia (103) Special pruning is not necessary except for thining out every third year, or the shrubs may be clipped moderately each year as soon as the flowering period is over. When forsythia is grown as a bush, the main branches should be cut back to the same height each year. This method stimulates the formation during the summer of long shoots which will be in full bloom from end to end the following spring.

Hawthorn (77–80) No special pruning required.

Holly (122–129) Do not clip back the shoots, since they are naturally stiff and erect; instead, clean out some of the laterals of the shoots to accentuate them. Holly hedges may be clipped back at the middle or end of summer.

Honeysuckle, bush (161–164) The true shrub species should be thinned out every 3 to 4 years. If overgrown, the longer shoots should be cut back, in summer if possible, and not every year. The climbing species requires very little formal pruning if the plants have room to develop, but if they are growing under restricted conditions, they may be cut after the flowering period.

Ivy (112) Grown in the form of a bush, ivy may require a little shaping each year, merely removal of a branch here and there. Old plants can be invigorated by cutting back in spring. Where it is grown against walls, ivy should be cut back as close as possible to the walls in February or March. On the sides of buildings, cut back the upper shoots well below the roof or gutters. Also examine and cut the plants toward the beginning of July, removing long shoots that are protruding away from the wall.

Jasmine (131–132) The bushy species requires occasional thinning but no other formal treatment. The winter jasmine (*Jasminum nudiflorum*) and the primrose jasmine (*J. primulinum*) should have the flowering shoots cut back to within two buds of the base as soon as the flowers fade, but no further pruning should follow.

Laurel (143) This species has no need of formal pruning.

Leucothoe (150) Plants treated as shrubs should have their older stems removed and the younger shoots shortened in late February before the spring season starts. Shrubs grown for the color effect of their bright green bark should be cut close to the ground in March.

Lilac (269–276) If the plants are flowering freely, no regular pruning is needed. If flowers are sparse, and growth is weak, thin out the branches in April, removing some of the inside wood and weak shoots. Inspect shrubs again early in June, and remove weaker shoots. All new growth should be removed from the base of the plant at least once a year.

Locust (108–109, 233) The shrubby locusts should be cut back a little in summer to prevent branches from becoming too long and rank.

Magnolia (165) The shrubby species does not require regular pruning.

Mock orange (183–184) This shrub needs no formal pruning, and in fact does best if left untouched; it may be thinned out a little at intervals of a few years.

Privet (151–157) Shrubs need no special pruning; hedges should be clipped several times during the summer.

Periwinkle (326) Formal pruning is not necessary, though the big-leaf periwinkle may be cut back occasionally.

Quince (45) When grown as a bush, quince requires no pruning. If grown as a hedge, it may be cut back when the flowering period is over.

Redbud (43–44) Shape the plants when young but prune as little as possible when plant is mature. Remove only deadwood as plant matures.

Rhododendron (221–222) Needs no regular pruning except for the removal of the flower heads as soon as the flower fades. However, young plants should be clipped occasionally to induce sturdy growth. Overgrown plants that are old can be cut back severely without serious injury. Such cutting should be done in March or April.

Rose (234–243) Ramblers and climbers should have all the old flowering canes removed as soon as the flowers fade. Bush roses should have all weak wood removed, and vigorous young canes from the root should be encouraged. This general pruning is best done in March.

Shadblow (15) No specific pruning is necessary.

Snowball (318) No special pruning is necessary.

Spirea (253–259) Needs very little pruning. The Thunberg spirea (*Spiraea thunbergi*) and some others may be slightly winter-killed on the tips; such injured shoots should be removed.

Spurge, Japanese (180) No specific pruning is necessary.

Sumac (225–231) When sumac is grown for the large compound leaves and autumn coloration, the young shoots must be cut down to within a few inches of the ground in February or early March. If the plants are grown for shrubbery or mass effects, no special pruning is required.

Sweet shrub (37) No specific pruning is necessary.

Willows (244) If they are grown for colored-bark effects, cut willows back in February; otherwise no regular pruning is required.

Witch Hazel (111) Prune only to shape the plants, particularly when they are young; older plants have no need for further formal pruning.

PLANTING METHODS

Dig the pits for trees and shrubs before the plants arrive, so that the plants are out of the ground no longer than necessary. Large balled-and-burlapped plants should be placed in the holes directly from the truck.

If the plants are left out of the ground for a few days, cover the balls of earth with soil to prevent the roots near the surface from drying out. Cover the roots of all bare-root trees and shrubs with wet burlap or similar material as soon as they are unloaded if planting is to take place within a few hours.

Heel in all other bare-root trees and shrubs at once in a trench deep enough to accommodate the roots of the plants. Place them at a 45° angle, and cover the roots with soil or sawdust to prevent drying. When shrubs or trees are delivered in bundles, keep the bundles intact to facilitate future handling. Avoid injury to plants by rough treatment. When removing plants from the heeling-in trench, uncover roots carefully. Do not grasp the top of the plants and pull them out of the trench without removing the covering soil. Locate the heeling-in ground as near the final planting site as possible, preferably where water is available. Water heeled-in stock periodically if the plants are to stay in the trench longer than normal. Do not wash the soil away from the roots when watering.

Planting Pits

In digging planting pits for trees, separate the soil into three piles: sod, topsoil, and subsoil. Use the salvaged sod elsewhere to repair grassed areas. Arrange the piles to keep open the side of the pit from which the tree will be placed.

The planting pits should be dug wide enough to accommodate all roots without crowding or twisting. Dig tree pits at least 1 ft wider than the spread of roots or ball of earth. Prepare all planting pits with straight sides. Dig tree pits just deep enough to allow for a 6 in. cushion of topsoil in the bottom and to permit the top of the ball to be flush with the existing grade. Deeper planting hinders air from reaching the roots and may kill the tree. Shape the pit bottom with the center slightly raised for proper drainage. Place about 6 in. of compacted topsoil in the bottom of the pit.

Setting Plants

If the tree is delivered on a platform, tip the ball on its side by pushing against the ball after it is set in the hole. Do not crack or damage the earth ball. Cut the ropes holding the platform and remove the platform from the pit. Carefully right the tree by lifting against the ball. Cut the rope lacing and cut away as much burlap wrapping as possible. Leave the burlap in place under the ball because it helps to hold the ball together and will soon disintegrate in the soil. To prevent crumbling, do not cut rope lacing while the tree is tipped. Placing trees and shrubs without a platform follows the same general procedure. The plant is set directly into the pit, with a minimum of movement after it reaches its final level.

Set all plants plumb before backfilling. Avoid straightening trees or shrubs after the backfill has been placed. Damage to plants may result from air pockets formed under the roots when the tree or shrub is moved. See Fig. 3.7.

Backfill the space between the ball and the side of the planting pit with good loam topsoil. Work soil under the ball to eliminate air pockets. Place backfill in 6-in. layers, using the salvaged topsoil. Firm each layer by tamping until the pit is half filled. If the soil is wet, use a light wood tamper to avoid heavy compaction, which reduces air spaces too much. It is always best to avoid using wet soil. If the soil is reasonably dry, fill the top half of the pit with water to settle the backfilled soil. Allow the water to be absorbed and fill the remainder of the planting pit with topsoil, tamping lightly as it is filled. Settle the soil with water to prevent tight compaction. See Fig. 3.8.

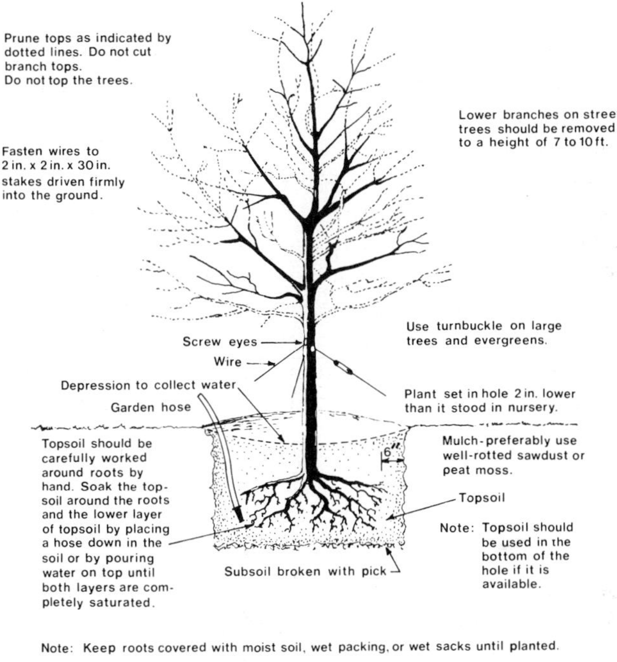

Fig. 3.7 Method of planting bare-root trees and shrubs.

Bare-Root Plants

Before setting bare-root trees and shrubs, shape the bottom of the pit so that the center of the pit is slightly higher than the sides, forming an inverted cone. The plant should then be set on this cone so that the center of the plant is resting on the highest portion, and the roots are carefully spread out along the sides. Prune all broken roots before backfilling. Plumb the plant so that it is standing straight and hold it in place by backfilling enough topsoil to cover the roots. Add water until the soil becomes a thick liquid. Gently raise and lower the plant to allow the soil to fill between the fibrous roots. Continue adding soil and water until the planting pit is filled to grade. It is not a good idea to do too much tamping on bare-root plants for fear of damaging the roots.

Settlement After the water has drained away, check all planting pits for settlement and add enough soil to bring them up to grade, keeping the surface sloped slightly toward the tree.

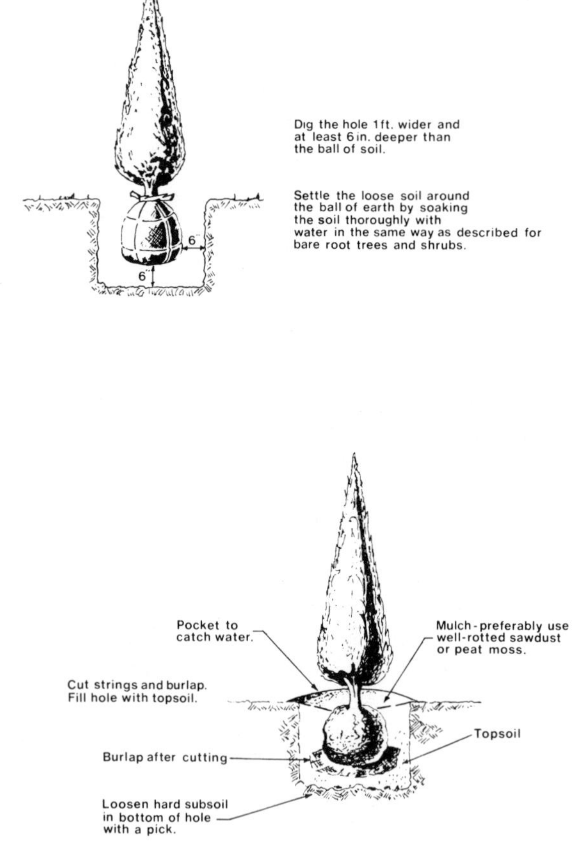

Fig. 3.8 Method of planting balled-and-burlapped trees and shrubs.

Earth Ring If planting is done in the spring, make an earth ring about 3 in. high around the plant. This ring should vary in size with the size of the plant. A good rule of thumb for the diameter of the ring is to make the ring extend to the outer edge of the spread of the branches. Omit earth rings around trees and shrubs planted in the late fall; level all existing rings in the fall because water collecting inside the rings may freeze the plants.

Dry Planting If water is not available at planting time, carefully work the loose soil around the roots by raising and lowering the tree or shrub slightly. Cover the roots with soil, backfill, and tamp the topsoil in 6-in. layers.

Vines

Plant field-grown vines by digging individual soil pockets wide enough to hold the roots without crowding. Place about 2 in. of topsoil under the plant. Firm the soil around the roots until the planting pocket is filled.

Remove pot-grown vines from the containers carefully to avoid breaking the soil around the roots. Set 2- to 3-in. pot-grown vines in planting pockets about 6 in. wide; proceed as in planting field-grown vines.

Planting Broadleaf Evergreens in Limestone Regions

Normally it is not a good practice to plant acid-loving plants such as the azaleas, rhododendrons, laurel, andromedas, etc., in soils which are high in lime or have pH readings above 5.0. However, it has been done successfully by following these rules:

1. Do not set plants in individual holes but first excavate the entire bed to a depth of 2 ft.
2. Fill excavation with water to test for drainage. If the water drains away within 2 to 3 hours no further measures need be taken. If, however, the water continues to stand in the hole for periods up to 12 to 24 hours, a French drain should be dug. Broadleaf evergreens will not stand poor drainage situations.
3. Place 4 lb powdered sulfur per 1000 ft^2 of area in the bottom of this excavation.
4. Backfill with composted oak leaves or acid peat moss. Bring backfill to top of excavation and settle thoroughly by watering.
5. Place the plant on top of the backfill and fill around it with acid peat moss or composed oak leaves. Do not hesitate to bring the backfill well up into the plant a foot or more. This type of plant thrives in deep mulches and likes to keep its roots cool.

6. Replenish the mulch each year. It is essential to maintain this mulch at least 1 ft deep at all times.
7. It usually is not necessary to anchor the plants when they are planted in groups. Single plants can be staked with one stake.

Staking and Guying

Stake or guy all trees and treelike shrubs immediately after planting. Unless they are staked or guyed at once, newly planted balled and burlapped trees are loosened from the ball by the wind; both bare-root and balled-and-burlapped plants may be pushed out of alignment and need to be pulled back to a vertical position. If a tree is straightened after planting, not only may air pockets be formed around the roots but all the strain will be placed on one stake or guy wire. Keep tension on all stakes or guy wires equal. Do not use guy wires where pedestrians may trip over them.

STAKING STREET TREES

Stake street trees up to 3-in. caliper with two stakes on opposite sides of the tree, about 18 in. from the trunk and parallel to the curb. Use cedar stakes with the bark attached, if available. Select stakes 8 ft long with a diameter of about 2 in. at the top and about 3 in. at the butt. Stakes must be this long in order to provide the proper stiffening to the tree at least one-quarter of the way up the trunk. Drive the stakes 3 ft deep at a slight angle away from the tree.

Stake street trees of 4- to 5-in. caliper with four stakes 10 ft long, driven 4 ft into the ground. Place the stakes in box formation at equal distances 18 in. from the tree.

Place scrap rubber hose, 1 to 2 in. in diameter, around the tree trunk near the top of the stakes to prevent damage to bark by supporting wires. If scrap rubber hose is not available, use fairly thick cloth wrappings or laths cut 6 in. long, where the wire makes contact with the tree.

Use 12-gage wire between the stakes and the tree. Cut the wire in proper lengths and draw it through the rubber hose or around the protective collar until the cut ends meet. Pull the ends of the wire around the stake near the top until taut. Wrap the cut ends around the stake and twist them together on the inside of the stake. Secure the tree to the second stake in the same way. To give added tension, insert a stick between the strands of double wire and twist until the wire is tight.

STAKING SHRUBS AND SMALL TREES

Stake treelike shrubs and small trees with single stakes placed on the side toward the prevailing winds. Set the stake about 1 ft from the trunk and about 2 ft deep. When planting bare-root stock, drive the stake before setting the plant to prevent injury to the roots. Use scrap rubber hose and 12-gage wire as described above. If ½-in. rope is used instead of wire and hose, cross the rope between stake and tree, wrap loose ends around the stake, and tie in place with a square knot.

GUYING

In nontraffic areas, guy trees up to 4-in. caliper from three directions (Fig. 3.9). Drive three equally spaced 4-ft stakes of cedar or scrap

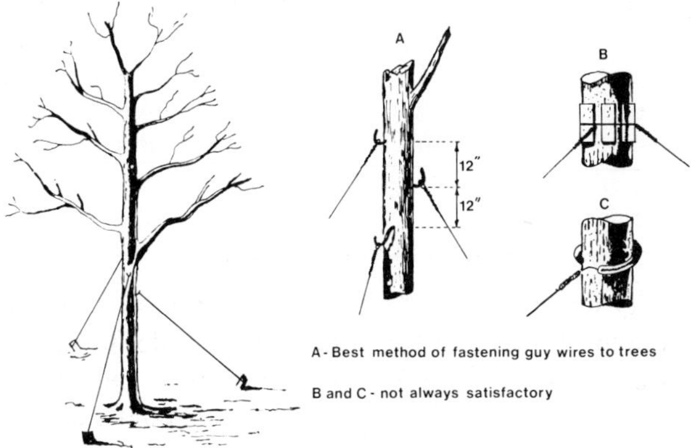

Fig. 3.9 Method of bracing trees.

lumber around the tree outside the planting pit. Place the stakes so that guy wires will not interfere with the lower limbs. Notch the stakes near the top on the side away from the tree and drive them to within 6 in. of the top at a slight angle away from the tree. Place scrap rubber hose or protective collar around the trunk, about 6 ft from the ground. Another method is to screw small but heavy lag screws with a hook into the trunk of the tree. The guy wires can be fastened to these hooks without damage to the tree. After the tree has become firmly anchored and fully established, remove guy wires and lag screw hooks from the tree. The holes left by the screws should be treated with a good tree-wound paint and filled with wood putty.

If the protective-collar method is used, put the wrapping slightly above the lower limbs for street trees. Run a single strand of wire through or around the protective collar and back to the stake. Cut the wire free from the coil, allowing enough slack to fasten the wires securely and to permit driving the stake below the ground level. Repeat for the other two stakes. Get the same tension on all guys to give proper alignment. If the tree settles, tighten the guys by driving the stakes deeper or inserting a stick between the two strands of wire and twisting until the wire is tight.

Guy 5-in. caliper trees with two double strands of 12-gage wire attached to three 2- by 4-in. stakes, 4 ft long, in the method shown (Fig 3.9) for 2- to 3-in. caliper trees.

Remove identification tags and labels from trees to prevent wire or cord from constricting the limb or trunk as the tree grows.

Remove guy wires and stakes the second year after planting. The root growth by that time is anchored firmly, and failure to remove the wires may cause total or partial girdling as the tree grows against constricting wire.

WRAPPING

Newly planted trees of 2 in. caliper and over should always have the trunk and the lower parts of the first limbs wrapped with burlap or kraft crepe paper 6 in. wide to reduce the amount of water given off by the tree through the bark while the roots are becoming established.

Start at the lower part of the bottom branches and wrap spirally to the ground. Overlap half of each spiral to form a double wrapping. Secure the last wrapping with twine, winding the twine in wide spirals up the trunk and tying above the lower branches.

WAXING

Another way to reduce the amount of water given off through the bark pores is to spray newly planted trees with a paraffin-base preparation, which takes the place of burlap or crepe-paper wrappings. Prepare the material according to the manufacturer's directions and apply as a fine spray. Limit the spray to heavy limbs and trunk; do not cover entire tree. Do not use these sprays for trees with thin bark, such as dogwood and sugar maple, unless the ingredients are known to be harmless.

Watering after Planting

The water needs of newly planted trees, shrubs, and vines depend on temperature, water-holding capacity of the soil, drainage, and normal rainfall. Generally, plants do not need watering in cold weather. During the first few years after planting, artificial watering is necessary in hot, dry periods.

Too much watering in clay soils may reduce soil temperatures and retard plant growth. It also may drown the plant by preventing air from reaching the roots.

To determine the need for watering, dip up a shovelful of earth and test the soil below the first few inches. Squeeze it in the hand, and if it keeps the shape of a ball, watering is not necessary.

QUANTITY

When watering is required, soak the soil thoroughly. About 27,000 gal of water per acre equals 1 in. of rainfall, or a little over $\frac{1}{2}$ gal/ft^2. Clay soils generally require $\frac{1}{2}$ gal/ft^2, while sandy soils require 2 gal; soils between these two extremes require about 1 gal.

WILT-PRUF

Wilt-Pruf is a water stabilizer for plants. By substantially reducing water loss during periods of high water transpiration, it protects plants from desiccation. Wilt-Pruf NCF is not an insecticide, fungicide, or pesticide. It makes it possible to transplant at any time of the year when the ground is not actually frozen. In addition, it minimizes transplant losses even during optimum transplanting weather.

Wilt-Pruf NCF acts as a protective blanket over plant surfaces to slow down the transpiration rate demanded of it from searing winds and hot, dry air. It is a film that produces a lower rate of moisture-vapor transpiration. At recommended dilution rates it does not stop all water loss or passage of oxygen and carbon dioxide but tends to balance the rate of water loss with the water-gathering capacity of the roots. Maintaining this balance is critical for balled-and-burlapped as well as bare-root plants until new feeder roots are produced.

It provides additional protection as a physical barrier against drying winds. This mechanical barrier under some conditions protects against air pollution and toxic materials such as salt spray, dog urine, city soot, etc. There are three major uses for this plastic coating:

1. As an antitranspirant to prevent moisture loss in hot-weather planting. By applying the coating before digging, one can transplant practically all types of nursery material at any time of the year, with very little wilt or setback.
2. As a fall spray to prevent winter burn and sun scorch.
3. As a sticker for insecticides and fungicides. The combination of a plastic spray with insecticides and fungicides prolongs the life of such materials and makes fewer applications necessary.

Transplanting Shrubs and Trees from Native Stands

The safest procedure in transplanting or collecting deciduous shrubs from native stands is to dig them with a ball of earth on the roots. In clay or clay loam soils this is a simple process because the soil is heavy enough to stay around the roots. The ball of earth for an average size shrub should be about one-half the spread of the branches.

Shrubs growing in sandy or gravelly soils are more difficult to move because it is difficult to keep the soil from falling away from the roots. Use a pick to dig the plants and comb the soil away from the roots, without damaging or destroying them. Prepare a soupy mixture of soil and water and dip the roots into the mixture to puddle the mud around the roots and keep them from drying out. Cover the roots with wet burlap or some other suitable material for further protection from the sun and wind.

DECIDUOUS TREES

In collecting deciduous trees from native stands it is wise to select trees of 3-in. caliper or less. Such trees are easier to move and will frequently

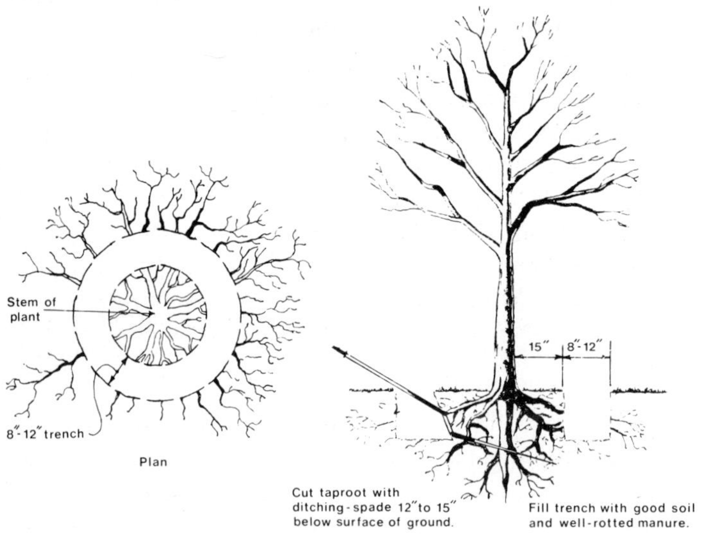

Fig. 3.10 Root pruning before transplanting.

catch up to trees of a larger size transplanted at the same time. Transplant only with a ball of earth, allowing 1 ft in its diameter for each inch of tree-trunk diameter taken 1 ft above the ground surface.

A large tree should be root-pruned at least one growing season before it is moved from its natural site. To do this, dig a trench during the dormant season, about 3 ft in diameter for a 3-in. caliper tree, deep enough to sever all roots extending into the trench. A trench 2 ft deep will usually suffice. This trench should then be backfilled with good soil, preferably mixed with peat moss or well-rotted sawdust. This mixture should be about 75 per cent soil and 25 per cent humus. Prune the tree back about one-fourth, by pruning only its side branches.

The tree will produce new fine roots during the following year within this trench. To dig for transplanting, dig a trench outside the trench previously dug, being careful not to damage the new roots (Fig. 3.10). Protect the ball by wrapping with burlap. This method will reduce the size of the ball considerably, making it easier to handle.

Evergreens are transplanted in much the same manner, except that they must always be moved with a ball of earth.

Preserving Existing Trees When Grades Are Changed

When the grade is raised around existing good trees, a dry well should be constructed. Increasing the depth of soil over tree roots makes it difficult for air to reach the roots and may smother the tree. There are three general methods of protecting the tree:

1. Construct a dry well 1 to 3 ft from the trunk of the tree, using flat fieldstone or brick, with open (uncemented) joints. If the fill is over 1 ft deep, place a layer of crushed stone from the outer drip of the branches to the dry well. Place vertical tile at intervals at the outer drip range of the tree, to admit air to the root system.
2. Use the same method described above but bring the crushed stone up to finished grade to form a ring around the tree under the outer drip of the branches (see Fig. 3.11).
3. Place a coarse rock fill up to the trunk of the tree. This rock fill should cover an area 10 ft in circumference around the tree (see Fig. 3.12).

Reforestation

Many parks or publicly owned lands have areas which cannot be developed for recreational use. Such areas are usually well removed from the major area of activity and would serve little purpose as grass or meadow areas. They may include slopes on which the erosion problem is acute. Land of this kind can be reforested to native trees at a very nominal cost and will serve to reduce maintenance costs, control erosion, supply cover for wildlife, and provide a future crop of timber and pulpwood.

Because the kind of tree to plant for this purpose will vary from one

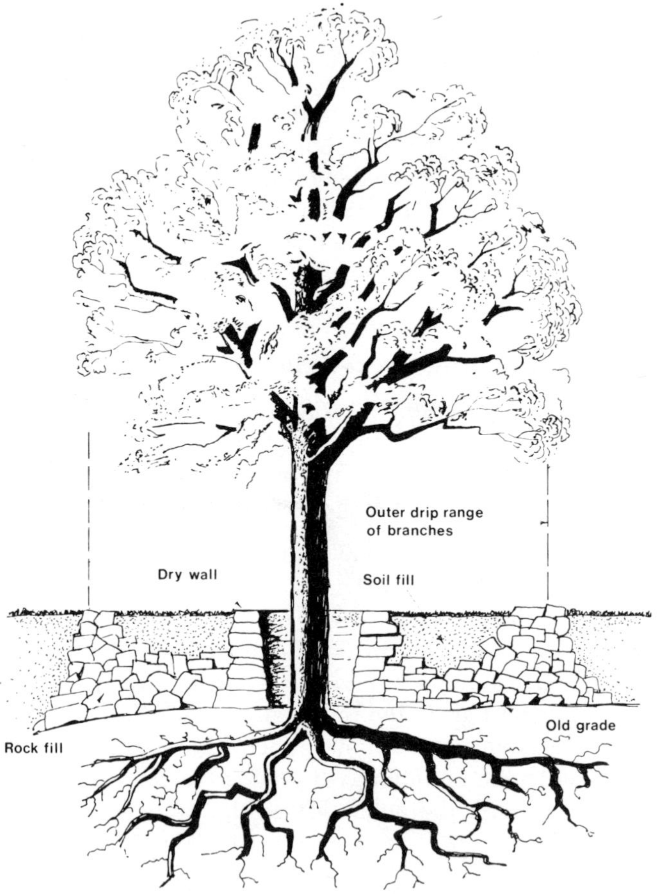

Fig. 3.11 Method of preserving trees when grades are changed.

locality to another, it is best to consult your local state forester before making a selection. He will also be able to add detailed advice on your particular problem to the planting information given below.

SEASON TO PLANT

In most locations the time to plant seedlings is in the spring, beginning as soon as the frost is out of the ground. The length of the planting season will vary with the year and the locality, but seedlings must always be started early enough to become established before hot weather.

CARE OF TREES

Seedling trees usually arrive from the nursery in bundles, cartons, or crates, with the roots packed in sphagnum moss. They should be taken

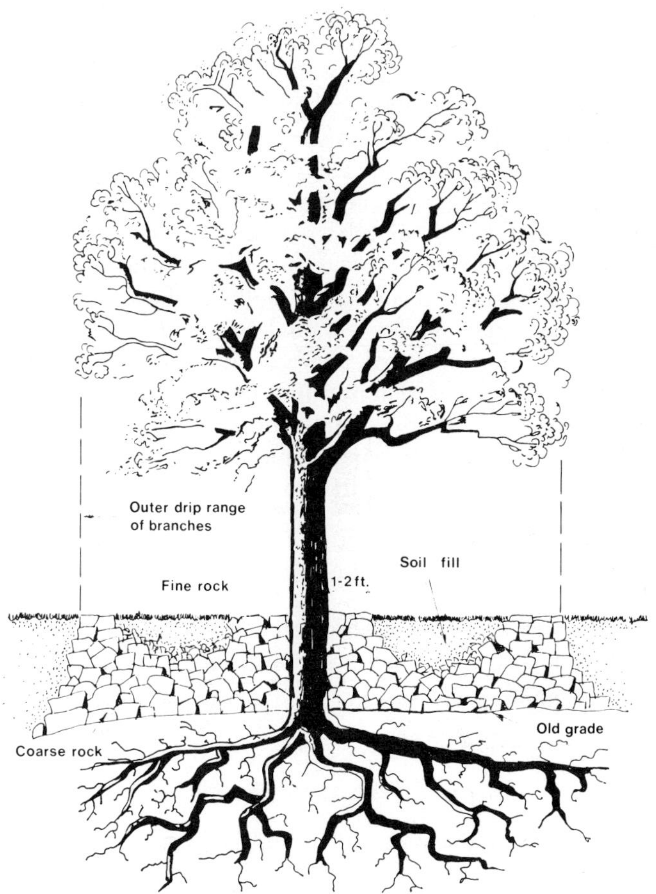

Fig. 3.12 Method of preserving trees when grades are changed.

out of the container immediately after arrival and heeled in. The heeling-in trench (about 8 in. deep and as wide as the ordinary shovel blade) should be prepared beforehand in a moist, shaded area, or in an area where brush can be cut to shade the seedlings. The trees should be placed in the trench and the roots covered with loose soil. Do not let the roots dry out; water if the trees remain in the trench for any length of time.

PLANTING

Planting may be done either by hand or by machine. In planting by hand use a mattock or grub hoe. Strike the hoe into the ground, press downward and to one side to open a slit in the ground or sod, whip the tree roots into this slot, remove the blade, and press the soil or sod firmly about the roots with the heel of your boot. Carry the trees in a pail with enough water in it to keep the roots moist. A two-man team, one planting and one carrying and tamping, should be able to plant from 800 to 1500 trees per day, depending on the weather, ground conditions, and the physical stamina of the men (Table 3.7).

Machine planting is being done more and more, especially on large areas where the land contour allows a farm tractor to be used with safety. Tree-planting machines come in various forms and operate on one of three principles: (1) scooping out a clump of sod by lugs mounted on a tractor or on a pair of wheels pulled as a trailer; (2) cutting a continuous slit by a tractor-mounted, hydraulically operated, single-bottom plow, and (3) the same operation by a unit manufactured specifically for tree planting, mounted either on small wheels or on runners, and towed behind a tractor with the man who is planting the trees riding the unit. Machine operators have claimed that they can plant up to 10,000 seedlings per day with two men.

SPACING

Spacing of seedling plantings will vary with the type of tree used. Table 3.10 shows the number of trees per acre at various spacings.

CARE OF PLANTINGS

The most serious hazard to forest plantings is fire. Firebreaks should be provided around all plantings less than 10 acres in size, and for larger areas there should be a system of fire lines as breaks. Protection from grazing animals is also necessary. A thinning program should be instituted when the plantings are 15 to 20 years old. Consult the local state forester for detailed plans for forest control and management.

White pine plantations must be protected from the spread of the white pine blister rust. This disease must spread from *Ribes* plants (currant and gooseberry), and therefore a program of intensive eradication of these plants must be carried forward.

TABLE 3.7
Average Time for Digging and Planting*

Height of shrub in feet	Time to dig (min.)	Time to handle (min.)	Time to plant, prune, water and clean up	Total time, (min.)	No. one man can move per day
Shrubs with bare roots					
2 to 3	5	5	20	30	18
3 to 4	6	5	25	36	15
4 to 5	8	6	31	45	12
5 to 6	10	8	42	60	9
6 to 8	20	10	60	90	6
Shrubs with soil, burlapped but not laced					
2 to 3	8	6	31	45	12
3 to 4	10	8	42	60	9
4 to 5	20	10	60	90	6
5 to 6	30	15	90	135	4
6 to 8	60	30	180	270	2

* Compiled by Owen B. Schmidt, Superintendent, F. D. Moore & Sons, Landscape Contractors and Nurserymen, and reproduced by his permission.

TABLE 3.8
Average Time for Planting 1000 ft² with Ground Covers*

Number and kind of plants	Labor to dig bed 10 in. Deep	Labor (spread manure and peat and prepare bed†)	Time to plant	Total labor (time)
500 Ivy	9 hr.	9 hr.	5 hr.	23 hr.
4000 Pachysandra	9	9	18	36
750 Sarococca	9	9	7½	25½
4000 Ajuga	9	9	18	36
334 Roses	9	9	18	36
334 Honeysuckle	9	9	9	27
1000 Vinca minor	9	9	10	28

* Compiled by Owen B. Schmidt, Superintendent, F. D. Moore & Sons, Landscape Contractors and Nurserymen, and reproduced by his permission.

† On each bed was spread four bales of peat moss 1 in. deep and 1 ton of rotted manure, also 1 in. deep.

TABLE 3.9
Average Time for Digging, Handling, Planting, Watering, Pruning, Guying, and Wrapping Trees

Ball size diam. depth, in.	Soil in ball, ft^3	Weight of ball, lb	Time to dig and lace, minutes	Time to handle ball, minutes	Size hole required, in.	Soil in hole to excavate, ft^3	Time to dig hole, minutes	Soil displacement, ft^3	Time to plant and prune, minutes	Time to water, wrap, guy, and clean up, minutes	Topsoil handled in moving, ft^3	Total time in moving
12 × 12	7/10	56	15	10	24	3 3/4	20	3	15	4	10 1/2	64 min
18 × 16	2	160	30	20	30	7 1/2	28	5 1/2	21	5	21	1 2/3 h
24 × 18	4	320	60	40	36	13	65	9	49	12	38	3 2/3 h
30 × 21	7 1/2	600	114	76	48	26 1/2	133	19	100	25	76	7 1/3 h
36 × 24	12 1/2	980	189	126	54	38	190	25 1/2	143	36	114	11 1/3 h
42 × 27	19	1520	285	190	66	64	320	45	240	60	185	18 1/2 h
48 × 30	28	2040	420	280	72	85	360	57	270	68	254	23 1/3 h
54 × 33	38 1/2	3060	579	386	84	127	635	88 1/2	476	119	370	36 1/2 h
60 × 36	52	4160	780	520	90	159	795	107	596	149	474	47 1/3 h
66 × 39	68	5440	1020	680	96	196	905	128	679	168	596	57 1/2 h
72 × 42	87	7160	1305	870	108	267	1240	180	930	233	795	76 h

Protection and Control of Street Trees

The installation and care of street trees are complicated by the interests of a variety of departments of town and city government. The safety of the public, space requirements, traffic, utilities, and many other factors must be considered. The hazards and inconveniences that result when these factors are ignored can be seen today in many cities where the older trees were planted before controlling ordinances were enacted.

It is important, first of all, to select the right tree for the spot available. A tree that requires a space of 40 to 50 ft within which to mature should not be forced to crowd itself into a 20-ft space. Trees with surface roots and trees that require a great deal of moisture should not be placed where the roots will be cramped or can interfere with sewer lines. Large trees should not be planted where there are overhead power lines, as anyone will appreciate who has seen an avenue of trees with branches on only one side, or the tops cut out, or even with holes cut out among the branches. Smaller flowering trees are suitable for planting under power lines: dogwood, crabs, mountain ash, redbud, fringe tree, hawthorns, flowering cherry, and other similar species. Any of these may be spaced 20 ft apart, and will grow successfully in a strip of lawn 4 ft wide. Larger shade trees should be planted a minimum distance of 40 ft apart and only where the lawn between sidewalk and curb is at least 8 ft wide.

TABLE 3.10
Trees per Acre at Various Spacings

Spacing (ft)	No. trees per acre
5	1,740
6	1,210
7	890
8	680
9	538
10	436
12	303

Below is a list of common regulations governing the planting and care of street trees. These regulations should become a part of the city or town ordinances:

1. Posting signs on trees should not be allowed.
2. Hitching animals to trees should not be allowed.
3. Anchoring ropes and chains to trees should not be allowed.
4. Adequate guards should be provided around trees in construction areas.

5. No chemicals, including salt, should be placed in contact with trees.
6. No cement or stone paving should be placed around the trunks of trees.
7. No excavations should be permitted within 20 ft of a tree.
8. Heavy equipment should not be permitted to operate within 20 ft.
9. Gas leaks should be repaired immediately.
10. Electric lines and poles should be safeguarded during trimming operations.
11. Branches should be trimmed to allow a minimum clearance of 8 ft if they overhang sidewalks or streets.
12. Branches of trees should not be permitted lower than 5 ft at street corners in order to allow motorists a full view of the intersection.
13. Trees should be planted or spaced 20 to 40 ft apart, depending upon the species.
14. No trees should be planted closer than 20 ft to a sewer line.
15. All diseased trees, including elms with the Dutch elm disease, should be removed immediately. No diseased trees should be planted.
16. Several species of trees should never be used for street or city use because their habits of growth create problems of maintenance repair to streets and sidewalks. Some have excessively large leaves and seed pods difficult to clean up; with others thorns and brittleness of branches create a safety problem; others are too spreading in growth, and some have shallow root systems which get into sewer lines and break up sidewalks. The most common of these undesirable trees are poplar, box elder, willow, catalpa, tree of heaven, soft maple, chestnut, black locust, Chinese elm, ash, basswood or linden, and cottonwood.

In order to make the proper selection of plant materials for various conditions, uses and requirements, the following list has been prepared (see Table 3.11). The number following the common name refers to the scientific name found in the master list in Table 3.41.

POISONOUS PLANTS

Table 3.12 lists plants known to be harmful. Care should be exercised with all these plants to prevent accidental contact with them, particularly where small children are concerned.

TABLE 3.11
Plant Materials for Specific Conditions

Screens—quick-growing

Trees	Shrubs
Arborvitae, pyramidal (290)	Buckthorn, glossy (220)
Douglas fir (209)	Honeysuckle, bush (161)
Hemlock, Canada (300)	Nannyberry (313)
Maple, silver (10)	Ninebark (186)
Pine, scotch (193)	Olive, Russian (87)
Pine, white (192)	Privet, ibota (153)
Poplar (197)	Privet, California (155)
Cypress, Sawara (46)	Photinia, oriental (185)
Spruce, Norway (187)	Wayfaring tree (312)
Willow (244)	

Hedge—formal clipped

Trees	Shrubs
Arborvitae, American (289)	Barberry, Japanese (27)
Hawthorn, cockspur (79)	Boxwood (33)
Hawthorn, English (80)	Buckthorn, common (219)
Hawthorn, Washington (78)	Buckthorn, glossy (220)
Hemlock, Canadian (300)	Euonymus, dwarf winged (91)
Hornbeam, American (40)	Euonymus, winged (90)
Maple, Amur (5)	Firethorn, Laland (210)
Maple, hedge (4)	Holly, convex leaved (124)
Pine, white (192)	Holly, littleleaf Japanese (125)
Spruce, Norway (187)	Privet, California (155)
Yews (280)	Privet, Ibolium (152)
	Wintercreeper, bigleaf (97)

Hedge—Informal

Shrubs, flowering, fruiting or evergreen	
Althea, shrub (114)	Lilac, common white (276)
Arrowwood (310)	Quince, Japanese flowering (45)
Barberry (26)	Rose, hugonis (235)
Deutzia, lemoine (84)	Spirea, Anthony Waterer (254)
Deutzia, slender (82)	Spirea, Kashmir False (249)
Euonymus, spreading (96)	Spirea, thunberg (257)
Forsythia, showy border (103)	Spirea, vanhoutte (259)
Honeysuckle, bush (161)	Sweetbrier (240)
Hollygrape, Oregon (166)	Viburum, doublefile (323)
Juniper, pfitzer (133)	Wayfaring tree (312)
Kerria, white (144)	Yew, Brown's (286)
Lilac, common (275)	Yew, Hatfield (287)

Wet locations

Trees	Shrubs
Arborvitae, American (289)	Arrowwood (310)
Cedar, white (47)	Buttonbush (42)
Elm, American (302)	Chokeberry, red (18)
Hemlock, Canadian (300)	Cranberrybush, American (308)

TABLE 3.11 (Continued)

Hornbeam, American (40)	Cranberrybush, European (316)
Linden, American (294)	Dogwood, Tatarian (52)
Maple, red (9)	Dogwood, red osier (62)
Maple, silver (10)	Dogwood, silky (54)
Oak, pin (216)	Fringetree, white (48)
Poplar (197)	Hardhack (258)
Shadblow, downy (15)	Inkberry (126)
Sourgum (177)	Nannyberry (313)
Sweetbay (165)	Rose, swamp (239)
Sweetgum (160)	Rose, Virginia (242)
Sycamore, American (195)	Summersweet (50)
Willow (244)	Willow (244)
	Winterberry (129)
	Withe rod (309)

Dry locations

Trees	Shrubs
Ash, green (105)	Aralia, five leaved (3)
Birch, gray (32)	Bladder-senna, common (51)
Elm, dwarf asiatic (303)	Blackhaw (319)
Hackberry (41)	Buckthorn, glossy (220)
Locust (109)	Cinquefoil, shrubby (201)
Maple, amur (5)	Dogwood, gray (59)
Maple, hedge (4)	Eleagnus, cherry (88)
Oak, mossycup (215)	Honeysuckle, Tatarian (164)
Oak, scarlet (214)	Indigobush (16)
Pine, scotch (193)	Juniper, Douglas (138)
Pine, white (192)	Juniper, Sargent's (134)
Scholartree, Chinese (248)	Locust, black (233)
Tree of Heaven (13)	Olive, Russian (87)
Goldenrain-tree (145)	Pea tree, Siberian (38)
	Plum, beach (206)
	Privet (151–157)
	Sumac (225)
	Tamarix, Algerian (278)
	Tamarix, five-stamen (279)

Berry-bearing

Red berries

Ash, European mountain (252)	Cotoneaster, willowleaf (75)
Barberry, Japanese (27)	Crab, Sargent's (173)
Cherry, cornelian (58)	Cranberrybush, American (308)
Chokeberry, red (18)	Cranberrybush, European (316)
Coralberry (268)	Dogwood, flowering (55)
Cotoneaster, Diels, (69)	Dogwood, kousa (57)
Cotoneaster, ground (73)	Eleagnus, cherry (88)
Cotoneaster, Franchet (71)	Euonymus, winged (90)
Cotoneaster, rock (72)	Euonymus, dwarf winged (91)
Cotoneaster, Simons (76)	Firethorn, Laland (210)
Cotoneaster, spreading (70)	Hawthorn, cockspur (79)

TABLE 3.11 (Continued)

Hawthorn, thicket (77)
Hawthorn, Washington (78)
Holly, American (128)
Honeysuckle, Morrow (163)
Honeysuckle, Tatarian (164)
Photinia, Oriental (185)
Rose, meadow (234)
Rose, swamp (239)
Sweetbrier (240)
Snowberry, Chenault (265)
Sweetbay (165)
Viburnum, linden (311)
Viburnum, tea (322)
Viburnum, Wright (324)
Winterberry, common (129)
Wintercreeper, bigleaf (97)

Black berries

Barberry, warty (29)
Blackhaw (319)
Buckthorn, common (219)
Buckthorn, glossy (220)
Chokeberry, black (19)
Cotoneaster, Peking (68)
Holly, convex-leaved (124)
Holly, Japanese littleleaf (125)
Inkberry (126)
Kerria, white (223)
Nannyberry (313)
Privet, ibota (153)
Privet, regal (156)
Shadblow, downy (15)
Viburnum, Siebold (321)
Viburnum, mapleleaf (307)
Wayfaring-tree (312)

White berries

Bayberry, northern (175)
Coralberry (268)
Dogwood, gray (59)
Dogwood, Tatarian (52)
Dogwood, red osier (62)
Spurge, Japanese (180)

Blue-black berries

Arrowwood (310)
Barberry, wintergreen (25)
Barberry, three-spined (28)
Beautyberry, American (35)
Beautyberry, Chinese (36)
Dogwood, silky (54)
Viburnum, Kentucky (314)
Withe rod (309)
Withe rod, smooth (315)

Small or dwarf plants

Abelia, glossy (1)
Almond, flowering (205)
Andromeda, mountain (189)
Arborvitae, globe and dwarf (288)
Azalea, amoena (20)
Azalea, Hinodegiri (21)
Barberry, three-spined (28)
Barberry, warty (29)
Boxwood, common (33)
Cinquefoil (202)
Cotoneaster, ground (73)
Cotoneaster, rockspray (74)
Deutzia, Lemoin (84)
Deutzia, slender (82)
Goldflower (121)
Hollygrape, Oregon (166)
Holly, convex leaved (124)
Holly, Japanese littleleaf (125)
Honeysuckle, Southern bush (86)
Juniper, Sargent's (134)
Leucothoe, drooping (150)
Rose, bristly (238)
Snowball, Japanese (318)
Snowberry (264–267)
Spirea, Anthony Waterer (254)
Spirea, thunberg (257)
Spurge, Japanese (180)
Stephanandra, cutleaf (260)
Wintercreeper (98)
Yellowroot (328)
Yew, dwarf Japanese (284)

TABLE 3.11 (Continued)

Smoky, dusty, city situations

Trees

Corktree (182)
Hackberry (41)
Hornbeam, European (39)
Locust, honey (108)
Maidenhair tree (107)
Maple, Norway (6)
Pine, Austrian (191)
Pine, Scotch (193)
Plane tree, European (196)
Poplar, Carolina (199)
Poplar, Japanese (200)
Scholar tree, Chinese (248)
Thorn, cockspur (79)

Shrubs

Aralia, five-leaved (3)
Barberry, Japanese (27)
Bladder-Senna, common (51)
Forsythia (103)
Holly, Japanese (122)
Holly, Japanese littleleaf (125)
Honeysuckle, winter (162)
Kerria, white (223)
Lilac, common (275)
Ninebark, common (186)
Privet (151–157)
Snowberry (264–267)
Spirea, vanhoutte (259)
Thorn, Washington (78)
Withe rod (309)

Street Trees

Tall, formal and heavy

Linden, American (294)
Maple, Norway (6)
Maple, sugar (11)
Oak, red (217)
Sycamore, American (195)
Tulip tree (159)
Oak, pin (216)
Oak, scarlet (214)

Tall, medium to light textured

Ash, green (105)
Ash, white (104)
Elm, American (302)
Honeylocust, thornless (108)
Maidenhair tree (107)
Maple, red (9)
Maple, silver (10)

Medium height for narrow residential streets

Ash, European mountain (252)
Birch, European white (30)
Corktree, Chinese (181)
Golden rain-tree (145)
Hackberry (41)
Linden, European littleleaf (295)
Maple, columnar Norway (7)
Maple, hedge (4)
Scholar tree, Chinese (248)
Sweetgum (160)

Seashore locations

Trees

Holly, American (128)
Maple, sycamore (8)
Plane tree, London (194)
Poplar, Bolleana (198)
Poplar, Carolina (199)
Shadblow, downy (15)
Sourgum (177)

Shrubs

Althea, shrub (114)
Arrowwood (310)
Bayberry (176)
Chokeberry, red (18)
Eleagnus, autumn (89)
Hydrangea, otaksa (116)
Inkberry (126)
Juniper, Andorra (139)
Juniper, Bar Harbor (137)
Lilac, common (275)
Olive, Russian (87)
Plum, beach (206)
Privet, California (155)
Rose, meadow (234)
Rose, wichurian (243)
Sumac (225)
Summersweet (50)
Tamarix (277)

TABLE 3.11 (Continued)

Partial shade

Trees

Dogwood, pink-flowering (56)
Dogwood, white-flowering (55)
Fringetree, white (48)
Hemlock, Canadian (300)
Holly, American (128)
Maple, amur (5)
Sweetbay (165)
Shadblow, downy (15)
Silverbell, great (110)
Sourwood (179)

Shrubs

Abelia, glossy (1)
Aralia, five-leaved (3)
Barberry, wintergreen (25)
Blackhaw (319)
Buttonbush (42)
Cherry, cornelian (58)
Chokeberry (17)
Cinquefoil, shrubby (201)
Cranberrybush, European (316)
Euonymus (90–99)
Firethorn, Laland (210)
*Hollygrape, Oregon (166)
Holly, Japanese littleleaf (125)
Honeysuckle, Morrow (163)
Honeysuckle, Southern bush (86)
Honeysuckle, winter (162)
Hydrangea, oak leaf (118)
Hydrangea, snowhill (115)
Inkberry (126)
*Ivy, English (112)
Kerria, white (223)
*Laurel (143)
*Leucothoe, drooping (150)
Nannyberry (313)
*Periwinkle (326)
Privet, California (155)
Privet, regal (156)
Redbud, American (43)
Redbud, Chinese (44)
*Rhododendron, rosebay (222)
*Snowberry (264–267)
Spurge, Japanese (180)
Stephanandra, cutleaf (260)
Summersweet (50)
Sweet shrub (37)
Viburnum, mapleleaf (307)
Winterberry, common (129)
*Witchhazel (111)
Yellowroot (328)
Yew, spreading Japanese (282)

Steep Slopes

Small shrubs and vines

Bayberry (176)
Bearberry (329)
Broom (330)
Canby pachistima (331)
Creeping juniper (134, 137–139)
Crown vetch (332)
Drooping leucothoe (150)
Fragrant sumac (226)
Grape ivy (333)
Heath (334)
Heather (335)
Honeysuckle, Hall's (336)
*Ivy, English (112)
Japanese fleece vine (337)
*Japanese spurge (180)
Jasmine (131, 132)
Matrimony vine (338)
Natal plum (339)
Periwinkle (326)
Red osier dogwood (62)
Rosemary (340)
Rose spp. (234–243)
Southern bush honeysuckle (86)
Sweet fern (341)
Wintercreeper (98)

* Tolerates dense shade.

TABLE 3.12
Harmful Plants*

Hay fever:	Flowering trees, especially
Grasses	*Alnus* (alder) and
Ragweeds	*Quercus* (oaks)
Dermatitis and skin rashes:	
Buttercup	Jimsonweed
Cactuslike euphorbias	Lady's slipper
Carrots	Nettles
Crown of thorns	Parsnips
Datura	Poinsettia
Dictamnus	Poison ivy
Dill	Poison sumac
Fennel	Rock poppy
Gas plant	Snow-on-the-mountain
Iris	
Plants that harm when eaten:	
Abrus	Ivy, English
Amanita	Jack-in-the-pulpit
Amaryllis	Jequirity bean
Autumn crocus	Jerusalem cherry
Baneberry	Lantana
Belladonna	Lily-of-the-valley
Bittersweet	Lupine
Black locust	Marijuana
Bleeding heart	Marsh marigold
Bloodroot	Mayapple
Boxwood	Mistletoe
Caladium	Monkshood
Castor bean	Morning glory
Celastrus	Mountain laurel
Cherry, jerusalem	Mushrooms, death angel
Cherry, wild black	Nightshade
Crocus, autumn	Oleander
Daffodil	Peyote
Daphne	Philodendron
Datura	Poison hemlock
Dieffenbachia	Pokeweed
Digitalis	Privet
Dumb cane	Rhododendron
English ivy	Skunk cabbage
Euonymus	Taxus
Glory-lily	Tomato
Golden chain tree	Water hemlock
Holly	Wisteria
Hyacinth	Yew

* Data from Arnold Arboretum, Jamaica Plain, Mass.

DEICING SALT ON HIGHWAYS*

Deicing compounds on highways in winter consist of sodium chloride and/or calcium chloride, both of which are toxic to plants, including trees. These salts penetrate to the root system even though the ground is frozen. Construction and other activities, which may have previously created adverse conditions for roadside trees, compound the injury caused by deicing salts. Salt also tends to make drought injury worse, and drought makes salt injury worse.

Avoid the use of salt around your trees. When planting near areas to be exposed to salt spray from traffic or salt in water runoff, use salt-tolerant trees, such as:

Austrian pine
Bigtooth aspen
Birches
Black cherry
Black locust
Japanese black pine
Pitch pine
Quaking aspen
Red cedar
Red oak
White ash
White oak
White spruce
Yews

Avoid planting these salt-intolerant trees where they will be exposed to salt:

American elm
Basswood
Eastern white pine
Hemlock
Ironwood
Red maple
Red pine
Shagbark hickory
Speckled alder
Sugar maple

PARK WOODLAND CLEANUP AND CLEARING

In most areas there are many woodlands that require a certain amount of cleanup or clearing before they can be made useful and available to the public for general use. This cleanup can be classified into four general types: general cleanup, clear cutting, selective cutting, and pruning.

Cleanup

Areas usually requiring cleanup are those which are in general park use, such as picnic areas, overlooks, areas adjacent to structures, and (if

* Shade Tree Laboratories, Department of Plant Pathology, University of Massachusetts, Amherst, Mass.

time and funds permit) all other areas serviced by foot or horse trails or otherwise made accessible to the public.

1. All areas designated as requiring cleanup should be cleared of dead, dying, or structurally dangerous standing trees, all flammable material on the ground, and all undesirable underbrush.
2. Dying trees should include all trees which will not survive if left in their present condition and which cannot be saved by normal maintenance pruning and care. Any tree with a 25 per cent dead crown, unless otherwise marked for saving, should be considered a dying tree and removed.
3. All trees to be removed should be cut as close as possible to the ground (no higher than 5 in.) and felled so as to avoid damaging adjacent material. In order to control regrowth of undesirable material, remaining stumps 3 in. or more in diameter should be painted or sprayed within two weeks after cutting with a mixture of 1 part herbicide (such as 2,4-D or 2,4,5-T) and 19 parts fuel oil. Do not use kerosene because of its toxicity to desirable plants and its flammability.
4. All undesirable underbrush, including vines and all scrubby growth such as blackberry and locust, should be removed.
5. Debris, including fences, wire, cans, junk, rubbish, or other types of refuse, should be removed or disposed of.

Clear Cutting

Areas usually requiring clear cutting are those designated for opening views or vistas, to provide open lawns or playfields, or to vary the tree line along roads or highways by cutting bays at appropriate intervals.

1. All trees and underbrush, except those specifically marked as specimen plants, should be completely removed.
2. In areas where it is desirable to maintain a lawn or grass cover, the stumps should be removed and disposed of. In all other areas the trees should be cut flush with the ground and the stump treated with herbicide to prevent resprouting.
3. All ruts, holes, and scars caused by the removal of logs, trees, or stumps should be filled in and the grade restored.

4. No heavy equipment which would in normal operation injure desirable material should be used. Any equipment in operation should stay far enough away from permanent trees to avoid damage to large roots close to the trunks.

Selective Cutting

Areas to be cut selectively include picnic areas, the borders of access roads or highways, and other areas where an open-woods effect is desired close to buildings.

1. Specifications applicable to cleanup also apply to the areas to be cut selectively. In addition, trees should be removed to provide adequate room for more desirable material to grow. Enough trees should be left to allow their crowns to touch after normal growth. For instance, elm should be thinned to approximately 30-ft spacing; maple to 25 ft; ash to 40 ft; oak to 35 ft; linden or basswood to 20 ft. Other species of trees should be spaced proportionally. Such cutting of trees should apply only to trees up to 6 in. in caliper.
2. Avoid an even spacing of trees in any wooded area. Small clumps of the better trees scattered throughout the cutting area will produce a more attractive appearance.
3. Clear away all growth from mature specimen trees for a distance of approximately 35 ft.

Pruning

Areas to be pruned should be limited to the areas designated for selective cutting. If funds permit, some pruning can be done on the better specimen trees in the cleanup areas if such pruning will prolong the life of the tree. Specimen trees are those which stand out above all others, full grown and healthy.

> All deadwood and rubbing branches 1 in. or more in diameter, measured 6 in. out from the base, should be removed, as well as all borer-infested and structurally weak branches, stubs from broken branches, and old rotted stubs. The cuts should be made flush with the trunk or branch and painted with an acceptable tree-wound paint.

Disposal of Materials

1. All waste should be removed from the site of the work or burned completely. The burning of such waste should never be allowed to harm or damage growing material in any way.
2. All trash to be burned should be piled and burned when in a suitable condition. Burning should be so thorough that the trash is reduced to ashes. Piling for the burning should be done where it will cause the least fire risk and with all possible fire precautions. Ashes should be scattered, and the burned sites obliterated.
3. Every precaution should be taken to prevent fires from spreading. A supply of axes, saws, mattocks, shovels, rakes, and other fire-fighting equipment should be available at all times for use in preventing and suppressing fires.
4. Material which cannot be burned should be buried in pits and covered with a minimum of 3 ft of earth.
5. An approved type of brush shredder is useful in disposing of brush and tree limbs up to 10 in. in diameter. Stumps of all sizes can also be disposed of easily with a stump chipper which removes the stump cleanly 10 in. below the ground surface. The chips thus produced from both types of machines are useful for mulching trees and shrubs.

SAFETY FOR TREE WORKERS*

Rules of Safe Practice

The purpose of these rules is to bring out the following facts: (1) the man who is to avoid accidents and reduce loss of life and human suffering must exert every personal effort; (2) all tree workers, especially those who are inexperienced, should be informed of the dangers incident to tree-preservation work, so far as it is possible to do so in a set of rules; (3) precautions must be taken by all tree workers, experienced or inexperienced, to reduce the hazards of their work to a minimum; and (4) experience with causes and prevention should be applied to future work.

* The best information available today on rules for safe practice for tree workers is Tree Preservation Bulletin No. 2 written by A. Robert Thompson, Forester, National Park Service. These rules, slightly adapted, are reproduced on the following pages by permission of the Government Printing Office.

The rules have been established not from one person's ideas of safety but from the accumulated experience and observations of many individuals and organizations over many years. Each rule, without exception, has evolved directly from one or more accidents caused by failure to observe proper safety principles. These safe practice rules apply generally wherever tree-preservation work is done.

General

1. Every tree worker should know these safety rules. It is his duty to observe them at all times. He should have a good working knowledge of first aid and resuscitation.

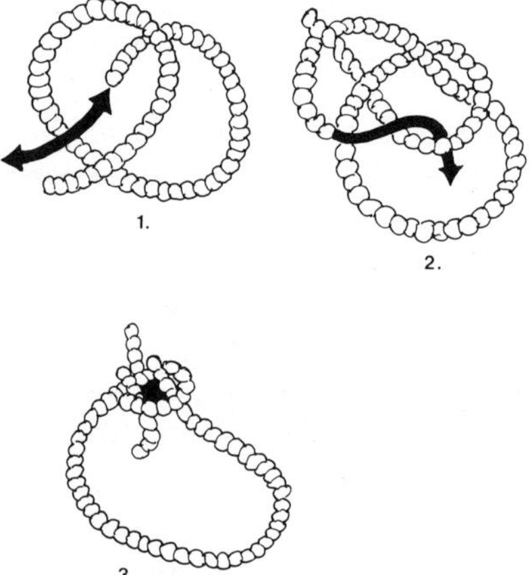

Fig. 3.13 Bowline.

2. No man should engage in any phase of tree work until he is able to tie the following knots readily and knows when to use them: bowline, bowline on a bight, running bowline, square knot, clove hitch, timber hitch, taut-line, and figure-of-eight knot (see Figs. 3.13 to 3.18).
3. Before any man attempts to do actual work in a tree, he must be trained in the use of rope and knots and must spend sufficient time in practice climbing and knot tying to become proficient.
4. Before any tree operation is started, all necessary time should be taken to find out if any local danger exists. Haste causes accidents; it pays to take time to be careful.
5. Except under exceptional circumstances, trees should not be climbed or worked in when wet. It is impossible

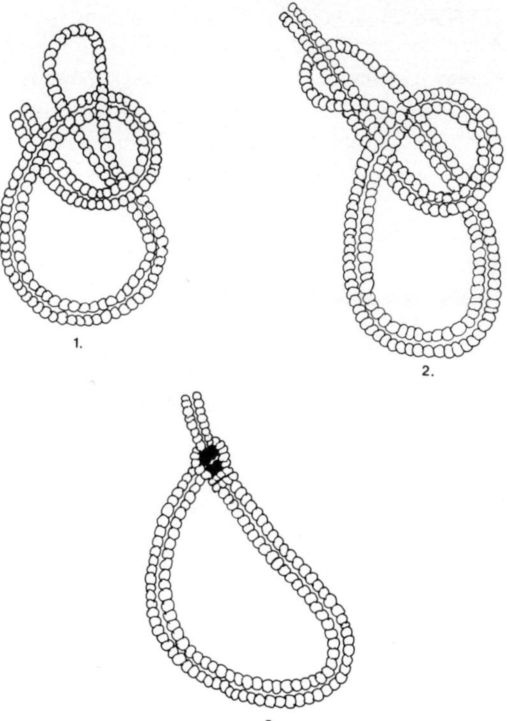

Fig. 3.14 Bowline on a bight.

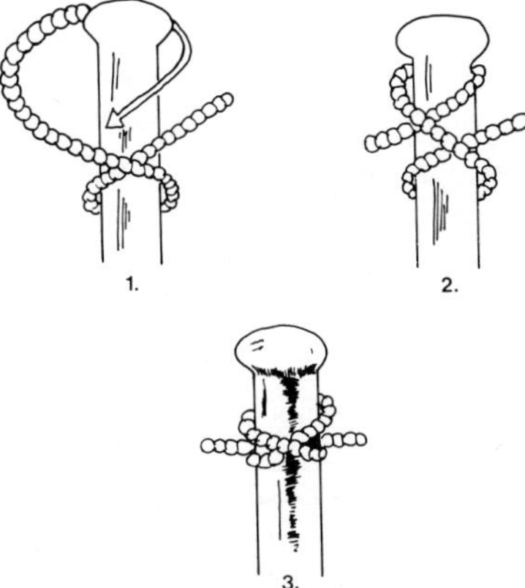

Fig. 3.15 Glove hitch.

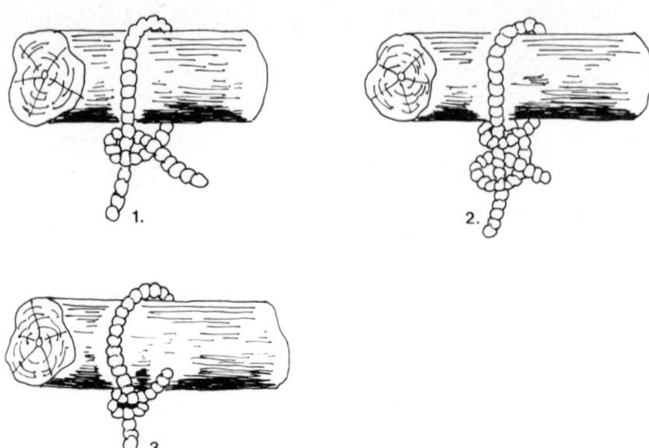

Fig. 3.16 Timber hitch.

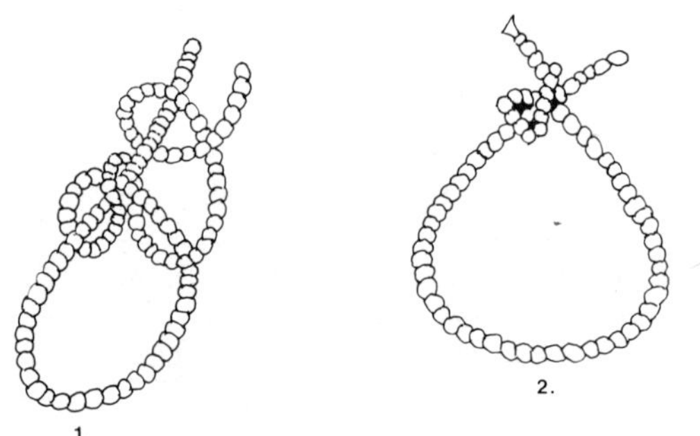

Fig. 3.17 Tautline hitch.

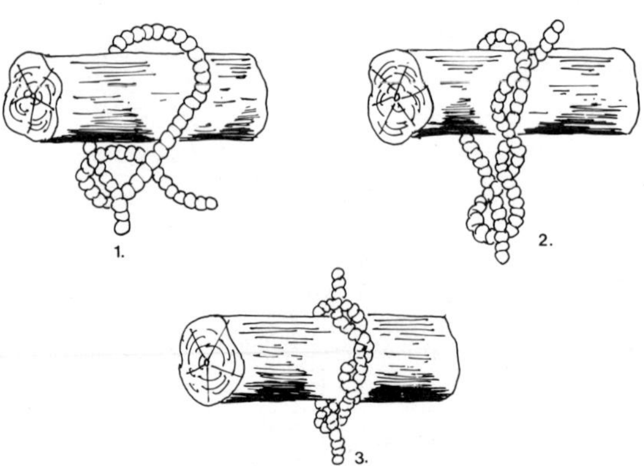

Fig. 3.18 Double half hitch.

to get a good foothold on slippery bark, and knots are likely to slip if the rope is wet.

6. Men should stay out of trees in high winds, except in emergencies.
7. Only men who are physically fit should be allowed in trees. Men suffering temporary ill health should be sent home.
8. There is no place for intoxicating liquors on a tree-preservation operation. Men suffering from aftereffects of alcohol must not be allowed on the job.
9. A tree is not the place for a person with an exhibitionist complex. Men who persist in taking unnecessary risks or in showing off should be released from the job.
10. As a general rule, only one man should work in a tree at a time, especially during pruning operations.
11. Workmen should request assistance only from men working directly on the job, never from passersby or casual observers, regardless of how simple the assistance temporarily required.
12. Danger signs or red flags or both should be placed on sidewalks, roadways, or streets where any tree work is to be done. Dangerous areas should be roped off, and ground men used to divert traffic when necessary.
13. The foreman should exercise close supervision over his men at all times. He should satisfy himself that the men working under him are competent to perform their work with safety. He should outline safe methods and see that his instructions are obeyed implicitly.
14. The foreman must make a daily inspection of all tools, rope, and other equipment before use and condemn or destroy all tools, etc., which in his opinion are unsafe. Each tree worker must also inspect all tools, rope, etc., before using them.
15. Foremen are held responsible for observance of all safety rules.

Clothing

Ordinary street or work clothes are unsuitable for tree work. For tree workers a cap is preferable to a hat because it offers less obstruction when passing between limbs and thick foliage. For ground workers a hard hat is better protection than a cap. High-topped leather shoes with composition or rubber soles are preferable to ordinary shoes with leather soles. Hobnailed shoes should never be used for climbing, and nailed soles should be avoided. Special tree-climber's boots with instep flaps and steel stays are sometimes preferred. Breeches of strong, dark-colored material are preferable to long trousers, which are easily caught and torn. They should be fairly loose in the leg and knee to give freedom in cramped positions. A long overcoat is unsuitable for tree work. Long underwear and snug-fitting wool or leather jackets or extra shirts are preferable when cold weather requires extra warmth. An athletic strap with a wide abdominal band should be worn by all men engaged in tree work. For protection of the hands and wrists, gloves of the gauntlet type are generally considered satisfactory for tree work. Sleeves should be kept rolled down to protect forearms and wrists.

Rope

The standard safety rope for tree work is a first-grade, three-strand, rot-treated, ½-in.-diameter manila rope not less than 120 ft and preferably 150 ft in length. The ½-in. nylon rope is coming into wider use and is acceptable as a standard rope where preferred. Standard power rope consists of first-grade, three-strand, rot-treated, ¾-in.-diameter manila rope in lengths of not less than 150 ft. It is often desirable to have a number of longer lengths as well. A 1-in.-diameter manila rope is recommended for pulling trees over. Cheap substitute ropes should be avoided.

TABLE 3.13
Federal Standards for Manila Rope (Three-Strand)

Diameter,* in.	Length of coil,* ft	Gross weight of coil,* lb	Maximum weight per ft, lb	Length per lb, ft	Minimum breaking strength, lb	Safe load (⅛ max), lb
¼	2750	55	0.020	50.0	600	75
½	1200	90	0.075	13.3	2650	331
¾	1200	200	0.167	6.0	5400	675
1	1200	324	0.270	3.71	9000	1125

* Approximate.

Table 3.13 gives the breaking strength and safe loads of different sizes of manila rope. This table may be used in estimating stresses for manila rope used for tree work.

Under average conditions the working load on a rope should not exceed one-sixth of the breaking load, but under the best conditions if the rope is new, the working load may be one-fourth the breaking load.

Under unfavorable conditions where rope is used frequently and for indefinite periods, as with a climbing rope, the working load should not exceed one-eighth of the breaking load.

Every rope must be thoroughly inspected for cuts or abrasions before each use. Occasionally the strands should be separated and the inside of the rope examined to see that the yarns are bright and unbroken. There is no positive way of testing a rope by subjecting it to an overload; this may weaken it so that it will soon break under normal use.

If the rope end becomes worn at the knot or at the saddle, it should be cut off immediately. Do not try to make the rope last too long. A man's life is worth more than the price of a new rope.

Kinking is one of the main causes of injury to manila rope and should be avoided, especially when the rope is wet. To avoid kinks in new rope, uncoil from the inside of the coil, never from the outside.

A rope should not be "burned" by being allowed to run through a crotch too rapidly. Great care should be used to avoid dropping cigarettes on rope. Rope should be kept away from fire, excessive heat, acids, and such sources of acid fumes as storage batteries.

Since rope deteriorates rapidly when it is saturated with water and improperly dried, unnecessary wetting must be avoided and wet ropes must be dried properly before storing. Rope should not be allowed to freeze after wetting, as frozen rope breaks easily. Rope should not be left in a tree overnight when there is reason to expect a heavy dew or rain or where it might be stolen or injured.

All rope should be kept coiled when not in use. It should never be stored or transported where it can be cut by sharp tools. Rope should not be dragged in the dirt, over rough surfaces, or across itself. Avoid sharp bends over unyielding surfaces.

Climbing

All limbs should be inspected before the weight of the body is allowed to rest on them. Do not trust your weight to a dead limb. If possible, all dead limbs should be broken off as the climber comes in contact with them.

Trees are of varying strengths, but it is necessary to remember that no matter how tough the wood of the tree or how large the diameter of a limb, a rotten or decayed limb is never safe. The limbs of old cherry and apple trees are likely to be weak because of heartrot, and black locusts are likely to be weakened by borer attack. All old or diseased trees may have invisible decay which makes them more hazardous than young trees.

Trees may be grouped according to strength:

1. Very easily broken: willow, poplar, aspen, box elder, catalpa, ailanthus, soft maple, white pine, and sassafras
2. Split easily: linden, ash, red elm, persimmon, magnolia, and tulip tree
3. Rather hard to break: apple, pear, plum, most conifers, hackberry, birch, oak, walnut, hickory, sycamore, hard maple, American elm, black locust, and osage orange

Trees with thorns which cut and scratch and may also set up infection are honey locust, osage orange, black locust, and hawthorn.

When climbing without a rope, the climber should rarely entrust his full weight to one limb. A better practice is to keep one arm around the trunk or to keep the hands on separate limbs, so that if one limb breaks the body can be supported by the trunk or the other limb. A rope should not be climbed hand over hand unless a footlock is used or the legs are gripping the tree. Shinning a tree over 15 ft is an unsafe practice. Climbs over 30 ft should be made by using a safety sling. Fatigue and cramps should be avoided. Feet, hands, and rope should be kept out of tight crotches.

A bowline on a bight tied into a safety line, a standard tree worker's belt, or a saddle with or without separate leg straps, in combination with a tautline hitch, constitutes the safety sling (Fig. 3.19). The saddle is preferred by many because it is more comfortable and permits free action of the legs. The ordinary lineman's belt and strap are neither safe nor practical for tree work.

The safety sling must always be used for tree work, even if a ladder or scaffold is also used. Many men have been injured or killed by failing to observe this cardinal rule. The safety sling should be tied immediately after the climber has crotched his rope. The crotch should be as high and as close to the trunk as possible. Tight crotches which will bind the rope should be avoided. When practicable, the rope should be crotched on the side of the tree opposite that to be worked, so as to avoid accidentally slipping the rope out along the limb to a point where the limb cannot support the climber's weight. The climber should check the location of the entire length of the safety sling and the taut-line hitch before swinging free.

A figure-eight knot should always be tied in the ground end of a safety rope to prevent accidental pulling of the end through the taut-line hitch when the climber is coming down the rope. If someone else ties the knots, the climber should check them himself before trusting his weight to them.

The ground end of a safety rope must not be left dangling over roadways or walks, and it must be kept free from obstructions, tight crotches, and fallen brush. All slack must be kept out of the safety rope.

The safety rope may be recrotched whenever this will make the work safer or quicker. To be absolutely safe, the climber should tie himself to a convenient limb while making the change.

The climber should stay in the safety sling until he is on the ground again. He should never release the taut-line hitch before coming out of a tree. A climber should not slide down a limb or tree trunk without carefully inspecting it for projecting stubs, nails, or loose bark. Severe gland injuries have occurred through failure to observe this rule. At the end of a working day all knots should be removed from the rope. To leave knots tied for a prolonged period or to tie knots repeatedly in the same point in a rope will cause kinking and undue wear. Remember: a good safety rope is the tree worker's most important accident insurance policy.

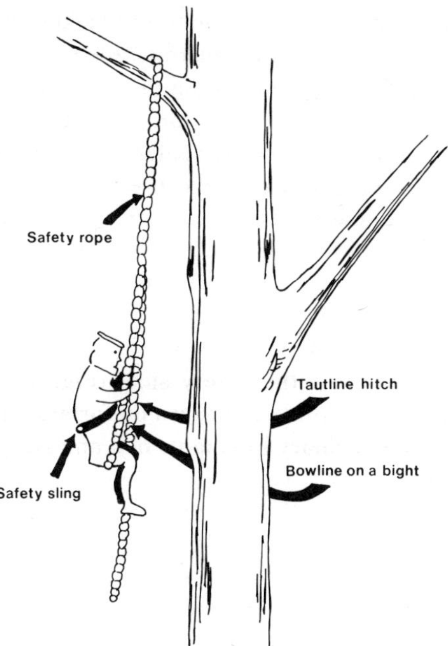

Fig. 3.19 The safe way to climb a large tree.

Ladders

Ladders are used in tree work primarily for climbing into trees. If any trimming or other work is done from a ladder, a safety sling should also be used.

Ladders should not be used in tree work unless the base can be set on a firm foundation. They should never be used in trees with the bottom rung or rail bases resting in a crotch. A ladder should never be set on a truck or other object which can be moved while a man is working on it. If it is absolutely necessary to place a ladder in a street or on a walk and no other footing can be obtained, it should be guarded by a ground man and lashed in place with hand lines. The foot of the ladder should be moved out of the perpendicular by one-fourth the length of the ladder; i.e., if the ladder is 12 ft long, the foot of the ladder should be 3 ft from the base of the trunk of the tree, provided the top of the ladder rests against the trunk and the trunk is perpendicular.

Ladders should be inspected frequently to make sure they are sound. Ladders with broken or cracked rungs or rails should be discarded or immediately repaired, and protruding slivers should be removed. Ladders used against trees where the limbs will not support the weight of the climber should be secured with hand lines. Lashings should pass over the rails and the ends of the rungs, not the center of the rungs. When a ladder is leaned against a tree, the weight should be distributed equally on both rails and not against the top rung unless this has been especially braced. The ladder should be lashed in place if there is any danger of slipping.

Ladders should be placed in proper racks or on the ground after use and not left leaning against trees or buildings. They should not be left on the job at the end of a working day unless they are secure from tampering or use by unauthorized persons.

Pruning

Tree pruning or other work in the crowns of trees should be performed only when weather conditions are favorable. Branches are more apt to snap off on a cold day than on a warm one. Branches wet by rain or snow or covered with ice are dangerous to the climber.

Before any tree job is started, the program should be worked out carefully with the foreman if possible. This planning may eliminate extra climbing and additional hazards.

Automobiles that are found under trees where overhead work is being done should be pushed clear, or the owners should be asked to move them to a safe place. When possible, "No Parking" signs should be placed the day before the work is to begin.

Warning should always be given when a limb is about to be dropped from a tree. The shouts "Timber!" "Heads up!" or "Look out below!" are common signals for this purpose. Dropping limbs or stubs should be permitted only when there is no danger to men or objects beneath.

Ground men should wear hard hats painted with bright colors, which can readily be seen by men in the trees.

A limb which cannot be controlled by hand while being severed from the tree should have a line or lines attached before it is cut off, to permit controlled lowering. The end of the safety sling should never be used for this purpose. Lowering ropes should be snubbed to prevent injury to the holder. It is well to remember that a snubbed rope does not hold so well on wet limbs or trunks as on dry wood. A man should hold only one rope at a time. Never allow ground men to wrap a bull line around their hands or bodies.

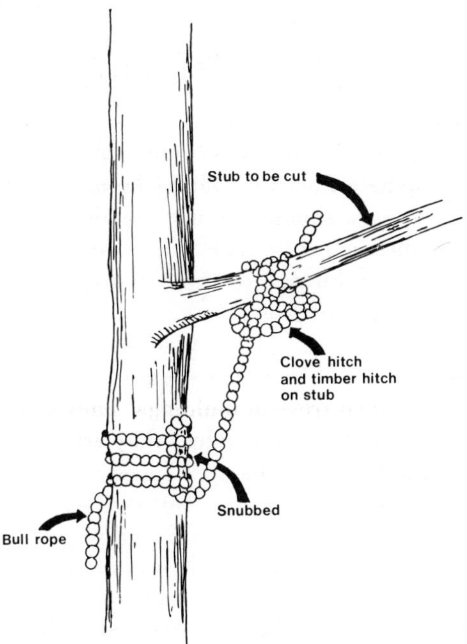

Fig. 3.20 Method for tying stubs to be cut to main trunk.

The trimmer should never cut a large limb above him except as a last resort. When large limbs or parts of the trunk of a tree are to be sawed off and no suitable crotch is available for passing the support rope, the limb should be snubbed to the lower portion of the trunk and lowered when completely severed (Fig. 3.20). The climber should be sure that he is in a safe position or on the ground before the stub or branch is finally swung clear. Be sure the bull line being used is large enough to handle the weight of the limb being lowered. A sudden jerk may break the line if it is too light.

Care should be used in pulling branches out of trees by hand or by means of pole pruners; the limbs may fall and cause injury. The worker should stand in a place to the side, or if possible above the limb, in order to allow it to fall without striking him.

Never leave "hangers" or anything not securely fastened in the tree. If a tree is not completely pruned at the end of a working day, all hangers, tools, and ladders should be removed, since they might become dislodged during the night and fall on someone. If a climbing rope must be left in a tree overnight, it should be tied up out of reach.

Electrical Hazards

Special care must be exercised when work is being done close to charged wires or electrical apparatus. Only men who are thoroughly familiar with the dangers involved should be allowed to do this work, and only insulated tools should be used under such conditions. In manipulating aerial lifts close to limbs and wires, the trimmer must be very careful not to bring himself or the equipment in contact with the wires.

Before work is undertaken in trees that are close to or touching live wires, the power company concerned should be notified so that if possible they can deenergize and ground the lines locally. In any event, lines should be declared safe by a qualified power company employee before men are allowed to work in trees touching wires.

Wet materials are conductors of electricity—even materials which are nonconductors when they are dry. If clothing, rope, equipment, or the trees are wet or even damp, no work should be done in trees near or touching wires. The use of weatherproof rope and periodic shellacking of poles and wooden handles are worthwhile practices.

The climber should never pass between wires unless authorized by the foreman and never until rubber guards such as hoods, snakes, or blankets are placed on the wires by a thoroughly experienced man. No one should ever stand on conductor or guy wires.

Special care must be used to avoid dropping limbs or branches on wires, but if they accidentally fall or are resting on wires, they should be removed by means of a dry rope slung over the branch or a long-handled pruner equipped with a rope pull. Rope or pruner should be handled with rubber gloves. Fallen wires should not be touched. The power company should be called at once and the wires guarded from passersby until the company responds to the call. Even if the wires are known to be dead, they should be brushed lightly with the back of the hand before they are touched. If a person does come in contact with live wires, do not allow the victim to be touched. The wire may be lifted from him, or he may be lifted off the wire by using dry, nonconductive materials such as clothing, rope, boards, or rubber materials. After rescue, the back-pressure–arm-lift method of artificial respiration should be applied if the patient has stopped breathing, and a doctor or the emergency squad should be called.

During thunderstorms, trees, especially those standing alone, should be avoided.

Tools

Tools should be raised or lowered by means of a hand line or the free end of the safety rope. They must never be thrown into or dropped from a tree.

Tools should not be left where they may be tripped over or stepped upon or in a leaning position from which they may fall. Rope and rope ends should be kept free.

Handsaws with teeth on only one edge should be used for general tree work. They should be kept sharpened and properly set so that they will not jump out of the cut and cause injury. Each handsaw and bull-saw and other small-handled tool should be provided with a leather or wire loop through the handle.

Handsaws should not be carried on the belt or in the hand when a worker is climbing. A saw may be attached to the end of the safety line or hand line before the tree is climbed and then pulled up. When temporarily out of use, a saw should not be laid on a limb or in a crotch but should be securely hooked on the belt or over a branch of sufficient size to hold it securely. There are scabbards or sheaths which are hooked to the belt in which saws are safely carried when not in use. Pole saws should be as light in weight as possible and of sufficient length to allow the trimmer to reach his work readily. They should be made with a one-piece wooden handle, angular in cross section, and provided with a hook just below the blade.

Pole saws should be raised or lowered by means of a rope tied below the blade. When temporarily out of use in a tree, they may be hooked over limbs of sufficient size to hold the weight. They should never be laid on limbs or in crotches or hung on wires.

Pole pruners should be as light in weight as possible and of sufficient length to allow the trimmer to reach his work readily. They should be made with a one-piece wooden handle and be provided with a rope pull leading from the lever arm to the end of the handle. Poles which are hexagonal or square in cross section are easier and safer to handle than round ones.

Pole pruners should never be raised or lowered by placing a finger in the hook, but by means of a rope tied under the head of the tool, never over the jaw, as the cutting edge may close on the rope and cut it. They should never be thrown by a ground man to a trimmer in the tree. A pole pruner temporarily out of use in a tree may be hooked over a limb of sufficient size to hold the weight securely. They should never be hooked over wires, laid on limbs or in crotches, or used for lifting other equipment.

Chisels, gouges, and other sharp-edged tools should never be carried in the boot. A leather kit with a wooden bottom is a convenient way to carry such tools. Chisel kits should be made so that they prevent the tools from falling out if the kits are accidentally tilted. When working in awkward or confined places, the operator should use long chisel handles to prevent bruising his hands. When using a chisel or gouge, he should keep his head out of the line of swing to prevent possible injury of the face from the rebound of the mallet. Chisel handles should be provided with iron ferrules to prevent splitting. Operators should remember that chisels and gouges are cutting tools and should not be used as levers or wedges. They should be kept sharp.

Axes are, of course, necessary on tree operations for felling and bucking, but they should never be used as wedges or for pruning or trimming shade trees. They should not be used for driving wedges. They should be kept sharp.

Steel wedges should be provided on each felling operation. They should be kept free from burred edges, and should be driven only with a sledgehammer.

Spurs or climbing irons should never be used on live trees except possibly during tree-removal operations. Use of spurs at any time is a questionable practice and should be discouraged, since the gaffs are apt to tear out of the bark and cause the climber to slip, fall, or spur himself. The tree climber has so little occasion to use spurs that he rarely becomes expert and consequently should avoid them.

Toolboxes should provide special places for saws, chisels, and other sharp-edged tools so that they will not come in contact with other tools and rope. After use, saws, rope, small tools, picks, shovels, etc., should be placed inside the toolbox in their designated places. When not in use, tools should be kept covered with light machine oil or easily removed metal protector to prevent rust.

Pneumatic pruners and saws are coming into wider use, particularly with aerial lifts. They should be handled with care. The pruner or saw should not be handed from one trimmer to another unless it is disconnected from the air hose. The trimmer should not try to catch the pruner or saw if it falls and is still connected to the air hose. The pruner should not be laid down with air hose attached since it may be tripped with the foot.

The use of electric or gasoline chain saws in trees is common but also hazardous. The trimmer must place himself in the tree so that the saw cannot fall against him. The saw should be suspended from a line crotched at a point other than where the climber's safety line is crotched and if possible so that if the saw should be released by the trimmer for any reason, it will swing away from him. A special carrier is available for use with a chain saw in a tree.

Tree Felling

Before any tree is felled, the crew should be properly instructed by competent authority in the proper manner of notching and wedging, so that the tree will fall where desired. Space immediately around the tree should be cleared of all brush.

Before each tree is felled, it should be carefully studied by a competent man taking the following factors into consideration: (1) height of tree, (2) soundness, (3) direction of lean, (4) slope of ground, (5) species of tree, (6) top-heaviness, (7) direction of wind, (8) proximity to other trees, structures, and wires, and (9) dead limbs or stubs which may break off and fall, endangering workmen.

If there is danger that the trees being felled may damage property, block and tackle should be used. In most cases in shade-tree felling guidelines will be necessary to avoid damage. Guidelines should be tied and snubbed around other trees before any cutting is done at the base of the tree. Winch line, block and tackle, or pull lines assist in controlling the direction of the fall. It may sometimes be necessary to fell a tree by lowering it in sections instead of simply cutting it off at the ground. If this is done, careful study must be given to the size and position of limbs, location and order of making cuts, and methods of snubbing and guiding. Great care must be exercised to avoid severing any guide ropes or power lines. Special precautions in roping rotten or split trees are important because they may fall in an unexpected direction even though the cut is made on the proper side.

Not more than two men at a time should be allowed to work on the base of a tree being felled. Both should know where the tree is to fall and where they are to go when the tree starts to fall. All persons should be kept away from the butt of a tree starting to fall. It may kick back or take an unexpected roll. Just before the tree is ready to fall, the shout "Timber!" should be given, and all who are working in the vicinity should immediately move to a place safely out of range.

Felling operations, once started, should be finished before the crew leaves the job for lunch or at the end of the working day. It is especially important to complete such operations when roots have been excavated or cut or when the base cut has been started.

Additional precautions are necessary in felling trees with a chain saw. If there is loose bark on the trunk where the cut is to be made, it is best to remove it with an ax; otherwise the saw may throw it into the face of the operator. An undercut should be made to the proper depth on the side of the desired direction of fall and notched out with an ax. All but small trees should be undercut. When trees must be cut flush to the ground, it is safer to make the first cut at a stump height above the swell of the roots and a second cut flush with the ground after the tree is down.

As the cut proceeds, the saw operator should check to see that the cut on the tailstock end is even with the depth of cut on the saw end. If any binding occurs, wedges may be used, but care must be taken not to drive them in against the chain. Sometimes the pull rope may be sufficient to prevent binding. When the final cut is to the proper depth for felling, the tree should be pulled or wedged over. If there is danger of driving the wedge into the saw, a wooden wedge should be used. Extreme care must be exercised not to make the final cut too deep and beyond the wood controlling the direction of fall. Because of the speed with which the saw cuts, some trees have been cut clear off, so that there was no control over direction of fall.

Small brush should not be cut with a power chain saw, as the saw may either throw the operator or throw the butt of the brush back at the operator. Special power brush saws are made for cutting brush. On very steep slopes a one-man saw is much the safest, because one operator can abandon the saw quickly if the tree should fall in the wrong direction. Where the tree leans in the opposite direction to that of its intended fall, and where there is not enough room to drive a wedge back of the saw, it is safest and best to go back to the old crosscut saw. With most two-man and one-man saws, the operators should be very careful that the hand does not slip over the edge of the outboard handle. Especially when gloves are worn, the hand can be very easily pulled into the chain. On one-man saws, this is true when the saw is used in a horizontal position and the guard, where the hand is placed, is on the underside of the saw.

Brush and Wood Removal

Brush and logs should not be allowed to accumulate at the site of the operation but should be cleared away as rapidly as possible. Pending removal, debris should be piled so it will not interfere with the operation or where men might stumble over it.

Ground men handling brush should not attempt to pick up the brush or limbwood from under that side of a tree where the climber is working.

A ground man having his attention called by workmen in a tree should first step out from under the tree before looking up, in order to avoid falling brush.

Men should not try to lift logs or other loads that are too heavy. A large number of tree accidents result from strains. The loads should be reduced by the use of skids, by cutting logs into shorter lengths, by use of winch equipment, etc.

The man on the truck who is loading the brush should stand between the brush and the cab—never on or straddling a load of brush. Brush should be kept within the bed of the truck and held down tightly by rope lattice. This gives a better vision to cars passing around the truck and prevents the brush from scraping cars or striking pedestrians. Whenever brush extends beyond the confines of the truck, red flags should be placed on the ends.

When disposing of brush by burning, the truck driver should not back his truck close to the fire but should dump the brush some distance to one side where it can be fed to the fire by hand. On large clearing jobs these brush piles can safely be pushed into the fire by small tractors with a rake attachment. Care must be exercised to keep the fire under control. Be sure that there is no chance of the fire's spreading to fields, fences, woods, or buildings. Fires must never be left unattended, and all fire must be extinguished before the crew leaves for lunch and before the work is finished for the day. Every crew required to burn brush should be equipped with a few suitable fire tools. Fire rakes and swatters are especially designed for brush, grass, and leaf-litter fires. Fire pumps, which contain 5 gal of water and are carried on the back, are also useful. Brush must never be burned except in places that have been designated by competent authority and then only when burning conditions are satisfactory and safe. Locate the fires in open areas well away from trees. Why prune the trees only to scorch them later in the burning operations? Ordinarily, poisonous vines should not be burned because the smoke is likely to affect susceptible persons. If it is absolutely necessary to burn such material, care should be taken to keep workmen and passersby out of the smoke, which carries the poison.

If brush is piled on a public dump, the foreman should make sure that he complies with all the requirements of that particular dumping ground.

Transportation

Truck drivers should qualify under all rules which apply to licensing, driving, and maintenance of motor vehicles.

All persons should get on and off the truck on the right (or curb) side of the truck or the rear. No one should get on or off when the truck is in motion. The driver should be the last one to get on and before starting the truck must make certain that all riders are safely within the truck bed.

No person should be allowed to ride on any part of the truck except within the cab or bed. No part of the body should extend beyond any part of the truck when it is in motion. Stake sides and tail gates must be in place in trucks carrying persons.

Tools and equipment must not be carried loosely on the truck beds but in proper boxes or receptacles provided for them. Every truck should be equipped with a fire extinguisher and a good first-aid kit properly stocked with suitable materials. Crewmen should be instructed in the use of both.

Spraying

All spray materials must be used with extreme caution. Arsenic in any form is a deadly poison, and serious injury or discomfort may result from careless use of many materials. Cautions and instructions for any commercially prepared spray material should be carefully read and observed.

Insecticides, fungicides, and their containers must not be left within reach of children or animals. Spray wastes should be buried or drained into a sewer, and containers should be burned or otherwise destroyed as soon after emptying as possible. Sprayer drippings and materials accidentally spilled should be washed off lawns, walks, and roads.

Although it is questionable whether lead arsenate in concentrations normally deposited in ordinary operations is lethal to birds and stock, it is safer to use nonpoisonous substitutes when spraying in or near bird runs and pastures. Spray materials are especially deadly to fish, and extreme care must be exercised to avoid pollution of ponds, streams, and sources of drinking water.

Stomach poisons, such as lead arsenate, should not be used for insect control on fruits or garden vegetables if there is a possibility that poison residues in harmful concentrations may remain until the time of consumption.

To avoid the hazards of poisoning from lead, arsenic, and other spray materials, the following rules should be observed:

1. If possible, every workman should have a medical examination, including a complete blood analysis, before working with spray materials. Workers having blood diseases should not work with lead.

2. Teeth should be brushed daily after work.
3. Hands and face should be well washed before eating and after work.
4. A shower should be taken and clothes changed as soon after work as possible.
5. Lunches should be kept and eaten away from spray materials.
6. When mixing dry spray materials, the worker should keep the nostrils and mouth covered with a respirator or wet cloth. Most spray materials are especially dangerous in concentrated form.
7. During the spraying season, workers should drink plenty of milk to counteract arsenic poisoning.
8. Operators should wear raincoats, hats, and goggles while spraying and keep out of the drift as much as possible.

Spray crews using lead arsenate may be subjected to both lead and arsenic poisoning. Symptoms of lead poisoning include headache, dizziness, colic, constipation, loss of weight, convulsions, blood changes, anemia, palsy, neuritis, weakness, blue line on gums, joint pains, twitching, and paralysis. Arsenic poisoning symptoms include skin ulceration; loss of nails and hair; inflammation of the nose, mouth, throat, and lungs; brown discoloring of the skin; perforation of the bonelike part of the nose; muscular weakness; paralysis; and diarrhea. Persons suspecting either type of poisoning should consult a doctor immediately.

Care must be exercised, especially when using a solid-stream nozzle, to avoid contact of the spray stream or the nozzle with electric wires. Spray apparatus should be kept as clean as possible at all times, not only for general reasons of good management but to avoid falls of persons from slippery surfaces. Cleats should be attached to the floors of trucks to prevent slipping on slick surfaces. Hose connections on hydraulic sprayers should be checked and tightened before use to prevent blowing. Extreme care is necessary in cranking motors on sprayers; watch for kickback. There should be no smoking around or on mist blowers when oil solutions are being mixed or used.

Fumigation

Fumigation is the practice of killing pests by means of a gas. The gas may be applied directly from suitable containers or formed from chemicals introduced into the area requiring treatment, which may be tree cavities or soil. Special techniques are required in treatments of this kind.

The chemicals employed are usually very poisonous and should be handled and used only upon the advice of and by persons thoroughly familiar with the individual properties of each. Operators should make sure that they comply with all local laws and regulations covering fumigation.

First Aid and Poisonous Plants

Each member of a tree-preservation crew should be trained in first aid and the back-pressure–arm-lift method of resuscitation. First-aid kits should be provided for each crew.

Small cuts, scratches, and blisters must be attended to immediately. Even the most minor scratch may easily become infected and lead to serious complications.

A common source of lost-time accidents among tree workers is contact with poisonous plants such as poison ivy, poison oak, and poison sumac. Susceptibility to the poison varies with individuals, but it is never safe to assume immunity from it.

Learn to know the poisonous plants on sight and then avoid contact with them. If contact cannot be avoided, the hands, arms, and face should be washed as soon as possible after exposure with strong yellow soap or washing powder, which will often prevent infection or at least retard it.

There is danger of reinfection through handling or wearing clothes which have been in contact with poisonous species, even after the passage of months or years. Susceptible persons should avoid wearing such clothes.

Poison ivy remedies are numerous, but most are of doubtful value as preventives or cures. They may relieve itching and burning, but frequently a remedy that will give relief to one person may not help another. Some of the newer treatments are reported to be superior to older remedies. However, avoid promiscuous use, particularly with home remedies, as they may tend to spread rather than cure the infection. Susceptible persons should investigate through proper medical channels the latest immunization treatments. A physician should be consulted in all cases of severe poisoning.

Duties of the First-Aid Man

The trained man possesses the ability to render first aid, and should immediately assume charge of the situation. He should:

1. Keep the patient lying down.
2. Determine the nature and extent of the injuries. Serious bleeding, stoppage of breathing, and internal poisoning demand immediate treatment and take precedence over everything else.
3. Keep the patient warm.
4. Send for a physician or ambulance immediately and do not move the patient unless absolutely necessary in more serious cases. For less serious injuries, prepare the patient for transportation and get him to a doctor.
5. Keep calm.
6. Never give an unconscious person anything to drink.
7. Keep onlookers away from the injured.
8. Make the patient comfortable and cheer him as much as possible.
9. Avoid letting the patient see his own injury.

NURSERY STOCK STANDARDS*

There are many times when it becomes necessary to purchase various types of plant materials, either as replacement stock or for expansion of existing plantings. At such times it is necessary to know the relationship between the height, spread, caliper, and branching habits of trees and shrubs. Since all reputable nurseries adhere to grading standards as established by the American Association of Nurserymen, it is best to prepare specifications for purchasing plant materials based on these standards.

DECIDUOUS SHADE AND FLOWERING TREES

General Specifications

Caliper and Height Measurement

In size grading balled-and-burlapped trees, caliper shall take precedence over height.

In size grading bare-root trees, height shall take precedence to 8 ft; thereafter caliper takes precedence.

The caliper of the trunk shall be taken 6 in. above the ground level up to and including 4-in.-caliper size and 12 in. above the ground level for larger sizes.

Where a minimum and maximum size, i.e., size range, is specified, the average of the lot should approximate the midpoint of the specified size range.

* The standards given here are adapted, by permission of the American Association of Nurserymen, Inc., from American Standard for Nursery Stock, ANSI Z60.1–1973.

Height of Branching: Street Trees

Unless otherwise specified trees are to be suitable for planting as street trees and are to be free of branches to a point about 50 per cent of their height. Height of branching should bear a relationship to the size and kind of tree also, so that the crown of the tree will be in good balance with the trunk as the tree grows.

Examples

Acer platanoides, 2 to 2½ in. caliper, 12 to 14 ft, branched 6 to 7 ft
Quercus borealis Maxima, 3½ to 4 in. caliper, 14 to 16 ft, branched 7 to 9 ft

Trees with ascending branches, e.g., *Ulmus americana* and *Tilia tomentosa*, may be branched 1 ft or more below the standard height and still provide proper clearance, which is the purpose of this specification.

Height Relationship to Caliper by Types

It is recognized that climate conditions in different sections of the country produce trees of different caliper-height proportions. Trees from one region of the country may have less caliper in proportion to height while trees from another section may have greater caliper in proportion to height than shown in Table 3.14.

Type 1: Shade Trees Table 3.14 shows the average height range and also maximum heights permitted (Fig. 3.21).

TABLE 3.14

Caliper, in.	Height range, ft	Maximum height, ft
½–¾	5–6	8
¾–1	6–8	10
1–1¼	7–9	11
1¼–1½	8–10	12
1½–1¾	10–12	14
1¾–2	10–12	14
2–2½	12–14	16
2½–3	12–14	16
3–3½	14–16	18
3½–4	14–16	18
4–5	16–18	22
5–6	18 and up	26

Sizes under 1 in. may be calipered if desired.

Examples

Acer rubrum, A. saccharinum
Betula
Fraxinus americana, F. pennsylvanica
Ginko
Gleditsia
Liriodendron
Platanus
Populus
Quercus borealis, Q. macrocarpa, Q. palustris, Q. phellos
Salix
Tilia americana
Ulmus americana

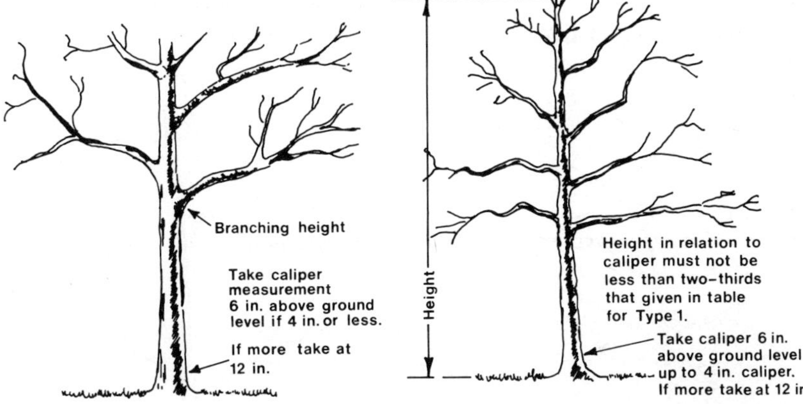

Fig. 3.21 Type 1: shade trees. (*Redrawn by permission from American Association of Nurserymen, American Standard for Nursery Stock, ANSI* Z60.1–1973.)

Fig. 3.22 Type 2: shade trees. (*Redrawn by permission from American Association of Nurserymen, American Standard for Nursery Stock, ANSI* Z60.1–1973.)

Type 2: Shade Trees These trees of slower growth will not usually attain the height measurement in relation to caliper as in type 1; however, the height should be not less than two-thirds the height relationship given for type 1 (Fig. 3.22).

Examples

Aesculus
Celtis
Cladrastis lutea
Fagus sylvatica
Koelreuteria
Laburnum
Liquidambar
Nyssa
Quercus alba
Sorbus
Tilia cordata, T. euchlora

Type 3: Small Upright Trees (Fig. 3.23) This is a broad group including small upright trees which may be grown as a clump or shrub. Height shall be the governing measurement. For single-stem plants, the minimum relationship of caliper and branching will usually be as follows:

2 to 3 ft, $^5/_{16}$ in. caliper, three or more branches
3 to 4 ft, $^7/_{16}$ in. caliper, four or more branches
4 to 5 ft, $^9/_{16}$ in. caliper, five or more branches
5 to 6 ft, $^{11}/_{16}$ in. caliper, six or more branches
6 to 8 ft, $^7/_8$ in. caliper, seven or more branches

Examples

Acer campestre, A. circinatum
Cercis
Crataegus
Halesia
Malus (most crabapples)
Prunus cerasifera Thundercloud
Prunus serrulata, P. subhirtella
Styrax
Syringa amurensis Japonica

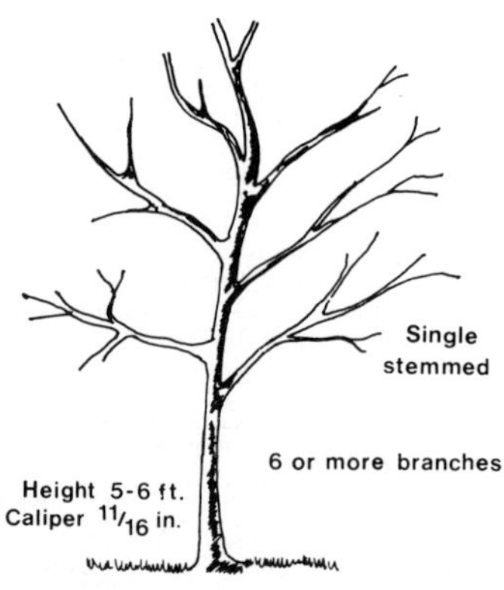

Fig. 3.23 Type 3: small upright trees. (*Redrawn by permission from American Association of Nurserymen, American Standard for Nursery Stock, ANSI* Z60.1–1973.)

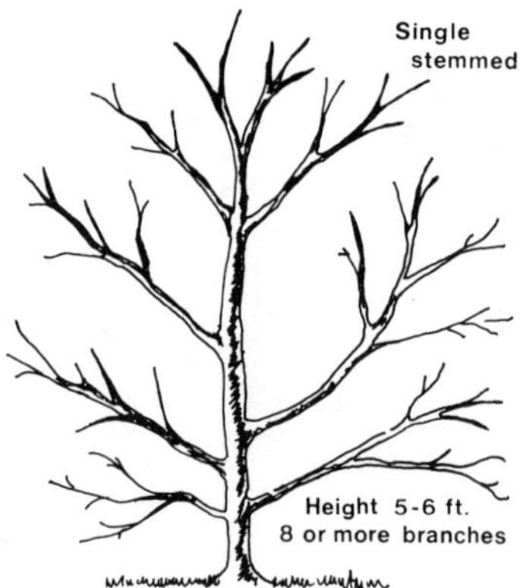

Fig. 3.24 Type 4: small spreading trees. (*Redrawn by permission from American Association of Nurserymen, American Standard for Nursery Stock, ANSI* Z60.1–1973.)

Type 4: Small Spreading Trees (Fig. 3.24) This is a broad group including small spreading trees of dwarf habit of growth and certain large shrubs grown in tree or multistemmed form. Height shall be the governing measurement. For single-stem plants, the minimum branching will be as follows:

2 to 3 ft, four or more branches
3 to 4 ft, five or more branches
4 to 5 ft, seven or more branches
5 to 6 ft, eight or more branches
6 to 8 ft, eight or more branches

Examples

Acer palmatum, A. griseum
Cornus
Lagerstromia indica
Magnolia soulageana, M. stellata
Malus sargentii
Viburnum prunifolium

Deciduous Trees for Other Uses

Trees for special uses should be branched or pruned naturally according to type. Where a form of growth is desired which is not in accordance with a natural growth habit, this form should be so specified.

Examples

Bush form Trees which start to branch close to the ground in the manner of a shrub.
Clumps Trees with two or more main stems starting from the ground, with the number of stems specified.
Cut back or sheared Trees that have been pruned back to multiply the branching structure and develop a more formal effect.
Topiary Trees sheared or trimmed closely in a formal geometric pattern.

Bare-Root Specifications

Spread of Roots

Nursery-grown All bare-root trees shall have a well-branched root system characteristic of the species. Table 3.15 represents the approved minimum root spread for nursery-grown shade trees.

TABLE 3.15

Caliper, in.	Height range, ft.	Minimum root spread, in.
½–¾	5–6	12
¾–1	6–8	16
1–1¼	8–10	18
1¼–1½	8–10	20
1½–1¾	10–12	22
1¾–2	10–12	24
2–2½	12–14	28
2½–3	12–14	32
3–3½	14–16	38

Collected Trees collected from native stands or established plantings must be so designated. The spread of roots for bare-root trees shall be one-third greater than the spread of roots for bare-root nursery-grown trees, as tabulated above.

Trees collected from wild or native stands may be considered nursery-grown when they have been successfully reestablished in the nursery row and grown under regular nursery cultural practices for a minimum of two growing seasons and have attained adequate root and top growth to indicate full recovery from transplanting into the nursery row.

Balling-and-Burlapping Specifications

Ball sizes should always be of a diameter and depth to encompass enough fibrous and feeding root system for the full recovery of the plant.

Nursery-grown

Table 3.16 represents the recommended minimum sizes of balls for trees which are being grown in the nursery under favorable growing conditions and

TABLE 3.16

Single-stem trees, types 1 to 3		Small spreading trees, type 4	
Caliper, in.	Minimum diameter ball, in.	Height, ft	Minimum diameter ball, in.
1/2–3/4	12		
3/4–1	14	2–3	10
1–1 1/4	16	3–4	12
1 1/4–1 1/2	18	4–5	14
1 1/2–1 3/4	20	5–6	16
1 3/4–2	22	6–7	18
2–2 1/2	24	7–8	20
2 1/2–3	28	8–9	22
3–3 1/2	32	9–10	24
3 1/2–4	38	10–12	26
4–4 1/2	42		
4 1/2–5	48		
5–5 1/2	54		

which have received the proper cultural treatment to develop a well-branched root system (Fig. 3.25). These specifications are for plants dug with the ball of earth in which they are growing. It is recognized that plants which have a coarse or widespreading root system because of natural habit of growth, soil condition, or infrequent transplanting practice or which are moved out of season require a ball larger than the recommended sizes.

Collected

It is generally recognized that plants growing in their native state will sustain a much more severe shock when transplanted than the same kinds of plants when nursery-grown. If collected material is moved, a considerably larger ball than that recommended for transplanted nursery stock is required because of the unrestricted root development and the varying conditions of the soil in which such material is found.

The minimum ball sizes shall be equal to those specified above for the next larger size nursery-grown stock.

Trees collected from wild or native stands may be considered nursery-grown when they have been successfully reestablished in the nursery row and grown under regular nursery cultural practices for a minimum of two growing seasons and have attained adequate root and top growth to indicate full recovery from transplanting into the nursery row.

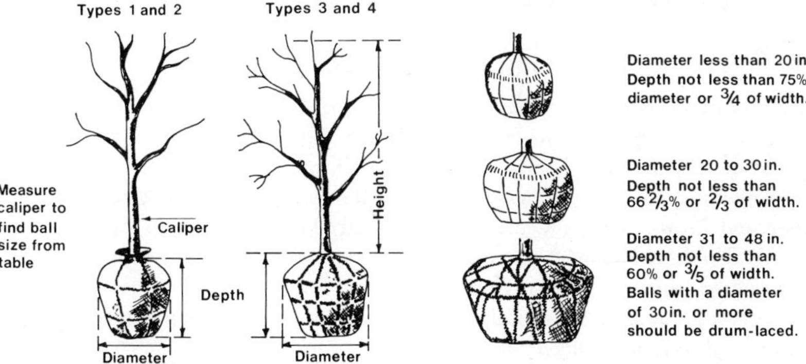

Fig. 3.25 Balling-and-burlapping specifications. (*Redrawn by permission from American Association of Nurserymen, American Standard for Nursery Stock, ANSI* Z60.1–1973.)

Fig. 3.26 Ball-depth ratio. (*Redrawn by permission from American Association of Nurserymen, American Standard for Nursery Stock, ANSI* Z60.1–1973.)

Plantation-grown Stock

These are plants which have been systematically planted in fertile, friable soil relatively free of stones and foreign matter but with a minimum of aftercare.

The minimum ball sizes shall be equal to those specified above for the next larger size nursery-grown stock.

Ball Depths (Fig. 3.26)

Under certain soil and regional conditions, plants have root systems of proportionately less depth and greater diameter. These require a shallower but wider ball to encompass the roots properly. Conversely in other soils and in certain regions roots develop greater depth and less spread, requiring an exceptionally deep ball, which may be smaller in diameter and greater in depth than the size recommended.

For the greater part of the country ball depths will carry the following ratios:

Balls with diameters less than 20 *in.* Depth not less than 75 per cent of diameter

Balls with diameters of 20 *to* 30 *in. inclusive* Depth not less than 66⅔ per cent of diameter

Balls with diameters of 31 *to* 48 *in. inclusive* Depth not less than 60 per cent of diameter.

The percentage of depth of larger balls will scale down proportionally.

Container-grown Specifications

All container-grown trees shall be healthy, vigorous, well-rooted, and established in the container in which they are sold. They shall have tops which are of good quality and in a healthy growing condition.

An established container-grown tree shall be a tree transplanted into a container and grown in that container sufficiently long for the new fibrous roots to have developed enough for the root mass to retain its shape and hold together when removed from the container.

The container shall be sufficiently rigid to hold the ball shape protecting the root mass during shipping.

Dwarf and light-growing varieties may be one or two sizes smaller than standard for a given size container.

Table 3.17 gives tree sizes and acceptable container sizes.

TABLE 3.17

Tree height	Container size
12–18 in. 18–24 in. 2–3 ft. 3–4 ft	1 gal (trade designation): minimum of 5½ in. across top and height of 6 in. or equivalent volume
2–3 ft 3–4 ft 4–5 ft	2 gal (trade designation): minimum of 7 in. across top and height of 7½ in. or equivalent volume
4–5 ft 5–6 ft 6–8 ft	5 gal, egg can, or square can (trade designation): minimum of 9 in. across top and height of 10 in. or equivalent volume

Balled and Potted

Balled and potted plants are field-grown nursery plants, dug with a ball of earth still intact in which they are growing; in lieu of burlapping, they are placed in a container to retain the ball unbroken.

Ball sizes shall always be a diameter and depth to encompass enough fibrous and feeding root system for the full recovery of the plant.

The minimum ball size specification for balled-and-potted plants shall be the same as for balled-and-burlapped plants.

DECIDUOUS SHRUBS

General Specifications

Height Measurement

Dwarf and Semidwarf Shrubs State height in inches up to 24 in., over 24 state in feet. Size grade in 3-in. series to 18 in., 6-in. series for 18 to 24 in., and ½-ft series for over 24 in.; for example, 12 to 15 in., 15 to 18 in., 18 to 24 in., 2 to 2½ ft, 2½ to 3 ft.

Strong-growing Shrubs Grade in 6-in. series up to 24 in.; for example, 12 to 18 in.; over 24 in. by single feet up to 6 ft; in double feet above 6 ft; for example, 8 to 10 ft.

Quality Definitions

If a plant is well grown with single stem, well shaped, and bushy and has sufficient well-spaced side branches to give it weight and good bud qualities, it should be an acceptable plant.

A cane shall be considered a primary stem which starts from the ground or close to the ground at a point not higher than one-fourth the height of the plant.

Grading Tolerance

The growing of plant material cannot be rigidly standardized because of varying conditions of growth and methods of handling preferred or necessitated by climate, soil, and other conditions beyond the control of the grower. Judgment should therefore be exercised and allowances made in the above definitions to agree with those which are recognized by the trade as typical of acceptable plants in that region.

Recommended Grades

Lots or groups of plants of a given grade should have an approximate average height as shown in Table 3.18.

TABLE 3.18

Grade of plant	Approximate average of lot
18–24 in.	21 in.
2–3 ft	2½ ft
3–4 ft	3½ ft
4–5 ft	4½ ft

TABLE 3.19
Types of Shrubs

Subtype	Size	Minimum number of canes	Minimum length of live top	Examples
		Type 0		
		Shrubs having a tendency not to mature all top growth*		
0–1	6–9 in.	2	6 in.	
	9 in. and up	3	9 in.	*Hydrangea macrophylla*
0–2	9–12 in.	2	9 in.	*Caryoptis; Herpericum* (shrubby types)
0–3	12–18 in.	2	12 in.	*Hydrangea arborescens; Buddleia; Vitex*
	18 in. and up	3	18 in.	
		Type 1		
		Dwarf and semidwarf shrubs (Fig. 3.27)		
	12–15 in.	4	12 in.	*Berberis thunbergii; atropupurea* Crimson Pigmy; *Deutzia gracilis; Euonymus kiautschovica* Jewell; *Potentilla fruticosa; Ribes alpinum; Spiraea bumalda* Anthony Waterer
	15–18 in.	4	15 in.	
	18–24 in.	5	18 in.	
	2–2½ ft	6	2 ft	
	2½–3 ft	7	2½ ft	
		Type 2		
		Fig. 3.28		
	1½ ft	3	1½ ft	*Azalea* (deciduous); *Cephalanthus occidentalis; Cornus alba, C. sibirica, C. racemosa, C. stolonifera; Diervilla sessilifolia; Itea virginica; Kolkwitzia amabilis; Lespedeza thunbergii; Philadelphus lemoinei; Rhodotypos scandens; Rosa multiflora, R. setigera; Stephanandra incisa*
	2–3 ft	4	2 ft	
	3–4 ft	5	3 ft	
	4–5 ft	6	4 ft	

Type 3 Fig. 3.27			
1½ ft 2–3 ft 3–4 ft 4–5	3 3 4 5	1½ ft 2 ft 3 ft 4 ft	*Acanthopanax sieboldianus; Alnus rugosa; Amelanchier; Aronia arbutifolia, A. melanocarpa; Calycanthus floridus; Chaenomeles speciosa; Clethra alnifolia; Cornus amomum, C. sanguinea; Corylus americana, C. avellana; Cotoneaster acutifolia; Deutzia* (tall-growing species); *Euonymus americanus; Forsythia; Hamamelis; Hibiscus syriacus; Hydrangea paniculata grandiflora* (Peegee H); *Ilex laevigata, I. verticillata; Kerria japonica* (single and double); *Lingustrum obtusifolium regelianum; Lonicera* (bush form); *Myrica pennsylvanica; Philadelphus virginalis; Prunus amygdalus, P. cistena, P. cerasifera, P. triloba* (bush forms); *Rhus canadensis; Rosa blanda, R. rugosa; Sambucus canadensis, S. nigra* (variegated forms); *Sorbaria aitchisonii, S. arborea, S. sorbifolia; Spiraea* (tall-growing varieties); *Symphoricarpos chenaultii, S. mollis, S. occidentalis, S. albus, S. orbiculatus; Syringa chinensis, S. amurensis japonica, S. josikaea, S. persica, S. villosa; Vaccinium corymbosum, V. stramineum; Viburnum cassinoides, V. dentatum, V. lantana, V. molle, V. opulus, V. plicatum, V. tomentosum, V. trilobum; Weigela floribunda, W. florida*
Type 4 Fig. 3.27			
1½–2 ft 2–3 ft 3–4 ft 4–5 ft	2 2 3 4	1½ ft 2 ft 3 ft 4 ft	*Amorpha fruticosa; Baccharis halimifolia; Caragana arborescens; Chionanthus virginica; Colutea arborescens; Cotinus americanus, C. coggygria; Cornus alternifolia, C. mas; Elaeagnus angustifolia, E. commutata, E. umbellata; Euonymus alatus, E. atropurpureus, E. bungeanus, E. europaeus; E. yedoenis; Exochorda racemosa; Halesia carolina; Lespedeza bicolor; Lindera benzoin; Rhamnus carthartica, R. frangula; Rubus odoratus; Sambucus pubens; Syringa vulgaris; Tamarix; Viburnum lentago, V. prunifolium*

TABLE 3.19 (Continued)

Type 5

Fig. 3.27

Height	Minimum cane height	Caliper	Examples
1 1/2 ft	1 1/2 ft	5/16 in.	*Rhus copallina, R. glabra, R. typhina*
2–3 ft	2 ft	3/8 in.	
3–4 ft	3 ft	1/2 in.	
4–5 ft	4 ft	5/8 in.	
5–6 ft	5 ft	7/8 in.	

Type 6

Barberry (*Berberis thunbergii*) (Fig. 3.27)

Height	Minimum number of canes	Minimum cane height
12–15 in.	3	12 in.
15–18 in.	3	15 in.
1 1/2–2 ft	4	1 1/2 ft
2–2 1/2 ft	4	2 ft
2 1/2–3 ft	5	2 1/2 ft
3 ft	6	3 ft

Type 7

Privet (hedging) (Ligustrum) (Fig. 3.27)†

Height	Minimum number of canes	Minimum cane height
1 1/2–2 ft	3	1 1/2 ft
2–3 ft	4	2 ft
3–4 ft	5	3 ft
4–5 ft	6	4 ft

* It is accepted nursery trade practice to prune the top growth of these shrubs back to live wood.

† For *Lingustrum obtusifolium regalianum* see type 3.

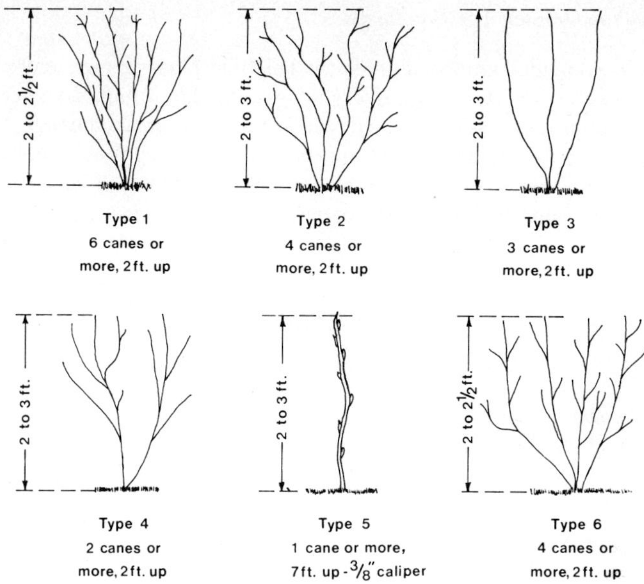

Fig. 3.27 Various types of deciduous shrubs. (*Redrawn by permission from American Association of Nurserymen, American Standard for Nursery Stock, ANSI* Z60.1–1973.)

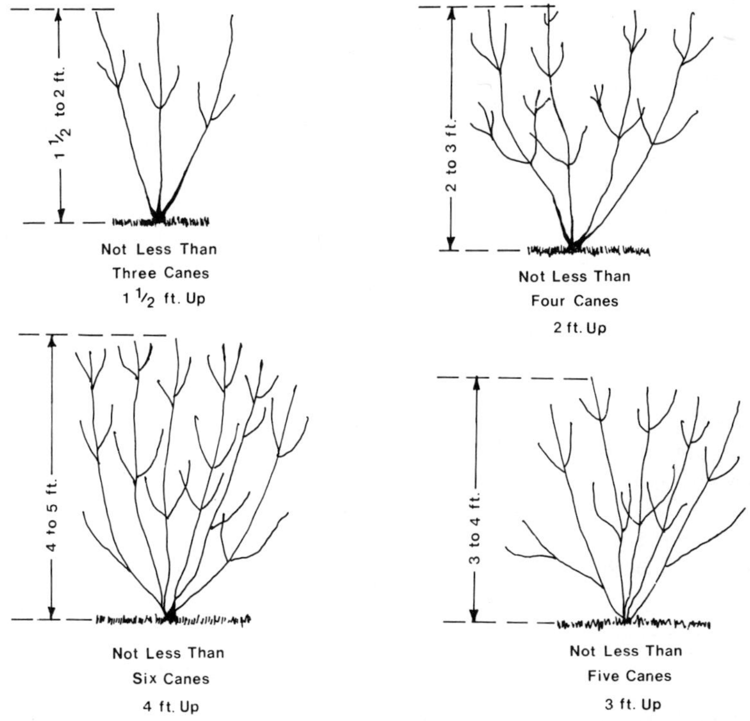

Fig. 3.28 Typical grades or sizes in type 2, deciduous shrubs. (*Redrawn by permission from American Association of Nurserymen, American Standard for Nursery Stock, ANSI* Z60.1–1973.)

The recommended grades apply to the height of plants grown under average soil and climatic conditions in nursery beds and fields, which have been transplanted, root-pruned, and trimmed according to regular nursery practice. Judgment must be exercised in interpreting and adapting these general classifications to any particular species or variety and consideration given to the normal growth habit under conditions peculiar to the region.

Bare-Root Specifications

Spread of Roots

Nursery-grown Roots of deciduous shrubs shall be well branched and fibrous, and bare-root shrubs shall have minimum root spreads shown in Table 3.20 as follows:

TABLE 3.20 Minimum Root Spread for Strong-Growing Shrubs

Height of plant	Minimum root spread
18–24* in.	10 in.
2–3 ft	11 in.
3–4 ft	14 in.
4–5 ft	16 in.
5–6 ft	18 in.
6–8 ft	20 in.

* Including dwarf types up to 24 in.

Collected Shrubs collected from native stands or established plantings must be so designated. The spread of roots for bare-root collected shrubs shall be one-third greater than the spread of roots of nursery-grown shrubs as given in in Table 3.20.

Shrubs collected from wild or native stands may be considered nursery-grown when they have been successfully reestablished in the nursery row and grown under regular nursery cultural practices for a minimum of two growing seasons and have attained adequate root and top growth to indicate full recovery from transplanting into the nursery row.

Balling-and-Burlapping Specifications

Ball sizes should always be of a diameter and depth to encompass the fibrous and feeding root system necessary for the full recovery of the plant.

Nursery-grown

Table 3.21 represents the recommended minimum sizes of balls for shrubs which are being grown under favorable growing conditions and which have received the proper cultural treatment to develop well-branched root systems.

These specifications are for plants dug with the ball of earth in which they are growing.

TABLE 3.21
Deciduous Shrubs (Fig. 3.29)

Height	Minimum ball diameter, in.
12–18 in.	8
18–24 in.	9
2–3 ft	10
3–4 ft	12
4–5 ft	14
5–6 ft	16
6–7 ft	18
7–8 ft	20
8–9 ft	22
9–10 ft	24
10–12 ft	26

Collected

The minimum sizes of ball shall be equal to those specified in Table 3.21 for the next larger size nursery-grown stock.

Shrubs collected from wild or native stands may be considered nursery-grown when they have been successfully reestablished in the nursery row and grown under regular nursery cultural practices for a minimum of two growing seasons and have attained adequate root and top growth to indicate full recovery from transplanting into the nursery row.

Plantation-grown Stock

These are plants which have been systematically planted in fertile, friable soil relatively free of stones and foreign matter but with a minimum of aftercare.

The minimum ball size shall be equal to that specified in Table 3.21 for the next larger size nursery-grown stock.

Ball Depths (Fig. 3.30)

For the greater part of the country ball depths will carry the following ratios:

Balls with diameters less than 20 *in.* Depth not less than 75 per cent of diameter

Balls with diameters of 20 *to* 30 *in. inclusive.* Depth not less than $66\frac{2}{3}$ per cent of diameter

Under certain soil and regional conditions, plants have root systems of proportionally less depth and greater diameter. These require a shallower but wider ball to encompass the roots properly. Conversely in other soils and in certain regions roots develop greater depth and less spread, requiring an exceptionally deep ball, which may be smaller in diameter and greater in depth than the size recommended.

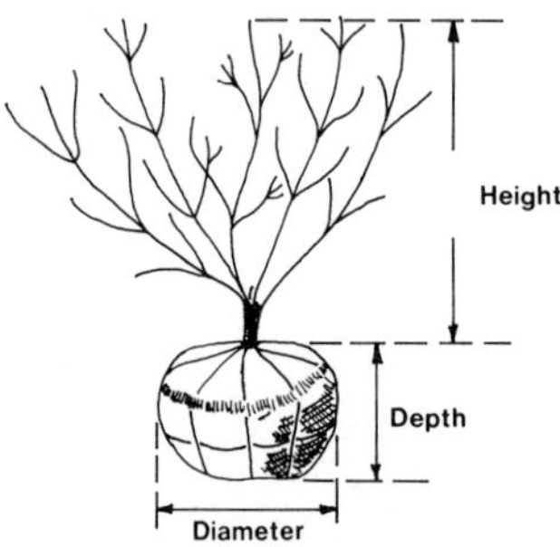

Fig. 3.29 Balling-and-burlapping specifications for deciduous shrubs. (*Redrawn by permission from American Association of Nurserymen, American Standard for Nursery Stock, ANSI* Z60.1–1973.)

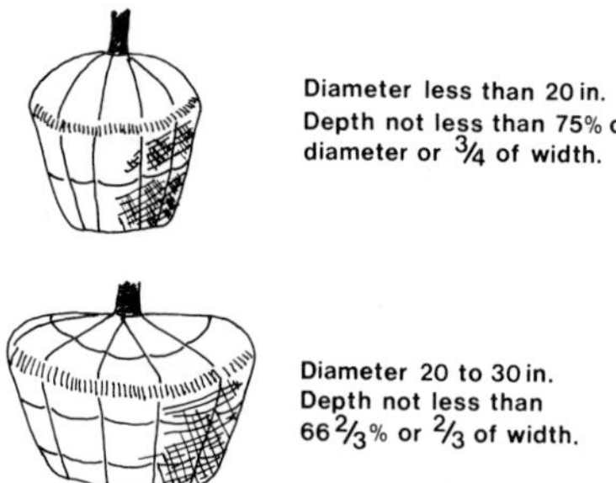

Fig. 3.30 Ball-depth ratio for deciduous shrubs. (*Redrawn by permission from American Association of Nurserymen, American Standard for Nursery Stock, ANSI* Z60.1–1973.)

Container-grown Specifications

All container-grown deciduous shrubs shall be healthy, vigorous, well-rooted, and established in the container in which they are sold. They shall have tops of good quality and in healthy growing condition (see Table 3.22).

An established container-grown deciduous shrub shall be a deciduous shrub transplanted into a container and grown in that container long enough for the new fibrous roots to have developed so that the root mass will retain its shape and hold together when removed from the container.

The container shall be sufficiently rigid to hold the ball shape protecting the root mass during shipping.

Dwarf and light-growing varieties may be one or two sizes smaller than standard for a given size container.

Balled-and-Potted

Balled-and-potted plants are field-grown nursery plants, dug with a ball of earth still intact, in which they are growing. In lieu of burlapping they are placed in a container to retain the ball unbroken.

Ball sizes shall always be of a diameter and depth to encompass enough fibrous and feeding root system for the full recovery of the plant.

The minimum ball size specification for balled-and-potted plants shall be the same as for balled-and-burlapped plants.

TABLE 3.22
Deciduous Shrub Sizes and Acceptable Container Sizes

Height	Container size
6–9 in. 9–12 in. 12–15 in. 15–18 in. 18–24 in. 2–3 ft	1 gal (trade designation): minimum of $5\frac{1}{2}$ in. across top and height of 6 in. or equivalent volume
12–15 in. 15–18 in. 18–24 in. 2–3 ft	2 gal (trade designation): Minimum of 7 in. across top and height of $7\frac{1}{2}$ in. or equivalent volume
18–24 in. 2–3 ft 3–4 ft 4–5 ft	5 gal, egg can, or square can (trade designation): minimum of 9 in. across top and height of 10 in. or equivalent volume

CONIFEROUS EVERGREENS

General Specifications

Quality Definitions

The quality of evergreens offered is assumed to be normal for the species or variety unless otherwise designated as:

Specimen (Spec.) This designation may be used to indicate exceptionally heavy, well-shaped plants and is usually applied to the larger commercial sizes and plants which have been cut back or trimmed to form a perfectly symmetrical, tightly knit plant. The letters X, XX, or XXX may be used to designate the degree of heavy grades in place of using the word "specimen" (spec.)

Collected (Coll.) Natural seedling plants dug from native stands or forest plantings must be so designated.

Types of Conifers

Type 1: Creeping or Prostrate Type Measurement designates spread (height not considered).

Use 3-in. intervals up to 18 in.
Use 6-in. intervals from 18 in. to 4 ft.
Use 1-ft intervals from 4 ft up.

Measurement should be average of plant and not the greatest diameter. Plants properly trimmed and transplanted should measure the same in any direction. If a plant is uneven, for example, 15 in. the widest way and 9 the narrowest, it should be classified as 12-in. stock.

Examples

Juniperus horizontalis cultivars, *J. procumbens Pinus mugo* Mughus

Type 2: Semispreading Type (Fig. 3.31) Measurement designates spread.

Use 3-in. intervals up to 18 in.
Use 6-in. intervals from 18 in. to 4 ft.
Use 1-ft intervals from 4 ft up.

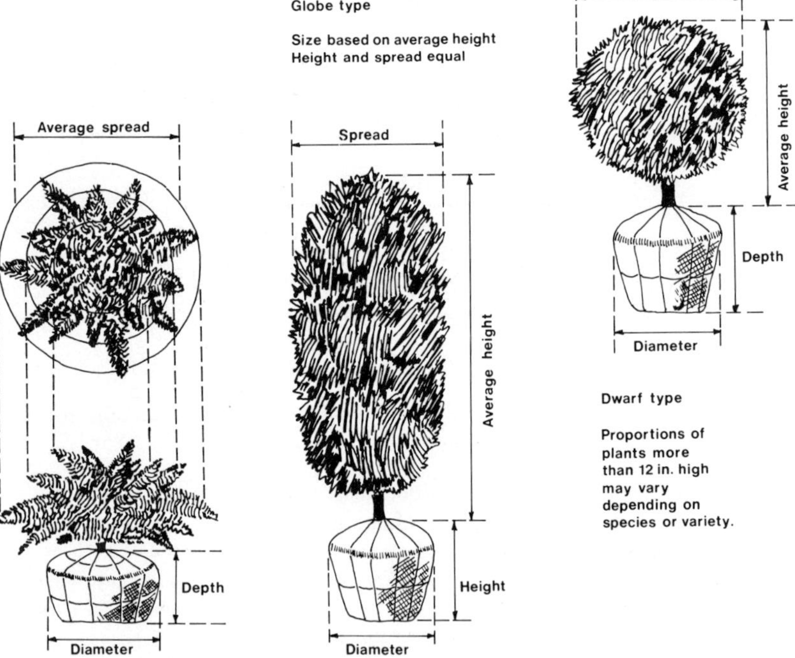

Fig. 3.31 Type 2 conifers, semispreading type. (*Redrawn by permission from American Association of Nurserymen, American Standard for Nursery Stock, ANSI* Z60.1–1973.)

Fig. 3.32 Type 3 conifers, broad spreading, globe, and upright dwarf types. (*Redrawn by permission from American Association of Nurserymen, American Standard for Nursery Stock, ANSI* Z60.1–1973.)

Measurement should be average as in type 1.

Height of first-class material will be at least one-half of the spread. Above 3 ft the height will be less than spread, varying somewhat according to natural growth of the particular species and method of handling.

TABLE 3.23

Spread	Height	Examples
6–9 in. up to 3 ft	Same as spread	*Juniperus chinensis pfitzer, J. sabina;*
3–4 ft	$2\frac{1}{2}$–$3\frac{1}{2}$ ft	*Taxus cuspidata, T. cuspidata* Nana,
4–5 ft	3–4 ft	*T. media* Densiformis

Type 3: Broad-spreading, Globe, and Upright Dwarf Types (Fig. 3.32) Measurement designates height.

Use 3-in. intervals up to 18 in.
Use 6-in. intervals from 18 in. to 4 ft.
Use 1-ft intervals from 4 ft up.

Spread will usually be equal to height in well-grown material up to 12 in. From there on there will be a variation of spread to height depending on the variety.

TABLE 3.24

Height	Minimum spread, in.
6–9 in.	6
9–12 in.	9
12–15 in.	10
15–18 in.	12
18–24 in.	15
2–$2\frac{1}{2}$ ft	18
$2\frac{1}{2}$–3 ft	21
3–$3\frac{1}{2}$ ft	24

Many broad-spreading and globe types included in this classification will usually have the same spread as height (or a greater spread) even in the larger sizes.

Examples

Chamaecyparis obtusa Nana, *C. pisifera* Plumosa Nana
Juniperus virginiana Globe
Picea abies Nidiformis
Taxus media Brownii
Thuja occidentalis Globe, Little Gem

Upright growing dwarf types may approach the minimum dimensions above.

Examples

Chamaecyparis obtusa Gracilis
Juniperus squamata Meyeri, *J. excelsa* Stricta
Thuja occidentalis Hovey, Parsons, Woodward, *orientalis* Goldbush

Type 4: Cone Type (Pyramidal) (Fig. 3.33) Measurement designates height.

Use 3-in. intervals up to 18 in.
Use 6-in. intervals from 18 in. to 3 ft.
Use 1-ft intervals from 3 ft to 10 ft
Use 2-ft intervals from 10 ft up.

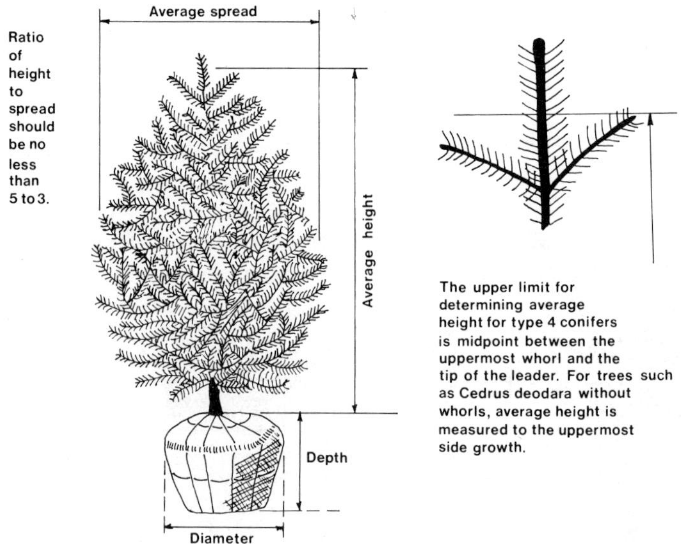

Fig. 3.33 Type 4 conifers, cone type (pyramidal). (*Redrawn by permission from American Association of Nurserymen, American Standard for Nursery Stock, ANSI* Z60.1–1973.)

The ratio of height to spread of properly grown material should not be less than 5:3.

TABLE 3.25

Height	Spread	Examples
12–15 in.	8–12 in.	*Abies; Cedrus deodara; Chamaecyparis*
15–18 in.	9–15 in.	*pisifera* and varieties (except dwarf
18–24 in.	12–18 in.	types); *Picea abies* (conical types); *Pinus*
2–2½ ft	15–21 in.	(except dwarf types); *Pseudotsuga*
2½–3 ft	18–24 in.	*menzeisii; Taxus cuspidata, T. capitata;*
3–4 ft	21–30 in.	*Thuja occidentalis, T.* orientalis
4–5 ft	2½–3 ft	(clonical types); *Tsuga canadensis,*
5–6 ft	3–4 ft	*T.* caroliniana

Type 5: Broad Upright Type (Fig. 3.34) Measurement designates height.

Use 3-in. intervals up to 18 in.
Use 6-in. intervals from 18 in. to 3 ft.
Use 1-ft intervals from 3 to 10 ft.
Use 2-ft intervals from 10 ft up.

This group includes all the broader, upright-growing evergreens, which develop a straight-sided form with many upright branches or leaders.

The ratio of height to spread of properly grown material should not be less than 2:1.

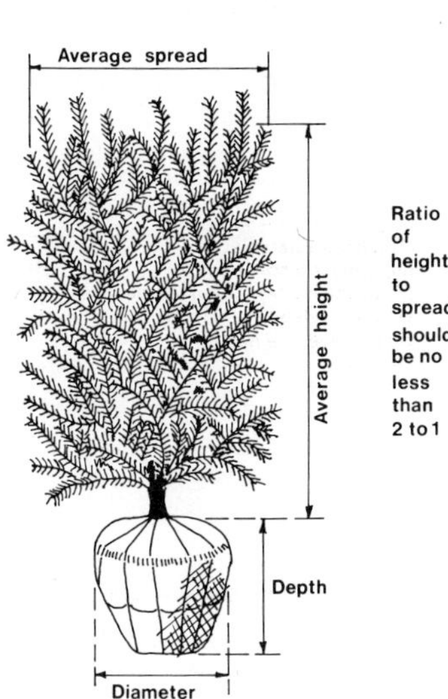

Fig. 3.34 Type 5 conifers, broad, upright type. (*Redrawn by permission from American Association of Nurserymen, American Standard for Nursery Stock, ANSI* Z60.1–1973.)

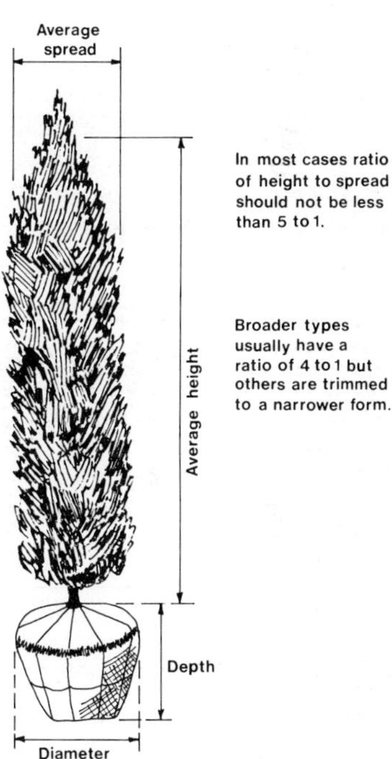

Fig. 3.35 Type 6 conifers, columnar type. (*Redrawn by permission from American Association of Nurserymen, American Standard for Nursery Stock, ANSI* Z60.1–1973.)

Type 6: Columnar Type (Fig. 3.35) Measurement designates height.

Use 3-in. intervals up to 18 in.
Use 6-in. intervals from 18 in. to 3 ft
Use 1-ft intervals from 3 to 10 ft
Use 2-ft intervals from 10 ft up

This group includes all the upright-growing evergreens which naturally develop a straight-sided form or one that tapers only slightly from the ground to a point more than half the height.

TABLE 3.26

Height	Spread	Examples
12–15 in.	8–12 in.	*Chamaecyparis lawsoniana* Alumii
15–18 in.	9–15 in.	*Juniperus chinensis* Keteleeri, *J. scopulorum*
18–24 in.	12–18 in.	*Taxus baccata* Irish
2–2½ ft	15–21 in.	*T. media* Hicks, Hatfield
2½–3 ft	18–24 in.	
3–4 ft	21–30 in.	
4–5 ft	2½–3 ft	
5–6 ft	3–4 ft	

The broader types will usually have a ratio of height to spread of 4:1. Many forms, however, will not attain this ratio, and even those of broad habit may be trimmed to advantage into a narrowed form. However, in most cases the ratio of height to spread should not be less than 5:1.

TABLE 3.27

Height	Spread, in.	Examples
12–15 in.	3–6	*Cupressus sempervirens; Juniperus communis, J.* virginiana
15–18 in.	4–7	(columnar type varieties); *Thuja occidentalis,*
18–24 in.	5–8	*T. orientalis* (columnar type varieties)
2–2½ ft	6–9	
2½–3 ft	7–10	
3–4 ft	9–12	
4–5 ft	12–15	
5–6 ft	15–18	
6–7 ft	18–21	
7–8 ft	21–24	
8–10 ft	24–30	

Balling-and-Burlapping Specifications

Ball sizes should always be of a diameter and depth to encompass the fibrous and feeding root system necessary for the full recovery of the plant.

Nursery Grown

Table 3.28 represents the recommended minimum sizes of balls for conifers which are being grown in the nursery under favorable growing conditions and which have received the proper cultural treatment to develop a well-branched root system. These specifications are for plants dug with the ball of earth in which they are growing.

It is recognized that plants which have a coarse or wide-spreading root system because of natural habit of growth, soil condition, or infrequent transplanting practice or which are moved out of season will require a ball larger than the recommended size. It is also recognized that special handling of certain material, e.g., stock grown in pots or other containers, field plants recently planted out from containers or with smaller balls, or material which has been frequently transplanted or root-pruned, constitutes cases where the sizes recommended may be excessive.

TABLE 3.28

Spreading, semispreading, and globe or dwarf conifers, types 1 to 3		Cone and broad upright conifers, types 4 and 5	
Spread, ft	Minimum ball diameter, in.	Height, ft	Minimum ball diameter, in.
1½–2	10	1½–2	10
2–2½	12	2–3	12
2½–3	14	3–4	14
3–3½	16	4–5	16
3½–4	18	5–6	20
4–5	21	6–7	22
5–6	24	7–8	24
6–7	28	8–9	27
7–8	32	9–10	30
8–9	36	10–12	34
		12–14	38
		14–16	42
16–18	46	18–20	50

Columnar conifers, type 6

Regular-growing kinds		Rapid-growing kinds*	
Height, ft	Minimum ball diameter, in.	Height, ft	Minimum ball diameter, in.
1½–2	10	1½–2	8
2–3	12	2–3	9
3–4	13	3–4	11
4–5	14	4–5	12
5–6	16	5–6	14
6–7	18		
7–8	20		
8–9	22		
9–10	24		
10–12	27		
12–14	30		
14–16	33		
16–18	36		
18–20	40		

* Such as *Thuja orientalis* (oriental arborvitae); *Juniperus communis* Stricta (Irish junipers).

Collected

The minimum sizes of ball shall be equal to that specified above for the next larger size nursery-grown stock.

Plants collected from wild or native stands may be considered nursery-grown when they have been successfully reestablished in the nursery row and grown under regular nursery cultural practices for a minimum of two growing seasons and have attained adequate root and top growth to indicate full recovery from transplanting into the nursery row.

Plantation-grown Stock

These are plants which have been systematically planted in fertile, friable soil which is relatively free of stones and foreign matter but with a minimum of aftercare.

The minimum ball sizes shall be equal to that specified above for the next larger size nursery-grown stock.

Ball Depths (Fig. 3.36)

For the greater part of the country ball depths will carry the following ratios:

Balls with diameters less than 20 *in.* Depth not less than 75 per cent of diameter

Balls with diameters of 20 *to* 30 *in. inclusive* Depth not less than 66⅔ per cent of diameter

Balls with diameters of 30 *to* 48 *in. inclusive* Depth not less than 60 per cent of diameter

Balls with diameters over 48 *in.* Depth scaled down proportionally

Under certain soil conditions, plants have root systems of proportionately less depth and greater diameter. These require a shallower but wider ball to encompass the roots properly. Conversely, in other soils and in certain regions roots develop greater depth and less spread, requiring an exceptionally deep ball, which may be smaller in diameter and greater in depth than the size recommended.

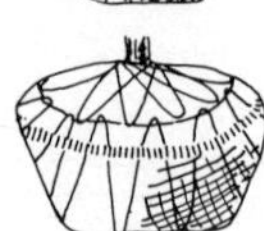

Fig. 3.36 Ball-depth ratio for conifers. *(Redrawn by permission from American Association of Nurserymen, American Standard for Nursery Stock, ANSI* Z60.1–1973.)

Container-grown Specifications

All container-grown conifers shall be healthy, vigorous, well rooted, and established in the container in which they are sold. They shall have tops of good quality and in a healthy growing condition.

An established container-grown conifer shall be a conifer transplanted into a container and grown in that container sufficiently long for the new fibrous roots to have developed so that the root mass will retain its shape and hold together when removed from the container.

The container shall be sufficiently rigid to hold the ball shape protecting the root mass during shipping.

Dwarf and light-growing varieties may be one or two sizes smaller than standard for a given size container.

Table 3.29 gives conifer sizes and acceptable container sizes.

TABLE 3.29

Types 1 to 3	
Spread (type 1, spreading, and type 2, semispreading conifers) or Height (type 3, globe or dwarf conifers)	Container size
6–9 in. 9–12 in. 12–15 in.	1 gal (trade designation): minimum of 5½ in. across top and height of 6 in. or equivalent volume.
12–15 in. 15–18 in.	2 gal (trade designation): minimum of 7 in. across top and height of 7½ in. or equivalent volume.
1½–2 ft	5 gal, egg can, or square can (trade designation): minimum of 9 in. across top and height of 10 in. or equivalent volume
Types 4 to 6*	
Height	Container size
6–9 in. 9–12 in. 12–15 in. 15–18 in. 18–24 in.	1 gal (trade designation) minimum of 5½ in. across top and height of 6 in. or equivalent volume
12–15 in. 15–18 in. 18–24 in. 2–2½ ft.	2 gal (trade designation): minimum of 7 in. across top and height of 6 in. or equivalent volume
18–24 in. 2–2½ ft 2½–3 ft 3–3½ ft 3½–4 ft	5 gal, egg can, or square can (trade designation): minimum of 9 in. across top and height of 10 in. or equivalent volume

* Except for extreme columnar types as *Cupressus sempervirens* (Italian cypress), which is acceptable one or two sizes taller than standard for a given container.

Balled-and-Potted

Balled-and-potted plants are field-grown nursery plants dug with a ball of earth still intact, in which they are growing; in lieu of burlapping they are placed in a container to retain the ball unbroken.

Ball sizes shall always be of a diameter and depth to encompass enough fibrous and feeding root system for the full recovery of the plant.

The minimum ball size specification for balled-and-potted plants shall be the same as for balled-and-burlapped plants.

BROADLEAF EVERGREENS

General Specifications

Quality Definitions

The quality of evergreens offered is assumed to be normal for the species or variety unless otherwise designated as:

Collected (Coll.) Natural seedling plants dug from native stands or forest plantings must be so designated.

Grading Tolerance

The growing of plant material cannot be rigidly standardized because of varying conditions of growth and methods of handling preferred or necessitated by climate, soil, and other conditions beyond the control of the grower. Judgment should therefore be exercised and allowances made in the above schedules to agree with definitions which are recognized by the trade as typical of acceptable plants in that region.

Where a minimum and maximum size, i.e., size range, is specified, the average of the lot shall approximate the mid-point of the specified size range. Plant lots of a given height shall have an approximate average as in Table 3.30.

TABLE 3.30

Height of plant	Average of lot
18–24 in.	21 in.
2–3 ft	2½ ft
3–4 ft	3½ ft
4–5 ft	4½ ft

Types and Measurement Designation

Measurement of height should begin at the ground line and continue up to where the main part of the plant ends and not to the tip of a thin shoot.

Five general types or groups are considered separately as follows:

Type 1: Spreading Type (Fig. 3.37) Measurement designates spread (height not considered).

Use 3-in. intervals up to 18 in.
Use 6-in. intervals from 18 in. to 4 ft.
Use 1-ft interval over 4 ft.

Examples

Calluna vulgaris (and cultivars)
Carissa grandiflora Green Carpet
Cotoneaster dammeri, C. horizontalis (and cultivars)
Cytisus Lydia
Plex crenata Helleri
Mahonia nervosa, M. repens

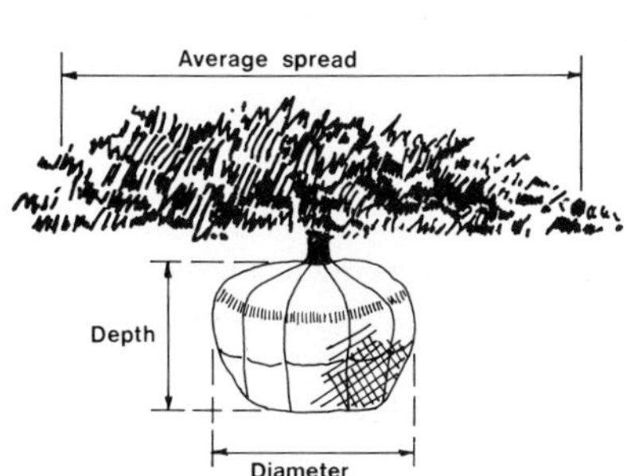

Fig. 3.37 Type 1 broadleaf evergreens, spreading type. (*Redrawn by permission from American Association of Nurserymen, American Standard for Nursery Stock, ANSI* Z60.1–1973.)

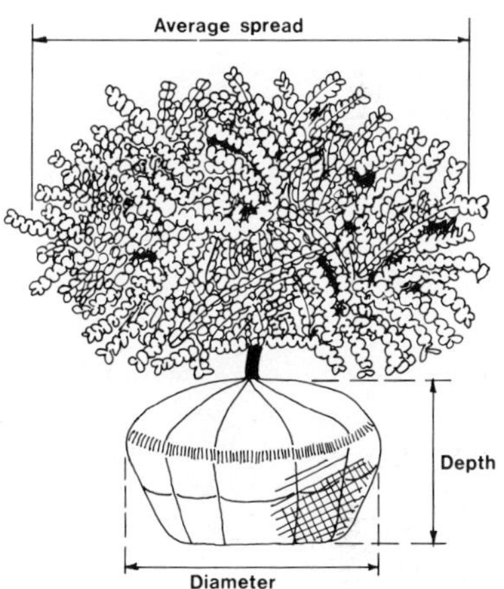

Fig. 3.38 Type 2 broadleaf evergreens, semispreading type. (*Redrawn by permission from American Association of Nurserymen, American Standard for Nursery Stock, ANSI* Z60.1–1973.)

Type 2: Semispreading Type (Fig. 3.38) Measurement designates spread (height not considered).

Use 3-in. intervals up to 18 in.
Use 6-in. intervals from 18 in. to 4 ft.
Use 1-ft intervals over 4 ft.

Examples

Berberis verruculosa
Cotoneaster franchetii, C. salicifolia
Daphne odora

Ilex crenata Convexa, Hetzii
Leucothoe axillaria, L. catesbaei
Raphiolepis umbellata
Rhododendron (*Azalea*) *obtusum* Amoenum, Gumpo and Kurume types, *impeditum*

Type 3: Globe or Dwarf Type (Fig. 3.39) Measurement designates height.

Use 3-in. intervals up to 18 in.
Use 6-in. intervals from 18 in. to 4 ft.
Use 1-ft intervals from 4 ft.

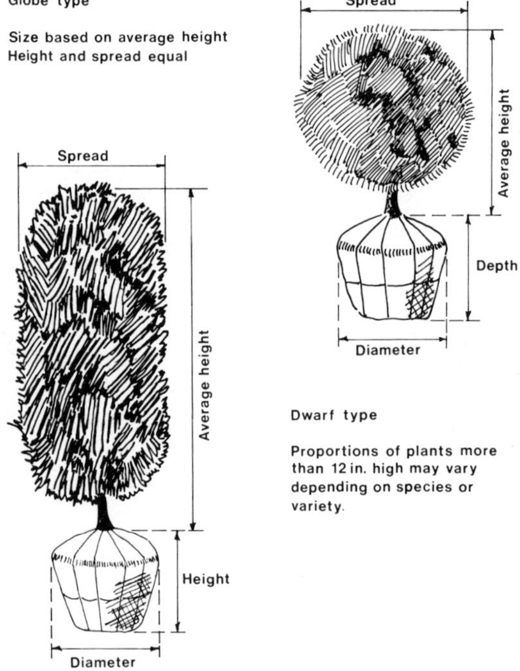

Fig. 3.39 Type 3 broadleaf evergreens, globe or dwarf type. (*Redrawn by permission from American Association of Nurserymen, American Standard for Nursery Stock,* ANSI Z60.1–1973.)

Spread will usually be equal to or only slightly less than the height up to 12 in. From there on the spread may be less than the height, but in no case will the ratio be more than 2:1 or height more than twice the spread. Both dimensions may be given.

Type 4: Broad Upright Type (Fig. 3.40) Measurement designates height.

Use 3-in. intervals up to 18 in.
Use 6-in. intervals from 18 in. to 3 ft.
Use 1-ft intervals from 3 ft up.

This group includes all of the larger-growing upright broadleaves, which vary considerably in ratio of spread to height. Well-grown material will in most cases have a height equal to if not greater than the spread. However, the spread should not be less than two-thirds of the height.

TABLE 3.31

Height	Minimum spread, in.	Examples
6–9 in.	5	*Buxus microphylla* (dwarf cultivars), *B. sempervirens*
9–12 in.	6	Suffruticosa; *Ilex cornuta* Rotunda, *I. vomitoria*
12–15 in.	7	Nana; *Leiophyllum buxifolium*
15–18 in.	9	
18–24 in.	10	
2–2½ ft	14	

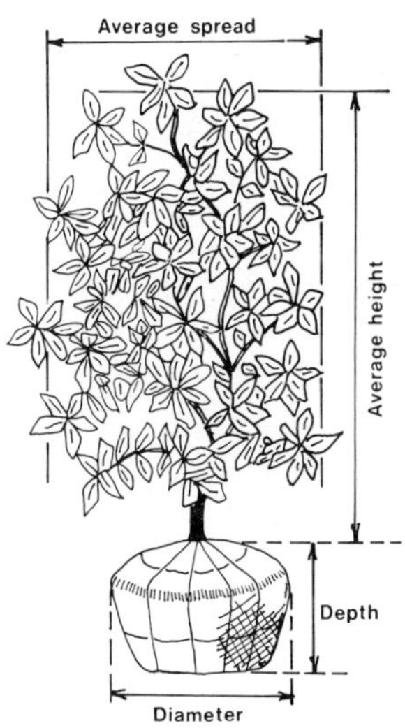

Fig. 3.40 Type 4 broadleaf evergreens, broad, upright type. (*Redrawn by permission from American Association of Nurserymen, American Standard for Nursery Stock, ANSI* Z60.1–1973.)

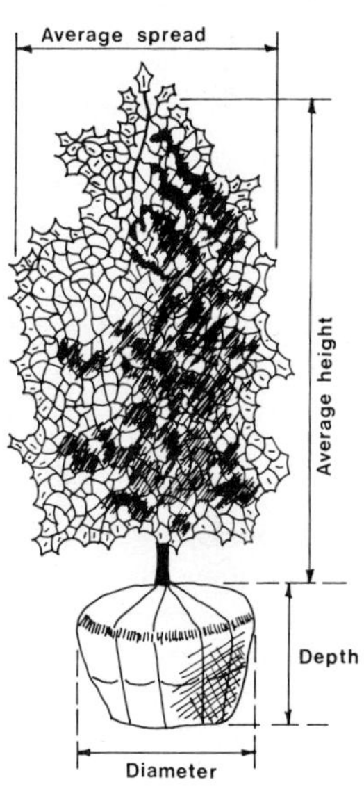

Fig. 3.41 Type 5 broadleaf evergreens, cone type. (*Redrawn by permission from American Association of Nurserymen, American Standard for Nursery Stock, ANSI* Z60.1–1973.)

Type 5: Cone Type (Fig. 3.41) Specifications identical to Type 4.

This type includes all upright-growing broadleaf evergreens which naturally develop into a conical form. Well-grown material will have a ratio of height to spread of 3:2, but a greater spread is acceptable.

Examples

Ilex aquifolium, I. opaca
Camellia japonica, C. sasanqua (cone types)
Illicium anisatum
Prunus caroliniana, P. laurocerasus, P. lusitanica

TABLE 3.32

Height	Minimum spread, in.	Examples
12–15 in.	8	*Abelia grandiflora; Aucuba japonica* (and cultivars); *Azalea* Rosebud; *Berberis julianae; Cytisus* Burkwood; *Elaeagnus pungens; Gardenia jasminoides; Ilex cornuta* (and cultivars), *I. crenata* Rotundifolia; *Kalmia latifolia; Ligustrum lucidum, L. texanum; Mahonia aquifolium; Pieris japonica; Rhododendron* (cultivars); *Viburnum rhytidophyllum, V. tinus*
15–18 in.	10	
18–24 in.	12	
2–2½ ft	16	
3–4 ft	24	
4–5 ft	28	

Balling-and-Burlapping Specifications

Ball sizes should always be of a diameter and depth to encompass the fibrous and feeding root system necessary for the full recovery of the plant.

Nursery-grown

Table 3.33 shows the recommended minimum size of ball for broadleaf evergreens being grown in the nursery under favorable growing conditions and which have received the proper cultural treatment to develop an average or better than average root system.

These specifications are for plants dug with the ball of earth in which they are growing.

It is recognized that plants which have a coarse or wide-spreading root system because of natural habit of growth, soil condition, or infrequent transplanting practice or which are moved out of season will require a size of ball in excess of the recommended sizes. It is also recognized that special handling of certain material, e.g., stock grown in pots or other containers, field plants recently planted out from containers or with smaller balls, or material which has been frequently transplanted or root-pruned, constitutes cases where the sizes recommended may be excessive.

Collected

The minimum size of ball shall be equal to that specified above for the next larger size nursery grown stock.

Plants collected from wild or native stands may be considered nursery-grown when they have been successfully reestablished in the nursery row and grown under regular nursery cultural practices for a minimum of two growing seasons and have attained adequate root and top growth to indicate full recovery from transplanting into the nursery row.

TABLE 3.33

Spreading, semispreading and globe or dwarf broadleaf evergreens, types 1 to 3		Cone and broad upright broadleaf evergreens, types 4 and 5	
Spread, ft.	Minimum diameter ball, in.	Height, ft	Minimum diameter ball, in.
1½–2	10	1½–2	10
2–2½	12	2–3	12
2½–3	14	3–4	14
3–3½	16	4–5	16
3½–4	18	5–6	20
4–5	21	6–7	22
		7–8	24
		8–9	27
		9–10	30
		10–12	34
		12–14	38
		14–16	42
		16–18	46
		18–20	50

Plantation-grown Stock

These are plants which have been systematically planted in fertile, friable soil which is relatively free of stones and foreign matter but with a minimum of aftercare.

The minimum ball sizes shall be equal to that specified above for the next larger size nursery-grown stock.

Ball Depths (Fig. 3.42)

For the greater part of the country ball depths will carry the following ratios:

Balls with diameters less than 20 *in.* Depth not less than 75 per cent of diameter

Balls with diameters of 20 *to* 30 *in. inclusive* Depth not less than 66⅔ per cent of diameter

Balls with diameters of 30 *to* 48 *in. inclusive* Depth not less than 60 per cent of diameter

Balls with diameters over 48 *in.:* Depth scaled down proportionally

Under certain soil and regional conditions, plants have root systems of proportionately less depth and greater diameter. These require a shallower but wider ball to encompass the roots properly. Conversely, on other soils and in certain regions roots develop greater depth and less spread, requiring an exceptionally deep ball, which may be smaller in diameter and greater in depth than the size recommended.

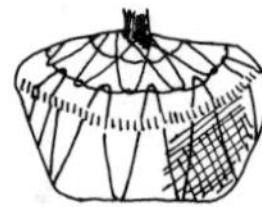

Fig. 3.42 Ball-depth ratio for broadleaf evergreens. (*Redrawn by permission from American Association of Nurserymen, American Standard for Nursery Stock, ANSI* Z60.1–1973.)

Container-grown Specifications

All container-grown broadleaf evergreens shall be healthy, vigorous, well-rooted, and established in the container in which they are sold. They shall have tops which are of good quality and are in a healthy growing condition (see Table 3.34).

An established container-grown broadleaf evergreen shall be a broadleaf evergreen transplanted into a container and grown in that container sufficiently long for the new fibrous roots to have developed so that the root mass will retain its shape and hold together when removed from the container.

The container shall be sufficiently rigid to hold the ball shape protecting the root mass during shipping.

Dwarf and light growing varieties may be one or two sizes smaller than standard for a given container.

ROSE GRADES

General

The standards specified apply only to field-grown 2-year roses when sold either bare-root or individually wrapped and packaged or in cartons.

All grades of roses must have a well-developed root system and have proportionate weight and caliper according to grade and variety. Roses shall be graded by size, number, and length of canes, and proper consideration should be given to weight and caliper of canes, depending upon grade and variety.

The specifications outlined for length of canes are applicable before pruning in preparation for sale.

Rose bushes that do not meet these standards for the individual grades are defined as *culls.*

TABLE 3.34
Broadleaf Evergreen Sizes and Acceptable Container Sizes

Broadleaf evergreens, types 1 to 3	
Spread (type 1, Spreading, and type 2, semispreading) height (type 3, dwarf or globe)	Container size
6–9 in. 9–12 in. 12–15 in.	1 gal (trade designation): minimum of 5½ in. across top and height of 6 in. or equivalent volume
12–15 in. 15–18 in.	2 gal (trade designation): minimum of 7 in. across top and height of 7½ in. or equivalent volume
1½–2 ft 2–2½ ft 2½–3 ft	5 gal, egg can, or square can (trade designation): minimum of 9 in. across top and height of 10 in. or equivalent volume
Type 4, broad upright type, and type 5, cone type* broadleaf evergreens	
Height	Container size
6–9 in. 9–12 in. 12–15 in. 15–18 in. 18–24 in.	1 gal (trade designation): minimum of 5½ in. across top and height of 6 in. or equivalent volume
12–15 in. 15–18 in. 18–24 in. 2–2½ ft	2 gal (trade designation): minimum of 7 in. across top and height of 6 in. or equivalent volume
18–24 in. 2–2½ ft 2½–3 ft 3–3½ ft 3½–4 ft	5 gal, egg can, or square can (trade designation): minimum of 9 in. across top and height of 10 in. or equivalent volume

* Except for such extreme columnar types as *Prunus laurocerasus* (cherry laurel) and *Lingustrum japonicum* (Japanese privet), which are acceptable one or two sizes taller than standard for a given container.

Hybrid Tea, Tea, Grandiflora, Hybrid Perpetual, Moss and Miscellaneous Bush Roses (Fig. 3.43)

Grade 1

Three or more strong canes, two of which are to be 18 in. and up, with the exception of a few of the light-growing sorts,* which are to have three or more canes, two of which are to be 16 in. and up, and one cane to be 18 in. and up, branched not higher than 3 in. above the bud union.

Grade 1 ½ or Medium

Two or more canes, to be 15 in. and up with the exception of a few of the light-growing sorts,* which are to have two strong canes 13 in. and up, branched not higher than 3 in. above the bud union.

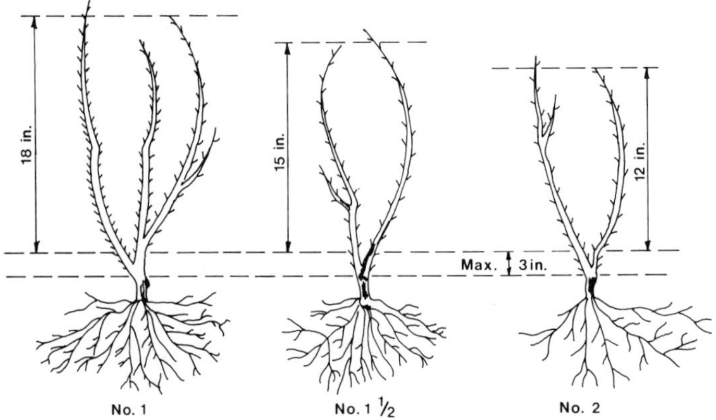

Fig. 3.43 Rose grades for hybrid tea, tea, grandiflora, etc., roses. (*Redrawn by permission from American Association of Nurserymen, American Standard for Nursery Stock, ANSI* Z60.1–1973.)

Grade 2

Two or more strong canes 12 in. and up, with the exception of a few light growing sorts,* which are to have two or more canes, 10 in. and up, branched not higher than 3 in. above the bud union.

* Many varieties of Hybrid Tea roses express varying growth characteristics in different parts of the country. Some varieties may be generally known to be less vigorous in some regions than in others. Therefore the term light-growing sorts cannot be used in a universal or rigid sense. Examples of varieties generally to be considered to be light-growing are President Hoover, Étoile de Hollande, The Doctor, and Mojave. Other examples that are often considered in some areas as light-growing varieties are New Yorker, Charlotte Armstrong, and Helen Traubel.

Floribunda Roses (Fig. 3.44)

Grade 1

Three or more strong canes, two of which are to be 15 in. and up branched not higher than 3 in. above the bud union.

Grade 1½ or Medium

Two or more strong canes to be 14 in. and up, branched not higher than 3 in. above the bud union.

Grade 2

Two or more strong canes to be 12 in. and up, branched not higher than 3 in. above the bud union.

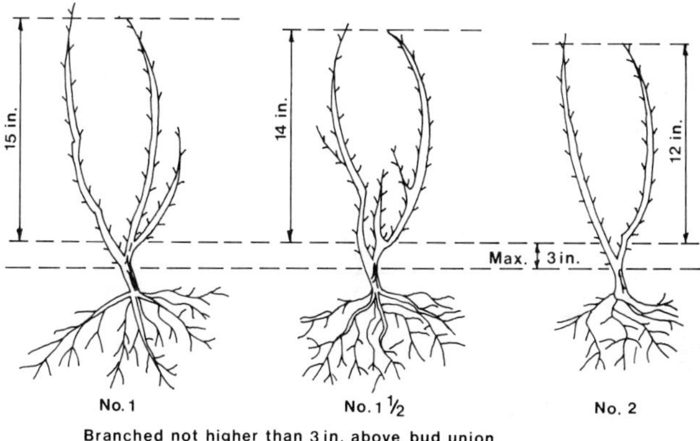

Fig. 3.44 Rose grades for floribunda roses. (*Redrawn by permission from American Association of Nurserymen, American Standard for Nursery Stock, ANSI* Z60.1–1973.)

Polyantha, Dwarf, and Light-growing Floribunda Roses (Fig. 3.45)

Grade 1

Four or more canes, all to be 12 in. and up, branched not higher than 3 in. above the bud union.

Grade 1½ or Medium

Three or more canes, all to be 10 in. and up, branched not higher than 3 in. above the bud union.

Grade 2

Two or more strong canes, both to be 10 in. and up, branched not higher than 3 in. above the bud union.

Climbing Roses (Fig. 3.46)

Grade 1

Three or more strong canes, 24 in. and up, branched not higher than 3 in. above the bud union or crown.

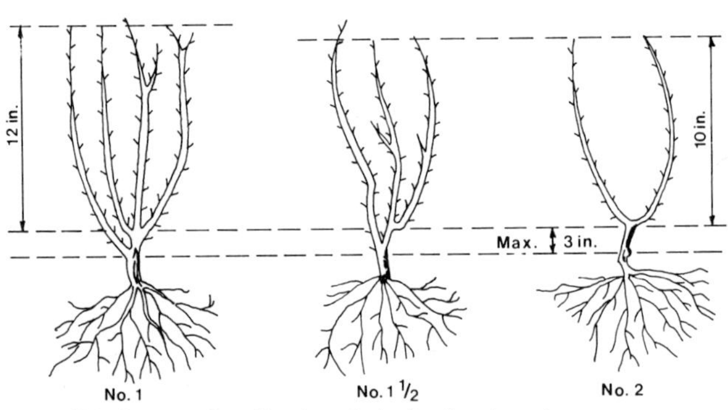

Fig. 3.45 Rose grades for polyantha roses. (*Redrawn by permission from American Association of Nurserymen, American Standard for Nursery Stock, ANSI* Z60.1-1973.)

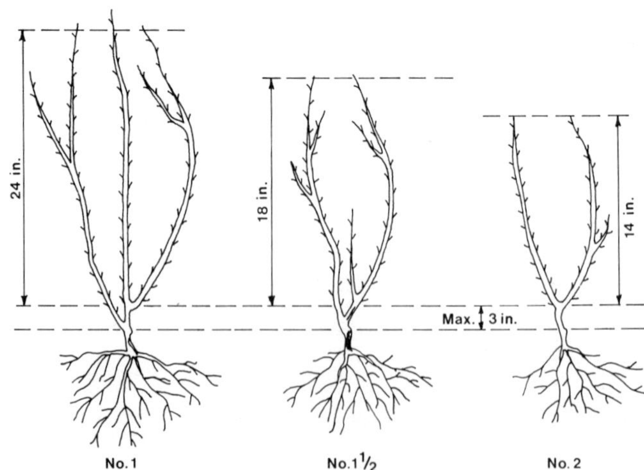

Fig. 3.46 Rose grades for climbing roses. (*Redrawn by permission from American Association of Nurserymen, American Standard for Nursery Stock, ANSI* Z60.1-1973.)

Grade 1½ or Medium

Two strong canes, each 18 in. and up, branched not higher than 3 in. above the bud union or crown.

Grade 2

Two strong canes each 14 in. and up, branched not higher than 3 in. above the bud union or crown.

Container-grown Roses

All container-grown roses shall have been growing in the container in which they are marketed for a minimum of 1 month of active growing season and for a maximum of two growing seasons. Roses may be cut back to a minimum of 4 in. above the bud union at the time they are potted and still comply with the grades in which they were classified prior to pruning in preparation for potting.

TABLE 3.35

Grade of roses	Minimum container size
1	2 gal (trade designation): minimum of 7 in. across top and height of 7½ in. or equivalent volume
1½ and 2	1 gal (trade designation): minimum of 5½ in. across top and height of 7½ in. or equivalent volume

VINES AND GROUND COVERS

Type 1: Fast-growing Vines

The fast-growing vines which normally produce a number of vigorous woody runners in 1 or 2 years shall be graded and designated as follows:

2-year, no. 1 shall have heavy well-branched tops with not fewer than three runners 18 in. and up and vigorous, well-developed root system.

2-year, no. 2 lighter grade below number 1 standard but without serious defects, three runners 12 in. and up and a root system commensurate with the top.

Older vines should be designated according to age, heavy or light grade, length of runners, and other characteristics such as standard, grafted, potted, or tubbed.

Examples

Celastrus orbiculata, C. scandens
Lonicera japonica, L. japonica halliana, L. sempervirens
Parthenocissus quinquefolia, P. engelmannii
Rosa wichuriana
Wisteria

Type 2: Medium-growing Vines

Woody vines usually starting with a single cane or runner should be designated by age and grade (heavy and light).

2-year, no. 1 shall have a heavy, well-branched top and vigorous well-developed root system.
2-year, medium is lighter grade than the above without serious defects; top not as well branched. However, root system must be in proportion to top.

Older vines should be designated according to age, heavy or light grades, length of runners, and other characteristics such as standard, grafted, potted, or tubbed.

Examples

Actinidia
Aristolochia
Campsis (Bignonia) radicans
Parthenocissus tricuspidata veitchii
Vitis

Type 3: Clump Type

Clump type shall be designated by age and heavy or light grade. Dormant plants may or may not have live runners. In this group a well-developed root system and healthy well-developed crown are the important considerations.

Examples

Clematis
Pueraria (Kudzu)

Type 4: Ground Covers

Dwarf vines and ground covers are to be designated or described by age, size of clump, length of runners, and other characteristics peculiar to the particular species offered.

Examples

Arctostaphylos uva-ursi
Cornus canadensis
Cotoneaster dammeri
Hedera helix (and cultivars)
Euonymus radicans minimus
Pachysandra teminalis
Vinca minor

Type 5: Ground Cover: Crown vetch

Clump type should be designated by age, runner length, and container. Dormant plants may or may not have live runners. In this type a well-developed root system and healthy, well-developed crown are the important considerations.

Field-grown crown vetch shall be whole crowns, at least one growing season old. The overall length of the plant shall be 6 to 9 in., including ½ in. of top growth and the root caliper 1 in. below the root collar shall measure no less than ⅛ in.

Crown vetch produced in pots or other media-holding containers will be grown in sizes adequate for the age and grade and will be acclimated to conditions befitting the planting season.

Vines in Pots and Containers

Ground covers supplied in pots or similar containers shall be thrifty, well-balanced plants, well established in the containers.

Table 3.36 gives suggested minimum specifications.

LINING-OUT STOCK

General

Lining-out stock shall include all plant material coming from propagating houses, beds, or frames and young material of suitable size to plant out in nursery rows.

Designation

Age Should be given by number of years since propagated or (in case of seedlings) since growth started.

Transplanted The number of times transplanted to be represented by using for each transplanting the letter T.

Seedling Stock to be represented by the letter S.

Cuttings To be represented by the letter C.
Grafted Stock to be represented by the letter G.
Size Should be given in accordance with the intervals recommended for each plant class.

Example

"Koster Spruce G, 6 to 8 in., 4 yr TT" means Koster Spruce graft, 6 to 8 in. high, 4 years old, and twice transplanted.

TABLE 3.36

Variety	Size of pot	Min. no. of runners	Min. length of runners, in.
Ajuga reptans and cultivars	2¼ in., 4 in., gal		
Euonymus fortunei and cultivars	2¼ in.	2	8
	3 in.	3	10
	4 in.	4	12
	gal	6	12
Hedera helix and cultivars	2¼ in.	2	8
	3 in.	2	10
	4 in.	3	10
	gal	4	10
Lonicera japonica halliana	2¼ in.	2	4
	3 in.	3	6
	4 in.	4	8
Pachysandra terminalis	2¼, 3, 4 in.		
Vinca minor, V. major, and cultivars	2¼ in.	3– 6	6– 8
	3 in.	6– 8	8–10
	4 in.	10–12	8–10

Collected (Coll.) Plants collected from the wild must be so designated.

Size Designation

In grading use 2-in. intervals up to 12 in; 3-in. intervals up to 24 in.; 6-in. intervals for larger sizes.

Recommendations for Evergreen Lining-out Stock

Evergreens should be transplanted frequently enough to create a good root system, which will ensure a minimum of transplanting loss, and to give the top room enough to start the branch framework properly, making a well-shaped specimen when placed in the nursery row.

In order to produce a fibrous root system it is recommended that species like firs, pines, and similar sorts, which normally make a few coarse roots, be transplanted every 2 or 3 years, and that species such as *Arborvitae* and *Retinospora* be transplanted every 3 or 4 years, as they naturally make better roots.

Broadleaf evergreen species such as *Pyracantha lalandi,* which normally make a few coarse roots, should be transplanted every year, while those producing a good system of fibrous roots may be transplanted every second year only.

Trimming is also necessary to ensure a proper foundation for good shape in the finished plant, although frequent transplanting will usually eliminate the need for severe trimming.

SEEDLING TREES AND SHRUBS

General

Forest, game-refuge, erosion control, shelterbelt, or farm woodlot plantings under natural conditions shall come under the following classifications. Actual conditions of soil, climate, and environment will necessarily govern the minimum size for a particular species that is required.

Tolerance of not more than 10 per cent under grade should be accepted so long as it is not intentional and the ones under grade are close to the grade required.

Deciduous or Hardwoods

When caliper is important, measurements are taken at root collar or ground line (Table 3.37). Tops or roots will not be trimmed unless specified by grower or requested by purchaser. When height is important, measurements are taken from root collar or groundline (Table 3.38). These measurements are suggested for commercial nurseries furnishing or purchasing stock for the retail trade, while complying with demands for calipered stock.

TABLE 3.37

Caliper, in.	Minimum height, in.	Minimum root length, in.
$\frac{1}{4}$ and up	12	10
$\frac{3}{16}$–$\frac{1}{4}$	10	10
$\frac{1}{8}$–$\frac{3}{16}$	8	8
$\frac{1}{16}$–$\frac{1}{8}$	6	8

It should be understood that when heights are to govern, the caliper specification is minimum and when caliper is to govern, the height specification is minimum.

TABLE 3.38

Height, in.	Minimum caliper, in.	Minimum root length, in.
24–36	1/4	12
18–24	3/16	10
12–18	1/8	10
6–12	1/16	8

TABLE 3.39

Height, in.	Minimum caliper, in.
12–15	3/16
9–12	1/8
6–9	1/16

Conifers, Evergreens

Age is not important when height or caliper is specified; however, it may be used in listings or demanded by purchaser (Table 3.39). The following key is for use in indicating seedling, root-pruned, or transplants:

- S Seedling
- RP Root-pruned (should not be root-pruned deeper than 6 in. when applying to conifers)
- T One T for each time transplanted

General

All plants are to have well-developed root systems, to be free of insects, diseases, and mechanical injuries, and in all respects be suitable for field planting. All conifers must have dormant buds (except in the South) and secondary needles.

At the option of the purchaser other special restrictions may be specified.

BULBS, CORMS, AND TUBERS

General

Bulbs and corms are generally sold under grade names such as forcing size, top-size, large, etc. In the case of narcissus and daffodils, the designations

TABLE 3.40
Bulb Sizes

Designated by centimeters or inches of circumference

Grade	Circumference	
	cm	in.
Tulips*		
Top	12 and up	4¾ and up
Large	11–12	4¾–4¾
Medium	10–11	4–4⅜
Small	9–10	3⅝–4
Hyacinths		
Top exhibition forcing size	19 and up	7⅝ and up
Large exhibition forcing size	18–19	7¼–7⅝
Medium exhibition forcing size	17–18	6¾–7¼
Top bedding or garden size	16–17	6⅜–6¾
Large bedding or garden size	15–16	6–6⅜
Medium bedding, miniature, or garden size	14–15	5½–6
Grape hyacinths		
Top	9–11 and up	3⅝–4⅜ and up
Large	8–9	3⅛–3⅝
Medium	7–8	2¾–3⅛
Crocus		
Top	9 and up	3⅝ and up
Large	8–9	3⅛–3⅝
Medium	7–8	2¾–3⅛
Small	6–7	2–2¾
Narcissus, paper-white†		
Top	16 and up	6⅜ and up
Large	15–16	6–6⅜
Medium	14–15	5½–6
Small	12–14	4¾–5½

Narcissus and daffodils‡

Grade	Explanation
Top size round Large size round Medium size round	Round means single-nosed bulbs which are fairly circular in cross section and which show evidence of producing one flower; slabs not permitted in this grade

TABLE 3.40 (Continued)

Narcissus and daffodils‡	
Grade	Explanation
Top size double nose Large size double nose Medium size double nose	Double nose means bulbs that show evidence of producing two or more flowers; double character of bulb means that circumference measurements are variable

Designated by inches in diameter

Grade	Diameter, in.
Gladioli§	
Jumbo	Over 2
No. 1	1½–2
Large:	
No. 2	1¼–1½
No. 3	1–1¼
Medium:	
No. 4	¾–1
No. 5	½–¾
Small:	
No. 6	⅜–½
No grade name:	
No. 7	Under ⅜
Amaryllis	
Fancy	3½ and up
Top	3½–3½
Large	3–3¼
Medium	2¾–3
Small	2¼–2¾
Not acceptable	Under 2¼
Caladium (fancy-leaved)	
Giant	3½ and up
Large	2½–3½
Standard	2–2½
Medium	1½–2
Small	1–1½
Tuberous begonias and gloxinias	
Giant	2½ and up
Extra large	2–2½
Large	1½–2
Medium	1¼–1½
Small	1–1¼

TABLE 3.40 (Continued)

Designated by inches in diameter

Grade	Diameter, in.
Callas	
Top	2½ and up
Large	2–2¼
Medium	1½–2
Small	1¼–1½
Ranunculus	
Giant	1 and up
Extra large	⅞–1
Large	¾–⅞
Medium	⅝–¾
Small	½–⅝
Freesia	
Extra large	⅞ and up
Large	¾–⅞
Medium	⅝–¾
Small	½–⅝
Anemones	
Extra large	⅞ and up
Large	¾–⅞
Medium	⅝–¾
Small	½–⅝

Designated by inches of circumference

Grade	Circumference, in.
Lilies (Regal and Easter)	
Giant	10 and up
Fancy	9–10
Extra large	8–9
Large	7–8
Standard	6–7
Medium	5–6
Tuberoses	
Top size	4–6
First size	3–4

TABLE 3.40 (Continued)

Designated by eyes, or buds, per division	
Peonies and bleeding heart	
Grade	Number of eyes, or buds, per division
Select	5–7
Standard	3–5
Small	2–3
Cannas	
The number of eyes, or buds, per root to be indicated; e.g., roots with 2–3 eyes; roots with only one eye are not to be offered to the public (they are suitable for growing on in nursery or for potting or bedding purposes)	
Dahlias	
The nature of divisions from different varieties makes it impossible to list size designations; each division must have portion of live crown and at least one eye, or bud	

* Some botanical and species tulips are smaller than above designated sizes. Bulbs of botanical and species tulips should be so identified and sizes given.

† This type of bulb is normally smaller than other narcissus varieties and consequently is listed separately.

‡ Certain varieties normally have smaller bulbs than others. Until size grades are established, name grade designations as indicated and accepted by the trade (as bulbs are purchased) should be used.

§ According to Fair Trade Practice Rules adopted by Gladiolus Growers.

double nose to indicate a split bulb with probably two flower buds, and *rounds* are used.

With some groups, e.g., hyacinths, the grade names indicate special usage, such as exhibition and forcing sizes and sizes more suitable for outdoor bedding purposes.

Some grade measurements have normally been given in centimeters of circumference, since this measurement allows closer grading. This system is in vogue and is generally accepted in the trade for the smaller bulbs, e.g., crocus and grape hyacinth, while for larger and particularly for the flat corms, inches in diameter is the generally accepted measurement, e.g., for gladioli, tuberous begonias, and caladiums.

For such items as peonies, bleeding heart, and cannas, the number of eyes or buds on the tuber is designated.

The grades in Table 3.40 conform in substance to generally accepted trade usage. Both grade names and sizes in inches or centimeters should be given; size in inches or centimeters must be designated.

Offers of bulbs, corms, and tubers (except peony divisions) which cannot reasonably be expected to bloom in the season after planting should not be made to the public unless they are clearly indicated as *nonblooming* sizes for naturalization or other plantings for which nonblooming sizes might be acceptable.

TABLE 3.41
A Master List of Trees and Shrubs

Key	Botanical Name	Common Name
1.	*Abelia grandiflora*	Glossy abelia
2.	*Abies* species	Fir
3.	*Acanthopanax pentaphyllum*	Five-leaved aralia
4.	*Acer campestre*	Hedge maple
5.	*Acer ginnala*	Amur maple
6.	*Acer platanoides*	Norway maple
7.	*Acer plantanoides columnare*	Columnar Norway maple
8.	*Acer pseudo platanus*	Sycamore maple
9.	*Acer rubrum*	Red maple
10.	*Acer saccharinum*	Silver maple
11.	*Acer saccharum*	Sugar maple
12.	*Aesculus* species	Horsechestnut
13.	*Ailanthus glandulosa*	Tree of heaven
14.	*Alnus rugosa*	Smooth alder
15.	*Amelanchier canadensis*	Downy shadblow or shadbush
16.	*Amorpha fruticosa*	Indigobush
17.	*Aronia* species	Chokeberry
18.	*Aronia arbutifolia*	Red chokeberry
19.	*Aronia melanocarpa*	Black chokeberry
20.	*Azalea amoena*	Amoena azalea
21.	*Azalea hinodegiri*	Hinodegiri azalea
22.	*Azalea obtusa*	Hiryu azalea
23.	*Azalea kaempferi*	Torch azalea
24.	*Baccharis halimifolia*	Groundsel-bush
25.	*Berberis julianae*	Wintergreen barberry
26.	*Berberis* species	Barberry
27.	*Berberis thunbergii*	Japanese barberry
28.	*Berberis triacanthophora*	Threespine barberry
29.	*Berberis verruculosa*	Warty barberry
30.	*Betula alba*	European white birch
31.	*Betula papyrifera*	Canoe birch
32.	*Betula populifolia*	Gray birch
33.	*Buxus sempervirens*	Common boxwood
34.	*Buxus suffruticosa*	Dwarf English box
35.	*Callicarpa japonica*	American beautyberry
36.	*Callicarpa purpurea*	Chinese beautyberry
37.	*Calycanthus floridus*	Sweetshrub, Carolina allspice
38.	*Caragana arborescens*	Siberian pea-tree
39.	*Carpinus betulus*	European hornbeam
40.	*Carpinus caroliniana*	American hornbeam
41.	*Celtis occidentalis*	Hackberry
42.	*Cephalanthus occidentalis*	Buttonbush
43.	*Cercis canadensis*	American redbud
44.	*Cercis chinensis*	Chinese redbud
45.	*Chaenomeles japonica*	Japanese quince
46.	*Chamaecyparis pisifera*	Sawara cypress
47.	*Chamaecyparis thyoides*	White cedar
48.	*Chionanthus virginicus*	White fringe-tree
49.	*Cladrastis lutea*	Yellow-wood
50.	*Clethra alnifolia*	White-alder, summersweet
51.	*Colutea arborescens*	Bladder-senna
52.	*Cornus alba*	Tatarian dogwood
53.	*Cornus alternifolia*	Pagoda dogwood

TABLE 3.41 (Continued)

Key	Botanical Name	Common Name
54.	*Cornus amomum*	Silky dogwood
55.	*Cornus florida*	Flowering dogwood
56.	*Cornus florida rubra*	Pink flowering dogwood
57.	*Cornus kousa*	Kousa dogwood
58.	*Cornus mas*	Cornelian cherry
59.	*Cornus paniculata*	Gray dogwood
60.	*Cornus sanguinea*	Red dogwood
61.	*Cornus sibirica*	Coral dogwood
62.	*Cornus stolonifera*	Red-osier dogwood
63.	*Cornus stolonifera lutea*	Yellowtwig dogwood
64.	*Corylus americana*	American hazel
65.	*Corylus avellana*	European hazel
66.	*Cotinus americanus*	American smoke-tree
67.	*Cotinus coggygria*	Common smoke-tree
68.	*Cotoneaster acutifolia*	Peking cotoneaster
69.	*Cotoneaster dielsiana*	Diels cotoneaster
70.	*Cotoneaster divaricata*	Spreading cotoneaster
71.	*Cotoneaster francheti*	Franchet cotoneaster
72.	*Cotoneaster horizontalis*	Rock cotoneaster
73.	*Cotoneaster horizontalis perpusilla*	Ground cotoneaster
74.	*Cotoneaster microphylla*	Rockspray cotoneaster
75.	*Cotoneaster salicifolia*	Willowleaf cotoneaster
76.	*Cotoneaster simonsii*	Simons cotoneaster
77.	*Crataegus coccinea*	Thicket hawthorn
78.	*Crataegus cordata*	Washington hawthorn
79.	*Crataegus crus-galli*	Cockspur thorn
80.	*Crataegus oxyacantha*	English hawthorn
81.	*Daphne odora*	Winter daphne
82.	*Deutzia gracilis*	Slender deutzia
83.	*Deutzia gracilis rosea*	Rose panicle
84.	*Deutzia lemoinei*	Lemoine deutzia
85.	*Deutzia* (tall growing varieties)	Deutzia
86.	*Diervilla sessilifolia*	Southern bush honeysuckle
87.	*Eleagnus angustifolia*	Russian olive
88.	*Eleagnus longipes*	Cherry eleagnus
89.	*Eleagnus umbellata*	Autumn eleagnus
90.	*Euonymus alata*	Winged euonymus
91.	*Euonymus alata compacta*	Dwarf winged euonymus
92.	*Euonymus americana*	Brook euonymus
93.	*Euonymus bungeana*	Winterberry euonymus
94.	*Euonymus europaea*	European burningbush
95.	*Euonymus fortunei*	Fortune euonymus
96.	*Euonymus patens*	Spreading euonymus
97.	*Euonymus radicans vegeta*	Bigleaf winercreeper
98.	*Euonymus radicans*	Wintercreeper
99.	*Euonymus yedoensis*	Yeddo euonymus
100.	*Exochorda racemosa*	Common pearlbush
101.	*Fagus americana*	American beech
102.	*Fagus sylvatica*	European beech
103.	*Forsythia*, all varieties	Forsythia
104.	*Fraxinus americana*	White ash
105.	*Fraxinus pennsylvanica*	Green ash
106.	*Gaylussacia*	Huckleberry

TABLE 3.41 (Continued)

Key	Botanical Name	Common Name
107.	*Ginkgo biloba*	Maidenhair-tree
108.	*Gleditsia triacanthos inermis*	Thornless honeylocust
109.	*Gleditsia* varieties	Honeylocust
110.	*Halesia tetraptera*	Great silverbell
111.	*Hamamelis*	Witchhazel
112.	*Hedera helix*	English ivy
113.	*Hibiscus,* bush form	Hibiscus, rose mallow
114.	*Hibiscus syriacus*	Shrub-althea
115.	*Hydrangea arborescens grandiflora alba*	Snowhill hydrangea
116.	*Hydrangea macrophylla Otaksa*	Otaksa hydrangea
117.	*Hydrangea paniculata grandiflora peegee*	Peegee hydrangea
118.	*Hydrangea quercifolia*	Oakleaf hydrangea
119.	*Hydrangea petiolaris*	Climbing hydrangea
120.	*Hypericum kalmianum*	Kalm hypericum
121.	*Hypericum moserianum*	Goldflower
122.	*Ilex crenata*	Japanese holly
123.	*Ilex crenata rotundifolia*	Round leaved holly
124.	*Ilex crenata convexa (bullata)*	Convex leaved holly
125.	*Ilex crenata microphylla*	Littleleaf Jap. holly
126.	*Ilex glabra*	Inkberry
127.	*Ilex laevigata*	Smooth winterberry
128.	*Ilex opaca*	American holly
129.	*Ilex verticillata*	Common winterberry
130.	*Itea virginica*	Sweetspire
131.	*Jasminum floridum*	Summer flowering jasmine
132.	*Jasminum nudiflorum*	Winter jasmine
133.	*Juniperus chinensis pfitzeriana*	Pfitzer juniper
134.	*Juniperus chinensis sargenti*	Sargent juniper
135.	*Juniperus communis*	Common juniper
136.	*Juniperus communis hibernica*	Irish juniper
137.	*Juniperus horizontalis Bar Harbor*	Bar Harbor juniper
138.	*Juniperus horizontalis douglasii*	Douglas juniper
139.	*Juniperus horizontalis plumosa*	Andorra juniper
140.	*Juniperus squamata Meyeri*	Meyer juniper
141.	*Juniperus virginiana*	Red cedar
142.	*Juniperus virginiana globosa*	Globe red cedar
143.	*Kalmia*	Mountain laurel
144.	*Kerria japonica*	White kerria
145.	*Koelreuteria paniculata*	Golden rain-tree
146.	*Laburnum*	Laburnum
147.	*Leiophyllum*	Sandmyrtle
148.	*Lespedeza bicolor*	Shrub bushclover
149.	*Lespedeza thunbergii*	Thunberg lespsdeza
150.	*Leucothoe catesbaei*	Drooping leucothoe
151.	*Ligustrum amurense*	Amur privet
152.	*Ligustrum ibolium*	Ibolium privet
153.	*Ligustrum ibota*	Ibota privet
154.	*Ligustrum lucidum*	Glossy privet
155.	*Ligustrum ovalifolium*	California privet
156.	*Ligustrum regelianum*	Regel privet
157.	*Ligustrum vulgare*	European privet

TABLE 3.41 (Continued)

Key	Botanical Name	Common Name
158.	*Lindera Benzoin*	Spicebush
159.	*Liriodendron tulipifera*	Tuliptree
160.	*Liquidambar styraciflua*	Sweetgum
161.	*Lonicera* (bush forms)	Bush honeysuckle
162.	*Lonicera fragrantissima*	Winter honeysuckle
163.	*Lonicera Morrowii*	Morrow honeysuckle
164.	*Lonicera tatarica*	Tatarian honeysuckle
165.	*Magnolia glauca*	Sweetbay
166.	*Mahonia aquifolium*	Oregon hollygrape
167.	*Malus arnoldiana*	Arnold crabapple
168.	*Malus atrosanguinea*	Carmine crabapple
169.	*Malus baccata*	Siberian crabapple
170.	*Malus coronaria*	Wild sweet crabapple
171.	*Malus floribunda*	Japanese flowering crabapple
172.	*Malus ioensis plena*	Bechtel crabapple
173.	*Malus sargenti*	Sargent crabapple
174.	*Malus scheideckeri*	Scheidecker crabapple
175.	*Myrica caroliniensis*	Northern bayberry
176.	*Myrica pennsylvanica*	Bayberry
177.	*Nyssa sylvatica*	Tupelo, sourgum
178.	*Ostrya virginiana*	American hophornbeam
179.	*Oxydendron arboreum*	Sourwood
180.	*Pachysandra terminalis*	Japanese spurge
181.	*Phellodendron chinense*	Chinese corktree
182.	*Phellodendron* species	Corktree
183.	*Philadelphus coronarius*	Sweet mockorange
184.	*Philadelphus lemoinei*	Lemoine mockorange
185.	*Photinia villosa*	Oriental photinia
186.	*Physocarpus opulifolius*	Common ninebark
187.	*Picea abies (excelsa)*	Norway spruce
188.	*Picea* (dwarf)	Dwarf spruce
189.	*Pieris floribunda*	Mountain andromeda
190.	*Pieris japonica*	Japanese andromeda
191.	*Pinus nigra austriaca*	Austrian pine
192.	*Pinus strobus*	White pine
193.	*Pinus sylvestris*	Scotch pine
194.	*Platanus acerifolia*	London planetree
195.	*Platanus occidentalis*	American sycamore
196.	*Platanus orientalis*	European planetree
197.	*Populus*	Poplar
198.	*Populus alba Bolleana*	Bolleana poplar
199.	*Populus eugenei*	Carolina poplar
200.	*Populus maximowiczii*	Japanese poplar
201.	*Potentilla fruticosa*	Shrubby cinquefoil
202.	*Potentilla* varieties	Cinquefoil
203.	*Prunus amygdalus*	Almond
204.	*Prunus cerasifera*	Myrobalan plum
205.	*Prunus glandulosa*	Flowering almond
206.	*Prunus maritima*	Beach plum
207.	*Prunus triloba*	Flowering plum
208.	*Prunus subhirtella pendula*	Weeping Japanese cherry
209.	*Pseudotsuga taxifolia*	Douglas fir
210.	*Pyracantha coccinea Lalandii*	Laland firethorn

TABLE 3.41 (Continued)

Key	Botanical Name	Common Name
211.	*Quercus alba*	White oak
212.	*Quercus bicolor*	Swamp white oak
213.	*Quercus borealis*	Northern red oak
214.	*Quercus coccinea*	Scarlet oak
215.	*Quercus macrocarpa*	Mossycup oak
216.	*Quercus palustris*	Pin oak
217.	*Quercus rubra*	Common red oak
218.	*Quercus velutina*	Black oak
219.	*Rhamnus cathartica*	Common buckthorn
220.	*Rhamnus frangula*	Glossy buckthorn
221.	*Rhododendron*	Rhododendron
222.	*Rhododendron maximum*	Rosebay rhododendron
223.	*Rhodotypos kerrioides (scandens)*	Jetbead, white kerria
224.	*Rhus Cotinus*	Common smoke tree
225.	*Rhus* in variety	Sumac
226.	*Rhus aromatica (canadensis)*	Fragrant sumac
227.	*Rhus copallina*	Shining sumac
228.	*Rhus glabra*	Smooth sumac
229.	*Rhus glabra laciniata*	Cutleaf sumac
230.	*Rhus typhina*	Staghorn sumac
231.	*Rhus typhina laciniata*	Shredded sumac
232.	*Ribes alpinum*	Mountain currant
233.	*Robinia hispida*	Black locust
234.	*Rosa blanda*	Meadow rose
235.	*Rosa hugonis*	Hugonis rose
236.	*Rosa lucida*	Virginia rose
237.	*Rosa multiflora*	Japanese rose
238.	*Rosa nitida*	Bristly rose
239.	*Rosa palustris*	Swamp rose
240.	*Rosa rubiginosa*	Sweetbrier
241.	*Rosa setigera*	Prairie rose
242.	*Rosa virginiana*	Virginia rose
243.	*Rosa wichuriana*	Wichurian rose
244.	*Salix* in variety	Willow
245.	*Sambucus canadensis*	American elder
246.	*Sambucus nigra*	European elder
247.	*Sambucus pubens*	Scarlet elder
248.	*Sophora japonica*	Chinese scholartree
249.	*Sorbaria aitchisonii*	Kashmir false spirea
250.	*Sorbaria arborea*	Tree spirea
251.	*Sorbaria sorbifolia*	Ural false-spirea
252.	*Sorbus aucuparia*	European mountain ash
253.	*Spiraea bumalda*	Bumalda spirea
254.	*Spiraea bumalda Anthony Waterer*	Anthony Waterer spirea
255.	*Spiraea japonica Fortunei*	Fortune spirea
256.	*Spiraea*, tall varieties	Spirea
257.	*Spiraea thunbergii*	Thunberg spirea
258.	*Spiraea tomentosa*	Hardhack
259.	*Spiraea vanhouttei*	Vanhoutte spirea
260.	*Stephanandra flexuosa*	Cutleaf stephanandra
261.	*Stephanandra incisa*	Stephanandra
262.	*Styrax japonica*	Japanese snowball
263.	*Styrax obassia*	Fragrant snowball

TABLE 3.41 (Continued)

Key	Botanical Name	Common Name
264.	*Symphoricarpos albus (racemosus)*	Common snowberry
265.	*Symphoricarpos chenaultii*	Chenault snowberry
266.	*Symphoricarpos mollis*	Spreading snowberry
267.	*Symphoricarpos occidentalis*	Western snowberry
268.	*Symphoricarpos orbiculatus (vulgaris)*	Coralberry
269.	*Syringa amurensis*	Manchurian lilac
270.	*Syringa chinensis*	Chinese lilac
271.	*Syringa japonica*	Japanese tree lilac
272.	*Syringa josikaea*	Hungarian lilac
273.	*Syringa persica*	Persian lilac
274.	*Syringa villosa*	Late lilac
275.	*Syringa vulgaris*	Common lilac
276.	*Syringa vulgaris alba*	Common white lilac
277.	*Tamarix* species	Tamarix
278.	*Tamarix parviflorum*	Algerian tamarix
279.	*Tamarix pentandra*	Five stamen tamarix
280.	*Taxus*	Yew
281.	*Taxus baccata*	English yew
282.	*Taxus cuspidata*	Japanese yew
283.	*Taxus cuspidata capitata*	Upright yew
284.	*Taxus cuspidata nana*	Dwarf Japanese yew
285.	*Taxus cuspidata Hicksii*	Hicks yew
286.	*Taxus media Browni*	Brown's yew
287.	*Taxus media Hatfieldii*	Hatfield yew
288.	*Thuja* (globe and dwarf forms)	Globe and dwarf arborvitae
289.	*Thuja occidentalis*	American arborvitae
290.	*Thuja occidentalis pyramidalis*	Am. pyramidal arborvitae
291.	*Thuja occidentalis Rosenthalii*	Rosenthal arborvitae
292.	*Thuja orientalis*	Oriental arborvitae
293.	*Thuja plicata*	Giant arborvitae
294.	*Tilia americana*	American linden
295.	*Tilia cordata*	Littleleaf European linden
296.	*Tilia euchlora*	Crimean linden
297.	*Tilia europaea*	Common linden
298.	*Tilia platyphylla*	Bigleaf European linden
299.	*Tilia tomentosa*	Silver linden
300.	*Tsuga canadensis*	Canada hemlock
301.	*Tsuga caroliniana*	Carolina hemlock
302.	*Ulmus americana*	American elm
303.	*Ulmus pumila*	Dwarf Asiatic elm
304.	*Vaccinium corymbosum*	Highbush blueberry
305.	*Vaccinium stamineum*	Deerberry
306.	*Veronica*, evergreen types	Speedwell
307.	*Viburnum acerifolium*	Mapleleaf viburnum
308.	*Viburnum americanum*	American cranberrybush
309.	*Viburnum cassinoides*	Withe rod
310.	*Viburnum dentatum*	Arrowwood
311.	*Viburnum dilatatum*	Linden viburnum
312.	*Viburnum lantana*	Wayfaring tree
313.	*Viburnum lentago*	Nannyberry
314.	*Viburnum molle*	Kentucky viburnum
315.	*Viburnum nudum*	Smooth withe rod

TABLE 3.41 (Continued)

Key	Botanical Name	Common Name
316.	*Viburnum opulus*	European cranberrybush
317.	*Viburnum opulus nanum*	Dwarf cranberrybush
318.	*Viburnum plicatum*	Japanese snowball
319.	*Viburnum prunifolium*	Blackhaw
320.	*Viburnum rhytidophyllum*	Leatherleaf viburnum
321.	*Viburnum Sieboldii*	Siebold viburnum
322.	*Viburnum theiferum*	Tea viburnum
323.	*Viburnum tomentosum*	Doublefile viburnum
324.	*Viburnum wrightii*	Wright viburnum
325.	*Vitex*	Chaste-tree
326.	*Vinca minor*	Periwinkle
327.	*Weigela Eva Rathke*	Red Flowering weigela
328.	*Zanthorhiza apiifolia*	Yellowroot
329.	*Arctostaphylos uva-ursi*	Bearberry
330.	*Cytissus* species	Broom
331.	*Pachistima canbyi*	Canby pachistima
332.	*Coronilla varia*	Crown vetch
333.	*Cissus rhombifolia*	Grape ivy
334.	*Erica* species	Heath
335.	*Calluna vulgaris*	Heather
336.	*Lonicera japonica* halliana	Hall's honeysuckle
337.	*Polygonum cuspidatum*	Japanese fleece vine
338.	*Lycium halimifolium*	Matrimony vine
339.	*Carissa macrocarpa*	Natal plum
340.	*Rosmarinus officinalis*	Rosemary
341.	*Comptonia peregrina*	Sweet fern

THE SELECTION, USE, AND MAINTENANCE OF EQUIPMENT

The selection, use, and maintenance of all types of grounds equipment are important to all park or grounds maintenance programs. Good equipment, plus a well-rounded supply of materials and an efficient maintenance program, determines the difference between economical and efficiently operated programs and costly and inefficient programs utilizing old and outmoded methods.

The best maintenance is, of course, preventive maintenance. A program of preventive maintenance reduces the number and extent of repairs and in the long run will save money. Many budgets are less than adequate when it comes to purchasing new equipment. It therefore is necessary to get as much use out of a piece of equipment as is possible. By efficient preventive maintenance the life of most equipment can be extended considerably.

SELECTION OF EQUIPMENT

There is a wide variety of equipment on the market today, all designed to speed up the job of grounds maintenance. The following descriptive material gives some indication of the type of equipment required to do an efficient job. This list is designed as a general outline of the kinds of equipment available. The management of each individual area or plant must determine which of the equipment is suitable for its particular use and make its own selection of make or manufacturer.

Spraying Equipment

The invasion of new insects and diseases each year adds to the already heavy burden of park maintenance. The development of spraying and dusting equipment has therefore taken on greater significance. Fortunately there have been many recent advances in chemical control.

Spraying and dusting equipment must be selected to suit the conditions and problems involved. There is no one size of sprayer or duster which will meet all control needs of any one specific area or park. There is, however, a wide variety of models and sizes of equipment and accessories available to meet most anticipated needs.

The first consideration in selecting the equipment to be used is the jobs for which the equipment will be used. The following list presents some of the jobs the spraying equipment is expected to perform:

1. Weed control
2. Brush control
3. Plant-disease control
4. Insect-pest control on trees and shrubs
5. Insect-pest control for flies, mosquitoes, chiggers, etc.
6. Application of liquid fertilizers
7. Application of wood preservatives
8. Control of grass, brush, and forest fires

In order to select the proper model of sprayer or duster, the extent or frequency of use must first be determined. For jobs in which the equipment will be in almost constant seasonal use, heavy-duty models should be selected for the most economical operation. Certain types of chemicals may affect the selection of equipment. Application of spray materials such as wettable-powder insecticides, some of the common fungicides, whitewash, or water-base paints will require a unit with enough mechanical agitation to keep the spray material properly mixed in the tank. The sprayer must have a pump which will withstand the resulting abrasive action.

Another consideration in selecting the proper sprayer is the amount of coverage required. Tall shade trees require hydraulic sprayers with pump capacities of 20 to 50 gal/min at pressures from 500 to 800 lb/in.^{2} to cover them with the required spray material. On the other hand, for weak spraying a pump capacity of 4 to 10 gal/min at pressures under 100 lb/in.^{2} is sufficient.

Hand equipment will be required for small spraying jobs, for spraying in areas inaccessible to power equipment, and for fighting grass, brush, or forest fires. Hand-operated dusters are used in greenhouses and nurseries and in protecting floral displays.

POWER SPRAYERS

The three most commonly used types of power sprayers used in grounds maintenance work are (1) conventional hydraulic sprayers, (2) mist blowers or concentrate sprayers, and (3) aerosol generators or fogging machines. The conventional hydraulic sprayer is the mainstay of most spraying programs. The mist blower or concentrate sprayer is used primarily for shade-tree work and to a lesser degree for fly and mosquito control. The aerosol generator, or fogging machine, is used for applying space sprays in the control of adult flies, mosquitoes, and other pests.

HYDRAULIC SPRAYERS

There is a wide selection of types and models of hydraulic sprayers now available, differing primarily in size of tank, size and type of pump, method of agitation, power source, and type of mounting. The con-

Fig. 4.1 General-purpose sprayer. The gun makes it possible for the operator to direct the spray to areas particularly susceptible to plant diseases. (*Buffalo Turbine.*)

ventional unit of this type consists of a tank containing an agitator, a pump, a power source, a combination pressure regulator and relief valve, and a discharge system consisting of one or more hand guns or a multiple-nozzle boom.

A surge tank or air chamber is provided with these pumps to assure a constant pressure at the nozzle, and a mechanical agitator keeps the spray materials properly mixed in the tank.

A common type of hydraulic sprayer in use today is the truck-mounted (Fig. 4.1) sprayer. A convenient model weighs about 220 lb, with a Wisconsin 4½-hp engine and an 11-gal stainless-steel tank. This type of sprayer will cover more area with less chemical load and equipment, cut handling and labor costs, prevent heat degradation of the chemicals, reduce air pollution by using lower volumes of material, and reduce a source of fire hazard.

Another hydraulic sprayer (Fig. 4.2) which is applicable to many turf-management control requirements is a machine which can be pulled by a tractor or truck. This machine is so versatile that it is used by many municipal park departments to smooth the surface of ice-skating rinks in the winter. The pump provides 10 gal/min at 500 lb/in.^{2} for full-range chemical applications. The engine is a 7-hp 4-cycle air-cooled Kohler. The tank is 200-gal, made of 12-gage steel and mounted with a 21-ft boom having 13 Teejet nozzles spaced 20 in. apart. The boom will fold to 7 ft 8 in.

A handy type of sprayer for small jobs is the Back-pack mistblower, a small portable power unit producing a fine mist spray which penetrates 40 ft horizontally and reaches 33 ft vertically. The mist spray covers fast—up to 10 times faster than hydraulic spraying (Fig. 4.3).

Fig. 4.2 An ideal sprayer for many turf-management application control requirements. (*F. E. Myers & Bros. Co.*)

The estate, or small wheel-mounted, sprayer has a tank capacity of 15 to 50 gal, with piston-type pump discharging from 1 to 4 gal/min at pressures up to 250 to 300 lb. Standard equipment with this type of sprayer is a hand gun with a 25-ft length of hose.

The skid models are made in a wide range of sizes suitable for transporting in a jeep, truck, or trailer. The smallest of this class is the estate, or small wheel-mounted, sprayer. The largest skid models range in capacity from 500 gal up and have a pump capacity of 50 gal/min with pressures up to 800 lb. The power plant ranges in size from 1 to about 30 hp.

The most versatile of the skid or wheel-mounted models is a multiple-use sprayer commonly available with a pump of 4 to 8 gal/min capacity, developing pressures in the range of 30 to 250 or even 800 lb, and tank capacity of 50 to 250 gal. Most are equipped with field booms for turf-insect and weed control and hand guns and hose for selective area spraying. If they are equipped with oil- and chemical-resistant hose and gaskets plus a mechanical agitator, these sprayers will apply almost any spray material successfully.

The tractor- or jeep-mounted type of hydraulic sprayer has proved satisfactory in applying sediment-free sprays (such as certain weed-control chemicals) in the low gallonage range at pressures under 100 lb. Such sprayers (Fig. 4.4) are commonly equipped with a rotary gear pump operated by the power takeoff on the tractor or jeep.

Fig. 4.3 Back-pack mistblower, a small, portable power unit that can handle all spraying jobs up to 33 ft in height. (*Vandermolen Corporation.*)

Mist Blowers or Concentrate Sprayers

Concentrate sprayers are used primarily for treating shade trees and for residual and larvicidal treatment of large areas for mosquito control. The effective coverage is from 50 to several hundred feet, depending upon the size of the machine, the terrain, density of foliage, and the direction and velocity of the wind.

The use of concentrates, of course, requires lesser volume of water to be handled, and therefore may result in some operating economies. The concentrate sprayer consists essentially of a low-volume, low-pressure sprayer which is incorporated with an engine-driven fan or blower. The spray material is pumped under relatively low pressure to an outlet side of a fan, where it is sprayed into the air stream. The air blast aids in breaking up the liquid, and carries the small droplets to the surface to be covered.*

The smaller models are usually mounted on wheelbarrow or cart chassis and have high-velocity, low-volume blowers delivering about 5000 ft^3/min at over 150 mi/h. The larger models have velocities from 5000 to 25,000 ft^3/min at velocities from 100 to 150 mi/h. Such models are usually mounted on skids for ease in transport by truck, trailer, or boat.

Fig. 4.4 Multipurpose mist sprayer; an ideal pesticide applicator for air spraying in shade trees, air spraying on greens and fairways, and for gun spraying. (*F. E. Myers & Bros. Co.*)

Aerosol or Fog Generators

Temporary control of adult mosquitoes in restricted areas such as picnic grounds, ball parks, and camping areas is the chief use for aerosol or fog generators.

A unit of this type dispenses liquid insecticides in the particle size range classified as aerosol or fogs [1 to 50 μm (1 μm = 1×10^{-6} m)]. They are usually operated at a time when the most favorable temperature, humidity and wind conditions prevail. . . . The essential parts of the typical machine consist of a self-contained power source, a tank for insecticides, a means of breaking up the liquid into the desired droplet size either mechanically or thermally, and a

* National Sprayer and Duster Association, Chicago.

force to impart an initial velocity to fog as it leaves the machine. This may be either skid or wheel-mounted. The smallest units are suitable for treating a few acres—the largest several square miles. The net effective width of coverage is usually 400 to 500 ft maximum, depending upon the wind movements which are relied upon to carry the fog over the area.*

Power Dusters

There are now available tractor-mounted power dusters light enough to be carried on small farm tractors and powerful enough to cover a

Fig. 4.5 Back-pack sprayer-duster. Ideal for spraying, dusting, and granular applications. (*Buffalo Turbine.*)

swath several times the tractor width. They can be used with a multiple-nozzle boom or with a single-nozzle outlet on the fan case.

A Back-pack duster is ideal for use in areas inaccessible to larger equipment (Fig. 4.5). It weighs $21\frac{3}{4}$ lb, sprays at the rate of 0 to 1 gal/min, and dusts at the rate of 0 to 4 lb/min. Its liquid capacity is

* National Sprayer and Duster Association, Chicago.

$3\frac{1}{2}$ gal, and the dust capacity is $\frac{1}{2}$ ft^3. A duster of this type is used for control of turf insects, dusting on ornamental plantings, and for distributing insecticide pellets for mosquito control.

Hand Equipment

There is always room for hand-operated equipment to supplement the power equipment. The common compressed-air sprayer is available in several different sizes ranging in capacity from 1.5 to 5 gal. Some of the latest models are equipped with rechargeable electric batteries, which eliminate hand pumping.

The knapsack sprayers have capacities of 4 to 6 gal and have lever, pump, or telescopic operation. Both types of sprayers are supplied with oil- and chemical-resistant hose and gaskets. Multiple-nozzle booms, also available, will speed up many hand-spray jobs. Hand dusters are useful for quick application of insecticides and fungicides on floral or other ornamental plantings.

Fig. 4.6 A tractor mower for highway slope work. (*Massey-Ferguson.*)

Power Mowers

The wide selection of power mowers on the market today ranges from the small 18-in. mower, used principally for small areas, to the larger tractor-drawn rotary or gang mowers. Practically all mowers are the rotary, sickle-bar, or reel type, and it is a matter of judgment which type is best suited to the particular use (Figs. 4.6 to 4.12).

Generally speaking, the rotary mower is used and built for rough and heavy work. It will cut weeds and grasses so coarse that the reel type of mower will hardly touch them. The rotary mower should be used in meadows, where a close, even cut is not essential, or on large grass areas, such as golf fairways. The sickle-bar mower is generally found

Fig. 4.7 The wide assortment of rotary mowers on the market today ranges in cutting widths from 18 in. to over 76 in. (*Massey-Ferguson.*)

Fig. 4.8 A rotary mower and trimmer which will also serve as a leaf mulcher, a V-plow for snow, a 48-in. two-stage snow thrower, or a rotary broom. (*The Toro Company.*)

in use on highway shoulders and slopes, or in meadows or pastures if a hay crop is desired. The reel type, single or gang, is used principally on lawns, in parks, on golf courses, and on industrial grounds, where a smooth even cut is desired.

Soil Shredders

Soil shredders are useful in any grounds maintenance program. They come in sizes to suit practically every type of job for greenhouses, nurseries, golf courses, parks, college campuses, and municipal

Fig. 4.9 An efficient seven-gang hydraulic power-driven reel mower. This unit mounts on Ford 2000 and 3000 all-purpose tractors. Drive power for the reels is taken directly from the tractor engine, eliminating the need for excessive drawbar pull and requiring minimum weight for traction. Hills and banks can be mowed easily regardless of soft or wet turf conditions; the cutting swath is 15 ft. (*Roseman Mower Corporation.*)

sewage-treatment plants. Soil shredders are used principally for preparing topdressing materials. They produce a topdressing that is loose, fluffy, and of small particle size, free of sticks, stones, roots, and other trash. They are also used to prepare compost for flower and shrub beds, shred composted leaves, prepare topsoil, blend commercial fertilizers with topdressing and topsoil, and sterilize topsoil by blending in weed seed posions.

In cities where the disposal of leaves becomes a problem, the shredder

Fig. 4.10 A small rotary mower. Small areas and strips adjoining walls can be trimmed with this 18-in. rotary mower. Height of cut can be adjusted from 1 to 3 in., and mowing capacity is 21,000 ft^2/h at 3 mi/h. (*International Harvester.*)

Fig. 4.11 A cordless electric trimmer. More powerful edgers and trimmers are also available. (*International Harvester.*)

will clean and shred them so they can be bagged and sold for leaf mold. Sewage sludge can also be ground or shredded and sold for fertilizer.

Power Saws

All grounds maintenance programs need some power-saw equipment. The power saw is useful in clearing brush and dead, down, and diseased timber from forest areas. It is useful in cutting wood for picnic areas and in clearing away storm damage. The one-man chain saw will cut practically all size timber found in most wooded areas and is

Fig. 4.12 A Rake-O-Vac machine, which effectively cleans, rakes, and sweeps turf areas. It comes with separate hard-surface brush and a thatching reel. The hopper has a capacity of 5¾ yd^3. Cleans or rakes a 5-ft swath. (*The Toro Company.*)

probably the most useful piece of equipment. Extremely useful for park or any type of grounds maintenance work is the lightweight shoulder unit. It is extremely versatile as it will cut grass, weeds, briars, brush, and trees, will cultivate shrub beds, and edge walks and around shrub and specimen trees.

Aerating Equipment

As stated previously, aerating turf areas is becoming increasingly common, especially on golf courses and more recently on large industrial and government reservations. Proper aerifying of the turf will do many things—all beneficial to the turf.

There are several types of aerifiers all designed for specific purposes. The small power aerifier suitable for home and industrial lawns, athletic field, school grounds, smaller golf courses, and some landscape work has a cultivating width of 18 in., operational speed up to 4 mi/h, and cultivation depth up to 3 in.

A larger model is the junior aerifier for use on golf greens and for fast coverage of large turf areas in parks, athletic fields, golf course fairways, military installations, and lawns around industrial plants and institutions. It uses a unit cultivating a width of 6 ft and is powered by standard farm tractor. A new type of mower, the Verti-Cut, has come into general use in connection with the aerification principle.

Regular mowers make a horizontal cut, removing the tips of grass blades to control the height of grass. But close to the soil, the surface

Fig. 4.13 Brush chipper. Larger chippers, which permit loading directly into a truck, are used by street-cleaning departments and power companies. (*International Harvester.*)

stems and old grass leaves accumulate, and this excess growth is removed by the Verti-Cut. The blades cut down into the turf, trim through runners and outspread leaves. There is no pulling or tearing such as occurs when material is torn out with rakes.

Brush Chippers

More and more cities, towns, parks and industrial plants—especially highway departments, utility companies and line-clearance contractors—are finding the brush chipper useful in fast and economical disposal of brush and tree limbs. The chipper will reduce brush to chips up to 4 in. in diameter (Fig. 4.13). Brush chips can be either loaded directly into trucks and hauled to a central location for use later as a mulch or spread in place as the chipper moves along. The chips can be used for many things: mulching, erosion control, soil conditioners, weed control in shrub beds, and as cushion material under slides and swings in playground areas. After severe storms, when cities and towns find their streets clogged with broken branches and trees, the chipper will dispose of such hazards much faster than the conventional methods of loading, hauling, and burning. You can load many more trees to a truck as chips than as brush. At Christmas time the chipper permits faster and more economical disposal of Christmas trees and provides useful

Fig. 4.14 A Chiparvestor in action: feeding bundles of trees and limbs into chipper and loading chips into a truck for transportation to another site. (*Morbark Industries, Inc.*)

mulching material for acid-loving plants such as rhododendrons and laurels. The larger chippers will cut trees and brush up to 10 in. in diameter.

Total Wood Chippers

A new system of combatting the environmental despoliation of clear cutting in forest areas, right-of-way clearing, land clearing, street and highway clearing, and maintenance has been developed. This involves the total utilization of the harvested tree—limbs, tops, trunk, leaves, and all. This in turn produces a totally new source of wood fiber. Figures 4.14 and 4.15 demonstrate the machine in use. A companion machine, known as the *feller-buncher,* will cut the tree off at ground level, pick up the whole tree, carry it to the chipping machine, and insert it.

There are several advantages to this system:

1. The entire tree is used.
2. The machine may be used for selective cutting.
3. It protects the environment by eliminating burning and clogging landfills and provides good erosion control.
4. The by-products (wood chips) can be used to improve the environment, for mulch, land covering, or nature trails, or as raw material in pulp and papermills.

Fig. 4.15 A Chiparvestor in action: feeding entire trees, up to 18 in. in diameter, into the chipper and distributing chips over eroded areas. (*Morbark Industries, Inc.*)

Posthole Digger

Like an electric drill in any workshop, a posthole digger is a real saver of time and muscle power. There are several types: the tractor equipped with an auger extension, the jeep equipped similarly, and a power tool for earth boring and tunneling. The tractor and jeep equipped with an auger can bore holes for fence posts, guard posts, power and telephone poles, holes for planting trees and shrubs, and practically anything that requires a hole in the ground. Most of this equipment is hydraulically operated from the power-takeoff shaft. Control levers to raise and lower the auger are within easy reach of the operator.

Portable Generators

Portable generators are ideal for operating tools for contractors, public utilities, ground maintenance work in cemeteries and parks, yard maintenance in industrial plants, and for police and fire departments, campers, etc. To determine the size of generator needed use Table 4.1. These recommendations take into account starting and operating loads normally imposed by the equipment listed.

TABLE 4.1
Approximate Power Requirements*

Power tool	Power required, W
Drill, ¼-in.	400–600
½-in.	700–1200
¾-in.	1000–1500
1-in.	1400–2000
Hole-a-matic	1700–2200
Portable floor planner	700–1200
Radial saw, 1½-hp	3000–3500
3-hp	3600–5000
7½-hp	8000–12,000
Electric saw, 6-in.	1200–1700
7-in.	1400–2000
8-in.	2000–2500
10-in.	2400–3000
Pipe-threading machine	2200–2500
Portable router	600–1500

* Information from the Gen-A-Matic Corporation, Van Nuys, Calif.

Mulch Spreader

New equipment is constantly being introduced on the market. In the past few years, methods of seeding, fertilizing, and mulching steep slopes and large areas have undergone radical changes. For instance, the old methods of applying straw and hay mulches by hand and then staking and tying the mulch down became so expensive that it was rapidly becoming necessary to stop mulching altogether or to devise more economical ways of getting the job done. As a result, new machines were invented that did the job quickly and economically.

Since mulching of newly seeded slopes was essential in most areas, the mulching machine was developed first. The mulch spreader is simply a machine equipped with a chute into which bales of hay or straw are fed. The straw is forced into a hopper, where it is beaten apart and blown by a powerful fan into a discharge tube. The straw emerging from the end of the discharge tube is distributed evenly over the ground, with a minimum of bunching. To hold the mulch in place on the ground, the spreader is equipped with three jets at the end of the discharge tube. These jets are connected to a drum of asphalt mounted on the side of the machine. The operator of the discharge tube can control the amount of asphalt discharged through the jets by means of a lever which opens or closes the jets. The asphalt is applied to the straw as it comes out of the discharge tube. Just enough asphalt adheres to the straw to form a mat after it falls on the ground. Approximately 100 gal of asphalt per acre is required to do an effective holding job on

Fig. 4.16 Power mulcher, a truck-mounted machine which is ideally suited for commercial or residential turf work. May be used for blowing tree seeds, sprigs, fertilizer, limestone, or spray mists. Discharges 150 lb/min at a velocity of 150 mi/h and has a 360° horizontal and 60° vertical boom rotation; 4 tons of mulch per hour can be spread to distances of up to 60 ft in calm air. (*Reinco.*)

mulch spread at the rate of 2 tons/acre. Normally the mulch can be spread to a distance of 50 to 75 ft effectively (see Fig. 4.16).

Hydrograsser

The Hydrograsser is basically a truck-mounted tank into which a slurry of fertilizer and seed is mixed. The mixture is sprayed upon the areas to be seeded. The tank has a volume of 800 gal, a spray range of 80 ft maximum, 20 ft minimum, with fan nozzle. For fast, economical seeding and fertilizing of slopes, ditches, shoulders, and large open areas this method is unsurpassed. Combined with the power mulcher, it can do the entire operation of liming, fertilizing, seeding, mulching, and anchoring the mulch in two operations (see Fig. 4.17).

Hydraulic Boom

One piece of equipment that has proved extremely useful to the tree pruner on large-scale jobs is a hydraulically operated boom for carrying workers aloft and maintaining them on constant work base at any required level (Fig. 4.18). It rotates upon a turret mounted on a truck, dolly, trailer, or tractor. It provides a working height above ground of up to 41 ft. The turret is equipped with power tools, and all positions of the turret can be controlled by the operator in the turret. Some of the work that can be performed from this machine is as follows:

1. Trimming for proper distribution of new light system
2. General tree pruning
3. Pruning and topping Dutch elm–diseased trees
4. Trimming city trees from power and telephone lines
5. Telephone line work
6. Electric utility work

Fig. 4.17 A Hydrograsser, which saves time and money in establishing grass areas. Other models range from 250- to 2500-gal capacity. (*Reinco.*)

Soil-Preparation Equipment

New methods of preparing the ground for seedbeds, renovating old turf, and general maintenance work are constantly being introduced, but perhaps one of the most reliable, efficient, and inexpensive is one that has been in use for many years, the flexible tine harrow (Fig. 4.19). The *tine harrow* has a year-round use:

Spring good for seedbed preparation; also rakes established turf areas to stimulate healthy plant growth.

Fig. 4.18 An ideal aerial tower for tree-trimming work. This machine is fitted with a chip box which provides a fast and economical removal of debris from line-clearing and shade-tree-trimming operations. (*Mobile Aerial Towers, Inc.*)

Fig. 4.19 Flexible tine harrow, a practical, low-cost tool that does a variety of jobs. It comes in widths of 8 to 24 ft. The Mini-Harrow is $4^1/_2$ ft wide. (*Fuerst Brothers, Inc.*)

Summer breaks up and scatters soil cores following aeration. If crabgrass is a problem, the harrow will lift the runners so the mower can cut them.

Fall pulverizes dry leaves; seedbed preparation; when set to a maximum penetration, opens up turf before overseeding and fertilizing for the winter.

Winter multiple uses on ski slopes.

Fig. 4.20 A York rake, ideal for final preparation of a seedbed, can also be used for small grading jobs. (*York Modern Corporation.*)

The tine harrow has specialized uses on golf courses, horse paddocks and pastures, race tracks, athletic fields, beaches and picnic grounds, ski slopes, and highways.

The *York rake* (Fig. 4.20) is another tool for final grading in preparation for seeding. This piece of equipment operates off the power take-off of a tractor. It smooths the grade, fills in indentations, pulverizes clods of earth, and generally establishes a good, viable seedbed.

The *stone picker* is a useful machine to have in preparing a good seedbed, for beach cleaning, race-track preparation, root-crop cultivation, and clearing grassland or pastures of stones (see Figs. 4.21 and 4.22).

The stone picker is designed to pick stones $1\frac{1}{2}$ to 9 in. in diameter from the *surface* of the ground. For efficient operation of the machine stones should be brought to the surface by discing or harrowing the soil first. Best results are obtained in ground that is fairly dry and friable. Normally one machine will pick 2 to 4 acres/day. The picker is a two-wheel

Fig. 4.21 A stone picker (Pixtone) operating on a beach. (*Bridgeport Implement Works, Inc.*)

Fig. 4.22 The stone box on a stone picker. At the dumping area the rope from catch lever is pulled to tilt the box and let the load slide out. (*Bridgeport Implement Works, Inc.*)

trailer machine that can be efficiently handled by any two-plow tractor. No power takeoff or hydraulic mechanism is required.

Normal maintenance of the machine is as follows:

1. Engine air cleaner should be emptied, cleaned, and refilled at least once a day when in use.
2. Engine oil should be changed at least every 24 hours of operation.
3. Use regular gasoline only, and add about 1 tbsp of upper-cylinder oil to each tank of gas.

4. Always close gas valve on bottom of gas tank and let carburetor run out of gas when finished each day.
5. When storing the machine always be sure the fuel tank is either completely full or empty to prevent water accumulation.
6. Although the roller chain is self-lubricating, when the machine is not in use for a month or more, it is advisable to cover the chain with grease to eliminate rusting.
7. Tire pressure should be maintained between 27 and 32 lbs.

Fig. 4.23 A walk-behind tiller with a 26-in. cut. This tiller has adjustable tilling depth, adjustable row width, which can be narrowed to 11 in., and tine-extension kit, which can be used to extended tine length to 32 in. (*International Harvester.*)

A *rotary-tiller* is another piece of soil-preparation equipment which serves a useful purpose (Fig. 4.23). The tiller will thoroughly loosen the soil to a depth of 6 to 8 in., leaving a very loose and friable surface with most of the heavy clods of earth well pulverized. The tiller is useful for cultivating around trees and under shrubs and for mixing mulch and soil. The tiller can also be obtained as an attachment to a tractor for easier and more efficient operation on large areas (Fig. 4.24).

A cultipacker is constructed of heavy, solid disks about 12 in. in diameter, with sufficient weight to break up soil clods, smooth and firm the seedbed, and, when combined with a seeding attachment, to cover and roll the seed to the proper depth, thereby ensuring maximum germination.

Tractors

The most important and most versatile piece of equipment used today is the tractor, available in all sizes and with all types of attachments (Fig. 4.25). Every efficient grounds maintenance program must have one or more tractors, depending upon the size of the area to be maintained.

Fig. 4.24 A tractor-operated rotary tiller with 6-in. extension and safety shield. (*International Harvester.*)

Fig. 4.25 Some of the tractors in use today. (*Massey-Ferguson.*)

The tractor is a very versatile machine, and with attachments it can perform almost every conceivable job of grounds maintenance, including moving earth from one place to another, light grading and scarifying, drilling holes in earth, cutting grass, asphalt paving, loading with forklift, hauling, rolling, trenching, logging, sweeping, sawing wood, turf seedbed preparation, snow removal, spraying, and many others.

Some of the attachments available to do the above work are disc plows, disc tillers, subsoilers, harrows, cultivators, combines, balers, mowers, cranes, rakes, front and rear loaders, lime and fertilizer spreaders, scoops, wagons, cordwood saws, posthole diggers, and rotary cutters.

Stump Removers

Two types of stump removers are available, the stump razor and a stump cutter. The stump razor operates on a horizontal rotary motion, slicing away even the toughest hardwood stumps to 6 in. below ground level. It is a compact machine which can easily be transported from place to place (see Fig. 4.26). The stump cutter is a much larger machine, operating on a vertical, circular motion. The machine is towed to the site by a small truck or tractor (see Fig. 4.27). Both machines efficiently remove the stump, leaving nothing but a hole in the ground and a pile of chips. They eliminate long hours of expensive digging and chopping.

Fig. 4.26 A stump remover that permits one man to remove a tree stump or runner root of any diameter standing 5 in. or less above ground. It will remove the stump to 6 in. below ground level. (*Hesston Corporation.*)

Trenching Equipment

Good trenching equipment is a valuable asset to any maintenance program. All types and sizes are available, and it is only necessary to determine how large or how difficult the job will be to decide on the right piece of equipment. The three types described here will in all probability be the ones most needed for maintenance or installation work in parks and recreation areas.

1. A self-contained vibratory plow which buries wire, cable, and plastic or copper tubing up to $^3/_8$ in. in diameter with full 12-in. cover without trenching (see Fig. 4.28). Turf damage is kept to a minimum, thereby eliminating costly and time-consuming restoration work. This machine is ideal in installing service lines and sprinkler systems in

Fig. 4.27 An efficient stump cutter which will effectively remove stumps of any size. (*Vermeer Manufacturing Co.*)

   already landscaped areas. The machine is compact enough to work in tight areas and can be loaded by one man into a truck or pickup.
2. A small trencher compact enough to deliver straight trench in places too tight for other larger models. Self-propulsion keeps the trencher on the move and does not require constant operator attention (see Fig. 4.29). This trencher will cut trenches from 4 to 6 in. wide and 6 to 24 in. deep.
3. An earth saw (see Fig. 4.30) may not be practical in many areas where the soil is suitable for operation of smaller types of equipment, but where rock, coral, or frozen earth abound, the earth saw becomes very useful. It can cut through most types of asphalt and concrete roadways.

Fig. 4.28 A self-contained vibratory plow. (*The Charles Machine Works.*)

Fig. 4.29 A small trencher. (*The Charles Machine Works.*)

Depth of cut varies with the size of the machine or from 24 to 30 in.

Sweepers

Various types of sweepers are useful maintenance tools for both inside and outside work. Three types, each performing a different kind of task, are described as follows:

1. A power sweeper ideal for both outside and indoor work (see Fig. 4.31).
2. An all-purpose grounds maintenance tractor that will ef-

Fig. 4.30 An earth saw. (*The Charles Machine Works.*)

Fig. 4.31 A 66-in.-path power sweeper that covers up to 200,000 ft²/h. It is powered by a gas engine, LP-gas engine, or diesel engine and sweeps at speeds up to 10 mi/h. The hydraulic-dump debris hopper holds 1800 lb. (*Tennant Company.*)

fectively sweep lawn areas of leaves and trash (see Fig. 4.32).

3. A sweeper which is very effective at loosening and removing thatch in lawn areas (see Fig. 4.33).

Transplanter

Every park department, street department, golf course, and recreational area must transplant trees and shrubs at one time or another. Old

Fig. 4.32 An all-purpose grounds maintenance tractor that will adapt to mowing swaths of 48, 60, or 80 in. has hydraulic-controlled blades for earth moving and scraping, snowplowing, sweeping, plowing, discing, and cultivating. (*Hesston Corporation.*)

Fig. 4.33 A multipurpose sweeper which will remove thatch, sweep snow, backfill ditches, sweep dirt and debris, and sweep pea-gravel roofs. (*Sweepster.*)

methods of hand labor to dig large trees and shrubs are too expensive today to be seriously considered. Fortunately, there is equipment that will do the job economically and efficiently. Some kinds are primarily an adaptation of the front-end loader or the backhoe with the cutting blade shaped like a scoop, which digs under the root system and lifts the tree or shrub out of the ground for transporting to its new site. This machine will dig an 18-, 24-, 30-, or 36-in. bottom to obtain the desired

Fig. 4.34 A root pruner and plant digger that is attached to any three-point-hitch tractor. (*Schutts Equipment Co.*)

root ball. It will also dig and move a 4½-in. caliper tree (see Fig. 4.34).

Another type of transplanter is designed to be attached to a loader, the same as the loader bucket. It uses the loader hydraulic system with quick disconnect and is simple and safe to operate (see Fig. 4.35). It operates on the principle of three spades to dig around and under the plant to form a good ball. The center spade is hydraulically opened and closed for positioning the transplanter without requiring the operator to leave the machine. The control of the individual spades allows the operator to alternate between the three spades in order to hold the frame on the ground. If one spade strikes a tough root or stone, it can be worked in and out. The blades are inserted as far as possible to anchor the machine.

Miscellaneous Equipment

Laborsaving machines are important wherever large acreages are to be maintained. Many of these have been discussed above, but still others will be needed, e.g., discs, cultivators, seeders, fertilizer and lime spreaders, road-repair equipment, utility vehicles, road stripers and line removers, sod cutters, snow-blowing equipment, and an assortment of small tools, shovels, picks, axes, and pruning equipment. Some of this equipment is shown in Figs. 4.36 to 4.40.

Fig. 4.35 The CareTree Transplanter provides tree- and shrub-digging capability that is fast and dependable. (*CareTree Systems.*)

TRACTOR-BATTERY CARE*

General

The most important point in lengthening battery life in your tractor is keeping the liquid at the proper level. It should be checked regularly, in most cases about once a week. Since the charging process has a tendency to evaporate the water but not the acid, more water must be added at intervals to maintain the correct level. Unless some of the

* Based on information from International Harvester, Chicago.

solution is accidentally spilled, it is not necessary to add acid. Distilled water is best for use in batteries. Next best is clean, soft water, i.e., without dissolved minerals. Least desirable is ordinary well water.

Most batteries have some sort of a marker to indicate the proper liquid level. Do not fill above this mark. Otherwise the solution may

Fig. 4.36 A spreader and seeder which broadcasts all fertilizers, seeds, powders, herbicides, granular chemicals, salt, and sand. The swath width (depending on material) is up to 50 ft. The rate of work is up to 40 acres/h, and travel speed is up to 10 mi/h. Material discharge is 10 to 2500 lb/acre for fertilizer and 3 to 360 lb/acre for seeds. (*Vandermolen Corporation.*)

Fig. 4.37 A utility vehicle that will carry a 1000-lb load. (*The Toro Company.*)

overflow when the battery is charging. This causes loss of some of the acid. Check the holddown arrangement. It should hold the battery firmly but not injure it. If the battery is not securely fastened, the case may be damaged when the tractor is operated over rough ground.

Cranking capacity is especially critical in cold weather. A fully charged battery has only 40 per cent of the capacity at 0°F that it has at 70°F, yet it takes at least twice as much power to start the engine at this low temperature. So keep the battery fully charged. The amount of charge is best checked with an inexpensive hydrometer.

A *trickle charger* that operates on 110 V ac can be used to keep a battery fully charged. The charger is plugged into an electrical outlet, and two small wires are clamped to the battery terminals. It charges slowly and should be left attached for some time, even overnight.

If a good battery needs frequent recharging, check on the generator and regulator performance. Do not expect a battery to give dependable service for much longer than the guarantee period, especially in cold weather.

Fig. 4.38 A snow blower with enclosed cab. (*Hesston Corporation.*)

Most manufacturers provide heavy-duty batteries for use in tractors. The cases of these batteries are designed to withstand the extra jolting and bouncing of tractor service.

An accumulation of corrosion products, or fuzz, at the terminals of a tractor battery indicates two things: poor maintenance and a battery that is unable to deliver its full contribution to tractor performance.

When the battery is charged by the generator, the hydrogen gas given off escapes from the cells. It carries along with it a very slight amount of acid. This vapor settles on the battery top and provides a damp surface to which dust and dirt cling. The acid attacks the metal of the battery terminals, the cable clamps, and the frame that holds the battery in place. The corrosion products form a path that permits the battery to discharge itself. All batteries not being used have a tendency to discharge, but if corrosion has collected on top of the battery, the rate of discharge is much faster. If allowed to continue, other corrosion products may eventually form an insulating layer between the battery terminals and the cable clamps. This tends to increase circuit resistance and prevents full battery capacity from reaching the starter motor. To prevent the increased rate of self-discharge and poor starter performance, battery terminals and cable connectors should be cleaned at regular intervals.

Fig. 4.39 An efficient and economical paint striper that comes with interchangeable rollers for various widths, 1, 2, $2\frac{1}{2}$, 3, and 4 in. It can be used on natural grass, artificial turf, tennis courts, ice-hockey rinks, parking lots, safety lanes, and many other areas. (*R. E. Muncey, Inc.*)

Procedure

1. Disconnect the ground strap at the end opposite the battery. This important first step eliminates the danger of accidentally grounding the other terminal of the battery and producing an unexpected spark.
2. Loosen the cable clamp after scraping away enough of the fuzz to find the clamping nut. If the corrosion is well advanced, it may have eaten away so much of the nut that a standard wrench will no longer fit. In this case, you will need to use pliers to turn the nut. Usually, the nut will be so severely damaged by this method of removal that the cable and clamp will have to be replaced after the battery is cleaned.
3. Brush away the corrosion products around the battery terminal and from the top of the battery.
4. Prepare a pastelike mixture of ordinary baking soda and water. Apply this with a paint brush to the terminals and surrounding area. The soda neutralizes the acid and

helps clean up the terminals. Continue applying until the solution no longer fizzes.

5. Wash terminals and battery top with warm water. The vent holes in the filler caps should be plugged so that none of the soda solution gets into the cells themselves.
6. If the terminals are badly corroded, it may be necessary to repeat the soda-and-rinsing treatment until there is no more fizzing.

Fig. 4.40 Traffic-line remover. (*Tennant Company.*)

7. Clean the battery terminals and the cable clamps to ensure good electrical contact. There are several satisfactory ways of doing this:
   a. One handy tool combines a wire brush that can be rotated over the battery terminals to clean them with a second cylindrical wire brush that can be used to clean the inside of the cable clamps.
   b. The battery terminals can be cleaned with a conventional wire brush, and sandpaper can be used to clean the inside of the cable clamps.
8. Apply a light coating of grease to the battery terminal and the cable clamps to help reduce future corrosion. Then reinstall and tighten the battery cables. Avoid hammering the clamps into place on the battery post. Doing so may crack the cell cover or break the seal around the battery terminal.
9. If the jaws of the clamp meet before the clamp grips the

post firmly, cut a small amount of metal from between the jaws with a pocket knife.

10. Reconnect the end of the ground strap to the tractor frame and remove the plugs from the vent openings in the filler caps.

HAND TOOLS

Winter Care for Hand Tools*

Hand tools are the easiest of all to prepare for winter. The basic winterizing job is rust avoidance, but there are some other tasks you can attend to at this time that will prolong hand-tool life.

1. Survey your hand tools for irreparable damage or wear. Discard the summer casualties. It makes good sense to replace the discarded tools at this time.
2. Survey the remaining tools. Wooden handles can often be glued with a suitable epoxy or wood cement if the damage is merely a crack. Then rub a coat of boiled linseed oil into handles of all implements.
3. Use either a commercial rust remover or a pad of steel wool and clean the rust off. You can protect against more rust by painting the tool, but adequate protection is provided by a thick coat of heavy oil on the metal parts.

EQUIPMENT

Preparation for Winter Operation*

GENERAL GUIDELINES

Lubricants For effective winter operation, the engine of a tractor or other outdoor machine may need a different lubricant from that used during the summer. If so, switch to a lightweight lubricant during the winter, following the directions in your operator's manual.

On older tractors, it was frequently recommended that the gear-train lubricant be changed for winter operation also. Recommendations for an earlier era were that the lubricant be drained, the gear case flushed, and a lubricant diluted with kerosene added. Advances in lubricants in the last few years, however, have made this step unnecessary. So even if your older tractor manual suggests this step, check with your

* Based on information from International Harvester Co., Chicago.

dealer to see if he has a modern transmission lubricant that can be used year-round without diluting. Note that if your tractor has a hydrostatic transmission, you *must* use the hydraulic fluid specified in the manual year-round. Typically, your warranty will be voided if you substitute fluids, dilute the fluid, or otherwise tamper with its composition.

Air Cleaner Check the air cleaner on your tractor to see if it is the replaceable dry type or the oil-bath type. The replaceable filter should be replaced for winter. An oil-bath filter should be cleaned and the oil replaced by a lubricant of the same weight as used in the engine crankcase.

Electrical System Winter places harsh demands on the electrical system of the tractor or other powered machines. Lights may be used more often, starting is more difficult and more protracted; it is therefore important to make sure the electrical system is in topnotch condition. It is a good idea to give the system a visual check first, to make sure the cables are not frayed or cracked; if any are, replace them. Check the battery to make sure the electrolyte is at the required level. Then put a battery charger on the battery, charge it fully, and make sure it is always fully charged. A weak battery can fail to deliver enough energy to start the tractor on a cold day, and a discharged battery can easily freeze during a cold snap.

Spark Plugs Check the spark plugs. If they were installed new the spring before, you can probably get by with removing them, cleaning, gapping, and replacing them. If they are older than that, or if there is any doubt about their condition, they should be replaced. Set distributor points, following step by step the instructions listed in your operator's manual.

Preparation for Winter Storage*

GENERAL

Winterizing is simplified considerably if you are not going to be using powered equipment during the winter. Then you need only prepare the tool for winter storage. The type of winter-storage service you give on a tractor is the level of service you should give such equipment as mowers, power edgers, and trimmers.

* Based on information from International Harvester Co., Chicago.

Procedure

1. The first step in winterizing is a thorough cleaning. Then inspect the paintwork closely. Use steel wool or sandpaper to clear rust spots from the painted surfaces. Use an aerosol spray primer and paint to touch up the surfaces and restore the implement to like-new appearance.
2. Now look at the engine. If you feel that your equipment will need a tuneup or major service, this is the time to get it in the shop. If no tuneup is needed, you can be content with simple winterizing. For machines with a separate cooling system, like water-cooled tractors, check the coolant level and freezing temperature. If it does not provide adequate protection for the temperature expected in your area, add the necessary coolant or drain the coolant. Remember, there are taps both on the bottom of the radiator and on the engine block; both must be opened for complete draining. Place a tag in a highly visible spot noting that all coolant has been removed from the implement and the drains are open. This step can avoid damage if someone else tries to start it in the spring without checking to make sure that the tractor has a proper coolant supply.
3. Drain the oil from the engine crankcase. Some manufacturers recommend that you immediately refill the crankcase with oil that will be used next season. Others recommend that you refill with a flushing mixture that can be left in during the winter. If you leave the crankcase empty or refill with a flushing solution, it is imperative that you place another tag near the control area so that the tractor will not be inadvertently started without the proper lubricant.
4. It is also a good practice to drain the fuel system, including the tank, carburetor, and fuel lines. Leave the drains open and let the system dry naturally.
5. For best protection of the battery remove it from the tractor, recharge it fully, and store it in a dry place where the temperature is above freezing. If the battery is left on the tractor in freezing temperatures, keep it fully charged to prevent freezing.
6. The last step for winter storage is to protect the exterior painted surfaces and brightwork of your implement for winter. A good heavy coat of wax will keep it looking good

during the winter and will furnish considerable rust protection. Or a more effective commercial rust preventive can be applied at greater cost and effort. The rust preventive should be kept from coming in contact with tires because it can damage rubber.

SNOW-BLOWER MAINTENANCE*

Procedure

1. If the fuel was not drained from the machine at the end of the last season, it should be drained. Fuel left over from last season may contain gum and varnish that will stick carburetor parts, such as the float valve and main jet.
2. The engine oil should be drained and refilled at the end of the season of use. After the oil has been changed, the engine should be run for a few minutes to ensure that the new oil has circulated through the engine. If engine oil was not changed at the end of last season, it should be changed now before the machine is used. Use of engine oil of the proper viscosity is important, as it affects starting as well as engine lift. Refer to the operator's manual for oil-viscosity recommendations based on expected ambient temperatures.
3. If the engine fails to start after several attempts, the spark plug should be removed. If the spark plug is fouled or wet with oil, a new spark plug should be installed. The spark gap should be set properly before the spark plug is installed.
4. Most snow blowers do not use engine air cleaners as there is virtually no airborne dust when there is a layer of snow on the ground and snow would have a tendency to plug air-cleaner elements. As a result, most snow blowers do not require any air-cleaner maintenance.
5. Drive belts should be inspected before each season of use. Belts that are cracked or frayed should be replaced.
6. Drive chains and gears should be lubricated. Gearboxes should be checked for lubricant. The operator's manual should be referred to for recommendation of the proper lubricant.
7. It is important that the auger, blower, and discharge chute be kept clean and free of rust. Rust spots should be sanded clean and the area repainted. It is advisable to use an aerosol can of silicone and spray the auger, blower, and discharge chute before each use of the machine. This is especially important if the machine is used in wet snow.
8. If the discharge chute becomes plugged with snow, always be sure to shut the engine off and disconnect the spark-plug wire before attempting to clear the chute.
9. Electric starting attachments are available on some snow blowers. This

* Adapted from statement by James D. Coulson, Service Supervisor, International Harvester, Chicago.

attachment helps take the effort out of cold-weather starting and makes the machine more reliable.

10. Preventive maintenance is the key to dependable snow-blower operation.

THE BASIC FACTS ABOUT OILS*

The first job an oil does is lubricate. It must also remain at the right thickness across a broad temperature range, without "wearing out" too soon, allowing the metal surfaces to rust, or turning into a gooey sludge.

Viscosity

The first important measure of oil performance is a measure of an oil's thickness, or *body*. An oil must be thin enough to run freely through tiny passages in the tractor or mower engine, yet it must be thick enough to resist scuffing and abrasion. A basic fact about oils is that they tend to be thicker (have higher viscosity) at low temperatures and thinner at high temperatures. Viscosity is the "weight" listed on the top of the can, usually as SAE 5, 10, 20, or 30. Oils of 5 and 10 weight are low-viscosity oils. Oils in the 30 and 40 weight range are of comparatively high viscosity. If two numbers are shown, for instance, 10W30, they mean that the oil is a multiple-viscosity grade; it behaves like a thin SAE 10W at low temperatures and like thicker SAE 30 oil at high temperatures. The only safe rule to follow in selecting a weight is to choose the oil recommended by your implement manufacturer. Be sure to use the exact grade of oil that is listed in your owner's manual.

Service Classifications

These are listed on oil cans and tell you what kind of duty the oil manufacturer designed it for. Obviously, an oil designed for service in a lawn mower, for example, would not work well in a diesel-truck engine. The manufacturers have therefore developed a series of service grades that help steer you to the right oil.

About two decades ago, the American Petroleum Institute (API) sponsored the development of a series of API engine service classifications: ML, MM, MS, DG, DM, DS. About 1970, a new system of API service classifications was devised. It includes nine classes, five for spark-ignition engines and four for diesel engines. Comparison of the new and old systems is shown in Table 4.2.

* Based on information from International Harvester Co., Chicago.

Additives to Engine Oil*

Several additional ingredients are put in oils in order to meet the service-classification requirements:

1. Pour-point depressants improve the ability of an oil to flow at a low temperature.
2. Detergents loosen deposits on internal parts and keep them clean during operation.

TABLE 4.2
Oil Classifications*

New API service class	Previous API service class	Typical duty
	Service-station classes	
SA	ML	Gasoline and diesel engines in utility service
SB	MM	Gasoline engines in minimum-duty service
SC	MS (1964)	Engine-warranty maintenance service for 1964 through 1967 gasoline engines
SD	MS (1968)	Engine-warranty service for gasoline engines beginning with 1968 models
	Commercial and fleet-engine services	
CA	DG	Diesel engines in mild to moderate duty with high-quality fuels
CB	DM	Diesel engines in mild to moderate duty with lower-quality fuels
CC	DM	Lightly supercharged diesel engines in moderate to severe duty and certain heavy-duty gasoline engines
CD	DS	Severe operating conditions; supercharged diesel engines in high-speed, high-output duty

* Data from 1974 news release of International Harvester, Chicago.

* Based on information from International Harvester Co., Chicago.

3. Corrosion inhibitors coat metal surfaces with a film that fights off attacks of corrosive compounds.
4. Antifoamants prevent accumulation of air bubbles in the oil and thus improve its lubricating and wear-resistance properties.
5. Oxidation inhibitors reduce the rate of oxidation and thus slow the formation of sludges and harmful compounds.
6. Extreme-pressure agents allow some oils to take extremely heavy operating loads.

Engine-Oil Requirements*

Inside your tractor or mower engine, oil lubricates, cleans, transfers heat from hot parts, holds dirt in suspension, and protects against corrosion. Before operating any engine, check the oil level. On tractors, oil is usually measured with a dipstick that has two marks. The top mark indicates that the oil is full, and the bottom mark indicates that it is low. Never operate the tractor with the oil level below the bottom mark on the dipstick. Always fill it until the oil is between the two marks.

On lawn mowers, the oil level is often measured by removing a plug and observing the oil height. Again, if the oil is low, do not operate the machine unless oil has been added to the indicated level.

When you are changing oil, follow the instructions your operator's manual gives for change intervals and procedures. After the initial period of use, the oil should be changed every 30 hours of operation. The viscosity of the oil used is specified in the owner's manual. Before changing the oil, run the engine until it warms to a normal operating temperature. This procedure agitates the oil and gathers up the contaminants and dirt in the crankcase so that most of them are removed with the oil.

Transmission and Drive Lubricant*

Another type of oil needed by more sophisticated tractors is hydraulic fluid. It is used in the hydrostatic transmissions and for implement operations, such as lift cylinders and three-point hitches. Like an engine oil, this hydraulic fluid must lubricate, protect against corrosion, and retard foaming. It must carry extreme forces at high pressures to perform work. It is a hard-working oil and deserves the very best treatment.

* Based on information from International Harvester Co., Chicago.

The fluid used must be very carefully selected to exactly match the fluid in the tractor. Since this fluid will be changed rather infrequently, you will be topping up the existing fluid and the fluid you add must blend without problems with the fluid in the tank. For this reason, it is a good practice to purchase hydraulic fluid of the type recommended from the machinery dealer. Most manufacturers regard this matter seriously and warn implement buyers that warranties will be invalidated if the user adds any brand of fluid other than the type recommended.

TILLERS AND SHREDDERS*

Tillers

Tillers are used for preparing the soil for planting. A tiller has a small gas engine, a driving set of rotary tines that cut through the soil, chopping and pulverizing it to prepare a suitable seedbed in which the young plants can grow and thrive. When the plants are well under way, tillers are used for cultivating between the rows to keep weeds to a minimum. After the plants are harvested, the tillers can be used to mulch crop refuse back into the soil.

Tillers are available in two major types. The most common type has the rotating tines at the front of the tiller. The tines are powered by the engine and literally pull the tiller along so that you do not have to push it from place to place. The second type of tiller has the tines mounted at the rear, with the front wheels driven by the motor. This configuration is normally found only in extremely large tillers, more suited for the multiacre garden than the small back lot.

The front-tined tiller will permit plowing to within 1 or 2 in. of a walk, foundation, or established shrub. The rear-tined tiller can plow only within 8 or 10 in. of such surface.

Tillers for average home use are driven by gasoline engines of 3 to 5 hp. A tiller with a 5-hp engine will allow extra power for the tough tilling jobs. Width of the tines ranges up to 26 in., although extender tips are available so that a strip 32 in. wide can be prepared in a single pass. The tiller should have a reversing arrangement, so that it can be backed away from obstacles. Controls should be convenient to the operator to allow instant shifts into neutral or reverse if a dangerous situation arises.

Be sure that the tiller you select can dig deep enough to prepare a suitable seedbed. Some tillers can only stir the surface soil, but better ones can prepare a finely pulverized seedbed as deep as 9 in. The seed-

* Based on information from International Harvesters Co., Chicago.

bed depth should be determined by a depth guide at the rear of the tiller. In some models, the depth guide can be replaced by a furrowing attachment, so that the tiller makes a small furrow for seed planting during its cultivation pass.

A tiller should be used at a steady, comfortable pace for effective tilling. Speed is determined by the adjusted depth of tilling and also by the soil depth. Heavy, wet soil or sod requires a slower speed than a light sandy soil. If you go too fast, the motor bogs down and may stop. High grass, twine, or other similar obstructions may also wrap around the tines, stopping the motor. When this type of blockage occurs, stop the motor, clear the tines, and proceed at a slower pace.

Shredders

Shredders are used to grind leaves, grass, weeds, roots, twigs, and crop residue into a fine mulch. Selection of a shredder should be based on the intended use. In each of the two major types available, leaves and crop refuse are fed through the top of the shredder into a chamber where they are pulverized by the grinder.

In the more common type of shredder, the pulverized refuse is then blown out through the side into a bag. This type of light-duty shredder is suitable for dry refuse, such as leaves, but has a hard time coping with damp refuse, wet leaves, spoiled vegetables, and other wet products. Fairly small, it is typically powered by a 3-hp gasoline engine and is commonly used with a bagging attachment for packing the shredded refuse in large plastic bags.

The second type of shredder is larger, huskier, and able to handle wet refuse. The chief difference is that it has a more powerful engine, of up to 5 hp, and material fed into it is processed slightly differently. Instead of being blown through the shredder, material is forced through, hammered into small shreds, and then forced out through a mesh screen. Because wet, soggy materials cannot reliably be moved by a blowing action, they are much more easily handled by the second type of shredder. Instead of being blown into a plastic bag, refuse fed through the second type of shredder is deposited on the ground where it is to be used.

The final screen of this type of shredder can be replaced by optional screens for different tasks. The typical screen for the average gardening job has 1-in. mesh. For fine powdering of dry materials, a screen with a ½-in. mesh can be used. If extremely wet, soggy materials are to be forced through, a screen with larger openings is available. Some screens have openings as large as 2 by 7¼ in.

Attachments

Low-cost tiller and shredder attachments can also be purchased as options for a lawn and garden tractor. If you have such a tractor, your implement dealer can probably fit a shredder or tiller attachment to it. Not only will it handle the shredding and tilling, with proper attachments, but it can mow the grass, plow snow, and handle a wide variety of other tasks that neither a shredder nor a tiller can tackle.

Both shredders and tillers made today are equipped with a wide variety of safety devices. Nevertheless, they should be treated with the respect afforded any piece of powered machinery.

Shredders are usually capable of pulverizing small branches trimmed from trees or bushes. Typically, the larger the shredder, the bigger a branch it can handle, perhaps up to $1\frac{1}{2}$ in. in diameter. The shredder is designed to pulverize leaves and stalks only, rather than branches. A large branch may jam the shredder, requiring it to be stopped and freed before operation can continue.

Even though the tiller or shredder may be equipped with a clutch, never try to free obstructions while the motor is running. Safety experts recommend that you not only stop the mower but remove the spark-plug wire so that the engine cannot be started accidentally while your hands are near operating parts. When you start the machine to continue, be sure to keep hands and feet away from operating areas while the engine is running.

Do not fill the gasoline tank while the engine is running or hot. Wait until the engine has cooled, then use a funnel and avoid spillage. Keep smokers and flames away to avoid the possibility of a fire or explosion.

MAINTENANCE PROCEDURES AND SCHEDULING

Maintenance designed to prevent costly breakdowns contains two basic activities: (1) a periodic inspection of equipment to uncover conditions which may lead to breakdowns or excessive depreciation and (2) upkeep to remedy such conditions while still in a minor stage. By following these two basic activities through proper lubrication, job planning, and scheduling of repairs, certain major returns can be expected—fewer breakdowns, with a corresponding decrease in production downtime; fewer large-scale or repetitive repairs; lower costs for simple repairs made before breakdowns (because less manpower, fewer skills, and fewer parts are needed); less overtime pay on ordinary adjustments and repairs than for breakdown repairs; and less standby equipment.

The best way to achieve a maintenance program based on preventive maintenance is through periodic inspections to discover and correct unsatisfactory conditions. Frequency of inspections depends upon the amount and degree of use and will vary from one area to another. To establish the best frequency cycle, begin with an analysis of the equipment based on such factors as age, condition, value, amount of use, safety requirements, number of hours or mileage operated, and susceptibility to wear, damage, and loss of adjustment.

Most maintenance programs can be divided into three groups: routine upkeep, periodic inspections, and contingent work. The latter includes work at irregular intervals when the equipment is down for other reasons; the more work which can be squeezed into this category, the less costly it will be.

Routine upkeep of vehicular equipment includes such chores as lubrication, oil change, checking tires and batteries, washing, tune-up, checking spark plugs and points, brake inspection, etc. Most of these chores should be the responsibility of the operator, and if he finds anything which should be corrected, he should report it to the main service garage.

Periodic inspections should be done at the garage by personnel trained in this kind of work. During these inspections, every moving part of the equipment should be checked and worn parts removed and replaced. Following inspection the equipment should be thoroughly cleaned and lubricated.

Contingent work consists of repairs for major breakdowns or general overhaul of the equipment. At this time the equipment should be inspected as for a regular inspection period, and all worn or broken parts removed and replaced.

Scheduling maintenance work can be done by the use of overall charts for all equipment and individual cards for each piece of equipment. The overall chart will give a quick picture of the workload. The chart should list the days or months across the top border and an itemized list of the equipment down the left side. A system of symbols to show various types of repairs, adjustments, etc. should be devised so they can be marked under the date and opposite the piece of equipment (see Table 4.3). The individual cards (Table 4.4) should provide more details for each piece of equipment. Both major and minor repairs should be listed on the card, plus the time and materials used.

One important factor in achieving good maintenance practices or in making preventive maintenance effective is the proper training of the driver or operator. Improper driving or operation is a major factor in mechanical failures of motor vehicles. Carelessness can nullify all efforts at proper maintenance. Wherever it is practicable, a regular driver or operator should be assigned to each piece of equipment. The operator should be made responsible for such preventive maintenance as daily checks on fuel, oil, and water levels, on tires for inflation, unusual wear, and penetration of foreign objects; on lights, horns, windshield wipers, and other equipment accessories; and on indications of fuel, oil, water, gear-oil, or brake-system leaks. While the equipment is in operation, the operator should observe the operation of the various instruments, brakes, steering, engine, and power-driven units and report any defects immediately to his foreman or supervisor. The operator should also make weekly checks on the carburetor, generator, regulator, starter, water pumps, fan and drive belts, battery, and battery connections.

TABLE 4.3
Sample Overall Chart for Vehicle Maintenance

	January											
Truck No.	1	2	3	4	5	6	7	8	9	10	11	12
1			wa		o.c.				tu			
	√		lu									
2								sp				
			√	tu				wa				
3												
							√					

Symbols

√	inspection	o.c.	oil change
wa	wash	sp	spark plugs
lu	lubrication	tu	tune-up

Operating Rules

The operator of any power unit should know a few fundamental principles in order to get the best service possible:

1. All excess grease, oil, and dust should be wiped clean from the unit before it is placed in operation after a long period of idleness.
2. The crankcase should always have a sufficient supply of the recommended grade of oil. The oil should be changed periodically or after every 25 hours of operation. Oil depth in the crankcase should be checked after every 5 hours of operation to make sure it is at the recommended level.
3. All moving parts should be properly lubricated. Lubrica-

TABLE 4.4
Sample Card for Individual Vehicle Maintenance

Material used		Name of park					
Name or no. of part	Amount						
		Unit no.	Description			Mileage in	
		Date start	Job ordered			Mileage out	
		Date finish	by			miles	
		Oper. no.	Repair order instructions				
		Tires and batteries		Item	Quantity	Amount	Total
		Ticket no.	Amount	Gasoline			
				Diesel oil			
				Lube oil			
				Grease			
				Parts			
				Tires			
				Item	Hours	Amount	
		Total		Labor			
		Processed by		Overhead on labor			
		Cost		Overhead on stores			
		Foreman		Total labor and overhead			

tion should not be overdone, however, since an excess of grease will collect dirt and do more harm than good.

4. Use only the regular commercial gasoline mixtures as fuel. High-test gas or special fuel mixtures should be used only if specifically recommended by the manufacturer.
5. Always allow the motor to warm up after first starting it and before placing it in operation. If the engine runs smoothly with the choke wide open (not pulled out), it is warm enough for safe operation. On cold or damp days,

an engine that is difficult to start can be started more easily by priming.

6. After the unit is placed in operation, the motor should be run at the proper speed for the conditions and job to be done. The operator should never strain the unit by running it at excessively high speeds when the extra power is not needed.
7. All power tools are designed to do the work. An operator need only guide the power tool he is using and should not force it.
8. The operator should clean up the unit immediately after it has been used. Dirt and grime can be removed more easily at this time than if they are allowed to dry and harden.
9. When the unit is not in use, it should be stored in a dry, level, dirt-free area and covered with a protective cover to keep out dust and dampness.
10. If the unit is equipped with different attachments, the attachments should receive as good care as the unit itself.

Safety Rules

The operator of power mowers and similar equipment should know a few basic safety rules:

1. Keep feet and hands away from the moving blades.
2. With self-propelled models, hold the mower down firmly with the foot, safely placed before starting the engine; disengage the clutch, and then be careful not to engage it accidentally.
3. Do not touch the spark plug of a running mower; it can give you a nasty shock.
4. Keep your hold on the handle at all times when the mower is going or in a position to start moving.
5. Stop the engine when you leave the mower or equipment.
6. Do not add fuel while the engine is hot.
7. Before starting to mow, rake the area free of loose objects that might be thrown by the blades.
8. Treat a running rotary mower as you would a gun; never allow its discharge opening to point at anyone. The fewer people around when a mower is used, the less chance that someone will be injured by a flying object.

9. If you are going to move the blade of a rotary mower by hand for any reason, disconnect the spark plug wire and make sure it cannot touch the plug while you are near the blade. Rotating the blade cranks the engine, and if the plug is connected, the mower could conceivably start running.

DISEASE AND INSECT CONTROL

The control of diseases and insects of trees and shrubs is a constant problem on public lands of all categories. A well-rounded maintenance program should have the skills, materials, and equipment to control all kinds of diseases and insects. Many new chemicals are proving effective, and many of the old standby formulas are still good. Pests and diseases to which shrubs, evergreen trees, and deciduous trees are prone are listed in Appendix Tables A.5, A.6, and A.7, respectively.

CONTROL OF DISEASES

The control of diseases in trees and shrubs is based largely on eradication and protection. For example, collecting and burning fallen leaves from diseased plants will eliminate one source of trouble. Pruning infested branches and burning them also removes a source of subsequent infections. Spraying with dormant or delayed dormant sprays at the point where infection occurs is another common method of control. The removal of decayed wood from trees is only partially successful in eradicating disease, since the fungi usually extend well beyond the zone of decay.

Spraying

The successful control of disease by spraying depends upon three factors:

1. Sprays must be applied at the proper time. All protective sprays must be applied before rainy periods, because fungi and bacteria penetrate plant tissues when the plants are wet.
2. The spray must be applied as a fine mist in order to cover

the plant. Complete coverage by an even protective film is essential for effective control.

3. The sprays must contain the proper ingredients. Copper and sulfur are the two chemical elements most often used in protective sprays. They can be used safely on plants without injury to the tender leaves.

COPPER SPRAYS

The most commonly used copper spray is bordeaux mixture, which adheres well to most shade tree leaves without the addition of a spreading and sticking agent. When copper sprays are used on conifers, however, casein soap or fish-oil soap should be added at the rate of 2 lb in 50 gal of spray. Surplus spray should not be stored for future use, since it deteriorates rapidly.

There are two objectionable features about bordeaux mixture: (1) it forms an unsightly residue on the leaves, and (2) it may burn foliage during extended periods of cool, wet weather.

Other copper sprays which may be used are Bardow, Basicop, Copocil, Copper Hydro 40, copper phosphate, Cupracide 54, Cupro-K, Pyrox, and Triogen. Complete instructions for use are given by manufacturer. Since most copper sprays are corrosive to metals, spraying machines and accessories should be thoroughly cleaned with water after each operation.

SULFUR SPRAYS

Sprays containing sulfur as the active ingredient are also used for disease control. The most common is a lime sulfur solution, which is used also as a contact insecticide and as a disinfecting spray. When it is used as a dormant disinfecting spray, a strength of 1 part in 10 parts water is recommended. The powdered form should be mixed at the rate of 20 lb in 50 gal water. For a protective spray on leaves, use 1 gal of the concentrated liquid or 4 lb of powder in 50 gal of water. Never use a lime sulfur spray on trees near a house, since it reacts very strongly on house paint.

Other sulfur compounds, known as wettable and flotation sulfurs, are Flotex wettable sulfur, Kolofog, Koppers flotation sulfur, micronized wettable sulfur, Mike sulfur, sulfocide, and Sulfrox. Sulfur sprays are used to treat mildew, rust diseases, and the diseases of the rose family. Do not use a sulfur spray when the air temperature is 90°F or higher.

COMBINATION SPRAYS

Protective sprays can be combined with insecticides to control fungus or bacterial diseases and insects in one operation. However, care should be taken to mix compatible materials together in order to avoid injuring the plant or reducing the efficiency of one or several of the materials in the mixture. The following rules for mixing should be observed:

1. Copper sprays and bordeaux mixture may be mixed with lead arsenate for chewing insects and with nicotine sulfate for sucking insects.
2. Lime sulfur may be mixed with calcium or lead arsenate and nicotine sulfate. To prevent burning the foliage, be sure the quantity of lime added is equal to that of the calcium or lead arsenate.
3. Do not mix lime sulfate with paris green, soaps, bordeaux mixture, or oil emulsions.
4. Wettable sulfurs may be mixed with arsenicals or nicotine sulfate.
5. Do not mix wettable sulfurs with oil emulsions or soaps.

CONTROL OF INSECTS

Insects are usually classified into five categories: leaf-chewing, sucking, leaf-mining, borers and bark beetles, and root-infesting.

Stomach poisons are generally most effective against chewing pests. The most widely used stomach poison is arsenate of lead. For use as a spray, mix as follows:

Large quantity	2 to 3 lb arsenate of lead to 50 gal water
Small quantity	2 to 3 level tablespoons arsenate of lead to 1 gal water

For use as a dust, mix one part of arsenate of lead to nine parts of dusting sulfur, hydrated lime, or other suitable carrier.

Other common stomach poisons are paris green, calcium arsenate, magnesium arsenate, and sodium fluosilicate.

Pyrethrum sprays are contact sprays, but some are effective against chewing pests. Rotenone is effective both as a stomach poison and as a contact insecticide. Both rotenone and pyrethrum are nonpoisonous to man and warm-blooded animals. They should not be used near water, as they may kill fish. The directions of the manufacturer should be followed.

Insecticides for Sucking Insects

Contact sprays are usually used for sucking insects. They kill by acting on the nervous system, clogging the breathing pores, or producing caustic action on body tissues. The most common of these sprays are made with nicotine, pyrethrum, rotenone, soap, oil, or lime sulfur as the active agent.

Nicotine spray Ordinarily nicotine is used 1 part to 500 to 800 parts water. Add 2 to 5 lb of soap to each 50 gal of spray to increase its effectiveness. For small quantities, use 1 to 1½ tsp of nicotine and 1 oz of soap to each gallon of water.

Nicotine dust Effective against aphids and leafhoppers.

Pyrethrum and rotenone Follow manufacturer's recommendations on the package.

Soap Applications of fish-oil soap or other good soaps in mixtures of 1 lb in 20 to 40 gal of water are effective on some soft-bodied insects.

Oil Summer-oil emulsions are oils with most of the chemically active material removed and are safe on most foliage. Summer oils (white sulfonated oils) may be used in concentrations of up to 2 per cent actual oil and may be applied to plants in foliage.

Dormant-spray oils are not safe on foliage, and should be used for dormant spraying only. Dormant-spray oils may be either miscible oils or oil emulsions. Miscible oils are diluted 1 part to 15 parts water for scale-insect control. Oil emulsions are diluted so that the final spray will contain 3 per cent actual oil. Most oil emulsions contain from 66 to 80 per cent oil.

Insecticides for Borers and Bark Beetles

Borers are hard to control because they attack only weak and devitalized trees. The best preventive is to keep the trees in good health and vigor.

Carbon Bisulfide This compound can be injected into the burrow with an oil can. After the injection the burrow should be closed with putty or some similar substance. The fire hazard of carbon bisulfide can be avoided if a mixture of ethylene dichloride and carbon tetrachloride is used instead.

Pine Oil Effective control of boring insects and bark beetles has been obtained with a soluble pine oil containing 1 lb of paradichlorobenzene to the quart. Paradichlorobenzene is dissolved in the pine oil by heating it to 120°F. To use, dilute this mixture with 2 qt water and paint on the infested bark.

Repellent Washes One formula for a repellent wash consists of 1 gal soft soap dissolved in 1 gal hot water, with 1 pt crude carbolic acid stirred in. The mixture is left overnight and then diluted with 8 gal water and applied to the trunk. Another formula consists of 25 lb potash soap, 1½ gal water, 12 lb naphthalene, and 1 lb flour. Soap and water are heated together to 180°F, and the flour is stirred in, followed by the naphthalene. After being reheated to 180°F and stirred until thoroughly mixed, it can be removed from the fire, cooled quickly with occasional stirring, and painted on tree trunks. Best results with washes are obtained when trees are painted in late spring (May or June, or at the time adults are emerging) and applications repeated at several 2-week intervals.

Protectors Damage by borers can be prevented by wrapping trees with protectors made of newspaper, building paper, or another suitable paper. Cylinders of fine-meshed wire screen give protection if the tops are plugged with cotton.

Sprays Spraying with arsenicals is helpful in the control of adult borers that chew foliage. Spraying should be done when the adults are emerging and before they lay eggs.

Carbon Bisulfide This compound is useful in killing ants and other insects in the soil. Make several holes about 4 in. apart in the infested area and place in each hole a tablespoonful of the material; close with soil. This mixture is extremely flammable and should be handled with great care.

*Other Insecticides to Kill Bark Beetles** Mix 1 gal lindane (20% concentrate) and 15 gal of fuel oil, or mix 1 pt ethylene dibromide (83% concentrate) and 4⅞ gal fuel oil. It takes about 1½ qt of lindane or 2 gal of ethylene dibromide spray to treat an average-sized ponderosa pine.

* Adapted from Protect Your Pines from Bark Beetles, *USDA Forest Serv.* PA 1011, 1972.

Insecticides for Leaf-mining Insects

Leaf miners are insects, mostly Lepidoptera and Diptera, which in the larval stages burrow in and eat the parenchyma of leaves. Leaf-mining insects are not easily controlled because neither contact nor stomach poisons can be used against them. Some may be controlled by fumigation with cyanide and treatment with hot water. Hand picking infested leaves is also of value.

Insecticides for Root-infesting Insects

Carbon Bisulfide Emulsion This emulsion can be prepared by mixing (parts by volume) 1 part of rosin fish-oil soap (other soaps may be used), 3 parts water, and 10 parts carbon bisulfide. Place soap and water in container and stir until mixture is uniform. Add carbon bisulfide and agitate until mixture is creamlike. Mix 1 qt emulsion in 50 gal water and apply this mixture to the soil at rate of 1 qt/ft^2. Avoid fires of any kind, and do not smoke when using this mixture. This treatment kills Japanese beetle grub, white grub, earthworms, and burrowing bees.

Arsenate of Lead Use 5 to 15 lb per 1000 ft^2 of surface, depending on the degree of infestation. Spread evenly over the surface of the ground by mixing the material with 25 times its volume of moist sand or soil. Wash material into the soil by running water sprinkler in one spot for ½ to 1 hour. This application will protect the lawn for years against root-infesting insects.

To grub-proof a lawn during construction, use 35 lb of lead arsenate per 1000 ft^2 of surface. Apply as above and mix into the soil to a depth of 3 in.

USE OF CHLORDANE FOR SUBTERRANEAN CONTROL OF TERMITES

For fast initial control and extended protection against reinfestation, 0.5 to 1.0% chlordane-water emulsions are recommended. The strength of insecticide required varies with the soil: sandy soils require the least, clays and loams more, and peats and mucks the most (see Table 5.1).

This solution will not damage nearby foliage, and a water emulsion eliminates the fire hazard of oil sprays, but care should be taken not to contaminate wells or other water supplies. Annual inspection of the treated areas is recommended, to check for reinfestation.

Treatment of Exposed Soil Areas

Outside surfaces of foundation walls are usually exposed by trenching to a soil depth of 1 or 2 ft, but no lower than the footings. Both trench and backfill should be treated with 2 gal of the chlordane emulsion per linear foot. Exposed soil areas under porches and other structures should be treated with 1 gal of the chlordane emulsion per 10 ft^2.

Treatment of Unexposed Soil Areas

Under sidewalks and driveways which border foundation walls, the emulsion can be applied through shrinkage cracks or through specially drilled holes.

TABLE 5.1
Chlordane Dilution Guide*

Chlordane in finished formulation, %	Volume of finished formulation, gal	Required amount of chlordane emulsifiable concentrates			
		40% concentrate	44–46% concentrate	60–62% concentrate	72–75% concentrate
1.00	5	1.00 pt	14.00 fl oz (or 0.875 pt)	9.00 fl oz	7.00 fl oz
	50	1.50 gal	4.25 qt	5.5 pt	4.25 pt
	100	2.25 gal	8.50 qt	11.00 pt	4.25 qt
0.50	5	8.00 fl oz	7.00 fl oz	4.00 fl oz	3.00 fl oz
	50	2.50 qt	4.25 pt	2.75 pt	2.125 pt
	100	1.25 gal	4.25 qt	5.50 pt	4.25 pt

* To obtain 5, 50, or 100 gal of a 1.00 or 0.50 formulation (columns 1 and 2) measure out amount of concentrate specified in columns 3 to 6, and add water to make up desired volume.

Under structures the inside surface of the foundation should be treated wherever the soil is exposed. Dig a shallow trench about 6 in. wide and treat as described for other trenching. Depth of penetration will depend upon the relationship between inside and outside soil level. If the soil is not exposed, remove or drill through the covering, treat with chlordane emulsion, and replace the covering.

Other contact points to be checked and treated are tree stumps and fence posts, wooden stairs, stoops, supports, trellises, and possible termite entrances around basement windows and pipes, chimney bases and supporting piers, and points where beams, joists, and sills rest on foundations.

Concrete-Slab Construction

Termites have been found infesting baseboards, partitions, closets, and all types of interior wood construction in many houses built on concrete slabs. They gain access through cracks in the slabs and through wooden stakes or forms not properly removed during construction.

The best way to prevent such infestations is to treat the fill beneath the slab with a 1% chlordane-water formulation before the concrete is poured.

Architectural Plans

Termite protection should start with the design of the building. The architect can indicate on the plans the spots where entrances may develop and chlordane treatment should be applied. He can also design termite shields and other barriers.

NOTES OF GENERAL INTEREST

1. Neither highly alkaline soils nor high-alkaline plaster and plasterboard scraps found at building sites affect the stability of chlordane (see Table 5.2).

TABLE 5.2
Dilution Guide for 20% Chlordane Liquid Concentrates*

Chlordane in finished formulation, %	Add to 1 gal 20% chlordane concentrate		
	In kerosene		In no. 2 diesel oil
	Kerosene IBO,† gal	No. 2 diesel oil IBO, gal	No. 2 diesel oil IBO, gal
1	21.0	18.0	20.0
2	10.0	8.50	9.50
2.5	7.75	6.50	7.50
5	3.25	2.75	3.125

Example To prepare 2.5% chlordane oil solution from 20% chlordane concentrate in deodorized kerosene using no. 2 diesel oil, mix 1 gal of the 20% concentrate with 6.5 gal of no. 2 diesel oil.

When using 40% chlordane oil concentrate, use 0.5 gal of concentrate to the same amount of IBO. The approximate weight of kerosene is 6.6 lb/gal, and no. 2 diesel oil is 7.8 lb/gal.

* By permission of the Velsicol Chemical Corporation.

† Insecticide base oil.

2. Chlordane water-emulsion formulations have been recommended for soil treatment because experimental field tests and practical applications have shown no harmful phytotoxic effects to plants and shrubbery. Such formulations also eliminate fire hazard.
3. Chlordane formulations properly applied to the soil do not produce obnoxious odors.
4. One application at proper concentration and satisfactorily applied will control termites for 5 years or longer. Case histories of over 10 years of continuous effective control are on record.
5. Reference: "Protection against Decay and Termites in Residential Construction" No. 448, NAS, 1956, The Building Research Advisory Board,. National Academy of Science, National Research Council, 2101 Constitution Avenue, Washington, D.C. 20418.
6. Consult pest control operators on termite problems.

DIRECT CONTROL METHODS*

Chemical treatment of the soil around or under the foundation of buildings is one method of preventing termite attack for many years. Soil treatment, however, should be used as a supplement to good construction, not as a substitute for it. The use of chemically treated and naturally resistant woods also reduces the susceptibility of wooden structures to termite attack. Again, however, use of such materials is a supplement to good construction practices.

Chemical Soil Treatment

Formulations of four materials (aldrin, dieldrin, chlordane, and heptachlor) are currently registered for use in treating soils to control native subterranean termites. In tests in south Mississippi, these chemicals, applied at the prescribed rates and methods, have provided complete protection for 17 to 21 years. To date, no alternative materials have been found that will provide comparable long-term, economical protection.

Preparation of Chemicals

A soil chemical is economical and most easily prepared when purchased in the form of a *liquid-concentrated solution*. The concentrate is sold according to

* Adapted from Subterranean Termites: Their Prevention and Control in Buildings, *USDA Home Gard. Bull.* 64, 1972.

the percentage, or weight in pounds per gallon, of the toxicant it contains. These percentages and weights vary according to the amount of toxicant present in the concentrates of the different chemicals. Each concentrate contains an emulsifier to make it miscible with water and *must be diluted before it is ready for use.*

Directions for diluting the concentrated solutions to the strength of the finished emulsion recommended are usually given on the container. If they are not, the following directions should be used in preparing each chemical for soil treatment.

Aldrin, 0.5% in Water Solution Aldrin is usually sold as a liquid concentrate containing either 2 or 4 lb of the technical grade chemical per gallon. To prepare a 0.5% water emulsion, ready for use, dilute 1 gal of the 2-lb concentrate with 47 gal of water or 1 gal of the 4-lb material with 95 gal of water. This makes 48 gal of the 0.5% water emulsion from the lower concentrate and 96 gal from the higher one. The rate of dilution is 1:47 and 1:95, respectively, regardless of the unit of measure used (gallon, pint, etc.).

Chlordane, 1.0% in Water Emulsion Chlordane is sold as 46 to 48 or 72 to 74% liquid concentrate. To prepare a 1% water emulsion, ready for use, dilute 1 gal of the 46% concentrate with 48 gal of water, or 1 gal of the 72% material with 99 gal of water.

Dieldrin, 0.5% in Water Emulsion Dieldrin is usually sold as a liquid concentrate containing 1.5 lb/gal of the technical grade chemical. To prepare a 0.5% water emulsion, ready for use, dilute 1 gal of the concentrate with 36 gal of water.

Heptachlor, 0.5% in Water Emulsion Heptachlor is sold as a liquid concentrate containing 2 or 3 lb of the actual chemical per gallon. To prepare a 0.5% water emulsion, ready for use, dilute 1 gal of the 2-lb concentrate with 48 gal of water or 1 gal of the 3-lb concentrate with 72 gal of water.

Rates and Methods of Application

The object of chemical treatment of the soil is to provide a barrier through which termites cannot pass to reach a building. The rates and methods of application vary with the type of construction and the area to be treated as follows.

Slab-on-Ground Buildings

Soon after the gravel or dirt fill has been made and tamped, treat the soil with a chemical before the concrete is poured. The chemical may be applied either with a power sprayer or tank-type garden sprayer. The soil is treated as follows:

1. Apply 4 gal of chemical per 10 lin ft to the soil in critical areas under the slab, e.g., along the inside of foundation walls, along both sides of interior partition walls, and around plumbing.
2. Apply 1 gal of chemical per 10 ft^2 as an overall treatment under the slab and attached slab porches and terraces where the fill is soil or unwashed gravel.
3. Apply $1\frac{1}{2}$ gal of chemical per 10 ft^2 to areas where the fill is washed gravel or other coarse absorbent material, such as cinders.
4. Apply 4 gal of chemical per 10 lin ft of trench for each foot of depth from grade of footing along the outside edge of the building after all grading is finished. This is accomplished by digging a trench 6 to 8 in. wide along the outside of the foundation. Where the top of the footing is more than 12 in. below the surface, make crowbar holes in the bottom of the trench as described below for basement houses. Mix the chemical with the soil as it is being replaced in the trench.

Crawl-Space and Basement Houses

To treat the soil along the exterior and interior walls of foundations with shallow footings, use the method described above for treating the exterior of slab-on-the-ground houses.

Where the footings are more than 12 in. deep, and where large volumes of the chemical must be applied, make holes about 1 ft apart in the bottom of the trench, using a crowbar, pipe, metal rod, or power auger. Punch or drill these holes down to the top of the footing (Fig. 5.1). This permits better distribution of the chemical. The holes may need to be closer together in hard-packed clay soils than in light sandy soils.

The soil under or around crawl-space houses should be treated as follows:

1. Apply 4 gal of chemical per 10 lin ft of trench along the inside of foundation walls, along both sides of interior partitions (Fig. 5.1), and around piers and plumbing. Do not apply an overall treatment in crawl spaces.
2. Apply 4 gal per 10 lin ft of trench for each foot of depth from grade to footing along the outside of foundation walls, including the part beneath entrance platforms, porches, etc.
3. Apply 4 gal per 10 lin ft along the inside and outside of foundation walls of porches.
4. Apply 1 gal per 10 ft^2 of soil surface as an overall treatment only where the attached concrete platform and porches are on fill or ground.

To treat the soil under and around basement houses, apply chemicals as recommended for slab-on-ground construction. Treat the basement floor in the same way as a slab-on-ground house (Fig. 5.2). Voids in masonry foundations should be treated with at least 2 gal of chemical per 10 lin ft of wall, at or near the footing.

Chemical Movement within the Soil

Analysis of soil adjacent to treated plots has shown that aldrin, chlordane, dieldrin, and heptachlor have moved only a few inches laterally or downward through sandy loam soil after two decades of heavy rainfall and weathering. However, there is risk of contamination if the insecticides are applied near a water well on soil that contains layers of gravel or that tends to crack severely during periods of drought. In the latter cases, the soil should not be treated with chemicals.

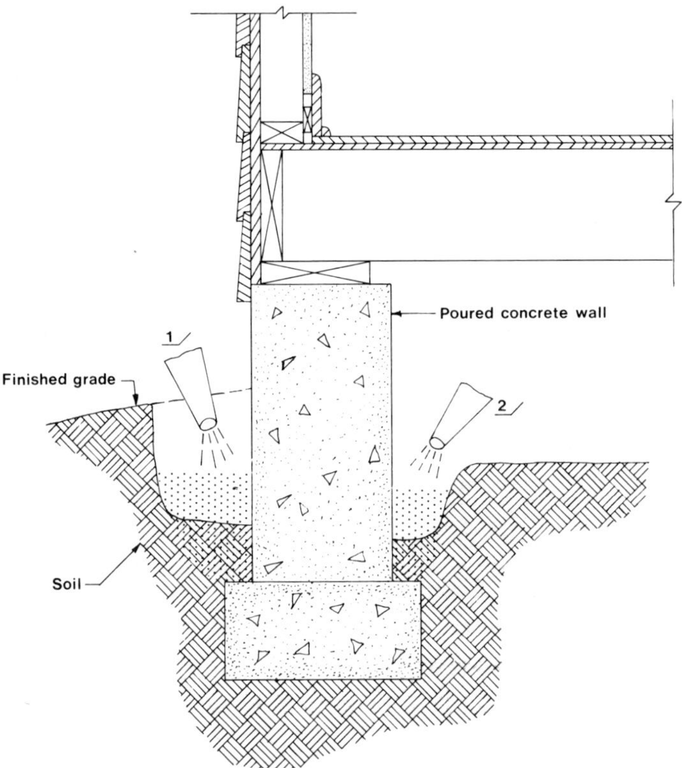

Fig. 5.1 Application of chemical to crawl-space construction. Soil treatment (1) outside and (2) inside foundation wall. (*USDA*.)

Chemically Treated and Naturally Resistant Woods

Chemically treated wood is an additional safeguard against damage by termites and decay. For maximum protection the wood should be pressure-impregnated with an approved chemical by a standard process. Vacuum treatment gives adequate protection where conditions are less severe. Brush, spray, or short-period soak treatments give limited protection to wood above ground. The chemicals and their uses are given in (1) Federal Use Specification TT-W-571d (current revision), (2) Standards of the American Wood Preservers Association, and (3) Standards of the National Woodwork Manufacturers Association.

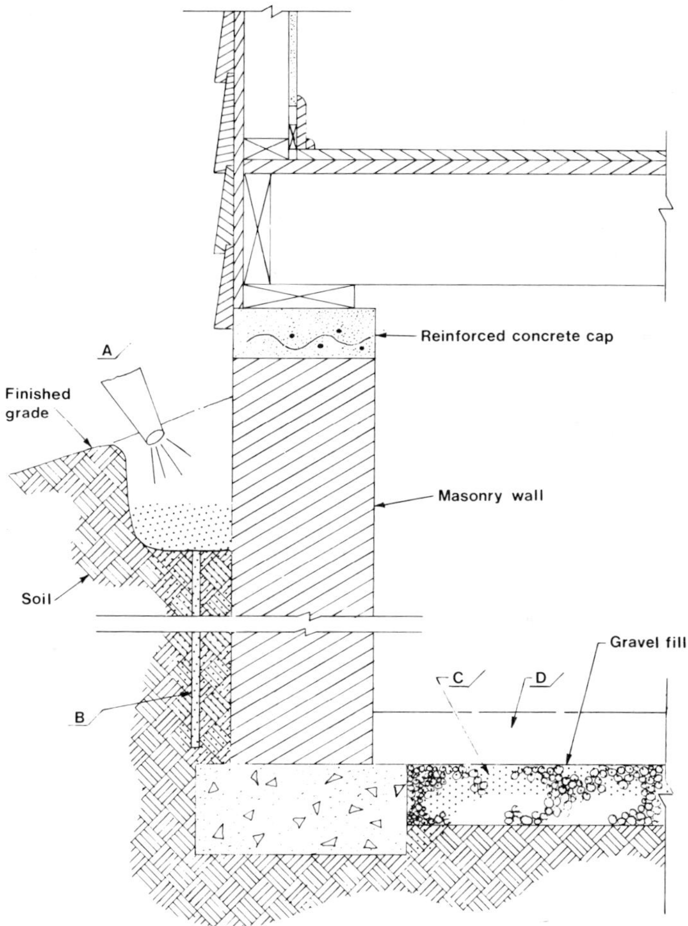

Fig. 5.2 Application of chemical to the soil in and around a structure with a full basement: *A*, soil treatment along outside of the foundation; *B*, pipe and rod hole from bottom of trench to the top of the footing to aid distribution of the chemical; *C*, treatment of fill on soil beneath a concrete floor in basement; *D*, position of concrete slab after chemical has been applied. (*USDA*.)

The slow-growing heartwood of some of the native species of wood is quite resistant to termites, but it is neither immune nor as resistant as pressure-treated wood. So far as is known, the following kinds and grades of lumber are the most resistant to native termites:

1. Foundation-grade California redwood
2. All-heart southern tidewater red cypress
3. Very pitchy southern pine lightwood
4. Heartwood of eastern red cedar (less resistant than the above)

SAFETY IN CHLORDANE HANDLING*

Chlordane, when given to laboratory animals in sufficient quantities, may produce an acute toxic state, recognized by signs of irritation of the central nervous system. Symptoms of chronic intoxication are usually not so clearly defined as those of acute, but in general are similar and slowly progressive. In addition, a history of the loss of appetite, loss of weight, and headaches may be noted. If intoxication, either acute or chronic, is suspected, a detailed history of conditions of exposure must be obtained, as well as information on the components of the formulations exposed. The above symptoms are in general typical of chlordane exposure, but not necessarily of other components of a formulation. Solvents may produce symptoms such as nausea and vomiting, and irritation to the skin, eyes, throat, and lungs.

Precautionary Measures

1. Personal hygiene
   a. Remove materials spilled on the skin immediately by thorough washing, but not scrubbing, with soap and water.
   b. After routine contact with chlordane, wash the face and hands before eating in order to avoid repeated ingestion of small quantities.
2. Clothing
   a. Avoid wearing clothing contaminated with chlordane. Do not wipe chlordane on clothing where it could soak through and come into contact with the skin.
3. Protective equipment
   a. Respirators provide protection against inhalation of sprays, fogs, or dust. The extent to which they should be used depends upon the conditions and methods of insecticide application, but respirators are recommended for persons treating confined areas.
   b. Gloves are suggested if there is danger of unsuspected exposure to chlordane during formulation or application.

Treatment

1. If chlordane is spilled on the skin, wash thoroughly, without scrubbing, with large amounts of soap and water. Always change if clothing has been contaminated.

* Adapted, by permission, from a publication of the Velsicol Chemical Corporation.

2. If chlordane is splashed or spilled into the eyes, wash repeatedly with water.
3. If chlordane has been swallowed, induce vomiting immediately by inserting fingers into throat or by drinking a tumbler of warm water containing 1 tbsp of salt or 1 tsp of mustard. If patient is unconscious, do not give anything by mouth.
4. Persons exhibiting symptoms of chlordane intoxication following excessive exposure should be given a doctor's care immediately. The doctor must be told what materials the formulation contained, how it was applied, and how long the patient was exposed.

TABLE 5.3
Dilution Guide for Chlordane Emulsifiable Concentrates*

		Amounts of chlordane emulsifiable concentrate (balance of final volume is water)	
Chlordane in finished formulation, %	Amount of finished formulation, gal	Using 44–46% chlordane emulsifiable concentrate (4 lb technical chlordane per gallon)	Using 72–75% chlordane emulsifiable concentrate (8 lb technical chlordane per gallon)
	5	0.875 pt	7 fl oz
1	50	4.25 qt	4.25 pt
	100	8.5 qt	4.25 qt
	5	1.75 pt	0.875 pt
2	50	8.5 qt	8.5 pt
	100	17.0 qt	8.5 qt
	5	1.0 qt	17 fl oz
2.5	50	10.5 qt	10.5 pt
	100	5.25 gal	21 qt
	5	2 qt	1 qt
5	50	5.25 gal	10.5 pt
	100	10.5 gal	21 qt

Example To make 100 gal of 2% chlordane using 72% chlordane emulsifiable concentrate, mix 8.5 qt of 72% concentrate with sufficient water to make 100 gal of finished formulation (water used would be 97.875 gal). For liquid equivalents, see Appendix Table A.2.

* By permission of the Velsicol Chemical Corporation.

Note to Attending Physician

Treatment for chlordane intoxication is primarily symptomatic. The following measures have been suggested:

1. An attempt should be made to control nervous symptoms and convulsions by use of sedatives and anticonvulsants. Suggested mate-

rials are phenobarbital, sodium pentabarbital, chloral hydrate plus magnesium sulfate, and cannabis. Use at levels that relieve symptoms but do not interfere with eating or excretion.

2. Definite measures should be taken to encourage appetite. Parenteral feeding should be given if patient is comatose.
3. In cases of intoxication by ingestion, oily laxatives and enemas should be avoided.
4. Provide a quiet place as free from noises or other sources of irritation as possible.
5. Supportive treatment should be given consistent with that used in liver or central-nervous-system impairment.

USE OF DDT AND CHLORDANE

DDT has been banned for use in the United States by the Environmental Protection Agency. Many states have followed the lead of the EPA and have also banned or restricted the use of DDT. However, there seems to be considerable doubt in some scientific quarters that this total ban was either necessary or wise. There are still advocates for the limited use of DDT for special purposes.

We are therefore continuing to include the information and tables on DDT in this publication, without any recommendation for the indiscriminate use of DDT or any other pesticide.

In August 1975, the EPA announced an intention to suspend chlor-

TABLE 5.4
Forms of DDT and Methods of Use with Mist Sprayers

Technical (100 per cent) DDT powder (commercial)

Cannot be added directly to water. Must first be dissolved in a solvent, and then combined with an oil soluble emulsifier (like Triton X-100).

Solvents: Sufficient amounts of kerosene, No. 2 fuel oil, xylene, benzene and other DDT solvents.

***Wettable DDT powders containing 25–50 per cent DDT** (commercial)*

Add directly to water to make a suspension for mist blowers or for hydraulic sprayers. Do not add oil.

***Wettable DDT powders containing 10 per cent DDT** (commercial)*

Use as a dust. Do not use in sprays.

Emulsifiable DDT containing 25–40 per cent DDT (commercial or homemade)

For general use. Add to water or to oil to make any concentration desired for mist blowers or for hydraulic sprayers. Dilute to 4–12 per cent DDT concentration for mist blowers. For hydraulic sprayers use 1–2 pt per 100 gal water. These DDT solutions are ones to which an emulsifier has been added.

DDT solutions containing 4–40 per cent DDT (commercial or homemade)

Do not add directly to water. Do not use "as is" in hydraulic sprayers. Can be added directly to oil for use in mist blowers at 4–12 per cent DDT concentration. Can be diluted with water for mist blowers or hydraulic sprayers after adding one part by volume of emulsifier to each 20 parts of the solution before adding the water.

dane from further production and sale for most uses. This could mean that sometime in the near future a total ban on the manufacture and use of chlordane will be imposed. However, it seems appropriate to continue to include the information on chlordane since we cannot tell how extensive the proposed ban will be and since the handbook is sold in many foreign countries where restrictions imposed by the United States government do not apply. It seems reasonable for these chemicals to be used under strict regulation where safer, shorter-lived, or more efficient alternatives are not available.

Before either DDT or chlordane is used, a check should be made with the local health authorities concerning current laws affecting the use of DDT, chlordane, or any other chemical.

Control of Mosquitoes, Flies, and Small Flying Insects

To control mosquito larvae in standing water, apply Malathion emulsifiable liquid at rate of 13 fl oz (approximately 0.5 lb actual Malathion) per

TABLE 5.5
Quantities of Materials to Use in Making Given Concentrations of DDT for Mist Blowers

Type of DDT spray	Ingredients	Quantities of material for		
		1 gal	10 gal	100 gal
6 per cent suspension	Water	1 gal	10 gal	100 gal
	Wettable powder (50 per cent DDT)	1 lb	10 lb	100 lb
5 per cent solution	Kerosene	1 gal	10 gal	100 gal
	100 per cent technical DDT powder	6.4 oz (0.4 lb)	4 lb	40 lb
6 per cent solution	No. 2 fuel oil	1 gal	10 gal	100 gal
	100 per cent technical DDT powder	0.5 lb (8 oz)	5 lb	50 lb
12 per cent emulsion	Xylene	2.25 pt	2 gal 3 qt	28 gal
	100 per cent technical DDT powder	1 lb	10 lb	100 lb
	Triton X-100	2 fl oz	1.25 pt	12.5 pt
	Water	5.33 pt	6.66 gal	67 gal
6 per cent emulsion	Xylene	1 pt 2 fl oz		14 gal
	100 per cent technical DDT powder	0.5 lb	11.25 pt	50 lb
	Triton X-100	1 fl oz	10 lb	6 pt
	Water	6.5 pt	3 gal	83 gal

acre. Mix in sufficient water or oil to obtain even coverage when applied by air or ground equipment. For control outdoors, use 2% Malathion fog, aerosol, or space spray. For spray. dilute 1 part 57% emulsifiable liquid in 28 parts of a mixture consisting of 4 parts Kerosene solvent and 1 part aromatic hydrocarbon solvent. Repeat applications as necessary.

TABLE 5.6
Dilution Table for DDT Solutions and Emulsions Made from 25% Emulsifiable DDT Solution for Mist Blowers

Per cent	Ingredients	Quantities for			
		1 gal	10 gal	50 gal	100 gal
4	DDT solution (water or oil)	1.25 pt 6.75 pt	11 pt 8 gal 3 pt	6 gal 6 pt 43 gal 2 pt	13.5 gal 86.5 gal
5	DDT solution (water or oil)	1 pt 10 oz 6 pt 6 oz	2 gal 8 gal	10 gal 40 gal	20 gal 80 gal
6	DDT solution (water or oil)	1 qt 3 qt	2.5 gal 7.5 gal	12.5 gal 37.5 gal	25 gal 75 gal
10	DDT solution (water or oil)	3 pt 3 oz 4 pt 13 oz	4 gal 6 gal	20 gal 30 gal	40 gal 60 gal
12	DDT solution (water or oil)	4 pt 4 pt	5 gal 5 gal	25 gal 25 gal	50 gal 50 gal

TABLE 5.7
Preparation of Emulsifiable Stock Formula Containing 0.37 lb of DDT per Pint or 32% DDT by Weight

Ingredient	Quantity for lots of		
	1 gal	10 gal	100 gal
Xylene (xyolo)	6.75 pt	8.5 gal	84.4 gal
100 per cent technical DDT powder	3 lb	30 lb	300 lb
Triton X-100	6 fl oz	3 pt 12 oz	4 gal 5.5 pt

Avoid applying oil-based formulations to valuable ornamental plants; they may be injured. Malathion may be toxic to certain species of fish, particularly in shallow water.

WARNING*

Most pesticides are poisonous! Spray only when pest control is essential and when the pesticide used will not harm people or useful forms of life in the

* Adapted from Subterranean Termites: Their Prevention and Control in Buildings, *USDA Home Gard. Bull.* 64, 1972.

vicinity. Read and follow all directions and safety precautions on labels. Handle carefully and store in original containers with complete labels, out of reach of children, pets, or livestock. Chemicals used for control of pests of shade or ornamental trees and shrubs should be applied in manner that precludes contamination of any agricultural commodity, food, or feed product.

TABLE 5.8
How to Prepare Sprays to Control Adult Mosquitoes Outdoors*

Insecticide	Formulation† Residual spray	Formulation† Space spray	Formulation† Fogs	Preparation‡
Lindane	1% EC			Mix $1\frac{1}{2}$ fl oz of 20% lindane EC with enough water, kerosene, or fuel oil to make 1 qt of spray
	1% WP			Mix $1\frac{1}{4}$ oz of 25% lindane WP with enough water to make 1 qt of spray
		0.5% EC	0.5% EC	Mix $\frac{3}{4}$ fl oz of 20% lindane EC with enough water, kerosene, or fuel oil to make 1 qt of spray
Malathion			3% EC	Mix $1\frac{3}{4}$ fl oz of 55% Malathion EC with enough kerosene or fuel oil to make 1 quart of spray
		2% EC	2% EC	Mix $1\frac{1}{2}$ fl oz of 55% Malathion EC with enough water, kerosene, or fuel oil to make 1 qt of spray §

* From Controlling Mosquitoes: In Your Home and on Your Premises, *USDA Home Gard. Bull.* 84, 1972.

† EC = emulsifiable concentrate; WP = wettable powder

‡ When mixing a wettable powder with water, first make a paste by mixing the powder with a little of the liquid; when lumps disappear, continue to stir and add rest of liquid. Strain before spraying.

§ For use as fogs, mix with kerosene or fuel oil; do not mix with water.

Precautions in Use of Chemicals*

In handling any insecticide, avoid repeated or prolonged contact with skin and inhalation of mists or vapors. Wear clean, dry clothing, and wash hands and face before eating or smoking. Wear freshly laundered clothing daily.

Avoid spilling the insecticide on the skin, and keep it out of the eyes, nose, and mouth. Wash it off the skin immediately with soap and water. If spilled on

* Adapted from Subterranean Termites: Their Prevention and Control in Buildings, *USDA Home Gard. Bull.* 64, 1972.

clothing, remove clothing and wash the contaminated skin thoroughly. Launder clothing before wearing again. If the insecticide gets into the eyes, flush with plenty of water for 5 minutes and get medical attention.

Insecticides should be kept in closed well-labeled containers—never in a soft-drink bottle or other food container. Do not store opened containers of chemicals or leave them unguarded where children or pets can get to them. They should be stored in a dry place where they will not contaminate food or feed and out of reach of children and animals.

TABLE 5.9
Portions of Emulsifiable Stock Formula to Use with Water to Make Given Concentrations of DDT

Per cent of DDT in finished spray	Quantity for lots of			
	1 gal	10 gal	50 gal	100 gal
12	2.7 pt solution 5.3 pt water	3 gal 3 pt solution 6 gal 5 pt water	16.87 gal solution 33.13 gal water	33.3 gal solution 66.25 gal water
10	2.25 pt solution 5.75 pt water	2.8 gal solution 7.2 gal water	14 gal solution 36 gal water	28 gal solution 72 gal water
6	1.35 pt solution 6.65 pt water	13.5 solution 8.5 gal water	8.5 gal solution 41.5 gal water	17 gal solution 8 gal water
5	1.125 pt solution 6.875 pt water	11.25 pt solution 8.6 gal water	7 gal solution 43 gal water	14 gal solution 8 gal water
4	0.9 pt (14.4 oz) solution 7 pt 16 oz water	9 pt solution 8.78 gal water	5.62 gal solution 44.4 gal water	11.25 gal solution 88.75 gal water

When treating soil near buildings, be sure to leave no puddles of treating solution on hard soil surfaces. Also, check children's playthings that may be contaminated and endanger children who may enter the area later.

Do not apply chemicals to the soil where there is a possibility of contaminating drinking water.

Because of the increasing concern for environmental quality, the Federal Environmental Protection Agency and most state regulatory agencies are actively reviewing the need for, and safety of, many pesticidal chemicals. Therefore, anyone planning to use the insecticidal chemicals recommended in this publication should check with local authorities on the current status of federal regulations and state restrictions regarding their use.

PROPER USE OF PESTICIDES*

Whenever there is a choice between chemicals listed for control, the relative hazard and toxicity of a chemical should be considered before deciding which chemical to use. Hazard is the probability or likelihood that harm or injury may occur. Toxicity is the capability to injure living organisms and is an inherent characteristic of the material. Toxicity varies according to the particular organism being considered.

The type of precautionary statement on the label of a pesticide can be used as a general guide to toxicity. The words caution, warning, or poison serve as a quick indicator of the potency of the chemical.

TABLE 5.10
Gallons of 6% DDT Solution or Emulsion to Apply per Acre (Mist-Blower Application)

Insect Species	Gal per acre
Sawflies on pines	2
Green birch leaf aphid	10
Brown-tail moth	2
May beetles	2
Lace bugs on oak and sycamore	2
Green-striped maple worm	3
Tussock moth	2
Fall webworm	1
Orange-striped oak worm	3
Forest tent caterpillar	2
Eastern tent caterpillar	2
Spiny elm caterpillar	2
Gypsy moth	2
Japanese beetle	3
Cankerworm	2
House fly (out of doors)	3
Horn fly (out of doors)	2
Black fly (out of doors)	2
Mosquito (out of doors)	2

Caution Pesticides bearing the word caution as the strongest precautionary indication are relatively low in toxicity and hazard. Protective clothing and and other devices are desirable under conditions of continual or prolonged use but not essential when handling dilute sprays or dusts. If concentrates are absorbed through the skin in large quantities or swallowed, they may be harmful.

Warning Although the word caution may appear on the label, the word warning is also present on labels of more toxic or hazardous materials. They

* Adapted by permission from Clifford S. Chater and Francis W. Holmes, "Insect and Disease Control Guide for Trees and Shrubs," University of Massachusetts and USDA Cooperative Extension Service, 1973.

TABLE 5.11
Amounts of 12% DDT Solution or Emulsion* per Tree for One Mist-Blower Application

Insect	Tree height (ft)						Dates for application (Northeastern states)
	90–80	80–65	65–50	50–35	35–20	20–10	
Brown-tail moth				1 pt	8 oz	4 oz	Aug. 10–25 April 25–May 20
May beetles	2 pt	1 pt 8 oz	1 pt	11 oz	8 oz	4 oz	As soon as adults are abundant
Lace bugs on oak and sycamore	3 pt	2 pt	1 pt	11 oz	8 oz	4 oz	As soon as nymphs are abundant
Green-striped maple worm	1 pt 8 oz	1 pt 8 oz	1 pt	1 pt	1 pt	8 oz	July 15–31
Tussock moth	2 pt	1 pt 8 oz	1 pt	1 pt	8 oz	4 oz	Start treatment when eggs start hatching
Fall webworm	1 pt	1 pt	8 oz	4 oz	2 oz	1 oz	Aug. 1–30
Orange-striped oak worm	1 pt 8 oz	1 pt 8 oz	1 pt	1 pt	1 pt	8 oz	Aug. 1–Sept. 10
Japanese beetle	2 pt	2 pt	2 pt	1 pt	11 oz	8 oz	(a) July 1–15 (b) Aug. 15–30
Forest tent caterpillar	1 pt 8 oz	1 pt	11 oz	8 oz	4 oz	2 oz	Apr. 20–June 7
Eastern tent caterpillar	2 pt	1 pt 8 oz	1 pt	1 pt	8 oz	5 oz	Apr. 5–June 7
Spiny elm caterpillar	2 pt	1.5 pt	1 pt	8 oz	8 oz	4 oz	May 15–June 15
Gypsy moth	1 pt	1 pt	2 pt	4 oz	8 oz	2 oz	Apr. 20–June 10
Canker worm	2 pt	1.5 pt	1 pt	1 pt	5 oz	3 oz	Apr. 25–May 20
Elm leaf beetle	4 pt	3 pt	2 pt	1 pt	8 oz	4 oz	May 1–June 15

* When using 6 per cent DDT concentration, double the volume of liquid given.

may be absorbed through the skin in harmful quantities. In diluted or concentrated form, repeated or prolonged contact with skin, eyes, nose, and mouth should be avoided. Proper protective clothing and devices must be used during mixing and spraying. A respirator should have the proper filter, and the cartridge should be changed frequently. Within this category some chemicals may be more hazardous than others, with the difference due to type of poisoning mechanism, the rapidity with which the chemical is absorbed through the skin, the necessity for ingestion or inhalation, or the tendency for cumulative effects.

Poison Pesticides bearing the word poison on the label must display the skull and crossbones. They are extremely poisonous and may be fatal if swallowed, absorbed through the skin, or inhaled, even in small quantities. All pesticides should be applied only by experienced persons thoroughly familiar with their hazards who will assume full responsibility for their proper and safe use and will comply with all the precautions on the label. Specified protective clothing and equipment must be worn.

Formulations

Emulsifiable concentrates (liquid formulations) are generally preferred because of their ease of handling and mixing and because they do not settle out. Emulsions spread and stick well and usually combine easily with other pesticides although various combinations must be checked for compatibility. They provide the longest residual deposits and resist washing off. Also they perform well in all types of sprayers. However, the solvents in emulsions are more likely to injure plants than the wettable powders or dusts. Of the common materials used to dissolve pesticides, solvents of the xylene type are the safest to plant foliage.

Wettable powders are safer for plants than emulsions because the diluents are inert. However, they cannot be used in mist blowers, and they must be continuously agitated while they are in the sprayer. Wettable powders leave a residue which is sometimes objectionable, and often the powders require extra spreader-sticker to wet the foliage and insects properly. Also, wettable powders do not have as long a residual action on the plants as the emulsifiable concentrates.

Wetting Agents and Spreader-Stickers

Wetting agents and spreader-stickers are incorporated in pesticide formulations by the manufacturer, but often additional wetting material is required to wet plants that have a glossy or waxy surface, e.g., holly and rhododendron, and insects such as mealybugs, scales, and wooly aphids. Most spray mixes will benefit from the addition of a proprietary wetting agent, following directions on the label. Care should be taken to avoid using too much since this may cause excess foaming in the tank and also may produce more runoff on the plant, resulting in less pesticide deposit.

Mist Blowers and Hydraulic Sprayers

Mist blowers are used mostly by municipalities because of their greater speed and lower application cost per tree, and yet they control many pests as well as a hydraulic sprayer. Hydraulic spraying is used mostly by commercial arborists for estate spraying because hose can be extended for some distance from the sprayer. Hydraulic sprayers also do a better job of control on mites and aphids since coverage is more complete. The more concentrated deposits from a mist blower are not so effective against a sucking pest that does not move around much.

Rates for hydraulic spraying are often furnished in volume units per 100 gal. The tree is then sprayed evenly until the spray mix starts to drip off the leaves.

Rates for mist blowers are often furnished in per cent and vary according to the pest to be controlled and the pesticide being used. The rates vary from about 1 to 2% for mites and aphids upward to 12% for dormant elm spraying with methoxychlor for elm bark beetle control.

For general defoliators such as cankerworm or elm leaf beetle, methoxychlor is applied at the concentration of 6%. Large trees are sprayed with a mist blower adjusted to deliver about $\frac{1}{2}$ gal/min. The trees are sprayed for $\frac{1}{2}$ minute to apply the proper amount of deposit. Lower percentages such as 3% carbaryl for elm leaf beetle control are used by simply doubling the application time to 1 minute per tree. Malathion is commonly used at the 2% rate for the pests it controls.

While mist blowers are faster, they are also more sensitive to wind than hydraulic sprayers. A blower cannot operate satisfactorily at wind speeds over 5 m/hr. Night spraying, making use of spotlights, is ideal since there is more likelihood of windless conditions. Also traffic offers less interference in street-tree spraying, and honeybees are not likely to be about.

Toxicity of Pesticides to Bees

Chemicals used to kill harmful insects and other pests are also capable of killing beneficial insects. Foremost among beneficial insects are honeybees, wild bees, and flies, which are necessary for fruit and seed-crop pollination. By understanding the toxicities of various pesticides to bees and following a few basic rules when making pesticide applications, accidental bee poisoning can be reduced or eliminated (see Table 5.12).

1. Bees forage on open flowers; therefore do not apply insecticides to trees or shrubs in full bloom. Avoid drift of sprays and dusts to neighboring areas where bees may be foraging. Often there are annual or perennial flowers in bloom near trees and shrubs which may attract honeybees. White clover is a favorite honey plant that often flowers in lawn areas. Check your area before applying pesticides.
2. Bees require large amounts of fresh drinking water and may be killed in large numbers when they drink from pesticide-contami-

TABLE 5.12
Toxicity of Pesticides to Bees*

High toxicity			
Severe bee kill will result if these pesticides are used during bee activity; remove colonies before application			
Aldrin	Chlordane	Guthion	Phosdrin
Arsenicals	Ciodrin	Heptachlor	phosphamidon
Azodrin	Diazinon	Imidan	Pyramat
Banol	Dicapthon	Isodrin	Sabadilla
Baygon	Dieldrin	Lindane	Sumithion
Baytex	Dimethoate (Cygon)	Malathion	Telodrin
Benzene	Dinitro-*o-sec-*	Metacil	(TEPP)
chloride (BHC)	butylphenol	Methyl parathion	Vapona, DDVP
Bidrin	EPN 300	Methyl trithion	Zectran
Bomyl	Ethyl guthion	Naled (Dibrom)	Zinophos
Carbaryl (Sevin)	Famophos	Parathion	
Moderate toxicity			
These pesticides may be used if dosage and timing are correct; never spray directly on foraging bees or colonies			
Carbophenothion	Di-Syston	Endrin	Phosalone
(Trithion)	Endosulfan	Methyl demeton	tartar emetic
Chlorobenzilate	(Thiodan)	Mirex	
Co-Ral	Endothion	Phorate (Thimet)	
Low toxicity			
These pesticides may be used with minimum danger			
Allethrin	Dexon	Herbisan	Randox
Amitrole	Dicamba (Banvel D)	IPC	Rhothane (TDE)
Aramite	Dichlone (Phygon)	Karathane	Rotenone
Bacillus	Difolatan	Kepone	Ryania
thuringiensis	DiLan	Maneb	Schradan (OMPA)
Binapacryl	Dimite (DMC)	MCPA	Sesamin
(Morocide)	Dinitrocyclohexylphenol	Menazon	Sesone
Bordeaux	(DNOCHP)	Methoxychlor	Silica gel (SG-78)
mixture	Diquat	Monuron	Simazine
Captan	Dodine (Cyprex)	Morestan	Strobane
Chlorbenzide	Dylox (Dipterex)	Mylone	Sulfur
(Miltox)	Dyrene	Nabam (Parzate)	Sulphenone
Copper oxychloride	Eptam	Nemagon	tetradifon (Tedion)
sulphate	Eradex	Neotran	Tetram
Copper 8-	Ethion	nicotine sulfate	Thiram (Arasan)
quinolinolate	Fenson	NPA (Alanap-1)	Toxaphene
Copper sulfate	Ferbam	Olancha clay	Trysben-200
(monohydrated)	Folpet (Phaltan)	Ovex (Ovatran)	2,4,5-T,
Cryolite	Genite 923	Paraquat	2,3,6-TBA
Cuprous oxide	Glyodin (Glyoxide)	Phostex	Vegadex
2,4-D		Pyrethrins	Zineb
Dalapon		Pyrolite	Ziram
Demeton (Systox)			

* Adapted by permission from Clifford S. Chater and Francis W. Holmes, "Insect and Disease Control Guide for Trees and Shrubs," University of Massachusetts and USDA Cooperative Extension Service, 1973.

nated puddles, rainwater, dew on foliage, or honeydew from sucking insects. Bees also may gather water for their colony from a contaminated source.
3. Bees are most active during daylight hours, when temperatures are above 55°F. Applications made at night, in early morning or evening, or during cool cloudy weather when bees are not foraging are less hazardous to bees.
4. Inform the beekeeper and remove colonies from the spray area before applications are made.
5. Dusts are more toxic than sprays, while granular applications are the least hazardous to bees.
6. Aerial application of pesticides is more hazardous to bees than ground application.
7. Do not use carbaryl (Sevin) in any prebloom spray.
4. Clean up spilled chemicals promptly. Keep an inventory of all chemicals. Mark containers with the year the material was purchased. Make certain all labels stay intact on each container.
5. Inform your local fire department of any agricultural chemicals (including fertilizer) stored in quantity.
6. Check the label for any storage instructions or precautions.
7. Post a list of Poison Control Centers near the storage site. Make sure all members and employees are aware of it.

Disposal of Pesticides

1. Check the label for special instructions.
2. Pesticides may be discarded in a refuse disposal area assigned by the local board of health or in a municipal incinerator. The pesticide should be buried at least 18 in. deep under compacted soil. In this way the pesticide is less likely to leach out into water courses and will be out of reach of people and animals. When disposing of pesticides in a dump, select an area that is unlikely to be disturbed by further dump operations.

Organophosphate or hormone-type (2,4-D; 2,4,5-T) pesticides should never be burned since injury to people and/or plants may result. Other pesticides may be burned if they are in a solvent. The burning should be restricted to 1-gal lots at any one time, and care should be taken to avoid the smoke and to avoid drift of this smoke into areas occupied by people. Open burning will not destroy the toxicity of all pesticides. Burning in small amounts under proper atmospheric conditions will lessen the hazards and create less of a problem in the matter of atmospheric pollution with the pesticides and with combustion products of the pesticides and their carriers.

Toxicity of Pesticides to Fish

Pesticides often are much more toxic to fish and the aquatic environment than they are to insects or other animals. It is important to avoid pollution of streams and ponds. The emulsion formulations of pesticides are the most toxic and dusts are least toxic to fish.

The information in Table 5.13 will serve as a guide where fish toxicity is of particular concern.

TABLE 5.13
Toxicity of Pesticides to Fish*

Group 1: Highly toxic		
Concentrations of pesticides from 0.007 to 0.099 ppm (parts per million) in water will cause about 50% mortality of young fish in 1 day		
Azinphosmethyl (Guthion)	Endosulfan (Thiodan)	Perthane
Binapacryl	Lindane	Phorate (Thimet)
Carbophenothion (Trithion)	Methoxychlor	Pyrethrum
Chlordane	Mevinphos (Phosdrin)	Rotenone
Group 2: Moderately toxic		
Concentrations of pesticides from 0.1 to 12 ppm in water will cause about 50% mortality of young fish in 1 day		
Abate	Dicofol (Kelthane)	Methyl trithion
Carbaryl (Sevin)	Di-Syston	Morestan
Chlorobenzilate	Ethion	Naled (Dibrom)
Ciodrin	EPN	Parathion
Demeton	Fenthion	Phosphamidon
Diazinon	Malathion	Tetradifon (Tedion)
Dichlorvos (DDVP)	Methyl parathion	
Group 3: Slightly toxic		
Concentrations above 12 ppm in water will cause about 50% mortality in young fish in 1 day		
	Dimethoate (Cygon)	
	Trichlorfon (Dylox, Dipterex)	

* Adapted by permission from Clifford S. Chater and Francis W. Holmes, "Insect and Disease Control Guide for Trees and Shrubs," University of Massachusetts and USDA Cooperative Extension Service, 1973.

Storage of Pesticides

1. Store in a clean, cool, dry, well-ventilated building. Keep the building locked. The emulsion concentrations should not be exposed to freezing temperatures. This may destroy the emulsion properties, resulting in loss of toxicity and/or serious plant injury. *Do not store weed killers with pesticides.* Mark the storage *Pesticides—keep out.*
2. Do not store pesticides where food, feed, seeds, or water can be contaminated.
3. Keep all pesticides in original containers. *Never put pesticides in empty food or drink containers.*

TABLE 5.14
List of Spray Formulas*

Spray Formula No. 1: 2 gal dormant miscible oil (Sunoco or Scalecide), 1 pt nicotine sulfate (Black Leaf 40) mixed in 100 gal of water. Apply before the buds open. Caution: Do not drench plants, and do not repeat dormant oil sprays. Do not use when temperature is below 40°F or over 70° in the sun.

Spray Formula No. 2: 6 gal dormant miscible oil mixed in 100 gal water. Caution as above.

Spray Formula No. 3: 2 gal summer oil emulsion, or 4 oz Vatsol, 1 pt nicotine sulfate, mixed in 100 gal of water.

Spray Formula No. 4: 10 gal lime-sulfur (liquid) mixed in 100 gal water. Caution: Do not use this formula near buildings, because it will discolor painted surfaces as well as stone and brick. Do not use after an oil spray has been applied to the same plant in the same season.

Spray Formula No. 5: 25 lb dry lime-sulfur in 100 gal water. Caution: Do not use near buildings; see No. 4.

Spray Formula No. 6: 4 lb DDT 50 per cent wettable powder, 2 lb Ovotran 50 per cent wettable powder, 8 oz sticker and spreader (Filmfast) mixed in 100 gal water. Apply just before buds open in the spring. Caution: Heavy applications of DDT may injure the buds and result in a thinning of the foliage.

Spray Formula No. 7: 1 qt DDT 25 per cent emulsion mixed in 100 gal of water. Apply when main leader elongation begins.

Spray Formula No. 8: 1 gal Dinitro Slurry mixed in 100 gal water. Caution: Do not use on evergreens.

Spray Formula No. 9: 3 lb lead arsenate powder, 8 oz spreader and sticker, mixed in 100 gal of water.

Spray Formula No. 10: 5 lb lead arsenate powder, 8 oz spreader and sticker (calcium caseinate) mixed in 100 gal of water. Caution: Magnolias, hemlocks, and box are susceptible to injury by heavy sprays of lead arsenate. Keep away from pastures.

Spray Formula No. 11: 5 lb lead arsenate powder, 1 pt nicotine sulfate, 1 gal summer oil emulsion (Nursery Volck) mixed in 100 gal water. Two sprays are needed for New England conditions, the first about the middle of June and the second 10 days later. The spray should be applied forcibly downward into the bud and needle clusters.

Spray Formula No. 12: 2 lb DDT 50 per cent wettable powder, 2 lb Ovotran 50 per cent wettable powder (or 1 lb 8 oz Aramite 15 per cent wettable powder), 8 oz sticker and spread, mixed in 100 gal water. Caution: Do not use DDT near pools or streams; it is very toxic to fish and aquatic animals. Also keep spray away from grazing animals. Substitute Aramite for Ovotran where dogwood, holly, roses, or privet are included.

Spray Formula No. 13: 4 lb DDT 50 per cent wettable powder, 2 lb Ovotran per cent wettable powder (or 1 lb 8 oz Aramite 15 per cent wettable powder). 8 oz sticker and spreader, mixed in 100 gal water. Two sprays are necessary, the first in May, the second three weeks later, when eggs are hatching. Apply the spray to the underside of leaves

TABLE 5.14

List of Spray Formulas (*Continued*)

where larvae of beetles are feeding. The use of DDT is likely to build up a mite population; therefore include a miticide where necessary.

Spray Formula No. 14: 1 pt nicotine sulfate, 6–8 qt summer oil or 7 lb soap flakes, or 8 oz Vatsol mixed in 100 gal water. Vatsol should be used where insects with a protective covering are to be controlled, or hairy-leaf trees or shrubs are involved. Caution: Do not use oil if the temperature is over 85°F. When soap is used as a spreader, do not apply this combination where there is an arsenical residue on the foliage. It is safer to spray conifers with the above solution during a cool and cloudy day.

Spray Formula No. 15: 2 lb Ovotran 50 per cent wettable powder, or 1 lb 8 oz Aramite 15 per cent wettable powder mixed in 100 gal water. Caution: Foliage may be injured if Ovotran is used on dogwood, holly, roses, or privet. Aramite is fast-acting and is recommended for a quick clean-up of a heavy infestation. Ovotran is slow acting but has a residual action of a month or more.

Spray Formula No. 16: 1 lb lindane 25 per cent wettable powder mixed in 100 gal of water.

Spray Formula No. 17: 16 lb Bordeaux mixture, 8 oz spreader and sticker (potassium oleate), mixed in 100 gal of water. Two or three applications are usually required: first as buds are breaking; second, two weeks later; and third, when leaves are half grown. Caution: Do not use on fruit trees.

Spray Formula No. 18: 3 lb methoxychlor 50 per cent wettable powder, 2 lb DDT 50 per cent wettable powder, 1 lb Ferbam 50 per cent wettable powder, 5 lb micronized sulfur, 1 pt nicotine sulfate, mixed in 100 gal water. Caution: Do not add the nicotine sulfate until time to use the spray.

Spray Formula No. 19: 4 lb chlordane 50 per cent wettable powder mixed in 100 gal water.

Spray Formula No. 20: 8 oz chlordane 50 per cent wettable powder mixed in 100 gal water, to 1000 sq ft of soil, or 5 lb of chlordane 5 per cent dust to 1000 sq ft of soil. This is the soil treatment for grubs and black vine weevil larvae.

Spray Formula No. 21: 6–8 lb toxaphene 25 per cent wettable powder mixed in 100 gal water.

Spray Formula No. 22: Carbon bisulfide (disulfide) or Cyanogas (a calcium cyanide compound). Use carbon bisulfide to control borers tunneling below entry point. Close opening with putty, gum, or plastic wood, after fumigant has been injected. Caution: Carbon bisulfide is highly flammable and explosive. Cyanogas releases hydrocyanic gas, one of the fastest and most powerful poisons known.

Spray Formula No. 23: 1 teaspoonful emulsifiable liquid Malathion per gal water. Thorough, full-coverage applications should be made and repeated as necessary.

Spray Formula No. 24: 2 teaspoonfuls emulsifiable liquid Malathion per gal water. Thorough, full-coverage applications should be made and repeated as necessary.

Spray Formula No. 25: 4 teaspoonfuls emulsifiable liquid Malathion per gal water. Thorough, full-coverage applications should be made and repeated as necessary.

---

* Refer to "a selected List of Pesticides . . ." on page 355 for additional information.

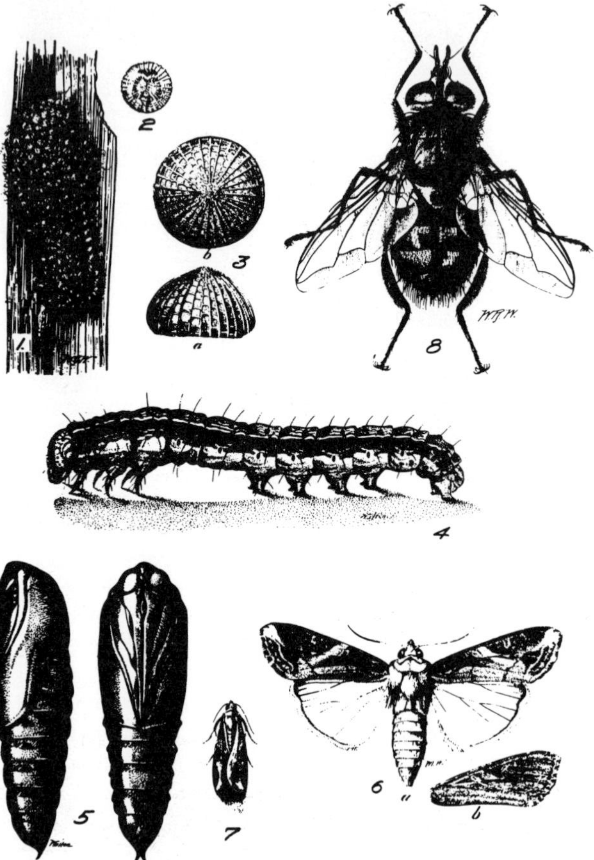

Fig. 5.3 Army cutworm: (1) egg mass; (2) egg about ready to hatch, larva showing through shell; (3)*a*, side view of egg; *b*, egg from above; (4) larva; (5) pupa; (6)*a*, male, *b*, front wing of female; (7) moth in resting position; (8) parasite. (*USDA*.)

Fig. 5.4 Bagworm: larva, pupa, and adult. (*USDA*).

Fig. 5.5 Black vine weevil. (*USDA.*)

Fig. 5.6 Cabbage looper. (*USDA.*)

Fig. 5.7 Carpenter worm. (*USDA*, ***Bureau of Entomology and Plant Quarantine.***)

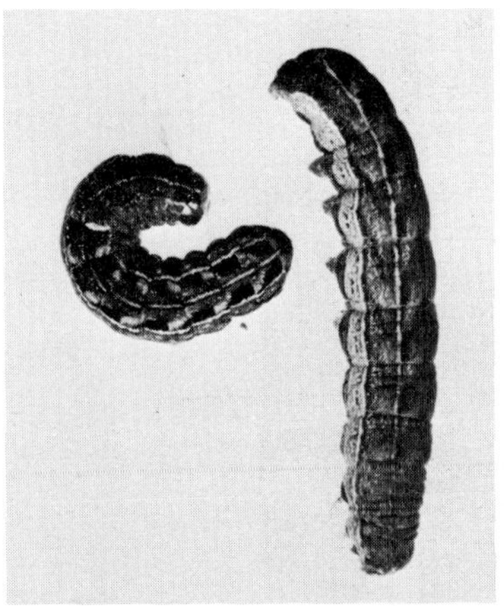

Fig. 5.8 Cutworms. (*USDA*.)

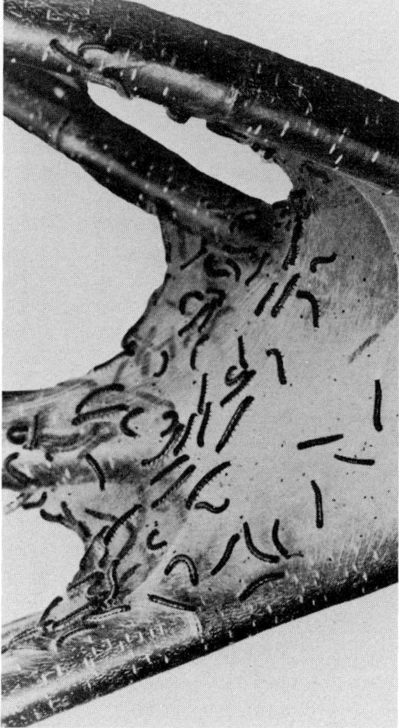

Fig. 5.9 Eastern tent caterpillar on wild cherry. (*USDA.*)

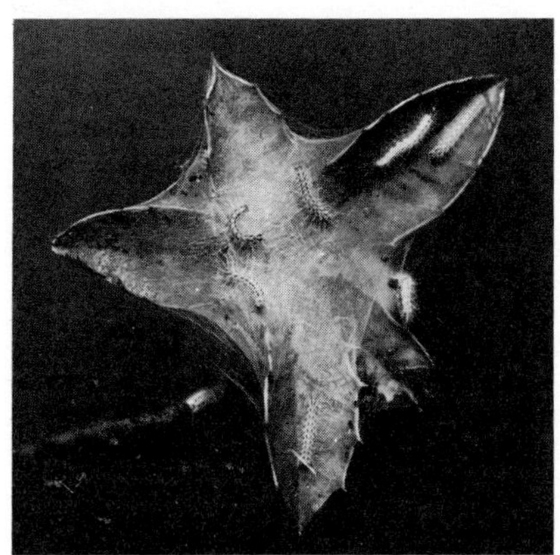

Fig. 5.10 Fall webworms. (*USDA.*)

Fig. 5.11 Fuller's rose beetle. (*USDA.*)

TABLE 5.15
Description and Control of Insects and Disease

Name	Description	Treatment and control
Abbott's pine sawfly	Larvae yellowish, black-headed, black-spotted, and nearly 1 in. long when full grown	*Control* Spray formula 10, 12, or 18
Alder blight aphid	In downward-folded leaves large woolly masses cover bluish-black aphids	*Control* Spray formula 14 when aphids are young
Ambrosia beetle	About $\frac{1}{8}$ in. long; attacks trunks of soft maples, making a vertical gallery about $\frac{1}{16}$ in. in diameter, which extends directly into the wood for several inches and then divides into several branches	*Control* Spray formula 4, 5, or 14; formula 22 also effective in galleries
Antlered maple caterpillars	Caterpillars, which hatch about mid-July and attain full growth in September, are about $1\frac{1}{2}$ in. long, greenish, and variably marked with reddish brown	*Control* Spray formula 10, 11, 12, or 18
Ants		*Treatment* Any type of oil solution, water-emulsion dust, or wettable powder at 2% concentration can be used to control the Argentine ant, crazy ant, fire ant, lawn ant, red harvester ant, and pharaoh ant; since chlordane does not repel ants, complete destruction of the colonies may be obtained; A 3% concentration applied to the nests of the mound-building prairie ant has given 100% control of the entire colony
Aphids	Small, soft-bodied insects, generally wingless; green, yellow, red, or black; produce a sweetish liquid known as honeydew	*Treatment* Treat crevices of bark on twigs of most deciduous plants or undersides of leaves of elm, linden, maple, oak, and many other plants; also twigs; also needles of some conifers

TABLE 5.15
Description and Control of Insects and Diseases (*Continued*)

Name	Description	Treatment and control
		Control Spray formula 2, 5, 11, 14, 18, 23 or dimethoate, Meta-Systox-R, Malathion, or diazinon
Arborvitae leaf miner		*Treatment* Treat all foliage and soil surfaces with carbaryl
Arborvitae weevil		*Treatment* Treat foliage and soil surface of arborvitae, chamaecyparis, and juniper with chlordane
Army cutworm	(Fig. 5.3)	*Treatment* Apply 5% chlordane dust at the rate of 20 to 30 lb/acre; spray of 1 lb chlordane per 100 gal of water also effective
Ash borer	Works just a little below surface of soil, frequently producing irregular dead areas surrounded by deformed bark tissues; young borers work first in sapwood and later enter hardwood	*Control* Spray formula 22; cut and burn all infested shoots
Ash timber beetle	Females usually tunnel the cambium in opposite directions from the entrance point and quickly girdle infested limb; young grubs make slender longitudinal galleries from ½ in. to nearly 2 in. long	*Control* Trim all weak branches and burn infested wood
Asiatic garden beetle	Less than ½ in. long, dull chestnut brown, and looks somewhat like a coffee bean; adults hide in soil during the day and appear at dusk, feeding only at night; foliage becomes ragged; sometimes only midribs are left	*Control* Spray formula 10, 12 or 18; apply 10 lb actual chlordane per acre as a dust or spray and work into soil by cultivation or watering
Azalea bark scale		*Treatment* Treat bark of twigs and branches of azalea, rhododendron, andromeda

TABLE 5.15
Description and Control of Insects and Diseases (*Continued*)

Name	Description	Treatment and control
		Control Spray with Malathion, dimethoate, Meta-Systox-R, or diazinon
Azalea leaf miner	Small yellowish caterpillar, about 1/2 in. long when full grown; until nearly half grown it mines inside the leaves; later folds over the tip or margin of leaf and feeds on surface within this fold; mined leaves turn yellow and drop; the small moths, yellow with purplish markings, deposit their eggs on leaves	*Treatment* Treat foliage, larvae within rolled leaves of azalea *Control* Spray formula 10, 14, 18 or diazinon or Malathion
Bagworms	Can be recognized by spindle-shaped bags hanging on tree each inhabited by a worm; young (one brood per year) appear in May; adults are moths (Fig. 5.4)	*Control* Spray formula 10, 18, 21, or 24; small infestations can be handpicked and destroyed
Balsam twig aphid		*Treatment* Treat twigs of balsam fir and spruce; spray on warm days *Control* Spray with dimethoate or Malathion
Banded ash borer	Beetle about 1/2 in. long, mostly dark purple with narrow yellow lines on the thorax and three yellow bands on the wing covers; grub bores in dying trees and logs of black ash	*Control* Spray formula 22
Barberry aphid	Small yellowish-green aphid usually found on undersides of leaves and tender shoots, where it sucks the sap and weakens the plant; has soft, pear-shaped or nearly globular body and three pairs of comparatively long legs; usually not over 1/8 in. long	*Control* Spray formula 11, 12, 14, or 18

TABLE 5.15
Description and Control of Insects and Diseases (*Continued*)

Name	Description	Treatment and control
Barberry worm	Caterpillars black with white spots; when full grown are about $1\frac{1}{2}$ in. long; form webby, excrement-filled masses on the tips of the shoots, which remain through the winter; moths fly about the first of July, and caterpillars feed on leaves in late summer and fall	*Control* Spray formula 10, 11, or 18
Bark beetle	Seepage of balsam from the trunk, reddening of the needles, and death of the upper parts of the tree result from attacks by this beetle, which is about $\frac{1}{10}$ in. long	*Control* Prune and burn infested parts; spray formula 6 may also give some control
Beech blight aphid	Blue insect covered with white cottony substance; it punctures the bark and extracts the juices	*Control* Spray formula 2, 14, or 18
Beech leaf miner	Larvae small, white worms; adult is small black sawfly	*Control* Spray formula 19, or 23
Beech scale		*Treatment* treat bark of trunk and branches in August and September *Control* Spray with dimethoate, Meta-Systox-R, or Malathion
Birch leaf miner		*Treatment* Treat foliage of white, gray, yellow, and European white birch in May and July; also surface of soil beneath trees to drip line in April and May *Control* For foliage treatment use dimethoate or Meta-Systox-R; for soil treatment use Di-Syston
Black-banded leaf roller	Moth is light brown with dark brown bands obliquely across the forewings; at rest it is flat, somewhat triangular	*Control* Spray formula 10 or 11

TABLE 5.15
Description and Control of Insects and Diseases (*Continued*)

Name	Description	Treatment and control
	and about ½ in. long; larvae feed within rolled or folded leaves	
Black spot	Spots produced by this parasite lead to defoliation and retarded growth	*Control* Spray formula 5 or 18
Black vine weevil	White, grublike larvae feed on rootlets and later strip or girdle bark from outer roots; adults about ⅖ in. long and black, with patches of yellowish hair scattered over the otherwise roughened body; wingless adult females emerge in June and July (Fig. 5.5)	*Control* Spray formula 10, 18, or 20
Black walnut curculio	Pale, reddish weevil is ¼ in. long and covered with a grayish pubescence; causes dropping of young nuts in June, each with a crescent-shaped scar	*Control* Collect and destroy infested nuts
Bladder gall mite	Globular, bladderlike galls about ⅒ in. in diameter, on the upper leaf surfaces produced by white, pink, or red mites, which are 1/125 in. long; galls first green, then red, and finally black; mites live in galls and leaf tissues and winter in scars and wounds on bark	*Control* Spray formula 4 or 5
Bladder maple gall	Small bladderlike galls about ⅒ in. in diameter, green at first, later turning red, produced by a tiny plant mite; sometimes practically cover the upper surface of the leaves	*Control* Spray formula 4 or 5 during or immediately after blossoming period
Blight	Sudden browning and death of single leaves in spring is first blight symptom; later, brown, dead areas along and between veins appear in	*Control* Collect and burn all fallen leaves and twigs; infected parts should also be cut and burned; apply formula 4 in spring before the buds

TABLE 5.15
Description and Control of Insects and Diseases (*Continued*)

Name	Description	Treatment and control
	other leaves; leaves fall prematurely, and the disease completely defoliates the tree	break; fertilize tree heavily to increase its vigor
Blue pine borer	Bluish flattened beetle about ½ in. long bores into dead branches of pine	*Control* Cut and burn badly infested wood
Box-elder bug	Adult is stout grayish-black bug ½ in. long, with three red lines on the back; all stages clustered on bark and branches in the early fall; eggs deposited in bark crevices in the spring	*Treatment* Treat foliage and twigs in June *Control* Spray formula 14 or 18 or carbaryl
Boxwood leaf miner	Injury denoted by oval swelling on underside of leaves, each containing one or more small yellowish-white maggots about ⅛ in. long; adults small yellowish-orange flies resembling gnats or mosquitoes, appearing in early May; leaves show mottled appearance above and below; blister-like effect, which may be light yellow or brown; plants lose leaves first year, become undernourished, have thin foliage, make poor growth, and have an unsightly appearance	*Control* Spray formula 14, 16, 18, or 24; keep plants covered with spray during the period adults emerge, usually in May; treat undersides of leaves in June; also use diazinon or Malathion
Boxwood psyllid	Adult a small dark greenish insect ⅛ in. long, with transparent wings; young covered with a white, waxy material; leaves cupped	*Treatment* Treat undersides of leaves in June *Control* Spray formula 14, or 18 or Malathion
Broad-necked prionus	Full-grown grubs 3 in. long, ½ in. or more in diameter, legless, and white with brown head; infested shoots easily broken off at or a little below the	*Control* Remove and destroy all infested plants

TABLE 5.15
Description and Control of Insects and Diseases (*Continued*)

Name	Description	Treatment and control
	surface of the ground or pulled out; base of stem and thicker roots full of large, irregular, blackened galleries	
Bronze birch borer	White, legless larva, ¾ in. long; adult bronze-colored beetles ½ in. long appear in June	*Treatment* Treat bark of uppermost branches especially; also bark of trunk and main stem, especially white and European white birch *Control* Spray formula 11 or 22 or lindane
Brown-tail moth	Small, firm-webbed nests on tips of twigs in midwinter are characteristic; small reddish caterpillars, about ¼ in. long, begin feeding as leaves push out from buds	*Control* Spray formula 10, 11, 12, or 18
Brown wood borer	Winding galleries in the wood made by white-bodied, black-headed borers, 1¼ in. long; tiny holes in the bark made by emerging shiny brown beetles, ¾ in. long	*Control* Treat all open wounds and avoid mechanical injuries to bark; use formula 22 in galleries
Buck or maia moth	Caterpillars black and shiny; feed on leaves of various oaks, especially in swampy places	*Control* Spray formula 10, 11, 12, or 18
Bud gall	Hard, globular, woody galls in vicinity of buds; formed by small jumping louse	*Control* Spray formula 14 with soap when leaves are one-quarter grown and adults are about
Bull's-eye spot	Spots show distinct target pattern with layers of concentric rings occurring on red, sugar, and silver maples	*Control* Spray formula 17; gather and burn all diseased leaves in fall
Butternut curculio	About ¼ in. long, reddish-brown, ornamented with golden and silvery hairs; grubs work in young shoots and stems in early summer; nuts drop after grubs have fed about 10 days or 2 weeks	*Control* Collect and destroy infested nuts; cut off and destroy infested shoots

TABLE 5.15
Description and Control of Insects and Diseases (*Continued*)

Name	Description	Treatment and control
Cabbage looper	Caterpillar delicate pale green when first hatched; full grown, it is about 1$^3/_8$ in. long and green with a white stripe along each side of the body; adult is medium-sized, grayish-brown moth (Fig. 5.6)	*Control* Spray formula 10, 11, or 18
California oak moth	Longitudinally striped olive green, black, and yellow caterpillars measure 1 to 1$^1/_2$ in. long; moths appear in May and June; second brood in November	*Control* Spray formula 10, 11, 12, or 18
Callous borer	Causes ugly scars on trunks and produces irregular, blackish, gall-like growths on smaller branches; moths in flight from latter part of May to middle of June; full-grown caterpillars whitish, brown-headed, and about $^1/_2$ in. long	*Control* Keep trunks and limbs as smooth as possible; borers should be dug out and the wound treated; formula 22 may also be used
Canker	Most obvious symptom is reduction in number and size of leaves; tree usually dies within a year or two; elongated cankers or sunken areas in the bark cause girdling; wood beneath the cankers marked by reddish-brown to bluish-black streaks	*Control* Diseased trees should be removed and burned; avoid injuries to sound trees
Carpenter worm	Large scars along the trunk and irregularly circular galleries about $^1/_2$ in. in diameter produced by 3-in. pinkish-white caterpillar; the adult moth has wingspread of nearly 3 in. and deposits eggs in crevices or rough spots on bark during June and early July (Fig. 5.7)	*Control* Use formula 22 in tunnels; seal openings; spray the trunks and branches in fall with $^1/_4$ lb sodium arsenite and 1 qt miscible oil in 50 gal water; carbaryl or Imidan may also be used

TABLE 5.15
Description and Control of Insects and Diseases (*Continued*)

Name	Description	Treatment and control
Case bearer	Caterpillar light yellow to green, 1/5 in. long with a black head; adult is brown moth with a wingspread of 2/5 in.; caterpillars mine and shrivel leaves	*Control* Spray formula 5, 12, 16, 18, or 19
Caterpillars	Caterpillars green with pale spots and lines along back and spinelike projections at each end	*Control* Spray formula 10, 12, 16, or 18
Cecropia moth	Larvae 4-in. bluish-green caterpillars with rows of red, yellow, and blue tubercles along body; adult moth has wingspread of nearly 7 in.; brown wings have red-bordered white crossband	*Control* Spray formula 10, 11, or 18
Chiggers		*Control* Water and emulsifiable concentrates have given excellent control of chiggers when used at the rate of 2 lb chlordane per acre; dust applications have also given equivalent control results
Chinch bugs		*Control* Dusts or sprays have given control of chinch bugs when 1 lb actual chlordane is applied per acre; false chinch bug can be controlled in lawns or turf by an application of 6 lb of 5% chlordane dust per 100 ft^2
Citrus whitefly	Adults tiny, pale yellow, with white-powdered wings, similar to those of the greenhouse whitefly; larvae thin, flat, oval, and about 1/8 in. in diameter; nearly transparent; excrete honeydew, upon which an	*Control* Spray formula 14, 18, or 23; 2 or 3 applications at weekly intervals

TABLE 5.15
Description and Control of Insects and Diseases (*Continued*)

Name	Description	Treatment and control
	unsightly mold grows and spoils appearance of leaves	
Cloaked knotty horn	Dark blue beetle, base of the wing covers orange-yellow; about 3/4 in. long; grubs work in stems	*Control* Cutting out and burning infested wood is most practical control
Clover mite		*Treatment* Treat foliage and twigs of honeysuckle, elm (especially English elm) in May and June; *Control* Spray with dicofol or diazinon
Cockroach		*Treatment* A 2% chlordane spray gives approximately 100% kill within 24 to 48 hours; this spray provides a residual surface for 60 to 90 days and is nonrepellent
Cockscomb gall	Feeding of wingless, yellowish-green aphids causes these elongated galls, resembling the comb of a rooster, to form on leaves	*Control* Spray formula 1, 5, 14, or 18
Cone gall	Cone-shaped galls at branch tips produced by small maggots; adult is a small fly and deposits eggs in opening buds	*Control* Spray formula 3 or 14; spray when buds are swelling in the spring; remove and burn galls in fall
Cooley spruce gall aphid		*Treatment* Treat crevices of bark on terminal twigs and bases of buds, principally on blue and Norway spruce and Douglas fir in May and in mid-October *Control* Spray with Malathion, carbaryl, dimethoate, or Meta-Systox-R
Cottonwood borer	Small borers cut bark and prevent sap flow, while larger ones tunnel wood and weaken tree; beetle is 1 1/4 to 1 1/2 in. long, stout, black, with	*Control* Screen base of trees during July and August and treat soil at base with formula 20

TABLE 5.15
Description and Control of Insects and Diseases (*Continued*)

Name	Description	Treatment and control
	irregular strips and patches of cream-colored scales and slender antennae longer than body	
Cottonwood leaf beetle	Beetles are yellowish, about ½ in. long, and variably marked with elongated black spots; dark blackish grubs are about ⅜ in. long; beetles appear in early spring and feed on tender shoots	*Control* Spray formula 10, 12, 16, or 18
Cottony maple scale	¼ in. long, with cottony egg masses protruding from brown scale; sucks undersides of the branches, weakening the tree; adult female appears in late May or June; winter is passed in adult stage	*Treatment* Treat twigs of maple, honey locust, and other deciduous trees in June and July *Control* Spray formula 4, 5, 14, or 18; use only the soap in 14, as oils are not recommended for soft maples; Malathion, carbaryl, dimethoate, or Meta-Systox-R may also be used
Crepe myrtle aphid	Foliage attacked by this aphid becomes unsightly, sticky, and blackened; tree may be completely defoliated	*Control* Spray formula 14 or 18
Cutworms Fig. 5.8		*Treatment* Apply 30 lb of 5% chlordane dust per acre to soil surface or around base of plant; sprays containing chlordane have given equal control, as have 2 oz chlordane added to 50 gal of water; chlordane formulations may also be used in preparing baits
Datana caterpillar	Leaves chewed by the black, yellowish-white striped larva, 2 in. long; adult female cinnamon-brown with dark lines across wings; wingspread is 1½ in.; eggs deposited	*Control* Spray formula 10, 11, 12, or 18

TABLE 5.15
Description and Control of Insects and Diseases (*Continued*)

Name	Description	Treatment and control
	on undersurfaces of leaves	
Dieback	Upper branches progressively die back; cause not known	*Control* Prune affected branches to sound wood and fertilize and water heavily to revitalize tree
Dogwood bark borer	Works in cambium of older bark; occasionally infested area may be over 2 ft long and contain possibly 50 borers; caterpillars winter in outer dead bark; moths appear late in June or July	*Control* Remove and burn old, dead bark after leaves start and before moths appear; bark should not be removed in early spring, when dogwood bleeds
Dogwood borer	Flat-headed borer makes flattened galleries just beneath bark, often completely girdling tree; adults lay eggs in bark crevices in June and July; caterpillars of the clear-winged moth may be encountered working in cambium of limbs and trunk; adults lay eggs in May and June; twig girdler is indicated by cracked and shrunken areas on bark and dying twigs	*Control* Keep trees in good state of vigor; cut out and burn infested twigs and branches; use Formula 22 in burrows; lindane may also be used
Dogwood club-gall	Spindle-shaped or tubular swelling, from $\frac{1}{2}$ to 1 in. long, found at tips or along stems of small twigs, caused by a tiny, two-winged fly or club-gall midge, which deposits eggs in bark in spring; maggot develops inside swelling and deserts gall late in summer	*Control* Cut off and destroy galls soon after formulation
Dogwood sawfly		*Treatment* Treat foliage of wild, shrubby types of dogwood in July and August

TABLE 5.15
Description and Control of Insects and Diseases (*Continued*)

Name	Description	Treatment and control
		Control Spray with carbaryl
Dogwood scale	Trunks and limbs heavily infested with dogwood scale have whitish, scurfy appearance; female scales roughly pear-shaped, grayish, about 1/10 in. long; male scales narrow, with parallel sides; pure white	*Control* Spray formula 1, 3, or 4
Dutch elm disease	Early symptoms are wilting of leaves on one or more branches, followed by yellowing, curling, and dropping of all but a few of leaves at the branch tips about midsummer; in winter tufts of dead, brown leaves adhere to tips of curled twigs; this fungus penetrates tree only through wounds, most commonly made by the bark beetles that carry the disease	*Control* Prune and burn infested wood promptly; strip and burn bark from felled trees; spray with formula 6 just before emergence of beetles in early spring; repeat in midsummer
Eastern spruce gall aphid	Small, conelike swellings or galls produced by this aphid on bases of new shoots; galls usually about 3/4 in. long and resemble miniature pine-apples; tiny, bluish-gray young aphids winter on twigs at base of buds; in spring they develop into wingless adults, about 1/16 in. long, which are soon covered with a white cottony secretion; in August galls turn brownish, and each cell opens, permitting maturing aphids to escape	*Treatment* Treat crevices on ends of twigs and bases of buds in April *Control* Spray formula 1, 3, 5, 14; measure 1 lb of actual chlordane per 100 gal of water; carbaryl, dimethoate, or Meta-Systox-R may also be used
Eastern tent caterpillar	Construct tents in tree forks or crotches in early spring and often	*Treatment* Treat foliage of wild cherry, or choke-cherry, in late April and

TABLE 5.15
Description and Control of Insects and Diseases (*Continued*)

Name	Description	Treatment and control
	strip leaves; reddish-brown moths emerge in early summer and lay eggs in a dark-brown collarlike band that encircles small twigs; eggs hatch following spring; full-grown caterpillar nearly 2 in. long; black to light brown, some with white and blue markings and a white stripe along middle of back (Fig. 5.9)	early May *Control* Spray formula 10, 12, or 18; carbaryl, diazinon, or methoxychlor may also be used
Eight-spotted forester	Reddish, black-ringed caterpillars about 1½ in. long when full-grown; parent insect is black moth with eight large lemon-yellow spots on wings; wings about 1½ in. wide	*Control* Spray formula 10, 12, or 18
Elm bark beetles		*Treatment* Treat bark of twig crotches in tops of trees, also bark of trunks in April *Control* Spray with methoxychlor on suitable days in March and April
Elm borer	White grub, 1 in. long, burrows into inner bark and sapwood and pushes sawdust out through bark crevices; adult a grayish-brown beetle, ½ in. long, with brick-red bands and black spots	*Control* Remove and burn severely infested branches or trees, and fertilize and water weakened trees; use Formula 22 in burrows
Elm case bearer	Tiny larva chews small holes in leaves and mines angular spots between leaf veins; adult a small moth with ½-in. wing-spread	*Treatment* Treat upper and lower surfaces of leaves of English, Scotch, and American elms in May and June *Control* Use spray formula 5, 10, 11, Malathion, or carbaryl
Elm cockscomb gall		*Treatment* Treat foliage of American and slippery

TABLE 5.15
Description and Control of Insects and Diseases (*Continued*)

Name	Description	Treatment and control
		elm when fully expanded in May *Control* Spray with Malathion
Elm leaf beetle		*Treatment* Treat upper and lower surfaces of leaves in June *Control* Spray with carbaryl
Elm leaf miner	Larvae of this small sawfly produce irregular, circular blister mines; shining black sawflies, about $^1/_8$ in. long, deposit eggs in leaves the latter part of May; legless grubs work between upper and lower surfaces of the leaves, emerging in late June or very early in July	*Treatment* Treat foliage of English, Scotch, and Camperdown elms in late May and early June *Control* Spray formula 12, 14, 16, 18, 24 or carbaryl, dimethoate, diazinon, or Meta-Systox-R
Elm sawfly	Cylindrical, coiled, yellowish-white worm with a black line down middle of back; coil has a major diameter of about 1 in.; larva is full-grown in late July or August; winter passed in tough, coarse, silken cocoon at or just below surface of the ground; large wasplike female, about 1 in. long with wingspread of 2 in., has black head and steely blue body	*Control* Spray formula 10, 12, 16, or 18
Elm spanworn	Brownish-black, yellow-marked, looping caterpillars, or measuring worms, with dull reddish or reddish-brown heads; feed early in summer, sometimes defoliating large areas; moths snow white, appearing in July	*Control* Spray formula 10, 11, 12, or 18; Imidan, carbaryl, or methoxychlor may also be used
English walnut scale	Full-grown female scale circular, with a diameter	*Control* Spray formula 2, 4, 5, or 14

TABLE 5.15
Description and Control of Insects and Diseases (*Continued*)

Name	Description	Treatment and control
	of about 1/8 in.; young stay in circle around mother scale	
Euonymus scale	Reddish, woolly-bordered scale insects attack bark; winter as partially developed larvae; young emerge in June and settle on the leaves, where they develop until fall and then migrate to bark; usually not over 1/4 in. long; infestation causes yellow spots on foliage and gives twigs and branches a slate-gray color; severe injury causes leaves to drop off early	*Treatment* Treat twigs and stems of euonymus, bittersweet, and pachysandra in April *Control* Spray formula 2, 5, 8, 14, or 24; ethion oil may also be used
European bark beetle	Adult female, reddish-black beetles 1/10 in. long, deposits eggs along gallery in sapwood; small white larvae tunnel out at right angles to main gallery; tiny holes visible in bark when adult beetles finally emerge	*Control* Remove and burn severely infested branches or trees and fertilize and water weakened trees; use formula 22 in galleries
European canker	Scattered, often numerous, rough, sunken or flattened cankers form prominent ridges of callus wood on trunks and branches; some cankers reach length of 4 ft and width of 2 1/2 ft and have as many as 24 ridges	*Control* All badly infested trees should be felled and cankered tissue cut out and burned; specimen trees may be saved by removing the canker, shellacking edges of wound, and coating wound itself with good wound dressing; fertilize and water to build up resistance to other insects
European elm scale	Elliptical, greenish-brown scale, 1/12 in. in diameter, with woolly fringe around edge; causes yellowing and premature defoliation; young scales	*Treatment* Treat bark, branches, and main trunk of elms in July *Control* Spray formula 2, 3, 5, or 14; Malathion, dimethoate, or Meta-

TABLE 5.15
Description and Control of Insects and Diseases (*Continued*)

Name	Description	Treatment and control
	appear on foliage in June and move to bark in fall	Systox-R may also be used
European fruit lecanium		*Treatment* Treat bark of twigs and small branches of elm, oak, arborvitae, and other hosts in April and foliage in July *Control* Use ethion oil on bark and spray foliage with diazinon or dimethoate
European pine mite	Tiny mites within basal sheath of the needle clusters; infestation can be recognized by thinner crown of paler foliage and distinct orange-brown color of fallen needles	*Control* Spray formula 1, 3, or 15
European pine shoot moth	Brown-bodied, black-headed caterpillar, $^2/_3$ in. long, feeds on lateral shoots of pine, causing them to wilt; adult moth has silvery-banded, reddish-orange frontal wings and brown hind wings, which have a spread of $^3/_4$ in.	*Treatment* Treat small area between buds on terminals and laterals in April; also treat foliage and bark of twigs on Scotch, mugho, and Japanese black pine in July *Control* Remove and burn infested shoots in fall, winter, or early spring; two sprays of formula 11 are recommended for New England conditions, the first about the middle of June and the second about 10 days later; the spray should be forced downward into the bud and needle clusters; use formula 23.
European red mite		*Treatment* Treat twigs and bark of crabapple, mountain ash, and English elm in April; also treat foliage of English elm and flowering fruits in June

TABLE 5.15
Description and Control of Insects and Diseases (*Continued*)

Name	Description	Treatment and control
		Control Use 60- or 70-second oil on bark and dicofol, tetradifon, or chlorobenzilate on foliage
European willow gall midge	Yellowish, jumping maggots cause swollen, distorted twigs; adults appear in early spring	*Control* Prune and burn infested twigs; spray formula 14 or 15
Fall canker worm	Wingless females deposit dark-gray flowerpot-shaped eggs on bark in irregular clusters of 10 to 50 or more; eggs hatch when leaves begin to push out of bud; caterpillars complete growth end of May and are about 1 in. long, mostly black, usually with three narrow white stripes and a broader lemon-yellow stripe on each side; they have three pairs of prolegs	*Control* Spray formula 10, 12, or 18
Fall webworm	Caterpillars spin tent-like web at ends of branches, enclosing foliage, on which they feed; caterpillars are hairy, with long grayish-brown hairs arising from black and orange spots and shorter hairs between; fully grown, they are about 1 in. long, with a broad brownish stripe along back; two generations per year, in late spring and late summer; cocoons spun in protected locations or in soil; satiny white moths which emerge from them lay their eggs in masses on leaves (Fig. 5.10)	*Treatment* Treat foliage of many deciduous trees and shrubs in late July and early August; caterpillar general feeder when populations are high but usually prefers wild cherry *Control* Spray formula 10, 12, 18 or carbaryl, trichlorfon, or diazinon
False pine webworm	About $^{3}/_{4}$ in. long when full-grown and greenish or yellowish-brown; con-	*Control* Cut out worms and webs and use spray formula 10

TABLE 5.15
Description and Control of Insects and Diseases (*Continued*)

Name	Description	Treatment and control
	spicuous antennae and well-developed anal filament; in late summer form webbed masses of greenish or brownish excrement on terminal twigs	
Flatheaded apple tree borers	Slender white grubs have greatly enlarged anterior portion of the body; make wavy flattened galleries in wood; parent insect an inconspicuous, metallic-colored, grayish, flattened beetle about $\frac{1}{2}$ to $\frac{5}{8}$ in. long; it is in flight from latter part of May into September	*Control* Cut out and burn infested or dying wood; use formula 22 in galleries
Flatheaded borer	Adult beetles emerge in late spring and early summer and are attracted to weakened trees, where they lay eggs in bark crevices; grubs make broad, irregular tunnels filled with boring dust; when nearly full-grown, in late fall or spring, they bore into the wood; yellowish-white and legless grub about 1 in. long when mature; body is flattened, and first segment back of head is much broader than rest of body; adult brownish, metallic, flattened beetle about $\frac{1}{2}$ in. long, blunt at anterior end and more pointed at posterior end	*Control* Wrap trunks of newly planted trees with burlap or heavy paper to prevent egg laying on bark; apply wrapping first of May and maintain during first season or two; if borers have entered wood, use formula 22
Flea beetles	Gnaw small holes through leaves from underside, giving shot-hole appearance; when disturbed, they jump away like fleas; most are dark metallic color, about $\frac{1}{5}$ in. long	*Control* Spray formula 12 or 18
Fleas		*Control* Chlordane very toxic to fleas; 0.25%

TABLE 5.15
Description and Control of Insects and Diseases (*Continued*)

Name	Description	Treatment and control
		spray or dip has proved very effective in flea control; chlordane dust (2 or 5%) may also be used
Fletcher scale		*Treatment* Treat foliage and twigs of taxus and arborvitae in April and again in July and September; *Control* In April use 60- or 70-second oil and in July and September use diazinon or dimethoate
Flies		*Control* A 2½% chlordane concentration recommended for general fly control; apply around baseboards, windows, doors, and other appropriate parts of buildings; applications to surface of breeding media have given very good control of larvae
Flower thrips	Thrips enter developing flower buds and feed on tender flower parts, causing petals to become flecked and discolored and flowers deformed; adult tiny, slender, brownish-yellow insect with featherlike wings; extremely active; young lemon-colored	*Control* Spray flowers with tartar emetic solution prepared as follows: 1 oz tartar emetic, 2 oz brown sugar, and 3 gal water; repeat applications twice a week until insect is controlled; use spray formula 23 for additional control
Forest tent caterpillars	Leaves chewed by caterpillar 1½ in. long, bluish-black, with white spots down back; caterpillars mass in large numbers on trunk during day; adult female a brown moth with two dark lines across wings and span of 1½ in.	*Treatment* Treat foliage of maple, elm, and other deciduous trees in May *Control* Spray formula 10, 11, 12, 18, or 24; carbaryl or methoxychlor may also be used
Fuller's rose beetle	Adult beetle feeds mostly at night; larva attacks	*Control* Spray or dust application containing

TABLE 5.15
Description and Control of Insects and Diseases (*Continued*)

Name	Description	Treatment and control
	roots, and beetle feeds on foliage, buds, and flowers; beetle brown or grayish, about 3/8 in. long, with short snout and white diagonal stripe across each side (Fig. 5.11)	50% barium fluosilicate or cryolite or use spray formula 18
Fusiform maple gall	About 1/5 in. long, tapers at both ends, and sometimes very abundant on upper surface of leaves	*Control* Spray formula 4 or 5 just after or during blossoming period
Giant hornet	About 1 in. long, hairy, and black with dark yellowish-orange markings; tears bark from stems and feeds upon sap flowing from wounds	*Control* Locate nests and destroy with formula 22, carbaryl, or lindane
Gloomy scale	Similar to San Jose scale but larger and does not cause reddish discoloration of green tissue; insect very prolific and can encrust a limb in a relatively short time	*Control* Spray formula 2, 4, 5, or 14
Golden oak scale	Infested trees have ragged, untidy appearance; shallow pits formed in bark by circular, greenish-gold scales, 1/16 in. in diameter	*Control* Spray formula 1 or 2
Grasshoppers		*Control* Use 1/2 to 1 lb chlordane per acre as a spray, and 3/4 to 1 1/2 lb per acre as a dust; also 1/2 lb chlordane per 100 lb of wet or dry bait
Green maple worm	Full-grown caterpillars smooth, from 1 to 1 1/2 in. long, rather stout, and light green with yellowish-white stripes along the body and a pale, yellowish-green head; are not usually observed until May or early June, when they are about half-grown	*Control* Spray formula 10, 11, 12, 18, carbaryl, or trichlorfon
Gypsy moth	Fig. 5.12	*Treatment* Treat foliage of oaks, elm, linden,

TABLE 5.15
Description and Control of Insects and Diseases (*Continued*)

Name	Description	Treatment and control
		maples and pines in May *Control* Spray with carbaryl, trichlorfon, Imidan, or *Bacillus thuringiensis*
Hackberry psylla		*Treatment* Treat bark, twigs, or branches in May *Control* Spray with diazinon or carbaryl
Hawthorn leaf miner		*Treatment* Treat upper surface of leaves of the hawthorn in June *Control* Spray with carbaryl, dimethoate, diazinon, or Meta-Systox-R.
Hemlock looper		*Treatment* Treat foliage by spraying with carbaryl or trichlorfon in June
Holly leaf miner	Injury easily recognized by the yellowish or brown serpentine mines in leaves caused by very small fly larvae; larvae winter in leaves; pupation begins around first of April; adults begin to emerge middle of May	*Treatment* Treat upper and undersides of leaves in June *Control* Spray formula 11, 12, 14, 16, 18, or 19; dimethoate or Meta-Systox-R may also be used
Holly scale	Circular and flattened, about $^1/_{16}$ in. in diameter, like other scale insects	*Treatment* Treat leaves and twigs of hollies in April and May *Control* Spray formula 2, 3, 4, or 14; dimethoate or Meta-Systox-R may also be used
Honey locust mite		*Treatment* Treat undersides of leaves on honey locust and moraine locust in July and early part of August *Control* Spray with dicofol or tetradifon
Honeysuckle sawfly	Occasionally strips leaves in spring; larvae resemble hairless caterpillars about 1 in. long when full-grown; somewhat grayish,	*Control* Spray formula 10, 12, or 18

TABLE 5.15
Description and Control of Insects and Diseases (*Continued*)

Name	Description	Treatment and control
	with several yellowish stripes along body and row of black spots down the back; after feeding is completed, they spin cocoons in the soil and remain until spring, when wasplike adults emerge to lay eggs	
Imperial moth	Large, thick, pale green caterpillar about 3 to 4 in. long when full-grown, with pale-orange head and legs and six yellowish spined tubercles behind the head; moth is yellowish, spotted with purplish-brown, and has wingspread of 5½ in.; appears late in August through September	*Control* Spray formula 10, 11, 12, or 18
Imported willow leaf beetle		*Treatment* Treat upper and lower surfaces of leaves of most willows in late May and early June *Control* Spray with carbaryl
Io moth	Caterpillar large and pale green, with delicate markings of yellowish-red; has uniform, rather thick, groups of irritating, sharp, poisonous spines; full length (late summer) about 2 in. (Fig. 5.13)	*Control* Spray formula 10, 11, 12, or 18
Ivory-dotted longhorn	Pale brownish-yellow beetle ½ to 1 in. long, with four double ivory-like spots on wing covers; grubs white and over 1 in. long when full-grown; burrow deeply into limbs and enter heartwood	*Control* Cut out and burn sick or dying wood; use formula 22 in burrows
Japanese beetle	About ½ in. long, approximately size of potato bugs; head and thorax shining brownish-green or	*Control* Spray formula 10 (increased to 6 lb), 12, 18, or 23; carbaryl may also be used; see page

TABLE 5.15
Description and Control of Insects and Diseases (*Continued*)

Name	Description	Treatment and control
	coppery; wing covers brown, tinged with green at edges; conspicuous whitish spots, usually not concealed, on side and at tip of hind body, or abdomen; adults emerge from ground in late June and continue abroad until early October; grubs winter in earthen cells $1\frac{1}{2}$ to 12 in. below the surface (Fig. 5.14)	73 for more details
Japanese beetle larva	Fig. 5.15	*Control* To secure protection for long time 10 lb of chlordane per acre is recommended; if only initial kill is desired, use 5 lb of chlordane per acre
Japanese scale insect	Narrower than the common oystershell scale, only about $\frac{1}{16}$ to $\frac{1}{12}$ in. long, and dull grayish-white	*Control* Spray formula 2, 4, 5, or 14; diazinon, dimethoate, or Meta-Systox-R may also be used
June beetle		*Control* Adults have been controlled by spraying foliage of plants with a chlordane spray consisting of 1 lb per 100 gal of water
Juniper webworm	Larvae small and light brown, striped lengthwise; moths (or adults) appear in June and lay eggs which hatch within 2 weeks; only one brood per year; twigs and needles webbed together, as larvae feed on plants and web them throughout summer, fall, and early spring	*Control* Spray formula 10, 11, 12, or 18; trichlorfor or carbaryl may also be used
Kermes scale	Globular, light-brown scale, $\frac{1}{8}$ in. in diameter; infests terminal twigs and leaves; young scales covered with white down	*Control* Spray formula 2, 4, or 5; carbaryl, diazinon, or Meta-Systox-R may also be used

TABLE 5.15
Description and Control of Insects and Diseases (*Continued*)

Name	Description	Treatment and control
Lace bug	Small, flattened sucking plant bug has white lace-like wings and grayish body underneath; young flattened like adult but lack wings; eggs winter in leaves and bark, hatching in May or early June; upper surface of leaves where they feed takes on a mottled grayish-green color and may become almost white; lower surfaces usually disfigured by black specks	*Control* Spray formula 14, 16, 18, or 23 or carbaryl
Larch case bearer	Affected leaves turn first yellow, then brown, and finally die from attacks of this dark-brown-bodied, black-headed larva, $^1/_5$ in. long; adult female, silvery gray moth with wingspread of $^1/_3$ in., lays cinnamon-colored eggs on leaves in June; larvae winter in tiny cases on branches	*Control* Use Spray formula 4 or 5, trichlorfor, or carbaryl
Larch sawfly		*Control* Spray foliage of larches with carbaryl
Laurel psyllid	Leaves of affected shrubs curl and thicken, galls form, and growth is stunted; young covered with white, cottony, waxy layer; adult $^1/_{12}$ in. long, yellowish-brown; eggs laid in March or April on leaves	*Control* Spray formula 3, 4, or 18
Leaf beetle	Soon after leaves unfurl in spring, rectangular areas are chewed in them by brownish-yellow beetles, $^1/_4$ in. long; later leaves are skeletonized, curl, and dry up as a result of attacks on lower surfaces by black grubs with yellow markings	*Control* Spray formula 10, 12, 13, or 18; use formula 20 to kill masses of grubs around base of tree

TABLE 5.15
Description and Control of Insects and Diseases (*Continued*)

Name	Description	Treatment and control
Leaf blister	Circular, raised areas, ranging up to $^1/_2$ in. in diameter, scattered over upper leaf surfaces; upper surface of bulge is yellowish-white; lower, yellowish-brown	*Control* Gather and burn infected leaves; use formula 17 before rainy periods in spring
Leaf blister fungi	Round galls or blisters formed on leaves; surface of gall or blister becomes reddish or purplish and covered with whitish bloom	*Control* Pick off diseased leaves and burn them or use spray formula 17
Leaf blotch	Small, irregular, slightly discolored, water-soaked spots appear on leaves in spring; later centers of spots become reddish-brown, surrounded by yellow zone that merges into healthy green portion; numerous minute black specks appear in center of the spot on upper surface of the leaf; tree appears as if scorched by fire, and affected leaves drop prematurely	*Control* Spray formula 17; all leaves should be gathered and burned in fall
Leaf cast	Affected needles turn yellow, then brown, and drop prematurely; disease is a fungus, producing elongated black bodies along the middle vein of lower leaf surface	*Control* Spray formula 17
Leafhopper	Slender, delicate insects, usually $^1/_8$ in. long; vary from brown to pale green; eggs laid in leaf tissue or stalks with two or more broods annually (Fig. 5.16)	*Treatment* Treat undersides of leaves in June, July, and August *Control* Spray formula 12, 18, or 23; carbaryl, diazinon, or methoxychlor may also be used
Leaf miner	Yellow or brown serpentine mines or blotches in leaves produced by a small yellowish-white maggot, $^1/_{16}$ in. long;	*Control* Spray formula 11, 12, 14, 16, 18, 19, or 24

TABLE 5.15
Description and Control of Insects and Diseases (*Continued*)

Name	Description	Treatment and control
	adult small black fly that emerges about May 1 and makes slits in the lower leaf surfaces, where it deposits eggs	
Leaf mottle	In spring, small translucent spots surrounded by yellowish-green to white areas appear on young unfurling leaves; spots turn brown and dry; within a few weeks browned areas multiply until the entire leaf looks scorched and leaves drop prematurely	*Control* Provide adequate fertilization to combat disease; protect defoliated branches from sun until second set of leaves develops
Leaf roller	Larvae of several species may be found feeding upon the terminal leaves; roll and bind the leaves together with a silken web, preventing leaves from developing properly (Fig. 5.17)	*Control* Injured twigs should be cut off and burned; use spray formula 12 or 14
Leaf skeletonizer	Lower leaf surface chewed and leaf skeletonized, turning brown; larvae yellowish-green, $^3/_4$ in. long; adult moth has white-lined, brown wings with spread of $^3/_8$ in.	*Control* Spray formula 11, 12, or 14
Leaf spot	Small, gray to brown spots, usually surrounded by purple margin; occur almost entirely on 2-year-old leaves and always more numerous on trees that suffered from drought previous year or growing in unfavorable soil	*Control* Spray formula 17; improve soil conditions
Leaf tier	Leaves tied and matted together by small larvae	*Control* Spray formula 10, 14, or 18 before leaves are matted together
Lecanium scale	Branches and twigs covered with brown, downy half-round scales, $^1/_{16}$ in. in diameter	*Treatment* Treat twigs and small branches in April; treat foliage, upper and undersides

TABLE 5.15
Description and Control of Insects and Diseases (*Continued*)

Name	Description	Treatment and control
		of most trees, in July *Control* Spray formula 2, 3, 4 or 5; 60- or 70-second oil may also be used on twigs and small branches; diazinon or dimethoate may be used on foliage
Leopard moth	Pinkish-white black-spotted larvae, about 2 in. long, tunnel and girdle trunks and branches; adult female has white wings with metallic blue spots and wingspread of $1\frac{1}{2}$ in.; life cycle completed in 2 years	*Control* Prune and burn severely infested branches; use spray formula 22.
Lilac borer	Whitish caterpillar about 1 to $1\frac{1}{4}$ in. long when full-grown; bores in stem, usually near base; moths appear in July or August; larvae tunnel beneath bark and through stems, often girdling or weakening stem so that it dies or breaks off	*Control* Cut out and burn infested shoots; use spray formula 22 in tunnels
Lilac leaf miner	Young caterpillars mine leaves early in June; toward end of month mines are deserted and caterpillars web leaves into curled masses and skeletonize them; first generation completes its development about second week of July; second continues into September	*Treatment* Treat foliage of lilac and privet in May or early June and again in latter part of July and early August *Control* Spray formula 12, 14, 16, or 18; Malathion or carbaryl may also be used
Linden borer	Slender white larva, 1 in. long, making broad tunnels beneath bark near the trunk base or roots; adult is yellowish-brown beetle, $\frac{3}{4}$ in. long, with three dark spots on each wing cover; feeds on green bark	*Control* Spray formula 22 in tunnels

TABLE 5.15
Description and Control of Insects and Diseases (*Continued*)

Name	Description	Treatment and control
Locust borer	Trunks and branches scarred and gnarled, and tunnels mined in the sapwood and heartwood by white larva 1 in. long; adult, black beetle with yellow lines crossing back, emerges in August or September; severely infested trees die back from top	*Treatment* Treat trunk and oldest branches every 3 years in late August and early September *Control* Infested areas on trunk may be treated in late fall or early spring with formula 22 or when new growth starts in the spring; trunk and branches may be sprayed with solution of 4 oz sodium arsenite in 5 gal of water; lindane may also be used in late August or early September
Locust gall maker	Elongated, gall-like swellings, 1 to 3 in. long, produced on twigs by feeding of these pale yellow larvae; adult female is grayish-brown moth with wingspread of $^3/_4$ in.	*Control* Prune and burn infested twigs in August and gather and burn fallen leaves in fall
Locust leaf beetle	Holes observed in leaves in late April may be caused by the locust leaf beetle, black-headed, orange-red beetle, $^1/_4$ in. long, with black stripe down back; leaves turn brown and fall in summer	*Control* Spray formula 10, 11, 12, or 18
Locust leaf miner		*Treatment* Spray foliage of black locust with diazinon, dimethoate, or Malathion in late May or early June and the middle of July
Long-tailed mealybug	About $^1/_5$ in. long when full-grown; oval or elongated bodies covered with white waxy or mealy excretion and usually found in clusters along veins or undersides of leaves or in crevices	*Control* Spray formula 3, 14, 18, or 23

TABLE 5.15
Description and Control of Insects and Diseases (*Continued*)

Name	Description	Treatment and control
	at base of leaf stems; excrete copious quantities of sticky honeydew, in which black sooty mold grows; infestations cause loss of color, wilting, and death of affected parts	
Luna moth	Produces stout apple-green caterpillar about 3 in. long when full-grown and with six rows of small pink hairy tubercles; caterpillars appear in midsummer feeding on tree leaves; moth is light green and long-tailed, with wing-spread of about 4 in.	*Control* Spray formula 10, 11, 12, or 18
Magnolia scale	Underdeveloped leaves and generally weak trees result from attacks by this brown, varnishlike hemispherical scale, $\frac{1}{2}$ in. in diameter, with white waxy covering; young scales appear in August	*Control* Spray formula 1, 3, 5, or 24; second application 2 or 3 weeks after first may be necessary; carbaryl may also be used in early fall
Maple leaf cutter	Irregular oval holes $\frac{1}{10}$ in. in diameter produced in foliage by this little caterpillar, which feeds between the upper and lower surface of the leaf; damage occurs from July until September	*Control* Burn old fallen leaves; use spray formula 11 or 14 in late June or early July
Maple leaf stem borer	Dropping of sugar maple leaves in June results from the work of this yellowish, nearly legless, sawfly larva; about $\frac{1}{3}$ in. long when full-grown, and tunnels leaf stalks, causing leaves to drop from lower branches	*Control* Pick and destroy infected leaves about mid-June; gather infested stems and burn them
Maple nepticula	Causes heavy dropping of Norway maple leaves in June; very lowest part of	*Control* Spray formula 1, 3, or 14

TABLE 5.15
Description and Control of Insects and Diseases (*Continued*)

Name	Description	Treatment and control
	affected leaf stem has variable sooty-black discoloration, and at a point almost exactly ½ in. from the base of leaf stem is minute, elevated, white oval object; insect winters in a pale orange-yellow cocoon about 3/16 in. in diameter, which is spun mostly on bark	
Maple and oak twig pruner	White, cylindrical, conspicuously segmented grub girdles branches 1 in. or less in diameter; adult is slender, grayish-brown, longhorn beetle, ½ in. long; eggs deposited inside twigs in July; larvae winter in fallen twigs	*Control* Collect and burn all fallen twigs in summer and fall
Maple phenacoccus	Cottony masses sheltering the females of this insect abundant in midsummer on undersurfaces of sugar maple leaves; full-grown males migrate to trunk; when numerous, may give it a characteristic chalky appearance; three generations: first brood hatches in June, second in August, and third wintering	*Control* Spray with tobacco-soap preparation when young are crawling in numbers
Maple trumpet skeletonizer	Leaves of red maple folded loosely in August and September; larva lives in a long black, tapering, trumpetlike tube near adjacent skeletonized areas	*Treatment* Treat undersides of leaves in late July and early August *Control* Spray formula 10, 11, 14, 16, or 18; carbaryl may also be used
Mildew	Tips of growing canes are halted in growth and leaves distorted and covered with white spores	*Control* Spray formula 5 or 18
Mosquito		*Control* Chlordane applied at the rate of 0.2 to 0.4 lb/acre has given control of both larvae and adults

TABLE 5.15
Description and Control of Insects and Diseases (*Continued*)

Name	Description	Treatment and control
Mottled willow borer	White legless larvae, ½ in. long, eat through the cambium and wood, producing swollen and knotty limbs; adult beetle, ⅓ in. long, has long snout and grayish-black, mottled wing covers	*Treatment* Treat bark in August and September *Control* Paint injured area in May or early June with paradichlorobenzene and pine oil mixture or treat with lindane or trichlorfon in August and September
Mountain ash sawfly		*Treatment* Spray foliage of the mountain ash with trichlorfon in June
Mourning cloak caterpillars	Clusters strip terminal branches; caterpillars over 2 in. long when full-grown, and spiny, with dull red markings; species also known as spiny elm caterpillar	*Control* Spray formula 10, 12, 16, or 18
Mulberry whitefly	Foliage discolored by these pests, found mostly on lower leaf surfaces; nymphs oval, black, scale-like, with a fringe of white waxy filaments around edges, approximately size of pinhead; adults resemble tiny white moths; attacks may occur from spring to fall	*Control* Spray formula 14, 18, or 23
Native holly leaf miner		*Treatment* Spray foliage of inkberry with dimethoate in August
Needle and twig blight	Needles of current season's growth turn red and shrivel; new twigs blackened and stunted; severely infected trees appear as if scorched by fire or damaged by frost	*Control* Prune and burn infected twigs and apply formula 17 as leaves develop in spring
Needle rusts	In late May or early June some new leaves turn yellow; within 2 weeks shoots turn yellow and droop; most needles then drop from the shoots; branch tips look as if they had been scorched by fire; waxy red linear	*Control* Spray formula 5 but reduce to 4 lb to 50 gal of water; apply at weekly intervals in May

TABLE 5.15
Description and Control of Insects and Diseases (*Continued*)

Name	Description	Treatment and control
	fungus bodies occur on the lower leaf surface, shoots, and cones	
Northern brenthian	Slender grub about $^{3}/_{4}$ in. long and not quite $^{1}/_{20}$ in. thick; bores into solid wood of white oak	*Control* Cut out and burn sick or dying wood; use formula 22 in burrows
Norway maple aphid	Large, hairy, greenish-marked aphids appear on undersides of leaves, and excrete large amounts of honeydew; leaves become badly wrinkled, blackened, and only two-thirds normal size; heavy midsummer leaf drop follows	*Control* Spray formula 11, 14, or 18
Norway maple leafhopper	Numerous small yellow hoppers infest foliage of Norway maples and cause cankerous swelling on twigs; twig damage caused by abundant deposition of eggs just under tender bark, in small oval cells about $^{1}/_{25}$ in. long; surface of such twigs is slightly ridged with numerous small openings	*Control* Spray formula 12, 14, or 18
Oak blotch leaf miner		*Treatment* Treat foliage of red oaks and white oaks with carbaryl or Malathion in June
Oak leaf tier		*Treatment* Treat new opening buds of oaks as larvae hatch with carbaryl in April
Oak mite	Mottled yellow foliage; mites are yellow, brown, or red, and have eight legs	*Control* spray formula 1, 3, 5, 14, or 15
Oak skeletonizer		*Treatment* Treat foliage of red oak group with two applications at 10-day intervals in June and August *Control* Spray with

TABLE 5.15
Description and Control of Insects and Diseases (*Continued*)

Name	Description	Treatment and control
		carbaryl, Imidan, or trichlorfon
Oblique-banded leaf roller	Caterpillar conceals itself by rolling leaf upon which it is feeding and tying terminal leaves together; varies from yellow to pale green and is $^3/_4$ in. long when mature; two generations per year, one in spring and other in late summer	*Control* Dust plants with a mixture of equal parts tobacco dust and pyrethrum powder; make two successive applications, separated by a $^1/_2$-hour interval; first application drives caterpillars from hiding places and second kills them
Obscure scale	Tiny, circular, dark-gray scales, about $^1/_{10}$ in. in diameter, cover bark of twigs and branches	*Control* Spray formula 2, 4, 5, or 14
Ocellate maple leaf gall	Disfigures red maple leaves; galls circular, yellow, eyelike spots about $^3/_8$ in. in diameter, with the center and margin cherry-red	*Control* Spray formula 4 or 5
Oleander scale	Heavily infested plants lose vigor, turn pale, and die; scales usually circular, somewhat flattened, about size of pinhead; male scales tiny and pure white; female scales light buff with a faint tinge of purple, and 2 to 3 times as large as males	*Control* Spray formula 2, 3, 5, or 14
Orange-striped oak worm	Spiny black caterpillars, with four orange-yellow stripes on the back and two along each side, about 2 in. long when full-grown; commonly occur in clusters and appear in midsummer	*Control* Spray formula 10, 11, 12, or 18
Oriental moth caterpillar	Sluglike caterpillars appear in midsummer; about $3^2/_5$ in. long when full-grown, and yellowish, red-marked, blue-spotted, green, and grayish-brown, with groups of large spiny processes at both	*Control* Spray formula 10, 12, or 18 when caterpillars are small

TABLE 5.15
Description and Control of Insects and Diseases (*Continued*)

Name	Description	Treatment and control
	ends; winter in oval cocoons, about 3/4 in. long and with somewhat irregular broad white markings; moths appear in late June or early July	
Oystershell scale	Has shape of miniature oystershell, about 1/8 in. long; brown to brownish-gray; eggs winter under female and hatch into crawling stage about when apple blossoms are falling; second generation produced in July-August (Fig. 5.18)	*Control* Spray formula 2, 3, 5, 14, or 24
Pacific oak twig girdler	Produces small areas of fading yellow-red or brown on the foliage; makes a gallery only a few inches long first year, which may be extended 1/2 ft or more in second year; burrow spirals around branches not over 1/2 in. in diameter, killing part beyond	*Control* Cut out and burn infested twigs about April; use spray formula 14 in June to kill beetles before they deposit eggs
Pales weevil		*Treatment* Treat tender bark of seedling white pine and other conifers up to 18 in. high with lindane in April or September
Pear leaf blister mite	Tiny elongated pest, 1/125 in. long, causes tiny brown blisters on the lower leaf surfaces and premature defoliation	*Control* Spray formula 4 or 18
Peony scale	Usually thin bark grows over these tiny sucking insects, leaving small bumps or swellings on the bark surface; circular, convex, grayish-brown scales, each about 1/10 in. in diameter, found when swellings opened; when	*Control* Spray formula 2, 14, or 18

TABLE 5.15
Description and Control of Insects and Diseases (*Continued*)

Name	Description	Treatment and control
	swellings removed, thin layer of white wax remains; young start hatching about last of March and continue for over a month, remaining exposed for about 4 weeks before bark covers them; only one generation each year	
Pine bark aphid	Causes white woolly patches on trunks and limbs; adult females winter under woolly material; attacks white, Scotch, and Austrian pines	*Control* In April and May spray formula 12, 14, 16, or 18; Malathion, dimethoate, or diazinon may also be used
Pine leaf miner	Full-grown brown larva, about 1/5 in. long, mines the tips of pine needles; injured tips turn yellow and dry up; three generations per year, first appearing in June	*Control* Spray formula 12, 14, 16, or 18
Pine looper		*Treatment* treat foliage of pitch pine with carbaryl latter part of June and in July
Pine needle scale	Tiny elongated white scales appear on the needles during the summer and winter as purplish eggs under female scales; appear on needles of white, red, Scotch, Austrian, mugho, and spruce pines	*Control* In April spray formula 2, 4, 5, 25, dimethoate, or Meta-Systox-R
Pine pitch borer	White larva 1 in. long causes bark to exude masses of pitch; adult is moth; its clear wings have spread of 1 in.	*Control* Remove pitch in early May and crush borers; use formula 22 or paint injured bark with pine oil and paradichlorobenzene (moth balls) mixture
Pine root collar weevil		*Treatment* Treat bark at base of trunk and soil surface 8 in. out from trunk of Scotch, red, and

TABLE 5.15
Description and Control of Insects and Diseases (*Continued*)

Name	Description	Treatment and control
		Austrian pines; treat in June and latter part of August and early September *Control* Spray with lindane
Pine sawfly	Full-grown larva about 1 in. long; head black and body greenish-yellow, with double stripe of brown down the middle of the back, and on either side yellow stripe broken with transverse brown; adults appear in the latter part of April; two broods of larvae, first in May and June and second in August and September	*Treatment* Treat latter part of May, in June, and the early part of July *Control* Spray formula 10, 12 or 18; carbaryl may also be used
Pine spittlebug Fig. 5.19		*Treatment* Treat needles (need long residual) especially white pine, also Scotch, red, Japanese red pine *Control* Use methoxychlor in May and in latter part of July and in August
Pine tortoise scale		*Treatment* Treat twigs on Scotch, Austrian, jack and mugho pines; treat in latter part of May *Control* Use diazinon, dimethoate, or Meta-Systox-R
Pine tube moth	Larvae produce cylindrical tubes of needles webbed together, eating off terminal third of needles almost to uniform height; moths emerge from last of April to middle of July	*Control* Spray formula 11 or 12, carbaryl may also be used in May or July
Pine webworm		*Treatment* Treat needles on red, pitch, white pine and usually on seedlings and in plantations *Control* Use carbaryl in latter part of June, in July, and early in August

TABLE 5.15
Description and Control of Insects and Diseases (*Continued*)

Name	Description	Treatment and control
Plant mites	Cause flower galls, irregular in size and ranging from about $1/4$ to $3/4$ in. in diameter, which eventually dry and remain on the twigs with start of growth in spring	*Control* Spray formula 2, 3, 14, or 15
Poplar borer	Blackened and swollen scars on limbs and trunk and sawdust at base of tree; white larvae $1\frac{1}{4}$ to $1\frac{1}{2}$ in. long at maturity; upper and lower parts of the body have horny points; female is bluish-gray beetle approximately 1 in. long with black spots and yellow patches	*Control* Remove and burn badly infested trees; use formula 22 in tunnels
Poplar curculio	Full-grown borer or grub about $1/2$ in. long, fleshy, white, and legless; ordinarily works within $1/2$ in. of the surface of the branch or trunk; beetle about $1/3$ in. long and black with peculiar tufts of black scales or hairs; tips of the wing covers, sides of the thorax, and portions of the legs pinkish white	*Control* Cut out and burn badly infested trees; use spray formula 3 in midsummer
Poplar sawfly	Orange-yellow larvae black-spotted and nearly 1 in. long when full-grown; broods hatch in June and August	*Control* Spray formula 10, 12 or 18
Privet mite	Small mites swarm on foliage; blood-red eggs usually deposited with the long axis perpendicular to leaf; life cycle completed in 3 weeks, with six or seven generations per year; infestation causes yellowing or fading of leaves	*Control* Spray formula 5, 14, or 15

TABLE 5.15
Description and Control of Insects and Diseases (*Continued*)

Name	Description	Treatment and control
Promethea moth	Large, delicate, bluish-white caterpillars 2½ in. long when full-grown; have four large yellowish or red tubercles on the posterior segments and large ones on eighth abdominal segment; web leaves firmly to stem, draw edges together, and spin firm cocoon	*Control* Pull off and destroy the cocoons; use spray formula 11, 12, 14, or 18
Red cedar bark beetle	Light brown or black beetle about $^1/_{16}$ in. long; excavates vertical galleries	*Control* Control by liberal watering and feeding
Red-headed pine sawfly	Larvae red-headed, dirty yellowish, black spotted, about 1 in. long when full-grown; feed in clusters near tips of branches; first brood occurs in July and second in September	*Control* Spray formula 10, 12, or 18; wet needles thoroughly when spraying with carbaryl in June, July, and August
Red-humped caterpillar	Yellowish and black-striped with red heads and red humps; adult is grayish brown moth with a wingspread of 1¼ in.; caterpillars chew leaves	*Control* Spray formula 10, 11, 12, or 18
Red spider	Leaves assume gray or yellow cast when severely infested by these tiny green, yellow, or red mites, $^1/_{50}$ in. long; infested leaves and twigs occasionally covered with fine silken webs	*Control* Spray formula 1, 5, 14, 15, or 18, or dust with sulfur
Rhododendron clearwing	Leaves wilt as a result of mining inner bark and sapwood of branches and stems by this yellowish-white borer ½ in. long; adult female clearwing moth with wing expanse of ½ in.	*Control* Prune and burn dead or dying stems in fall or winter
Ribbed bud gall	Conical, strongly ribbed, and about $^3/_{16}$ in. long;	*Control* Spray formula 1 or 3

TABLE 5.15
Description and Control of Insects and Diseases (*Continued*)

Name	Description	Treatment and control
	occurs in crowded masses in longitudinal cracks of bark; sweetish secretion exudes from galls in early summer, attracting many bees and flies	
Ribbed pine borer	Grub white, broad-headed, and common under the bark of dead trees; follows work of sawyer beetles; beetle is stout, about $\frac{1}{2}$ in. long, and common in partly rotten bark	*Control* Protect logs by barking or placing in water
Rose aphid	Small greenish lice, clustering on buds, stems, and shoots; deform and kill leaves, buds, and branches	*Control* Spray formula 11, 14, or 18
Rose chafer	Long-legged grayish-brown beetles, about $\frac{1}{2}$ in. long, appear in swarms about when grapes are in bloom; young are grubs and feed on roots and grass	*Control* Difficult to control; spray consisting of 4 lb arsenate of lead and 1 gal molasses in 50 gal of water is recommended or 5% chlordane dust; thoroughly wetting foliage with a residual spray such as carbaryl also effective
Rose curculio	Black-snouted beetle about $\frac{1}{4}$ in. long, bright red above; snout and under portions of body black; injures roses by puncturing buds and eating numerous holes in them	*Control* Spray formula 10, 11, or 18; injured rosebuds should be collected and destroyed before Sept. 1
Rose leaf beetle	Shiny green beetle, about $\frac{1}{8}$ in. long, eats buds and partly opened flowers	*Control* Spray formula 10 or 18
Rose midge	Fragile, two-winged fly about $\frac{1}{16}$ in. long, yellowish, with the head and anterior of body brownish; tiny, white maggots distort leaves and blast buds	*Control* Nightly fumigations with nicotine or cyanide will help; also keep soil covered with layer of tobacco dust about $\frac{1}{4}$ in. deep

TABLE 5.15
Description and Control of Insects and Diseases (*Continued*)

Name	Description	Treatment and control
Rose slugs	Several species of small greenish sluglike or coiled larvae; some species feed on upper surfaces of leaves; others on lower; adults four-winged flies, and because some have more than one brood, damage may occur throughout summer	*Control* Spray formula 10, 11, 14, or 18; carbaryl may also be used on upper and lower surfaces of foliage in May and June
Rose stem girdler	Elongated stem swellings frequently marked with longitudinal lines; leaves of infested canes turn yellow and finally wither, and stem dies; beetle is metallic-colored and is abroad during June and July	*Control* Spray formula 14 or 18; infested canes should be cut and burned as soon as detected
Rust mites		*Treatment* Treat upper and lower leaf surfaces of elm, oak, maple, honey locust, and lilac in June, August, and September *Control* Use dicofol, chlorobenzilate, or tetradifon
Saddleback caterpillar	Leaves chewed by black, yellowish-white striped larva, 2 in. long; adult female is cinnamon brown with dark lines across the wings and wingspread of $1\frac{1}{2}$ in.; upper wings dark reddish-brown; lower, light grayish-brown	*Control* Spray formula 10, 11, 12, or 18
San Jose scale	Twigs, branches, or stems covered with grayish layer of tiny overlapping waxy scales; injury indicated by dead or dying branches, poor vigor, and thin foliage; waxy scale covering the female insect is circular,	*Control* Spray formula 2, 3, 5, or 14; use 5 in spring before the buds open and 14 in late spring or summer

TABLE 5.15
Description and Control of Insects and Diseases (*Continued*)

Name	Description	Treatment and control
	grayish, about $^{1}/_{16}$ in. in diameter, with slight elevation, or nipple, near center; male scale smaller and more oval; insects winter in partly grown condition, when scale is nearly black; two to six generations produced annually (Fig. 5.20)	
Sassafras weevil		*Treatment* Treat foliage of sassafras and magnolia with carbaryl in May and June
Satin moth	Moths winter in small very inconspicuous silken pockets on the bark of the branches and trunk; full-grown caterpillars about 2 in. long, with a bluish-black head and a black body, with irregular white markings and spots down middle	*Control* Spray formula 10, 12, or 18; carbaryl may also be used on foliage in June and August
Sawfly	Leaves chewed by olive-green larvae, $^{3}/_{4}$ to 1 in. long, covered with small brown spines; adult is wasplike fly with wingspread of $^{4}/_{5}$ in.	*Control* Gather and burn fallen needles; use spray formula 10, 12, or 18
Sawyer	Large white fleshy grubs, about $1^{1}/_{2}$ to 2 in. long, work in the inner bark, sapwood, and heartwood of dying pines; grayish beetles about $^{3}/_{4}$ to $1^{1}/_{2}$ in. long, and the antennae measure from 2 to 3 in. additional	*Control* Protect logs by barking or placing in water
Scotch pine scale insect	Cherry-red to reddish-brown, about $^{1}/_{8}$ in. long	*Control* Spray formula 2 or 4
Scurfy scale	Irregular white oval, about $^{1}/_{10}$ in. long; insects winter in egg stage	*Control* Spray formula 2, 3, or 24; two applications should be made of 3, one just when young are appearing and another 10 days later

TABLE 5.15
Description and Control of Insects and Diseases (*Continued*)

Name	Description	Treatment and control
Sitka spruce gall	Exceed ½ to 3 in. in length and usually include entire new shoot; galls open early in July and cause yellow spots and bend in needles	*Control* Spray formula 1, 3, 5, or 14
Snowball aphid		*Treatment* Treat foliage of viburnum with diazinon, dimethoate, or Meta-Systox-R in May
Sod webworm	See fall webworm for description	*Control* Use 4 lb of 50% chlordane wettable powder in 100 gal of water; apply at rate of 6 to 7 gal per 1000 ft^2
Soft scale, also known as soft brown scale	Soft, greenish-brown or yellowish-green, often with marbled or ridged effect across back; oval, rather flat, nearly ⅛ in. long; twigs and leaves encrusted and take on a lumpy appearance; scales produce large quantities of honeydew, on which sooty fungus develops	*Control* Spray formula 2, 5, 14, or 24
Sphinx caterpillar	Two types: (1) brown, with black and yellow dottings and short rough tail horn; (2) either green or brown, with spot resembling eye at posterior end; both types about 3 in. long when full-grown	*Control* Not usually abundant enough to make control measures necessary; however, spray formula 10, 12, or 18 will control
Spider mites	Tiny, yellow, green, or red eight-legged mites about 1/64 in. long; foliage of injured plants takes on grayish, mottled appearance (Fig. 5.21)	*Control* Spray formula 18 or 24 or thoroughly dust or spray with sulfur compounds
Spiny elm caterpillar	Spiny, black with reddish markings, about 2 in. long when full-grown, with conspicuous rows of spines; parent butterfly maroon, with blue-spotted black wings bordered with yellow	*Control* Spray formula 11, 12, or 18

TABLE 5.15
Description and Control of Insects and Diseases (*Continued*)

Name	Description	Treatment and control
Spiny oak worm	Caterpillar bright tawny or orange with dusky stripe along back and prominent spines on thoracic segments	*Control* Spray formula 10, 11, 12, or 18
Spittlebug	Spittlelike substance covering needles and twigs produced by young of spittlebug, a frog-shaped brown insect, ⅜ in. long; eggs deposited the fall; young hatch following spring	*Control* Spray formula 3 or 14
Spotted hemlock borer	Wide, shallow galleries in inner bark and sapwood result from boring by white larvae ½ in. long; adult, flat metallic-looking beetle with three circular, reddish-yellow spots on each wing cover, deposits eggs in bark crevices	*Control* Prune and burn badly infested branches; keep tree vigorous by fertilizing and watering
Spring cankerworms	Yellowish-green oval eggs deposited in early spring by wingless females in irregular piles or clusters on trunks and branches; eggs laid about when leaves begin to push out of bud; caterpillars complete growth end of May; about 1 in. long, vary in color from light mottled yellowish-brown to dull black, with only two pairs of prolegs	*Control* Spray formula 1, 3, or 5
Spruce bud scale	Globular red scales, about ⅛ in. in diameter, occasionally infest twigs of Norway spruce	*Control* Spray formula 1, 3 or 5; also treat bark of twigs with diazinon, dimethoate, or Meta-Systox-R in late June and early July
Spruce budworm	Mature caterpillar about ⅛ in., rather thick, dark-brown body with yellowish-white parts;	*Control* Spray formula 10 or 11 as soon as new shoots begin to develop in spring or while cater-

TABLE 5.15
Description and Control of Insects and Diseases (*Continued*)

Name	Description	Treatment and control
	moth dull gray with brown or red markings on wings; flies during June and July; caterpillars feed by boring into opening buds and later on needles, which are cut off and held together with silken threads	pillars are still feeding on needles
Spruce cone worm	Cones disfigured with masses of webbed borings; occasionally a bunch of cones may be fastened together	*Control* Collect and burn diseased cones
Spruce gall aphid	Two different galls occur on spruce, the spruce cone gall (1) and Sitka spruce gall (2); (1) occurs as many-celled gall at base of Norway spruce shoots; galls about ¾ in. long and resemble miniature cones; (2) occurs on blue, Sitka, and Engelmann spruce; also many-celled but found on terminal shoots rather than at base of shoots	*Control* Spray formula 1, 3, 5, 14, or 18
Spruce mite		*Treatment* Thoroughly wet the needles and bark of arborvitae, hemlock, spruce, juniper, retinospora, and pines in April with dicofol or tetradifon
Spruce needle miners	Mature caterpillars about ⅓ in., reddish-brown or green, with shiny yellow-brown heads; small brown adult moths appear in May and June, bore into and mine the needles, and later cut off mined needles and web them together into a nest of silken strands	*Control* Spray formula 11 or 12; wash the webs loose from the tree with strong stream of water; begin at uppermost webs and work downward; treatment should be made in March, before leaf buds begin swelling, or in late fall before cold weather sets in

TABLE 5.15
Description and Control of Insects and Diseases (*Continued*)

Name	Description	Treatment and control
Spruce sawfly	About ½ in. long, dark green, striped with darker green, and has dark head; defoliates trees in midsummer and early fall	*Control* Spray formula 10, 12, or 18
Spruce spider mite	Plants have a rusty and unhealthy appearance caused by mites sucking juices; abundant accumulation of webbing; mite resembles common red spider; young pale green, adults dark green or nearly black; particularly injurious and abundant during hot dry seasons and often most serious in spring and fall	*Control* Spray formula 1, 11, 18, or 24
Stem borer	Grubs yellow, less than 1 in. long, with a swollen thoracic region; top of thickened first segment has a crown of short, conspicuous, dark-brown spines; beetles fly about the time plants in bloom; tips of the stem girdled, usually after plants bloom; young larvae hollow out stem and push borings out through surface holes	*Control* Cutting out and burning infested stems is most practical method of control; formula 22 may also be used
Sugar maple borer	Wide channels in inner bark and sapwood of the trunk and larger branches made by pinkish-white larvae 2 in. long; adult beetle 1 in. long, velvety black with yellow markings; bark above infested area dies, leaving large scars	*Control* Prune and burn infested parts by June 1 and inject a nicotine paste into remaining tunnels; lindane may also be used by thoroughly wetting bark in August
Tar spot	Yellow spots appear on the leaves during late May, then turn reddish-brown and finally black by fall; narrow border of yellow	*Control* Preventive sprays of formula 17 applied at 2-week intervals in late spring should keep this disease in check

TABLE 5.15
Description and Control of Insects and Diseases (*Continued*)

Name	Description	Treatment and control
	tissue remains around darkened spots	
Taxus bud mite		*Treatment* Treat twigs and buds of taxus in May and June with diazinon
Taxus mealybug		*Treatment* Treat bark of trunk, large branches, small branches and twigs in May and June *Control* Use ethion oil for trunk; carbaryl or Malathion for small branches and twigs
Tent caterpillars		*Treatment* Treat foliage immediately following bud break on wild cherry, maple and oaks *Control* Spray in April and May with methoxychlor or carbaryl
Termites		*Treatment* Use 1 gal of 0.5–2.0% chlordane–water solution per linear foot; apply to soil in trench 1 to 2 ft deep; treat soil as trench is refilled
Terrapin scale	Clusters of reddish-brown, terrapin-shaped female scales, $\frac{1}{8}$ in. long; sooty mold develops on secretions	*Control* Spray formula 4, 5, or 14; do not use oil on soft maples
Thorn-leaf aphid	Usually pink or yellow-green, attacks young leaves early in spring, causing them to curl; soft, with pear-shaped or nearly globular bodies and three pairs of comparatively long legs	*Control* Spray formula 14, 18, or 23
Thorn limb-borer	Oval swellings, about 1 in. long, and marked with four or five longitudinal scars, appear on small limbs and stems; cinnamon-brown, white-marked beetle appears in last week of May or early	*Control* Prune out diseased parts and burn them

TABLE 5.15
Description and Control of Insects and Diseases (*Continued*)

Name	Description	Treatment and control
	June; grub bores in outer layer of wood	
Thrips	Fig. 5.22	*Control* Sprays using 1 lb chlordane in 100 gal water have been very effective in control of various species of thrips; equivalent control results have been obtained by dust applications
Tick		*Control* Applications of 1 to 2 lb chlordane dust or sprays per acre have proved very effective in controlling ticks; complete coverage bordering paths and roadways is necessary
Trunk decay	Trunks often show a white or brown decay of the heartwood; hard, gray, hoof-shaped fruiting bodies up to 8 in. wide form along the trunk in vicinity of decay; latter forms soft, fleshy, shelf-like fruiting structures, orange-red above and bright yellow below; fruiting bodies become hard, brittle, and dirty white with age	*Control* Clean out the badly decayed portions and apply good wound dressing; maintain vigor by fertilizing and watering
Tulip scale	Trees may be killed by heavy infestations of oval, turtle-shaped, often wrinkled, brown scales, $\frac{1}{3}$ in. in diameter; secretion from scales drops on leaves and soon is covered by sooty-black fungus growth	*Control* Spray formula 1 or 2; diazinon, dimethoate, or Meta-Systox-R may also be used on foliage in April
Tulip spot gall	Minute gall midge or fragile, yellow gnatlike fly about $\frac{1}{8}$ in. long	*Control* Spray formula 1, 14, or 15
Tussock moths	Fig. 5.23	*Treatment* Treat foliage with carbaryl in May and June

TABLE 5.15
Description and Control of Insects and Diseases (*Continued*)

Name	Description	Treatment and control
Twig blight	Tips of the twigs die, turning light tan; minute black fruiting bodies pushed through epidermis of leaves and twigs and spread from there; blight prevalent in wet periods	*Control* Spray formula 17; prune off and burn dying twigs
Twig girdler	Larvae ½ in. long girdles twigs, causing them to be broken off by wind; adult is reddish-brown beetle ¾ in. long (Fig. 5.24)	*Control* Gather and burn severed branches and twigs in autumn or early spring
Two-lined chestnut borer	White, flat-headed larvae, ½ in. long, form tortuous galleries underneath bark; adult is slender, greenish-black beetle ⅜ in. long, appearing in late June	*Control* Cut down and burn all badly infested trees. Increase vigor of remaining trees by fertilizing and watering
Two-marked treehopper	Numerous snow-white frothy masses approximately ¼ in. long and ⅛ in. wide appear on smaller stems as protective matter placed over the point where eggs are laid; adults brownish-black with two white spots; when resting upon shoots they look like thorns; eggs hatch in May	*Control* Spray formula 5, 12, 14, or 18
Two-spotted spider mite		*Treatment* Treat undersides of leaves on elm, linden, rose, ornamental fruit trees *Control* Spray latter part of May and early June and latter part of July and early August with dicofol or tetradifon
Walnut aphid	Light-yellow plant louse with black markings on antennae, legs, and abdomen; winter passed as eggs, which hatch in February and March	*Control* Spray formula 11, 14, 18, or 23

TABLE 5.15
Description and Control of Insects and Diseases (*Continued*)

Name	Description	Treatment and control
Walnut datana	Trees defoliated by a black caterpillar (growing to 2 in. long) covered with long white hairs; adult female moth has a wingspread of 1½ in.; dark-buff wings crossed by four brown lines	*Control* Spray formula 10, 11, or 18
Walnut husk maggot	Produces blackened hulls which are slimy within and contain numerous whitish maggots; parent fly dark yellow with brown-banded wings, about size of housefly	*Control* Spray formula 10, 11, 12, or 18
Walnut scale	Round brown scales, ⅛ in. in diameter, appear in masses; adult female frequently encircled by young scales	*Control* Spray formula 2 or 4
Wasps (hornets, yellow jackets, and mud daubers), white grubs		*Treatment* Use a 5 or 6% chlordane dust, 2% oil spray, or 2 tbsp of 75% emulsifiable chlordane solution in 1 qt of water; apply to nest openings at night; at rate of 5–10 lb/acre chlordane has given control of white grubs; amount of insecticide required depends upon type of soil
White-banded elm leafhopper		*Treatment* Treat undersides of leaves with methoxychlor in June and July
White blotch oakleaf miner	Larva ⅓ in. long feeds between leaf surfaces, producing white, blotched patches on leaves; adult female is small moth with white forewings and silvery hindwings, with a spread of ¼ in.	*Control* Gather and burn leaves; use spray formula 11, 14, 16, or 18
Whitefly	Leaves usually sticky from honeydew secreted by tiny black young, which look like oval scales	*Control* Spray formula 14 or 18

TABLE 5.15
Description and Control of Insects and Diseases (*Continued*)

Name	Description	Treatment and control
	about $1/35$ in. long; adults tiny white flies that dart away when leaves are disturbed	
White-marked tussock moth	Full-grown caterpillar, nearly 2 in. long, has a red head and is marked with yellow and black; three long black tufts, two at front end and one at rear; insects winter in conspicuous egg masses, which are covered by a white frothy substance about $1/2$ in. in diameter	*Control* Spray formula 10, 11, 12, or 18
White peach scale	Bark covered with tiny white scales; female scale circular, nearly $1/10$ in. in diameter, and gray with a yellow center; male scale smaller, more oval, elongated, and pure white; clusters of white male scales often noticeable near base of branches	*Control* Spray formula 2, 3, or 5; dimethoate, diazinon, or Meta-Systox-R may also be used in June and July on bark and twigs
White pine aphid		*Treatment* Treat twigs and small branches of white pine with diazinon or Malathion in May
White pine weevil	Leader shoot wilts and dies as a result of girdling inner bark by a white, legless form, $1/3$ in. long; adult is reddish-brown beetle, about $1/2$ in. long, mottled with brown and white scales; adult hibernates in ground litter	*Control* Spray formula 5, 7, or 18; remove and burn infested leader shoots in spring; lindane may also be used in April
Willow flea weevil		*Treatment* Treat upper surface of willow foliage mined by larvae in May and June with carbaryl
Willow leaf beetle	Holes chewed in the leaves by blue, metallic adult form, $1/8$ in. long; leaves are skeletonized by black larvae, $1/4$ in. long	*Control* Spray formula 3, 4, 5, or 14

TABLE 5.15
Description and Control of Insects and Diseases (*Continued*)

Name	Description	Treatment and control
Willow scale	Pear-shaped white scale, ⅛ in. long; eggs winter under scale of female	*Control* Spray formula 3, 4, 5, or 14
Willow scurfy scale	Purplish-red eggs carry insect over winter, young appearing in late May or early June	*Control* Spray formula 1, 4, or 5
Willow-shoot sawfly	Adult is wasplike insect which lays eggs in shoots in early spring, then girdles shoot below point of deposition; larva feeds in pith, causing terminal shoots to wilt	*Control* Prune and burn infested twigs; use formula 10 or 12
Willow twig aphid		*Treatment* Treat small twigs and branches of willows in August with diazinon, dimethoate, or Meta-Systox-R
Wilt	Leaves on one limb or several suddenly wilt and die and usually fall; infection of entire tree may result in small, sparse, sickly foliage; sometimes entire side of a tree is killed during winter and fails to leaf out in spring; presence in sapwood of bright green streaks, turning to bluish-black and brown, is positive identification of wilt	*Control* Trees showing a severe infestation cannot be saved and should be cut down and burned; mild cases can be corrected by judicious pruning and application of high-nitrogen fertilizers
Wireworm		*Control* Chlordane applied at ½–5 lb/acre gives control of wireworms; correct dosage depends upon type of soil; in some areas, side dressing has been sufficient to give control; a solution of 2–4 oz of chlordane per 50 gal of transplant water has given protection; chlordane can be incorporated with fertilizers
Witches'-broom	Visible on buds during winter; affected buds are	*Control* Prune back all infected twigs to sound

TABLE 5.15
Description and Control of Insects and Diseases (*Continued*)

Name	Description	Treatment and control
	larger, more open, and hairier than normal ones; branches break off more readily, exposing wood to decay	wood and spray with 1 part sulfur in 10 parts water in early spring
Woolly aphids	Clusters on tips of new shoots kill tips back to 6 or 8 in.	*Control* More difficult to kill than most common aphids; make sprays stronger and apply as coarse driving spray in order to penetrate waxy covering on body of aphid; use formula 14, 18, or 23
Woolly beech aphid	Leaves curled and blighted by an insect with cottony cover; cast skins adhere to lower leaf surface	*Control* Spray formula 2, 14, or 18; treat undersides of leaves with diazinon, Malathion, dimethoate, or Meta-Systox-R
Woolly elm aphid		*Treatment* Treat bark, buds, and foliage of elm; migrates in June to apple, pear, quince, and hawthorn *Control* Spray in May with Malathion
Woolly larch aphid	White woolly patches adhering to needles hide adult aphids	*Control* Spray formula 4, 5, 14, 18, or 23; Malathion may also be used
Yellow-spotted willow slug	Greenish-black sawfly or false caterpillar, ½ in. when full-grown, with heart-shaped yellow spots on each side; first signs of infestation are blister-like swellings containing eggs on upper surface of leaves; young slugs eat small holes and usually feed near each other; growth completed in 10 days to 3 weeks; full-grown caterpillars slaty-black with lighter spots on sides; change to adult occurs in dark-brown cocoons on or near surface of ground	*Control* Spray formula 10, 11, 16, or 18

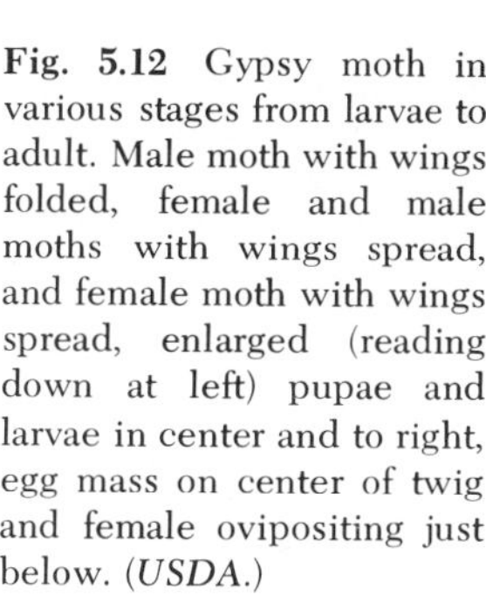

Fig. 5.12 Gypsy moth in various stages from larvae to adult. Male moth with wings folded, female and male moths with wings spread, and female moth with wings spread, enlarged (reading down at left) pupae and larvae in center and to right, egg mass on center of twig and female ovipositing just below. (*USDA*.)

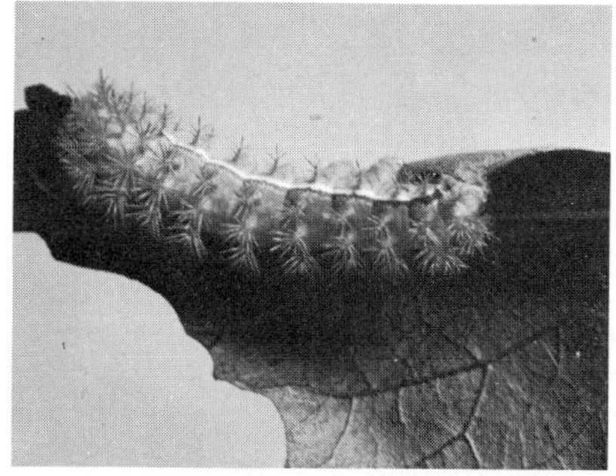

Fig. 5.13 Io moth: (*a*) caterpillar, (*b*) pupa, (*c*) adult male, (*d*) adult female. (*USDA*.)

Fig. 5.14 Adult Japanese beetle. (*USDA.*)

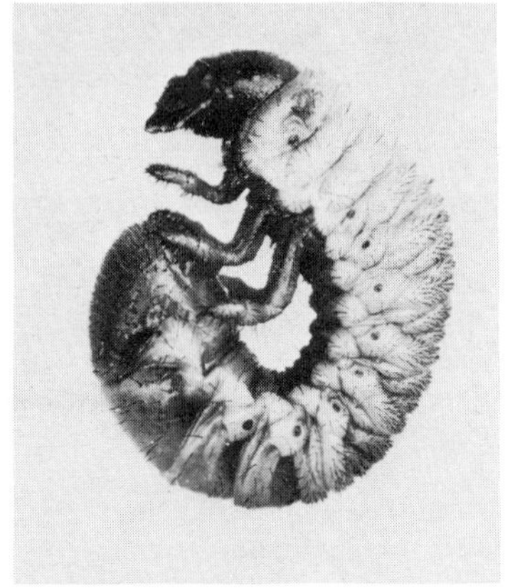

Fig. 5.15 Japanese beetle larva. (*USDA.*)

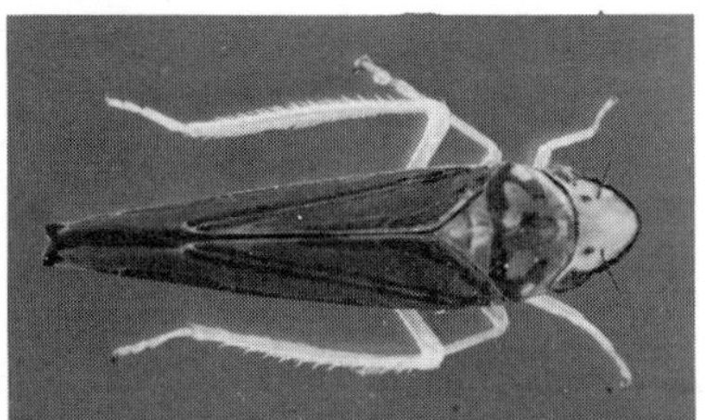

Fig. 5.16 A leafhopper, greatly enlarged. (*USDA.*)

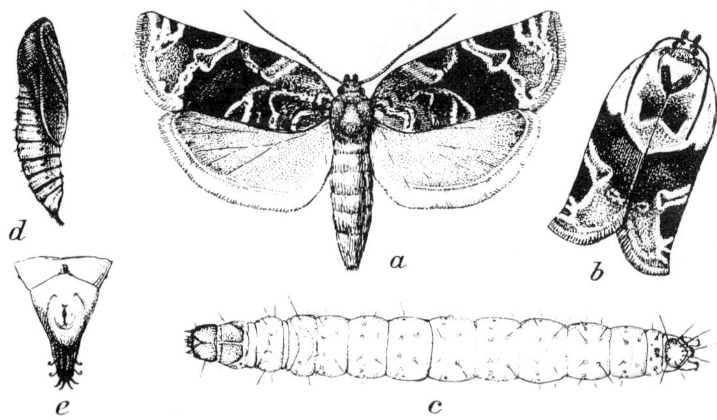

Fig. 5.17 Red-banded leaf roller. (*USDA.*)

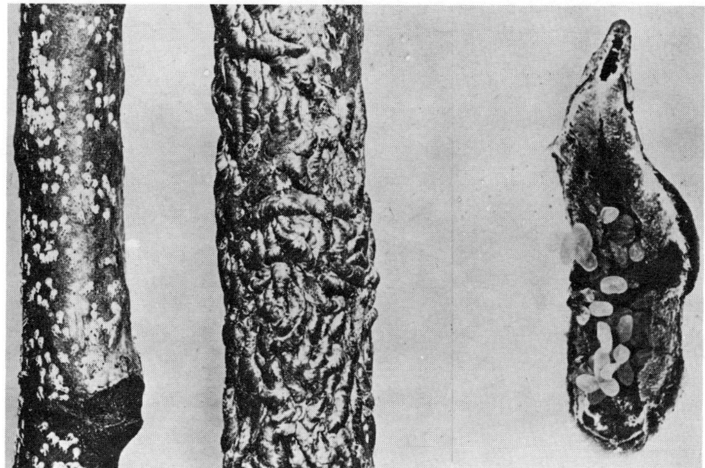

Fig. 5.18 Young and mature oystershell scales and scale turned over to show eggs. (*USDA.*)

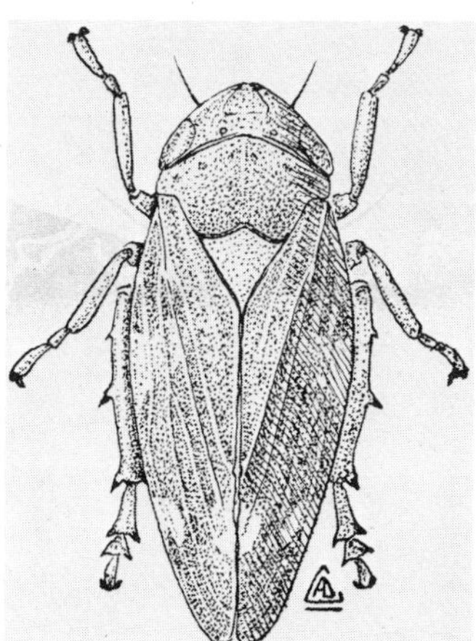

Fig. 5.19 Adult spittlebug. (*USDA.*)

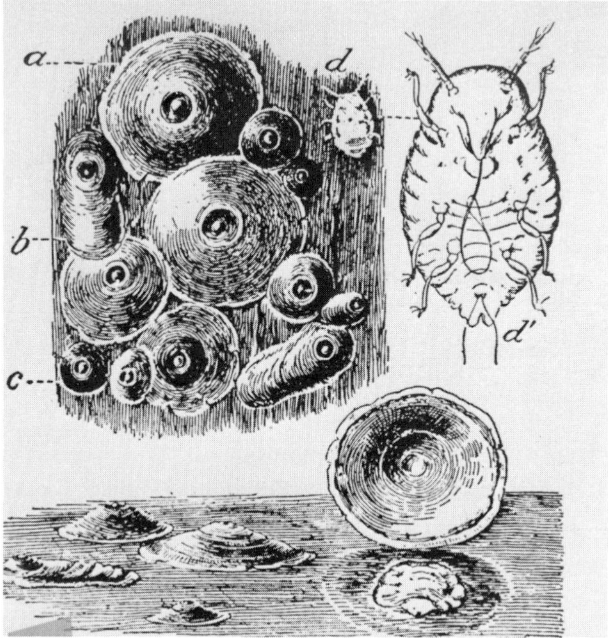

Fig. 5.20 San Jose scale: *a*, adult female scale; *b*, male scale; *c*, young scales; *d*, larva just hatched; *d*, same highly magnified, *e*, scale removed, showing body of female beneath. All much enlarged. (*Quaintance*) (*USDA*.)

Fig. 5.21 Common red spider mite. (*USDA*.)

Fig. 5.22 A typical flower thrip. These tiny insects feed on opening flowers, causing them to turn brown. (*USDA*.)

Fig. 5.23 Tussock moth. Larva. (*USDA*.)

Fig. 5.24 Twig girdler. (*USDA*.)

A SELECTED LIST OF PESTICIDES REGISTERED AND PERMITTED FOR USE ON TREES AND SHRUBS IN MASSACHUSETTS*

INSECTICIDES

Biologicals

Bacillus thuringiensis (Thuricide) A microbial insecticide which is nontoxic and nonpathogenic to man and warm-blooded animals, fish, and honeybees but which is capable of inducing fatal disease in certain insects, mostly caterpillars. On the basis of evidence to date, this bacillus is harmless to parasitic and predatory insects and other forms of life. Useful against such insects as cankerworms, fall webworms, linden looper; also gives some control of tent caterpillars. Has occasionally given erratic performance. Insects stop eating promptly but require a few days to die. May be used in a mist blower.

Chlorinated Hydrocarbons, Long-lasting

Chlordane Not permitted for use on foliage pests but may be used against Japanese beetle and other turf insects, carpenter ants, black vine weevil, and other principally boring insects.

Endosulfan (*Thiodan*†) Labeled to prohibit drift in residential areas. May be used in nurseries, etc., or applied by paintbrush in residential areas. One of

* For other states check your local health board. Adapted by permission from Clifford S. Chater and Francis W. Holmes, "Insect and Disease Control Guide for Trees and Shrubs," University of Massachusetts and USDA Cooperative Extension Service, 1973.

† Trade name.

the longest-lasting aphicides available. Also effective against many borers, e.g., dogwood, rhododendron, lilac, and peach. Will control many leaf defoliators, beetle larvae, and eriophyid mites. Highly toxic.

Lindane Use limited to white pine weevil, turpentine beetles, bronze birch borer, rhododendron borer, and other borers. Not approved for foliage application.

Methoxychlor The only material currently available for elm bark beetle control, but complete coverage is essential. May cause staining of cemetery headstones. Highly polished stone is more susceptible than rough-finished stone. Also may be very difficult to remove from car finishes. Staining and spotting may be largely eliminated through greater care in application. Effective against elm leaf beetle, white-banded elm leafhopper (which is the vector of phloem necrosis), and many other chewing insects.

Organic Phosphates, Short-lived

Diazinon Effective against a wide range of insects with some action against mites. Controls aphids, leafhoppers, pine-shoot moths, webworms, whiteflies, and scale crawlers.

Dimethoate (Cygon)* A contact systemic insecticide-miticide for control of holly leaf miner, birch leaf miner, and some other kinds of miners, spruce gall aphid, scale crawlers, Nantucket pine-tip moth, and other insects, and some mites. Will not prevent unsightly egg-laying punctures by holly leaf miner flies, but the mines will not develop. Some foliage injury has been reported at higher dosages on some kinds of ornamentals.

Disulfoton (DiSyston)* A highly toxic systemic insecticide useful for the control of aphids, birch leaf miner, lace bug, leafhoppers, mites, pine-tip moths, and thrips. These are principally granular formulations intended for ground application. A 10% granular formulation is available which is restricted to commercial use.

Imidan Newly registered for shade-tree use to combat gypsy moth, elm spanworm, spring cankerworm, and other pests.

Trichlorfon (Dylox)* A nonpersistent phosphate insecticide of moderate toxicity to people. Kills insects mainly as a stomach poison and therefore has little effect on other beneficial predatory insects. Dylox is most effective against caterpillars or worm-type insects and may be used as an alternate material for carbaryl (Sevin) or lead arsenate for many pests. Should not promote aphid or mite buildup, as many pesticides do. Has given effective con-

* Trade name.

trol of the oak leaf skeletonizer. *Caution:* Use only at the lower recommended dose rate to avoid possibility of burning.

Malathion Effective against many kinds of insects, including aphids, mealybugs, scale crawlers, lace bugs, some leaf miners, and young stages of caterpillars. Has short residual action, and so timing of applications must be very accurate. Relatively *ineffective* against mites. Does not keep well in storage and breaks down very rapidly when mixed with water.

*Meta-Systox-R** A contact systemic insecticide-miticide now widely available under a number of brand labels; effective against mites and a wide range of insects including aphids, leafhoppers, birch and holly leaf miners, and scale insects. Used mainly as a spray. For limited use against defoliating caterpillars.

Petroleums

Petroleum Oil Dormant application is often useful against most scale insects, mite eggs, and some insect eggs. Use dormant oils when spray will dry quickly and when temperature is between 40 and 75°F and not expected to go to 32°F within 24 hours. If one cannot be sure of nonfreezing night temperatures, morning applications are preferred. *Blue spruce and Douglas fir are particularly sensitive to applications of oil.* All evergreens are somewhat sensitive to oil, and overdosage is hazardous. Also, trees in poor condition are likely to be susceptible to oil injury. Never make more than one dormant application per season. Apply only while trees are still dormant; late application of oils designed for dormant use injures trees of many species. Not practical for use in a mist blower. Oils with a viscosity of 60 to 70 seconds are effective and have a greater margin of safety than oils of 100 or more seconds viscosity. Application every third year on some trees may be considered desirable.

Ethion Oil A 60-second oil containing a small percentage of ethion. Ethion is a highly toxic phosphate insecticide-miticide that is very effective against mites, aphids, and scale insects. Combined with oil for dormant use, it is very effective against these pests. Do not mix with other materials.

Carbamates, Fairly Long Lasting

Carbaryl (Sevin)* Useful against many kinds of insects, including lace bugs, periodical cicada, caterpillars, earwigs, and some scale crawlers, some aphids, and some leaf miners. Particularly effective against Japanese beetle adults, elm leaf beetle, and birch leaf miner. Very toxic to honeybees. Avoid application to blossoms, particularly white clover and linden. Produces severe injury or death to Boston ivy and Virginia creeper. May injure tender foliage of

* Trade name.

annuals, perennials, and some shrubs under poor drying conditions. Contributes to a buildup of mites.

Acaricides (For mites only; will not kill insects)

Chlorobenzilate*	Ovex (Ovotran*)
Dicofol (Kelthane*)	Tetradifon (Tedion*)
Genite*	Morestan*

Fungicides†

Benomyl (*Benlate*‡) A new systemic fungicide having both curative and preventive properties. Reported to be effective for a number of diseases, including certain leaf diseases of trees and ornamentals. Currently being tested for control of Dutch elm disease. Water-soluble derivatives are not currently available for use.

Captan Useful against many leaf and stem diseases, brown rot, and sooty mold but ***not*** powdery mildew or rusts.

Copper, fixed A preventive fungicide useful against nursery blight on juniper and pine-tip blights.

Cycloheximide (*Acti-dione-TFG*‡) An antibiotic systemic fungicide available in various formulations. Use the formulation designed for use on trees and shrubs. May be used both as a preventive and restrictive treatment against hawthorn leaf blight disease. Applications made to immature leaves may cause defoliation. Handle with caution, and follow all label recommendations.

Dodine (*Cyprex*‡) Mainly a preventive fungicide with some curative values. Useful for hawthorn leaf blight and for scab control on ornamental crabapples.

Ferbam A preventive carbamate fungicide. Effective against many leaf spots. Especially useful against rusts.

Folpet (*Phaltan*‡) A preventive fungicide. Useful in controlling many leaf and stem diseases.

Karathane‡ Very effective against powdery mildew of ornamental plantings. Some action against mites. Useful instead of sulfur in hot weather to avoid plant injury.

* Trade name. Apply pesticides only to plants listed on labels to avoid injury.

† For use with insecticides or separate application; consult the labels.

‡ Trade name.

Streptomycin An antibiotic fungicide useful in control of bacterial diseases, such as fireblight and bacterial blight of lilac.

Sulfur An inorganic material effective against powdery mildew. May cause injury in hot weather. Do not use on *viburnum*. Darkens house paints that contain lead.

Thiram Useful against many leaf spots, rots, and rusts. It also has some deer- and rabbit-repellent properties, but to remain effective long, it must be applied with a sticking agent.

Zineb A preventive carbamate fungicide. Useful in controlling many leaf and stem diseases. Will control hawthorn leaf spot.

PESTICIDES NOT PERMITTED FOR USE ON TREES AND SHRUBS IN MANY AREAS OF THE COUNTRY

Aldrin
DDD
DDT
Dieldrin
Endrin
Heptachlor
Toxaphene

Lindane and chlordane are not permitted for use against pests which are principally leaf defoliators but may be used against boring insects. Chlordane may be used on turf. Since endosulfan (Thiodan) is labeled only for use where it will not drift onto people or dwellings, its use is largely limited to nonresidential areas.

Tables of Equivalents

From Appendix Table A.2 equivalent amounts can be read or calculated in terms of standard units of liquid measure, or measuring units such as cups, tablespoons, and teaspoons. For accurate measurements of small quantities, a graduated cylinder should be used and amounts determined in milliliters.

Table 5.16 can be used to determine equivalent amounts of liquid concentrate to be used in making up various quantities of spray. If the recommendation states the number of pounds of pure insecticide in a certain number of gallons, look on the label of the container for the number of pounds of actual toxicant per gallon. Convert this amount to the number of pints, quarts, or gallons in order to use the table.

To determine how much liquid concentrate is necessary for treating various surface areas, follow the procedure above. For example, if 10 lb of actual chlordane is required per acre and your 75% chlordane concentrate contains 8.0 lb of actual chlordane, 5 qt of 75% chlordane concentrate will be required per acre. For lesser amounts, the amount to use can be determined from the table.

TABLE 5.16
Equivalents for Various Dosages of Liquid Concentrates*

Spray, gal	Amount† of concentrate recommended for 100 gal or 1 acre						Portion of acre	Ft²
100	½ pt	1 pt	1½ pt	1 qt	1½ qt	3 qt	1	43,560
50	½ cup	1 cup	1½ cup	2 cups	3 cups	3 pt	½	21,780
25	¼ cup	½ cup	¾ cup	1 cup	1½ cups	3 cups	¼	10,890
12	2 tbsp	4 tbsp	6 tbsp	½ cup	¾ cup	1½ cups	⅛	5,445
6	1 tbsp	2 tbsp	3 tbsp	4 tbsp	6 tbsp	¾ cup	1/16	2,722
3	½ tbsp	1 tbsp	1½ tbsp	2 tbsp	3 tbsp	6 tbsp	1/32	1,361
1½	¾ tsp	1½ tsp	2¼ tsp	1 tbsp	1½ tbsp	3 tbsp	1/64	680
	1½ tsp	2¼ tsp	3½ tsp	5 tsp	2½ tbsp	5 tbsp		1,000

* Adapted by permission from Clifford S. Chater and Francis W. Holmes, "Insect and Disease Control Guide for Trees and Shrubs," University of Massachusetts and USDA Cooperative Extension Service, 1973.
† Amounts given are approximations for general field use.

Rules of thumb for quick field calculations:

100 gal of water weighs about 800 lb (1 gal weighs 8.34 lb).
1 tsp of EC in 1 gal is equivalent to 1 pt of EC in 100 gal.
1 tbsp of WP in 1 gal is equivalent to 1 lb of WP in 100 gal.

Use Tables 5.17 and 5.18 for convenient conversion to percentages of active material in a desired spray.

TABLE 5.17
Dilution for Wettable Powders (WP)*

For numerous pesticide formulations it is often more convenient to make recommendations in percentage than to list each formulation with recommended amounts. To prepare a spray of a desired percentage of active material only the formulation is needed to use the chart. For example, a 0.125% methoxychlor spray may be wanted for elm leaf beetle control. To make a 0.125% spray using a 50% WP, mix 2 lb in 100 gal of water.

Formulation, % WP	Amount of spray, gal	Actual chemical wanted							
		0.313%	0.625%	0.125%	0.25%	0.5%	1.0%	2.0%	3.0%
15	1	2 1/2 tsp	5 tsp	10 tsp	7 tbsp	1 cup	2 cups	4 cups	5 cups
	100	1 2/3 lb	3 1/3 lb	6 2/3 lb	13 1/3 lb	26 2/3 lb	53 1/3 lb	106 2/3 lb	160 lb
25	1	1 1/2 tsp	3 tsp	6 tsp	12 tsp	8 tbsp	1 cup	2 cups	3 cups
	100	1 lb	2 lb	4 lb	8 lb	16 lb	32 lb	64 lb	96 lb
40	1	1 tsp	2 tsp	4 tsp	8 tsp	5 tbsp	10 tbsp	1 1/4 cups	2 cups
	100	5/8 lb	1 1/4 lb	2 1/2 lb	5 lb	10 lb	20 lb	40 lb	60 lb
50	1	3/4 tsp	1 1/2 tsp	3 tsp	6 tsp	4 tbsp	8 tbsp	1 cup	1 1/2 cups
	100	1/2 lb	1 lb	2 lb	4 lb	8 lb	16 lb	32 lb	48 lb
75	1	1/2 tsp	1 tsp	2 tsp	4 tsp	8 tsp	5 tbsp	10 tbsp	1 cup
	100	1/3 lb	2/3 lb	1 1/3 lb	2 2/3 lb	5 1/3 lb	10 2/3 lb	21 1/3 lb	53 1/2 lb

* Reproduced by permission from Clifford S. Chater and Francis W. Holmes, "Insect and Disease Control Guide for Trees and Shrubs," University of Massachusetts and USDA Cooperative Extension Service, 1973.

TABLE 5.18
Dilution for Emulsifiable Concentrates (EC)*

For numerous pesticide formulations, it is often more convenient to make recommendations in percentage than to list each formulation with recommended amounts. To prepare a spray of a desired percentage of active material only the formulation is needed to use the chart. For example, a 2% methoxychlor spray may be wanted for elm bark beetle control for a Dutch elm disease control program using a hydraulic sprayer. To make a 2% methoxychlor spray using a 25% EC, mix 8 gal with enough water to make 100 gal of spray.

Formulation		Amount of	Actual chemical wanted							
% EC	lb actual/gal	spray, gal	0.0313%	0.625%	0.125%	0.25%	0.5%	1.0%	2.0%	3.0%
10–12	1	1	2 tsp	4 tsp	8 tsp	16 tsp	10 tbsp	2/3 pt	1 1/3 pt	1 qt
		100	2 pt	4 pt	1 gal	2 gal	4 gal	8 gal	16 gal	24 gal
15–20	1	1	1 1/2 tsp	3 tsp	6 tsp	12 tsp	7 1/2 tbsp	1/2 pt	1 pt	1 1/2 pt
		100	1 1/2 pt	3 pt	6 pt	1 1/2 gal	3 gal	6 gal	12 gal	18 gal
25	2	1	1 tsp	2 tsp	4 tsp	8 tsp	5 tbsp	10 tbsp	2/3 pt	3/4 pt
		100	1 pt	2 pt	4 pt	1 gal	2 gal	4 gal	8 gal	12 gal
33–35	3	1	3/4 tsp	1 1/2 tsp	3 tsp	6 tsp	4 tbsp	8 tbsp	1/2 pt	3/4 pt
		100	3/4 pt	1 1/2 pt	3 pt	6 pt	1 1/2 gal	3 gal	6 gal	9 gal
40–50	4	1	1/2 tsp	1 tsp	2 tsp	4 tsp	8 tsp	5 tbsp	10 tbsp	1/2 pt
		100	1/2 pt	1 pt	2 pt	4 pt	1 gal	2 gal	4 gal	6 gal
57	5	1	7/16 tsp	7/8 tsp	1 3/4 tsp	3 1/2 tsp	7 tsp	4 1/2 tbsp	9 tbsp	14 tbsp
		100	7/16 pt	7/8 pt	1 3/4 pt	3 1/2 pt	7 pt	1 3/4 gal	3 1/2 gal	5 1/2 gal

* Reproduced by permission from Clifford S. Chater and Francis W. Holmes, "Insect and Disease Control Guide for Trees and Shrubs," University of Massachusetts and USDA Cooperative Extension Service, 1973.

WEEDS AND THEIR ERADICATION

Weeds are objectionable plants or plants that are undesirable in cultivated land. Like other plants, they have their botanical classifications. For weed control under a maintenance program, however, both the botanical system and a practical system are used.

BOTANICAL CLASSIFICATION OF WEEDS

Botanists have based their classification of weeds on the natural differences in growth habits of plants and the time each requires to complete a life cycle. Plants fall botanically under the headings of annuals, biennials, and perennials.

Annuals are plants which complete their life cycle in 1 year. From a seed, the plant grows, matures, and produces seed, after which the plant dies. The two types of annuals are *summer annuals,* which germinate in the spring, grow during the summer, and die in the fall, and *winter annuals,* which germinate in the fall, grow slightly during the winter, blossom in the spring, and die about midsummer.

Biennials require 2 years for completion of the life cycle. The first year the roots and leaves are developed; the second year the flowers and seeds are produced, and the plant dies.

Perennials, the largest class of plants, live 3 or more years. They produce seeds abundantly, and may spread also from underground parts. The three types of perennials are *simple perennials,* which have a fibrous or fleshy root and reproduce only by seeds; *creeping perennials,* which are propagated by creeping rootstocks as well as seeds; and *bulbous perennials,* which reproduce by bulbs, bulblets, and seeds.

PRACTICAL CLASSIFICATION OF WEEDS

An easier and more practical way to classify weeds is in four groups:

Common weeds are most commonly found in fields under ordinary tillage and forage conditions.

Noxious weeds are unusually troublesome and detrimental when once established. They cause great damage in fields and crops and a loss in crop value.

Lawn weeds are most commonly found on lawns, courts, and walkways.

Poisonous weeds produce toxic effects in human beings or animals.

WEED CONTROL

Good weed control can be secured if several important practices are followed: proper management and fertilization of the soil, proper seed-bed preparation, and sowing of clean seed. Control of some of the more persistent weeds, however, depends upon special tools and methods.

Tools

The tools used for weed control may be simple hand implements or more or less complicated machines.

Hand Tools The common hoe and spade are used over small areas to cut weeds at the surface and to dig out deep roots.

Field Tillage Implements The common plow is used for deep and shallow plowing to turn under weeds. The disc harrow will cut and turn weeds under and is adapted to killing small weeds which spring up on plowed or fallow ground. Weeders and rotary hoes are also effective.

Sprayers Power or hand sprayers of any kind can be used to apply chemical weed killers.

Automatic Liquid Guns These are used to a limited extent to destroy individual weeds.

Weed Torches Torches burning gasoline or kerosene are used in the eradication of weeds by burning.

Seed Cleaners Fanning mills and other types of seed cleaners are effective in blowing out light weed seeds and sifting the small, heavier seeds.

Methods

Mowing Close mowing prevents many weeds from reseeding, thereby eliminating them.

Pasturing Pasturing an infested area is often effective, since some weeds are palatable to cattle.

Smothering Crops A number of quick-growing farm crops, e.g., alfalfa, soybeans, sorghums, Sudan grass, and the millets, if thickly sown, are useful in smothering weed plants.

Mulching Straw or mulch paper and other materials, if properly placed to shade weed plants, will finally kill them.

CHEMICAL WEED DESTROYERS

Numerous chemicals can be used advantageously if the type of chemical and its action on plants other than weeds are well understood. The most common chemical formulas used today are 2,4-D, 2,4,5-T, 2,4-DB, and silvex. A further discussion of the use of these will follow.

Selective weed chemicals, such as Sodar, Weedone L-850, Artox, Di-Met, Crab-E-Rad, Crag Herbicide I, and others are being used more frequently for weed control in turf and in shrub beds. They are especially effective against crabgrass and chickweed.

The chemicals most commonly used in weed control are the following:

Chlorates Calcium, sodium
Sodium chloride (Common salt)
Acids Carbolic (phenol), hydrochloric, nitric, sulfuric
Sulfates Iron, copper
Petroleum oils Crude, kerosene
Sodium arsenite
Ammonium sulfocyanate
Phenoxy herbicides (2,4-D, 2,4,5-T, MCPA, 2,4-DB, and silvex)

CHLORATES

Chlorates are used as weed killers in both liquid and dry form. They have the ability to kill tops, and at the same time they work down into the roots and destroy them. Sodium chlorate has been used the longest, but an objection to it is that it may create a dangerous fire hazard.

Sodium Chlorate Sodium chlorate, if applied as a spray, is made by dissolving 1 to 2 lb of the chemical in 1 gal water and spraying at the rate of 100 gal/acre. The foliage should be thoroughly covered, and within a few days the leaves will start to die and turn brown. It will work more efficiently on damp days or toward evening. Sodium chlorate can also be used as a dust and applied directly to the foliage of weeds. The application should be 100 to 200 lb/acre. If applied in sufficient quantities to destroy weeds completely, sodium chlorate will render the ground sterile for 6 to 18 months. The period of sterility can be lessened by the addition of small quantities of lime. The best time for application is in the latter part of October and November.

Calcium Chlorate Although it acts like sodium chlorate, calcium chlorate is preferred for two reasons: (1) it is not flammable, and (2) it does not render the soil sterile.

SODIUM CHLORIDE

Common salt is an old and tried remedy for weed destruction. It kills all vegetation with which it comes in contact, by absorbing and withdrawing the water from the roots. It should therefore be applied on a hot, dry day. It is especially effective in driveways and walkways. It will, however, make the soil sterile for a prolonged period.

Salt may be applied either dry or in the form of a brine. If applied dry, 2 to 10 tons/acre will be required. If a solution is to be used, dissolve 3 or 4 lb in 1 gal of water and apply 100 to 400 gal/acre.

ACIDS

There is limited use for acids, but they must be used with extreme care because they will burn clothing and flesh. They must never be used in spray form and must always be stored and carried in glass containers. They are most useful for destroying plants with permanent crowns, such as dandelions, plantains, and some mustards.

SULFATES

Both iron and copper sulfate have been widely used.

Iron Sulfate Used dry or as a spray, iron sulfate should be applied on a bright, clear day. It is used to advantage in grain fields, since grains seem to be resistant to the chemical. The rate of mixture is 100 lb to 1 barrel (52 gal) of water.

Copper Sulfate Most active on young tender growth, copper sulfate should be sprayed in a fine mist on clear days when there is no likelihood of rain for some hours. Rate of mixture is 10 to 15 lb to 1 barrel of water.

The rate of application of these sulfates is 60 gal/acre. Both act upon foliage and flowers and should be applied when they are at their height.

PETROLEUM OILS

Acting upon all vegetation alike, petroleum oils kill all plants in the area treated. The recommended rate is 300 to 400 gal/acre, applied in the form of a fine spray. Precautions should be taken against fire.

SODIUM ARSENITE

Sodium arsenite is very poisonous, and the greatest care should be taken when it is used around human beings and livestock. It acts upon the foliage of weeds and causes the starvation of the root system. For the usual succulent weeds, 1 lb of arsenite dissolved in 25 gal of water is sufficient, but the chemical must be mixed when strictly fresh; otherwise it will harden. For the hardier plants with heavy leaves and a perennial root system, 2 to 5 lb of the chemical should be used to 25 gal of water.

AMMONIUM SULFOCYANATE

A 20% solution of ammonium sulfocyanate is useful for the destruction of weeds in walks, driveways, and on walls.

THE USE OF PHENOXY HERBICIDES*

General

The phenoxy herbicides comprise chiefly 2,4-D, 2,4,5-T, silvex, MCPA, and 2,4-DB. These herbicides are registered for use; however, the federal registration for the use of 2,4,5-T around homes, lakes, ponds, on ditch banks and on food crops has been canceled. These chemicals are useful in controlling weeds in crops, on grazing lands, on lawns,

* Information from Using Phenoxy Herbicides Effectively, *USDA Farmers' Bull.* 2183, rev. May 1974.

and for the control of unwanted brush and trees. They are useful because:

1. They are very effective. Many species of weeds can be controlled by less than 1 lb of active ingredient per acre.
2. They are easy to use.
3. They are not harmful to man, domestic animals, or game when applied at the recommended rates.
4. They do not harm soil organisms or accumulate in the soil.
5. They do not corrode spraying equipment.

The common and chemical names of phenoxy herbicides are given in Table 6.1.

TABLE 6.1
Common and Chemical Names of Phenoxy Herbicides

Common name	Chemical Name
2,4-D	(2,4-Dichlorophenoxy)acetic acid
2,4,5-T	(2,4,5-Trichlorophenoxy)acetic acid
Silvex	2-(2,4,5-Trichlorophenoxy)propionic acid
MCPA	(4-Chloro-*o*-toloxy)acetic acid
2,4-DB	4-(2,4-Dichlorophenoxy)butyric acid

Plant Reaction

When plants are sprayed with these herbicides, the leaves, green stems, twigs, flowers, and fruits usually absorb the chemical. When the chemical is sprayed on the soil, the roots will absorb it. The herbicides are most effective when the plants are growing rapidly, which permits the rapid distribution of the chemical in the leaves, stems, and roots, causing the plants to die. Annual weeds are the easiest to kill when young. Perennial weeds are best killed while they are still seedlings; after they are established, most perennials are easier to kill when flower buds appear.

Types of Phenoxy Herbicides Commonly Available

Salts, such as:
- Amine
- Sodium
- Potassium
- Ammonium

Esters
- High-volatile, such as:
  - Ethyl
  - Isopropyl
  - Butyl
  - Amyl
- Low-volatile, such as:
  - Butoxyethanol
  - Butoxyethoxypropanol
  - Ethoxyethoxypropanol
  - Isooctyl
  - Propylene glycol butyl ether

Salt formulations are safest to use because they do not release enough vapors to cause damage; they are generally less expensive. However, they will be washed away if rain falls soon after their application, making them ineffective.

The esters are more potent, pound for pound than salts, for the following reasons:

1. Their penetration of leaves and other plant surfaces is more effective than salts.
2. They are more effective for killing weeds during periods of drought or cold weather or in areas of low humidity.
3. Because esters are formulated in oils, they can remain in contact longer and will penetrate better than salts, which are mixed with water.
4. Because they are oily, esters are less likely to be washed away if rain occurs soon after application.
5. *Caution* Vapors from ester formulations can kill susceptible plants growing near the area to which the formulations are applied.

Application

The application of phenoxy herbicides should be made carefully in order to avoid killing susceptible plants. For safe and effective control of weeds the following rules should be observed:

1. Use herbicides wisely: follow label precautions, and do not apply them for any use for which they are not registered.
2. Avoid spraying on windy days.

3. Do not apply ester formulations when the temperature is above 90°F.
4. Check output of the sprayer frequently to prevent over application.
5. Avoid sprayer skips or overlapping swaths.
6. Before using spray equipment for applying insecticides or fungicides, be sure it has been thoroughly cleaned; better yet, use a separate sprayer for each use.
7. To control or reduce spray drift the following procedures are advisable:

   Use nozzles that apply a coarse spray.
   Use low pressures: no more than 35 lb/in.^{2} for boom sprayers and 100 lb/in.^{2} for spray guns.
   Avoid spraying on windy days or spray when the wind is blowing toward the area to be sprayed and away from any area which may be susceptible to damage.

8. To apply herbicides on noncropland use a ground sprayer with boom. Apply low-volume broadcast spray for the control of weeds, brush, and trees on grazing land and on irrigation-canal banks.
9. Airplane spraying is often used to apply low-volume broadcast sprays in large areas which are too rough for ground equipment.
10. Apply high-volume directed spray to kill brush and trees along roads, utility lines, and fence rows, and aquatic weeds and brush along irrigation and drainage canals.
11. Apply sprays of ester formulations in diesel oil or kerosene to the bark at the base of small trees or to cuts in the bark at the base of large trees. Apply to the lower 6 to 12 inches of bark on trees with diameters up to about 4 inches. To kill trees above the 4-in. diameter, ring the base of the tree with ax cuts and spray into the cuts. The ax cuts must go through the bark and into the sapwood to be effective.
12. After spraying, clean the equipment thoroughly by filling the tank about one-third full of water. For each 10 gal of water add $\frac{1}{4}$ lb of activated charcoal and $\frac{1}{8}$ to $\frac{1}{4}$ lb of laundry detergent. Agitate vigorously to distribute the charcoal through the water. Wash for 2 min and pump some of the liquid through the hose and nozzles. Then drain and rinse the tank with clean water.

Precautions

Phenoxy herbicides are safe when stored, handled, mixed, and used in accordance with label instructions and sound agricultural practices. Most herbicides are low in toxicity. However, some can cause injury to man, many domestic animals, and fish and wildlife if improperly used.

Most herbicides are toxic to many crop plants and ornamentals. Many are volatile, and their vapors and spray drift will cause damage to desirable plants. Avoid spraying when windy conditions exist.

Keep herbicides away from children, livestock, and pets. Store herbicides in closed, well-labeled containers in a dry place where they cannot contaminate food, feed, or water.

When handling herbicides wear clean, dry clothing. Launder clothing after each spraying operation before wearing again.

Do not inhale herbicides, and avoid contact with spray mist and drift. Avoid repeated or prolonged contact of herbicides with the skin. Avoid spilling it on any part of the body, especially the eyes, nose, and mouth. If a spill is made, wash it off with soap and water.

To protect fish, wildlife, and livestock, do not clean spraying equipment or dump excess spray material near lakes, streams, or ponds.

Empty herbicide containers may be hazardous. Dispose of them in accordance with label instructions and the recommendations of the state extension weed-science specialist or other agricultural authorities. Do not burn herbicide containers.

Susceptibility Chart

Table 6.2 lists the effects of phenoxy herbicides when applied as foliage sprays on a number of common weeds. Rate of application for 2,4-D, 2,4,5-T, MCPA, or silvex is 1 lb/acre; rate of application for 2,4-DB is 2 lb/acre.

The control ratings for the herbicides are interpreted as follows:

Excellent One application at rate kills the weed.
Good Several applications at rate needed to kill the weed.
Fair Repeated applications at rate or application at higher rates needed to kill the weed.
Poor Weed kill is erratic, even at high rates of application.
None No visible effect.

TABLE 6.2
Susceptibility of Common Weeds to Control by 2,4-D, MCPA, 2,4,5-T, Silvex, and 2,4-DB*

Plant name	Type of plant†	Control‡				
		2,4-D	MCPA	2,4,5-T¶	Silvex	2,4-DB
Alder (*Alnus* spp.)	W	G	G	E	E	
Alligator weed (*Alternanthera philoxeroides*)	P	P	N	F	F	
Alyssum, hoary (*Berteroa incana*)	P	F	F	E		P
Amaranth, green (*Amaranthus hybridus*)	A	E	E	E	–	E
Palmer (*A. palmeri*)	A	E	E	E	E	
See also pigweed						
Arrowgrass, seaside (*Triglochin maritima*)	P	F	–	F		
Arrowhead, annual (*Sagittaria calycina*)	A	E	E	E	E	E
Perennial (*S. longiloba*)	P	F	F	P		
Ash (*Fraxinus* spp.)	W	N	N	P	P	N
Aster, many-flowered (*Aster ericoides*)	P	G				
Western (*A. occidentalis*)	P	P	–	P	–	N
White heath (*A. pilosus*)	P	F	–	F	F	N
Woody (*Xylorrhiza parryi*)	P	P	N	P	P	
Baccharis, coyote brush (*Baccharis salicina*)	W	E				
Baileya, desert (*Baileya multiradiata*)	P	G	–	G		
Bassia, five-hook (*Bassia hyssopifolia*)	A	F				
Cornflower, batchelor's button (*Centaurea cyanus*)	A	E				
Bedstraw, cleavers (*Gallium aparine*)	A	P	N	P	G	N
Smooth (*G. mollugo*)	P	N	N	P	G	N
Bee plant, Rocky Mountain (*Cleome serrulata*)	A	F				
Beggar-tick, devil's (*Bidens frondosa*)	A	E	E	E		
Florida betony (*Stachys floridana*)	P	P	–	P		
Bindweed, field (*Convolvulus arvensis*)	P	F	F	F	F	F
Hedge (*C. sepium*)	P	G	G	G		
Biscuit-root (*Lomatium leptocarpum*)	P	F	–	G		
Bistort, American (*Polygonum bistortoides*)	P	F	–	F	–	N
Blackberry (*Rubus* spp.)	W	N	N	G	F	N

TABLE 6.2
Susceptibility of Common Weeds to Control by 2,4-D, MCPA, 2,4,5-T, Silvex, and 2,4-DB* (*Continued*)

Plant name	Type of plant†	Control‡				
		2,4-D	MCPA	2,4,5-T¶	Silvex	2,4-DB
Blackeyed susan (*Rudbeckia serotina*)	P	G	–	G	E	
Bloodweed (*Ambrosia aptera*)	A	E	–	E		
Blueweed, Texas (*Helianthus ciliaris*)	P	F				
Bouncing bet (*Saponaria officinalis*)	P	P	N	P	P	N
Box elder (*Acer negundo*)	W	G	–	G	G	
Bracken (*Pteridium aquilinum*)	P	N	N	N	N	N
Broom, Scotch (*Cytisus scoparius*)	W	G	–	G		
Broomweed, common (*Gutierrezia dracunculoides*).	A	G	–	G	G	
Buckbrush (*Symphoricarpos orbiculatus*)	W	G	–	F	N	
Western (*S. occidentalis*)	W	F	N	P		
Buckeye, California (*Aesculus californica*)	W	F	–	P	N	
Buckwheat, Tartary (*Fagopyrum tataricum*)	A	P	E	F		
Wild (*F. convolvulus*)	A	F	F	G	F	G
Buffalo bur (*Solanum rostratum*)	A	N	N	N		
Bull nettle (*Cnidoscolus stimulosus*)	P	G	F	G		
Bulrush (*Scirpus* spp.)	P	F	F	F	F	N
Bur cucumber (*Sicyos angulatus*)	A	F	E			
Burdock, common (*Arctium minus*)	B	E	E	E	E	E
Burhead (*Echinodorus cordifolius*)	A	E	E	E	E	
Burroweed (*Haplopappus tenuisectus*)	P	G	–	E		
Buttercup, celery-leaved (*Ranunculus sceleratus*)	A	F				
Corn (*R. arvensis*)	A	G	E	E	E	E
Creeping (*R. repens*)	P	G	E	E	E	G
Tall (*R. acris*)	P	G	E	E	E	E
Campion, bladder (*Silene cucubalus*)	P	N	N	N	N	N
Carpetweed (*Mollugo verticillata*)	A	E	–	N	N	E
Carrot, wild (*Daucus carota*)	B	F	F	F	F	F
Catchfly, night-flowering (*Silene noctiflora*)	A	N	N	N	N	N

TABLE 6.2
Susceptibility of Common Weeds to Control by 2,4-D, MCPA, 2,4,5-T, Silvex, and 2,4-DB* (*Continued*)

Plant name	Type of plant†	Control‡				
		2,4-D	MCPA	2,4,5-T¶	Silvex	2,4-DB
Catnip (*Nepeta cataria*)	P	G	–	E		
Cat's-ear, spotted (*Hypochoeris radicata*)	P	G	E	E	E	E
Cattail, broadleaf (*Typha latifolia*)	P	F	P	F	F	P
Narrowleaf (*T. angustifolia*)	P	F	P	F	F	P
Ceanothus (*Ceanothus* spp.)	W	F	F	G	–	F
Wedge-leaf (*C. cuneatus*)	W	G	F	E		
Chamise (*Adenostoma fasciculatum*)	W	F	P	F	P	P
Chickweed, common (*Stellaria media*)	A	F	P	G	E	F
Field (*Cerastium arvense*)	P	F	P	G	E	P
Mouse-ear (*C. vulgatum*)	P	F	P	G	E	P
Chicory (*Cichorium intybus*)	P	G	G	G	G	F
Chokecherry (*Prunus virginiana*)	W	P	–	F	F	N
Cinquefoil, blueleaf (*Potentilla diversifolia*)	P	F	–	F		N
Common (*P. canadensis*)	P	G	F	F	F	
Rough (*P. norvegica*)	A§	E				
Sulfur (*P. recta*)	P	G	F	G	F	
Cockle, corn (*Agrostemma githago*)	A¶	P	P	N	N	N
White (*Lychnis alba*)	P	P	N	N	–	N
Cocklebur, common (*Xanthium pensylvanicum*)	A	E	F	E	–	G
Coffeeweed (*Daubentonia texana*)	W	E	–	E	G	
Coyote brush (*Baccharis pilularis*)	W	G	–	F		
Coyotillo (*Karwinskia humboldtiana*)	P	–	–	E	E	
Cranebill, cutleaf (*Geranium dissectum*)	A§	–	E			
Cress, hoary (*Cardaria draba*)	P	F	F	F	F	F
Croton, Lindheimer (*Croton lindheimeri*)	A	E	E	G	G	G
Texas (*C. texensis*)	A	E	–	E	E	
Woolly (*C. capitatus*)	A	E	–	E	E	E
Cudweed (*Gnaphalium peregrinum*)	A	N				
Daisy, oxeye (*Chrysanthemum leucanthemum*)	P	F	F	G	F	N
Dandelion (*Taraxacum officinale*)	P	E	E	E	E	G

TABLE 6.2
Susceptibility of Common Weeds to Control by 2,4-D, MCPA, 2,4,5-T, Silvex, and 2,4-DB* (*Continued*)

Plant name	Type of plant†	Control‡				
		2,4-D	MCPA	2,4,5-T¶	Silvex	2,4-DB
Dead nettle, red (*Lamium purpureum*)	A¶	P	P	–	–	P
Death camas (*Zigadenus gramineus*)	P	F	–	P		
Foothill (*Z. paniculatus*)	P	G	–	F		
Deerweed (*Lotus scoparius*)	W	E	–	E		
Devil's claw (*Proboscidea louisianica*)	A	E				
Dock, broadleaf (*Rumex obtusifolius*)	P	G	F	G	G	F
Curly (*R. crispus*)	P	G	F	G	P	F
Fiddle (*R. pulcher*)	P	E				
Pale (*R. altissimus*)	P	G	G	G	G	P
Veiny (*R. venosus*)	P	F				
Dodder, large-seed (*Cuscuta indecora*)	A	P	N	N	N	N
Small-seed alfalfa (*C. pentagona*)	A	P	N	N	N	N
Duckweed, common (*Lemna minor*)	A	P		N	N	
Elm (*Ulmus* spp.)	W	P	N	F	F	N
Evening primrose, common (*Oenothera biennis*)	B	E	–	G	E	
False flax, small-seeded (*Camelina microcarpa*)	A	E				
Fennel, dog (*Eupatorium capillifolium*)	A	G	–	E	E	N
Fiddleneck, coast (*Amsinckia intermedia*)	A	G	F	G	E	N
Filaree, red-stem (*Erodium cicutarium*)	A§	G				P
Fireweed (*Epilobium angustifolium*)	P	G		G	E	
Fleabane, annual (*Erigeron annuus*)	A	F	F	G	E	E
Oregon (*E. speciosus*)	P	F				
Rough (*E. strigosus*)	A§	G	–	E	E	
Flixweed (*Descurainia sophia*)	A	E	F	–	–	G
Franseria, bur (*Franseria discolor*)	P	F				
Woolly-leaf (*F. tomentosa*)	P	F	P	P	P	P
Galinsoga, hairy (*Galinsoga ciliata*)	A	G	E	E	E	
Garlic, wild (*Allium vineale*)	P	F	P	P	N	P
Geranium, Carolina (*Geranium carolinianum*)	A§	G	E	G	G	E

TABLE 6.2
Susceptibility of Common Weeds to Control by 2,4-D, MCPA, 2,4,5-T, Silvex, and 2,4-DB* (*Continued*)

Plant name	Type of plant†	Control‡				
		2,4-D	MCPA	2,4,5-T¶	Silvex	2,4-DB
Goat's rue (*Galega offinalis*)	P	F				
Goldenrod (*Solidago* spp.)	P	F				
Gooseberry, sierra (*Ribes roezli*)	W	E	–	G		
Goosefoot, Jerusalem oak (*Chenopodium botrys*)	A	F				
Nettleleaf (*C. murale*)	A	E	E	E		E
Oakleaf (*C. glaucum*)	A	E	E	E	F	E
Gooseweed (*Sphenoclea zeylanica*)	A	F	P	F	P	N
Gourd, buffalo (*Cucurbita foetidissia*)	P	P				
Goutweed, bishop's (*Aegopodium podagraria*)	P	N				
Grape hyacinth (*Muscari botryoides*)	P	–	P			
Greenbrier (*Smilax bona-nox*)	W	N	N	P	P	
Common (*S. rotundifolia*)	W	N	–	P	P	
Gromwell (*Lithospermum officinale*)	P	N				
Ground-cherry, clammy (*Physalis heterophylla*)	W	N	–	F	F	N
Purple flower (*P. lobata*)	W	E				
Smooth (*P. subglabrata*)	W	E	N	P	P	N
Wright's (*P. wrightii*)	A	E	–	E	E	
Ground ivy (*Glechoma hederacea*)	P	F	P	F	G	
Groundsel, arrow-leaf (*Senecio triangularis*)	P	F	–	F	–	N
Common (*S. vulgaris*)	A	P	P	N	N	N
Cress-leaf (*S. glabellus*)	A	E	E	E	G	G
Riddell (*S. riddellii*)	P	E				
Thread-leaf (*S. longilobus*)	P	F				
Gum, sweet (*Liquidambar styraciflua*)	W	P	–	G	F	
Tupelo, or black (*Nyssa sylvatica*)	W	N	–	F	F	
Gumweed (*Grindelia squarrosa*)	P	E				
Halogeton (*Halogeton glomeratus*)	A	F	P	P	P	N
Hawk's-beard, smooth (*Crepis capillaris*)	A§	P	P	N	N	P
Hawkweed, orange (*Hieracium aurantiacum*)	P	F	P	P		
Yellow (*H. pratense*)	P	F	P	P		
Hawthorn (*Crataegus* spp.)	W	N	N	F	P	N
Heal-all (*Prunella vulgaris*)	P	G	N	P	P	N

TABLE 6.2
Susceptibility of Common Weeds to Control by 2,4-D, MCPA, 2,4,5-T, Silvex, and 2,4-DB* (*Continued*)

Plant name	Type of plant†	Control‡				
		2,4-D	MCPA	2,4,5-T¶	Silvex	2,4-DB
Hellebore, false western (*Veratrum californicum*)	P	G				
Hemlock, poison (*Conium maculatum*)	B	G	E	F	E	E
Hemp (*Cannabis sativa*)	A	G	–	G	–	G
Hemp nettle (*Galeopsis tetrahit*)	A	P	F			
Henbit (*Lamium amplexicaule*)	A	P	P	F	G	P
Hickory (*Carya* spp.)	W	P	F	F	F	N
Hog peanut (*Amphicarpa bracteata*)	P	E				
Hog potato (*Hoffmanseggia densiflora*)	P	N	N	N	N	N
Honey locust (*Gleditsia triacanthos*)	W	P	–	F		
Honeysuckle (*Lonicera japonica*)	W	F	E	G	G	
Horsebrush, little-leaf (*Tetradymia glabrata*)	W	P	–	P		
Horse nettle, Carolina (*Solanum carolinense*)	P	P	N	F	–	P
Horsetail, field (*Equisetum arvense*)	P	P	F	P	P	
Horseweed, mare's tail (*Erigeron canadensis*)	A	F	F	G	G	F
Hound's-tongue (*Cynoglossum officinale*)	B	F				
Indian hemp (*Apocynum cannabinum*)	P	P	N	N		
Indian tobacco (*Lobelia inflata*)	A	F				
Iris, Rocky Mountain (*Iris missouriensis*)	P	F	–	P		
Ironweed, western (*Vernonia baldwini*)	P	G	–	G	N	P
Ivy, English (*Hedera helix*)	P	–	–	E		
Jerusalem artichoke (*Helianthus tuberosus*)	P	G	–	E		
Jewelweed (*Impatiens pallida*)	A	E				
Jimmyweed (*Haplopappus pluriflorus*)	P	F	–	F		
Jimsonweed (*Datura stramonium*)	A	G	E	G		E
Joint vetch, northern (*Aeschynomene virginica*)	A	F	F	E	F	N
Juniper, alligator (*Juniperus deppeana*)	W	N	–	N	N	N
One-seed (*J. monosperma*)	W	N	–	N	N	N
Utah (*J. osteosperma*)	W	P	–	P	N	N

TABLE 6.2
Susceptibility of Common Weeds to Control by 2,4-D, MCPA, 2,4,5-T, Silvex, and 2,4-DB* (*Continued*)

Plant name	Type of plant†	Control‡				
		2,4-D	MCPA	2,4,5-T¶	Silvex	2,4-DB
Knapweed, brown (*Centaurea jacea*)	P	F				
Diffuse (*C. diffusa*)	B	E	N	P	P	N
Russian (*C. repens*)	P	P	P	P	P	N
Spotted (*C. maculosa*)	B	F	E	F	G	
Squarrose (*C. virgata* var. *squarrosa*)	P	E				
Knawel (*Scleranthus annuus*)	A	N	N			
Knotweed, Japanese (*Polygonum Cuspidatum*)	P	P	–	P	E	
Prostrate (*P. aviculare*)	A	F	P	F	F	P
Sakhalin (*P. sachalinense*)	P	G				
Silver-sheath (*P. argyrocoleon*)	A	F				
Kochia (*Kochia scoparia*)	A	E	G	E	E	E
Kudzu (*Pueraria lobata*)	P	F	F	F	F	
Lamb's-quarters, common (*Chenopodium album*)	A	E	E	E	E	E
Larkspur, duncecap (*Delphinium occidentale*)	P	N	–	F	F	
Little (*D. bicolor*)	P	N	–	N	–	N
Menzies (*D. menziesii*)	P	F	–	F	N	
Tall (*D. barbeyii*)	P	N	–	N		
Lettuce, blue (*Lactuca pulchella*)	P	F	F	F	F	F
Wild (*L. scariola*)	A	E				
Loco, big-bend (*Astragalus earlei*)	A§	E				
Locoweed, white (*Oxytropis lambertii*)	P	F	–	F	F	
Locust, black (*Robinia pseudacacia*)	W	F	–	G	G	
London rocket, annual (*Sisymbrium irio*)	A	E	E	E	E	E
Perennial (*Franseria confertiflora*)	P	N	N	N	N	N
Lupine (*Lupinus rivularis*)	W	E	–	E		
Silvery (*L. argenteus*)	P	F	N	E	E	E
Tailcup (*L. caudatus*)	P	G				
Madrone (*Arbutus menziesii*)	W	F	–	F		
Mallow, common (*Malva neglecta*)	A§	P	N	P	P	
Dwarf (*M. rotundiflora*)	P	F				
Little (*M. parviflora*)	A	F	N			
Venice (*Hibiscus trionum*)	A	G	E	E		
Manzanita (*Arctostaphylos* spp.)	W	G	P	F	F	P
Maples (*Acer* spp.)	W	P	N	F	G	N

TABLE 6.2
Susceptibility of Common Weeds to Control by 2,4-D, MCPA, 2,4,5-T, Silvex, and 2,4-DB* (*Continued*)

Plant name	Type of plant†	Control‡				
		2,4-D	MCPA	2,4,5-T¶	Silvex	2,4-DB
Marsh elder (*Iva xanthifolia*)	A	E	G	G	E	E
Mayweed, dog fennel (*Anthemis cotula*)	A	F	P	F	P	N
Medic, black (*Medicago lupulina*)	A	F	F	F	G	P
Mesquite, honey (*Prosopis juliflora* var. *glandulosa*)	W	P	–	F	F	F
Velvet (*P. juliflora* var. *velutina*)	W	N	N	G	F	N
Mexican tea (*Chenopodium ambrosioides*)	A	E	E	E	G	E
Mexican weed (*Caperonia castaneaefolia*)	A	F	F	G	G	N
Milkweed (*Asclepias curassavica*)	P	G	–	E	–	N
Broadleaf (*A. latifolia*)	P	F	–	–	F	
Common (*A. syriaca*)	P	N	N	P	F	N
Eastern whorled (*A. verticillata*)	P	N	N	P	–	N
Showy (*A. speciosa*)	P	N	N	P	G	N
Mimosa, catclaw (*Mimosa biuncifera*)	W	–	–	P	–	P
Moneywort (*Lysimachia nummularia*)	P	E				
Morning glory, common (*Ipomoea purpurea*)	A	E	–	E	–	E
Ivy-leaf (*I. hederacea*)	A	E	–	E	–	E
Woolly (*I. hirsutula*)	A	E	E	E	E	
Mountain mahogany (*Cercocarpus montanus*)	W	–	–	P	–	P
Mud plantain (*Heteranthera limosa*)	A	E	G	G	G	F
Mugwort (*Artemisia vulgaris*)	P	P	N	N		
Mulberry (*Morus* spp.)	W	N	–	P	F	
Mule-ears (*Wyethia amplexicaulis*)	P	G	–	G		
Mullein, common (*Verbascum thapsus*)	B	P	P	F	–	N
Moth (*V. blattaria*)	P	F	–	F		
Mustard, black (*Brassica nigra*)	A	E	E	E	G	E
Blue (*Chorispora tenella*)	A	F	P	G	G	N
Hare's-ear (*Conringia orientalis*)	A	E	G			
Hedge (*Sisymbrium officinale*)	A	E	E	E	E	E

TABLE 6.2
Susceptibility of Common Weeds to Control by 2,4-D, MCPA, 2,4,5-T, Silvex, and 2,4-DB* (*Continued*)

Plant name	Type of plant†	Control‡				
		2,4-D	MCPA	2,4,5-T¶	Silvex	2,4-DB
Indian (*Brassica juncea*)	A	E	E	E	G	E
Tumble (*Sisymbrium altissimum*)	A	E	G	E	–	E
Wild (*Brassica kaber*)	A	E	E	E	G	E
Wormseed (*Erysimum cheiranthoides*)	A§	E	E	E	–	E
Nettle, stinging (*Urtica dioica*)	P	G				
Tall (*U. procera*)	A	G				
Niggerhead (*Rudbeckia occidentalis*)	P	G				
Nightshade, black (*Solanum nigrum*)	A	F	F	F	G	F
Cutleaf (*S. triflorum*)	A	F				
Silverleaf (*S. elaeagnifolium*)	P	P	–	P	P	
Norcal bean (*Sophora secundiflora*)	P	–	–	E	E	
Nu sedge, Purple (*Cyperus rotundus*)	P	P	N	N	N	N
Yellow (*C. esculentus*)	P	P	N	N	N	N
Oak, black (*Quercus velutina*)	W	P	–	F		
Blackjack (*Q. marilandica*)	W	P	N	F	F	N
Blue (*Q. douglasii*)	W	P	P	P	F	P
Gambel (*Q. gambelii*)	W	–	–	F		
Interior live (*Q. wislizenii*)	W	P	P	P	P	P
Post (*Q. stellata*)	W	F	N	G	G	N
Scrub (*Q. dumosa*)	W	P	P	F	F	P
Shinnery (*Q. havardi*)	W	F	–	E	E	
Turbinella (*Q. turbinella*)	W	–	–	P	–	P
White (*Q. alba*)	W	F	N	G	F	N
Onion, wild (*Allium canadense*)	P	F	P	P	–	P
Orache (*Atriplex hastata*)	A	G	–	E		
Osage orange (*Maclura pomifera*)	W	P	–	G	F	
Parsley, desert (*Lomatium grayi*)	P	E	E	–	E	E
Parsnip, wild (*Pastinaca sativa*)	B	E	–	E		
Partridge pea (*Cassia fasciculata*)	A	E	E	E	E	
Passionflower, maypop (*Passiflora incarnata*)	P	F				
Peavine (*Astragalus emoryanus*)	A	G	–	G		
Pellitory weed (*Parietaria floridana*)	A	N	N	E	–	N

TABLE 6.2
Susceptibility of Common Weeds to Control by 2,4-D, MCPA, 2,4,5-T, Silvex, and 2,4-DB* (*Continued*)

Plant name	Type of plant†	Control‡				
		2,4-D	MCPA	2,4,5-T¶	Silvex	2,4-DB
Pennycress, field (*Thlaspi arvense*)	A	E	E	E	G	G
Pennywort, lawn (*Hydrocotyle sibthorpioides*)	P	G	–	E	E	
Penstemon, Rydberg (*Penstemon rydbergii*)	P	F	–	P	–	N
Pepperweed, field (*Lepidium campestre*)	A	E	E	G	F	E
Perennial (*L. latifolium*)	P	F	–	F		
Virginia (*L. virginicum*)	A	E	E	–	–	E
Yellowflower (*L. perfoliatum*)	A	E	E	E	E	
Persimmon (*Diospyros virginiana*)	W	P	–	P	F	
Texas (*D. texana*)	W	E	–	–	E	
Pigweed, prostrate (*Amaranthus graecizans*)	A	E	E	E	–	E
Rough (*A. retroflexus*)	A	E	E	E	E	E
Tumble (*A. albus*)	A	E	E	E	E	E
Pineapple weed (*Matricaria matricarioides*)	A	F	P	N	P	N
Plantain, blackseed (*Plantago rugelii*)	P	E	E	E	G	E
Broadleaf (*P. major*)	P	E	E	E	E	E
Buckhorn (*P. lanceolata*)	P	E	G	E	E	E
Poison ivy (*Rhus radicans*)	W	F	F	E	E	N
Poison oak (*Rhus diversiloba*)	W	F	P	E	E	N
Pokeweed (*Phytolacca americana*)	P	F	F	G	G	
Pondweed (*Potamogeton* spp.)	P	F	N	P	P	
Ponyfoot (*Dichondra repens*)	P	E				
Poor joe (*Diodia teres*)	A	G	F	G	F	F
Poppy, Roemer (*Roemeria refracta*)	A	E				
Prickly ash, northern (*Xanthoxylum americanum*).	W	P	–	F		
Prickly pear (*Opuntia* spp.)	P	–	–	F		
Prickly poppy (*Argemone intermedia*)	A	E				
Puncture vine (*Tribulus terrestris*)	A	G	F	–	F	G
Purslane, common (*Portulaca oleracea*)	A	F	F	E	G	G
Pusley, Florida (*Richardia scabra*)	A	E				
Queen's delight (*Stillingia sylvatica*)	P	N				

TABLE 6.2
Susceptibility of Common Weeds to Control by 2,4-D, MCPA, 2,4,5-T, Silvex, and 2,4-DB* (*Continued*)

Plant name	Type of plant†	Control‡				
		2,4-D	MCPA	2,4,5-T¶	Silvex	2,4-DB
Rabbit brush, gray (*Chrysothamnus nauseosus*)	W	F	P	P	P	
Yellow (*C. viscidiflorus*)	W	F	P	P	P	
Radish, wild (*Raphanus raphanistrum*)	A	E	E	E	E	E
Ragweed, common (*Ambrosia artemisiifolia*)	A	E	E	E	E	E
Giant (*A. trifida*)	A	E	E	E	E	E
Western (*A. psilostachya*)	P	G	–	E	E	E
Ragwort, tansy (*Senecio jacobaea*)	P§	A	F	F	F	P
Rape, bird (*Brassica rapa*)	B	E	E	E	E	E
Raspberry (*Rubus* spp.)	W	P	N	G	G	N
Redbay (*Persea borbonia*)	W	P	–	G	P	
Redbud (*Cercis occidentalis*)	W	P	–	P		
Redvine (*Brunnichia cirrhosa*)	P	N	N	P	P	N
Redstem (*Ammannia coccinea*)	A	E	E	E	E	G
Rose, California (*Rosa californica*)	W	N	–	F		
Cherokee (*R. laevigata*)	W	F	–	F	E	
Macartney (*R. bracteata*)	W	F	N	G	G	
Multiflora (*R. multiflora*)	W	P	N	F	F	
Prairie (*R. pratincola*)	W	F	–	E		
Woods (*R. woodsii*)	W	N	–	F	N	N
Rubberweed, bitter (*Hymenoxys odorata*)	A	E				
Colorado (*H. richardsoni*)	P	G	–	F		
Rue, African (*Peganum harmala*)	P	–	–	F	F	
Sage, creeping (*Salvia sonomensis*)	P	G	F	G	F	F
Purple (*S. leucophylla*)	P	G				
White (*S. apiana*)	P	G				
Sagebrush, big (*Artemisia tridentata*)	W	G	P	G	F	N
California (*A. californica*)	W	E	–	G		
Sand (*A. filifolia*)	W	E	G	G	G	P
Saint-John's-wort (*Hypericum perforatum*)	P	P				
Spotted (*H. punctatum*)	P	F		F		
Salsify, common (*Tragopogon porrifolius*)	B	G				
Meadow (*T. pratensis*)	B	G				
Salt cedar (*Tamarix gallica*)	W	P	N	F	G	N
Sedge, umbrella (*Cyperus difformis*)	A	F	F	P	P	

TABLE 6.2
Susceptibility of Common Weeds to Control by 2,4-D, MCPA, 2,4,5-T, Silvex, and 2,4-DB* (*Continued*)

Plant name	Type of plant†	Control‡				
		2,4-D	MCPA	2,4,5-T¶	Silvex	2,4-DB
Sesbania, coffee bean (*Sesbania exaltata*)	A	F	G	G	E	F
Sorrel (*Rumex acetosa*)	P	G	F	G	F	F
Heartwing (*R. hastatulus*)	P	E				
Red (*R. acetosella*)	P	N	N	N	P	N
Shepherd's purse (*Capsella bursa-pastoris*)	A	G	G	E	G	G
Sicklepod, coffeeweed (*Cassia tora*)	A	E	E			
Skunk cabbage (*Symplocarpus foetidus*)	P	G	–	G	F	
Smartweed, lady's thumb (*Polygonum persicaria*)	A	G	F	G	G	G
Pennsylvania (*P. pensylvanicum*)	A	G	F	G	F	G
Swamp (*P. coccineum*)	P	P				
Snakeroot, white (*Eupatorium rugosum*)	P	F	–	F	P	
Snakeweed, broom (*Gutierrezia sarothrae*)	P	F	F	F	P	P
Threadleaf (*G. microcephala*)	P	G	–	G	G	
Sneezeweed, bitter (*Helenium tenuifolium*)	A	E	E	E	E	G
Snow-on-the-mountain (*Euphorbia marginata*)	A	F	–	G	–	F
Sow thistle, annual (*Sonchus oleraceus*)	A	E	E	E	–	E
Perennial (*S. arvensis*)	P	F	F	F	F	F
Spiny (*S. asper*)	A	E	–	E	–	E
Spanish needles (*Bidens bipinnata*)	A	E	E	E	E	
Speedwell, common (*Veronica officinalis*)	P	P	N	N	P	N
Corn (*V. arvensis*)	A	P	N	N	P	N
Purslane (*V. peregrina*)	A	F	N	F		
Spike rush (*Eleocharis palustris*)	P	F	F	P	P	P
Spurge, flowering (*Euphorbia corollata*)	P	P	–	G		
Leafy (*E. esula*)	P	P	N	P	F	N
Spotted (*E. maculata*)	A	P	–	P	F	
Spurry, corn (*Spergula arvensis*)	A	P	F	N	F	N
Squawberry (*Rhus trilobata*)	W	–	–	P	–	P
Star thistle, yellow (*Centaurea solstitialis*)	A	F	–	–	–	N

TABLE 6.2
Susceptibility of Common Weeds to Control by 2,4-D, MCPA, 2,4,5-T, Silvex, and 2,4-DB* (*Continued*)

Plant name	Type of plant†	Control‡				
		2,4-D	MCPA	2,4,5-T¶	Silvex	2,4-DB
Sticktight, European (*Lappula echinata*)	A	G			–	
Strawberry, wild (*Fragaria* spp.)	P	P	N	P	F	N
Spotted (*H. punctatum*)	P	F		F		
Sumpweed, rough (*Iva ciliata*)	A	E				
Sunflower (*Helianthus annuus*)	N	P	G	E	E	E
Sweet clover, annual yellow (*Melilotus indica*)	N	P	E	–	–	E
Tanoak (*Lithocarpus densiflora*)	W	P	–	P	P	P
Tansy (*Tanacetum vulgare*)	P	F	N	F		
Tansy mustard (*Descurainia pinnata*)	A	E				
Thistle, blessed (*Cnicus benedictus*)	A	E				
Blue (*Echium vulgare*)	B	F	F	F		
Bull (*Cirsium vulgare*)	B	E	E	E	E	E
Bristly (*C. horridulum*)	P	F				
Canada (*C. arvense*)	P	F	F	F	F	F
Russian (*Salsola kali*)	A	G	G	G	G	G
Tickseed (*Coreopsis tinctoria*)	A	G	–	E		
Toadflax, blue (*Linaria canadensis*)	P	P				
Yellow (*L. vulgaris*)	P	N	N	N	N	N
Toyon (*Heteromeles arbutifolia*)	W	G	F	F	F	F
Tree-of-heaven (*Ailanthus altissima*)	W	F	N	E	G	P
Trumpet creeper (*Campsis radicans*)	W	P	N	F	E	N
Velvet leaf (*Abutilon theophrasti*)	A	E	G	G	–	E
Vervan, blue (*Verbena hastata*)	P	E				
Hoary (*V. stricta*)	P	G				
Prostrate (*V. bracteata*)	P	E				
Roadside (*V. bonariensis*)	P	G				
Vetch, narrowleaf (*Vicia angustifolia*)	A	E	F	E		
Milk (*Astragalus* spp.)	P	G	F	G	E	
Two-grooved (*A. bisulcatus*)	P	E				
Wild (*Vicia* spp.)	A	E	E	E	E	E
Violet (*Viola* spp.)	P	P	N		G	
Walnut, black (*Juglans nigra*)	W	E	–	E		
Water hemlock, spotted (*Cicuta maculata*)	P	G	–	E		
Water hyacinth (*Eichhornia crassipes*)	P	G	–	E	E	
Water plantain (*Alisma triviale*)	P	E	E	–	E	G

TABLE 6.2
Susceptibility of Common Weeds to Control by 2,4-D, MCPA, 2,4,5-T, Silvex, and 2,4-DB* (*Continued*)

Plant name	Type of plant†	Control‡				
		2,4-D	MCPA	2,4,5-T¶	Silvex	2,4-DB
Waterweed, Canada (*Elodea canadensis*)	P	F	—	—	E	
Willow (*Salix* spp.)	W	G	G	G	G	
Witchweed (*Striga asiatica*)	A	E	E	E	E	E
Woodsorrel, yellow (*Oxalis stricta*)	P	P	N	—	E	
Wormwood, annual (*Artemisia annua*)	A	G	F	G		
Yankeeweed (*Eupatorium compositifolium*)	P	F	—	F		
Yarrow, common (*Achillea millefolium*)	P	P	P	P	P	N
Western (*A. lanulosa*)	P	F	—	F	—	N
Yellow-rocket (*Barbarea vulgaris*)	P	G	G	G	F	F
Yerba-santa (*Eriodictyon californicum*)	W	E	G	G	F	N
Yucca; soapweed (*Yucca glauca*)	P	N	—	P	F	

* From *Using Phenoxy Herbicides Effectively*, USDA Farmers Bull. 2183, rev. May 1974.
† W = woody; P = perennial, A = annual, B = biennial.

‡ E = excellent; G = good; F = fair, P = poor; N = none; for explanation of control ratings, see p. 371.

‡ See limitation on use of 2,4,5-T on p. 367.

¶ Sometimes biennial.

CRABGRASS CONTROL*

Crabgrass is the most common weed pest in turf areas. Its eradication is difficult, especially if the adjoining property institutes no control procedures. Crabgrass seed has been known to lie dormant for many years, buried deep in the ground; exposed to the light of day, it germinates.

There are two types of crabgrass treatment: (1) preemergence treatment, in which the herbicide is applied in the spring, before the seeds germinate; this is normally considered the best control and the easiest to apply; and (2) postemergence treatment, in which the herbicide is applied after the crabgrass emerges.

* Based on information in *USDA Home and Garden Bull.* 123.

Preemergence Treatment

The most common preemergence herbicides for crabgrass control are DCPA, benefin, bensulide, terbutol, and siduron. Apply only to established turf and not on areas which are about to be seeded or which have recently been seeded. An exception can be made for siduron, which can be applied to new bluegrass or fescue lawns, as well as to established lawns. The preemergence herbicides should be applied in April or early May before crabgrass germinates. See Table 6.3 for correct dosages and time to apply. The turf should be well watered after applying the herbicide in order to wash it off the leaves and onto the soil surface.

TABLE 6.3
Springtime Preemergence Crabgrass Control and Reseeding with Bluegrasses and Fescues*

Herbicide	Dose† per 1000 ft², oz	Time to reseed
DCPA	3.7	Fall, before or 60 days after
Bensulide	5.5	Fall, after spring treatment
Siduron	2.2	Any time
Benefin	0.7	Fall, after spring treatment
Terbutol	3.7	Fall, after spring treatment

* From *USDA Home Gard. Bull.* 123.

† These herbicides are usually sold prepackaged for a specific lawn area shown on the label.

Postemergence Treatment

DSMA and other arsonate materials will give good postemergence control of crabgrass. For effective control make three applications at 7- to 10-day intervals, the first coming shortly after the crabgrass emerges. In using DSMA be sure the soil is moist before applying. In hot, dry weather, water the soil thoroughly a few days before application and again a few days after each application. *Caution:* Do not treat St. Augustine grass with DSMA. Fine-leaved fescue should be treated only with the lower rates recommended by the manufacturer and only in early spring.

Broadleaf weeds can be controlled at the same time by adding 2,4-D or silvex to the DSMA solution at first application. Use only the rates recommended on the labels for broadleaf-weed control. After the first application make full-strength applications of DSMA at normal intervals.

BERMUDA GRASS CONTROL*

It is desirable in some locations and under certain conditions to control or eradicate Bermuda grass. Chemicals which will provide this control include methyl bromide, dalapon, metham, and dazomet. The use of any of these solutions requires the lawn to be reseeded.

Methyl bromide is the most effective in that it requires only one application and permits the treated area to be reseeded in 2 or 3 days' time. The other herbicides mentioned above always require follow-up applications and require a longer time before reseeding.

Methyl bromide

This herbicide is available in kits which contain equipment needed for proper application. For normal application air temperatures should be above 65°F. If the temperature is as low as 50°F, double the application rate.

There are three steps to be taken in applying methyl bromide: (1) cover the area to be treated with a gasproof covering sealed to the ground with soil, (2) release the methyl bromide under the covering at the rate recommended by the manufacturer, and (3) remove the covering after a 24-hour waiting period. *Caution:* methyl bromide gas is a deadly poison and should not be used near children or pets. Do not release it in a closed room.

The above technique can also be used to kill existing turf, which permits reseeding the area without having to turn the sod over.

Dalapon

Dalapon should be mixed with water at the rate of 8 tbsp (¼ lb) per gallon of water. Apply at the rate of 1 gal of mixture to each 1000 ft^2 of area to be treated. The first application should be made in late June and another 3 to 4 weeks later. The area can be reseeded 4 weeks after the second application provided the temperatures have been high and the area has been kept moist. Otherwise wait 6 weeks before reseeding.

Metham and Dazomet

Follow the manufacturer's directions in applying these herbicides. The first application should be made in early August and another 4 to 6

* Based on information in *USDA Home Gard. Bull.* 123.

weeks later. Reseeding may be done 3 to 4 weeks after the second application.

BROADLEAF-WEED CONTROL

Where bentgrass and clover are to be maintained, apply 2,4-D or MCPA at rate of 0.1 to 0.2 oz per 1000 ft^2. Silvex will kill white clover and dichondra, which is also sensitive to 2,4-D.

Apply herbicides in spring or fall when the temperature is above 60°F and the wind is still. Fall treatment is the most effective. See Table 6.2 for more information on the effectiveness of 2,4-D, MCPA, and silvex on weeds.

TABLE 6.4
Broadleaf-weed Control

Weed	Control
Chickweed, henbit, knotweed, ground ivy, oxalis	Use silvex alone or mixed with an equal amount of 2,4-D, both mixed half-strength; follow directions on label for proper dosages
Knotweed, ground ivy, clover, red sorrel, speedwell	Use mixtures of 2,4-D and dicamba as directed by manufacturer; excess dicamba may leach into the soil and damage trees and shrubs
Wild onion, wild garlic	Use low-volatile ester formulations of 2,4-D; apply at rate of 0.07 oz per 1000 ft^2; make treatment every year in March or early April and in October or November; 3 years of treatment may be necessary

Rules for Applying Herbicides

1. Apply herbicides according to manufacturer's instructions.
2. Do not overdose: overdoses are costly and may damage desirable plants.
3. For best results, apply herbicidal sprays only when
   a. Temperature is between 70 and 85°F.
   b. Little or no wind is blowing.
   c. No rain is expected for several hours.

SPOT INFESTATIONS

Spot infestations of weeds may be treated with dalapon or petroleum naphtha. If dalapon is used, mix 8 tbsp (1/4 lb) in 1 gal of water. Apply with a cane-type applicator, syringe, or similar device. Take care to keep the herbicide off desirable grasses. If petroleum naphtha is used, apply 1 gal per 1000 ft^2 as a coarse spray or wet the foliage well. This injures desirable grasses, but they will recover. This application is effective on all annual weeds.

Cleaning Sprayers

Clean the sprayer after each use by thoroughly washing with water and a detergent. If 2,4-D or silvex has been used, the sprayer should be cleaned with activated charcoal or household ammonia. The activated charcoal cleans rapidly and permits the sprayer to be used for insecticides and fungicides immediately.

To use activated charcoal, put 1 oz of it, together with 1 to 2 oz of household detergent, in 2½ gal of water and agitate thoroughly. The sprayer should then be operated with this mixture for about 2 minutes to be sure that it is clean.

To use ammonia prepare a solution of 2 tbsp of ammonia in a quart of water. Fill the sprayer with the solution and spray a small amount through the nozzle. Let the rest of the solution stand in the sprayer overnight. Then pour out the solution and rinse twice with clean water. Spray part of each rinse through the nozzle.

Trimec* Turf Herbicides

A newer and effective chemical for broadleaf weed control, known as Trimec, has been developed. This material:

Will control the widest range of broadleaf weeds.
Will get hard-to-kill species without repeated applications.
Will give a wide margin of safety to lawn grasses.
Has no vapor action after application.
Is effective within a wide range of temperature.
Is sequestered to overcome water-hardness problems.
Permits treated areas to be seeded within 2 weeks.
Is stable for several seasons but should be protected from freezing.

* Trade name.

The broadleaf weeds usually killed by Trimec are:

Bedstraw	Henbit	Ragweed
Bindweed	Knotweed	Sheep sorrel
Black medic	Lamb's-quarter	Shepherd's purse
Carpet weed	Milford (yarrow)	Smartweed
Clover	Morning glory	Sunflower
Common chickweed	Mouse-ear chickweed	Spotted spurge
Dandelion	Mustard	Thistle
Dichondra	Peppergrass	Wild garlic
Curled dock	Pigweed	Wild lettuce
Ground ivy	Plantain	Wild onion
Heal-all	Purslane	Yarrow

BRUSH CONTROL*

Increased emphasis has been placed on chemical control of brush and weeds during the past few years, mainly because of the need to find cheaper, faster, and more convenient ways of accomplishing the work previously done by hand. Use of herbicides is now almost universal except in specific small-scale areas.

Best results (which means better) are obtained if brush is chemically treated while still comparatively young. Since less spray volume is required, the cost of application is reduced. Tall brush is often treated by first cutting it and then treating the suckers or sprouts when they are 3 to 6 ft tall. When brush has reached 15 ft or more, only a thorough wetting of the leaves and stem will kill it, but the brownout is very noticeable.

A most important consideration is timing. Good results have been obtained during the period from the first full-leaf stage until 2 or 3 weeks before frost and whenever soil moisture is adequate to sustain good results. Actually research has shown that the movement of 2,4-D from the leaves to the stem and roots of the plant takes place most readily when the plant is translocating carbohydrates in the same direction. In the stem the 2,4-D moves both upward and downward. Obviously, large acreages cannot be treated economically by ground equipment within a short period, and so spraying operations must spread over a major part of the growing season. Both 2,4-D and 2,4,5-T have been effective against a wide variety of woody species. Some

* Based on information from Lawrence Southwick, Dow Chemical USA, Midland, Mich.

species are easy to kill; others show more resistance. Certain ones are more susceptible to 2,4,5-T than 2,4-D, including sweet gum, osage orange, some oaks, poison ivy, maple, blackberry, raspberry, hickory, ash, rose, ribes, basswood, and meadowsweet.

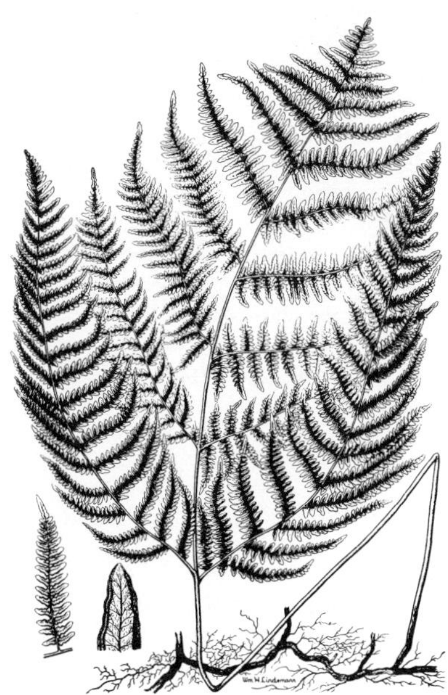

Fig. 6.1 Bracken fern (*Pteris aquilina*). This fernlike plant is rather widespread in pastures and meadows and is poisonous to horses and cattle. The plant varies in height, depending upon the location, but it may grow as high as 6 ft. It has a creeping black rootstock extending for many feet along the surface and penetrating 2 or 3 ft into the soil. Hay should not be cut from places where this fern grows. Clean cultivation for 2 or 3 years will destroy the deep-lying rootstocks by starving them out. Chemical control by Ammate. (*Seedburo Equipment Co.*)

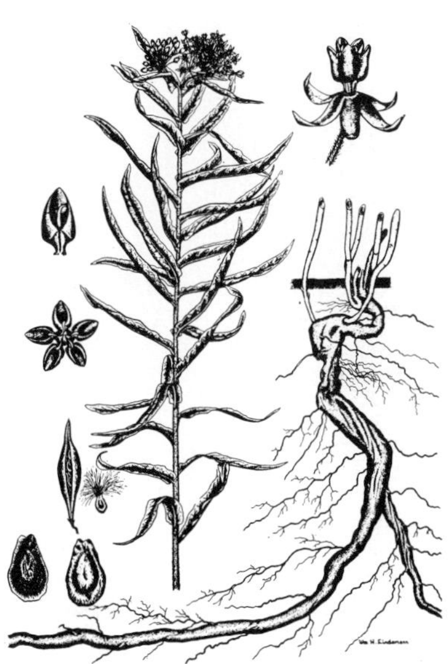

Fig. 6.2 Butterfly weed (*Asclepias tuberosa*). A mildly poisonous weed, tall, erect, and sturdy in habit, confined to sunny, dry open places along roadsides and in pastures. It comes from a thick tough perennial root, with many stems from the crown forming a bushy clump. It has many dark-green leaves, clasping the stem at their base. The flowers are orange and very showy and are followed by the characteristic milkweed pod with silky, flying seeds. Control by repeated spudding out below the crown followed by an application of common salt to the cut root surfaces. (*Seedburo Equipment Co.*)

Picloram is a newer herbicide that is more effective on many species than either 2,4-D or 2,4,5-T. Available in Tordon* products, this herbicide is used in foliage sprays, in pellet applications to soil (for root up-take), and in bark injections on larger trees.

* Trademark.

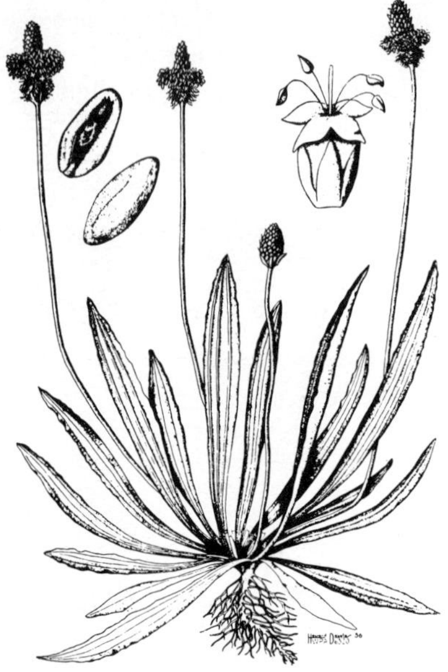

Fig. 6.3 Buckhorn (*Plantago lanceolata*). A very persistent perennial, reproduced by seeds in large numbers. Seed matures from May to November. Leaves are long, narrow, ribbed, and hairy. Flowers are small and form a collar around a short spike. Stem is 6 to 15 in. tall. Seeds are brown and boat-shaped, with a waxy coat. The most effective method of control is to prevent weeds from producing seeds. Small infestations can be dug out, or heavier infestations can be effectively sprayed with 2,4-D. Other chemical control by Weedar MCP or sodium salt at rate of 2 lb/acre. (*USDA*.)

Fig. 6.4 Canada thistle (*Cirsium arvense*). A perennial spreading by seed and rootstock. The long white roots lie deep in the ground and sometimes attain a length of 15 to 20 ft. They send up new plants at intervals, and stems reach 1 to 4 ft high. It has an erect, sturdy growth, with a bristly appearance. Leaves are cut and curled, spined, and with blooms much smaller than other thistles. Blooms are white to lavender. This weed forms dense patches to the exclusion of other plants. It is offensive to most grazing animals and reduces feeding value as well as market value of hay. The Canada thistle is very hard to control because of its spreading underground roots. Spray with a solution of calcium chlorate (½ lb per gallon of water) just before the bloom stage. Apply enough spray for a thorough wetting of all the aboveground vegetation and repeat when new growth begins. Two or three applications are usually required. Other chemical controls are, 2,4-D, sodium salt of 2,4-D (effective in spring and early summer), ester of 2,4-D foliage spray, 2,4-D postemergence spray (at 1 lb/acre), Eastern Brush Killer, and Weedar MCP. (*USDA*.)

Fig. 6.5 Clover dodder (*Cuscuta arvensis*). An annual weed of parasitic habit, spreading by seeds. This is a weak golden, leafless vine, subsisting by suckers which penetrate into the host plant, thereby reducing food supplies and retarding the development of clover. Once established, it rambles and twines rapidly, forming large patches in a field. Small rough-coated seeds are formed in large numbers from July to October. Of several control measures which may be taken the most effective is to burn the infested plants with a weed burner. This method also will kill dodder seeds on the ground. Infested plants may also be sprayed with oil, kerosene, sulfuric acid, ammonium thiocyanate (1 lb in 2 gal water), or sodium chlorate (1.5 lb in 1 gal water) and burned when dry. 2,4-D has also proved effective. (*Seedburo Equipment Co.*)

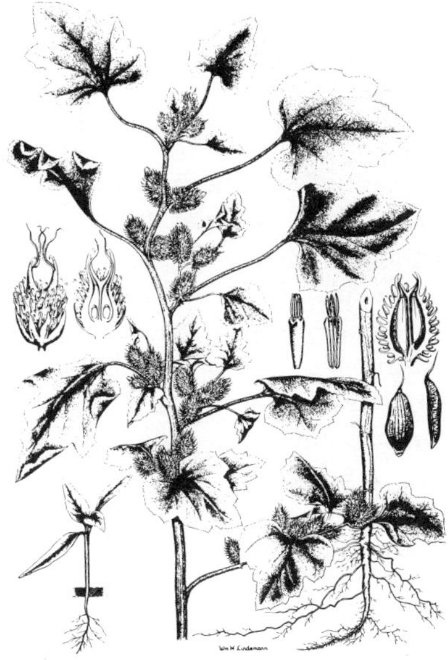

Fig. 6.6 Cocklebur (*Xanthium canadense*). A tough, hardy annual, 1 to 3 ft high, with rough-surfaced, alternate leaves. It reproduces by seeds. It is poisonous to swine feeding on the seedlings and does internal damage to other animals if found in hay. Keep animals away from infested spots. Hand pull, pile, and burn the plants while young. Chemical control can be achieved by spraying with 2,4-D. (*Seedburo Equipment Co.*)

Brush-Control Methods

To control brush generally, use 3 to 4 qt per 100 gal of water of an emulsifiable 2,4-D ester formulation (Esteron 99 concentrates) containing 4 lb of acid equivalent per gallon or an emulsifiable 2,4,5-T ester formulation (Esteron 245) containing 4 lb of acid equivalent per gallon. A combination of these two (Esteron Brush Killer) can also be used at the rate of 3 to 4 qt in 100 gal of water.

Fig. 6.7 Common Chickweed (*Stellaria media*). An annual, spreading by seeds and by rooting at the nodes of the stem. In sheltered spots it may bloom all year, producing seed in abundance. It is prostrate to upright in growth; the leaves are small and opposite, with small white flowers. It forms dense clumps or patches, choking out grass. For control, spray with iron sulfate and repeat if necessary. Small patches, however, should be removed by digging, especially in autumn, since this weed is capable of vigorous winter growth. Chemical control can be obtained with 2,4-D (high concentration as dust in soil), Weedar MCP, Dinitrol, Dow General Weed Killer (in oil emulsion), DN Dry Mix 1, or DN 111. (*USDA.*)

Apply the spray in sufficient quantity to wet the foliage and stems thoroughly. In order to get the best kill, it is necessary to have the herbicide absorbed and translocated within the plant. It may require as much as 100 to 400 gal of spray per acre to obtain adequate coverage. If the sprays are applied properly, a 75 to 90 per cent reduction in top growth may be expected. Do not expect 100 per cent kill. Apply one spray treatment the first season and a second the next season if needed. Subsequent applications will usually be limited to spot treatment. For determining cost of treatment, the program should be planned on a 5- or 10-year basis.

Brush-Control Equipment

The type of equipment to use will vary with the kind of job to be done. Power wagons equipped with 150- to 200-gal spray tanks and the orchard type of spray gun are useful. The spray guns should be adjustable in order to cover foliage both close and some distance away. In areas where the terrain will not permit use of mobile equipment an additional quantity of hose (1000 to 1500 ft) should be carried.

The problem of drift must be considered at all times. Adjoining property must be protected, since many crops, flowers, and ornamentals are very susceptible to herbicide sprays. Drift can be reduced by using low spray pressure. Also, special care must be taken to avoid spraying when crosswinds can carry spray particles off the target area. Most off-target injury has occurred because of spray drift. If there is any question about spray drift, the best decision is not to spray.

Fig. 6.8 Crabgrass (*Digitaria sanguinale*). An annual, sometimes called finger grass, spreading by seed and by rooting at the lower joints. Seed matures from August to October. Seed head contains three to six and sometimes as many as ten fingers several inches long and generally purplish or reddish-brown, arranged in a whorl like the fingers of the hand. Seed will remain alive in the ground for many years. Crabgrass is very difficult to eradicate or control. Preventing formation of seed heads by constant mowing or pulling will help to check its spread. Several chemicals have been used to control this weed, with varying degrees of success. Chemical solutions containing phenyl mercuric acetate will kill crabgrass, but it will also either kill other grasses or turn the grass brown for several weeks. Probably the most selective and best chemical to use is potassium cyanate. *Caution.* Do not confuse potassium *cyanate* with potassium *cyanide*, which is a deadly poison. Potassium cyanate is sold under several brand names, and full instructions for use are furnished. Briefly, these instructions are as follows:

1. Use a pump-up pressure garden sprayer in order to get a misty spray.
2. Apply when grass is green and lush. The chemical does not work well on dry ground. Wait for a good rain or give grass a good watering before spraying.
3. Spray early for best results, with the first application in early July to catch the first crop and the second in mid-August to kill crabgrass germinating later.

Crabgrass cannot be killed in one season because there will be seed from preceding years in the ground. It is necessary to fertilize, water, and cut the lawn properly for best results. (*Seedburo Equipment Co.*)

There are many areas where it is impossible for power-operated equipment to reach all portions to be sprayed. Here 2- to 5-gal knapsack sprayers can be used. The same amount of 2,4-D and 2,4,5-T per acre should be applied by this method as with the power equipment. Both water and oil have been used as carriers, and satisfactory results have been obtained. Uniform coverage is of utmost importance, but of course

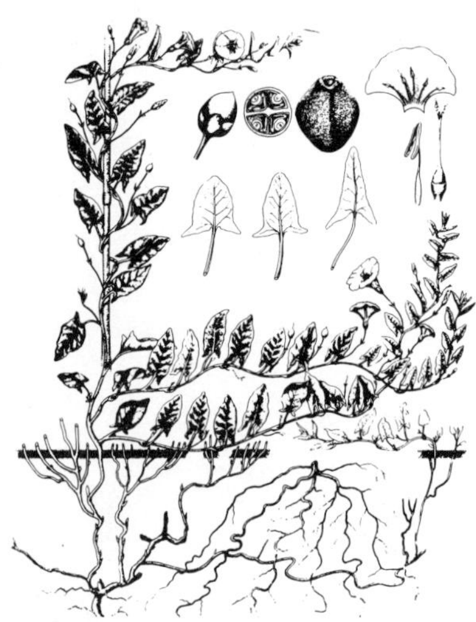

Fig. 6.9 Field bindweed (*Convolvulus arvensis*). A perennial, spreading by seed and root stocks. The root system is extensive and penetrates to great depths. Growth is prostrate, forming dense mats which choke and crowd out other plants. Leaves are usually shovel-shaped; flower usually white or pink, funnel-formed and single on the stems. An inch or two below the flower are two small leaflike appendages which distinguish it from the hedge type of bindweed, which carries two leafy bracts close to the flower. Spraying with 2,4-D will give adequate control. (*USDA*.)

Fig. 6.10 Field sorrel (*Oxalis stricta*). This plant likes a moist acid soil and frequently invades lawns. Leaves are similar to clover; the flowers are yellow, and the plant is prostrate to erect, sometimes creeping and spreading. Seeds are borne in a tight, eight-parted capsule. Control by preventing seed production. Chemical control can be obtained by using 2,4-D or (on the seedlings only) Weedar MCP. (*USDA*.)

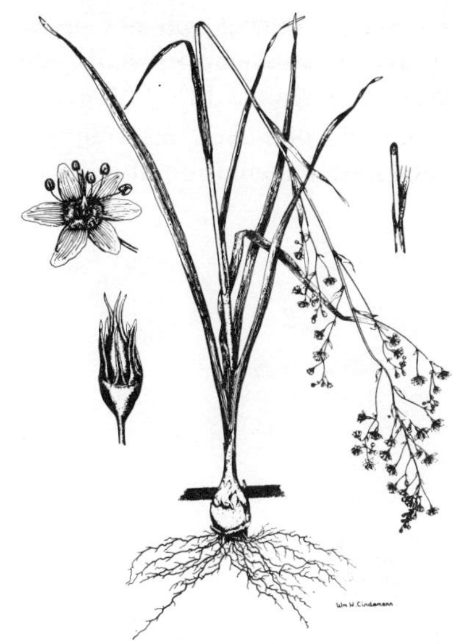

Fig. 6.11 Glaucus-leaved anticlea (*Zyadenus chloranthus*). A poisonous perennial coming from an onionlike bulb. All parts of the plant are poisonous, but the bulb is most poisonous of all. The plant reproduces by seeds. It is grasslike with long, narrow leaves surrounding an erect flower stem which bears numerous small yellowish flowers in a loose cluster. All animals should be kept away from infested areas, which should also be kept well salted to prevent them from forming an appetite for this weed. During the flowering period, grub out, pile, dry, and burn all plants. (*Seedburo Equipment Co.*)

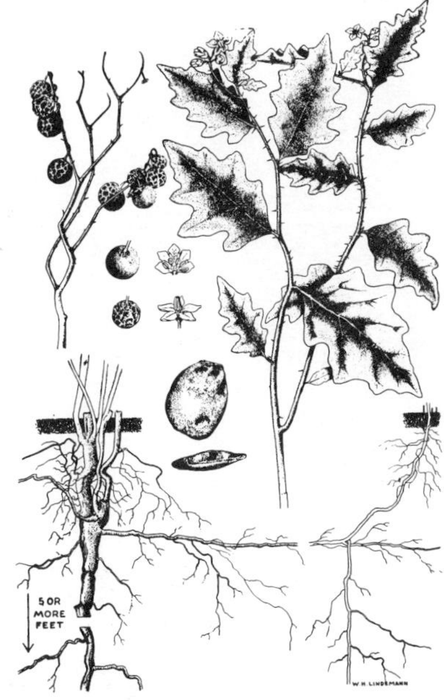

Fig. 6.12 Horse nettle (*Solanum carolinense*). A rugged perennial, hairy and prickly. The leaves are large, and similar to oak leaves. The flowers are like those of the potato, and the berries resemble small tomatoes, each of which may produce 40 to 60 seeds. The root system is deep, spreading, and tough. Seeds are oval, flattened, and yellowish. Horse nettle spreads vegetatively by means of creeping horizontal rhizomes up to 3 ft long and usually 6 to 10 in. below the surface. Vertical taproots extend as deep as 8 ft. A good sod of bluegrass will smother this weed out, as will regular cultivation. Several chemicals will give control: (1) salt applied at the rate of 1 lb/ft^2 after the shoots are cut in full bloom; (2) waste crankcase oil diluted with kerosene and applied as a drench when the first flower buds open; (3) sodium chlorate applied as a foliage spray in July and again in September; apply at rate of 1 to 1.5 lb chemical per gallon of water; (4) spraying with 2,4,5-T. (*Seedburo Equipment Co.*)

complete wetting will not be possible. The total volume of spray required will depend upon the density and height of vegetation. Under many conditions 10 to 25 gal of spray per acre will give satisfactory coverage, provided this volume is applied uniformly to the foliage and the solution contains sufficient amounts of the herbicides.

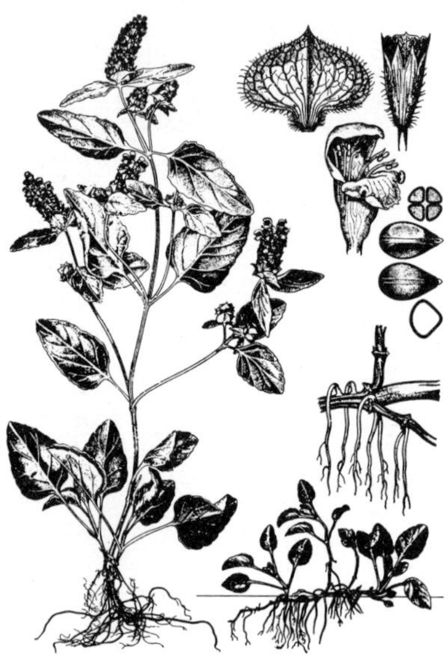

Fig. 6.13 Heal-all (*Prunella arelgaris*). A slender, leggy plant with pale violet flowers in moist, shaded situations. In open fields or on grassy roadside banks it is shorter and more compact, with darker-colored flowers. In lawns, where it is cut back severely and regularly, it develops horizontally and may form prostrate patches of considerable extent. The leaves vary from oblong to ovate, and the flowers range from purple to flesh color or even white. An application of a strong (8%) solution of iron sulfate will eliminate the weed without causing injury to other grasses. It may have to be treated at intervals of several weeks until all the plants disappear. Spraying with a high concentration of 2,4-D will also give control. (*Seedburo Equipment Co.*)

Fig. 6.14 Hemp (*Cannabis sativa*). An annual with palmately compound leaves composed of from five to seven narrow-tapering, coarsely toothed leaflets. It has small greenish flowers, with the two sexes developed on separate plants. This plant produces marihuana. It can easily be controlled by pulling or cutting close to the ground. (*Seedburo Equipment Co.*)

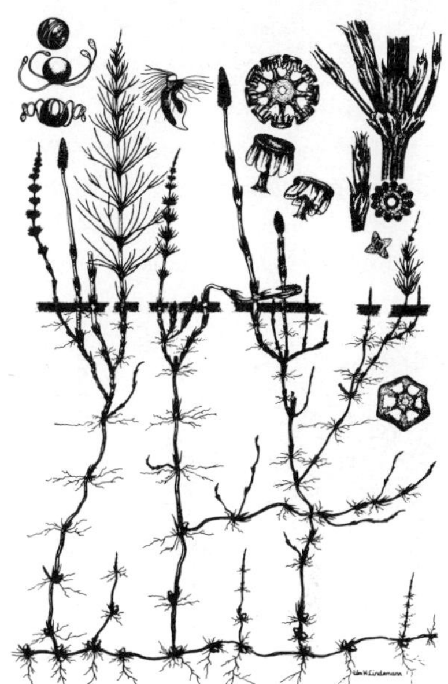

Fig. 6.15 Horsetail (*Equisetum arvense*). A poisonous perennial commonly found growing in gravelly soil, especially where there is ample water in the subsoil. There are two kinds of shoots, fertile and sterile, the fertile shoots appearing first, being unbranched, with nearly naked stems, sheathed at the joints. The sterile shoots appear later and are branched and taller. Drain and cultivate areas infested with this weed. Keep animals away. Spray with a high concentration of 2,4-D. (*Seedburo Equipment Co.*)

Fig. 6.16 Jimson weed (*Datura stramonium*). An annual with poisonous properties occurring most frequently on dumps, waste ground, and poor pastures. The plant has oaklike leaves, and stems and foliage give off an unpleasant scent when broken and bruised. The plant is coarse and ill-scented, with spiny pods. It is a source of atropine, and its long tabular flowers have a kind of exotic beauty. Hand pulling is an easy matter and should be done before the pods have matured. Chemical control can be obtained with 2,4-D or 2,4-D postemergence spray (at 1 lb/acre), Weedar MCP (sodium salt at 1 lb/acre). (*USDA*.)

Stump Treatment

For general stump treatment use 4 gal of an emulsifiable 2,4,5-T ester in 96 gal of oil or 6 gal of a combination of 2,4-D and 2,4,5-T in 96 gal of oil. For smaller quantities, use 1½ pt of the combination spray in 3 gal of fuel or diesel oil or 1 pt Esteron 245 in 3 gal of fuel or diesel oil. Tordon 101R is a ready-to-use product that is very effective.

Fig. 6.17 Knotweed (*Polygonum aviculare*). An annual with greenish-white flowers, ranging from a low, prostrate form to trailing and climbing forms. The most distinguishing feature is the somewhat cylindrical sheath at the base of each leaf, just where the petiole joins the stem. Many species are thickened at the nodes, giving them a jointed or "kneed" look. It can be controlled by hoeing and pulling or when it occurs in driveways, paths, or tennis courts, by the application of chlorate sprays or by salting. Other chemical controls are 2,4-D or 2,4-D postemergence spray (at 1 lb/acre); sodium TCA 90%. (*USDA.*)

Fig. 6.18 Frenchweed (*Thalspi arvense*). Sometimes called stinkweed. An erect, close-growing plant, sparingly leaved except near the soil; mustard-colored, with the entire top full of greenish-yellow bloom. Mature seedpods are like small winged capsules, with oval reddish-brown seeds marked by concentric ridges. It is an annual, appearing early and prolifically. Odor and taste are offensive. Spraying with 2,4-D as a postemergence spray at ½ lb/acre or as a sodium salt will give control. Dinitrol and Weedar MCP may also be used. (*Seedburo Equipment Co.*)

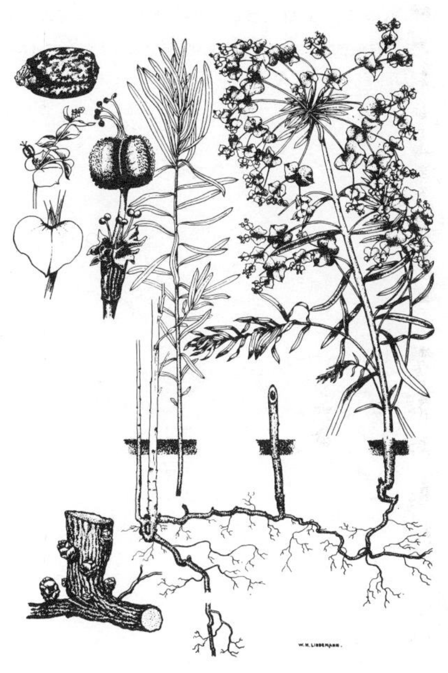

Fig. 6.19 Leafy spurge (*Euphorbia esula*). A perennial with deep, tough, woody roots, spreading both vegetatively and from matured seeds. It is an erect, branching plant with many buds at base of the crown, and forms tufts or dense clumps and patches. The entire plant is a yellowish green, leafy, and resembles a willow shoot. The flowers are small and surrounded by a group of leafy bracts resembling a flower head. Milky, poisonous sap causes blisters on skin. Seeds are mottled and smooth. Some roots have been found at depths slightly over 15 ft and are relatively numerous at 8 to 12 ft. Leafy spurge is very difficult to eradicate or control. 2,4-D has no effect, and since horses and cattle do not relish it, grazing is ineffective. Grazing by sheep, however, has been known to give some control. An application of from 2.5 to 4 gal per rod of the following solution has given some control: 1 lb sodium chlorate, 4 g (= 0.14 oz) animal glue, 3 m sulfuric acid, and 1 gal water. Apply when plants come into bloom and again just before first frost. Use of borax has given some control. (*Seedburo Equipment Co.*)

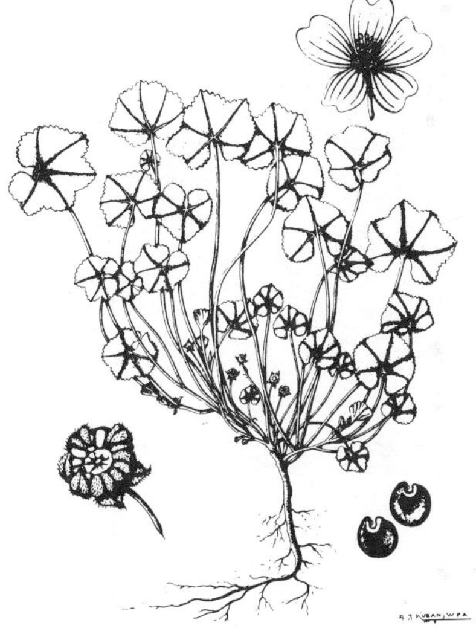

Fig. 6.20 Low or common mallow (*Malva rotundifolia*). A biennial or perennial plant producing vigorous, leafy stems from deeply embedded and extensive roots. Stems trail along the ground and cover a considerable area. The rounded, shallowly lobed and prominently veined leaves are borne on long petioles, from the axils of which arise the pale-pink five-petaled flowers. The small flattened circular fruit suggests miniature cheeses. Can be controlled by high concentrations of 2,4-D when plants are young and in active growth or with Weedar MCP, sodium salt, at 2 lb/acre. (*USDA.*)

The use of 2,4-D, 2,4,5-T, and picloram for stump treatment during winter, fall, spring, or summer adds tremendously to the versatility of the chemical control of woody vegetation. One man using a knapsack sprayer can spray all stumps and stubs that a good-sized crew can cut on an average right of way. There is very little hand labor in treating

Fig. 6.21 Marsh shield fern (*Dryopteris thelypteris*). A fern found in wet marshes and woods, rarely in dry soil. It comes from creeping, blackish rootstocks. The leaves are compound, divided into many distinct leaflets. It is poisonous to livestock, and if marsh hay is used, care should be taken in mowing. Control by grubbing out all rootstocks or by draining to prevent conditions suitable for growth of this plant. (*Seedburo Equipment Co.*)

Fig. 6.22 Night-flowering catchfly (*Silone noctiflora*). A tall, branched plant developing from a thick fleshy root. The stems are hairy and somewhat sticky, and leaves are opposite and lance-shaped. The flowers are perfect, with three styles. Stamens and carpels occur in the same flower, and petals are white. This weed can be controlled by spraying with 2,4-D. (*USDA*.)

stumps by this method, and the per acre cost of herbicides is low. In areas where susceptible crops are grown near the areas to be sprayed, stump treatment is less hazardous than foliage spraying.

A knapsack sprayer equipped with oil-resistant check values, pump leathers, and hose, is standard equipment for this job. Pressures of 15 to 25 lb/in.[2] are sufficient. The fan type of spray nozzle is held close to the stumps or stubs or close to the ground when spraying, in order to minimize spray drift. It is suggested that the spray be applied within 1 day after cutting, if possible. Various methods have been used for marking stumps that have been treated, and several organic oil-soluble dyes have been tested.

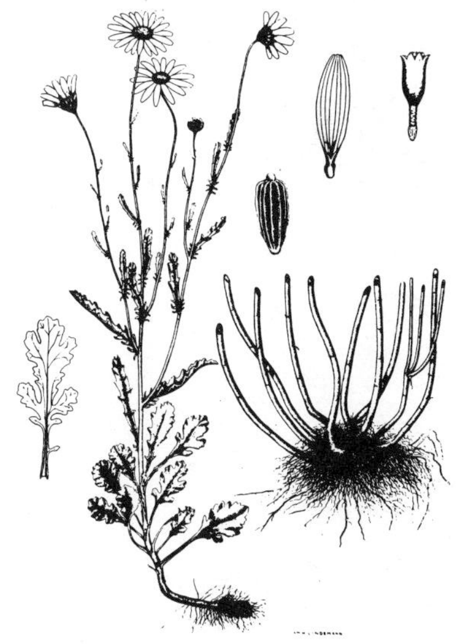

Fig. 6.23 Oxeye Daisy (*Chrysanthemum leucanthemum*). A perennial, spreading by seeds and by rootstocks from the thick, tufted crown. It is an early bloomer, with seeds maturing rapidly even after they are cut from the stalk. The flowers are single at end of stalk and white with yellow center. Leaves are crinkled and cut. The plant blooms from May to October and seeds from June to November. Control by preventing plants from going to seed and by working land in cultivated crops for several years. Chemical control may be obtained with 2,4-D (at high concentrations) or Weedar MCP (at high concentrations on young plants). (*USDA*.)

Fig. 6.24 Plantain (*Plantago major*). A perennial with a thickened crown and fibrous wiry roots. The leaves are smooth, broad, thick-veined, often red or purplish along the main stem. The flowers are small, borne on a long spike, and produce many small, black, irregular-shaped seeds. Chemical control can be obtained with 2,4-D, Dow General Weed Killer or Chipman General in oil emulsion, Weedar MCP (a sodium salt at rate of 2 lb/acre), or DN dry mix no. 1 or DN 111 in oil emulsion. (*USDA*.)

Substations and Pole Yards

A serious fire hazard is created if vegetation is left to grow unchecked in pole storage yards and substations. In addition to removing weeds, brambles, and woody vegetation from these areas, controlling grass is also desirable. This problem has usually been handled by means of

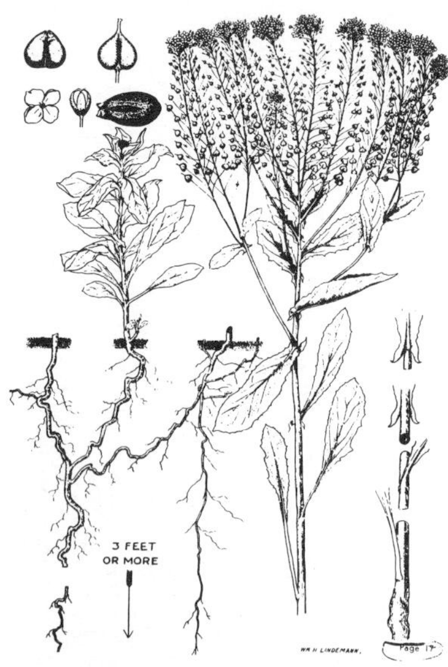

Fig. 6.25 Perennial peppergrass (*Lepidium draba*). A perennial which is reproduced by seeds and rootstock; forms large dense patches which choke and crowd out other vegetation. It is a rapid grower, blooming early and maturing many seeds. The leaves are hairy, clasping the stem at the base; are numerous at the crown and sparser above. The plant is much branched, carrying heavy flower stems with small white flowers. Seeds are oval, chocolate brown, and two in a pod. A postemergence spray of 2,4-D at 0.5 lb/acre will control. (*USDA.*)

Fig. 6.26 Poison ivy (*Rhus toxicodendron*). A widespread poisonous vine or shrub, climbing vine, or erect bush. The leaf is composed of three leaflets. Flowers are small and greenish, borne in drooping clusters, and followed by whitish, waxy-coated berries that remain after the leaves fall. All parts of the plant are poisonous at any time of year. Chemical control can be obtained with 2,4-D (several applications will completely eradicate); 2,4-D (as an ester or as an aqueous foliage spray); 2,4,5-T (foliage spray, esters or aqueous); ammate (1.5 lb dry per square yard or as aqueous foliage spray); borax; 2,4-D and 2,4,5-T (mixed esters, foliage spray); Esteron brush killer. (*USDA.*)

hand or machine cutting and by contact herbicides such as oils, pentachlorophenol, dinitrophenols, and others. These contact sprays kill the aboveground vegetation but do not affect the roots of perennial grasses to any extent.

An effective grass killer is sodium trichloroacetate, known commercially as TCA. The herbicidal action of TCA appears to be prin-

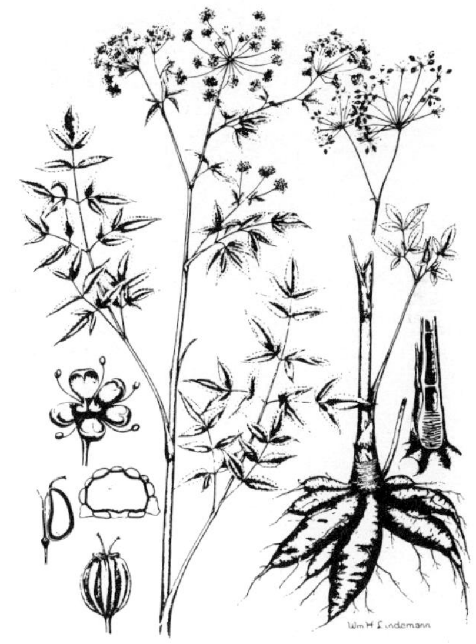

Fig. 6.27 Poison hemlock (*Circuta maculata*). A very poisonous perennial plant confined to low, wet pastures, creek banks, and ditches. The plant grows to a height of 2 to 6 ft. with swollen, hollow, dahlialike roots. The stems are stout and streaked with purple spots. The leaves are pale green, lacy, and much divided. The flowers are small, greenish white, and borne at the top of the branches forming flat clusters; in each cluster there may be from 15 to 30 small flowers. Grub out the root clusters, pile, dry, and burn. Chemical control can be obtained with 2,4-D, 2,4-D (high concentration or sodium salt), 2,4-D and 2,4,5-T (mixed esters), Esteron brush killer, or Weedar MCP. (*USDA.*)

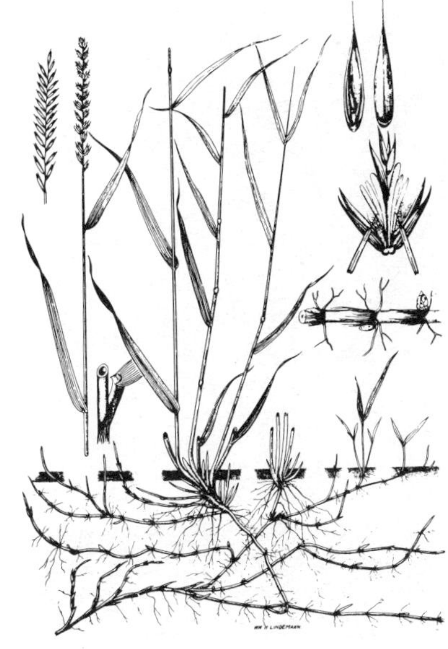

Fig. 6.28 Quack grass (*Agopyron repens*). A perennial grass spreading by creeping rootstock and by seed. It forms a dense sod, crowding out more valuable plants. It is erect, smooth, and dark green, with the seed borne on a spike, similar to two-rowed barley. This grass can be reduced if not eradicated by shallow plowing (4 to 6 in. deep) or digging infested areas during hot, dry summer weather. It can also be effectively crowded out with desirable grasses or white clover or by close mowing or grazing. A spray of 1.5 lb of calcium chlorate per gallon water just before the bloom stage is also fairly effective. Two or three applications are usually required. Other chemicals which have given control are 2,4-D, MH, and sodium TCA 90%. (*USDA.*)

Fig. 6.29 Giant Ragweed (*Ambrosia trifida*). An annual, growing to a height of 12 or 15 ft with numerous branches. The leaves are palmately divided into three or occasionally five lobes. The plant likes a moist, rich soil. Spraying with 2,4-D in the early stages of growth gives good control. Use at the rate of 1.25 in 100 gal water per acre, or 0.5 lb/acre, postemergence spray. Ammate will also give control. Common ragweed (*Ambrosia elatior*) (not shown) has leaves which are pinnately twice divided. Its seedlings somewhat suggest the marigold but lack the rank odor. The female flowers are borne in small clusters in the axils of the leaves, while the male, or staminate, heads are crowded into racemes at the top of the plant and the ends of the upper branches. Sprayed at the appropriate time, 2,4-D will give effective control at the rate of 2 lb/acre. (*USDA*.)

Fig. 6.30 Sow thistle (*Sonchus arvensis*). A persistent perennial spreading by seeds and rootstocks. It grows erect, forming dense patches to the exclusion of other plants. Leaves are dark green with edges spined and recurving toward the base; upper leaves are usually uncut but spined, clasping stem at base. Roots are yellowish and brittle. Plant is filled with a milky sap; flowers are similar to those of the dandelion. Cultural methods are the most practical means of control or eradication. One year of shallow cultivation will entirely eradicate perennial sow thistle.

1. In middle of June (or just before the plant begin to blossom) plow to a depth not greater than 3 or 4 in.; harrow or disc immediately to close the furrows.
2. During the following 12 weeks, keep the soil entirely free of top growth, employing a disc, duckfoot cultivator, or rod or wire weeder.

Chemical control can be obtained as follows: 2,4-D, high concentration applied to cut stem; 1 lb/acre, postemergence spray; sodium salt, high concentration; butyl ester, 1 lb/acre; Weedar MCP: sodium salt, 1 lb/acre, high concentration. (*USDA*.)

Fig. 6.31 Shepherd's purse (*Capsella bursa-pastoris*). The lower or rosette leaves are deeply toothed or lobed with long, tapering bases, while its stem leaves are arrow-shaped with entire or wavy margins and clasping bases. The most characteristic feature is the heart-shaped, flattened seedpod, which liberates innumerable small seeds. The plant may behave as a winter annual. It can be controlled by high concentrations of 2,4-D when plants are young and in active growth and by Dinitrol sodium salt, Dow General Weed Killer, or Chipman General and Weedar MCP. (*USDA.*)

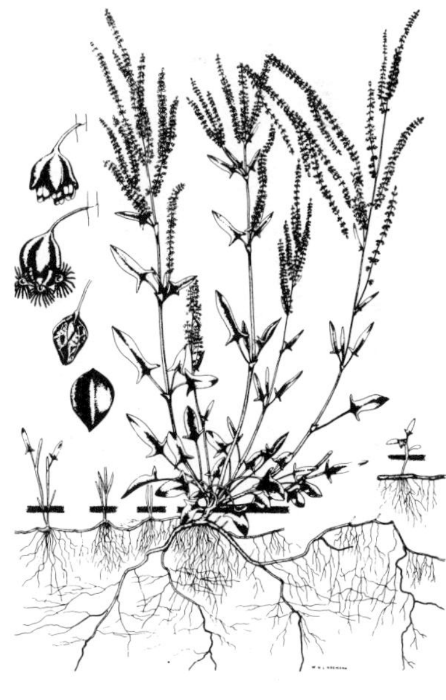

Fig. 6.32 Sheep sorrel (*Rumex acetosella*). A low, creeping perennial, producing a large number of small seeds. It has numerous creeping roots in the upper 8 in. of soil, parts of which may extend to a depth of 5 or 6 ft. Since sheep sorrel tolerates an acid condition, its presence may indicate an acid soil. However, it thrives best on rich, well-drained soils containing lime. Acid soils infested with sheep sorrel can be improved by treatment with ground limestone, 2 tons/acre, hydrated lime, 1.5 tons/acre, or quicklime, 1 ton/acre. Lime has no harmful effects on sheep sorrel but creates soil conditions that enable crop plants to compete with the weed. Selective sprays, such as iron sulfate, dilute sulfuric acid, and Sinox, will kill sheep sorrel and will not permanently harm pasture grasses except clover. Other means of chemical control are 2,4-D (sodium and amine salts; ammonium salt, high concentration); Dow General Weed Killer, Chipman General, DN dry mix no. 1, or DN 111 in oil emulsion; Weedar MCP, sodium salt as dust. (*Seedburo Equipment Co.*)

cipally through roots and is most effective when there is an abundance of soil moisture. When excessive rainfall occurs shortly after application, this herbicide may be subject to leaching, particularly on light-textured soils. TCA may retard or kill the following grasses: Johnson, Bermuda, para, quack, Kentucky blue, Canada blue, redtop, orchard, timothy, buffalo, and smooth brome. In addition, a number of winter annual grasses have been found to respond, often at lower dosages than

Fig. 6.33 Snow-on-the-mountain (*Euphorbia marginata*). This plant is used as an ornamental annual in some regions, but it is poisonous to some people. It is a tall, branching, strong-growing plant, pale green, and leafy at the top with leaf margins edged in white. Flowers are small, in loose clusters among the closely crowded leaves. It reproduces by seeds and thereby often escapes cultivation and becomes a weed. It can be readily controlled by hand pulling before it flowers. (*Seedburo Equipment Co.*)

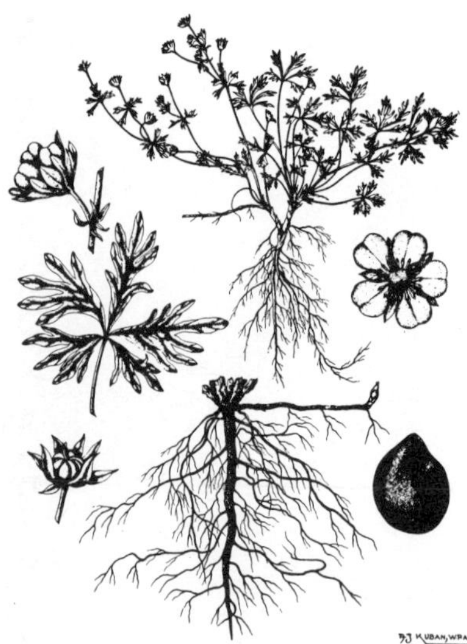

Fig. 6.34 Silvery or hoary cinquefoil (*Potentilla argentea*). A perennial silvery gray weed of creeping spreading habit. The leaves are finely cut, five-parted. The flowers are yellow, opening from May to September, and seeds are developed from June to November. *Control by frequent control* can be obtained as follows: Weedar MCP (sodium salt, 4 lb/acre); 2,4-D (foliage spray), 2,4-D and 2,4,5-T (mixed esters, foliage spray). (*Seedburo Equipment Co.*)

required for established perennials. Relatively small amounts applied to the soil often prevent the emergence of grass seedlings.

Soil sterility from TCA is usually of relatively short duration, that is, 1 to 3 months. Its toxicity is about the same as that of table salt, and it is compatible with 2,4-D and 2,4,5-T formulations in water sprays. In addition, it can be used with contact weed killers such as emulsifi-

Fig. 6.35 White snakeroot (*Eupatorium urticaefolium*). A shade-loving perennial plant which causes milk sickness or milk fever in cattle and people. It is erect, 2 to 3 ft high, and leaves are opposite, dark green, and strongly three-veined on the back. The flowers are borne at ends of branches in flat clusters; very small, white, and close-bunched. The roots are blackish, stringy, and tough, forming a thick crown or cluster, not deep or running in character. Hand pull, pile, and burn all plants found. Chemical control can be obtained by using mixed esters of 2,4-D and 2,4,5-T. (*Seedburo Equipment Co.*)

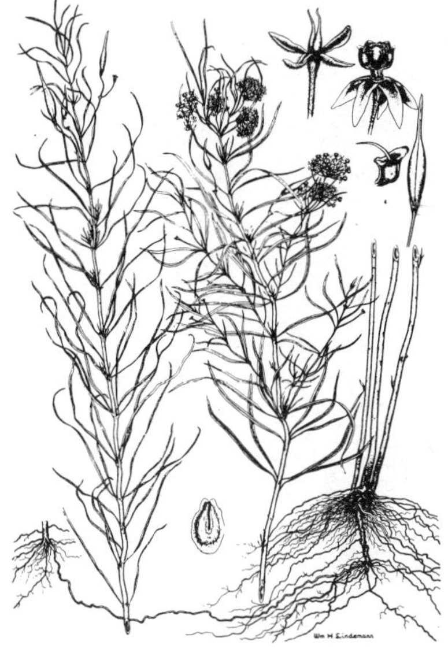

Fig. 6.36 Whorled milkweed (*Asclepias verticillata*). A perennial weed, poisonous to livestock, especially horses and sheep. The plant comes from a running rootstock or seed. It is pale green, with numerous small narrow leaves, almost like the blades of grass arranged in clusters around the stem. The flowers are small, greenish white, and borne at ends of branches in a compact cluster. They are followed by a long green pod filled with cottony seeds which are dispersed by the wind. The average height is about 2 ft. A system of clean cultivation and crop rotation will control this weed. Chemical control can be obtained with 2,4,5-T (35% solution) or 2,4-D and 2,4,5-T (mixed esters) stem painting. (*Seedburo Equipment Co.*)

Fig. 6.37 Wild lupine (*Lupinus perennis*). Plant is strong, erect, rather fleshy, and slightly hairy. The leaflets are usually in groups of seven to eleven, attached to a central stem. Flowers are pea-shaped and blue to white. The root is strong, penetrating the soil for several feet. This perennial is considered poisonous to livestock. Control by spading off below the crown several times during the season. (*Seedburo Equipment Co.*)

Fig. 6.38 Wild carrot (*Daucus carota*). A biennial coming from a thick boring taproot, similar to the common garden carrot. The leaves are lacy and fern-like, mostly at the crown, with the stem sparingly leaved and much branched. The flowers are small, white, and close bunched, forming a flat cluster. As the seeds form, the flower stems turn inward, so that when ripened, the entire flower head resembles a bird's nest. Seeds are ridged and spined so that they adhere. (*Seedburo Equipment Co.*)

able pentachlorophenol and dinitrophenol formulations. Its action is relatively slow when used alone.

Dalapon (Dowpon)* is an effective grass herbicide which is absorbed from foliar sprays better than TCA. This herbicide is widely used to

* Trade name.

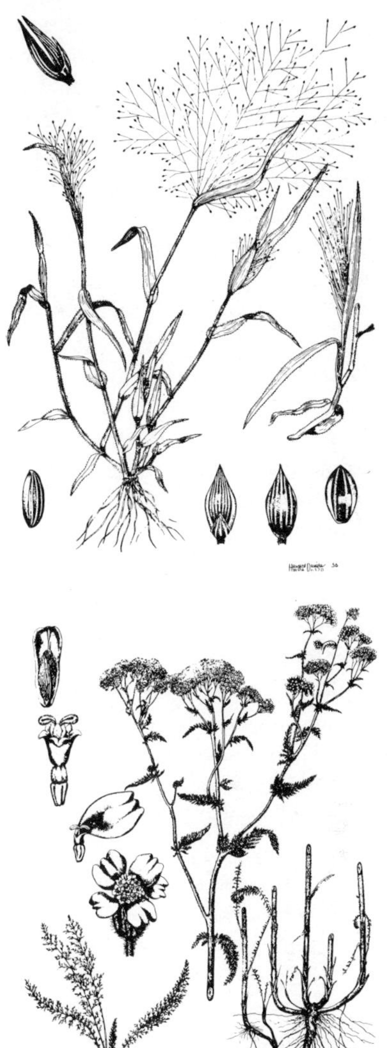

Fig. 6.39 Witchgrass (*Panicum capillare*). An annual, recognized by the small one-flowered spikelets with their very unequal glumes, the outer of which is much shorter than the inner. Fall panicum is a smooth-leaved, much-branching species. It may appear as a sprawling, prostrate specimen or as a vigorous, robust specimen up to 5 or 6 ft in height. It varies in color from bright green to blood red. It should be pulled out or cut back before flowers have a chance to form. Seeds are scattered by winds. Chemical control can be obtained with 2,4-D. 1.5 lb/acre, butyl ester, or preemergence sodium salt. (*Seedburo Equipment Co.*)

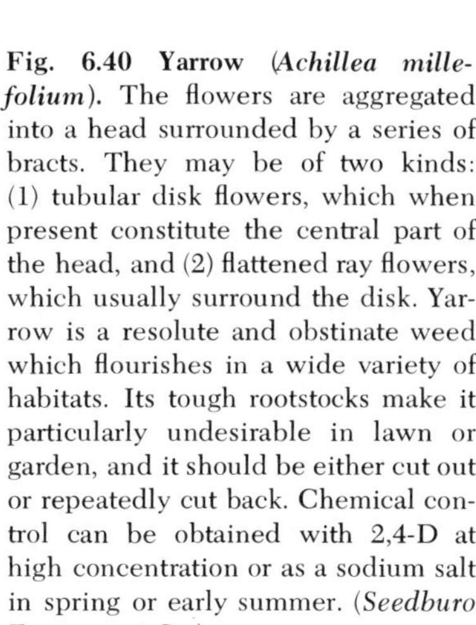

Fig. 6.40 Yarrow (*Achillea millefolium*). The flowers are aggregated into a head surrounded by a series of bracts. They may be of two kinds: (1) tubular disk flowers, which when present constitute the central part of the head, and (2) flattened ray flowers, which usually surround the disk. Yarrow is a resolute and obstinate weed which flourishes in a wide variety of habitats. Its tough rootstocks make it particularly undesirable in lawn or garden, and it should be either cut out or repeatedly cut back. Chemical control can be obtained with 2,4-D at high concentration or as a sodium salt in spring or early summer. (*Seedburo Equipment Co.*)

control annual and perennial grasses as well as cattails and tules. Its soil persistence is very low, and its toxicity is similar to that of TCA.

Highways

Chemical weed control along highways is an established and economically sound practice. Better knowledge of application methods and more efficient products now make chemical maintenance a wise choice for many highway weed-control problems. Where woody plants are desirable, herbaceous perennials are the chief problems, and combination sprays using 2,4-D and 2,4,5-T esters can be utilized. 2,4-D liquid amine salt sprays have proved effective against herbaceous weeds and some of the less resistant woody species. They are somewhat safer to use in areas bordering cropland ornamentals than ester formulations although spray drift is always a factor no matter what 2,4-D or 2,4,5-T formulation is used.

In most areas, especially where vegetation is dense, application with an orchard type of spray gun will prove efficient. There are many areas where vegetation should be controlled some distance from the road, e.g., at grade crossings and intersections, where brush or high weeds form a hazard in terms of obstructed vision. Several equipment manufacturers offer rigs with spray booms designed for, or readily adaptable to, highway work. Boom application is often quite satisfactory. A boom should be rigged to extend to the depth of the area to be sprayed, insofar as possible, and from the right side of the applying vehicle. It should be rigged so that it can be raised or lowered by the operator to conform with the slope of the shoulder or to avoid obstacles. Such a rig may have a jointed boom so that the outward section can be lowered or raised independently of the first section.

The volume and pressure required vary with the density of the weed growth to be controlled. For example, to control dandelion, thistle, and similar weeds in the attractive turf bordering our better highways, low pressure (40 lb/in.^{2}), low dosage rate (15 to 30 gal/acre), and nozzles giving a coarse spray are suggested. Here 2,4-D amine salt may be used at 2 to 3 lb of acid equivalent per acre in 20 gal or more of water. On the other hand, where weed growth is tall and dense, 2 to 3 lb of acid equivalent per 100 gal water may be used in sufficient spray volume to give adequate coverage, which means rather complete wetting of foliage. This may require 200 to 300 gal of spray per acre. 2,4-D low-volatile esters may also be used, especially if certain types of brush predominate. It should be stressed again that coarse, low-pressure sprays avoid the drift hazard of fine, high-pressure sprays.

Aerial Brush Control

The airplane is used extensively for spraying large areas for weed and brush control, for range-improvement purposes, and for the maintenance of transmission-line rights of way.

The main advantage of aerial spraying with herbicides is its speed and relatively low cost. Aerial spraying is also useful on areas which are difficult to reach with mobile or hand equipment, e.g., hilly or swampy terrain.

The principal disadvantage is the problem of drift. Aerial spraying must of necessity be restricted to nearly windless weather and to areas where there is no chance of injuring desirable stands of trees or crops on adjacent land. Use of low-spray pressure and large spray droplets minimizes the spray-drift hazard. Usually, wind velocity should not exceed 6 mi/h.

SPECIFICATIONS FOR CHEMICAL TREATMENT OF BRUSH*

Foliage Spray Method

A low-volatile ester brush killer composed of equal parts of 2,4-D and 2,4,5-T may be used as the active ingredient. The mixture often contains 2 lb of 2,4-D acid equivalent and 2 lb of 2,4,5-T acid equivalent per gallon of concentrate, or Tordon 101 mixture (picloram plus 2,4-D) may be chosen. Mix the herbicide with water at the rate of 1 gal of concentrate to 100 gal of water. Spray after the plants have acquired full leaf growth. The sprayer tank should be equipped with an agitator for thorough mixing. The spray solution must not be discharged into any stream. Any water, provided it is clean, may be used in preparing the spray solution. Provide sufficient hose to spray up to 1500 ft from the pumping equipment in areas which are inaccessible to mobile equipment. Use an orchard type of spray gun to apply the spray. Vary the gun setting from a fine mist to a semisolid stream to secure full coverage of the plants sprayed. Keep the spray gun within 25 ft of the plants being sprayed. The normal nozzle pressure should be between 150 and 200 lb/in.^{2} Maximum nozzle pressure should be 250 lb/in.^{2} In areas where complete drift control is essential, use lower spray pressures.

Woody plants, including briers, should be wet with the spray solution. Wet the entire leaf surface of the plants so that the solution just begins to drip from the leaves.

Basal Spray Method

This method utilizes a low-volatile phenoxy ester brush-killer (2,4-D plus 2,4,5-T) or 2,4,5-T alone. The herbicide should be mixed with

* Based on information from Lawrence Southwick, Dow Chemical USA, Midland, Mich.

no. 2 fuel oil, kerosene, or equivalent at the rate of 4 gal of concentrate to 96 gal of oil. Spraying may be done at any time when the lower 12 in. of the plant stems is accessible so that the spray mixture can run down to the root crown. Apply the spray mixture in sufficient quantity to wet the entire circumference of the stem and to allow the solution to flow down as described.

SOIL EROSION

The control of soil erosion is a major problem in many areas. Many maintenance problems stem from the original poor construction of roads and the inadequate attention given to slopes and drainage areas.

GENERAL PRINCIPLES OF EROSION CONTROL

Methods to correct these deficiencies are available and known but too often ignored. Briefly, these methods are as follows:

1. It is possible on most soils to establish good vegetative cover without the use of topsoil. This may seem a controversial point, but it has been done for several years in the TVA area, and the New York State Department of Public Works has reported similar success in its final report on Roadside Vegetative Cover. When topsoil is used, most grading operators try to finish a slope by leaving it as smooth as possible, instead of leaving it rough, with ridges along the contour to slow and catch the runoff water. Again, topsoil is usually dumped along the top of the slope and spread with a bulldozer. This leaves the heaviest deposit of topsoil at the top of the slope, and only a thin layer of soil at the bottom. Combine these two situations—a smooth surface and an unbalanced layer of topsoil—with a heavy rainfall, and no amount of mulch, seeding, brush, or grass will keep all that soil from sliding to the bottom.
2. Practically all soils can be made to support a vegetative cover by initial fertilization and liming and an adequate schedule of refertilization.
3. Rock outcropping should not be blasted away but should be left to appear as natural as possible.

4. Deep gullies should first be checked with adequate dams or heavy brush or rock.
5. Diversion ditches should be dug at the top to minimize the amount of runoff across the face of the slope.
6. Soil should be analyzed to ascertain the kind of grass it will support and the amount of fertilizer and lime needed.
7. On poor soils it may be necessary to add organic matter, such as straw or sawdust. Although costly as an initial expense, this operation is essential and will pay dividends in the long run.
8. Unless the steepness of a slope requires a fast-germinating seed like Italian ryegrass, it is a good idea to limit the varieties of grasses to one or two good ones.
9. If topsoil or other soils are added to a slope, the minimum uniform depth should be 2 in. This layer should be compacted into the existing soil by means of a sheepsfoot roller; before compaction the slope should be fertilized, limed, and mulched with hay or straw. Not more than 2 tons of mulch should be used per acre. At the same time that it compacts the topsoil into the slope, the sheepsfoot roller will mix the fertilizer and lime into the soil and anchor the straw in place. After rolling, the slope can be seeded.
10. A very economical method of stabilizing slopes is to use a seeding and mulching machine, which performs these operations in two steps. The machine first blows the seed and fertilizer mix onto the slope or, using an improved method, incorporates water into the mixture and forces it onto the slope hydraulically. In the second step, the mulch is blown onto the slope from the mulching machine and kept in place with asphalt sprayed onto the straw as it comes from the blower. As it settles on the slope, each piece of straw adheres to its neighbor. The effectiveness of this mat has been demonstrated many times. Labor and material costs have been reduced as much as 75 per cent by use of this machine.
11. A mulch is essential to controlling or stabilizing slopes. Sometimes the mulch alone is sufficient, but some protection must be given seeds, and water in the slope must be conserved.
12. Mowing should be done as needed, but the slope should never be cut closer than 2 in. and preferably 3 in.

KINDS OF SOIL EROSION

The two common forms of soil erosion are sheet erosion and gullying.

Sheet Erosion

In sheet erosion, or sheet washing, heavy rainfall loosens the soil on bare slopes and moves it down the slope by the flow of excess water. As the soil moves, its volume and velocity are increased, and it may appear to be moving in one continuous sheet. Such erosion is often not readily discernible, since it progresses slowly, removing the most fertile topsoil over a period of years. Sometimes it can be detected only by the gradual change in the color of the soil and by the appearance of "galled" spots in the field. Sheet-eroded areas can be treated by plowing, seeding, and mulching. If soil and moisture conditions are poor, fertilization and mulching are advisable. By discing the fertilizer and mulch into the soil before seeding, soil conditions can be greatly improved.

On long, easy slopes, contour furrows may allow greater absorption of water and also provide a planting site for trees. On long, steep slopes where terraces or diversion terraces are impractical, brush placed in strips along the contour of the slope and wired down will slow the flow of water. (See detailed control specifications at the close of this chapter.)

Gully Erosion

Gullies are continuous trenches cut through the surface structure of the soil, normally by continuous, heavy sheet washing. The first indication of gullying is frequently a concentration of rills in the natural depressions of the slope or a uniform spreading of rills over the slope.

Major gullies occur when erosion breaks through the surface soil and into the subsoil. Such gullies will increase in size and depth until bedrock or a nonerodable channel has been reached.

To plan successful control treatment of major gullies, the following steps are necessary:

1. A study of the drainage area
2. A computation of runoff into each gully
3. Diversion of runoff
4. Construction of channel control works

To control a major gully successfully, it is first necessary to stop the cutting in at the bottom and at the head of the gully. The control measures needed to accomplish this will depend upon the volume and velocity of water draining into the gully.

Sometimes minor changes in the drainage area will permit a simpler method of control in the gully. Such measures might include planting or seeding barren slopes above the gully, protecting the area from grazing, or constructing terraces or contour furrows. If it is possible to divert all the drainage from the gully, control measures may be limited to sloping the banks and seeding or planting or stabilizing the flow line of the channel with brush.

METHODS OF EROSION CONTROL WITH PERMANENT STRUCTURES

Soil-saving Dams

Soil-saving dams are used chiefly in large gullies or narrow draws. In order to justify their cost, a large basin should be created on the upstream side to catch and hold a substantial quantity of soil. A drainage area in excess of 50 acres should have a dam designed with a greater factor of safety than is usually needed for erosion-control measures.

EXCAVATION

All sod, stumps, roots, and large stones must be removed from the foundation of the dam before the fill is started, and the surface of the foundation should be scarified. If the dam is to impound water to a depth of more than 5 ft, or if the foundation of fill material contains a large proportion of sand or gravel, a trench 2 to 4 ft wide should be cut to a depth of 1 to 2 ft along the axis of the dam to prevent seepage and allow for construction of a core. The trench should be cut with vertical side walls to break the seam between the natural ground and the fill.

CONSTRUCTION

The dam should be not less than 2 ft wide at the top, with the side slopes constructed on a minimum slope of 2:1. The fill for the dam should be made of earth that is free from roots, large stones, stumps, and debris. It should be applied in well-compacted 6-in. layers. If the nature of the soil or the height of the dam requires the construction of a core, the core should be of impervious clay, tamped lightly in 6-in. layers. It should be kept slightly higher than the main body of the dam until the full height of the dam has been reached. Approximately 20 per cent should be allowed for shrinkage in the fill, and the downstream face of the dam should be sodded or seeded as soon as possible. The upstream face of the dam should be riprapped.

CONSTRUCTION OF SPILLWAY

Spillways, whether concrete or masonry, should be installed before the earth fill, and as the fill progresses, impervious clay should be packed tightly against the wing walls of the structure. Emergency spillways can be provided by the construction of a diversion channel leading from the upper side of the dam to a stabilized outlet in a heavily sodded or wooded area.

Concrete Dams

Concrete and masonry check dams are used in channels where watershed conditions do not permit controlling vegetation to be established. When properly located and constructed, permanent check dams provide an effective control of channels carrying a large volume of water. Such dams can be constructed to a height not exceeding 4 ft, measured from the top of the apron to the bottom of the spillway notch, without the use of reinforcing.

A 1:1 slope should be established along the gully banks for the entire length of the dam and apron and the sloping extended to the full height of the dam. The apron sloping should extend 2 ft up the banks at the dam, tapering to a minimum of 1 ft at the lip of the apron. The excavation for the dam should be 1 to 2 ft deep and should extend into the banks 2 to 4 ft. The thickness of the dam at the base should be equal to or greater than the thickness at the top (minimum 6 in.). The apron excavation should permit the top of the finished apron floor to be flush with, or slightly below, the normal gully floor. See Fig. 7.1.

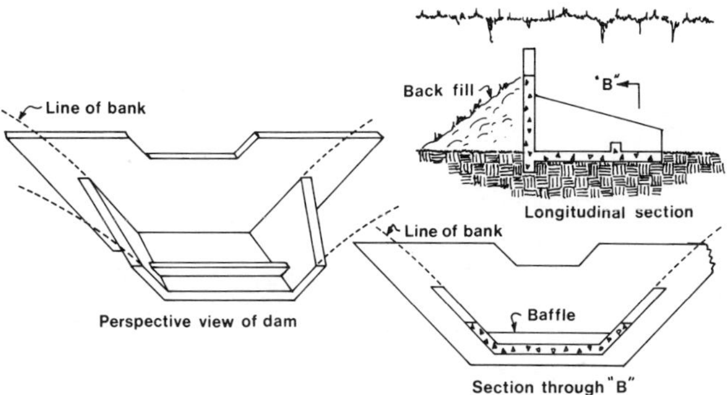

Fig. 7.1 Concrete dam. (*Tennessee Valley Authority.*)

CONSTRUCTION

Forms for concrete dams should be built of smooth plank, well braced and anchored to prevent spreading or sliding. The concrete, using a 1:2:4 mix, should be poured evenly and well tamped or "spaded" on both faces of the dam to eliminate voids. After the forms are removed, the surface of the concrete should be covered with moist straw, soil, or burlap for at least 7 days.

The upstream face and wings of the dam should be backfilled at a minimum slope of 2:1 immediately after the forms are removed. This backfill should be thoroughly tamped to prevent seepage.

If no reinforcing is used, the dam must be poured as a unit, and no part should be allowed to set before the next section is poured. The length of the apron should be at least 1½ times the height of the dam, measured from the top of the spillway notch, and at least as wide at the lip as at the base of the dam.

The side walls of the apron should be set below the surface of the gully banks on a slope of not less than 1:1. They should be at least 2 ft high at the dam, and may taper to a minimum of 1 ft at the lip. A stilling basin not less than 6 in. deep should be constructed across the apron. The baffle should be built as a part of the apron, at a distance from the dam equal to two-thirds the length of the apron. The entire apron, including the baffle, should be poured as a unit, and the finished concrete should be protected for not less than 7 days by a covering of moist straw, earth, or burlap.

Masonry Dams

Masonry dams require the same excavation as that described for concrete dams, but the minimum thickness at the top of the dam should be 12 in. See Fig. 7.2.

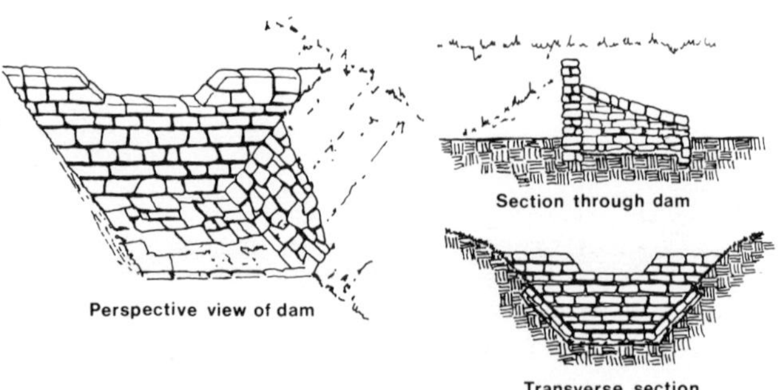

Fig. 7.2 Masonry dam. (*Tennessee Valley Authority.*)

CONSTRUCTION

The bottom of the excavation should be covered with a layer of mortar (1:3 mix) 1 to 2 in. thick. Masonry work is begun on the top of this layer of mortar and continued until top of dam is reached. As soon as the dam is completed, it should be covered with moist straw, earth, or burlap for not less than 7 days. Upstream face and wings should be backfilled as required for concrete dams.

The apron should be at least $1\frac{1}{2}$ times the height of the dam, measured from the top of the spillway to the normal gully floor. A toe wall should be set at the lip of the apron, extending 6 in. into the ground below the floor of the apron and into the banks not less than 1 ft beyond the width of the spillway of the dam. The top of the finished toe wall should be flush with or slightly below the normal floor of the channel. The apron floor should be at least 1 ft wider than the bottom of the spillway notch and should be at least as wide at the lip as at the base of the dam.

The side walls of the apron should be set below the surface of the gully banks on a slope of not less than 1:1, at least 2 ft high at the dam and tapering to a minimum of 1 ft at the lip. A stilling basin not less than 6 in. deep should be built by excavating sufficiently between the toe wall and the base of the dam to permit the floor of the apron to be 6 in. below the top of the toe wall or by constructing a 6-in. baffle across the apron.

Concrete and Masonry Checks

Checks are usually constructed of concrete and masonry from 6 to 8 in. thick and 12 to 18 in. high. They should be spaced so that the top of one check is slightly higher than the bottom of the one next above, thus eliminating the need for apron construction. Checks are useful in controlling broad, shallow gullies, highway ditches, and terrace outfall ditches of low gradient. They are seldom feasible for grades exceeding 6 per cent.

METHODS OF EROSION CONTROL WITH SEMIPERMANENT STRUCTURES

Check dams constructed of loose rock may be classed as semipermanent structures and are frequently used as substitutes for check dams of less durable materials. These dams are not recommended for use on areas that are to be restored to agriculture, since they may interfere with the use of agricultural implements. The average loose-rock dam is about 3 ft high and 8 ft long. See Fig. 7.3.

Crib Dams

Logs and fieldstone can be used to construct semipermanent structures called crib dams, which are generally used in controlling large gullies

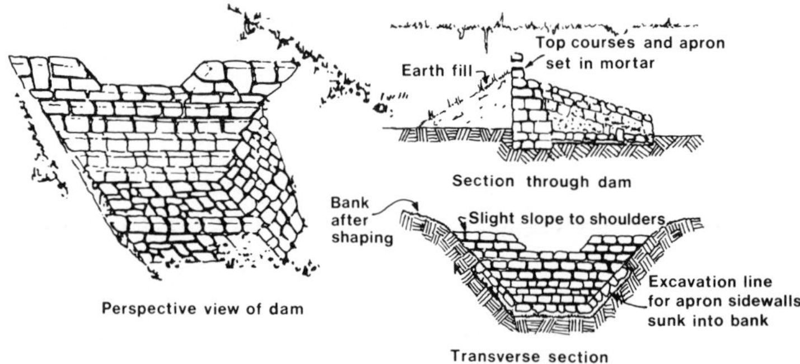

Fig. 7.3 Combination masonry and loose-rock dam. (*Tennessee Valley Authority.*)

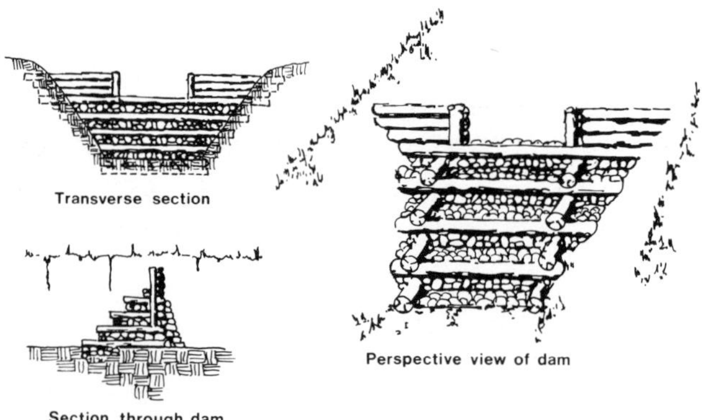

Fig. 7.4 Rock-filled log crib dam. (*Tennessee Valley Authority.*)

carrying a heavy runoff. The logs are used to hold the stones in place until they become settled and sealed into stable position by the collection of silt. An average rock-filled log crib is 8 ft high and 20 ft long, and contains 400 ft^3 of rock and 250 lin ft of logs not less than 8 in. in diameter. See Fig. 7.4.

All loose rock, soil, and debris should be cleaned out of the gully bottom at the site of the dam. Dig a trench of sufficient size and depth to hold two logs, laid one upon the other, across the gully at the toe of the dam. The top log should be flush with the normal gully floor. Extend the trench and logs at least 3 ft into the gully banks. Excavation for the first layer of straw and rock should be made for a distance of 3 ft behind the top log.

Building should be started from the front or toe. Place two logs, one on top of the other, in the excavation across the gully. Bedrock in straw behind the logs to the level of the top log. Secure two tie logs parallel to the gully to the top toe log. Place these tie logs against the gully bank. The space between tie logs should never be less than the width of the spillway. Place the first cross log back of the toe log at a distance equal to the diameter of the tie logs. This will produce a 1:1 slope on the face of the dam. Fill the space behind this log with rock, bedded in straw. Place the larger rocks in the face of the dam so that water action will not force them out between the logs.

Repeat this performance until the desired height of the dam is reached. Set upright posts in the rock base of the dam to a minimum depth of 4 ft in order to hold the logs of the spillway section. Attach logs for the spillway to the uprights and extend into the gully banks 2 to 4 ft, measured at right angles to the slope.

Do not place any backfill behind the dam; instead allow the water to filter through the layers of rock and straw, filling the voids with silt.

Concrete or Rock Paving

Erosion can be controlled in gullies carrying runoff at high speeds by lining the channel with concrete or rock. Such construction is especially useful in highway or terrace outfall ditches on steep grades and from high embankments. Loose rock paving without grouting can be used where the runoff does not reach a high speed or the grade does not exceed 15 per cent.

METHODS OF EROSION CONTROL WITH TEMPORARY STRUCTURES

Temporary structures are used primarily to establish vegetation in gullied areas. Their effective life must be consistent with the time required for the growth of vegetation on the site.

Log or Plank Check Dams

Log or plank dams are used in gullies which have large volumes of runoff but which can be stabilized by certain types of vegetation. Since vegetation eventually attains control, the spacing and height of these structures must be such that breaks will not occur in the gully bottom after the structure has decayed. A desirable height is 2 ft, measured from the top of the apron to bottom of the spillway notch. The maximum height should be 3 ft. See Figs. 7.5 and 7.6.

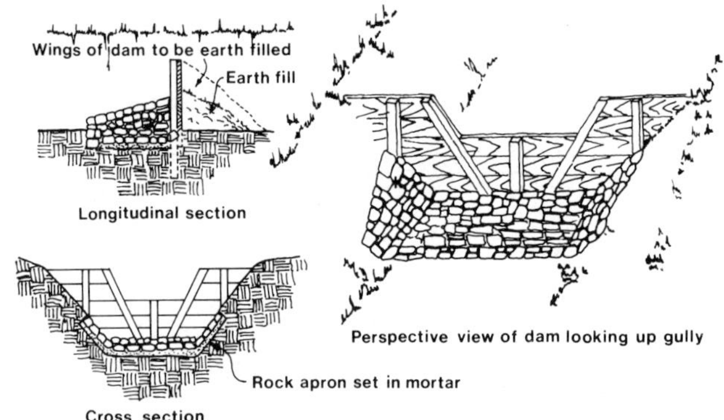

Fig. 7.5 Plank dam with rock apron. (*Tennessee Valley Authority.*)

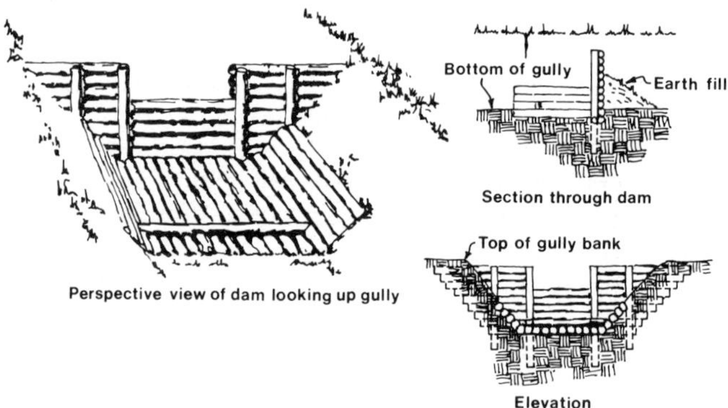

Fig. 7.6 Log dam with log apron. (*Tennessee Valley Authority.*)

EXCAVATION

Slope the gully banks to a 1:1 slope for the entire length of the dam and apron. Sloping should extend up the sides of the gully to the full height of the dam, tapering down to a minimum of 1 ft at the lip of the apron. The excavation for the dam should be 1 to 2 ft deep and should extend into the banks 2 to 4 ft, measured at right angles to the slope.

CONSTRUCTION

Set two upright posts to a minimum depth of 2 ft in the downstream edge of the excavation, in order to form the sides of the spillway notch of the dam. Set an additional post in the center if the width of the spillway notch exceeds 6 ft. Set additional posts, at intervals not exceeding 6 ft, between the spillway posts and the points where the top cross logs or planks enter the gully banks. Place a 2-in. layer of straw, grass, or leaves in the bottom of the excavation to prevent leakage under the dam. Place horizontal logs or planks of sufficient length to span the entire width of the gully on the upstream side of the posts. Short top logs or planks extending into the gully banks and fastened to the central upright posts form the spillway notch. If logs are used, the space between the logs should not exceed 0.5 in. and should be chinked tightly with straw or grass. Backfill, on a 2:1 slope, the upstream face and wings of the dam.

The length of the apron should be at least $1\frac{1}{2}$ times the height of the dam, measured from the top of the spillway to the normal gully floor, and should be at least 1 ft wider than the bottom of the spillway notch and at least as wide at the lip as at the base of the dam.

A toe log or wall should be set at the lip of the apron and extend into the ground 6 in. below the floor of the apron and into the bank not less than 1 ft beyond the width of the spillway of the dam. The top of the finished toe log should be flush with, or slightly below, the normal floor of the channel. The side walls should be set below the surface of the gully banks on a slope of not less than 1:1. They should be at least 2 ft high at the dam, and may taper to 1 ft at the lip of the apron.

Construct a stilling basin not less than 6 in. deep by excavating between the toe wall and the base of the dam sufficiently to permit the floor of the apron to be 6 in. below the top of the toe log or wall or build a 6-in. baffle across the apron. Build the baffle at a distance from the dam to equal to two-thirds of the length of the apron.

Brush or Wire Check Dams

The most general and effective use of brush or wire check dams is to collect and hold silt and moisture in gully bottoms, thereby providing favorable growing conditions for vegetation. The effective height should be held to approximately 18 in., with ample overfall protection provided. Height should never exceed 2 ft. See Fig. 7.7.

Failures of brush or wire dams are usually due to one of three causes: (1) improper packing of brush or backfill, which produces leakage through the dam; (2) insufficient spillway space, which produces end cutting, or (3) excessive height, which produces undercutting.

Single-Post Brush Dams

Slope the gully banks for the entire length of the dam and apron on a 1:1 slope and extend sloping up the sides of the gully to the full height of the dam. See Fig. 7.8.

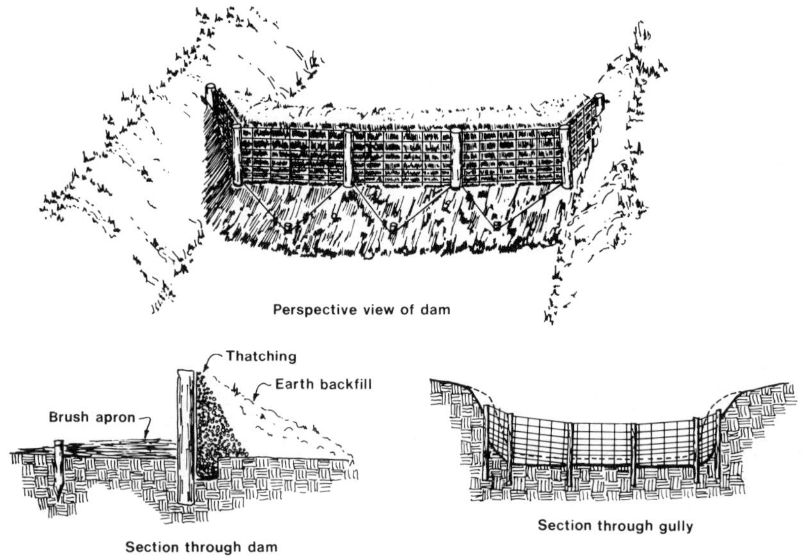

Fig. 7.7 Wire dam. (*Tennessee Valley Authority.*)

The base of the dam should usually be excavated 12 to 18 in. wide and never less than 6 in. The excavation should extend into the gully banks from 6 to 18 in. at right angles to the slope. The bottom of the excavation should be rounded to the curve desired in the finished dam, so that the finished structure will have a minimum weir depth of 9 in.

CONSTRUCTION

Space posts 2.5 ft apart and 18 to 24 in. deep in the downstream face of the excavation. A single wire should be fastened to each post near the base before it is set in the ground. This wire will be used in tightening brush. Cover the bottom of the excavation with a layer of straw, grass, or leaves 2 or 3 in. thick. Place the brush lengthwise in the excavation, placing the smaller branches near the bottom. Keep the brush at a uniform height for the full length of the dam, tamping each layer for compactness. After all the brush is in place, draw the wires attached to the base of the posts across the top of the dam as tight as possible and secure near the top of each post. Set or cut the posts so that they will not extend above the top of the dam.

For apron construction, excavate the gully bottom to the approximate shape of the dam. Extend the excavation up on the banks to the full height of the dam. The excavation should equal in length $1\frac{1}{2}$ times the height of the dam.

Construct the apron by placing a layer of brush 4 to 6 in. thick in the excavation below the dam. Lay the brush parallel to the gully with the butt ends extending into the base of the dam. Secure the brush by means of a wire to stakes set 12 to 18 in. apart in rows across the apron.

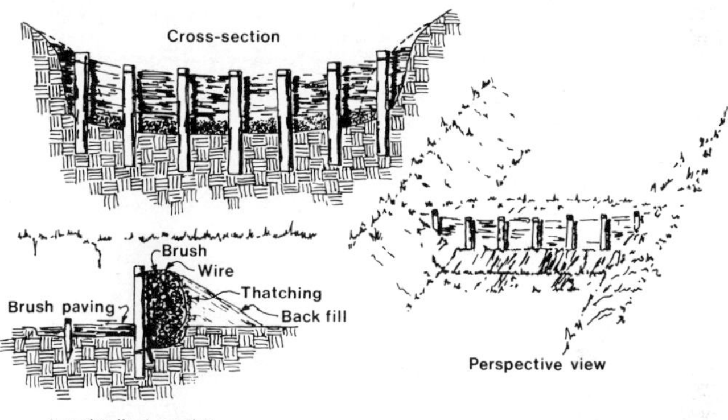

Fig. 7.8 Single-post brush dam. (*Tennessee Valley Authority.*)

Set the stakes and drive them partway in before the wire is attached. After the wire is fastened and the brush is in place, the stakes can be driven all the way, drawing the wire tight across the brush.

Double-Post Brush Dams

Double-post brush dams require the same excavation as single-post brush dams, with a minimum weir depth of 9 in. See Fig. 7.9.

CONSTRUCTION

Place a layer of hay, straw, or leaves, 2 to 3 in. thick, in the trench. Drive stakes along the bottom of the trench at intervals of 2 or 3 in. Drive stakes at intervals of 2 ft, set opposite each other, for the entire length of the dam. Place brush as for single-post dams. After all the brush is in place, fasten a wire securely to the top of the stakes and drive them to their final depth. Backfill as for single-post brush dams.

Wire Check Dams

Slope the gully bank for the entire length of the dam and apron on a 1:1 slope and extend sloping up the sides of the gully to the full height of the dam. Dig a trench 6 to 12 in. deep and 12 in. wide across the bottom of the gully. The wing trenches may be made upstream into the banks of the gully at a 45° angle to the cross trench, with a minimum depth equal to the height of the finished dam.

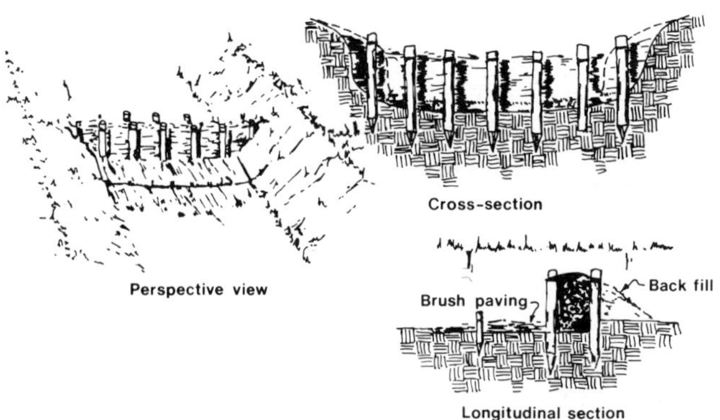

Fig. 7.9 Double-post brush dam. (*Tennessee Valley Authority.*)

CONSTRUCTION

Set posts 2.5 ft apart in the downstream edge of the excavation to a depth of 18 to 24 in. The wing or anchor posts should be set to a depth of 2.5 to 3 ft in the gully banks. Allow a minimum weir depth of 12 in. in the center of the dam. Fasten the wire to the upstream face of the posts and thatch with straw, grass, fine brush, or burlap or place a well-compacted layer of brush 12 to 18 in. thick on the upstream side of the dam. Backfill on a slope of 2:1 with clay or topsoil.

For apron construction, see single-post brush dams.

Brush Checks

In gullies carrying a very small amount of runoff, brush checks can be used. It is seldom necessary to do any excavation, and the checks serve as planting sites. The principal features of brush check construction are maximum height of construction, 1 ft, little or no excavation in the gully bottom, and simple devices for holding brush in place. All brush checks should be backfilled with clay or topsoil well compacted. See Figs. 7.10 and 7.11.

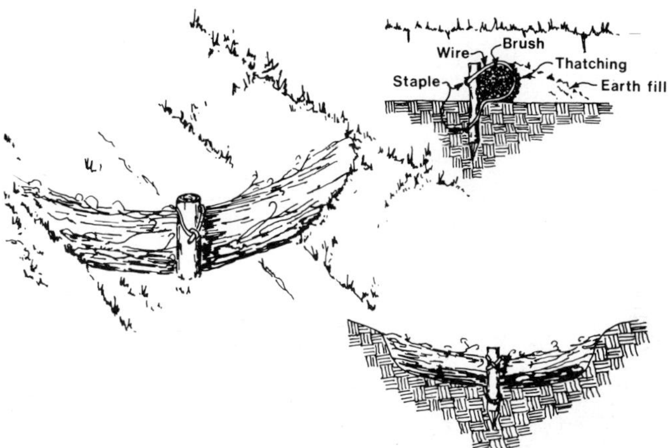

Fig. 7.10 Bundled brush check. (*Tennessee Valley Authority.*)

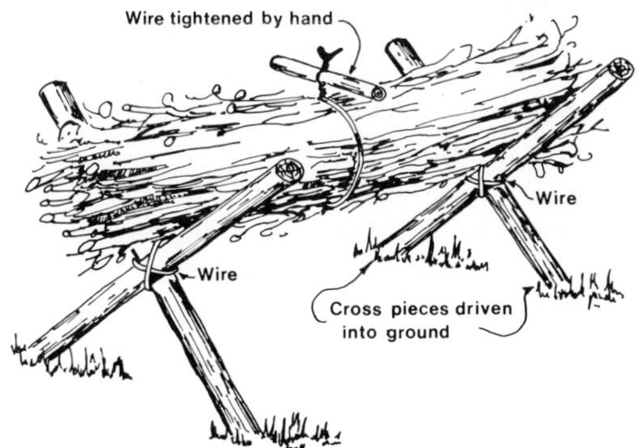

Fig. 7.11 Brush bundler. (*Tennessee Valley Authority.*)

Brush Paving

Brush paving is used largely in stabilizing gully channels to permit the growth of vegetation and is especially good for use on steep slopes in gullies carrying a considerable runoff. The effective life of brush paving is about 1 to 3 years, and vegetation must be established quickly. See Fig. 7.12.

The gully bottom should be rounded or flattened and the gully banks sloped to a minimum of 1:1 above the expected height of the water in the channel during storm periods. All loose earth in the channel should be removed or well compacted by tamping.

The materials for brush paving are green cedar or pine brush or hardwood, if cedar or pine is not available. Use only branches of 1-in. diameter or less; stakes 18 to 24 in. long of durable wood; straw, grass, or leaves; and 9- to 14-gage wire.

CONSTRUCTION

A 1-in. layer of straw, grass, or leaves should be placed in the gully for the full width of the paving. The brush should be laid with the butt ends

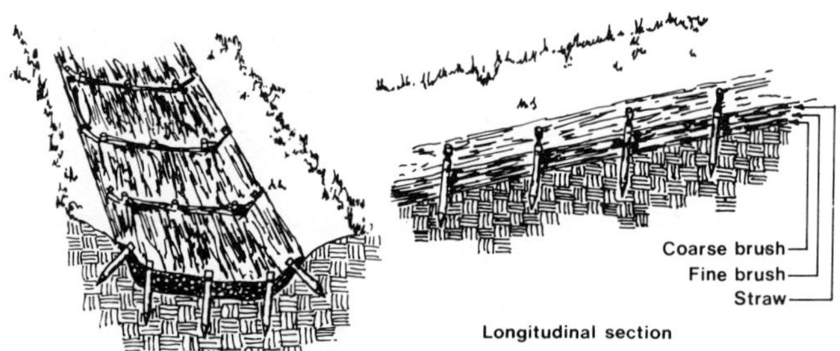

Fig. 7.12 Brush paving. (*Tennessee Valley Authority.*)

downstream, using the small branches in the bottom layer. Brush should be placed to provide a finished thickness of 1.5 to 2 in., after the paving has been wired down. The stakes should be set at intervals of 18 to 24 in. and partially driven. Wire should be fastened securely around each stake and the stakes driven in, to draw the wire down tight across the brush.

Flowline Staking

This is a variation of brush paving which can be used in gullies carrying less than 5 ft^3 per second of runoff. See Fig. 7.13.

Gullies adaptable to this method of control seldom require excavation.

Green cedar, pine, or hardwood brush, timber poles 1 to 2 in. in diameter, 18- to 24-in. stakes of durable wood, and 9- to 14-gage wire are the materials used.

CONSTRUCTION

Cover the bottom of the gully with fine brush and larger brush, placed in the same manner as for brush paving. Hold the brush down by timber poles laid across the gully and drawn down tight to a single stake set in the center of the channel, or stake and wire brush as in brush paving at intervals of 4 to 6 ft. If hardwood brush is used, the branches should be laid crosswise in the channel.

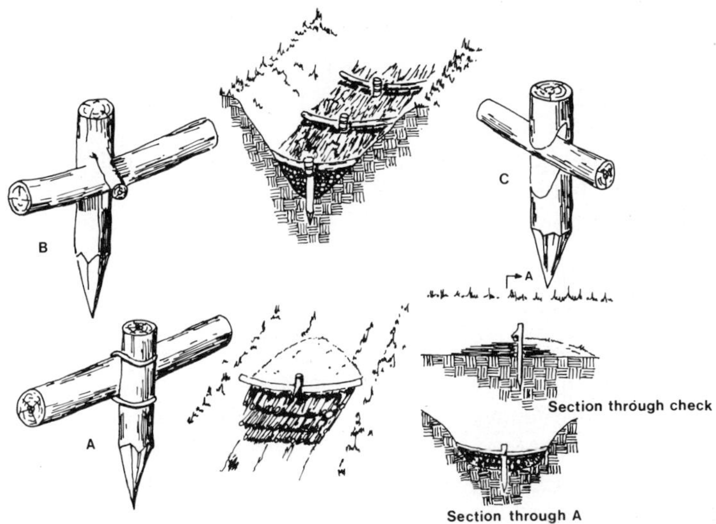

Fig. 7.13 Flow-line staking and brush checks. (*Tennessee Valley Authority.*)

Strip Matting

Strip matting may be used on steep, sheet-eroded hillsides to check runoff and to provide a protected area for planting. Construction procedure is to place layers of brush 1.5 to 2 in. thick and 4 to 6 ft wide at intervals along the contour, depending upon the length and steepness of the slope. The strip is formed by placing a 3- to 4-in. layer of brush with butt ends downhill. If a straw mulching is used, a 1-in. layer of brush is sufficient. The strip is then staked and wired at intervals of approximately 4 ft.

Diversion Ditches

Diversion ditches are used primarily for the reduction and control of runoff and as an aid to vegetative control. They are used to advantage in diverting runoff from major gullies or from critical gully heads and sheet-eroded areas, thereby permitting a simpler form of control. They should not be used unless they can be emptied into a safe and stabilized outlet.

CONSTRUCTION

The grade should not exceed 1 per cent. A fall of 4 to 6 in. per 100 ft is usually satisfactory. Where active gullies carrying a large volume of water enter the diversion ditch, the grade should be increased for a distance of several feet above the entrance of the ditch in order to prevent silt from piling up at the intersection point. The increase in grade should not exceed 1 per cent.

The ditch should be at least 2 ft wide, with sides sloped as much as possible. They should be constructed to carry 1½ times the computed runoff. The additional capacity will allow for silting in the channel.

Contour Furrows

Contour furrows create a series of basins to catch and hold water. The water thus caught reduces the runoff and permits a greater absorption of moisture for the use of vegetation. The furrows also serve as ground preparation for planting trees or sod. Their most practical use is in pasture or grassland which has a minimum of 60 per cent ground cover.

The effectiveness of contour furrows can be protected by raising the plow at intervals of 20 to 50 ft or by the construction of dams across the furrow at specified intervals. The advantage in so dividing the furrow is that if a break should occur in any weak sector, the entire furrow will not be drained to flood the furrow below.

Contour furrows are constructed with an ordinary turning plow or hillside plow. The furrow will function more efficiently if all the soil is turned downhill. Contour lines should be run with a level and stakes set at intervals of 25 to 50 ft, depending upon the slope.

Plowing and Mulching

In gullies which average less than 4 ft in depth the most effective method for quick control is to plow in the sides and fill the gully. The loose soil, when covered with a layer of protective straw, hay, or brush, makes an excellent planting or seedbed site.

GULLY-HEAD TREATMENTS

There are four classifications of gully heads, according to drainage area and depth of gully at the head. See Figs. 7.14 and 7.15.

Type A Gully heads less than 6 ft high and draining less than ½ acre. The head should be sloped to a 1.5:1 slope. Ground should be broken to a minimum depth of 6 in. for 5 ft back from the head and completely

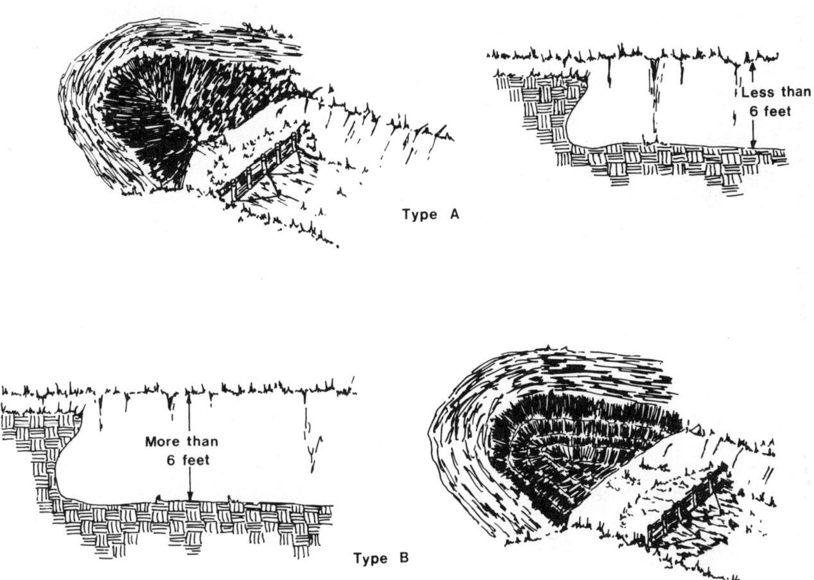

Fig. 7.14 Gully-head treatment for less than ½-acre drainage. (*Tennessee Valley Authority.*)

encircling it. The head should then be mulched with straw and light covering of cedar brush, with straw and a light covering of hardwood brush, or with hardwood brush alone. The 5-ft flat should be mulched with straw alone, finely chopped cedar brush alone, or finely chopped hardwood brush alone.

Type B Gully heads more than 6 ft high and draining less than ½ acre. The head should be sloped to a 1.5:1 slope, with the ground broken to a minimum depth of 6 in. for 8 ft back from the head and completely encircling it. The head should then be matted with straw and a covering of cedar brush, with straw and a covering of hardwood brush, with cedar brush alone, or with hardwood brush alone. This matting should be tied down by driving into it stakes 5 ft apart in rows 5 ft apart; wires fastened to the stakes should run both vertically and horizontally so that 5-ft squares are formed. The stakes should be long enough to reach into the ground. The mulching on the 8-ft flat above the head need not be fastened down. Mulching materials may be straw alone, finely chopped cedar brush alone, or finely chopped hardwood brush alone.

Type C Gully heads less than 6 ft high draining more than ½ acre. The treatment is the same as in type A, except for a flume constructed

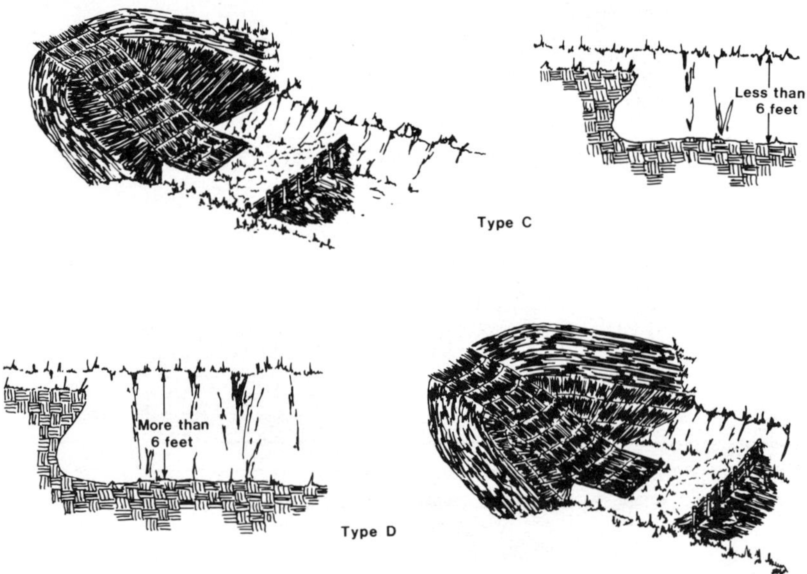

Fig. 7.15 Gully-head treatment for more than ½-acre drainage. (*Tennessee Valley Authority.*)

down the flow line, as follows. Excavation for flume should be made on a 2:1 slope, with the sides on a 1.5:1 slope. Excavation should be in hard soil. The bottom of the excavation is then broken to a depth of 2 to 3 in., and mulch and fertilizer are mixed with loose earth. Treat the sides in the same manner and sod sides and bottom with Bermuda. Hold sod in place with woven wire or brush. A wire or brush dam should be placed 6 ft from the bottom of the flume to form a 6-ft stilling basin 1 ft deep.

Type D Gully heads more than 6 ft high draining more than ½ acre. The treatment is the same as in type B, except that a flume of the same specifications as shown under type C is constructed.

EROSION CONTROL FOR HIGHWAY SLOPES

The maintenance of road slopes is an expensive item in general highway maintenance. Soil eroded from a cut slope is usually deposited in a position blocking drainage ditches, filling culverts and underground drains, or directly on the roadway, where it causes considerable damage to the pavement and creates serious traffic hazards. The cost of cleaning up this sloughed material is a considerable item in all road-

Fig. 7.16 Board-faced, undrained terraces on 1:1 cut slopes are subject to undermining. (*Department of Transportation, California.*)

maintenance budgets. In addition, an eroded cut slope is undesirable because it is unattractive. See Fig. 7.16.

Many methods of control have been tried, and some have proved successful. The most common methods are described below.

Diversion and Intercepting Ditches

The most common method of reducing the amount of runoff water pouring over a cut slope is to construct an intercepting ditch at the top of each cut slope. This restricts the amount of runoff water which could cause erosion on the slope and limits soil loss to the amount falling directly on the face. These ditches lose their value, however, if they are not kept clean to allow the free flow of water. See Figs. 7.17 and 7.18.

Low cuts are not subject to serious or rapid soil loss. Runoff water accumulating on low cuts does not attain the volume or velocity to move much soil, although the process of soil loss, while slow, is sure. If high cuts were broken up into a series of low banks or terraces, the same soil-loss characteristics would exist. The terraces must be so constructed that they will intercept runoff water and lead the water to one side, where it can be carried to the bottom of the cut in paved ditches or pipes.

The terrace method works very well provided the terraces are kept clean so that they drain at all times. The chief objection to this method is that the cost of construction is high for all but exceptional slopes.

Fig. 7.17 An unattractive ditch. Culverts may be clogged with eroded material when this type of soil loss occurs. (*California Department of Transportation.*)

Fig. 7.18 A broad, flattened intercepting ditch. Vegetation can easily be established here, and a large volume of water is carried without damage. (*California Department of Transportation.*)

Protecting Slopes by Hydro Seeding and Asphalt Mulching

New equipment is constantly being introduced on the market. In the past few years, methods of seeding, fertilizing, and mulching steep slopes and large areas have undergone radical changes. For instance, the old methods of applying straw and hay mulches by hand and then staking and tying the mulch down became so expensive that it was rapidly becoming necessary either to stop mulching altogether or to devise more economical ways of getting the job done. As a result, new machines were invented that did the job quickly and economically. These methods are described in detail in Chap. 2, page 61.

Use of Board Wattles on 1:1 Slope

This method has been common in the past but for the most part has been unsuccessful. Its main purpose was to establish favorable conditions for ground-cover plants. A ditch was dug in the slope, and faced with a length of 1- by 4-in. lumber held in place by stakes, and the space between boards was backfilled with topsoil and planted. Runoff water overtopping the board facings dropped to the slope below, eroding the steep slope between terraces. Such action caused the undermining of the board facings and subsequent loss of topsoil. In general, 1:1 slopes cannot be successfully protected without extremely high construction costs. See Fig. 7.16.

Establishment of Vegetative Cover

The most natural and attractive method of controlling erosion on cut slopes is to establish a solid vegetative cover. Since the angle of repose of loose soil is about 1.5:1, it first becomes necessary to flatten all slopes to a minimum of 1.5:1. The flatter the slope the more successful erosion-control methods will be. Details are given in Figs. 7.20 and 7.21.

A combination of 1.5:1 slope or a flatter, well-roughened cut face, and a relatively thin blanket of topsoil, seeded with good grass seed, properly mulched and with mulch secured to prevent blowing away, will give adequate protection under normal conditions. However, if a heavy and prolonged rainfall occurs (2 to 4 in. in 24 hours) before the grass is established, some slippage and erosion may occur.

CONTROL OF HIGHLY EROSIVE SOIL TYPES

On soils which have erosive tendencies, the above treatment is not sufficient. To solve this problem successfully, straw should be added on

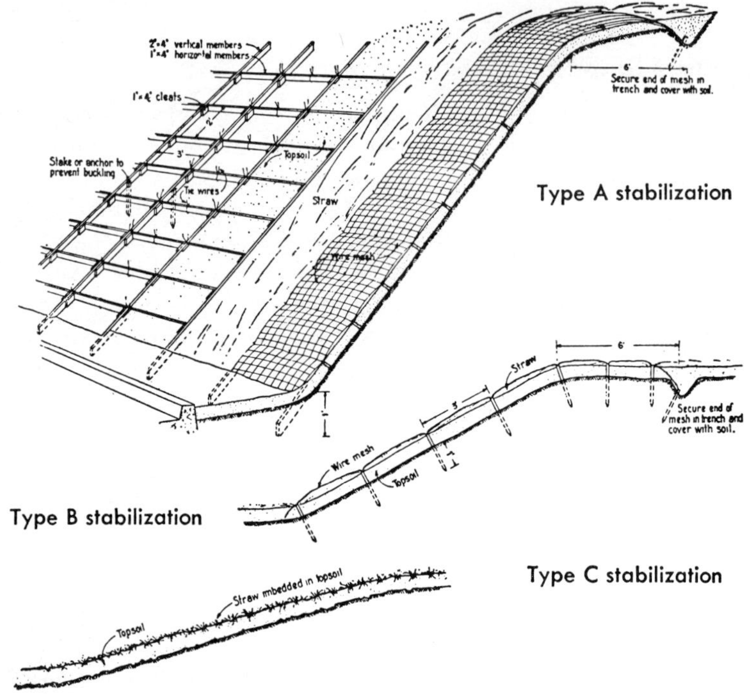

Fig. 7.19 Slope stabilization. (*California Department of Transportation.*)

Type A stabilization, for 1:1 or flatter slopes

1. Lay soil retaining frames on slope and nail securely. On slopes over 15 ft high (slope distance) anchor frames to slope to prevent buckling.
2. Attach 14-gage galvanized tie wires for anchoring wire mesh.
3. Fill frames with moist topsoil and compact the soil.
4. Spread straw about 6 in. deep over the slope.
5. Cover straw with 14-gage 4-in. mesh galvanized reinforcing wire. Secure mesh tightly to frames with tie wires.
6. Secure wire mesh at least 6 ft back of top of slope.
7. Plant ground-cover plants through straw into topsoil.

Type B stabilization, for 1.5:1 or flatter slopes

1. Cover slope with moist topsoil and compact to about 6-in. thickness.
2. Spread straw about 6 in. deep over slope.
3. Cover straw with 2-in. mesh galvanized poultry netting or 4-in. mesh galvanized reinforcing wire.
4. Anchor wire mesh to 18-in. 2 by 2 stakes spaced 3 ft apart in staggered rows with tie wires. Tying is preferred to nailing the stakes.
5. Plant ground cover through straw into topsoil.
6. If slope is to be seeded, sow seed before placing straw.

Type C stabilization, for 1.5:1 or flatter slopes

1. Roughen cut slopes on a rough contour with a scarifier or cultivator type of implement, in a series of longitudinal grooves or corrugations.
2. Cover cut slopes with about 3 to 6 in. of topsoil. If topsoil is not available, cultivate slope 4 to 6 in. deep and apply fertilizer. Fill slopes will not ordinarily require topsoil or cultivation unless very sterile or compacted.
3. Cover slope with straw at the rate of about 4 tons/acre. Embed straw into loose soil with a sheepsfoot roller.
4. Plant ground cover through straw into topsoil.
5. If slope is to be seeded, sow seed before placing straw.

Fig. 7.20 Well-roughened cut slope ready to be topsoiled. (*California Department of Transportation.*)

Fig. 7.21 Spreading and smoothing topsoil on a roughened slope. (*California Department of Transportation.*)

the topsoil before seeding, and a sheepsfoot roller should be used to compact the straw into the topsoil, thereby increasing its water-holding capacity. The older procedure of driving stakes through the topsoil layer into the subsoil, in an attempt to anchor the soil and straw in place, has produced the opposite effect of increasing the tendency toward saturation and consequent slippage of the topsoil. The method described above has given satisfactory control during periods of normal rainfall, and even when rainfall exceeds 3 to 4 in. in one storm, it has been successful in reducing slippage to a minimum. Detailed specifications for the most successful methods of slope erosion control are discussed at the end of this chapter, beginning on page 445.

Types of Seed and Ground-Cover Planting

The several kinds of grass and ground-cover plants which have been used successfully to control erosion on highway slopes may be classified as annual grasses, perennial grasses, and ground-cover plants.

ANNUAL GRASSES

There are two annual grasses in general use, Italian ryegrass and Korean lespedeza, which provide a quick cover under practically any condition. They are usually effective during the first year but do not provide permanent cover. They are useful as nurse crops for more permanent grasses or ground covers and in preventing soil erosion during periods when it is impossible to establish a permanent cover.

PERENNIAL GRASSES

The most common sod-producing grasses which can be used on highways, Bermuda grass, *Lespedeza sericea*, the fescues, Kentucky bluegrass and clover, are fully described in Chap. 2.

GROUND-COVER PLANTS

Where practical, various ground-cover plants have been used on slopes with varied success. Generally, planting road slopes to ground covers is confined to reservation roads, park roads, and freeways. The following plants do not require routine mowing or cutting back and have been used with success for this purpose.

Crown, vetch (*Coronilla varia*)
Honeysuckle, common Japanese (*Lonicera japonica*)
Honeysuckle, Hall's Japanese (*Lonicera japonica halliana*)
Ivy, English (*Hedera helix*)
Jasmine, winter (*Jasimum nudiflorum*)
Kudzu (*Kudzu*)
Periwinkle, bigleaf (*Vinca major*)
Periwinkle, common (*Vinca minor*)
Rockspray (*Cotoneaster horizontalis*)
Rose, prairie (*Rosa setigera*)
Rose, wichurian (*Rosa wichuriana*)

English ivy should be used only under good soil conditions and in areas where the surrounding grounds are well landscaped. Rockspray is a good ground cover where there is a preponderance of rock outcropping. It is uneconomical to use except where landscape work is a feature.

Kudzu, while a rapid grower, a good soil builder, and an effective erosion-control agent, should be used only under conditions where its growth can be controlled. It becomes a pest when allowed to spread into adjacent woods or farm lands.

EROSION CONTROL ON FILL SLOPES

Erosion on fill slopes generally goes on unnoticed until it reaches major proportions and begins to endanger the highway. By that time, extensive repairs are necessary in order to save the highway. Many methods have been tried, some successfully and others unsuccessfully. The following methods are the most common and have proved successful under certain conditions.

Control of Raw Fill Slopes

Many fill slopes which are not highly erosive or very infertile can be stabilized very cheaply and effectively by seeding the fill before rain has compacted the soil. Timing is all-important in this procedure, and unfortunately it usually cannot be attained. To counteract this element of time, straw mulches and fertilizer can be used to protect the slope until the grass is well established. Old fill slopes which have been consolidated and gullied by rainfall before being seeded generally produce poor results under the above treatment, until the gullies are filled up and straw or other humus worked into the gullies to prevent them from redeveloping before the seeds germinate.

Control of Highly Erosive Soils on Fill Slopes

Where fills are made of highly erosive soils, more elaborate measures of control must be taken. These are described in detail later, but in general they are as follows.

STRAW-AND-SHEEPSFOOT-ROLLER METHOD

After the degree of slope has been established, a straw covering is put in place. A sheepsfoot roller is then run over the completed slope in order to compact the soil and to incorporate the straw into the top layer of soil. The roller will leave a few inches of loose, uncompacted soil on the surface, but this loose soil is mixed with the straw, forming a food seedbed. Under normal conditions, a relative compaction of 89.4 per

Fig. 7.22 Rolling straw-covered 1.5:1 slope with sheepsfoot roller. (*California Department of Transportation.*)

cent is obtained below the top 4 in. This degree of compaction reduces the water-holding capacity of the soil, and the tendency of the soil to liquefy is substantially reduced. If the soil is poor in fertility, fertilizer should be added before either the straw or the rolling process is done. The same procedure is followed whether the slope is topsoiled or the existing fill is treated. See Figs. 7.22 and 7.23.

WIRE-MESH OR BRUSH-MAT METHOD

On deep-fill slopes composed of highly erosive material, an additional anchoring effect is needed. This is usually attained by the use of wire-reinforced brush mats, straw or wire-mesh mats, or brush layers, installed on the contour during fill construction. These mats and layers act as screens or filters in the event the surface straw protection breaks down. If gullies start to form, the mats or layers are exposed and by filtering the water and decreasing its velocity will tend to reduce the damage. The outer edge of the mat should be left flush with the surface of the fill slope to permit use of a sheepsfoot roller in compacting the loose surface material and embedding the straw in the soil.

It is important that the brush layers should not protrude beyond the slope face. Where brush is allowed to protrude 12 in. or more from the slope, the filtering action of the brush will cause terraces to build out to the point where runoff water, overtopping the terrace, will drop straight down and strike the slope below with considerable force, gouging out the slope below the layer.

EROSION CONTROL ON HIGHWAY SHOULDERS

On highway shoulders, erosion control is limited, depending upon the type of soil and grade. It is seldom a serious problem and generally occurs during the first year after construction and before the shoulder has become stabilized. Damage to road pavements caused by shoulder erosion may amount to a considerable sum if allowed to go unchecked. Asphalt or bituminous surfaces have a tendency to fray or deteriorate on the edges unless an adequate shoulder is maintained.

There are several ways by which erosion on highway shoulders can be controlled. The two most effective methods are (1) surface the shoulders with 2 to 3 in. of gravel and (2) mulch and seed the shoulder in order to establish a turf. The latter method is effective only in climates where there is adequate rainfall during the summer months. If rills develop, a thin coating of straw should be spread over the shoulder at the rate of approximately 3 tons/acre, run over by a sheepsfoot roller, and then seeded. This will stabilize the shoulder in a relatively short time. Korean lespedeza or fescues are best suited for this purpose.

Expensive treatments, such as topsoiling and planting of elaborate turfs, are not necessary except under extreme conditions or in highly developed public-use areas.

EROSION CONTROL IN DRAINAGE DITCHES

Erosion in intercepting and drainage ditches is potentially dangerous to highways and becomes very ugly. In the past, little attention has been

Fig. 7.23 Rolling 10-ft strip of fill slope after application of straw. (*California Department of Transportation.*)

paid to the proper construction of these ditches, and as result major erosion problems occur. Equipment is still being used that cuts a V-shaped ditch into the subsoil—an open invitation to erosion. Methods of control and construction are very simple and inexpensive, as follows:

1. The grade of drainage and intercepting ditches should never be steeper than 2 per cent. The steeper the grade the greater the velocity of the water and the greater the soil loss from the ditch.
2. Never cut a ditch in the V shape. Such ditches usually cut deeply into the subsoil, where it is difficult for vegetation to become established. As a result, each storm or rainfall cuts the ditch deeper and deeper, making control more and more difficult and expensive.
3. Wherever possible, form the ditch in a broad U shape. Such ditches do not cut deeply into the subsoil and reduce to a minimum the amount of water carried in a single channel. The bottom of the ditch should be cultivated, fertilized, and seeded with a quick-growing annual grain so that protection is provided the first year after construction. Native windblown seeds will be caught by the grain and will quickly establish a permanent cover.
4. Wherever it is impossible to construct a broad U-shaped ditch, an alternate method can be used. Scrape a thin layer of topsoil from the slope immediately above the top of the slope face, and form it into a low, rounded berm merging into the rounded brow of the cut. A motor grader can be used for this job. Cultivate the disturbed area and seed both the berm and the disturbed area. Again, the fescues and Korean lespedeza are satisfactory for seeding. If the soil conditions are such that topsoil is not available, use the existing soil and add fertilizer and mulch.
5. The construction of contour ditches at the ends of cut slopes will take runoff water into dispersal areas without any soil loss.
6. Where erosion has occurred in roadside ditches, the following control measures can be taken:
   a. Pack cut brush, supplemented with straw, into the ditch in order to filter the soil and slow up the runoff water to a point where it reduces the cutting action to a minimum.
   b. In deep erosion ditches, construct check dams placed in such a manner that the grade from the foot of one to the top of the next does not exceed 2 per cent. Such

dams may be made of concrete, stone, logs, or other available material.

c. Where right-of-way widths permit and the eroded ditches are not too deep, regrade into U shape and treat as described in item 4 above.

MAINTENANCE OF HIGHWAY SLOPES

Too often, maintenance crews forget or ignore highway slopes after the initial slope-stabilization treatment has taken hold. Unfortunately most slopes cannot be ignored for several years. A good maintenance program of fertilization is necessary until the slopes are completely stabilized. If rills and small gullies are caught in time, they can be prevented from developing into large gullies and causing subsequent damage, not only to the slope, but also the roadbed. Weak spots should be retreated with seed, fertilizer, and straw as they occur, and any damage caused by animals or fire should be repaired as soon as possible.

It is necessary to maintain constant vigilance in order to prevent streams of runoff water from running down over the slope face. Clogged culverts, or broken, clogged, or inadequate berms and intercepting ditches may allow a concentrated stream of water to pour down over the slope, forming large gullies very rapidly. Under such conditions, surface protection of the slope is of no value.

Sloughed material removed from gutters and shoulders should be disposed of in places where it will not cause damage to existing slopes. If such material is dumped on stabilized slopes, the entire stabilization treatment is wasted. It is usually possible to find some gully which needs filling within a reasonable hauling distance.

Since any form of slope stabilization treatment represents a sizable investment, sound economic practice justifies the expenditure of a proportionate amount to protect that investment.

DETAILED SLOPE STABILIZATION METHODS

TYPE A STABILIZATION, FOR 1:1 OR FLATTER SLOPES

The most elaborate and expensive method for stabilizing steep slopes (1:1) is the wooden grid system. This method, however, has been successful wherever tried and is useful in slope stabilization in highly developed urban areas where a wider right of way, to allow for flatter slopes, is either impossible or too expensive to obtain. Such slopes are too steep for economical mowing and should be planted to a ground cover instead of grass.

TYPE B STABILIZATION, FOR 1.5:1 OR FLATTER SLOPES

This type of stabilization is very effective where erosion must be controlled to prevent damage to the adjacent urban property or where a slope is constructed at the top of a retaining wall. This method is relatively expensive but gives effective protection. A thick layer of straw on top of a compacted topsoil layer, secured by anchored strips of wire mesh, effectively prevents the two types of soil movement, surface loss and slippage. Ground-cover plants can be planted through this layer and soon will provide a permanent cover.

TYPE C STABILIZATION, FOR 1.5:1 OR FLATTER SLOPES

Probably the most economical method of slope stabilization is that for type C (Fig. 7.19). On cut slopes the surface should first be roughened with a scarifier or cultivator type of machine. This roughened slope should show corrugations on a rough contour, which, when the soil becomes saturated, will tend to break up the smooth slippage plane which forms between the layer of topsoil and the subsoil. The topsoil blanket should be restricted to a thickness of 2 or 3 in. Thicker coverage will tend to become saturated and slip, and 2 or 3 in. will produce as dense a growth as a thicker layer. Over the topsoil blanket, a layer of straw is spread at the rate of 4 tons/acre. The slope is then compacted by rolling with a sheepsfoot roller. Several methods for rolling slopes with such a roller have been developed:

1. A single roller equipped with a yoke can be connected by wire cable to a power-operated drum unit on the back of a caterpillar tractor. The roller is lightened of ballast to the point where it will roll down the slope when the cable is slack but will not cause an excessive load on the power unit when it is being pulled back to the top of the slope. The tractor is positioned at the top of the slope, broadside to the slope face. The roller is let down, the speed of descent being controlled by the power-unit brake, and then pulled back. The tractor is then moved a distance equal to the width of the roller, and the process is repeated.
2. A truck crane has been used to roll low-fill slopes lengthwise. Two cables are attached to the roller, one to control the position of the roller on the slope and the other to pull it. Care must be taken to keep the axis of the roller at right angles to the direction of the pull, because a skewed roller has a tendency to pick up straw from the surface of the slope.

3. High-fill slopes can be rolled with a heavily weighted two-section sheepsfoot roller, provided a cable winch of sufficient power and braking capacity is available. A truck crane will roll slopes as much as 300 ft long. The roller, connected directly by cable to the winch, is stationed at the top of the slope, the crane boom cable is hooked to an eye attached to the roller frame, the roller is hoisted free of the slope, the truck is moved forward a distance equal to the width of the roller, the boom cable is unhooked, and the rolling is resumed.
4. When straw is spread on the completed portion of a fill slope at stages during the construction of the fill, a long-arched extension tongue has been used to connect a standard two-section sheepsfoot roller directly to the tractor drawbar. The tractor is backed to the top of the slope, and the roller is let down over the edge. The required number of round trips is made by moving the tractor forward away from the top of the slope and back for a distance equal to the length of the tongue.

After the slope has been compacted, spread fertilizer and lime in accordance with soil tests. In fact, it is better to spread the fertilizer and lime before rolling operations begin, so that these materials will be mixed into the soil. Seed the slope to the desired grass, depending upon local conditions.

The approximate cost of slope preparation for type C, roughing, straw, rolling, fertilizer, and seed, but exclusive of topsoil is about half that for type B.

TYPE D STABILIZATION FOR 1.5:1 OR FLATTER SLOPES, WHERE TOPSOIL IS NOT AVAILABLE

Many of the clay soils will, if properly prepared, support certain types of grass. Where such soils exist, it is not necessary to topsoil the slope before seeding. The same procedure of roughening the slope, spreading straw, and rolling with a sheepsfoot roller can be followed, with these exceptions:

1. The roughening of cut slopes should be more thorough and deeper, in order to ensure a fairly loose seedbed 2 to 3 in. deep.
2. Fertilize and lime the slope heavily. A soil test will determine the quantities and kind of fertilizer to use.
3. Increase the amount of straw from 4 to 6 tons/acre.
4. Roll by any of the methods previously described.

Brush-Layer Method for Stabilizing Fill Slopes

The brush-layer method (Fig. 7.24) is used in stabilizing fill slopes composed of highly erosive soils. Its principal function is to minimize the formation of gullies should the surface protection fail. Installation of brush layers or mats differs from type C methods in that a heavier appli-

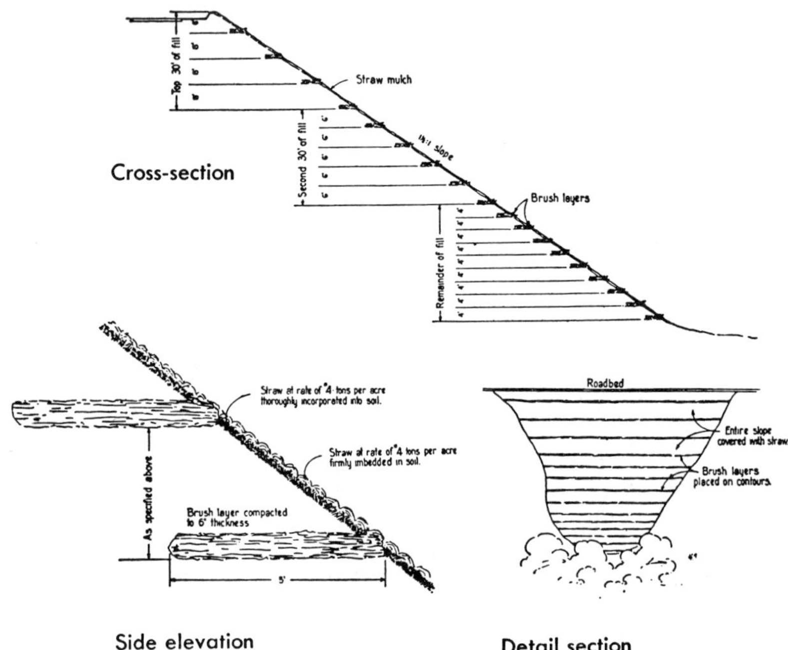

Fig. 7.24 Brush-layer method. (*California Department of Transportation.*)

1. At required fill elevation, smooth edge of fill bench on contour to width of mat.
2. Lay brush, leafy ends outward, flush with edge of fill to such depth that after compaction the finished mat will be approximately 6 in. thick.
3. Place additional fill material on top of brush and compact as for remainder of fill.
4. At convenient stages of fill construction, spread straw evenly over slope at rate of 4 tons/acre. Roll with a sheepsfoot roller operated vertically to the plane of the slope until straw is thoroughly incorporated into the soil. At least four round trips of the roller will be required.
5. Sow evenly over the slope a mixture of 50 per cent barley, 45 per cent rye grain, and 5 per cent alfalfa seed by weight at rate of 200 lb/acre.
6. Spread second application of straw at rate of 4 tons/acre. Repeat rolling operation until straw is firmly embedded in soil.
7. Plant live cuttings of baccharis and willow or cuttings and seed of hardy varieties of plants indigenous to the locality between mats for permanent vegetative protection.

The total quality of straw applied per acre will vary according to the character of fill material. Loose, granular, disintegrated granite soil usually requires more straw per acre for an adequate cover (6 to 10 tons/acre) than does soil of a loamy character (4 to 8 tons/acre).

cation of straw and additional rolling with a sheepsfoot roller are specified. The complete stabilization treatment should be given fill slopes at stages during fill construction, so that no extensive area of unprotected slope will be exposed to damage. Each portion of the slope should be thoroughly rolled in order to obtain the maximum compaction. When brush is not readily available, the following alternatives are possible:

Straw mat Lay 1-in.-mesh galvanized netting or fencing on the prepared fill bench surface. The mesh should extend into the fill about 5 ft. Spread straw on the mesh to such depth that after compaction the finished mat will be approximately 4 in. thick. Proceed as for brush layer.

Wire-mesh mat Lay 60-in.-wide 4-in.-mesh galvanized fencing on the prepared fill bench surface. On top of this lay several courses of small-mesh poultry netting. Proceed as for brush layer.

Wire-reinforced brush mat Lay 60-in.-wide 2- to 4-in.-mesh galvanized fencing on the prepared fill bench surface. Place brush on wire, leafy ends outward, to such depth that after compaction the finished mat will be from 4 to 6 in. thick. Lay wire mesh on top of brush and tie edges together at 1-ft intervals, with 16-gage galvanized wire. Tie along center and at quarter points, at 3-ft intervals. Proceed as for brush layer.

On low embankments and the upper portions of high slopes, every fourth brush layer is replaced by a wire-reinforced brush mat, and as the distance from the top of the fill becomes greater, this interval is reduced until every third, and finally every second layer consists of a reinforced mat (Fig. 7.25).

When wire mesh or fencing is used, the outer edge should be laid far enough inside the ultimate slope line not to be damaged during the rolling operation. Lengths of fencing should be overlapped and fastened together in order to take advantage of any structural strength and resistance to slumping which the wire may offer. The wire mat may then extend continuously for the full length of the fill, plus a short distance beyond the intersection of the embankment slope and original ground, where it should be secured.

The average cost per linear foot of these various methods, based on 1975 costs, is as follows:

Brush layers: $0.50 to $0.75
Wire reinforced brush mats: $2.20 to $2.50
Wire mesh mats (poultry netting): $2.50 to $2.75

Straw, furnished and spread in two applications at rate of 6 tons/acre, averages about $780 per acre.

Cost of rolling or compacting slopes averages about 30 cents per square yard, or $1450 per acre.

Repair of Failure on Newly Stabilized Slopes

The first winter after installation of the slope stabilization program is the critical one. Most failures occur at that time, before the vegetation has had a chance to consolidate the slope. The seriousness of the failure usually depends upon the intensity of the first severe storm. Prompt

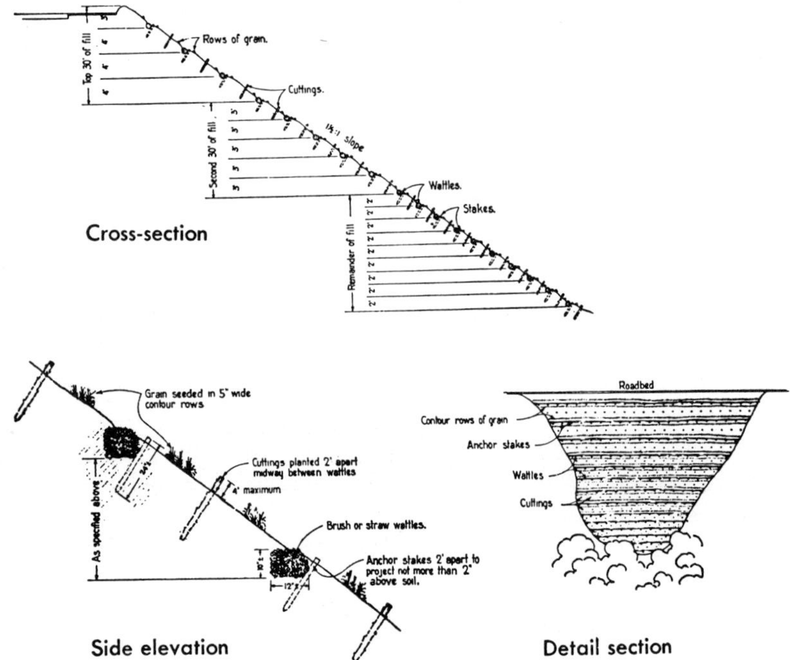

Fig. 7.25 Straw or brush wattle for fill-slope stabilization after construction. *(California Department of Transportation.)*

1. After fill is constructed, beginning at toe of fill, dig a trench approximately 12 in. wide and 10 in. deep following the contour.
2. Pack leafy brush, straw, or a combination of both into a cable about 12 in. wide and 10 in. thick and lay it in the trench.
3. Drive approximately 1 by 2 by 24 in. stakes at 2-ft centers below wattle and at right angles to the slope.
4. Partly cover wattle just placed with material excavated from next trench above.
5. After wattles are all placed, plant living cuttings not less than 1 in. in diameter and 24 to 30 in. long at 2-ft centers, in rows midway between wattles. Set cuttings in ground so that they protrude only 3 or 4 in.
6. Seed barley, rye grain, or alfalfa in rows 5 in. wide just above and just below each wattle, and broadcast additional seed evenly over surface of slope.

and effective repair of sections which have failed will forestall more serious trouble later.

The most frequent failure is surface slippage. If the slip starts at the top of the slope or near the top, it is possible that seepage or percolation of water from above through a porous layer of subsoil is causing the damage. It may be intensified by standing water in a poorly graded intercepting ditch. Saturation of this sort is caused by water originating elsewhere than on the slope face, and corrective measures must be taken to repair defective drainage systems.

If the slip starts on the lower two-thirds of the slope or below, it is usually caused by saturation of the soil due to lack of sufficient compaction before the rains start. Where cut slopes have had the subsoil insufficiently roughened before the topsoil is applied, the tendency toward slippage is often increased. If such slippage occurs only in minor section of the slope and remainder of the slope remains firm, only simple repair operations are necessary.

Failures appearing on slopes which have been given type C stabilization treatment need not be backfilled as part of the repair process. Such procedure would only tend to increase the saturation point. Such areas need only to be fertilized and reseeded or planted. The most economical and satisfactory method for repairing surface slips is to fertilize the exposed subsoil heavily, reseed or plant, and apply a straw mulch held in place with brush or a few shovelfuls of loose soil. The sooncr this method is employed, the better the chance for success.

Extensive gullies are caused by berm failures, plugged-down drains, or inadequate diversion ditches. Repairs are made only after the cause has been corrected. Usually it becomes necessary to backfill the gully, fertilize, seed, and mulch.

Repair of Old Eroded Slopes*

Old slopes which have never received a stabilization treatment and have eroded badly will require a light cultivation of the compacted soil before any other repair work can be undertaken. Such cultivation will smooth out small gullies and rills, break up channels of concentration, and make a more favorable seedbed. Cultivation should be followed by fertilization, seeding, and an adequate straw mulch.

Repair work on deeply eroded slopes is more or less a long-term proposition. Large gullies or slipouts in fill slopes usually require replacement of the material which has been lost in order to safeguard the roadbed. There are three methods which can be used which will provide

* Material from Erosion Control on California State Highways used by permission of the Department of Public Works, Division of Highways, State of California.

control in a relatively short time. The first of these methods will need subsequent treatment to take care of the slumping. All slumping should be stabilized within 2 or 3 years, however.

1. A crib of logs and coarse brush is constructed at the toe of the fill to provide a solid foundation against which backfill material can settle. Loose brush is placed in the slope gullies and covered with a thick layer of backfill material. Additional brush is spread over the surface and covered with soil, and the process is repeated until the original fill contour is restored. The surface should be protected with one of the various stabilizing methods described. Since the backfill material is not compacted, there will be a certain amount of settlement and slumping. Usually such settling is near the top and can be easily backfilled and re-treated.
2. Where immediate protection is needed in order to protect a roadbed, this method will give good results. A log and brush crib is constructed at the toe of the fill to give a solid foundation against which the backfill can be compacted. Backfill material is furnished from the top, and a bulldozer is used to spread, compact, and shape this material to the original fill contour. Brush layers are installed at suitable intervals as the fill is built up. (See the Brush-Paving Method, page 448.) The completed slope is then given surface protection as described previously.
3. Another method is to use metal cribbing into which the backfill can be dumped. This is probably the most efficient and lasting method.

MAINTENANCE OF ROADS AND PARKING AREAS

MAINTENANCE OF BITUMINOUS SURFACES

Practically all access roads, service roads, and parking areas on public grounds have a bituminous surface on a crushed-stone base. The proper maintenance of bituminous surfaces should consist mainly of preventive measures such as skin patching, spot sealing, or surface treating when the first signs of failure appear, and not of patching holes after they have formed. The most prevalent early sign of failure is map cracking, checking, or alligatoring of the surface. This usually begins in small areas, and unless repaired may extend over the entire road surface, producing potholes and finally destroying the road surface and damaging the base.

Careful watching and attention to checked or alligatored spots will nearly eliminate the formation of potholes and will result in much more effective maintenance, not only from the standpoint of cost but also from the standpoint of service to the public. Except in unusual circumstances, such as severe ice and snow conditions or after heavy storms, there should never be a pothole of any appreciable size in a bituminous surface.

In maintaining bituminous surfaces, the following points should be observed and considered: checking, alligatoring, or map cracking; surface deterioration and raveling; potholes; corrugations or sharp irregularities; settlements and deformations; completely failed sections; slippery surfaces; shoulders and ditches.

Checking, Alligatoring, or Map Cracking

Checking, alligatoring, or map cracking is caused by (1) soft subgrade material, (2) wet subgrade due to improper drainage, (3) drying out of the surfaces, (4) lack of sufficient thickness of the surface course, or (5) inadequate thickness of or lack of structural strength in the base course.

Repair by sealing with 0.15 to 0.25 gal/yd² medium-viscosity bituminous material and cover with 6 to 10 lb/yd² no. 12 (no. 8 to ⅜ in.) or no. 12-A (no. 100 to no. 4) aggregate. Rolling with a light roller is advisable but should be omitted if the base is inclined to be yielding.

Bituminous material may be applied on small areas with a hand spray. If areas are large, apply with pressure distributor, using bar widths as required. Care should be exercised not to apply an excess of bituminous material; it is always better to have too little than too much.

The principal rule about spot sealing map-cracked areas is that it should be done whenever the telltale cracks appear, regardless of the season of the year and regardless of whether the cracks are wet or dry. As long as the small sections of pavement surrounded by the cracks are reasonably dry, the treatment will hold and is effective in sealing out surface water.

Surface Deterioration and Raveling

Essentially the same defects as those described above for checking and alligatoring are responsible for surface deterioration and raveling. There is one additional cause of raveling, a deficiency of bitumen. Correction is also essentially the same, except that more bituminous material and a larger aggregate should be used, to replace lost material.

Potholes

Lack of proper surface maintenance or an uneven distribution of bituminous material may cause potholes. Also, movement of the base due to inadequate thickness of a yielding subgrade will cause the surface to break, thereby starting a pothole.

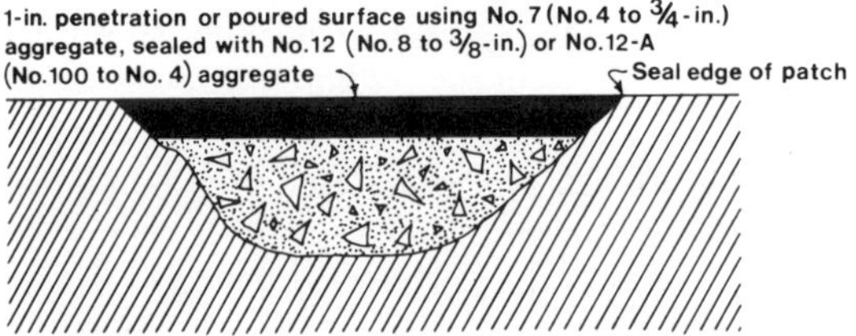

Fig. 8.1 Repairing deep potholes by restoring base to its original condition and then surfacing. Replacement to be comparable to original condition of base, containing the proper size of aggregate and filling material and to be thoroughly compacted in not over 3-in.-thick layers. Top of all layers to be parallel to finished grade. The top of the restored base should be cleaned and should be free of an excess of fine material before the bituminous surface course is placed. The application of a prime coat of bituminous material on the new base is advisable. Check the finished patch with a straightedge to ensure a smooth-riding surface.

There are three important considerations in patching potholes: (1) use essentially the same types of materials in the patch that are present in the base and the surface to be patched; (2) tie or blend the patch into the area surrounding the patch; otherwise, two new potholes will develop, one on each side of the new patch; (3) compact the material tightly into the cavity in approximately 3-in. layers, being careful to keep the surface of the layers parallel to the surface of the pavement. The surface of the completed patch must conform with the surrounding pavement surface.

The three methods of patching potholes are illustrated in Figs. 8.1 to 8.3.

Corrugations or Sharp Irregularities

There are four common causes for corrugations or sharp irregularities: (1) buildup of a mat of small aggregate, together with an excess of bituminous material, (2) a base or surface inadequate for the type of traffic, (3) structural obsolescence, and (4) poor subgrade soil conditions.

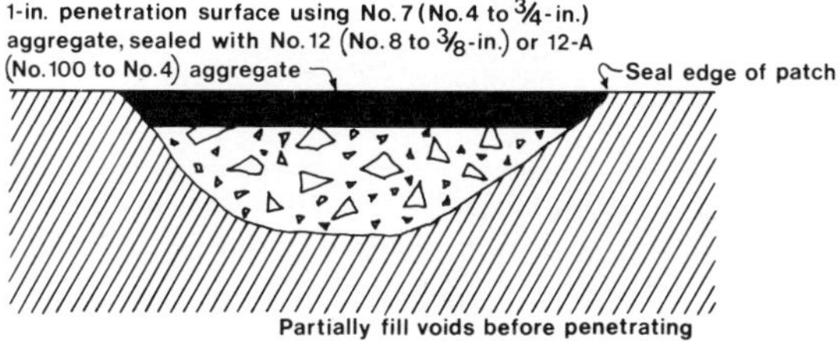

Fig. 8.2 Repair of deep potholes by penetration method. Place no. 1 (1- to 3½-in.) or no. 2 (1- to 3-in.) aggregate in layers approximately 3 in. thick when thoroughly compacted. Top of all layers to be parallel to finished grade. To save bituminous material and to obtain better mechanical bond, the voids in the no. 1 or no. 2 aggregate should be partially filled with no. 12 (no. 8 to ⅜ in.) aggregate before penetrating with bituminous material. Check the patch with a straightedge to ensure a smooth-riding surface.

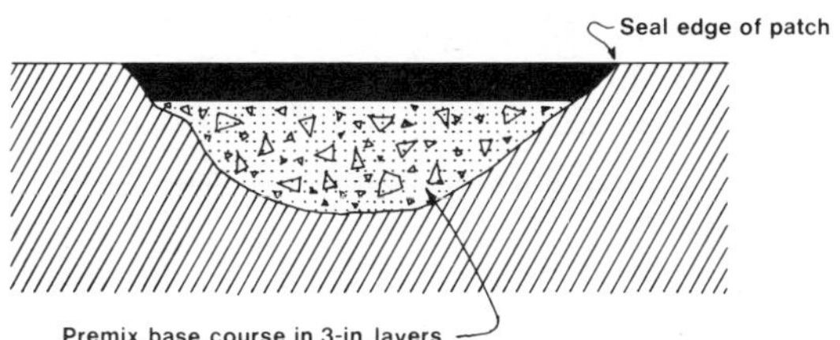

Fig. 8.3 Repair of deep potholes by use of premix base and top-course material 1- to 1½-in. premix surface course. Place premix base-course material in layers approximately 3 in. thick when thoroughly compacted. Top of all layers to be parallel to finished grade. Check the patch with a straightedge to ensure a smooth-riding surface.

A bituminous leveling course consisting of the following steps will be necessary to correct this situation:

1. Clean the surface thoroughly.
2. Patch potholes of surface breaks and spot-seal any cracked or alligatored sections. Care should be used in this operation, as an excess of bituminous material in patches or spot sealing will result in fat spots on the final surface.
3. Apply the appropriate grade of bituminous material in the correct amount (0.3 to 0.8 gal/yd^2) uniformly over the aggregate. (Avoid an excess of bitumen.)
4. Immediately after the application of bituminous material, grade with blade at right angles in such a manner that material will be dragged from the high spots and spilled into the depressions.
5. Roll thoroughly with a 10-ton three-wheel roller.
6. Correct any remaining depressions or irregularities by placing an additional course where necessary.
7. Place required surface treatment.

The weight of surface treatment required to cover and protect this type of leveling depends on the type of original surface leveled. A standard 25-lb treatment is sufficient for leveling a reasonably tight bituminous surface.

The gradation of the aggregate used in leveling course also affects the weight of surface treatment required. Where a leveling course in which no. 37 (no. 4 to 1½ in.) aggregate has been used and covered with a 25-lb surface treatment, the amount of the tack coat should be increased 0.15 to 0.20 gal/yd^2. This material for the leveling course should be crushed stone, slag, or 100 per cent crushed gravel which meets the standard specifications for concrete aggregate. The depth of irregularities filled with one course should not be more than 2 to 2½ times the maximum size of the aggregate. Courses of 30 to 60 lb/yd^2 placed over the entire surface require no. 7 (no. 4 to ⅜ in.) gradation, and courses of 60 to 100 lb require no. 37 (no. 4 to 1½ in.) gradation.

Bituminous materials should either be RT-7 to RT-9 tar, the grade depending on the temperature and weather conditions at the time of application, or asphalt cutback or emulsion having comparable viscosity and penetrating qualities.

Settlements and Deformation

The causes of settlements and deformation are (1) lack of adequate subgrade support, (2) slipping or movement of the fill, (3) inadequate thickness of base, and (4) structural obsolescence. Placing a patch affords only temporary relief unless the underlying cause of the subsidence is corrected. Lack of subgrade support is usually caused by a poor drainage condition, which should be corrected before the finished patch is placed.

Slipping or movement of a fill is generally caused by lack of stability in the soil upon which the fill was placed, lack of stability of the fill material itself, or settlement from lack of compaction. Corrective measures should be applied before patching.

If the base is too thin or is structurally obsolete, additional thickness should be provided before the patching.

If the settlement or deformation is not too pronounced, it can be corrected by placing a poured or premix patch; otherwise it may be necessary to bring the depression up approximately to grade with a base-course material and then resurface.

Completely Failed Sections

Poor drainage conditions, resulting in inadequate subgrade support, are responsible for completely failed sections. Remove the entire sec-

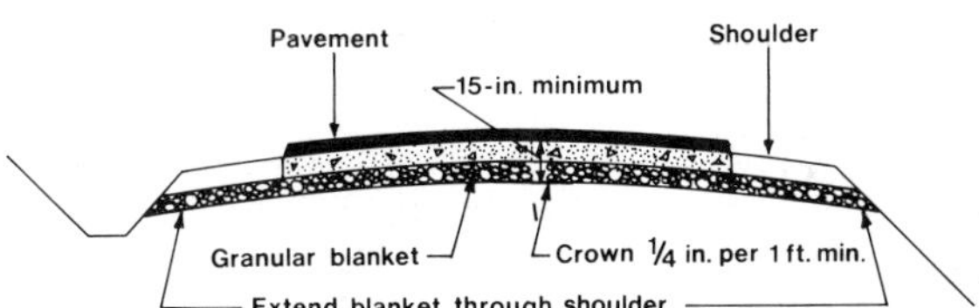

Fig. 8.4 Underdrainage for wet sections. Treatment as shown above is usually satisfactory for fill sections and for sections having wide ditches and flat, well-stabilized slopes. The granular blanket should be composed of a closely graded mixture of sand and gravel. Crushed stone or slag is not advisable because of the danger of clogging with subgrade soil, rendering the blanket ineffective for providing drainage and disrupting capillary action.

tion of surface and base, and correct the drainage condition by installing underdrains or French drains. Place a blanket of granular material from ditch line to ditch line, as shown in Fig. 8.4, and then place a new base and surface.

Slippery Surfaces

The causes of slippery surfaces are an excess of bituminous material or improper gradation of the aggregate. Fat spots can be prevented by exercising care in applying bituminous materials. It is better to have too little than too much, because if the surface lacks bituminous material more can be added, but if it is overbituminized, removal of the excess is difficult and costly.

There are two practical and effective methods for correcting slippery surfaces: (1) the application of a tack coat of tar or asphalt emulsion followed by an application of coarse, sharp sand and (2) the application of a new heavy open-graded road or plant-mix surface course.

Shoulders and Ditches

It is important to keep the shoulders dressed or smoothed in such a manner that there will be no holes, ruts, or high or low places to interfere with proper drainage of the edge of the pavement surface and the shoulders. High shoulders at the edge of the pavement allows surface water to soak down at the edge of the pavement. Ruts at the edge of the pavement also hold water, which soaks into and softens the subgrade, resulting in pavement-edge settlement.

Whenever practicable, the bottoms of the ditches should be below the subgrade elevation and should have sufficient fall to carry the water away quickly.

General

In placing patches of all types, extreme care should be exercised not to use an excess of bituminous material. An overbituminized patch will shove out of shape in hot weather and result in a fat, slippery spot and waste bituminous material. (Tables 8.1 to 8.3)

Patching just shead of resurfacing is important. The control of the bituminous material is particularly important; if an excess is used in the patches, it is likely to come up through the new surface to form unsightly blotches and slippery spots. The patches should therefore be on the lean side and not tightly sealed, because their only function is to fill a subsidence; the new surface will ensure the material's remaining in proper position.

Do not allow holes and broken places to accumulate in order to patch them all at once. This does not save costs but increases them. If repairs are neglected, the small holes and cavities develop into larger holes and cavities and require many times the material and labor to repair. Such lack of constant maintenance results in numerous holes at all times, and particularly during wet and cold seasons. A patch placed during wet or cold weather remains in place almost as well as one placed in dry weather. See Fig. 8.5 for proper method and Fig. 8.6 (sketches 1 and 2) for improper method. Figure 8.7 indicates the method of repair of a series of holes of different areas and depths.

TABLE 8.1
Use of Asphalt Emulsion

Type of work	Type and grade of bituminous material	Maximum application temperature (°F)	Minimum application temperature (°F)
Patching (late fall, winter, and early spring)	AE–1	130	70
Patching (summer)	AE–2	130	70
Light seals and light surface treatments	AE–3	130	70
	AE–5	130	100
Heavy surface treatments	AE–5	130	100
Road mixes	AE–4	130	70
Cold-laid plant mix	AE–3	130	70
Hot-laid plant mix	AE–3	130	70
Penetration macadam	AE–3	130	70
Crack filling (Impregnated with mineral flour)	AE–3	130	70
Primes:			
A. Knapped or macadam stone base	AE–6	150	100
B. Gravel base	AE–6	150	100
C. Traffic bound stone base	AE–6	150	100

MAINTENANCE OF GRAVEL OR TRAFFIC-BOUND SURFACES

A gravel surface road, if properly constructed, requires only ordinary drainage and grade maintenance common to all types of roads, together with the occasional blading of the surface. If chemicals are used, one or more light treatments will probably be required each spring. Blading a gravel surface, whether chemically treated or not, should always be done soon after a rain while more than the average moisture content is present in the top of the surface. If bladed while dry, some aggregate will be torn loose, leaving pits for the accumulation of water when rain

TABLE 8.2
Use of Tar

Type of work	Type and grade of bituminous material	Maximum application temperature (°F)	Minimum application temperature (°F)
Patching (late fall, winter, and early spring)	RT-6	150	80
	RT-7	225	150
Patching (summer)	RT-8	225	150
	RT-9	225	150
	RT-10	250	175
Light seals and light surface treatments	RT-6	150	80
	RT-7	225	150
	RT-8	225	150
	RT-9	225	150
	RT-10	250	175
Heavy surface treatments	RT-6	150	80
	RT-7	225	150
	RT-8	225	150
	RT-9	225	150
	RT-10	250	175
Road mixes	RT-6	150	80
	RT-7	225	150
	RT-8	225	150
	RT-9	225	150
	RT-10	225	175
Cold-laid plant mix	RT-8, 9 or 10		
	(8 and 9)	225	150
	(10)	250	175
Hot-laid plant mix	RT-12	250	175
Penetration macadam	RT-12	250	175
Crack filling (Impregnated with mineral flour)	RT-12	250	175
Primes:			
A. Knapped or macadam Stone base	RT-3, 4, or 5	RT-2:125	60
B. Gravel base	RT-2, 3, or 4	RT-3:150	80
		RT-4:150	80
C. Traffic bound Stone base	RT-2 or 3	RT-5:150	80

TABLE 8.3
Use of Asphalt

Type of work	Type and grade of bituminous material	Maximum application temperature (°F)	Minimum application temperature (°F)
Patching (late fall, winter, and early spring)	MC–2	200	150
	RC–2	175	100
	RC–3	200	150
Patching (summer)	RC–3	200	150
	RC–4	225	175
	MC–5	275	200
Light seals and light surface treatments	MC–3	250	175
	RC–2	175	100
	RC–3	200	150
Heavy surface treatments	MC–5	275	200
	RC–3	200	150
	RC–4	225	175
	AC–150–200 Penet.	300	200
Road mixes	MC–3	250	175
	MC–5	275	200
	RC–3	200	150
	RC–4	225	175
Cold–laid plant mix	AC–85–100 Penet.	340	275
Hot–laid plant mix	AC–85–100 Penet.	340	275
Penetration macadam (Impregnated with mineral flour)	AC–85–100 Penet.	340	275
	AC–150–200 Penet.	300	200
	RE–5	275	200
	AC–85–100 Penet.	350	275
Primes:			
A. Knapped or macadam Stone base	MC–1	125	80
B. Gravel base	MC–1	125	80
C. Traffic bound Stone base	MC–1	125	80
	MC–9	120	50

comes. Loosened material will not recompact while dry, and general raveling of the surface will be encouraged.

The regular use of a drag tends to cut away the crown and to dislodge aggregate, resulting in a flat, loose surface. The regular use of such

Fig. 8.5 Proper method of patching bituminous surfaces. Before the patch is placed, the cracked and broken area of the bituminous surface should be thoroughly primed and treated with a bituminous material of a viscosity low enough to penetrate the cracks thoroughly and to liven up the old surface. This will rebond the entire structure, giving it strength while cutting off both the surface and subgrade water. Care should be taken, however, to avoid an excessive amount of bitumen in sealing the failed surface before placing the patch. Too much bitumen will work up through the patch and result in a fat (slick) area on the surface. Furthermore, an excess of bitumen may cause the patch to shove.

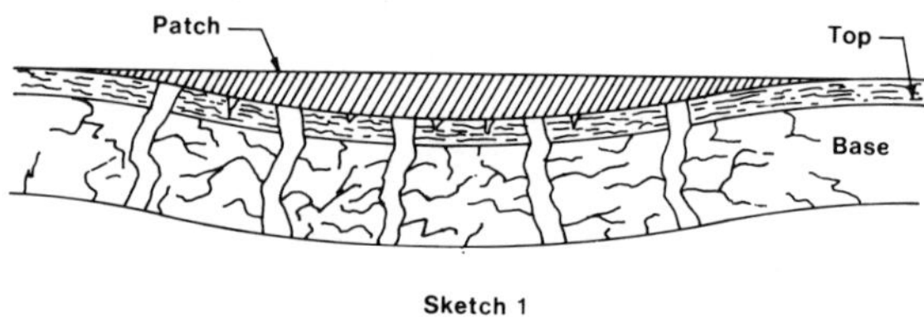

Sketch 1

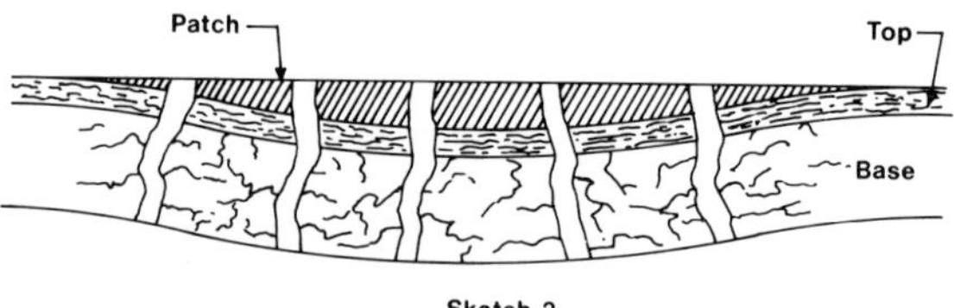

Sketch 2

Fig. 8.6 Improper method of patching bituminous surfaces. A patch like that shown in sketch 1, laid with premix material or paved with quick-setting or high-viscosity liquid bituminous material, will bridge over the cracks, with the result that the cracks, still open beneath the patch, will soon, under traffic, extend up through the patch (as shown in sketch 2), allowing surface water to seep into the surface and base. This process results in disintegration, particularly during freezing and thawing.

equipment is not recommended. The modern tandem-drive power grader, however, is a flexible unit capable of handling ditching and shoulder grading, as well as surface grading, and is highly recommended.

If the surface becomes badly pitted or potholed, it will be necessary to blade deep enough to remove the material at the bottom of the pits or holes. The material is placed in a windrow at the center of the road, then bladed to either side and recompacted to proper shape. This should always be done after a rain.

Treatment of Serious Failures

Serious failures or breakups caused by frost action or inadequate subgrade can be repaired by light blading to reshape the surface, as early and as often as moisture conditions will permit, and by adding aggregate to the sections that have completely failed. A crushed material is more effective than round gravel for the stabilization of very soft sections, because the angular crushed particles interlock much better, forming a mechanical bond which provides stability without the aid of cohesion.

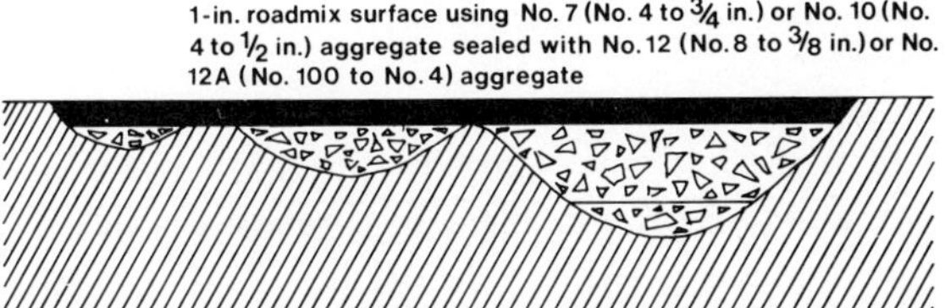

Fig. 8.7 Repair of a series of subsidences of different areas and depths. The subsidences are brought up to a point 1 in. below the finished grade with road-mix leveling course using no. 38 (no. 4 to ½ in.) aggregate. The courses are to be 2 to 3 in. thick, and the top of each course is to be parallel to the finished grade. Hot- or cold-laid bituminous concrete base course and surface course may be substituted for road-mix leveling and surface course.

Treatment to Prevent Dust

Calcium chloride is commonly used for retaining moisture on road surfaces. Used as a surface treatment, it has the property of absorbing moisture from the air as well as retaining moisture. Calcium chloride should be applied when the surface is damp, thoroughly compacted, and free of loose material. It should be placed in increments of 0.5 to 1.0 lb, and the entire treatment should total about 2.5 lb/yd^2. If it is necessary to apply calcium chloride during very dry weather, best results can be obtained by making the application at night or in the very early morning. Mechanical spreading gets better results than hand spreading. A lime spreader or chip or cinder spreader can be used.

Sodium chloride (common salt) can also be used. Its main function is to retain moisture, and since it will absorb moisture from the air only under certain conditions of humidity, the surface should contain the proper amount of moisture when treatment is made. If the surface does not contain enough moisture, it should be sprinkled just before treatment. Use the same method of application for salt as for calcium chloride. Another method of treating dry surfaces is to apply the salt in solution. This can be done with a pressure distributor or an ordinary sprinkling wagon. A total of about 3 lb/yd^2 is required for the salt treatment.

Light asphaltic oil is frequently used as a dust palliative on gravel roads. It partially waterproofs the surface, reducing evaporation, and aids in maintaining stability. The usual application is from $\frac{1}{4}$ to $\frac{1}{2}$ gal/yd^2.

General

The improvement of unsatisfactory gravel surfaces is accomplished by the addition of materials necessary to provide proper gradation and adequate thickness of surface; also, by proper shaping, by providing new or improvement of existing side ditches, and by installing underdrains where needed. Closer attention to requirements for stability and to proper drainage, and with a minimum of blading, will do much to improve the quality of the maintenance of gravel roads.

SHOULDERS AND DITCHES

The maintenance of shoulders and ditches is a type of work which must be carried on to some extent throughout the entire year. However, most work of this type is confined to the fall and spring cleanup. The fall cleanup is to ensure that the shoulders and ditches will go into the winter season in condition to effect proper drainage, and the spring cleanup is to dispose of the ravages of winter weather and its accompanying erosion and slides.

Shoulders

Shoulders are that portion of the roadway on each side of the pavement between the pavement edge and (1) the top of the inner ditch slope in cuts or (2) the top of the fill slope on fills.

The dressing of shoulders is important because (1) if the surface of the shoulder is smooth and properly sloped, it will drain properly, (2) a smooth shoulder adds to the safety of driving, and (3) a well-dressed shoulder adds to the appearance of a highway or access road.

Shoulders are to be maintained for their full width (except where the shoulders are unnecessarily wide) in a smooth condition, flush with the edge of the pavement at all times, and at a slope necessary to facilitate proper drainage of the roadway. As a general rule, slopes should be approximately $\frac{3}{4}$ in./ft for earth shoulders, approximately $\frac{1}{2}$ in./ft for stabilized shoulders, and approximately 1 in./ft for grass shoulders.

The regular blading of shoulders to keep them flush with the edge of the pavement is important because (1) if the shoulder is too high, water retained on the edge of the pavement causes surface deterioration or will soak down at the edge of the pavement and soften the subgrade, and (2) if the shoulder is too low, or if ruts and holes are permitted to remain in the shoulder at or near the edge of the pavement, a traffic hazard is created or, as in bituminous surfaces, raveling of the edges is induced.

Grass-covered shoulders invariably become "built up" to the point where they must be cut down to provide proper drainage. This should be done in the early spring, as soon as weather conditions permit, so that they will become grassed over again as quickly as possible. Cutting down must never be done in late summer and fall, because new ground cover will not have a chance to grow and the shoulder will be severely damaged by erosion during the late fall and early winter months.

Regular mowing of grass shoulders during the growing season not only improves appearances but causes grass to spread out from the base of the plants and give better cover. Regular mowing leaves relatively light cuttings that form a good mulch on the soil and hold moisture. Height of cut is determined by the area and specified on the plan of the individual area. Regular applications of fertilizer will improve both appearance and cover.

In blading and grading other than grass shoulders on fills which are protected with a guardrail, care should be exercised to leave no ridge of earth higher than the surface of the shoulder between, behind, or just in front of the guardrail posts, because a false ditch is formed and erosion of the shoulder will result. The slope of the surface of the shoulder should extend entirely out to the fill slope line, so that the surface drainage can run off uniformly for the entire length of the fill.

In numerous instances, pockets of water are impounded in low places on the shoulders at the edge of the pavement. Such places should be drained whenever observed. This applies also to earth or rock falls which block the ditch and interfere with proper drainage.

Ditches

The proper maintenance of ditches is of utmost importance. If the ditches are allowed to become filled with grass, weeds, leaves, earth, rock, and other debris, they cannot function properly and their effectiveness is definitely impaired.

During the winter, extensive ditch maintenance is very difficult. It is important, however, that rocks and slides which may block free drainage be removed as soon as they occur.

The leaves which fill ditches in woodland areas in the fall must be removed promptly; otherwise they will clog small pipe culverts. Furthermore, the presence of these leaves constitutes a definite fire hazard.

In blading ditches with a power grader, extreme care should be taken not to undercut the toe of the slope with the end of the blade because wherever the toe of the slope is undercut and the slope is left vertical, first the bottom of the slope and then material higher up will begin to slough into the ditch. Several points of maintenance require constant checking:

1. Late in fall, all weeds and tall grass should be cleaned from ditches so that drainage of excessive water will be expedited.
2. Ditches should be kept low enough to maintain the water table below the subgrade.
3. Ditches should be watched in particular during and immediately after hard, washing rains; a little grading work at the time water is moving in the ditches will make the force of the water do a great deal of ditch and pipe-culvert cleaning.
4. During the rainy seasons, inspections should be made at regular intervals to remove slides and debris.

Roadside Cleaning

The average visitor often does not observe good maintenance details and is only conscious of the overall effect. The general appearance of access roads and service drives therefore plays an important part in the first impression a visitor receives of an area.

The general appearance of these roads and drives within an area is improved by giving special attention to the following details:

1. Pavement surfaces should be free of holes and bad deformations.

2. Centerline strips should have good alignment and be kept well painted.
3. Signs should be kept properly placed and well painted.
4. Earth and traffic-bound shoulders should be free of ruts and well graded.
5. Grass shoulders should be kept well trimmed at all times.
6. Slopes should be kept trimmed reasonably close, careful attention being given to selective pruning of shrubs and trees.
7. Guardrails should be kept lined up and properly painted. Temporary guardrails should be replaced with permanent guardrails.
8. Trash and other refuse should be kept off the right of way.
9. Slides and falls of rock or earth onto pavements should be removed promptly.
10. Wooded areas close to the pavement should be cleared of dead, down, and diseased material and of vines and underbrush for a distance of approximately 50 ft on either side of the paved surface. This cleanup should gradually fade into the natural growth beyond.
11. No advertising signs should be permitted.
12. Eroded slopes and slopes with little or no cover should be regraded, fertilized, and planted. Steep slopes should either be mulched or have wattles built on them. The tops of such slopes should be rounded.
13. All important views should be preserved and cleared.

SPECIFICATIONS FOR CONSTRUCTION AND MAINTENANCE OF ROADS AND PARKING AREAS*

Excavation and Backfill for Concrete and Masonry Structures

Excavation should be made to the widths and depths necessary to provide satisfactory construction for the contemplated structure. Except where rock or unsuitable materials are encountered, the last of the excavation should be done by hand and should not be carried to its final depth until just before the construction of the footing or base course. The excavation should then be completed to a smooth surface and to exact grade, so as to provide a foundation of undisturbed earth. Wherever possible, any excavation below the elevation of the top of footing

* These specifications have been adapted from specifications used by the Tennessee Valley Authority.

or base course should be made to the neat dimension (exact size) of the footing.

Where rock is encountered, it should not be allowed to project within the lines of the structure shown on the drawings or established in accordance with the provisions of the drawings. Where rock exists under a portion of a footing which is otherwise to rest on an earth foundation, the rock should, when so indicated on the drawings or so directed, be removed to a depth of 6 in. below the underside of the footing and replaced with gravel or other approved fine materials.

All soft or unstable materials existing below the foundation elevation should be removed to the limits directed.

PREPARATION OF FOUNDATION

The foundation of the footing or structure will depend upon the condition and character of the material encountered. Test holes should be driven or drilled in the foundation material, whether rock or other material, to a depth sufficient to establish its suitability for use as a foundation. They should be sunk by jackhammer drills or other suitable equipment.

Where concrete or masonry is to be placed on the existing surface of rock, all dirt and loose or disintegrated material should be removed to provide complete contact with the solid rock. Where the rock is to serve as a foundation for bridge abutments or other structures requiring additional stability, its surface should be roughened or suitable anchors should be provided. Inclined surfaces of rock should be leveled in steps, as indicated on drawings or as directed, to prevent sliding. All dirt, mud, or loose material accumulating upon the foundation should be removed immediately before placing concrete. Any cracks or crevices in the foundation which are large enough to permit separation of the concrete materials should be filled with concrete or with suitable aggregate materials before concrete placing is begun.

Before concrete is poured in any footing of a foundation unit, all blasting necessary in excavating or shaping of all footings in the entire unit should be completed.

Any cavities resulting from excavation of either earth or rock below the foundation elevation should be backfilled with gravel, crushed stone, or other approved materials placed and thoroughly tamped in layers not more than 6 in. thick or should be backfilled with concrete, as directed. Whenever the excavation in rock below the elevation of the top of the footing is carried beyond the neat lines (exact dimensions) of the footing course, the space so formed should be filled with concrete.

BACKFILLING

That part of the excavation which is not occupied by the structure should be refilled with acceptable material to the normal surface of the ground, unless otherwise directed, in layers not more than 6 in. deep. Both sides of the opening should be carried up at equal elevations, and each layer should be tamped thoroughly before the succeeding layer is placed. When the material does not contain enough moisture for thorough compaction, sufficient water for this purpose should be added. No backfilling should be done until the concrete around which backfilling is to be placed is at least 14 days old.

Excavation and Backfill for Pipe Culverts

Excavation of trench for pipes shall be to the width necessary to provide space for thoroughly tamping the backfill material under the haunches and around the pipe, but where field conditions permit, the width should not be greater than required for this purpose. Except where rock or unsuitable foundation material is encountered, excavation of the trench should not extend below grade of the bottom of the pipe, and the bottom of the trench should be so excavated as to fit the lower part of the pipe exterior.

Where double lines of pipe are installed, they should be spaced at least $1\frac{1}{2}$ diameters center to center.

PREPARATION OF BED FOR PIPE

Whether in trenches or under embankments, the pipe should be bedded in an earth foundation of uniform density, carefully shaped to fit the lower part of the pipe exterior for at least 10 per cent of its overall height. This bed should be formed in undisturbed material wherever the nature of the site will permit. Where rock is encountered, in either ledge or boulder formation, it should be removed below grade and replaced with suitable materials in such manner as to provide a compact earth cushion having a thickness under the pipe of not less than 8 in. Where a firm foundation is not encountered at the grade established, because of the presence of soft, spongy, or other unsuitable soil, unless other special construction methods are called for, all of such unstable soil under the pipe and for a width of at least one diameter on each side of the pipe should be removed and replaced with gravel or other suitable material properly compacted to provide adequate support for the pipeline. Where drawings require that a portion of a pipe be on fill, the necessary fill should be built of approved earth materials and should have a top width of at least three diameters. The materials should be placed in 6-in. layers, each moistened just enough for maximum compaction and then thoroughly compacted by tamping.

Recesses of proper size to admit hubs or bells of pipe should be excavated across the trench so that the body of the pipe will rest upon the prepared bed.

BACKFILLING AROUND PIPE

Backfilling should be done with approved fine materials which should contain sufficient moisture to provide for compaction. Backfill material should be carefully tamped, in 6-in. layers or less, beneath and around the sides of the pipe but not directly over it. Care should be taken that thorough compaction of the material under the haunches of the pipe be obtained, that the backfill material provide a uniform support around all pipe, and that the joints and alignment not be disturbed.

Pipe laid in trenches should be protected against displacement or injury by backfilling to a minimum depth of 12 in. above the top of the pipe as laying progresses or as the entire line is laid. The remainder of the trench should be backfilled with material containing no stone exceeding 4 in. in diameter and compacted by tamping in 12-in. layers. All sheeting used in trenches should be removed, and cavities left by its removal should be carefully filled with tamped materials.

Backfilling around pipe culverts projecting into the embankment should be completed before the adjacent embankment is constructed. The work should be done in such manner that there will be on each side of the top of the pipe a berm of thoroughly compacted earth equal in width to the external diameter of the pipe and extending to a height of 18 in. above the top of the pipe.

DISPOSAL OF SURPLUS MATERIALS

All material excavated should be deposited or disposed of in such a way that it will not obstruct water courses or impair the function or appearance of the structure or other parts of the work. When the material is suitable, it should be used in the roadway embankment.

MEASUREMENT

The number of cubic yards of excavation for structures will be determined by measuring the volume of materials which lie within the limits defined hereunder, except that material required to be excavated in grading the roadway to its required limits in cut sections and that to be excavated within the finished limits of the channels beneath bridges will not be included.

The measurement of excavation for structures such as piers, abutments, box culverts, and headwalls will include the volume of all materials which lie between the surface of the underside of the structure and the normal surface of the ground and which is bounded by vertical planes situated parallel to, and 12 in. from, the neat lines of the footing or base course. In rock excavations the measurement will extend to a depth of 6 in. beneath the footing or base course. The measurement of excavation for pipe culverts, or similar structures, will include the volume of all materials which lie between the grade of the underside of the pipe and the normal surface of the ground and which are bounded at the sides of the pipe by vertical planes parallel to, and equidistant from, the axis of the pipe and at a distance apart which is 18 in. greater than the inside diameter of the pipe. Measurement along the pipe trench will extend to vertical planes 9 in. beyond the ends of the pipe or to the limits of headwall or inlet excavations. In rock excavation, the measurement will extend to a depth of 8 in. below the grade of the underside of the pipe.

Where excavation of unsuitable material other than rock is to be made below the structure or pipe, and where such material has not been rendered unsuitable through failure to protect the work properly, the measurement will include all material necessarily removed in the performance of such excavation to the limits directed.

Earth-borrow Excavation

Borrow pits should be excavated to regular lines as staked. The excavation should be carried only to the depth directed and should be as uniform as practicable throughout the pit. Side slopes should not be steeper than 2.5:1 unless otherwise indicated on drawings.

The pits should be completed so that they will drain properly and should be left in presentable and satisfactory condition. Solid rock or boulders may be found in the borrow pit. Such rock should be excavated and moved in order to obtain the required amount of material and leave the borrow pit of uniform or regular shape, with proper drainage.

MEASUREMENT

The volume of material excavated and disposed of, as specified or directed, should be measured in its original position and computed by the method of average end areas. Rock excavated as provided above should be included in this measurement.

Unclassified Excavation

Unclassified excavation refers to excavating cut sections of the roadway (including intersections and approaches), cutting or improving ditches and channels, constructing embankments, roadbed, and so on, from suitable materials thus excavated, removal and disposition of all unsuitable and surplus materials, and performing all other work necessary to shape, complete, and maintain the graded roadway thus constructed.

EXCAVATION AND DISPOSITION OF MATERIALS

Excavation should conform closely to the lines and grades given, and final slopes should be reasonably uniform and true to design requirements. Where changes in the character of materials or other unforeseen conditions make it necessary, the engineer may direct or permit the excavation to be made with slopes steeper than those originally indicated, but earth slopes should never be steeper than 2:1.

Changes in alignment or grade may be made by the engineer as the work progresses or if additional excavations such as ditches or turnouts are ordered. The engineer will then indicate lines, grades, and cross sections for the additional work. The engineer should likewise designate the limits of excavations indicated on the drawings but not fully designed.

Excessive blasting or oversheeting should be avoided. Necessary precautions should be taken to prevent damage from blasting to structures within 200 ft. All blasting necessary to excavation of channels or ditches within 100 ft of designated structure locations should be done before construction of structure and, when practicable, before completion of roadway cuts.

UNSUITABLE MATERIALS

All vegetation should be cut and removed from the site of excavations and embankments, including the slopes of existing embankments to be widened, before excavation or placement of materials is begun. Objectionable quantities of sod or leaves should not be placed in or left upon the site or an embankment 2 ft or less in depth between shoulder lines but should be removed as directed. Such materials should be disposed of in a presentable and satisfactory manner beyond the roadway limits.

Where soft, spongy, or otherwise unsuitable materials are encountered in the excavation or upon the embankment site, they should be excavated to the limits directed and disposed of in a presentable manner beyond the limits of the work.

ROCK BELOW SUBGRADE

The excavation of rock below roadbed elevation will not be required on any project unless called for on drawings. When called for, it should be excavated at the locations and to the limits and depths stipulated.

When excavation of rock below grade is called for on drawings, all stones of more than 4-in. size should be removed to the full width of roadbed and to the depths indicated on drawings so that no solid projections remain above these limits. The depth of excavation should be approved before backfilling is begun.

The cavities from which rock has been removed should be backfilled to the roadbed elevation with suitable earth or other acceptable material, all of which should pass a 3-in. sieve. The volume of rock excavated below roadbed elevation to the depths and limits designated should be measured.

DITCHES AND CHANNELS

Care should be taken in excavating to provide for proper drainage during construction, with a view to conformity with permanent drainage requirements. New ditches and channels should be cut and existing ones improved wherever indicated on drawings or directed; all should conform to the designated cross section and grade. Materials from ditch or channel excavation should be used in the embankment, if required. If they are not so used, they should be deposited a satisfactory distance from the ditch and shaped as directed to a neat and presentable appearance.

TERRACES, EXISTING ROADBEDS, AND STRUCTURES

Where embankments are to be constructed on existing ground slopes steeper than 1:3, contiguous deep steps or terraces at least 4 ft wide should be cut therein before placement of any material. Existing embankment slopes should be similarly terraced, except that the widths should be as directed by the engineer.

All portions of existing roadbed which are within 3 ft of the required surface of subgrade should be thoroughly broken up to a depth of not less than 6 in. Existing pavements within such depths, except those designated for removal under other items, should be broken up. If necessary, they should be removed and scattered through the embankment in such a manner that they will not interfere with its construction or be disposed of outside the limits of the work as directed.

All portions of structures within embankment limits should be completed and any concrete thoroughly cured before grading operations are begun. If grading must be authorized before such construction is finished, a large enough section of the embankment should be omitted to allow for completion of the structure.

EMBANKMENT MATERIALS

All embankments, including channels, approaches, and other appurtenances, should be formed with suitable materials excavated within the roadway and with necessary additional materials from borrow pits. Stumps, rubbish, sod, and other unsuitable materials should not be placed in embankments. Wasting material should be carefully avoided, but where suitable material in excess of filling requirements as designed or directed is excavated, such excess should be used to widen or flatten embankment slopes uniformly or distributed otherwise, as directed.

Frozen materials should not be placed in embankments, and objectionable quantities of snow and ice should be removed from the ground surface before work is begun.

FORMATION OF EMBANKMENTS

Embankments should be built to such height and width that after full shrinkage they will conform to the cross sections shown on the drawings. The materials should be deposited in uniform, successive level layers for the full width of the embankment. No side casting of material into embankments without spreading and compacting in layers in the specified manner is permitted. The top 12 in. of the embankment should always be built of earth, and no stone larger than 4 in. should be placed in this top layer.

In portions of embankments formed of materials which are principally rock, the thickness of the layers should not be greater than required by maximum size of stone and should never exceed 4 ft. All earth and fine materials should be well distributed into the interstices of the larger stones. All interstices within 3 ft of the upper surface of such fills should be well filled with small stones and earth. Mixtures of earth should not be used below reservoir surcharge elevation unless laid and tamped in 6-in. layers.

In the construction of earth embankments, the thickness of layers should not exceed 12 in. Earth embankments which will lie wholly or in part below reservoir surcharge elevation should be constructed in their entirety by depositing the material in uniform successive level layers not more than 6 in. thick, and the water content should be maintained within limits which permit the highest possible degree of compaction. The engineer will determine these limits from time to time, and when the material being placed contains insufficient moisture, sufficient water to bring the moisture content within the desired limits should be applied. Material containing excess moisture should not be placed in the fill until it has dried out so that the moisture content is within the proper limits. Water can be applied from a hose or similar equipment at the point where the material is being placed.

When new earth materials are placed against the slopes of an existing embankment, the hauling, spreading, and compacting operations over each layer should be conducted so that it may provide a thorough bond between the new and old materials.

Each layer of an earth embankment should be thoroughly compacted. For earth embankments having any portion below pool level, compaction by the use of a sheepsfoot roller will always be required for a distance of 5 ft from each edge of each layer. The roller should be operated along the edges so as to overhang the edge of the embankment as far as practicable, and as many passages should be made in this position as are necessary to produce the maximum practicable degree of compaction. If the portions of the layers of reservoir fills are more than 5 ft from either edge of the embankment, or if the entire layers of embankments which are entirely out of the pool are compacted by hauling all materials in vehicles weighing at least 8 tons when loaded, and the vehicles are operated so as to distribute their tracks uniformly over the entire layer, no further compaction of these portions will be required, except where special requirements for compaction are made on drawings. Wherever the above requirements for weight of hauling equipment and distribution of tracks are not met, compaction by the use of the sheepsfoot roller will be required.

When called for on drawings, compaction by use of sheepsfoot roller or by such other means as may be called for will be required on the embankments or portions of embankments in addition to those described above.

Wherever compaction by the use of sheepsfoot roller is required, the roller shall be operated uniformly over each layer as many times as necessary to obtain thorough compaction. The roller should pass over each portion of each layer at least 5 times, and the roller should weigh not less than 1000 lb per linear foot of tread.

If any portions of earth embankments adjacent to structures are not thoroughly and uniformly compacted in the manner specified, they should be constructed by depositing and tamping suitable materials in 6-in. layers. The backfilling should progress at equal elevations on each side of the structure and should be thus completed to sufficient height above the structure to protect the structure from injury by the equipment. These requirements should apply to the entire area of omitted sections of embankment which are of sufficient length to permit full compaction by the placement and compaction equipment.

Care should be taken to avoid damage to structures from impact of stones as well as from equipment. Any damage which does occur should be properly repaired to the satisfaction of the engineer.

COMPLETION OF GRADING

The completed roadbed should conform to the final grades given and to the cross sections shown on drawings. It should be carefully finished by blading its entire surface until it is smooth and of uniform appearance and should be maintained in such condition.

MEASUREMENT

The volume of excavation to be measured should be that of the material in its original position, computed in cubic yards by the method of average end areas. Each end area, whether of roadway cuts, channel, or ditches, etc., should be the cross-sectional area included between the original ground line and the theoretical lines of excavation, both as indicated on drawings. If any modifications or additional work are directed by the engineer, he should designate the lines, grades, and cross sections for such additional work, and they should be used in computing end areas, replacing the cross sections shown on drawings. The volume of any materials directed or permitted by the engineer to be left in place within these limits should be deducted from the quantities thus measured.

Metal-Plate Guardrails

All posts, blockings, and anchors should be set in compact soil. The holes for posts should be dug to the required grade, and their bottoms should be thoroughly compacted by ramming until a stable foundation is provided. The posts should then be set plumb to exact intervals and to the grade and alignment specified by the engineer. They should be set with front faces along a straight line on tangents and at a uniform distance from the edge of the pavement on curves, except where varied to conform to a bridge or roadway section or to the manufacturer's approved plan for construction of the guardrail. Suitable material should be placed in layers not exceeding 4 in. and each layer rammed thoroughly with hand tamps in such a manner that the posts are not displaced from true alignment.

Anchors, bracing, and blocking should be installed in accordance with the provisions of the plans of the rail-plate manufacturer so that the entire length of the rail plate will be maintained in uniform and taut condition. Anchors and blocking should be installed to the lines and grades given and backfilled around with material applied and tamped in 4-in. layers.

ERECTING STEEL RAIL PLATE

The rail plate should be erected to exact alignment and grade. It should be erected taut and firm and in full conformity with the provisions made in its design for maintaining its length and tautness under all temperature variations. After erection, the rail plates should be straight and should not vary more than ½ in. from a straight line along either edge in a 16-ft span.

All lap joints should be made so that the end of the plate next to traffic will point in the direction of travel.

When finally accepted, the entire length of steel rail should be uniformly taut and in true alignment, with all posts plumb and firmly tamped and all connections and fastenings neat and secure.

PAINTING

Pressure-treated and concrete posts will not be painted. All surfaces of posts and braces that will be in contact with the rail fittings should be brushed with two coats of white-lead paint before the fittings are erected. After erection of the guardrail is completed, all posts and braces should be painted to a uniform line below the rail plate, as indicated on plans or designated by the engineer, with two coats of white-lead paint. The remainder of the posts and braces to the surface of the ground should be painted with two coats of black carbon paint.

All metal parts of the guardrail, including rail plate and all supports and fastenings, should, after erection, be painted with two coats of white-lead paint.

The entire head of the package should be removed and the paint kept thoroughly stirred and mixed at all times while being applied. If congealing makes it necessary to thin the paint in cool weather, this should be done only by warming the paint. Paint should not be applied when the air temperature is below 40°F, when the air is misty, or when in the opinion of the engineer conditions are otherwise unsatisfactory for the work. It should not be applied upon damp or frosted surfaces.

Before any coat of paint is applied, surfaces to be painted should be thoroughly cleaned of dirt, oil, grease, and all other foreign substances. Bristle or wood-fiber brushes should be used for removing dust.

Before paint is applied to galvanized metal surfaces, they should be slightly etched with a dilute solution of vinegar, composed of 1 pt vinegar and 1 gal water.

Painting should be done in a thorough, neat, and workmanlike manner. Brushes should preferably be round or oval, but if flat brushes are used, they should not exceed 4 in. in width. The paint, when applied, should be so manipulated under the brush as to produce a uniform, even coating in close contact with the surface or with previously applied paint and should be worked into all corners and crevices. On surfaces which are inaccessible to paintbrushes, the paint should be applied with sheepskin daubers especially constructed for the purpose. Each coat of paint should be thoroughly dry before the next coat is applied; at least 24 hours should be allowed between coats. Metal guardrails are measured by the linear foot, from end post.

Wire-rope guardrails

The posts for wire-rope guardrails should be brush-treated, butt-dipped, or pressure-treated timber posts or concrete posts, according to specifications on the drawings. Round posts should be grouped to minimize noticeable variations in size between successive posts, with larger posts being placed at the ends of sections.

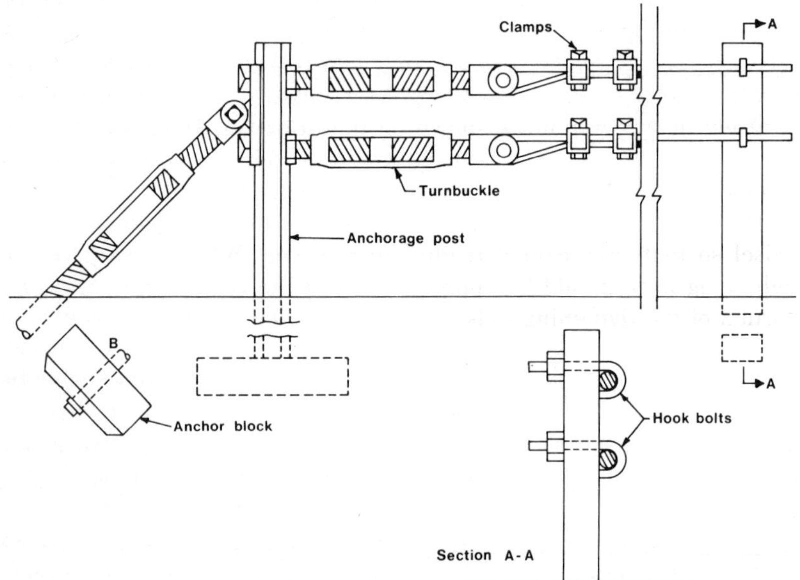

Fig. 8.8 Detail of wire-rope guardrail.

The posts should be set at a uniform distance from the edge of pavement, except where it is necessary to vary this distance at approaches to bridges or culverts. They should be set in a compacted soil, and the bottoms of the holes should be compacted by ramming to provide a stable foundation. They should be set plumb to the lines and grades given by the engineers and should be accurately aligned. Suitable backfill material should be placed in layers not exceeding 4 in. deep, and each layer should be rammed thoroughly with hand tamps in such a manner that the posts are not displaced.

The anchors should be accurately located and aligned and should be set with as little disturbance as possible of the material against which the anchor will bear. Holes should not be excavated larger than is necessary to permit installation of the anchors in the prescribed manner. The anchors should be backfilled around with materials placed and thoroughly tamped in 4-in. layers. If excavation of a trench is necessary for placing the anchor rods, the trench should be kept to the minimum width practicable (see Fig. 8.8).

PLACING ROPE AND FITTINGS

After the posts have been set true and rigidly to the line and grade given by the engineer, the wooden reel should be mounted so that it will revolve, and the wire rope run off by pulling straight ahead. Rope should be wired to prevent unravelling before being cut. The wire rope should be supported by the hook of the bolt, which should be loosely in place, and then drawn taut by means of rods attached to an anchor buried securely in the ground as shown on the drawings. Intermediate turnbuckles should be installed in accordance with the provisions of the drawings. After the rope has been drawn taut and anchored, the hook bolts should be tightened and the nuts set with a set punch or small chisel so that they cannot readily be removed. When taut, the cable-tightening nuts should be approximately at the center of the threaded portion of the tightening rods.

COMPLETION AND MEASUREMENT

When the guardrail is completed, all posts should be plumb, rigid, and accurately aligned. Each rope should be taut, held securely in position with all fittings snugly and securely fastened. The site should be left free of debris, and all excavated material should be neatly spread.

Wire-rope guardrail is measured by the linear foot from end post to end post.

Timber Guard Posts

Round posts should be grouped to minimize any noticeable variations in size between successive posts, with larger posts at the ends of sections.

Unless otherwise indicated on the drawings or directed, the posts should be spaced 6 ft center to center. They should be set at a uniform distance from the edge of the pavement except where it is necessary to vary this distance at approaches to bridges or culverts. They should be set in a compacted soil, and the bottom of the hole should be compacted by ramming to provide a stable foundation. They should be set plumb, to the lines and grades given by the engineer, and accurately aligned. Suitable backfilling material should be placed in layers not exceeding 4 in. in depth, and each layer should be rammed thoroughly with approved hand tamps in such a manner that the posts will not be displaced. Posts that are out of alignment should be realigned. Different types and shapes of posts should not be used on the same project unless so indicated on the drawings.

Posts should be painted in accordance with instructions on page 477.

Guard posts are measured by a report of the number of posts of each type within the limits designated.

GUTTERS AND CURBS

Standards for construction of several types of gutters and curbs are given in detail in the following pages.

Grouted Rubble Gutters

The lines, grades, and cross sections furnished by the engineer should be followed in the formation of subgrade. All soft and yielding or otherwise unsuitable material should be removed and replaced with fine material thoroughly tamped in thin layers. The excavation should be done by methods that will cause the least disturbance of the material outside required section. Special care should be exercised to avoid disturbing the material that will form the earth shoulders along and above each edge of the gutter.

GROUT

The grout should be composed of 1 part cement to $2\frac{1}{2}$ parts sand. It should be mixed to proper consistency and uniform color, using clean water. The mixing should be done in a suitable mechanical mixer or in a clean, tight mixing box. The mixture should be stirred at appropriate intervals to maintain proper consistency.

LAYING GUTTER

Construction of gutter should begin at its lower edge or should be integral with the toe wall when one is required. Just before the stores are set, a thick, plastic grout should be applied to the subgrade of the gutter to an approximate depth of 2 in. The stones should form a completed course not less than 6 or 10 in. thick, as called for on the drawings or directed. Each stone should extend entirely through the course, and the face exposed in the finished surface should be approximately flat. They should be set perpendicular to the slope and generally have the longer axis of the exposed face perpendicular to the centerline of the gutter. The stones should be set in contact, with all joints staggered, and should be worked or rammed to a firm bedding. The setting should be completed before initial set of the mortar begins. Chinking with spalls should be done as necessary. The finished surface should be reasonably smooth and regular, but local variations of not more than 2 in. from the surrounding surface may be permitted for 10-in. gutters.

As the setting of the stones is completed, grout of proper consistency should be poured and broomed or worked into the joints, to fill the spaces between the stones completely. Pouring should be done at stages and intervals to avoid overflow through the joints below. As the grouting proceeds, stone chips or gravel should be worked into the joints but should not be allowed to prevent the grout from penetrating and filling all the voids.

Joints need not be filled flush with the surface, but they should be filled to within 2 in. of the surface for 10-in. gutters and within 1 in. for 6-in. gutters.

Where toe walls are required, they should be constructed of stones specified for the gutter proper. The stones should be laid in courses with fully interlocked, spalled, and grouted joints.

WEATHER CONDITIONS

These gutters should not be constructed while the weather conditions are unfavorable or while the subgrade or materials are frozen. They should not be constructed when the air temperature in the shade is above 35°F and rising or below 40°F and falling. If freezing temperatures are expected after the grout has been placed and before it has fully set, the gutters should be protected against freezing.

SHOULDERS

As construction of the gutter progresses, the earth shoulder along and above the edges of the gutter should be formed by placing suitable material containing sufficient moisture to permit thorough compaction and carefully shaping and tamping until the shoulders conform to the typical cross section shown on the drawings and are thoroughly compacted throughout.

Gutters are measured by the square yard along the surface of the gutter to the limits designated for construction.

Stone Gutters

For construction of subgrade for stone gutters, see instructions for subgrade of grouted rubble gutters. All material unnecessarily excavated below the required subgrade should be replaced with gravel.

LAYING GUTTERS

The gravel course should be spread to the thickness shown on drawings and brought to a uniform surface. The stones should then be placed by hand and worked or rammed to a firm bedding in the layer of gravel. They should be set in close contact, with the joints approximately perpendicular to the finished surface. Joints should be broken satisfactorily, and the stone should present an approximately flat surface uppermost, with the long dimension of the exposed face at right angles to the centerline of the gutter. Use of too many stones may cause an excessive volume of joints, and should be avoided. The finished gutter should be full specified thickness and should present a reasonably smooth, uniform surface.

As the setting of the larger stones progresses, the spaces between them should be filled with smaller stones or spalls. Wherever practicable, each void should be filled with a single spall and each spall should be in contact with at least two of the adjacent larger stones. The spalls should be rammed firmly into place, with the upper surface of the spall below the top surface of the lowest adjacent larger stone. When complete, the gutter should be composed of a tightly keyed mass of stones.

Shoulders should be constructed as described for grouted rubble gutters, page 481.

Gutters are measured by the square yard along the surface of the gutter to the limits designated for the construction.

Concrete Curbs and Gutters

Subgrade should be constructed or excavated to required depth below the finished surface, in accordance with the cross sections shown on the plans. All soft, unyielding, or other unsuitable material should be removed and replaced with suitable material; the subgrade should be compacted thoroughly in layers not exceeding 4 in. in thickness, and finished to a firm, smooth surface.

BASE COURSE

If it is specified on the plans, or if soil conditions during construction make it necessary or desirable, a base course of approved sand, common pit gravel, broken slag, or common crushed stone or other material should be applied and consolidated beneath the curb, gutter, or combination curb and gutter.

DRAINAGE OPENINGS

Curbs or gutters should be provided with drainage openings as indicated or directed, and all castings, pipe, or other fittings should be set accurately as indicated. The curb or gutter should be depressed at openings if so indicated or directed. Where weep holes are installed, the engineer may require that an appropriate quantity of coarse aggregate be placed behind each opening.

FORMS

Either metal or wood may be used for forms. They should be straight and free from warp and of sufficient strength when staked to hold the concrete true to line and grade without springing or distorting. Wood forms should be of selected and dressed material at least 2 in. thick, except that on curves of short radius the thickness requirement can be waived to permit use of flexible material. Form boards for exposed curb surfaces should be at least as wide as the exposed surface. The facing board used for the front face of the curb in combined curb and gutter construction should be so constructed and shaped that its lower edge conforms to the radius specified on the drawings or by the engineer. Metal forms should be of approved sections and should have a flat surface on top. The depth of the forms should be equal to the depth of the curbing. Adequate means should be provided for securely fastening forms together at the tops. Forms should be securely staked, braced, and held together to the exact lines and grades established by the engineer and should be sufficiently tight to prevent the leakage of mortar.

Metal divider plates or templates should be not less than ⅛ in. thick and so designed that they will remain securely in place and produce a straight, smooth joint after they are removed. They should be of the full dimensions of the curb or gutter cross section. All forms should be thoroughly cleaned and oiled before each use.

REINFORCEMENT

If the use of reinforcing steel is required by the drawings, the steel should conform to requirements for design and spacing indicated. Approved methods of support and placement which will ensure maintaining the steel in correct position should be employed.

JOINTS

All curbs, gutters, or curb and gutter combinations should be constructed with ¾-in. expansion joints at intervals of 50 ft, except when other spacing or thickness of joints is indicated on the drawings. The expansion joints should be formed with premolded joint filler of the thickness of the joint. The filler should be cut to the full depth, length, width, and cross section of the joint, and any portion that protrudes from the finished concrete should be trimmed as directed.

Unless curbs, gutters, or curb and gutter combinations are reinforced, they should further be divided into sections not more than 10 ft in length or as otherwise indicated on the drawings. The length of the sections may be reduced to not less than 6 ft when necessary for closures. This division should be made by means of metal templates or divider plates, which would extend across the full width of the curb, gutter, or combination curb and gutter and at least 1 in. below its bottom surface.

Either an expansion joint or a metal template joint should be formed at all intersections at the point where the straight and curved sections meet.

All joints should be constructed truly perpendicular to the face and top of the curb or gutter, and all templates should be held securely and rigidly in place.

PLACING CONCRETE

Concrete should not be placed when air temperature in the shade is below 40°F and falling or until it is at or above 35° and rising. The subgrade should be clean, smooth, firm, and moist, but not wet or muddy, when the concrete is placed.

The concrete should be deposited in layers thin enough to permit thorough spading and consolidating. It should be spaded and tamped or vibrated sufficiently to produce a dense, homogeneous mass and to bring the mortar to the surface. Particular attention should be given to spading along the surfaces of the forms to eliminate voids. When the forms are filled, the surfaces should be struck off and then finished smooth and even with a wooden float. In striking off gutter surfaces, a template of the form and shape of the gutter should be used. Before the concrete is given the final finishing, the surface of the gutter and the top and face of the curb should be checked with a 10-ft straightedge, and all irregularities of $^1/_4$ in. or more should be eliminated.

While the concrete is still soft, the exposed edges of all curbs and gutters should be rounded with appropriate edging tools to the radius shown on the drawings or directed by the engineer. Unless otherwise indicated on drawings or directed, the back edge of curbs and the front edge of gutters should be rounded to a radius of $^1/_4$ in. The metal templates for the joints should be removed as soon as the concrete has set sufficiently to hold its shape, and the edges of these joints and of the expansion joints should be rounded to a radius of $^1/_4$ in.

FINISHING

The forms should be removed as soon as concrete is hard enough not to be easily injured and within 24 hours, unless otherwise directed. All minor defects should be eliminated by filling with a mortar composed of one part portland cement to two parts fine aggregate. Plastering should not be done, and all unsatisfactorily constructed sections should be removed and replaced with properly constructed substitutes. As soon as the defects are corrected and while the concrete is still green, all exposed surfaces of the curbs and gutters should be finished smooth and even, and all toolmarks should be removed by means of a wooden float, which should be kept moist by wetting.

Any exposed surfaces against which some rigid construction is to be made should be left smooth and uniform to permit free movement of the curb, gutter, or combination curb and gutter.

PROTECTION AND CURING

Immediately after the finishing operation is completed, the concrete should be covered with moist burlap or cotton mats and kept continuously moist for at least 5 days or longer if directed. Moist earth, sand, or other approved material may be substituted for the burlap or cotton mats after the concrete has set sufficiently. Whenever, in the opinion of the engineer, the air temperature is apt to fall below 35°F, adequate and approved means of protection should be provided to maintain temperatures around the concrete at not less than 45°F for a period of 5 days after placement of the concrete.

BACKFILLING AND CLEANING UP

After the concrete has set sufficiently, the spaces along the front and back of the curb or gutter should be backfilled to the required elevation with suitable material, which should be thoroughly consolidated in 4-in. layers by appropriate hand or mechanical tampers.

All waste or foreign materials should be disposed of as directed and the entire work left in a neat and presentable condition.

Curb, gutter, or combination curb and gutter are measured by linear foot along the curb or gutter to the limits designated for construction.

ROAD SURFACE TREATMENT

Specifications for construction and maintenance of aggregate, bituminous gravel, and crushed stone road surfaces are given below.

Aggregate – Stabilized Subgrade

This specification covers the stabilization of subgrades for pavements or bases by applying and mixing a suitable aggregate into the soil.

The length, width, and depth of stabilization and the quantity of stabilizer aggregate to be added should be as called for on the drawing or directed by the engineer.

MATERIAL

The stabilizer aggregate should consist of crushed stone, gravel, or sand unless otherwise indicated on the drawings or directed. It should be composed of sound, tough, and durable particles, which should meet suitable tests to demonstrate these properties when required by the engineer. The material should be free from schist, shale, and slate and from vegetable or other foreign matter. All stabilized aggregate should be well graded from coarse to fine, and should meet the following requirements:

Retained on ¾-in. sieve:	none
Retained on no. 8 sieve:	10 to 50 per cent by weight
Retained on no. 200 sieve:	90 to 100 per cent by weight

CONSTRUCTION METHODS

The stabilized mixture should be prepared in layers 4 in. thick. This is the maximum thickness, but the layers may be thinner if so required on the drawings.

The cut sections should be excavated and the embankment sections constructed to the elevation required to provide for stabilizing the subgrade or roadbed to the specified thickness, width, and finished elevation. Except where rock is encountered in cut sections, the surfaces thus graded should be a sufficient height above the required underside of the stabilization to provide sufficient soil for the first layer. In rock cuts, the excavation should extend to the full depth of stabilization.

The stabilizer aggregate should be spread uniformly over the entire area to be stabilized, to the thickness or at the rate specified for one layer. After the stabilizer aggregate is spread, it should be thoroughly and uniformly incorporated into the soil immediately thereunder, to the depth necessary to construct a compacted layer of the specified thickness, by scarifying, plowing, and harrowing with a satisfactory disc harrow having discs not less than 22 in. in diameter. The soil and stabilizer aggregate should be turned from 5 to 10 times, and more if required by the engineer. The existing soil should be loosened and harrowed before stabilizer aggregate is applied on any areas where satisfactory results are not obtained by performing this work after the aggregate has been spread.

After the materials have been mixed as specified above, the entire layer should be thoroughly compacted by means of a sheepsfoot or tamping roller. Additional sprinkling should be done if necessary to secure thorough compaction.

Sprinkling with water should be performed with an approved type of mechanical distributor, and the amount specified by the engineer. The distributor should be in first-class working condition and should be constructed and adjusted to control, by units, the amount of water being sprinkled.

Each successive layer should be constructed by uniformly spreading the required amount of soil, followed by the stabilizer aggregate, on the preceding layer. The materials should then be mixed, sprinkled, and compacted in the manner specified for the first layer. The final layer should be shaped to correct cross section and grade.

SHOULDERS

Where stabilization of the entire width of roadbed is required, the overlying shoulder material should also be stabilized unless otherwise shown on the drawings. Sufficient stabilized material for completion of the shoulders should be mixed at the same time as the remainder of the stabilized material. If construction of the pavement or base is not immediately to follow the stabilization construction, the material for the shoulders should be spread and compacted as a part of the final layer and later bladed to the shoulder before the construction of the base or pavement is started.

MAINTENANCE

The entire stabilized area should be maintained in a satisfactory manner and condition until preparation of the subgrade for the base or pavement is begun in accordance with specifications. Ditches should be kept open during the period of construction and maintenance so that the roadbed will be adequately drained.

The aggregate stabilized subgrade is measured by the square yard.

Bituminous Road Mix

Adequate and suitable equipment of such capacity and character as to ensure the completion of the work in proper manner should be provided. The equipment should be of approved design and should be maintained in first-class working condition at all times. The following requirements apply to equipment used.

The roller should be of such design, weight, and power as to ensure satisfactory compression. It should weigh not less than 8 nor more than 10 tons and should exert a pressure of not less than 175 lb per inch width of rear tread. The roller should be equipped with an approved device for wetting or oiling the wheels to prevent them from picking up the surface material.

The pressure distributor should be equipped with pneumatic tires having sufficient width of rubber in contact with the road surface to prevent breaking the bond of or forming a rut in the surfacing. If the distributor is mounted on a truck having only four wheels, it should not be loaded in excess of 800 gal of bituminous material. The distance between the centers of openings of outside nozzles of the spray bar should be the same width as the surface to be treated in one application. The outside nozzles at each end of the spray bar should have an area of opening not less than 25 per cent nor more than 75 per cent in excess of the other nozzles, which should have uniform openings.

The distributor should be so constructed and equipped that it will spread the bituminous material evenly, uniformly, and under the constant pressure specified over the entire surface being treated. It should be capable of being operated at the full required capacity both at the beginning and at the end of each spread.

The distributor should be equipped with a thermometer and suitable instruments for determining the rate of application, and with hand sprays consisting of a hose attached to the distributor and fitted with a proper nozzle.

The mixing equipment should consist of a blade grader either self-propelled or drawn by a tractor, a multiblade planer, or other approved equipment.

If a self-propelled blade grade is used, it should weigh not less than 8000 lb, and the tractor should be of adequate power and weight.

If a multiblade planer is used, it should be of an approved design which should weigh not less than 4800 lb and should be adequate and suitable for the work to be performed.

SEASONAL AND WEATHER LIMITATIONS

Road-mix construction should not be done between Oct. 15 and May 15. Mineral aggregate should be applied only when the base is dry, and bituminous material should be applied only when the aggregate is dry. Bituminous material should not be applied when the temperature of the air in the shade is below 50°F or has been below 45°F during the preceding 4 hours.

PROTECTION OF STRUCTURES

The surfaces of all structures should be protected by satisfactory methods or devices against disfigurement by bituminous materials. Any surfaces becoming disfigured should be restored to a satisfactory appearance.

APPLICATION OF MINERAL AGGREGATE

This construction should not be begun until the prime coat has completely dried and not until at least 48 hours after completion of the prime coat. The base coarse should be firm and smooth and the prime coat uniform and unbroken and free from caked or loose dirt or foreign matter when the mineral aggregate is applied.

Wooden forms constructed of straight, sound timber 1 in. thick and not less than 4 in. wide should be set accurately to line and grade along the required edges of the surface course and securely fastened and braced.

Mineral aggregate should be spread directly from trucks by means of approved mechanical spreaders and should be distributed uniformly between the forms at the rate of 100 lb/yd^2, on the basis of an aggregate weighing approximately 2650 lb yd^3 in the surface dry condition. To obtain approximately the same thickness with aggregates weighing appreciably more or less than 2650 lb/yd^3 surface dry, the weight of material to be applied per square yard must be correspondingly increased or decreased. The aggregate should be shaped to a uniform depth and surface.

Mineral aggregate should be spread uniformly between the forms directly from trucks by means of approved mechanical spreaders, at the rate of 100 lb/yd^2, and should be shaped to a uniform depth and surface.

APPLICATION OF THE BITUMINOUS MATERIAL

The mineral aggregate should be uniformly distributed when the bituminous material is applied. The bituminous material should be applied by means of a pressure distributor at a uniform rate of not less than 0.65 gal/yd^2 and not more than 0.80 gal/yd^2. The exact amount that will provide a sufficient and proper coating for the aggregate is to be determined by the engineer. The material should be applied at a uniform pressure of not less than 35 nor more than 75 lb/in.^{2} and at a temperature high enough to ensure proper distribution. However, cutback asphalt and emulsified asphalt should not be heated to a temperature above 150°F. Grade RT-6 tar should not be heated above 200°F, and grade RT-7 tar should not be heated above 250°F.

The material should be applied to the full width of the surface course in a single application. In beginning a succeeding application, care should be exercised to secure a proper junction with the preceding work. If necessary, building paper should be spread over the treated surface for a sufficient distance back to ensure that the nozzles will be operating at a full force when the untreated surface is reached. The building paper should then be removed immediately and destroyed.

Any excess of bituminous material where applications overlap should be removed and satisfactory correction made. Parts of the surface not reached or properly covered with bituminous materials directly from the distributor should be treated by means of a hand spray attached to the distributor or with approved hand-pouring pots. If at any time distribution within the specified limits is not uniform, the process should be stopped until satisfactory adjustment can be made or the operator replaced.

MIXING, SHAPING, AND ROLLING

Immediately after application of the bituminous material, it should be mixed with the aggregate until the latter is thoroughly coated and a homogeneous mixture is obtained.

If a blade grade is used, the materials should be bladed to a windrow in the center of the road. This windrow should then be evenly divided and the halves bladed successively to the quarter points, edge of surface course, and back again to the quarter points and center of the road. When no further mixing is required for proper coating of the mineral aggregate, the mixture should be allowed to stand in a windrow until the mixture begins to set up.

If the mixing is done by means of a multiblade planer, it should be continued until, in the opinion of the engineer, the materials are uniformly coated. During mixing, the equipment should be manipulated to mix the materials to their full depth without disturbing the underlying construction.

When, in the opinion of the engineer, the material has cured sufficiently, it should be spread to a uniform depth between the forms and shaped to the required crown and to a uniform surface. As the shaping is completed, the material should be compacted by rolling. Rolling should start at the edges of the pavement and progress toward the center, in passages parallel to the centerline of the pavement. Each passage of the roller should overlap the preceding passage by at least one-half the width of the rear wheel. Rolling should be continued until the entire surface has been covered at least 3 times daily for 3 consecutive days and until there is no appreciable movement in front of the roller wheels. The forms along the edges of the surface course should be removed before the final rolling.

As the rolling progresses, all depressions and areas containing voids should be filled with premixed material, until a uniform surface of the specified regularity and the crown is produced. The surface should be such that when a 10-ft straightedge is placed parallel to the center of the road, in any position, the surface will not deviate more than $^1/_4$ in. from the straightedge.

After completion of this course, and before the surface becomes dirty, stone chips should be spread uniformly over the road mix construction at the rate of not less than 5 nor more than 8 lb/yd^2.

The road-mix course should be maintained under traffic until the seal coat is applied. Side ditches should be kept open during the period of construction and maintenance, and all shoulders should be bladed and repaired as necessary to leave them in good condition with proper shape.

Bituminous Surface Treatment

Hot bituminous material is covered with coarse aggregate and a seal coat consisting of a layer of fine aggregate spread between two applications of lighter bituminous materials. The treatment should be constructed on a primed base in accordance with these specifications and in conformity with the lines, grades, and cross sections indicated or directed.

EQUIPMENT

Adequate equipment should be provided of capacity and character to ensure the completion of the work in proper manner. The equipment should be of approved design, and should be maintained in first-class working condition at all times. The following requirements apply to the equipment used.

The roller should be of a design, weight, and power to ensure satisfactory compression. It should weigh not less than 5 nor more than 8 tons and should exert a pressure of not less than 125 lb per inch width of rear tread. At least one roller should be supplied for each mile, or fraction thereof, of bituminous material applied in 1 day. The roller used in the seal-coat construction should be equipped with an approved device for wetting or oiling the wheels to prevent picking up of the surface material.

The pressure distributor should be equipped with pneumatic tires having sufficient width of rubber in contact with the road surface to avoid breaking the bond of or forming a rut in the surfacing. If the distributor is mounted on a truck having only four wheels, it should not be loaded in excess of 800 gal of bituminous material. The distance between the centers of openings of outside nozzles of the spray bar should be the same width as the surface to be treated in one application. The outside nozzles at each end of the spray bar should have an area of opening not less than 25 per cent nor more than 75 per cent in excess of the other nozzles, which should have uniform openings.

The distributor should be so constructed and equipped that it will spread the bituminous material evenly, uniformly, and under the constant pressure specified over the entire surface being treated. It should be capable of being operated at the full required capacity at both the beginning and the end of each spread.

The distributor should be equipped with a thermometer and suitable instruments for determining the rate of application, and with hand sprays, each consisting of a hose attached to the distributor and fitted with a proper nozzle.

The broom drag should be of a long base design suitable for distributing the aggregate as specified and should have means for its adjustment to the crown of the roadway at widths not greater than one-fourth the width of the surface course. It should be rigid enough and of such weight or adjustability as to afford proper planing action.

CONDITION OF BASE

The primed base should be properly cured and repaired and in a firm and uniform condition when construction of the surface treatment is begun. Before the bituminous material is applied, the entire primed surface should be swept with revolving brooms supplemented by hand brooms until cleaned of all loose or caked clay or other foreign matter.

APPLICATION OF BITUMINOUS MATERIALS

Weather conditions should be considered when applying bituminous materials. They should not be applied to a wet surface or when the temperature of the air in the shade is below 50°F or has been below 45°F during the preceding 4 hours.

The bituminous material should be applied uniformly at a pressure of not less than 35 nor more than 75 lb/in.[2] It should be applied to the full width of the treatment in a single application unless the engineer directs that the application be made to only one half width at one time, in order to permit movement of traffic. Where half-width applications are made, care should be taken to secure a complete coating of the area along the adjoining edges without an excess or deficiency of material.

The distributor should be operated at the full required capacity at both the beginning and the end of each spread. It should be stopped before the application begins to run light or whenever one or more nozzles becomes clogged. Before beginning a succeeding application, building paper should be spread over the treated surface for a distance sufficiently far back to ensure that the nozzles will be operating at full force when the untreated surface is reached. The building paper should be removed immediately and destroyed.

Any excess of bituminous material at transverse or longitudinal junctions of applications should be removed and correction made. Parts of the surface not reached or properly covered with bituminous materials directly from the distributor should be treated by means of a hand spray attached to the distributor or with approved hand-pouring pots. If at any time uniform distribution within the specified limits is not consistently obtained, the process should be stopped until the distribution is satisfactorily adjusted or the operator is replaced.

SPREADING MINERAL AGGREGATES

All mineral aggregates should have been satisfactorily air-dried before being applied. Seal-coat aggregate should contain no more moisture than will dry out satisfactorily before the second application of bituminous material is made. Each application of aggregate should be spread directly from trucks by approved mechanical spreaders. Trucks or spreaders should not pass over the uncovered bituminous material. If bituminous material is being applied to less than the full width of the treatment at one time, the aggregate should be spread to within 8 in. of the inner edge of the first application until the adjacent application has been made. The spreading of the aggregates should follow the application of bituminous material as closely as practicable. The application of bituminous material should never advance more than one distributor load ahead of the spreading of the aggregate. Hot bituminous material for mat course should be applied at a rate of not less than 0.40 nor more than 0.45 gal/yd^2.

APPLICATION OF COARSE AGGREGATE

The aggregate should be spread uniformly over the hot bituminous material at a rate of not less than 45 nor more than 50 lb/yd^2. It should follow the application of bituminous material closely enough to be embedded in the bituminous material while it is still hot.

Immediately after the aggregate has been applied, it should be dragged with a drag broom and manipulated with hand brooms until an even spread of uniform texture is obtained. Additional aggregate should be placed by hand on any areas not properly covered.

As soon as the aggregate has been uniformly distributed, it should be rolled with a power roller. The roller should work in a longitudinal direction beginning at the outer edges of the treatment and progressing toward the center, each trip overlapping the previous one by half the width of the roller. The first rolling should be completed within 1 hour after the application of the bituminous material. The rolling should be repeated as often as may be necessary to key the aggregate thoroughly to the bituminous material. When the aggregate has become sufficiently and satisfactorily embedded in the bituminous material, any loose aggregate remaining should be removed from the surface.

Slow-moving, light traffic may be permitted to use the road as soon as the coarse aggregate has been spread. The treatment should be maintained under traffic not less than 10 nor more than 60 days, as directed by the engineer. All defects occurring in the treatment from any cause should be corrected. The defective portions should be taken out and replaced or repaired in an adequate and workmanlike manner, as directed by the engineer, before construction of the seal coat is begun.

FIRST APPLICATION OF BITUMINOUS SEAL-COAT MATERIAL

Just before the first application of bituminous seal-coat material, the entire width of the surface should be thoroughly swept and cleaned until free of caked or loose dirt, dust, or other foreign matter. The surface should be firm, in satisfactory repair, and thoroughly dry.

The bituminous material should be applied in two approximately equal applications, which should produce a total deposit of not less than 0.30 gal/yd². The first application should be made before and the second after the seal-coat aggregate is spread. The first application should not advance more than two distributor loads ahead of the second unless otherwise directed by the engineer. Bituminous materials should be applied at the temperatures within the limits indicated in Table 8.4.

TABLE 8.4
Temperatures for Application of Bituminous Material

Material	Grade	Temperature °F
Tar	RT–6	80–150
	RT–7, RT–8	150–225
Cutback asphalt	RC–1	80–125
	RC–2	100–175

The first application of bituminous seal-coat material should receive at once a uniform covering of the seal-coat aggregate, at the rate of not less than 20 nor more than 25 lb/yd². The aggregate should be free from moisture when the final application of bituminous seal coat is made.

After the fine aggregate has been evenly spread, the final application of bituminous material should be made, according to the procedure described above for the first seal-coat application. Immediately after the final application of bituminous material, the seal coat should be dragged with a broom drag. The dragging should continue until all aggregate is thoroughly coated and is distributed to a smooth, even spread of uniform texture. The operations should be conducted so that mixing and spreading are completed before the mixture becomes stiff and difficult to place.

As soon as the mixing and spreading have been completed, the seal coat should be rolled with a power roller. The rolling should proceed in the manner specified for rolling coarse aggregate. Rolling should be repeated from time to time while the seal coat is setting up, as may be necessary to embed the aggregate firmly in bituminous material and produce a uniformly closed surface.

When finally completed, the surface should be such that when tested with a 10-ft straightedge, parallel to the center of the road in any position, the surface does not deviate more than ¼ in. from the straightedge.

Traffic should not be allowed on the seal coat while dragging and rolling are in progress nor until the engineer is of the opinion that the mat will not be deformed or injured thereby.

MAINTENANCE

The completed surface treatment should be maintained by the contractor for a period of not less than 30 days, and thereafter if necessary. All failures or defects that may develop should be fully and satisfactorily repaired and corrected, so as to leave an even-textured, uniform surface of correct shape.

Side ditches should be kept open during the period of construction and maintenance, and all shoulders should be bladed and repaired as necessary to keep them in good condition with proper shape.

GENERAL SPECIFICATIONS OF PROTECTIVE TREATMENT OF ASPHALTIC CONCRETE PAVEMENT (JENNITE J-16)

OBJECTIVE

1. To extend the service life of asphaltic concrete pavement by halting damage by the solvent action of petroleum derivatives, the drying and oxidizing effect of the sun, and the complex of troubles caused by water seepage, including frost action.
2. To provide the pavement with an attractive and easily cleaned surface.

MATERIAL

J-16 shall be thoroughly stirred in its container, preferably by power or with mortar hoe, so that a creamy homogeneous consistency of all J-16 in the container is assured for ready application. No adulterants of any nature should be necessary.

PREPARATION OF PAVEMENT

Areas to be sealed shall be cured, firm, and clean.

To be cured, the asphaltic concrete shall be oxidized on the surface so that there is no concentration of light oils at that level. This can often be determined by pouring a bucket of water on an area of the surface in question; if the water picks up a film of oil, the surface is not yet sufficiently cured for sealing.

To be firm, the pavement base must be sound, and there must not be any soft spots in the pavement proper. All soft or oil-soaked pavement material shall be removed and repaired with new paving material having aggregate of similar size and well compacted in place.

To be clean, the surface shall be free from sand, clay, dust, grease, and other foreign matter. Areas shall be swept thoroughly by hand or power broom, then flushed with clear fresh water and any additional small particles of embedded foreign matter removed. Any accumulations of oil or grease should be scraped off the pavement; then this section should be cleaned with caustic solution, the residue of which shall be thoroughly flushed with clear fresh water before application of J-16.

APPLICATION OF MATERIAL

Over damp pavement (free from standing water) prepared as described above, two uniform coatings of J-16 shall be applied. After the first coat has set, the second uniform application of J-16 shall be applied crosswise to the first application. The total application shall be equivalent to that provided by approximately 2 gal of J-16 per 100 ft^2, or 0.18 gal yd^2.

Generally, application may be made by long-handled 24-in. medium-soft rubber squeegee or long handled 18-in. nylon brush. Where pavement surface is unusually rough or very smooth, brush application is most suitable.

Application by distributor truck is most practical for sealing areas of over 40,000 yd^2.

Application by heavy-duty compressed-air spray equipment is not recommended for application of J-16 over areas where fuel or oil spillage is prevalent.

Allow J-16 seal coat to cure at least 24 hours before opening the roadway to traffiic.

NOTES

Weather J-16 shall not be applied outside when weather is foggy or rainy or when ambient temperature is below 45°F, nor shall J-16 be applied if such conditions are anticipated during the next 8 hours.

Curing Conditions J-16 sets in approximately 1 hour at 77°F and 50 per cent relative humidity where circulation of air is present. If application is inside a building, ventilation should be provided for proper curing.

Precaution Around fuel pumps, etc., where there may be intermittent gasoline or oil immersion, it is recommended that a third coat of J-16 be applied to cover any pinholes, voids, or holidays that may have been left inadvertently in the application of the first two coats.

Abrasive Finish If the surface texture of the pavement is such that a more abrasive treatment is desirable, the first coat application may be made with a homogeneous mix comprised of 2 to 4 lb of clean, sharp, well-graded sand for each gallon of J-16 distributed at the rate of approximately 0.1 gal/yd^2. The second coat of J-16 is then applied as described above, but without sand.

Cleaning Tools Application tools can be cleaned with water and/or coal tar benzene, xylene, or toluene.

Uses Jennite J-16 is excellent for playgrounds, tennis courts, driveways, airfields, paths, walks, and parking areas.

Compacted Gravel or Chert Surface Course

All equipment used should be of adequate capacity and suitable character to perform the several operations as specified. The shaping and blading operations shall be done with a motor grader weighing not less than 7 tons or with a blade grader weighing not less than 3 tons, which shall be drawn by a tractor of adequate power and weight. The blade of either grader shall not be less than 8 ft in length. Power rollers shall weigh not less than 8 tons.

SUBGRADE

The subgrade should be bladed and shaped true to line, grade, and cross section and to a smooth, true surface. It should be of firm bearing throughout. Any unsatisfactory materials in the subgrade should be removed and replaced with suitable materials. When so indicated on the drawings or directed, the subgrade should be channeled to provide material for the completion of the shoulders. Side ditches should be kept open, and the shaping should be conducted to ensure against ponding of water on the subgrade during construction.

The subgrade should be kept prepared at an appropriate distance in advance of the surface course construction. Each section should be firm and free from irregularities when surfacing materials are placed.

FORMS

Temporary wooden forms should be used where so indicated or directed in order to confine and compact the material properly.

SPREADING, SHAPING, AND ROLLING

The gravel or chert should be applied to such loose thickness that the total compacted thickness of the completed surface course will not be less than that called for on the drawings. For example, a loose thickness of 6 in. would be compacted to 4 in. The material should be applied in two or more equal layers, whenever necessary, to provide for satisfactory manipulation and compaction. The loose thickness of a layer should not be greater than 4 in., unless otherwise specifically directed by the engineer. The layer should be spread to a uniform depth and to the full width called for on the drawings by means of an approved spreading device or from the tailgate of trucks operated to produce uniform distribution.

If unsatisfactory areas are revealed due to a lack of reasonable uniformity in the material, mixing will be required to relieve this condition.

Where satisfactory results cannot be secured from mixing alone, coarse or fine material should be added or the unsatisfactory material should be removed and replaced with appropriately graded material, as required or directed.

All hauling over the layer should be distributed over its entire surface in a manner to secure uniform compaction. The material should be kept bladed to a smooth surface during the hauling operations.

Where construction of surface in two or more layers is being done, the first layer should be placed and compacted before placement of the second layer is begun. The layer should be continuously maintained in a smooth condition, compacted either by traffic or by rolling. Rolling should begin at the edges and progress toward the center of the roadway, each trip of the roller overlapping the course of the preceding trip by at least 18 in. The first trip along the edge of the layer should lap on the shoulder by at least 1 ft. Rolling should continue until thorough compaction has been obtained.

If rutting or segregation of the material or other failures should occur at any time, they should be corrected by reshaping, remixing, or removal and replacement of the material as required to secure a uniform and well-compacted surface.

Whenever the material does not contain sufficient moisture to provide proper compaction, it should be sprinkled. When the sprinkling is being done before compaction of the layer is started, the material should be harrowed or otherwise manipulated, as required, to distribute the moisture throughout the mass. Full advantage should be taken of weather conditions. The surface of the layer should be smooth and true to cross section and grade when shaping and compacting are completed. The completed surface course should be well bonded and consolidated, with no tendency to ravel or form ruts under traffic.

SHOULDERS

Shoulders should be shaped and completed as indicated on the drawing or as directed, with inner edges flush with the completed surface. If forms have been used, they should be removed and the spaces carefully filled with compacted material.

The completed surface course should be maintained in a smooth and firm condition until taken over by the agency or persons responsible for permanent maintenance.

Crushed-Stone Surface Course

If the stone does not contain sufficient fine materials having suitable binding properties to provide for a well-consolidated and bonded mass, additional binder should be added. This binder should consist of screenings, sand, clay, topsoil, other approved material. It should be clean material, of suitable gradation and binding value to correct deficiencies of these properties in the stone. The proportion of binder to be added to the stone will be determined by the engineer.

EQUIPMENT

The equipment used should be of adequate capacity and suitable character to perform the several operations as specified. The shaping and blading operations should be done with a motor grader weighing not less than 7 tons or with a blade grader weighing not less than 3 tons, which should be drawn by a tractor of adequate power and weight. The blade of either grader should be at least 8 ft long. Power rollers should weigh not less than 8 tons.

SUBGRADE

Subgrade should be bladed and shaped to true line, grade, and cross section and to a smooth, true surface. It should be of firm bearing throughout. Any unsatisfactory materials in the subgrade should be removed and replaced with suitable materials. When so indicated on the drawings or so directed, the subgrade should be channeled to provide material for the completion of the shoulders. Side ditches should be kept open and shaped to prevent ponding of water on the subgrade during construction.

The subgrade should be kept prepared an appropriate distance in advance of the surface-course construction. Each section should be firm and free from irregularities while surfacing materials are placed.

Temporary wooden forms should be used if required to confine and compact the material.

APPLICATION OF STONE

The stone should be applied at the rate called for on the drawings. This rate of application of stone should be maintained regardless of whether binder material is to be added. The stone should be spread uniformly upon the prepared subgrade from vehicles with approved spreading devices or from the tailgate of trucks if stone can be spread evenly and without segregation by this method. Material should never be unloaded on the subgrade in piles.

The material should be applied in two layers, whenever necessary, to provide for satisfactory manipulation and compaction. The loose thickness of any layer should not be greater than 4 in. unless otherwise specifically directed by the engineer.

Where the addition of binder material is necessary, it should be spread uniformly over the layer of stone at the rate directed. It should then be thoroughly mixed with the stone by blading, harrowing, or other appropriate methods. Or binder and stone may be mixed prior to application if appropriate equipment is available.

As the spreading of the material proceeds and after any mixing required to incorporate the binder has been completed, the layer should be shaped and smoothed to the required cross section and to a uniform surface. All hauling over the layer should be distributed over the entire surface to secure uniform compaction. The material should be kept bladed to a smooth surface, both during the hauling operations and while the layer is open to traffic. If rutting or segregation of material should occur at any time, it should be corrected by reshaping, remixing, or removal and replacement of the material as required.

The surface course should be maintained and compacted until it becomes firm and well bonded, with no tendency to form ruts under traffic, and with no loose stone that will be displaced by traffic. Rolling should be done wherever hauling operations or traffic will not secure full bonding and compaction. Sprinkling should be done as required to aid compaction, and full advantage should be taken of weather conditions. Where construction in two layers is being done, full compaction of the first layer should be completed before placement of the second layer is begun.

SHOULDERS

Shoulders should be shaped and completed as indicated on the drawings or as directed, with inner edges flush with the completed surface. If forms have been used, they should be removed and the spaces carefully filled with compacted material.

MAINTENANCE

The completed surface course should be maintained in a smooth and firm condition until taken over by the agency or persons responsible for permanent maintenance.

Hot Bituminous Seal Coat

This seal coat of hot bituminous material and stone chips is applied separately upon the bituminous road mix course or other designated surfaces, in accordance with the provisions of these specifications and in conformity with the lines, grades, and cross sections indicated or directed.

EQUIPMENT

Equipment of approved design and adequate to ensure proper completion of the work should be provided and should be maintained in first-class working condition at all times. The following requirements should apply to equipment used.

The roller shall be of such design, weight, and power as to ensure satisfactory compression. It shall weigh not less than 5 nor more than 8 tons and shall exert a pressure of not less than 125 lb per inch width of rear tread.

See specifications for pressure distributor as given under Bituminous Road Mix, page 488.

SEASONAL AND WEATHER LIMITATIONS

Seal-coat construction shall not be done between Oct. 15 and May 15.

The bituminous material should not be applied on a wet surface or when the temperature of the air in the shade is below 50°F or has been below 45°F during the preceding 4 hours.

The surface of all structures should be protected by satisfactory methods or devices against disfigurement by bituminous material. Any surfaces becoming disfigured should be restored to a satisfactory appearance.

APPLICATION OF BITUMINOUS MATERIAL

The entire surface to be covered should be swept and cleaned of all loose or caked foreign matter immediately before the application of bituminous material is started. The bituminous material should be applied uniformly at a pressure of not less than 35 or more than 75 lb/in.^{2} It should be applied to the full width of the treatment in a single application, unless the engineer directs that the application be made to only half the width at one time in order to provide for movement of traffic. Where half-width applications are made, care should be taken to secure a complete and even coating of the area along the adjoining edges of the applications.

The distributor should be operated at the full required capacity at both the beginning and the end of each spread. It should be stopped before the application begins to run light or whenever a nozzle becomes clogged. Before each succeeding application, building paper should be spread over the treated surface and so arranged that the nozzles will be operating at full force when the untreated surface is reached. The building paper should be removed immediately after the application and destroyed.

See specifications for treatment of excess bituminous material under Bituminous Road Mix, page 488.

The bituminous material should be applied at a uniform rate of 0.25 gal/yd^2. If asphalt cement is used, it should not be heated to a temperature greater than 350°F and should be applied at a temperature of not less than 300°F. If tar is used, it should not be heated to a temperature greater than 225°F and should be applied at a minimum temperature of 175°F.

APPLICATION OF STONE CHIPS

The stone chips should be satisfactorily air-dried before being applied.

The chips should be spread directly from trucks by means of approved mechanical spreaders. Trucks or spreaders should not pass over the uncovered bituminous material. If bituminous material is being applied to less than the full width of the treatment at one time, the chips should be stopped within 8 in. of the inner edge of the first application until the adjacent application has been made.

Stone chips should be spread uniformly over the hot bituminous material at a rate of not less than 20 lb/yd^2. They should follow application of the bituminous material as closely as necessary to ensure their being embedded in the bituminous material while it is still hot. They should be uniformly distributed over the surface by dragging with a drag broom, supplemented by hand brooming as necessary.

As soon as the chips have been uniformly distributed, they should be rolled with a power roller. The roller should work in a longitudinal direction, beginning at the outer edges of the seal coat and progressing toward the center, each trip overlapping the previous one by one-half the width of the roller. The first rolling should be complete within 1 hour after the application of bituminous material. The rolling should be repeated as many times as may be necessary to key the chips thoroughly in the bituminous material. The surface should be covered by the rear wheels of the roller at least 4 times.

During rolling, the surface should be broomed to secure even distribution, and any areas containing an excess of bituminous material should have additional chips added and rolled in until the surface is uniform in appearance and texture.

At such intervals as may be necessary to avoid loss of chips from the surface, all chips should be swept from the edges of the pavement to the center and spread uniformly over the surface. This operation should be repeated until all chips are embedded in the surface. The surface may be rolled to expedite the embedment of the chips.

When finally completed, the surface should not deviate more than ¼ in. from a 10-ft straightedge placed parallel to the center of the road in any position.

MAINTENANCE

The completed seal coat should be maintained for a period of not less than 30 days, and thereafter if necessary. All failures or defects that develop should be fully and satisfactorily repaired and corrected so as to leave an even-textured, uniform surface of correct shape.

Side ditches should be kept open during the period of construction and maintenance, and all shoulders should be bladed and repaired as necessary to leave them in good condition with proper shape.

Patching Existing Bituminous Surfaces

Existing bituminous surfaces are patched by applying and compacting a mixture of mineral aggregate and bituminous material after suitable surface preparation. Areas which show indications of early failure should be repaired, as well as those which have already failed.

Areas to be patched should be prepared by digging out and removing all dirt and fine material and all surrounding surfacing material which has ravelled or disintegrated or in which the bitumen has lost its bonding properties. These operations should be extended beyond the areas which have actually failed as far as necessary to obtain a firm, clean, well-bonded surface beneath and around the area to be patched. Apply patching material as soon as practicable after preparation of surface.

Patching material should not be applied when the surface to be patched is wet or when the temperature in the shade is below 65°F or has been below 55°F during the preceding 4 hours.

The surface to be patched and area of existing surfacing immediately adjacent thereto should be painted with a coat of tar of the grade specified above. When the tar has become tacky, the previously mixed patching material should be applied.

Patching material should consist of a mixture of tar of the grade specified above and of crushed stone. The proportions of the mix will be determined on the job by the engineer and should be such that the surfaces of all particles of the aggregate will be thoroughly coated but there will be no excess of bituminous material and the mixture will set up into a firm mass remaining stable under the conditions of temperature and traffic to which it will be subjected.

Mixing should be done in an approved type of mechanical mixer, except that mixing by hand methods may be permitted by the engineer when the amount of patching to be done is small. In any case, the mineral aggregate should be dry before mixing and the materials should be thoroughly mixed to ensure complete coating of the aggregate particles.

To keep the mixture from being displaced by traffic, the mixed materials should be kept in stockpiles long enough to permit the volatile solvents to evaporate.

The mixture should be thoroughly tamped into place and shaped to be flush with the adjacent surfaces and to conform to the grade and section of the roadway. Enough stone chips to cover the bitumen should be spread over the patch and the immediately adjacent areas which were painted with tar.

Single Bituminous Surface Treatment

Single surface treatment should consist of hot bituminous material and mineral aggregate in separate applications upon the primed base, in accordance with the provisions of the specifications and in conformity with the lines, grades, and cross sections indicated or directed.

See specifications for Hot Bituminous Seal Coat, page 502. The bituminous material should be applied at a rate of not less than 0.45 nor more than 0.50 gal/yd^2.

APPLICATION OF MINERAL AGGREGATE

The mineral aggregate should be satisfactorily air-dried before application. The aggregate should be spread directly from trucks by means of approved mechanical spreaders. In no instance should the application of bituminous material advance more than one distributor load ahead of the spreading of the aggregate.

The mineral aggregate should be spread uniformly over hot bituminous material at a rate of between 45 and 50 lb/yd^2. It should follow application of the bituminous material as closely as is necessary to ensure being embedded in the material while it is still hot.

Immediately after the aggregate has been applied, it should be dragged with a drag broom and manipulated with hand brooms until an even spread of uniform texture is obtained. Additional aggregate should be placed by hand on any areas not properly covered.

STABILIZED BASE

Construction of a stabilized base should consist of base courses composed of natural or artificial mixtures of stone, slag, chert or gravel, with soil to which should be added calcium chloride and water. The base courses should be constructed in layers to the lines, grades, and typical cross sections shown on the drawings or directed by the engineer and in accordance with the requirements of these specifications.

STONE AND SLAG

The stone or slag should be of such gradation that, when mixed with the soil to be used, it will meet the standards indicated in Table 8.5.

TABLE 8.5
Gradation of Stone and Slag in Base Mixtures

Size of sieve passed	Minimum per cent of weight	Maximum per cent of weight
1-in.	100	
¾-in.	80	100
⅜-in.	50	90
No. 4	35	65
No. 10	22	50
No. 40	15	30
No. 200	5	15

If as much as 40 per cent of the mixture passes the no. 10 sieve, the fraction passing the no. 200 sieve should not exceed 50 per cent of the fraction passing the no. 40 sieve. If less than 40 per cent of the mixture passes the no. 10 sieve and the plasticity index of the mixture is low, the fraction passing the no. 200 sieve may be not more than 65 per cent of the fraction passing the no. 40 sieve.

The fraction passing the no. 40 sieve should have a liquid limit of not more than 35 and a plasticity index of not more than 8.

TABLE 8.6
Gradations of Chert or Gravel in Base Mixtures

Size of sieve passed	Minimum per cent of weight	Maximum per cent of weight
2-in.		100
1½-in.	90	100
1-in.	75	100
¾-in.	60	95
½-in.	30	80
No. 4	25	60
No. 10	20	45
No. 40	15	35
No. 200	5	20

SOIL FOR BINDER

Soil for binder should be homogeneous material consisting primarily of fine soil particles and having binding properties to provide the physical structure and properties in the final mixture that are specified above. All soil should be obtained from sources approved by the engineer.

CHERT OR GRAVEL

Local sources of chert or gravel and soil should be selected to produce a mixture of high density similar to the specifications given in Table 8.6 and having a maximum size of not more than 2 in.

If as much as 40 per cent of the mixture passes the no. 10 sieve, the fraction passing the no. 200 sieve should not exceed 50 per cent of the fraction passing the no. 40 sieve. If less than 40 percent of the mixture passes the no. 10 sieve and the plasticity index of the mixture is low, the fraction passing the no. 200 sieve may be not more than 65 per cent of the fraction passing the no. 40 sieve.

The fraction passing the no. 40 sieve should have a liquid limit of not more than 35 and a plasticity index of not more than 8.

Calcium chloride should conform to the requirements of the Standard Specifications for Calcium Chloride, ASTM D-98-68, of the American Society for Testing Materials.

SUBGRADE

The subgrade should be cut to the elevations established by the engineer, which in general will produce sufficient material for construction of the shoulders. It should be prepared true to the grade and to the lines and typical cross sections shown on the drawings or to authorized modifications thereof and should be bladed and finished to a smooth and uniform surface. Adequate provisions should be maintained at all times to ensure removal of water without ponding on, or injury to, the subgrade.

When properly shaled, the subgrade should be compacted to a firm and uniform bearing with a roller weighing not less than 8 tons. If necessary for good compaction, the subgrade should be moistened while it is being rolled.

The subgrade should be kept prepared an appropriate distance in advance of the placement of base materials. Any irregularities such as ruts, holes, or the like which may develop should be corrected so that all material will be applied to a smooth, compact surface.

GUIDE PLANKS

Unless otherwise indicated on drawings, guide planks having a nominal thickness of not less than 2 in. and a width equal to the loose thickness of the layer should be set for each layer of the base. They should be set to exact lines along the edges of the base, with top edges at a height above the subgrade or the preceding layer which is equal to required loose thickness of the layer under construction.

MIXED-IN-PLACE CONSTRUCTION

The base should be constructed in approximately equal layers, the compacted thickness of which should not exceed 4 in. The base materials should be deposited along the subgrade or preceding layer in the quantities required for a complete layer and in the proportions fixed by the engineer. The calcium chloride should be spread uniformly over the soil in each layer at the rate of 1 lb/yd^2.

Water should be added to the materials in each layer of the base course before final mixing to secure maximum compaction when rolled. The total quantity to be added should be determined by engineer. At the time of compaction, the total moisture content should equal approximately 8 per cent, by weight, of the base materials or such other percentage as may be found appropriate from tests of the materials being used. The quantity added before mixing is begun should be sufficient to promote thorough and uniform moistening and proper workability without segregation of the materials.

The mixing should be done with a blade grader, which should weigh not less than 8000 lb. The grader should be drawn by a tractor of adequate power and weight. The materials should be turned from side to side until thoroughly mixed, the mixing equipment being manipulated to mix the materials to their full depth without appreciable disturbance of the underlying construction. When the mixing is completed, the mixture should be left in a windrow until it reaches the desired consistency, at which time it should be spread and shaped to a uniform depth and bladed to a smooth surface.

Before compaction of a layer is begun, shoulder material should have been placed adjacent to, and flush with, the guide planks to a width of not less than 2 ft and tamped and shaped to a smooth surface. After the layer of base material is spread, the guide planks should be removed and the spaces left vacant filled and tamped.

Compaction of each layer should be done with a self-propelled roller weighing not less than 8 tons. The rolling should begin at the edges of the base, the first course covering at least 1 ft of the shoulder, and should progress toward the center. Each track should overlap the preceding track by not less than 18 in. The rolling should continue until the entire surface of the layer is thoroughly and uniformly compacted. During rolling, the moisture content should be maintained at approximately 8 per cent and within such limits as the engineer may direct.

The surface of the final layer should not deviate more than $\frac{1}{4}$ in. from a 10-ft straightedge placed parallel to the centerline of the road.

PREMIX CONSTRUCTION

Base materials may be combined in any suitable mixer before they are placed on the road. Enough water should be added to the materials during mixing operations to promote thorough mixing and to obtain the desired workability for handling and spreading without segregation.

Calcium chloride should be added in the proportions specified above before mixing is begun. The mixed materials should be spread on the road in approximately equal layers which will compact to a thickness not more than 4 in. As soon as any excess moisture has evaporated and the moisture in the mixture amounts to approximately 8 per cent (or such other percentage as may be determined from tests of the material being used to be appropriate), the layer should be shaped and compacted as specified for mixed-in-place construction.

SHOULDERS

The shaping and compacting of the final layer of the base should be followed as closely as conditions will permit by construction of such portions of the shoulders as have not already been completed. The necessary material should be placed, shaped, and compacted until the shoulders are firm and true to the cross section shown on the drawings. The roller used for the base should be used to obtain thorough and uniform compaction of the entire shoulder.

MAINTENANCE

Machining, rolling, and sprinkling should be repeated frequently enough after completion of the base to maintain the surface smooth and compact. When maintenance is discontinued, both the base and the shoulders should be firm and smooth and true to the typical cross section shown on the drawings.

Stabilizing Subgrade with Sheepsfoot Roller

The subgrade and adjacent roadbed should be stabilized, where directed, by the use of a sheepsfoot roller in accordance with the methods herein specified. The engineer will determine the area to be treated after grading of the roadbed has been completed.

CONSTRUCTION METHODS

The section of roadbed to be stabilized should be shaped to conform to the subgrade on which the pavement is to be laid. The roadbed, to the width designed on the drawings or by the engineer, should then be loosened by scarifying or other means to a depth of not less than 6 in. below the final surface of the subgrade. The soil should be broken so that there will be no lumps more than 1 in. in diameter, and water should be added if necessary to bring the moisture content to that required by the engineer. The width of the roadbed being stabilized should then be compacted by rolling with an approved sheepsfoot roller until the roller will no longer sink into the soil. The soil should be so manipulated during the final stages of rolling that the subgrade under the proposed pavement will be at the proper lines, grades, and cross sections when the rolling is completed.

Tar Prime Coat

See specifications for equipment under Bituminous Surface Treatment, page 505.

PREPARATION OF BASE

The entire surface of the base should be firm, uniform, and of proper cross section when the tar is applied. The prepared surface should be swept and cleaned of all loose material, dust, dirt, caked clay, and foreign material to the full width to be treated immediately before being primed.

If the engineer so directs, the surface should be slightly damp when the priming is done but should have no signs of free moisture on the surface and should be firm enough not to show appreciable deformation under the rear tires of the distributor. If so directed, the base should be sprinkled for this purpose.

RATE OF APPLICATION

When the prime coat is constructed under the single application, the tar shall be applied at a uniform rate of not less than 0.30 nor more than 0.35 gal/yd^2. It shall be applied in a single application except on portions of the surface where two applications are directed to prevent the tar from running.

When the prime coat is constructed under the double application, two applications of tar shall be made to the entire surface. The first application shall be made at a rate of approximately 0.25 gal/yd^2 and the second at approximately 0.15 gal/yd^2. The two applications shall not total less than 0.40 nor more than 0.45 gal/yd^2.

METHOD OF APPLICATION

The tar should not be applied when the temperature of the air in the shade is below 50°F or has been below 45°F during the preceding 4 hours. The temperature of the tar when applied should not be less than 80°F nor more than 150°F and should be further limited if directed.

The bituminous material should be applied uniformly at a pressure of not less than 35 nor more than 75 lb/in.^{2} It should be applied to the full width of the treatment in a single application unless the engineer directs that the application be made to only one half width at a time, in order to provide for movement of traffic. Where half-width applications are made, care should be taken to secure a complete coating of the area along the adjoining edges of the applications without an excess or deficiency of material.

The distributor should be operated at the full required capacity at both the beginning and the end of each spread. It should be stopped before the application begins to run light or whenever a nozzle becomes clogged. Before beginning a succeeding application, building paper should be spread over the treated surface for a distance sufficiently back to ensure that the nozzles will be operating at full force when the untreated surface is reached. The building paper should then be removed immediately and destroyed.

Any excess of bituminous material at transverse or longitudinal junctions of applications should be removed and correction made in a satisfactory manner. Parts of the surface not reached or improperly covered with bituminous materials directly from the distributor should be treated by means of a hand spray attached to the distributor or with approved hand-pouring pots. If at any time uniform distribution within the specified limits is not consistently obtained, distribution shall be stopped until satisfactory adjustment of the distribution or replacement of the operator is made.

When the prime coat is being constructed in two applications, the second coat should not be applied until at least 48 hours after the first application and until all faulty distribution of the first coat has been corrected. The entire area should be free from dust, dirt, and other foreign matter and should be thoroughly dry when the second coat is applied.

REPAIRS

Any spots or areas that fail in any way after either prime-coat application should be thoroughly cleaned out and the spaces filled either with material similar to that used in the base or with a mixture of seal-coat aggregate and tar, as directed. The patching material should be thoroughly tamped as it is placed and should be smoothed flush with the surrounding surface. When so directed, the exposed areas should be sprinkled before the patching is done. If material similar to that in the base is used, it should contain the proper amount of moisture for maximum compaction.

After this material has been placed, the surface should be primed by means of hand-pouring pots or other suitable equipment. If a mixture of tar and aggregate is being used, it should be prepared in the proportions of from 10 to 15 gal of tar to each cubic yard of aggregate.

Traffic-bound Surface Courses

Traffic-bound surface courses should be prepared true to the lines, grades, and cross sections indicated or directed and should be of firm and uniform bearing. They should be prepared by blading and shaping the roadbed constructed during grading of the roadway and by replacing any soft or unstable materials with suitable materials. Side ditches should be kept open, and the shaping should be so conducted as to ensure against ponding of water on the subgrade during construction. The subgrade should be kept prepared an appropriate distance in advance of surface course construction. Each section should be firm and free from irregularities at the time of placing surfacing materials.

APPLICATION AND SHAPING

All hauling operations should be conducted to avoid rutting or displacement of the prepared subgrade or of surfacing material. Where such rutting or displacement occurs, it should be corrected by removal or reshaping of the disturbed materials so as to produce a finished surface course of uniform composition, stability, and thickness. The surfacing material should be applied at the rate specified on the drawings. It should be spread to proper width and thickness, and segregation and unequally compacted areas should be avoided.

All oversize material that may have been brought in should be exposed and either removed or broken down to meet the specification requirements. As the spreading of surfacing material progresses, the spread material should be leveled and planed to a smooth surface of the required cross section and crown.

MAINTENANCE

Until the end of the maintenance period, the surface course should be bladed as often as necessary to prevent the development of holes, ruts, or waves. Full advantage should be taken of weather conditions in the blading operations.

At the end of the maintenance period, the surface course should be properly shaped and crowned and should present a smooth, firm, and uniform surface.

MAINTENANCE OF RECREATION AREAS

PICNIC AREAS

Picnicking is an important part of all recreational activity. It is an activity in which persons of all ages indulge; unfortunately the public is generally lax in cooperating to keep the picnic premises clean and sanitary. The carelessness and vandalism that result add considerably to maintenance costs. Few seem to realize that all picnic areas on public grounds are tax-supported and by misusing them the public is penalizing itself for its own carelessness.

A picnic area includes many different types of facilities: structures such as shelters, comfort stations, and even refectories and bandstands; roads, parking spaces, walks, trails, steps, guard rails, drinking fountains, and signs; and the primary facilities such as water supply, tables, benches, fireplaces, and sanitary conveniences.

CARE OF GROUNDS

One of the most essential elements of proper care of picnic areas is the degree to which the grounds are maintained. The public is quick to recognize and respond to an efficient maintenance program and equally quick to criticize and aggravate a situation where the grounds remain littered with trash. Each area's maintenance crew should regulate its schedule so that during the summer season the picnic area is thoroughly cleaned early in the day—before 10 o'clock if possible. The schedule should provide for daily policing, depending upon the use and season. In addition, the schedule should provide for extra maintenance whenever the occasion demands, such as immediately following holidays and weekends or other periods of concentrated use. It is very important that trash and garbage not be permitted to accumulate over the weekend, or the grounds might conceivably become so littered as to be unsanitary as well as unattractive.

The preservation of existing ground cover, trees, and shrubs is highly important. It is much too expensive to provide extra picnic areas so that one badly deteriorated area can be retired from use until it is reclaimed and made serviceable once more. Also, it is impossible to replace full-grown trees. Therefore, the only alternative and the most economical method is to preserve the existing cover. All of the ground area of the intensive-use sections of picnic areas should receive annual light cultivation and fertilization. If the forest cover is dense and grass will not grow, a heavy mulching of leaves (held in place by well-rotted sawdust) after the area has been fertilized and cultivated will replace the normal ground cover worn thin by constant use. Another method, but more expensive, is to cover the area with tanbark or ground coconut

Fig. 9.1 A well-maintained picnic area. (*Tennessee Valley Authority.*)

hulls. This surface treatment is used in many city parks where there is a heavy concentrated use. This ground-cover replacement should be done after the picnic areas are no longer in heavy demand, usually in late fall or early winter (Fig. 9.1).

Care of Public Facilities

The old log or wood picnic table has proved to be a major maintenance and replacement problem. This problem has been met by the design of attractive concrete tables.

In order to reduce maintenance costs as much as possible, anchor all tables to the ground. Maintenance costs increase if the public is permitted to move the tables at will. In addition, each table should be placed on a paved level terrace in order to protect adjacent trees, prevent erosion, and make policing of the grounds easier.

Maintenance crews should make daily inspections of all picnic tables during the summer season. Such inspections should immediately reveal any need for repairs. A continuous repair and inspection program will greatly increase the life of the tables and reduce total maintenance costs.

CONCRETE TABLES

Maintenance costs are reduced by the use of concrete tables in picnic areas. These tables require periodic scrubbings with soap and water, frequency depending upon use. Concrete table tops can be treated with Amercoat solution no. 1254, clear or equal, to aid in cleaning. Such treatment reduces the amount of staining caused by grease, bottles, or food. Protect the wood seats with annual applications of a good wood preservative. Because it is toxic, do not use creosote or any preservative with a predominance of creosote. Treatment with Wood-Tox and two or three coats of marine varnish will give good protection.

WOOD TABLES

There are many designs of wood tables, but only those which provide a combination of stability, durability, reasonable cost, and an attractive appearance should be used. Low annual cost of maintenance should be the guide. The following points are offered as a maintenance guide:

1. Avoid using resinous woods such as yellow and Norway pines for replacement of seats and tops.
2. Norway pine is the most economical in the long run for legs and braces.
3. Use a good grade of lumber, such as redwood, cypress, or oak for tops and seats.
4. Treat all wood with a good wood preservative such as Wood-Tox, Cuprinol, etc. Do not use creosote.
5. Paint all tables with a good, durable grade of paint, preferably marine paint. Do not use stain, since stains are ineffective and shorter-lived than paint.
6. Use bolts for seats and at all important connections, with screws for the tops.
7. Separate top boards by $^3/_8$-in. cracks for drainage.
8. Chamfer or round all outside edges of the seats and tops.

FIREPLACES

The fireplace is an essential part of every picnic area. It need not be an elaborate arrangement of grates and fireboxes but should be efficient for cooking, safe against spread of fire, and reasonably inexpensive to maintain.

It is very difficult to build an outdoor fireplace which is entirely efficient for cooking. A fireplace built with an enclosed chimney provides too much draft, which draws most of the heat up the chimney and away from the cooking. In addition, fireplaces of this type are slow cookers and extravagant of fuel. A fireplace, to be most useful, should be built without a chimney and with the grate depressed between the sides. Such fireplaces confine the fire and decrease both the time and amount of fuel to prepare an outdoor meal.

Since most picnic areas are located in wooded areas, every precaution must be taken to eliminate fire hazards. A correctly built fireplace, protected from prevailing winds, will give this protection. To provide the maximum safety the fireplace should be enclosed on both sides and one end and located at right angles to prevailing winds.

Maintenance cost varies with the type of fireplace and degree of use. There are three general types now popular: the concrete type, the masonry type, and the round steel type. From a maintenance standpoint, the concrete fireplace is easy to maintain. Under most conditions the concrete fireplace is used until it has become so cracked and broken that it is unserviceable and unsightly, at which time it is removed and a new one installed. This type deteriorates rapidly under intense heat and probably needs replacement every 4 or 5 years.

The masonry type is generally built of stone, with the firebox lined with firebrick. Properly constructed, a masonry fireplace will last indefinitely because loose brick and stones can be replaced. The grate will tend to warp and twist under constant use, but it is so constructed that it can be removed and replaced when no longer of service. The maintenance crew should check each fireplace daily so that minor repairs can be made immediately. Such checking will help to reduce the need for major repairs.

In order to protect the existing forest cover from ravage by picnickers, firewood should be provided in convenient locations and in proper size. Most areas will have an abundance of dead and down trees and wood salvaged from power-line clearances to maintain a supply for many years.

Probably the most economical and easiest fireplaces to maintain are the upright steel charcoal burners. These are practically indestructible, except by rust. They have been used, regardless of treatment, for more than 6 years. As firewood grows scarce, installation of good charcoal burners will become essential.

Utilities

Water for drinking should be furnished at convenient locations in the picnic area. There are three types of water outlets in general use: the concrete, masonry, and upright hydrant types. The concrete fountain is used in areas where the predominant construction material is concrete. Very little maintenance is necessary except to check all working parts to be sure they are performing properly, to check for leaks, and to cut off water at proper time to ensure against freezing.

The masonry water outlet is used where the predominant construction material is stone and where the shelters and picnic area are entirely separate from major installations. The same type of maintenance is required as specified for concrete outlets.

The upright hydrant outlet, without fountain, is installed whereever a picnic area is close to a public building or to a parking area with drinking fountains installed. Maintenance on this type is essentially the same as specified above. Some areas have been experiencing maintenance difficulties with upright water hydrants, which develop leaks that are difficult to repair. The difficulty seems to be in the type of cutoff, which is metal-to-metal and requires a good hard turn. Most people using the fountain do not bother to apply the pressure needed, and as a result the hydrant drips or runs constantly.

Another problem has been the waste-water sumps at these fountains, which may fill up with water rapidly, indicating that the ground drainage from the sump is poor. There are several methods by which this can be corrected. One is to redig the sump and enlarge it to twice its size and depth. If the sump is in impervious clay, use a crowbar to break up the bottom. If the sump is in rock, it will probably be necessary to add a small drain field to take the water away from the hydrant or to pipe the waste water from the hydrant into a natural drain away from the hydrant or to a sump located in an area where good drainage can be obtained.

It may be advisable to install a cutoff valve at some convenient point in the water line servicing the picnic area. This cutoff should be provided with a drain and located at the lowest point of the line between the main line and the picnic line, permitting the picnic-area line to be thoroughly drained for the winter seasons. When it is cut on again in the spring, all water outlets in the picnic area should be opened wide in order to flush the line thoroughly. The line should be sterilized before it is put back into use. The local health and safety authorities should be consulted on this point.

POWER

Wherever possible, sufficient power should be provided to light the area adequately for night use. Lighting arrangements do not need to be extensive, but fixtures should be numerous enough to permit use of the area without endangering the safety of the public. Generally, lighting standards should be located adjacent to paths and parking areas. All service lines within the area should be underground. Where underground lines are impractical to install, overhead lines may be used, but they should be located so that they are inconspicuous.

Sanitary Facilities

There are two types of sanitary toilet facilities in use: dry-pit and flush type. The dry-pit privy, usually considered temporary, should be replaced as funds become available by the flush type. Maintenance of the flush-type sanitary facilities is as follows:

1. Keep lavatories, stools, and cell interiors clean and sanitary at all times. This means daily cleaning during normal summer use. During periods of intensive use (weekends and holidays) it may mean hourly checking and cleaning. The intensity of use will determine how often a facility must be cleaned in order to be neat and sanitary at all times.
2. Maintain an adequate supply of paper, soap, and towels.
3. Check all plumbing for leaks or faulty operation, and repair at once.
4. Keep interiors clean and neat.
5. Repaint all interiors and exteriors as needed. This will vary with locality, use, and weathering conditions. Repainting should never be deferred longer than 4 years under any conditions.
6. Maintain proper lighting.

The dry pit should be built in accordance with state's health department recommendations. It is essential that the privies be located in convenient places, sufficiently screened and marked. Do not hide them or place them in some out-of-the-way place where they may become useless. Maintenance of the dry-pit privy is simpler, but it is more difficult to keep clean. Periodic liming is necessary to keep down odors, and daily washings with soap and disinfectant water are necessary during the summer season. As the privies fill up, the simplest process is to move to a new location and seal the old pit. Since all pit privies are of frame construction, they require periodic painting and repair.

PLAY EQUIPMENT

Some suitable equipment—swings, seesaws, sandboxes and jungle gyms for the children, and horseshoe and badminton for adults—should be provided. Maintenance of such facilities is simple and inexpensive.

Trash and Garbage Disposal

Choosing the proper location and number of trash and garbage cans ensures (1) convenience to the public, (2) convenient truck access for efficient collection, (3) good appearance, and (4) maintenance of grounds in a sanitary condition.

All trash and garbage cans must be located where picnickers will use them instead of throwing everything on the ground. This may mean that every two or three tables will require a trash or garbage container, depending upon the spacing or grouping of the tables. Do not place the containers where they may detract from a view.

The design for the picnic area should provide a service drive for small trucks, with easy access for efficient collection of garbage. This drive should be located so that it comes within a relatively short distance of the trash and garbage containers. A wide trail will suffice for both truck and pedestrian access. Workmen sometimes have a tendency to disregard the design of the area and locate all containers at some central point, easily reached by truck, but every effort should be made to discourage this practice. In mountainous areas, where many of the picnic tables are inaccessible except by foot trail, small hand dollies can be used to reduce the number of trips and to make handling easier. Trash and garbage containers should be well labeled and in conspicuous places and should also be kept clean, well painted, and well maintained. Battered old cans make a poor appearance and are more difficult to handle.

The number of trash and garbage cans required for any particular picnic area depends upon the use of the area and the number of picnic tables. One method of estimating the required number in a new area is to place one container for three picnic tables and add more containers as demand or need increases.

Each garbage can should be placed in a permanent holder to prevent animals from tipping the can over and spreading the refuse over the ground. This holder may be a concrete base with four steel uprights holding the can in place or a concrete container large enough to hold a can. Both lids and cans should be fastened to the base by means of a chain or cable which can be locked.

MISCELLANEOUS

Barricades

Unless the area is designed for such use, no cars should be permitted to drive into the picnic area in order to park adjacent to a table. To prevent this, it is necessary to confine all cars to designated parking areas and to barricade entrances to service drives. Places where cars might be able to cross grass areas from access roads should be barricaded with posts or boulders, depending upon the locality.

There are several ways to confine cars to designated parking areas:

1. Curbs, either stone or concrete
2. A combination of guard rails and posts
3. Guard posts spaced close enough to prevent cars from driving between them
4. Boulders spaced as above

Guard posts should be constructed of concrete, and guardrails should be steel. Log construction should be avoided.

Barricades to service drives should be concrete or steel posts or masonry piers at either side of the drive with a chain or cable connecting the posts and securely locked. All posts should be anchored in the ground. Posts can be pulled from the ground by a car's pushing against them and loosening the post enough to let it be pulled out. This can be overcome by setting the posts in a concrete base or by setting them 3 to 4 ft in the ground.

If concrete posts are used, very little maintenance is necessary. Broken posts should be removed as soon as possible and new ones installed. Loose posts should be replaced as rapidly as possible with concrete posts and steel rails. Temporary wooden replacements should be treated as often as needed with creosote or other wood preservatives. Steel guardrails should be painted as often as necessary to maintain a good appearance.

Tree Maintenance

Since practically all picnic areas are located in heavily wooded areas, considerable attention should be given to the maintenance of existing trees. Under conditions where the natural litter of the woods is annually destroyed by continued use, trees will suffer, become diseased, and eventually die. It is therefore important that the soil-improvement program mentioned under Care of Grounds be followed. The picnic area should be checked at least once a year, and all dead and dangerous trees should be removed and all dead branches in good trees properly removed. This practice lessens one danger to the public—falling limbs and trees.

Some localities are subject to severe windstorms during the summer season. The picnic area should be ckecked immediately after each storm and all down trees removed and damaged trees repaired or removed. All debris left by such storms should be removed.

Roads and Parking Areas

The maintenance of roads and parking areas is covered in Chap. 8.

Structures

The most common structure found in picnic areas is the shelter, which varies from simple lean-to type to large recreation type, designed to accommodate large picnic groups. Many shelters have fireplaces and public toilets built in as a part of construction, whether log, stone, or some other type. In any event, maintenance should be based on the following principles:

1. Heavy use, requiring constant checking and policing. Trash and garbage must be removed promptly.
2. Painting, whether by a lead-base paint or by a creosote-base stain, should be done as often as required to keep the structure in good condition and good appearance. Log construction especially should be treated with a wood preservative annually.
3. Repairs to other wood sections should be done periodically. Broken or split members should be replaced as soon as the damage occurs. Parts which have rotted should be removed and replaced.
4. Masonry construction requires checking for cracks and broken stones. These should be repaired as they occur and not left until they become a major problem.
5. Shelters with fireplaces need to be checked constantly. A clogged or faulty flue may cause serious damage or complete loss.
6. Public toilets in shelters should be maintained in the same condition as described under Sanitary Facilities.
7. Shelters wired for lights need to be checked periodically. Faulty wiring or vandalism may cause serious damage or complete loss. Light bulbs should be replaced as soon as they burn out. Fixtures should be of a type to discourage vandalism as much as possible.
8. Tables and benches should be maintained as outlined under Care of Public Facilities.

9. Roofs, especially wood-shingle roofs, should be checked frequently. Repairs should be made as needed to prevent an accumulation of repairs leading to a major replacement. Winter accumulations of leaves should be cleaned off roofs to prevent rotting of shingles. Pine needles left on wood shingles are especially injurious (Fig. 9.2).

Trails

Maintenance of trails depends a great deal on their use. Even when not in use, trails should be maintained in order to repair damage from heavy

Fig. 9.2 A picnic shelter combining public toilets and shelter. (*Power Authority of the State of New York.*)

rainfall and frost and to remove fallen trees and branches (Fig. 9.3).

Constant horse travel tears up the surface, destroys the crown, impairs the drainage, and causes the surfacing material to disappear into the soil base. This requires regrading and resurfacing. In areas where trees and shrubs grow fast, overhanging or projecting branches must be trimmed annually to protect the equestrian.

Drainage ditches and culverts should be repaired and cleaned out annually for efficient operation. Wherever erosion has started to cut the drainage ditches deeper than necessary, check dams should be constructed to control the flow of water.

INSECT CONTROL IN RECREATION AREAS

All managers, park attendants, and those generally responsible for the efficient operation and safety of not only the public but employees as well should have a working knowledge of how to control and provide protection against insects in recreation areas. There is nothing more annoying than to have a picnic or camping trip spoiled by the insidious interference of the many forms of insect pests. Since many people are allergic to several forms of insect bite, those responsible for the management of the area must know have to combat insects.

The following information* on repellents, space sprays, and other methods will help the management personnel control or prevent insect annoyance.†

Fig. 9.3 A falls overlook and connecting stairway between upper and lower trails. (*Power Authority of the State of New York.*)

Repellents

Repellents are effective in varying degrees against mosquitoes, biting flies, gnats, chiggers, fleas, and ticks. They are not effective against wasps, spiders, and scorpions. Whenever a repellent is used, be sure to follow the directions carefully and heed all precautions on the label.

Materials To Use

Materials used as repellents fall into two general categories: general-use repellents, which may be applied to both skin and clothing, and repellents that may be applied to clothing only.

General-use repellents contain at least one of the following active ingredients: deet, ethylhexanediol, dimethyl phthalate, dimethyl carbate, or Indalone. They are available under various brand names, and the ingredients

* Be Safe from Insects in Recreation Areas, *USDA Home Gard. Bull* 200, October 1972.
† Mention of a proprietary product in this section is not a guarantee or warranty of the product by the USDA and does not imply its approval by the Department to the exclusion of other products that may also be suitable.

are listed on the label. When deet is an ingredient, it is sometimes listed under its chemical name, *N,N*-diethyl-*m*-toluamide.

Full-strength ethylhexanediol and dimethyl phthalate and a 50 per cent solution of deet in alcohol can be purchased from the local druggist or supermarket. Indalone is not widely available.

These repellents are also available in lower concentrations in liquid form, pressurized cans, and ordinary bottles. Some can be purchased as foams in pressurized cans. If a liquid in a pressurized can is selected, the repellent will be easier to apply if the container gives a coarse spray rather than a fine spray.

Deet is the best repellent to use for protection against most insects. It is very effective for most people. However, the effectiveness of any repellents varies from person to person. Deet repels more kinds of biting insects, ticks, and mites than other repellents.

The general-use repellents lose their effectiveness when the surface to which they are applied becomes wet or washed. Although general-use repellents are safe to use on the skin, as directed, they should never be taken internally.

Benzyl benzoate may be applied to clothing only, to control some kinds of insects. It is generally available from local druggists. Never apply benzyl benzoate to the skin.

Repellents dissolve or stain some kinds of paints and plastics, e.g., plastic lenses of glasses, fingernail polish, synthetic hairpieces, painted or varnished surfaces (such as an automobile body), and some kinds of rayon fabric. Plastic fountain pens and plastic watch crystals are particularly subject to damage. Of the general-use repellents, dimethyl phthalate is usually the most damaging. Ethylhexanediol and deet cause less damage to painted surfaces than the other repellents and usually cause no appreciable damage to most plastics.

Repellents will not damage nylon, polyester, acrylic, all-cotton, or all-wool cloth but may cause temporary stains.

Space Sprays

The number of flies, mosquitoes, and gnats in the air can be reduced if an insecticide space spray is used. Some of these sprays come in ready-to-use pressurized cans. Others must be applied with a hand sprayer that produces a fine mist.

Space sprays usually remain effective for at least 30 minutes, and if the insects are not migrating, effectiveness may last as long as several hours.

Space sprays are clearly labeled for use against flying insects. Follow the directions and heed all precautions on the labels. To use a space spray inside a tent, automobile, or trailer, spray for only a few seconds.

Precautions

Pesticides used improperly can be injurious to man, animals, and plants. Follow the directions and heed all precautions on the labels.

Store pesticides in original containers, out of reach of children and pets, and away from foodstuffs.

Apply pesticides selectively and carefully. Avoid prolonged inhalation of a pesticide spray.

After handling a pesticide, do not eat, drink, or smoke until you have washed. If a pesticide is swallowed or gets into the eyes, follow any first-aid treatment that is shown on the label and get prompt medical attention.

Dispose of empty pesticide containers by wrapping them in several layers of newspaper and placing them in the trash can.

It is difficult to remove all traces of any insecticide from a sprayer. Therefore, to prevent harmful exposure to insecticides, do not apply repellent sprays with equipment previously used for an insecticide.

TABLE 9.1
Recommended Repellents for Control of Insects

Insect	Repellent
Mosquitoes, biting flies, and gnats	Any of the general-use repellents mentioned in text
Chiggers	Any of the general use repellents mentioned in text
Fleas	Deet
Ticks	Indalone, deet, dimethyl carbate, and dimethyl phthalate

Some states have restrictions on the use of certain pesticides. Check your state and local regulations.

Other Methods

Do not overlook mechanical methods of protection against insects. Campers should make sure all of the windows in the tent are screened. To keep scorpions or spiders out of a tent, be sure camper has the floor tightly fastened to the sides.

Practice sanitation. A clean campsite or picnic area is less likely to attract most kinds of insects than a littered area.

If ticks are a problem, urge all participants in the area to wear slacks or long trousers tucked into the top of socks or boots.

Campsites should be cleared of dead leaves, twigs, and loose stones before the camper pitches a tent. Caution campers about camping near rockpiles or fallen trees in areas where scorpions and spiders are a problem.

ARTIFICIAL-TURF MAINTENANCE*

The establishment of turf and its high cost of maintenance invariably raises the question of using artificial turf, especially in the areas of high and intensive use. Artificial turf is primarily used for the following purposes:

Athletic fields: indoor and outdoor for all major sports (Figs. 9.4 to 9.6)
Playgrounds
Poolsides
Track
Landscaping
Home recreational areas
Tennis courts
Lawn bowling
Golf greens, tees, putting greens
Rooftop play areas
Highway median strips
Safety surfaces

Fig. 9.4 Leverone Field House, Dartmouth College. Installation includes both permanent and convertible grass like nylon stadium surface, plus a ⅛-mi track, tennis courts, and jump pits. Allows true multiuse athletic facility to be independent of climate. (*Monsanto Commercial Products Co.*)

* The following information and procedures for artificial-turf maintenance apply principally to AstroTurf stadium surfaces, manufactured by Monsanto. For more detailed information write to Monsanto Commercial Products Co., 800 N. Lindbergh Boulevard, St. Louis, Mo. 63166, Attention: AstroTurf Products Technology

Artificial turf, both indoor and outdoor, can be installed over asphalt, wood, concrete, metal, or any firm smooth surface. It is usually supplied in strips 3, 6, 12, or 15 ft wide that are seamed with adhesives. Seams are practically invisible. Depending on conditions or intended use, it may be permanently cemented to the subsurface or installed without any adhesive as a blanket. It can be maintained easily by cleaning with water or by vacuum cleaner. Stubborn stains can be removed with

Fig. 9.5 AstroDome interior installed in 1966; the same fabric was still in use in 1975. (*Monsanto Commercial Products Co.*)

Fig. 9.6 University of Nebraska football stadium. AstroTurf stadium surface installed in 1970. (*Monsanto Commercial Products Co.*)

mild detergents or recommended solvents. Repairs are made by match-patch piecing.

The advantages in using artificial turf are mainly economical maintenance and its ability to withstand increased traffic. It requires no weeding, seeding, resodding, watering, fertilizing, or mowing. It will dry faster than natural sod, and is therefore available for use sooner. It is always attractive, never suffering from the usual turf diseases causing failures, such as brown patch or mildew. It cushions footsteps, minimizes leg fatigue, and reduces bruises, burns, and sprains. Numerous artificial-turf areas are scheduled for occupancy for 1500 to 2000 hours/year.

Protection of Artificial Turf

Artificial turf should be protected from abuse or unnecessary exposure. Since it is expensive to install, the initial investment should be protected as much as possible. Protection is basically the process of keeping the turf clean, and in order to do this most effectively the following procedures and regulations should be established:

1. Keep adjacent areas free of dirt, mud, etc.
2. Fence the field for better control of access.
3. Prohibit smoking and carrying food onto the field.
4. Repair minor damage promptly.
5. Observe load limits.
6. Provide trash and litter cans.
7. Cover the artificial turf with a tarp when the area or field is not being used for several weeks.

FIELD COVERS

There are certain ways of extending the life of the artificial surface. For instance, using field covers minimizes exposure to the sun and helps keep the field clean.

There are several types of field covers available today. The most durable cover or tarpaulin is made of vinyl-coated nylon. This type is expensive ($12,000 to $15,000 to cover a football field), but it will last for many years.

The cheapest type of cover is a black, construction-grade polyethylene, available in rolls up to 40 ft wide and 200 ft long and costing a few cents a square foot. The disadvantage of this type is that it is subject to rips and tears and may have to be partially replaced each season.

Another material which is more expensive but will give several years' service is called Griffolyn. It is made by laminating two layers of polyethylene around a light-weight nylon scrim. The nylon gives it the added tear strength.

HOW TO CLEAN ARTIFICIAL TURF

The first aim in maintaining artificial turf is to keep it clean. It is essential to remove dirt and trash immediately and not let it build up to excessive levels which will endanger not only the turf but those who play or use the area. The cleaning process consists of:

1. Normal cleaning
2. Removal of stains
3. Snow and ice removal
4. Water removal
5. Paint removal

Normal Cleaning Normal cleaning procedures are best done with either a sweeper (Fig. 9.7) or a vacuum. The vacuum is an excellent machine to lift paper and trash from the artificial turf, but a combination vacuum-brush type of sweeper is more efficient in picking up finer foreign particles.

The sweeper selected should have synthetic fiber bristles such as nylon or polypropylene with a minimum length of $2\frac{1}{2}$ in. and a maximum bristle diameter of 0.030 in. There should not be any metal fibers

Fig. 9.7 A low-cost, efficient, walk-behind power sweeper that utilizes both a vacuum system and a revolving cylindrical brush. The vacuum system collects dust and helps pick up light litter while the brush dislodges clinging particles and handles heavier, bulky debris. This unit, model 140, sweeps a 29-in. path and covers up to 15,000 ft²/hr. (*Tennant Company.*)

in the brush, because they could fall out, damaging the playing surface and causing injuries to those using the area. The brush should be set so that it just touches the top of the turf surface, agitating the surface enough to permit the sweeper suction to pick up the resulting dust and trash. *Do not set the brush so low that it digs into the pile fiber or backing fabric.* Excessive amounts of dirt resulting from high water or dust storms are best removed with a high-pressure water hose. Since it is possible that any sweeping operation may require several passes, any sweeper weighing more than 300 lb should have pneumatic tires with a maximum tire pressure of 30 lb/in.^{2}

Exhaust fume stains and grease and oil spills should be cleaned up immediately. Such spots can be cleaned effectively by mopping up with a clean rag moistened with a suitable spot remover, e.g., an approved dry-cleaning fluid for nylon carpet, then washed with a mild detergent followed by a generous water rinse.

An electric-powered sweeper must be properly grounded for use on artificial turf.

An artificial turf should be cleaned as needed. A rule of thumb might be to clean at least once a week where the field is used regularly. A major wet cleaning may be required once or twice a season, depending upon use and exposure.

The artificial surface can be cleaned effectively by using a good neutral household detergent and plenty of hot water applied by means of a mechanical wet-type carpet-cleaning machine. Such cleaning should be followed with a thorough rinsing of hot water to remove all traces of the detergent. The solution should be made up of 6 oz of detergent to 1 gal of water or as specified by the maker of the cleaning equipment.

Following the above procedure, it is a good plan to scrub or sponge again with a 2% solution of ammonium hydroxide (household ammonia) in hot water. *Always rinse thoroughly after use of any cleanser or detergent.*

Removing Stains Most nonoily or nongreasy stains can be removed with a detergent and water mixture, followed by a clear water rinse and blotting dry with clean rags or paper towels. Such stains are:

Beer	Grape juice	Milk
Butter	Ice Cream	Mustard
Cocoa	Ketchup	Tea
Coffee	Margarine	Tomato juice
Cola	Merthiolate	Watercolor
Food Coloring		

Most oily or greasy stains can be removed with mineral spirits or dry-cleaning fluid by moistening a clean cloth with the solvent and then sponging the area. Sponge from the outside toward the center. ***Do not pour solvents directly on the turf, since excessive solvents will tend to spread the stain rather than remove it.*** Some solvents are flammable; proper precautions should be taken. Typical oily and greasy stains are:

Asphalt	Crayon	Rubber cleat marks
Ball-point ink	Floor wax	Shoe polish
Chewing gum*	Lipstick	Suntan oil
Cooking oil	Motor oil and grease	

The materials recommended for use in removing stains are a granular household detergent in water (Tide, All, Vel, Dreft, etc.), mineral spirits or a grease-spot remover, a commercial dry-cleaning fluid, or white distilled vinegar in equal amounts of water. This latter will neutralize animal wastes.

Snow and Ice Removal It is generally best to allow snow and ice to melt off naturally. However, there are times, e.g., when a football game is scheduled, when snow or ice must be removed. It should be done as close to game time as possible to prevent reaccumulation of more snow or ice. There are two methods in general use today, snow blowers and chemicals. If a snow blower is used, the following procedures should be observed:

1. The first pass of the blower should be down the center of the field.
2. The second pass is made at the edge of either side of the first pass and the snow deposited into a truck.
3. Continue down one side and up the other, loading the snow into trucks as you plow.
4. All remaining snow is cleaned off with a mechanical broom.

If a snowplow is used, equip one with a 4- to 6-in.-wide rubber tip. Wood, metal, or other rigid blades should not be used because of the danger of digging into the surface. The following procedure should be observed:

1. Adjust blade to proper height.
2. Push snow into windrows.
3. Load into truck with a front-end loader.
4. Use a mechanical broom to clean the remaining snow.
5. Ice can be removed by using a small lawn roller to break up the ice and then use the above procedure.
6. Use only pneumatic tires at 30 lb/in.^{2} or lower pressure on all mechanical equipment.

* Chewing gum is a common hazard and can be removed by using dry-cleaning fluid or by freezing with dry ice or an aerosol pack of refrigerant.

7. Keep tarps off field in freezing weather because they cannot be removed easily when frozen.

If chemical melter procedures are used, the residue must be washed off the field (weather permitting) before it is used. Many chemicals usually used for ice melting, e.g., rock salt, ammonium nitrate, and calcium chloride, could irritate players' skin, damage the surface, or corrode equipment. The only safe chemical is prilled urea, fertilizer grade. The spread rate is determined by the amount of ice present, but usually 100 lb per 3000 ft^2 is acceptable. The urea should be left in place for at least $\frac{1}{2}$ hour or until the ice melts and then removed from the field with water. This may leave behind a thin layer of urea and may cause more slippery conditions in wet weather. As soon as possible after the freeze, the field should be washed down with water to remove final traces of the urea.

Water Removal Usually most areas covered with artificial turf are shaped and sloped enough to provide good drainage. However, there are times when it may be necessary to remove water faster than normal drainage will provide. There are three methods in general use today, rubber squeegees for small areas, a water brush, and a water-removal machine.

A rubber squeegee is supplied in various sizes at mill or janitor-supply houses. Some are large enough to be fitted to a jeep or small tractor. Care must be exercised to avoid gouging the surface. Wood, metal, or rigid squeegee blades should not be used.

The water brush is a device designed by Monsanto for use with Astro-Turf fields. It will fit a standard three-point hitch on any farm tractor having a power takeoff (such as a Ford model 2000, or equivalent). This rotating brush will move water from the center of the field to the edges without throwing excessive spray.

The water-pressure machine (Astro Zamboni) is used in large stadiums for rapid water removal. It will remove standing water from a baseball field in less than 1 hour. The machine is a high-capacity wet vacuum system on a self-propelled vehicle. Holding tanks and discharge pumps throw the collected water approximately 40 ft to either side of the machine. This system is also used to remove soilage and debris that can be loosened from the turf with water.

Paint Removal The key to removal of paint from artificial turf is to control the initial application of the paint. Excessive amounts are wasteful and abrasive to players and require extra work in their removal. Paint-removal methods are determined by the type of paint used, and each turf supplier has its own types of paint and removal techniques.

For all types, however, the most important factor in removal is how the paint was applied. Consult the turf and paint suppliers for detailed application and removal techniques.

Repair of Artificial Turf Surfaces

LARGE-AREA REPAIR

Procedures have been developed for the repair of damaged artificial turf without requiring extensive replacement of the surfaces. The following procedures are recommended:

1. Identify area to be repaired and outline, using colored chalk.
2. Prepare a template of lightweight steel plate cut into a rectangular or square shape at least 3 in. wider than the damaged surface and place it over the damaged area, parallel to the direction of the roll of artificial turf.
3. Hold template firmly in place and with a sharp carpet knife or utility knife cut through the turf, using the template edge as a guide. The knife should be at right angles to the surface. Do not cut through into the padding.
4. After all four sides are cut through, begin to peel the surface off the pad starting at one corner. If it becomes difficult to peel the turf from the pad, use a 4-in.-wide sharp putty knife to assist in the peeling.
5. Inspect the underpad, and if spots have been damaged, cut them out and plug immediately.
6. Separate the turf surface from the pad around the four sides of the cut for a 4-in.-wide border by using a sharp knife or putty knife. Use sandpaper to smooth any rough spots on the pad.
7. Insert a strip of seaming tape under the separated area, letting 3 in. of tape project beyond the turf edges. Be sure that the seaming tape is flat and does not overlap at the four corners.
8. Remove seaming tape and apply adhesive (Tan Mastic* or Vorite 677-M-3) to the pad using a 4-in. notched trowel with $^{3}/_{16}$-in. teeth for a width of 7 in., ensuring that the adhesive is tight against the inside of the turf.

* Tan Mastic is made by H. B. Fuller Co., 315 South Hicks Road, Palatine, Ill. 60067. Vorite 677-M-3 is made by Industrial Chemicals Division, NL Industries, 40 Avenue A, Bayonne, N.J. 07002.

9. Next insert prefitted seaming tape onto adhesive and press firmly, using a 4-in. putty knife.
10. Cut a new piece of artificial turf by using the template. Cut on a smooth surface with the pile face down.
11. Fit the new piece of turf to the area to be repaired, trimming wherever necessary with scissors or razor knife. Remove fitted patch and apply adhesive to the seaming tape and the pad area, using a $^{3}/_{16}$-in. notched trowel.
12. Press the fitted patch firmly into place.
13. Apply sufficient weight to the patched area to hold the patch firmly against the pad. Allow the weight to stay in place for at least 18 hours. Place the weighted (cement blocks) object on top of plywood for this operation.

SMALL-AREA REPAIR

Minor damage can be repaired by a simple plugging procedure:

1. After identifying the area to be patched, cut out and remove the piece of damaged turf. The cut should be at least 3 in. in diameter. Do not cut into the pad.
2. Peel back the edge of the turf around the cut area for about 3 in., using a sharp putty knife. Sand off rough spots on pad.
3. Cut and fit seaming tape to the damaged area so that it covers the entire area including the peeled-back area.
4. After assuring a good fit, remove the tape and spread the adhesive (Tan Mastic) over the entire area.
5. Replace the tape and press into place.
6. Using a 3-in. round die cutter, cut a new patch from new material, place over tape, and fit properly in place.
7. Remove patch and apply adhesive over entire area, replace patch, and weight down for about 18 hours.

SEAM REPAIR

1. After determining the length of the open seam, separate the turf from the seaming tape 1 in. beyond the open seam and sand off rough spots.
2. Swab area to be rebounded with MEK (methyl ethyl ketone).
3. Spread adhesive on top of seaming tape with a narrow putty knife and press the loose turf back into place.
4. Weight down using a piece of $^{3}/_{8}$-in. plywood with cement blocks on top. Remove weights after 18 hours.

CUT SURFACES (SLIT)

1. Lift turf from pad 2 in. around cut and sand off rough spots.
2. Apply adhesive to the pad and insert a new piece of seaming tape which has been cut to fit the area.
3. Apply adhesive to the top of the seaming tape and press into place. Weight down for 18 hours using $^3/_8$-in. plywood and cement blocks.

Static and Rolling Loads

Artificial turf should not be overloaded at anytime. It is recommended that no static load of more than 50 $lb/in.^2$ be placed on artificial turf. It is acceptable to use rolling loads of up to 30 $lb/in.^2$ at occasional intervals.

If it becomes necessary to erect platforms or stages, it is recommended that long-term static loads be held to a maximum of 150 $lb/ft.^2$ Sheets of $^3/_4$-in. exterior plywood or pieces of 2 by 10 lumber may be used to spread major loads. The turf should be protected with a clean tarp under such load spreaders.

TENNIS COURT MAINTENANCE*

The emerging popularity of tennis places new strains upon the park superintendent, the maintenance supervisors, and all those responsible for the proper upkeep of the courts. Poor maintenance will affect the degree of play and could affect the safety of those using the courts. The following guidelines are presented to help those who do not have a detailed knowledge of the construction of tennis courts and to further high maintenance standards.

Caution These are only guidelines and may not be proper under all conditions. Each case should be examined on its own merits and the proper materials used as specified for that particular area.

Prior to the construction, refurbishing, or repair of damaged tennis courts, it may be necessary to determine the extent of minor or major damage to the base

* Information in this section was compiled with the assistance of the U.S. Tennis Court and Track Builders Association (USTC & TBA) and adopted from their copyrighted "Tennis Court Repair Guide, 1974" (approved May, 1975). Since information on the repair of tennis courts is so complex and differs greatly from one area to another, it is recommended that readers refer to the Association for the latest information.

construction, leveling course or surface course. This is normally accomplished by a soils/materials testing laboratory and/or soils engineer at the discretion and expense of the owner.†

General

Tennis courts may be divided into two categories, pervious-constructed courts and impervious-constructed courts.

PERVIOUS CONSTRUCTION

These are courts built of materials through which water can pass, e.g., clay and grass courts and Fastdry (fine crushed aggregate) courts.

IMPERVIOUS CONSTRUCTION

These are courts which are built of materials which do not permit water to pass through but permit it to run off into a drainage system. Courts of this type may be classified into noncushioned and cushioned construction.

Noncushioned Courts These are constructed of concrete or asphalt. The asphalt courts are constructed from several types of materials:

Hot plant mix
Emulsified asphalt mix
Combination hot plant and emulsified asphalt mix
Penetration macadam

Cushioned Courts These are constructed of asphalt-bound systems, such as:

Hot leveling course and hot cushion course
Hot leveling course and cold cushion course
Cold leveling course and cold cushion course

Before beginning any repairs of a court a thorough examination of the condition of the court should be made. This examination will assess the amount and degree of damage the court has sustained and permit a logical approach to the problem of determining the proper repairs required. It is always best to consult an *approved tennis court contractor and the manufacturer* of the material to be used in the resurfacing or patching operation.

† U.S. Tennis Court and Track Builders Association, "Tennis Court Repair Guide, 1974."

Since most tennis courts in use today are constructed from impervious materials, only repairs to such courts will be discussed here.

Surface Damage

Most of the breakdown or damage to a hard-surfaced court results from faulty construction, i.e., from poor materials improperly applied, poor base preparation, extremes of temperature changes, frost damage, etc. Damages resulting from these factors may be classified as follows.

ALLIGATOR CRACKS

These cracks (see Fig. 9.8), also known as checking or map cracking, are generally caused by (1) soft subgrade material, (2) improper drainage

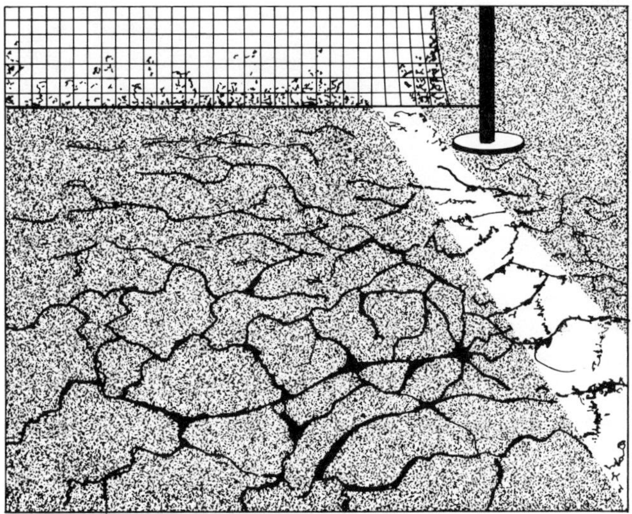

Fig. 9.8 Alligator cracks. (*USTC & TBA.*)

in the subgrade, (3) drying out of the surfaces, (4) surface course—that is too thin, or (5) a base course lacking in structural strength. Such cracks should be spot-sealed with the proper bituminous mixture as soon as the cracks appear regardless of the time of year. It is essential that the surface be sealed to prevent surface water from entering the subgrade and doing more extensive damage.

SURFACE DETERIORATION AND RAVELING

Raveling and spalling (Fig. 9.9) are essentially caused by the same defects as listed for alligator cracks with the added defect of inadequate or poor mix design. The loss of surface material caused by weathering and/or traffic abrasion is best described as an erosion of the fine aggregates first; as the erosion progresses, larger and larger aggregates are washed away, leaving a rough and jagged surface. Repairs are made essentially the same as for alligator cracks except that more bituminous material and larger aggregate is used. In severe cases of raveling a complete surface treatment should be used.

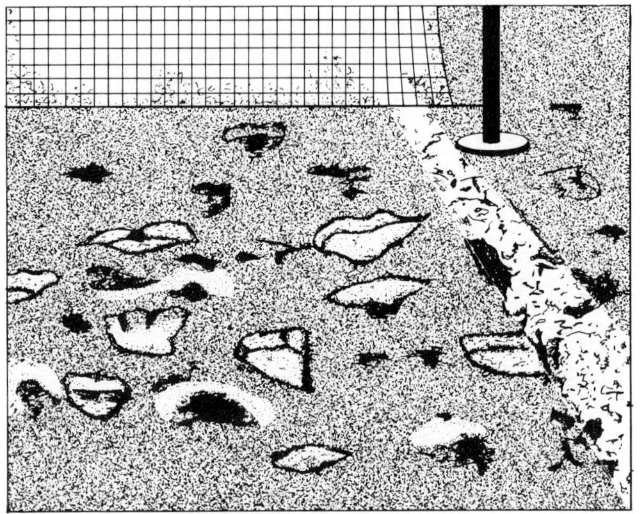

Fig. 9.9 Raveling. (*USTC & TBA.*)

POTHOLES

Potholes are caused by inadequate surface maintenance, by an uneven distribution of bituminous material, or by the movement of the base due to inadequate thickness of a yielding subgrade. Refer to Chap. 8 for the proper methods of repairing potholes. The materials to be used, however, should conform to those used for tennis court construction (see Figs. 8.1 to 8.3).

CORRUGATIONS OR SHARP IRREGULARITIES

Surface damage of this kind may be described as reflection cracks, shrinkage cracks, structural, upheaval, and hairline cracks.

Reflection Cracks (Fig. 9.10) These occur in asphalt overlays and reflect the crack pattern in the pavement structure underneath. They are caused by vertical or horizontal movements in the pavement beneath the overlay resulting from severe temperature fluctuations and/or earth movements.

Shrinkage Cracks (Fig. 9.11) These cracks frequently follow the construction joints of the original pavement. They may be caused by a volume change in the asphalt mix or in the base or subgrade.

Structural Cracks (Fig. 9.12) These cracks are usually due to a base failure or an improper mix design. The only way to keep them from reappearing is to rebuild the base and the surface treatment completely.

Fig. 9.10 Reflection cracks. (*USTC & TBA.*)

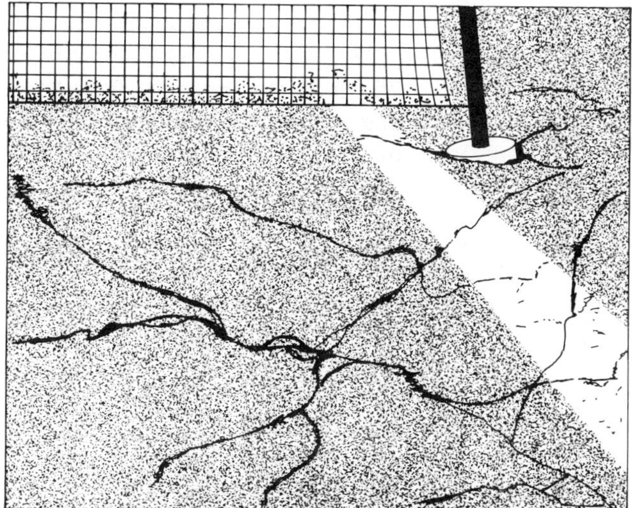

Fig. 9.11 Shrinkage cracks. (*USTC & TBA.*)

Upheaval (Fig. 9.13) Frost expansion in the subgrade is the common cause of an upheaval of the pavement, usually resulting from poor drainage below and around the court area.

Hairline Cracks (Fig. 9.14) As the name implies, these are very small cracks in the pavement surface; if left unrepaired, they may develop

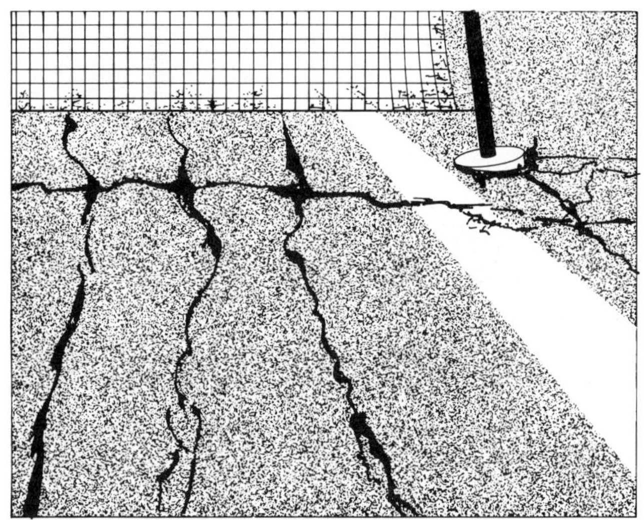

Fig. 9.12 Structural cracks. (*USTC & TBA.*)

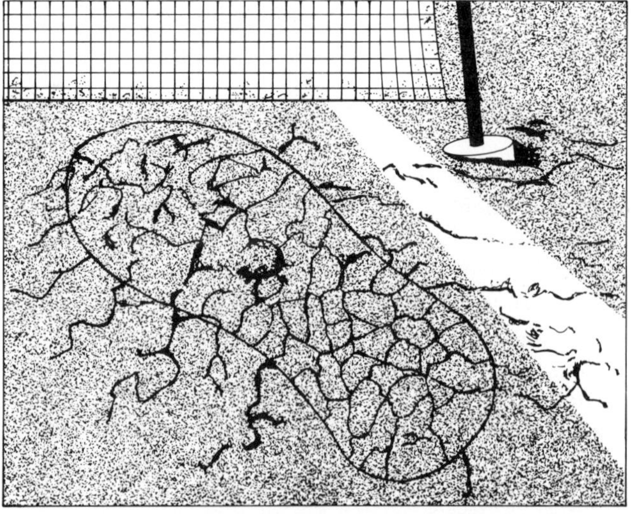

Fig. 9.13 Upheaval (movement of subbase). (*USTC & TBA.*)

into more significant cracks. They are caused by several factors, e.g., improper mix design, improper seal coats, solvent-type coatings, and the prevalance of foreign matter (leaves, worms, clay). It will usually require a leveling course of the proper bituminous mix to repair the above irregularities adequately. The existing surface should be thoroughly cleaned and surface breaks spot-sealed before the leveling course is applied.

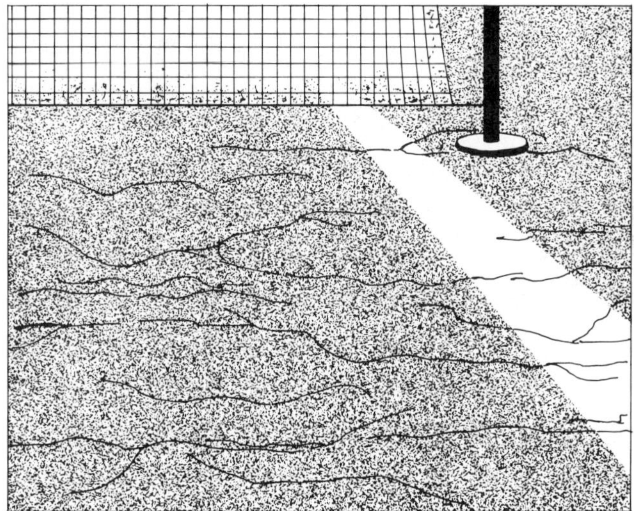

Fig. 9.14 Hairline cracks. (*USTC & TBA.*)

Settlements and Deformation

These are usually caused by (1) lack of adequate subgrade support, (2) slipping or movement of the fill, (3) inadequate thickness of the base, and (4) structural obsolescence.

A settlement or deformation may be defined as a "bird bath," a small depression in the surface which allows water to stand after a rain or flooding the courts, waiting until the surrounding areas have dried. Any remaining water which is deeper than a 5-cent piece is then considered repairable. Anything shallower is considered within tolerance and will evaporate within a reasonable amount of time.

The slope for nonporous outdoor courts should be 1 in. in 10 ft. To repair courts properly they must have the proper pitch to minimize the retention of water.

Repair Methods

HOT-ASPHALT OVERLAY METHOD

This system in combination with a tack coat can be done successfully over a court that has minor faults. It consists of placing a ½- to 2-in. hot plant asphalt mix over an existing deteriorated asphalt surface in accordance with USTC & TBA specifications type VI, section 8 for gradation recommendations. This system, however, will not prevent the reappearance of structural cracks.

PATCHING

Before doing any patching, clean the surface thoroughly of all loose material, dust, and dirt. All defective materials should be removed to

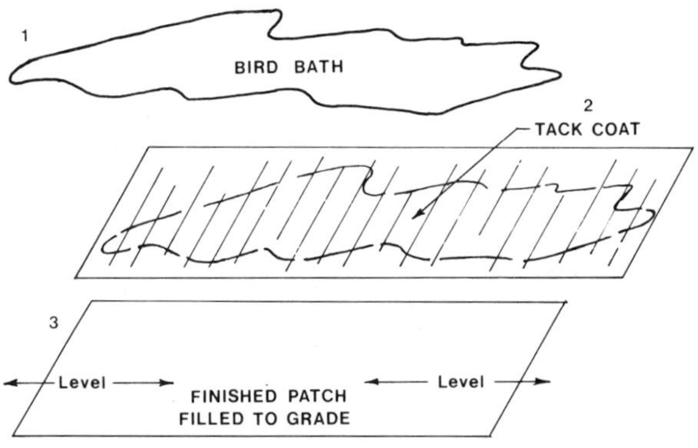

Fig. 9.15 Patching. (*USTC & TBA.*)

the full depth of the defect. If the underlying base course is also defective, it should be removed. If examination of the subgrade shows that it is also defective, it should be removed and replaced with the proper material and brought to specification requirements. The base-course material should then be replaced before patching any of the asphaltic courses supported by the base course. A tack coat should be applied to the bottom and the sides of the patch and allowed to cure thoroughly (see Fig. 9.15).

Patches Exceeding ⅜ in. in depth A patch which exceeds ⅜ in. in depth in old asphalt or portland cement concrete pavements can be repaired with hot plant asphalt concrete. For any patches which are deeper than 1 in., apply the patch in two lifts.

Any patch which is made in two lifts should have an additional tack coat applied to the surface of each lift. Compact each lift to its maximum density by tamping or rolling. Bring the final compacted lift to the elevation of the surrounding sound surface (see Fig. 9.16).

Patches $^3/_8$ in. or Less in Depth Outline with chalk all areas which retain enough water to cover a 5-cent piece; then sweep the water out. After the area is dry, apply a tack coat to the entire area within the chalkline.

Various emulsifying asphalt and acrylic materials can be used to patch the area. Apply the proper amount to the area and stroke off with a straightedge, the length of which is in excess of the dimensions of the patch. This strike-off should level the patch to the same elevation as the surrounding surface. Allow the patch to cure properly.

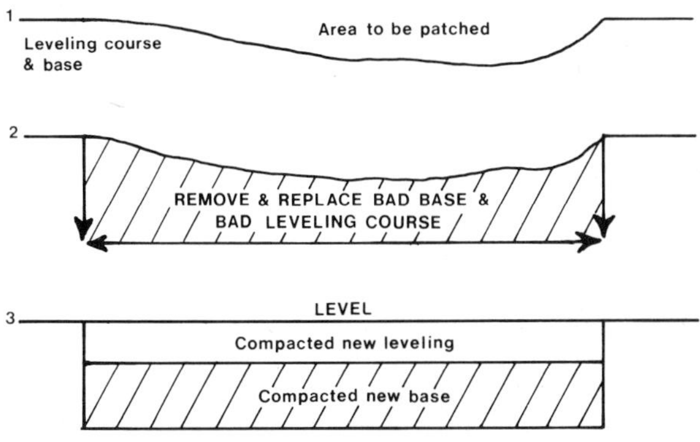

Fig. 9.16 Full-depth patch. (*USTC & TBA.*)

FIBER-GLASS AND/OR JUTE-MEMBRANE SYSTEMS

Several products, e.g., fiber glass or jute membrane, can be used to restore the surface of certain types of damaged courts and provide a smooth, dense, weathertight playing surface. These materials should be installed according to the manufacturer's specifications. These treatments, however, do not restore badly cracked or broken surfaces; nor do they permanently seal cracks subject to base movement.

GOLF COURSE MAINTENANCE

Golf courses have become increasingly popular as a means of relaxation and recreation. The degree of maintenance given a golf course affects how a person plays. Because of high costs and increasing materials costs it behooves all those responsible for the design of golf courses to use all available methods to eliminate time-consuming maintenance tasks.

Planning and Construction

A new golf course should be well planned beginning at its inception. A poorly sited or designed course will suffer from high construction costs and high maintenance costs. The initial steps are of great importance. For instance, before beginning construction the following information should be available:

1. General description of the area to be developed and its location
2. Data on soil conditions, tree removal, and the use of natural resources
3. Information on its effect on the environment and the local community
4. Yards of soil to be moved
5. Construction of necessary roads, parking areas, lakes, and bridges
6. Availability of power, water, and sanitary facilities
7. Capacity of water supply
8. Amounts of lime and fertilizer needed
9. Amounts of grass seed and bushels of stolons needed
10. Number and kinds of maintenance equipment needed
11. A rough layout of the course
12. Number and type of structures required
13. Preliminary estimate of cost of construction

Selection of Site

It is essential to engage the services of a competent golf course architect if it has been decided to proceed with the planning and construction of a golf course. The architect should have the opportunity of assisting in the selection of a site. He will be able to provide a great deal of information and assistance in selecting a site which can be obtained for a reasonable cost and which can be built for a minimum cost and properly maintained at minimum expense. Since most golfers are only average players, the layout or design of the course should be moderate but should be designed so that it can be adapted to all types of players.

An area which is naturally gently rolling with some tree cover is desirable. The minimum amount of land required for a nine-hole course is 50 acres, but 80 acres is much more desirable. The minimum acreage required for an 18 hole course is 110 acres, but 160 acres would be much better. The greater acreage will allow more room between fairways, thereby minimizing the danger to players and providing more opportunities for saving such natural features as trees, water, abrupt changes in grade, etc.

The area selected should have sufficient land to provide adequate space for the clubhouse, access roads, parking, a practice fairway,

Fig. 9.17 A golf course which has utilized a major construction site as its locale. Topography, layout, and planting were all man-made. Niagara Falls Municipal Golf Course. (*Power Authority of the State of New York.*)

putting greens, shops, and maintenance area (Fig. 9.17). The more elaborate courses now provide much wider recreational facilities such as tennis courts, swimming pools, and areas for picnicking and barbecues. Excess land around the course may be donated to the town or state for development or preservation as open space or for soil conservation.

SOIL FACTORS

In selecting a site for a golf course the condition of the soil should be taken into consideration. Since a golf course must maintain a good turf, it is essential that the site have a reasonably good soil as a base. For instance, a site which has been kept up as pasture land over the years is preferable to one which has been abandoned. Such a site may be developed at much less cost than one which takes poor land and tries to develop good turf or good playing conditions. The maintenance costs on the latter then become extremely high. Of course, the best soil for a golf course is a sandy loam, but unfortunately this cannot always be found. In any event, it is always a good idea to have a thorough soil analysis made before the property is purchased. The state agricultural departments of county agents can provide invaluable information and assistance. It is always wise to consult with them before acquiring a site.

ACCESSIBILITY

Another factor which should be taken into consideration when selecting a site is its accessibility. The course should be located on a good paved road, reasonably close to populated areas (taking into consideration the land cost), which will provide good access for not only the club members but for transients as well. Many courses depend heavily on greens fees to help defray the costs of maintenance, and so it is essential that the course have good access.

UTILITIES

Site selection involves the availability of power and water. Water supply is essential if the course is to be kept green and attractive at all times. A good supply of water must come from either municipal water-supply systems or from local sources, e.g., natural ponds, lakes, rivers, streams, or underground sources.

Electric power is usually available from the local power company.

Since disposal of sanitary wastes is always a problem, site selection again becomes an important factor. The location of a golf course close enough to tie into local sanitary systems is usually difficult, and the course must therefore provide its own sanitary system. To do this effectively the soil must be capable of providing good percolation.

Today it is possible to recycle the water effluents from the larger sanitary systems into the course irrigation system. This provides much-needed water without placing a strain on the supply of natural water. During periods of drought this becomes an important factor in keeping the course green. This program is still experimental and will be effective only if there are large quantities of water available from a sanitary system. In all probability, only municipal courses can take advantage of this type of system at this time.

NATURAL FEATURES

Site selection should look for possible natural golf features or hazards, e.g., rolling terrain, woodlands, creek valleys, ravines, and ponds. If the site lacks such features, artificial hazards must be provided at, of course, greater cost both initially and for maintenance.

Golf Course Design

After the site has been selected and all necessary data have been reviewed, the plans and design of the course should begin, approximately along the following lines:

1. Prepare strip plans showing all greens, fairways, tees, and other features of the entire course.
2. Locate the clubhouse, access road, and parking area.
3. Locate the practice fairways and putting green.
4. Locate all other features, such as tennis courts, swimming pool, picnic areas, etc.
5. Locate the turf nursery, maintenance, and work shops.
6. Prepare detailed irrigation and drainage plans.

Following the preparation of the final plans a procedure of project guidance should be set up as follows:

1. Appoint a construction supervisor and establish a headquarters of operation.
2. Prepare a guidance manual and time schedule.
3. Prepare a detailed construction budget.
4. Make arrangements for the use of construction equipment.
5. Determine the availability of manpower.
6. Obtain soil-test reports.

The next step is to determine the materials and documents needed for the operation and maintenance of the course.

1. Maintenance equipment
2. Maintenance programs for watering, fertilizing, mowing, pest control, aerification, and top dressing

Turfgrass Selection

The selection of the best turfgrass is very important for the normal improvement and maintenance of a golf course.

COOL-WEATHER GRASSES

The standard cool-weather grass used in all temperate climates has been Kentucky bluegrass, but the inherent problems of disease, mowing, and wear have always been troublesome. This old standby cannot be mowed closer than $1\frac{1}{2}$ to 2 in. if it is to thrive. Neither will it withstand constant wear of foot and cart traffic. It is also subject to many diseases, e.g., powdery mildew, rusts, leaf smuts, and leaf spots.

Over the past 20 years there has been a great improvement in Kentucky bluegrass through the development of many more serviceable cultivars. The following list of Kentucky bluegrass cultivars and their principal characteristics will provide a measure of selectivity for deciding which is the best grass to use under specific conditions:

Baron bluegrass This is a dark-green, medium-textured grass of low growth. It has a rapid establishment rate and greens up rapidly in spring. It has good resistance to disease.

Fylking bluegrass This is a dense, fine-textured, dark-green grass. It will tolerate a short cut but is best maintained at a cut of 1 to $1\frac{1}{2}$ in. It has good resistance to disease.

Merion bluegrass This is one of the earliest cultivars developed and has been in widespread use. It is a dense, dark-green, low-growing grass with a rather broad leaf. It will tolerate a rather short mowing height. Unfortunately it is susceptible to most turf diseases.

Newport bluegrass This cultivar is comparable to Merion in appearance. It is slow to establish but has excellent fall color. It has fair to good resistance to disease.

Pennstar bluegrass This cultivar is similar to Fylking and is a dense, dark-green, fine-textured grass. It will tolerate a rather short cut. It has a good to fair resistance to disease.

Warren A-20 bluegrass This is a medium-textured, dense, dark-green grass. It will withstand short mowing very well, which makes it ideal for tees. It has a good resistance to disease.

Windsor bluegrass This is a dense, dark green, vigorous and low-growing grass. It has a finer texture than Merion but unfortunately only fair to poor resistance to disease.

Other cool-weather grasses sometimes used in combination with the bluegrasses are the fine-leaved fescues. The most common of these is known as Pennlawn, which has a good tolerance to disease and is very adaptable to turf mixtures. Refer to Chap. 2 for further discussion on the creeping red fescues.

Two recently developed Chewings fescue grasses are also adaptable for use in turf mixtures:

Golfrood A narrow-leaved grass with good color, disease resistance, and turf quality.

Jamestown A dark-green grass which is tolerant to close mowing and resistant to some diseases, e.g., leaf spots.

New perennial ryegrasses are being developed which now blend well with the fine-textured grasses. There are three, Manhattan, Pennfine and Pelo, which are receiving wide use. These cultivars produce a leafy, fine-textured turf that will resist heat and drought and withstand a relatively short cut. They blend well with Kentucky bluegrass.

The Bent Grasses The finest and the most commonly used cool-weather grass for golf greens, putting greens, bowling greens, etc., is the bent grass. There are two species of bent grass in principal use today; Colonial bent grass (*Agrostis tenuis*) and creeping bent grass (*A. palustris*). A third species, velvet bent grass (*A. canina*), is limited in use because of its specific soil and climatic requirements. Refer to Chap. 2 for further information on the bent grasses.

There are several bent grass cultivars available today:

- Seeded creepers:
  - Emerald
  - Penncross
  - Seaside
- Colonial (seeded noncreepers):
  - Exeter
  - Astoria
  - Hofior
  - Boral
  - Highland
- Vegetatively propagated creepers:
  - Pennpar
  - Cohansey
  - Toronto

Disease control is the most important part of maintaining a bent grass turf. Brown patch, dollar spot, pythium, snow mold, and helminthosporium can cause severe damage or even complete loss of the turf unless properly controlled with chemicals.

The greatest challenge to bent grass is the very agressive inroads of annual bluegrass (*Poa annua*), which thrives under the close mowing and high fertilization and irrigation levels maintained for a bent grass turf. Control is difficult and spotty. Applications of arsenicals have been effective in the past but have become very expensive to use. The best economical cultural practice for the control of *Poa* is to irrigate only at the point of wilt and to use a low- (or no-) phosphorus fertilizer program.

WARM-WEATHER GRASSES

The warm-weather grasses are nearly all vegetatively propagated by shredded sprigs, sod, or plugs. The most popular varieties that are used in the south for tees, greens, and fairways are the Bermuda and zoysia grasses, discussed in more detail in Chap. 2.

Bermuda grass This is a deep-rooted grass which makes a good general-purpose turf where adapted. The common Bermuda grass is the most widely used mainly because it is more economical to establish and maintain. However, there are new cultivars which although they have higher maintenance requirements, have much better wear tolerance and a high recuperative potential.

Although there are many cultivars of Bermuda grass only four are discussed here:

Tifdwarf This is a dwarf, slow-growing grass which is very good on golf greens because of its close mowing tolerance. It has small, short, dark-green leaves and an excellent hardiness to low temperatures. It has good disease resistance but is susceptible to the sod webworm and smog injury.

Tifgreen This is a good, dark-green, fine-textured, disease-resistant grass which is widely used for golf greens and fine lawns in the southeast. It has a good low-temperature hardiness and greens up rapidly in the spring. Although it has good resistance to disease, it is susceptible to armyworms, sod webworms, and scale insects.

Tifway This is a dark-green, stiff-leaved grass which has a low-growing characteristic, making it good for use on fairways and tees. It does have a thatch problem.

Tifcote This is a vigorous, low-growing, stiff-leaved grass with a dark-green color. It is widely used on sports fields.

The Zoysias The zoysias are tough grasses that withstand heavy traffic and partial shade. This is used primarily for lawns and general-purpose turf on fairways and tees. Zoysia is a dense, slow-growing grass which turns brown with the first cool weather in fall. It is slow to be established, taking from 1 to 3 years, depending upon how close the plugs are planted. There are three varieties generally in use today:

Emerald This is a fine-textured, dark-green grass that forms a dense turf. It is an excellent hot-weather and drought-resistant grass with excellent wear qualities. It requires a high fertilizer application.

Meyer This is a dark-green, medium-textured grass with a good low-temperature hardiness. It is superior to Emerald in its drought-resistant qualities. It also requires high fertilizer applications.

Midwest This is a dark-green, medium-textured grass but has a better spring green-up rate and retains its color longer during low-temperature periods.

Early Maintenance Planning

The organization, operation, and maintenance of the completed course should be left up to the club officers and directors. The maintenance of the grounds is the responsibility of the golf course superintendent, who will be responsible for the efficient maintenance of the course. The procedure of keeping records, which was followed during construction, should be continued with the maintenance phase. Detailed records of all liming, fertilizing, weed control, irrigation, aerification, topdressing, and mowing should be kept.

The position of the superintendent is very important. He must:

1. Be responsible for area maintenance (golf course, roads, parking areas, driving range, etc.)
2. Be responsible for structure maintenance (buildings, fences, bridges, shelters, etc.)
3. Select and arrange for the purchase, storage, inventory, and maintenance of equipment
4. Select and employ all necessary personnel
5. Select and arrange for the purchase, storage, inventory, and use of all materials needed to maintain the course
6. Keep records of cost, weather, etc.
7. Prepare budgets
8. Make all necessary reports
9. Provide good landscape maintenance
10. Attend conferences of superintendents associations, turf conferences, USGA conferences, etc.

Factors Reducing Maintenance

There are many ways in which the design will affect the cost of maintenance. Such things as the size and shape of tees, greens, bunkers, etc., all have an effect on the degree of maintenance required.

TEES

Tees should be large. The elevated area should be made to blend into the surrounding terrain by means of long, gentle slopes. Tees should be long (generally more than 100 ft) in order to permit more flexibility and frequent rotation of the tee markers. Corners and sharp breaks in contour should be avoided and corrected. These considerations affect the ease of maintaining tees with larger units of power equipment and permit the use of such equipment without scalping. Space should be provided adjacent to the tee for parking of golf cars and carts to prevent their infiltration onto the tee.

FAIRWAY AND GREENS BUNKERS

Bunkers which do not affect the strategy of play and those which penalize the high-handicap golfer should be eliminated. Fairway bunkers should be built so that the sand is visible, well drained, and gently sloped. It is easier to maintain the areas surrounding bunkers if the edges are smooth rather than scalloped. The sand in the bunker should not pack down hard when wet or be so fine that it will blow away when dry.

GREENS

The green should be large enough to provide plenty of space for changing the location of the cup. Generally green sizes vary from 5000 to 8000 ft^2. The green should harmonize with the surrounding landscape, avoiding abrupt ridges, high knobs, steep slopes, and depressed, valley-like runways as a part of the construction. The location of the bunkers around the greens should be far enough from the putting surface to keep sand off the green and to allow sufficient room to turn mowing equipment. Drainage is very important. Avoid seepage of the green drainage into the trap. If water is allowed to stand in the trap above the level of sand, it makes an unsatisfactory playing condition. This can be avoided by constructing adequate drains in the bunker to take away surplus water.

FAIRWAYS

Fairways average about 60 yd in width, depending upon the site and the terrain. The fairway should be well drained so that play and maintenance equipment are not stymied by wet spots. The turf should be durable, well fertilized and limed, and properly mowed at the correct height. Refer to Chaps 2 to 6 for information covering the subjects of maintenance of turf, disease and insect control, weed control, and equipment maintenance. Plant materials should be used carefully to prevent their interference with maintenance and play. Trees should be spaced so that there is no necessity for small mowing equipment. Shrubs should not be used out on the course but should be restricted to use around the clubhouse, parking areas, etc.

Routine Maintenance Practices

Some maintenance procedures should be routinely performed by the course maintenance personnel:

1. Develop a regular fertilization program for the course which is based on the type of turf and on soil tests.
2. During dry periods establish a regular procedure of watering to maintain quality turf. The turf should be watered deep (6 to 8 in.) and only when absolutely necessary. Frequent light sprinklings, especially in late afternoon or early evening, do more harm than good.
3. Do not let thatch accumulate over ½ in. Remove excess thatch by using a vertical mower, power rake, or similar equipment. Thatch should be removed in spring or fall.
4. On closely mowed turfs, such as greens, control thatch by:

   Topdressing Topdressing with a soil mixture will encourage thatch decomposition and improve a poor green over a period of time.

   Coring Coring is the mechanical removal of soil plugs from the sod with spoons or tines. These soil plugs are left on the surface and then worked back into the sod. This method will greatly improve water and air penetration.

   Spiking and slicing This method is not particularly effective in thatch control, but it does result in a limited amount of thatch removal.

Clipping removal This has always been considered essential in controlling thatch, but studies have shown that grass clippings decompose rapidly and have little to do with thatch buildup.

Vertical mowing This is probably the most widely used of the methods of thatch control.

5. Cut the green, and in fact all turf, as often as necessary so that no more than one-third or one-fourth of the leaf surface is removed at one mowing.
6. Aerify compacted areas and protect them from traffic until they have become established.
7. Establish an insect- and weed-control program. See Chaps. 5 and 6 for further information.
8. Construct a good surface and subsurface drainage system. Fill in low spots where water may stand.
9. Use fungicides as recommended by the manufacturers. Turf fungicides which are presently available are Daconil 2787, Dyrene, Ortho Lawn and Turf Fungicide or Ortho Lawn and Disease Control, Fore, Tersan LSR, Actidione-Thiram, benomyl, and Kromad.
10. Mow greens at $^{3}/_{16}$ to $^{5}/_{16}$ in. in height; tees at $^{1}/_{2}$ to 1 in. in height; and fairways $^{1}/_{2}$ to $1^{1}/_{2}$ in. in height. The creeping grasses such as bents, Zoysia and Bermuda can be clipped at $^{1}/_{2}$ to $^{3}/_{4}$ in.

Fig. 9.18 A power riding greens mower which is equally effective as a spiker or thatcher, Toro Greensmaster 3. (*Toro Company.*)

Fig. 9.19 An efficient, versatile sprayer for golf course work. (*The F. E. Myers & Bro. Co.*)

Fig. 9.20 Toro Sand Pro, which rakes and conditions sand, spikes greens, does fine grading, scarifying, shaping, and contouring of seedbeds, edges around traps, incorporates top dressing, and breaks up aerifier cores. (*The Toro Company.*)

Maintenance Equipment

The amount and type of maintenance equipment considered essential for proper maintenance of 9- and 18-hole golf courses vary from area to area. Table 9.2 shows the recommended minimum.

TABLE 9.2
Minimum Maintenance Equipment for Golf Courses*

9-hole course	18-hole course
Tractors and trucks	
1 farm-type tractor 1 golf course tractor 1 Jeep or pickup truck 1 farm-type tractor with front-end loader	1 farm-type tractor 1 or 2 golf course tractors 3 or 4 turf trucksters 1 Jeep or pickup truck 1 construction tractor with front-end loader and backhoe or trencher attachment 1 dump truck
Mowing equipment	
3 power greens mowers or 1 riding mower 2 power tee mowers 1 3-unit power gang mower 1 24- or 30-in. rotary mower 1 or 2 18- or 21-in. rotary mowers 1 power lawn mower 1 5-gang or 7-gang fairway mower 1 5-gang rough mower 1 80-in. rotary mower with leaf-mulcher attachment 2 hand mowers	6 power greens mowers or 2 power riding greens mowers (Fig. 9.18) 3 power tee mowers 1 or 2 24- or 30-in. rotary mowers 1 or 2 3-unit power powers 2 or 3 18- or 21-in. rotary mowers 1 or 2 power lawn mowers 2 or 3 power vertical mowers 1 or 2 7-gang fairway mowers 1 5-gang or 7-gang rough mower 1 80-in. rotary-type mower with leaf mulcher attachment or 1 6-ft hammer-mill mower with leaf mulcher or 1 5-ft sickle-bar attachment for tractor 2 or 3 hand mowers 1 power edger and trimmer mower
Maintenance equipment	
1 power sprayer with 150-gal tank, 15 gal/min pump, 150-ft high-pressure hose, orchard gun, mistogun, and spray boom attachment 1 junior size power sod cutter 1 power air broom 1 power aerifying machine (green and tee) 1 power thatch-control machine 1 power shredder 1 power portable centrifugal pump with suction hose 1 power spike disc 1 16-in. electric hedge trimmer 1 hand or powered topdressing machine 1 topdressing mat	1 power sprayer with 200-gal tank, 15–25 gal/min pump, 150-ft high-pressure hose, orchard gun, mistogun, and spray boom attachment (Fig. 9.19) 1 power sod cutter 1 or 2 power air brooms 1 power sand rake (Fig. 9.20) 1 power aerifying machine (greens) 1 power aerifying machine (tees) 1 or 2 power thatch-control machines 1 power shredder 1 power portable centrifugal pump with suction hose 1 rotovator 1 power spike disc 1 16-in. electric hedge trimmer

* Compiled by Golf Course Superintendents Association of America and reproduced by their permission.

TABLE 9.2
Minimum Maintenance Equipment for Golf Courses (*Continued*)

9-hole course	18-hole course
Maintenance equipment	
1 8-ft fertilizer spreader	1 hand or powered topdressing machine
1 36-in. fertilizer spreader	2 topdressing mats
1 proportioner	1 8-ft or 10-ft fertilizer spreader
1 tractor-drawn aerifying machine	1 rotor-type fertilizer spreader
1 hand lawn mower	1 or 2 36-in. spreaders
1 hand leaf sweeper	1 or 2 proportioners
1 snow plow for Jeep or tractor	1 tractor-drawn aerifying machine
1 steel drag mat	1 or 2 tractor-drawn trailers
2 cyclone seeders	1 hand lawn roller
1 soil screen	1 hand or power leaf sweeper
1 power chainsaw	1 snowplow for Jeep or truck
	1 set of chains for Jeep or truck
	1 steel dragmat (Fig. 9.21)
	2 cyclone seeders
	1 soil screen
	1 power chainsaw
	1 grader blade
Golf course equipment and tools	
1 hole cutter	2 hole cutters
27 hole cups	36 hole cups
1 cup extractor	2 cup extractors
1 cup setter	2 cup setters
9 poles and flags	18 poles and flags
18 practice green markers	18 practice green markers
3 sets tee markers	3 sets tee markers
5 or 9 golf-ball washers	9 or 18 golf ball washers
6 dozen tee towels	6 or 12 dozen tee towels
5 or 9 waste retainers	9 or 18 waste retainers
9 tee benches	18 tee benches
1 divot repairer	1 or 2 divot repairers
1 4-in. plugger	1 or 2 4-in. pluggers
1 8-in. turf repairer	1 8-in. turf repairer
1 soil-sampling tool	1 soil-sampling tool
1 bundle bamboo poles	1 bundle bamboo poles
1 wheelbarrow	1 wood wheelbarrow
1 8-ft stepladder	1 steel wheelbarrow
1 20-ft extension ladder	1 8-ft stepladder
	1 20- or 30-ft extension ladder
	1 measuring wheel
	3 mole traps
	1 transit

Hand tools

Axes	Bilge pump	Bush hook
Crowbars	Cultivators	Five-prong forks
Garden hoes	Grape hoes	Grass shears

TABLE 9.2
Minimum Maintenance Equipment for Golf Courses (*Continued*)

9-hole course		18-hole course
Hand tools		
Hay rakes	Iron rakes	Lawn rakes
Lopping shears	Mattocks	Mortar hoes
Picks	Pole pruner	Posthole digger
Pruning saws	Pruning shears	Pushbrooms
Scales	Scoops	Scuffle hoes
Sickles	Sledgehammers	Sod lifters
Shovels, pointed	Shovels, square	Shovels, snow
Spades	Spading forks	Stone fork
Tamps	Turf edgers	Wedges
Wood rakes		
Shop tools		

1 portable steam cleaner
1 air compressor with 50-ft hose, spray paint gun, filter, regulator, tire gage, and blowgun
1 mower-reel grinder
1 bed-knife grinder
1 portable lapping machine with compound
1 bench grinder
1 1½-ton chain hoist or mobile hydraulic floor crane
1 1½-ton mobile hydraulic jack
1 3-ton hydraulic jack
4 axle stands
1 portable drum on stand for cleaning equipment
1 spark plug cleaner and tester
1 battery charger
1 electric and 1 acetylene welding unit
1 ¼-in. heavy-duty electric drill
1 ½-in. heavy-duty electric drill
1 drill stand with press
1 electric impact wrench with kit
1 6¼-in. skill saw
1 high-speed drill set
1 tap and die set
1 or 2 vises
Complete set of plumbing tools including wrenches, threaders, cutters, reamers, taps, soldering tools, blowtorch, etc.
Complete set of carpentry tools including hammers, saws, chisels, screwdrivers, levels, planes, bits, rulers, etc.
Complete set of machinery tools including screwdrivers, hacksaws, pliers, calipers, cold chisels, bolt cutters, punches, files, monkey wrenches, ignition wrenches, etc.
Complete set of socket, box-end, and open-end wrenches
Complete set of masonry tools including trowels, hammers, markers, mixer, etc.
Complete set of tools for engine repair including valve lifters, valve compressors, ring compressors, battery tools, pullers, etc.
Miscellaneous shop supplies and tools such as oil cans, grease cans, gas cans, paintbrushes, wire brushes, tire irons, funnels, etc.
4 drawer units for storage of bolts, nuts, screws, nails, washers, etc.
1 shelving unit for paints, etc.

TABLE 9.2
Minimum Maintenance Equipment for Golf Courses (*Continued*)

9-hole course	18-hole course
Watering system for tees, greens, and fairways, manual system only	
Pipe estimate:	Pipe estimate:
6-in., 1000 ft	6-in., 2150 ft
4-in., 5000 ft	4-in., 11,300 ft
3-in., 3000 ft	3-in., 10,000 ft
2-in., 2000 ft	2-in., 10,000 ft
$1\frac{1}{2}$-in., 10,000 ft	$1\frac{1}{2}$-in., 15000 ft
1 pump, capacity 500 gal/min (125 lb pressure)	2 pumps, for total of 1000 gal/min (125 lb pressure)
Sprinkler equipment:	Sprinkler equipment:
85 fairway valves	185 fairway valves
6 fairway sprinklers	12–18 fairway sprinklers (manual)
	200 fairway sprinklers (automatic)*
45 tee and green valves	95 tee and green valves (manual)
10 tee and green sprinklers	20–36 tee and green sprinklers
	120 tee and green sprinklers (automatic)*
5 hose sprinklers	12–18 hose sprinklers
	6–8 electric controllers (automatic system)*
9 50-ft sections 1-in. hose	1000–1800 ft 1-in. hose
2 drinking fountains	4 drinking fountains
Maintenance buildings	
Equipment storage building and shop, 4000 ft² (including office, 200 ft², locker lavatory for men 200 ft²)	Equipment storage building and shop, 6000 ft² (including office, 300 ft², and locker and lavatory for men 300 ft²)
Compost and fertilizer building 2000 ft²	Compost fertilizer building 3000 ft²
Office equipment	
1 office desk and chair	
3 chairs	
1 filing cabinet	
1 bookcase	
1 air conditioner or window fan	
1 map of golf course	
Supplies for the golf course	
Seed or vegetative material for greens	
Seed or vegetative material for tees	
Seed or vegetative material for fairways	
Seed for rough	
Fertilizer for greens, tees, and fairways	
Lime for greens, tees, and fairways	
Insecticides, fungicides, and herbicides	
Soil sterilizer	
Humus, topsoil, and coarse sand	
Topdressing	

* To convert a manual system to an automatic system these items should be added.

Use of Plant Materials

The use of plant materials on a golf course depends largely upon whether the course was constructed on open land or cut from wooded area. In some instances the course might have been constructed on part wooded and part open land.

A course with a natural tree growth will need very little in new planting. However, if a radical change has occurred, like cutting a fairway through a wooded area, it will in all probability create a change in the en-

Fig. 9.21 The drag mat used in combination with the Sand Pro. (*The Toro Company.*)

vironment. The water table will be effected, which in turn will tend to kill large trees. If this occurs, a program of removal of dead trees and a replanting of new trees should be planned.

A course planned and designed in open land will require new plantings of trees and shrubs which will eventually provide effective separation of fairways, sound and sight barriers, and aesthetic improvement of the course. Planting should use only materials indigenous to the area.

The following suggestions may be helpful in planning a planting program.

Sight and Sound Barriers There are areas which if planted to the proper combination of evergreen and deciduous trees will help to reduce the sight and sound effects of continuous play. These areas may be described as follows:

1. Separation of the course from adjoining private property
2. Separation of roads and parking lots from the course
3. Separation of the adjoining tee and green

In these areas it is advisable to use group plantings of evergreen and deciduous trees, with a mixture of small flowering trees to provide the type of screen which will be both useful and attractive. The type of plant to use depends upon the location, but as a general rule pines, spruce, and hemlock are the base for evergreen planting, oak, maple, beech, linden the base for deciduous planting, and the dogwoods, redbud, hawthorn, etc., the base for plantings of small flowering trees.

Functional Areas The functional areas are those which separate the active play areas from other activities provided.

Between Fairways Most fairways built in areas entirely devoid of trees need some planting of trees and shrubs in order to provide protection to players on adjoining fairways, for aesthetic reasons, and to delineate the direction and line of the fairway. These plantings should be informal groupings, planted in a naturalistic manner. The type of planting would be the plants indigenous to the area, which may include practically all species of evergreens, most species of large deciduous trees, the dogwoods, crabapples, goldenrain tree, cherry, redbud, etc., and the mountain laurels, rhododendrons, native azaleas, viburnum species, etc.

Between Clubhouse and Parking Lot Usually there is an open space which separates the clubhouse from the parking lot. It is always desirable to try to screen this area so that the parking lot is not visible from the clubhouse. The size of this area largely depends upon the layout of the area, and its size will therefore dictate what kind and size of material to use. This is a good place to use plant materials which provide color as well as a screen and for bird cover and feeding. This type of planting uses the berry and fruiting plants: firethorn, hawthorns, crabapples, Japanese barberry, buckthorn, cotoneasters, etc. Effective evergreens include the Japanese yews, junipers, laurel, rhododendron, and azalcas.

Play and Lounge Areas, Swimming Pool, Terraces Depending upon their design and location in the general plan, the areas would be planted with a combination of native and ornamental plants. Some shade trees would be used, but for the most part, the plantings would consist of low shrubs, ground covers, and an occasional flowering tree. The spreading junipers, dwarf yews, azaleas, hypericums, roses, holly, and boxwood are some suitable plants.

Background Some areas will require background plantings to screen out objectional views, to form a background to a green which is bordering a property line or highway, and to show off plantings of flowering trees and plants. Evergreens are generally used, e.g., hemlock, spruce, fir, and pine.

Enframement There will be areas which will require plantings to frame a distant view or provide a visual effect on an approach to the clubhouse or to a green. Many plants can be used, e.g., dogwood, crabapple, birch, magnolia, flowering cherry, Russian olive, goldenrain tree, amur maple, hawthorn, etc.

Shade For the course which does not have a natural tree growth there will be a need for shade trees near tees, terraces, and play areas. Trees to use would be those indigenous to the area, but as a general rule, the oaks, maples, sweet gum, and lindens (little-leaf) are the old standbys.

Average Course-Maintenance Costs for 18-Hole Course

The cost of maintaining a golf course will vary greatly from one area to another. To arrive at a reasonable cost, figures published in the 1975 February issue of *Golfdom* and actual cost figures of a local golf club were reviewed. The figures in Table 9.3 are *averages* established by the author.

TABLE 9.3
Average Golf Course Maintenance Costs

Item	High	Low	Average
Salary: superintendent	$ 20,000	$ 7,000	$15,500
Laborers	57,000	20,500	40,000
Sand and soil purchased	1,400	450	800
Chemicals	8,000	1,500	4,400
Fertilizer and seed	10,000	2,500	6,300
Gasoline, oil, and grease	3,750	1,000	2,500
Machinery and equipment, purchased	5,000	500	2,500
Repairs	5,200	900	3,500
New green or course rebuilding	6,000	200	2,500
Landscaping and flowers	3,500	300	2,000
All other grounds and greens expense	15,000	500	5,000
Total expenses	$134,850	$35,350	$85,000

GLOSSARY

Annual A plant that completes its life cycle in 1 year, germinating from seed, producing seed, and dying in the same growing season; *see also* winter annual.

Awn A slender bristle found at the ends of the lemmas or scales of some grasses.

Axil The angle between a branch or leaf and its stem.

Basal treatment An application to the stems of plants at and just above the ground line.

Berm A shoulder or flat area separating two steep slopes.

Biennial A plant that completes its life cycle in 2 years. The first year it produces leaves and stores food; the second year it blossoms and produces fruits and seeds.

Bract A leaf giving rise to a flower at its axil.

Broadleaf plants Plants with wider leaves than the grasslike plants.

Brush control Control of woody plants.

Bulb A subterranean bud with a short, thick stem, rootlets, and overlapping leaves.

Butt The larger end of a log.

Callus The tissue that forms over any wound on the surface of a stem.

Cambium The tissue that gives rise to new growth in the stems and roots of shrubs and trees.

Cant hook A wooden lever with an adjustable iron hook, for use with logs.

Carpel A modified leaf, which by the folding together and union of its edges forms a closed receptacle for the ovules.

Carrier The liquid or solid material added to a chemical or formulation to facilitate preparation, storage, shipment, or use in the field; *see also* diluent.

Chamfer To bevel the edges.

Chert An impure, flintlike rock.

Compatible Capable of being mixed without harmful effects; or two compounds or products that can be mixed without affecting each other's performance.

Concentrate A condensed formulation usually diluted with water or oil before use. Also, in a product name, the strongest commercially available formulation of the active ingredient.

Concentration The amount of active material in a given weight of a mixture or volume of a solution. Recommendations and specifications for concentration of agricultural chemicals are frequently given on the basis of pounds per unit volume of mixture or solution.

Contact herbicide A weed killer that acts primarily by contact with plant tissue rather than as a result of translocation, affecting only that portion of a plant with which it is in direct contact. Young seedlings are killed, but perennials may recover from the uninjured parts below ground.

Corm A bulblike stem, with scale leaves, which bears buds at the summit.

Course A horizontal layer.

Creosote An oily liquid used as an antiseptic and deodorizer.

Crown The top of a tree, including living branches and foliage.

Culm The jointed stem of a grass.

Deciduous Shedding leaves at the end of a growing period.

Decumbent Lying on the ground, but with vertical tips; used of stems or shoots.

Defoliant A material that causes the leaves to fall from plants; e.g., a spray used to remove leaves from cotton plants just before harvest.

Diluent Any liquid or solid material serving to dilute or carry an active ingredient or formulation.

Disc To cultivate with a disc harrow or disc cultivator.

Dormant spray A chemical applied in winter or very early spring before treated plants have started active growth.

Emulsifying agent A material that helps to suspend globules of one liquid in another, e.g., oil in water.

Emulsion A mixture in which one liquid is suspended in minute globules in another liquid, e.g., milk or an oily preparation in water.

Fibrous root system A system composed of profusely branched roots with many lateral rootlets and often with no main or taproot development.

Fumigant A chemical used in the form of a volatile liquid or gas to kill insects, nematodes, fungi, bacteria, seeds, roots, rhizomes, or entire plants; usually employed within an enclosure or in the soil.

Gall A swelling of a plant tissue caused by parasite attacks.

Germination The start of vegetative growth, usually from a seed.

Girdle A circle made by removing the bark around the trunk, usually fatal to the tree.

Glabrous Smooth and hairless.

Glume A bract, especially one at the base of a grass spikelet.

Grout Thin mortar used for filling in the joints of masonry, brickwork, or brick or stone pavements.

Heartwood The hard center wood of a tree trunk.

Herbaceous plant A plant that remains soft or succulent and does not develop woody tissue.

Herbicide A chemical for killing weeds.

Lemma The lower bract enclosing a grass flower.

Miscible Capable of being mixed; usually refers to liquids.

Neutral soil A solid neither acid nor alkaline, with a pH of 7.0.

Nonselective herbicides Chemicals or formulations which destroy or prevent plant life in general without regard to species.

Noxious weed A weed arbitrarily defined by law as undesirable, troublesome, or difficult to control.

Oils References are usually to aromatic or paraffinic oils used in formulating products as diluents or carriers for herbicides, or for direct use.

Palmate Having lobes placed about a common center.

Panicle Any pyramidal loosely branched flower cluster.

Peavy A lever ending in a sharp spike, similar to a cant hook.

Perennial A plant that continues to live from year to year. In many, in cold climates the tops die but the roots and rhizomes persist.

Pesticide Any substance or mixture of substances intended for controlling insects, rodents, fungi, weeds, and other forms of plant or animal life considered to be pests.

Petiole A stem supporting a leaf blade.

Pinnate Having parts arranged along the two sides of an axis.

Pith The spongy tissue within a stem.

Postemergence treatment Treatment made after plants emerge above the soil surface.

Preemergence treatment Treatment made after a crop is planted but before it emerges. Contact preemergency treatment is made after weed emergence but before crop emergence. Residual preemergence treatment kills the weeds as the seeds germinate or as they emerge, either before or after crop emergence. Application is made before crop emergence.

Pubescent Hairy. Pubescence affects ease of wetting of foliage and retention of spray on foliage.

Raceme A flower cluster.

Rate or *dosage* These terms are synonymous. Rate is the preferred term and usually refers to the amount of active ingredient material applied to a unit area (such as one acre) regardless of percentage of chemical in the carrier.

Residual Having a continued killing effect over a period of time.

Resistant Tolerant. Resistance of weeds determines the rates of weed-killer application required for control.

Rhizome Underground rootlike stem that sends out roots and leafy shoots.

Rootstock A rhizome.

Runner A decumbent branch that forms a new plant by rooting at the joints or end.

Sapwood The younger wood just beneath the bark.

Shoulder Either edge of a road, exclusive of pavement.

Slag The nonmetallic residue of smelted ore.

Spall A chip or fragment.

Spray drift The movement of airborne spray particles from the intended contact area to other areas.

Spud A sharp, narrow spade.

Spudding Digging, removing, or otherwise treating with a spud.
Square blading Blading at right angles.
Stamen The organ of a flower that bears the fertilizing cell.
Stem The part of a plant above ground that supports leaves, flowers, or fruit.
Stolon A runner or rootstock, or a piece of either, used to propagate a grass.
Style A prolongation of the ovary that supports the stigma, where pollen grains are received.
Sump A pit or depression serving as a drain or receptacle for fluids to be further disposed of.
Suspension A liquid or gas in which very fine solid particles are dispersed but not dissolved.

Template A pattern.
Tolerance In connection with pesticides, the amount of a pesticide chemical allowed by law to be present in or on a food product sold for human consumption.
Tolerant Capable of withstanding effects. For example, grass is tolerant of 2,4-D to the extent that this herbicide can be used selectively to control broadleaf weeds without killing the grass.
Toxic Poisonous; injurious to animals or plants through contact or systemic action.
Tuber A short, fleshy, usually underground stem or shoot bearing minute scale leaves with buds, or eyes, in the axils.

Volatility injury Injury from herbicide vapors.

Wattle A framework made of flexible rods.
Weed eradication The elimination from an area of all live plants, plant parts, and seeds of a weed infestation.
Winter annual A plant that starts from seed germination in the fall, lives over winter, and completes its growth, including seed production, the following season; *see also* annual.
Woody plants Plants that develop woody tissue.

APPENDIX

TABLE A.1
pH scale*

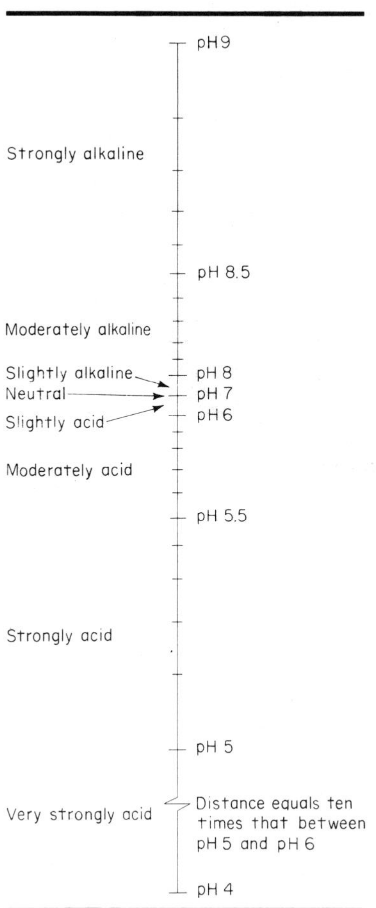

* The pH scale for soil reaction shows the tenfold increase in relative acidity or alkalinity for each unit change in pH. For example, pH 6.0 is 10 times more acidic than pH 7.0; pH 5.0 is 10 times more acidic than pH 6.0 and 100 times more acidic than pH 7.0.

TABLE A.2
Equivalents for Liquid Measure (Volume)

Gallons	Quarts	Pints	Fluid ounces	Cupfuls	Tablespoonfuls	Teaspoonfuls	Milliliters
1	4	8	128	16			
	1	2	32	4			
		1	16	2	32		
			1	1/8	2	6	30
				1	16	48	240
					1	3	15
						1	5

TABLE A.3
Land-Measure Equivalents

Ft^2	Acre
43,560	1
1,000	1/43
100	1/435

TABLE A.4
Metric Equivalents of Units in the U.S. Customary System

Unit	Metric equivalent	
	Approximate	Exact
	Length	
1 in.	2.5 cm	2.54 cm
1 ft	0.3 m	0.3048 m
1 yd	0.9 m	0.9144 m
1 rod	5 m	5.029 m
1 chain	20 m	20.117 m
1 furlong	200 m	201.17 m
1 mi	1600 m	1609.3 m
1 nautical mile	1850 m	1853.2 m
	Area	
1 in.^{2}	6.5 cm^2	6.451 cm^2
1 ft^2	0.09 m^2	0.0929 m^2
1 yd^2	0.83 m^2	0.8361 m^2
1 square rod	25 m^2	25.29 m^2
1 rood	1000 m^2	1011.7m^2
1 acre	0.4 hectare	0.4047 hectare
1 mi^2	258 hectares	258.99 hectares
	Volume	
1 in.^{3}	16.5 cm^3	16.387 cm^3
1 ft^3	0.028 m^3	0.028316 m^3
1 yd^3	0.76 m^3	0.7645 m^3
100 ft^3	2.8 m^3	2.8316 m^3
1000 board feet (M)	2.25 m^3	2.36 m^3
1 cord	3.6 m^3	3.624 m^3
1 pt (liquid)	0.47 l	0.473 l
1 qt (liquid)	0.9 l	0.946 l
1 gal (liquid)	3.7 l	3.785 l
1 peck	9 l	8.81 l*
1 bushel	36 l	35.24 l†
	Weight	
1 grain	0.0648 g	0.0648 g
1 oz (troy)	21 g	31.103 g
1 oz (avdp)	28 g	28.35 g
1 lb (avdp)	0.45 kg	0.4536 kg
1 wheat bushel (60 lb)	27 kg	27.216 kg
1 coal bushel (80 lb)	36 kg	36.287 kg
1 cental (100 lb)	45 kg	45.36 kg
1 hundredweight (112 lb)	50 kg	50.8 kg
1 net ton	0.9 metric ton	0.9072 metric ton
1 gross ton	1 metric ton	1.016 metric ton

* English 9.08 l.

† English 36.35 l.

TABLE A.5
Characteristics, Pruning, Insects, and Diseases of Evergreen and Deciduous Shrubs

Botanical and common name	Description	Conditions and habits of growth	Pruning and other remarks	Insects and diseases
Abela grandiflora—Glossy abelia	4–5 ft Flowers (pink): June–Nov.	Likes either sun or shade, in a light peaty soil. Pendulous growth. Foliage is small, glossy, and is evergreen in South.	Remove old flower heads and thin the plant out occasionally. The shrub needs no regular pruning.	No serious pests or diseases.
Amelanchier canadensis—Downy shadbush	20–25 ft Flowers (white): March–April in South May in North Fruit (purple): May–June	Likes either sun or ½ shade, limestone soil. Open spreading growth. Fruit is sweet.	No specific pruning is necessary.	Pear leaf blister Mite—willow scale
Ampelopis quinquefolia—Virginia creeper	30–40 ft Flowers inconspicuous Fruit (blue): Sept.–Oct.	Likes sun or ½ shade in good loam soil. Has aerial roots and twining stems.	Requires no specific pruning. Has scarlet fall foliage.	Eight-spotted forester. Sphinx caterpillars
Ampelopsis quinquefolia Engelmanni—Engelmann creeper	30–40 ft Flowers inconspicuous Fruit (blue): Sept.–Oct.	Likes sun or ½ shade in good loam soil. Has aerial roots and twining stems.	Requires no specific pruning. Has smaller foliage than type.	Eight-spotted forester. Sphinx caterpillars
Aronia melanocarpa—Black chokeberry	4–6 ft Flowers (white): Apr.–May Fruit (black): June–July	Both like either sun or ½ shade and a dry rocky soil. Upright growth. Good autumn color.	No specific pruning is necessary. Shape plant in winter by removing old or dead branches.	No serious pests or diseases..

Botanical and common name	Description	Conditions and habits of growth	Pruning and other remarks	Insects and diseases
Aronia arbutifolia Brilliantissima Red chokeberry	6–8 ft Flowers (white): Apr.–May Fruit (red): June–July	Both like either sun or ½ shade and a dry rocky soil. Upright growth. Good autumn color.	No specific pruning is necessary. Shape plant in winter by removing old or dead branches.	No serious pests or diseases
		Evergreen azaleas		
Azalea amoena— Amoena azalea	5–6 ft Flowers (purple): Apr.–May	Likes sun or ½ shade, woodsy, humus soil. Browns in winter in North.	Prune only to shape plant. Prune in winter. Where planted outside its native woods habitat, maintain acid soil condition by mulching with acid peat moss, well-rotted sawdust, or oak leaves. Also by application of an acid fertilizer.	Mulberry white fly
Azalea hinodegiri— Hinodegiri azalea	3–4 ft Flowers (carmine-pink): May	Likes sun or ½ shade. Woodsy, humus soil.	as above	Leaf blister fungi
Azalea hinomayo— Kurume azalea	3–4 ft Flowers (pink): May	as above	as above	Peony scale Lace bug
Azalea indica— India azalea	4–5 ft Flowers (pure white): May	as above	as above	Stem borer Azalea leaf miner
Azalea ledifolia— Snow azalea	2–3 ft Flowers (snow white): May	as above	as above	Spider mites

TABLE A.5
Characteristics of Shrubs (cont.)

Botanical and common name	Description	Conditions and habits of growth	Pruning and other remarks	Insects and diseases
		Deciduous azaleas		
Azalea calendulacea— Flame azalea	4–10 ft Flowers (yellow to flame): May–June	Likes sun or ½ shade. Woodsy loam soil. Has an open and delicate growth.	See Azalea amoena	Black vine weevil
Azalea kaempferi— Torch azalea	8–10 ft Flowers (red): Apr.–May	Same as above but with a dense and spreading growth.	as above	Fuller's rose beetle
Azalea mollis— Chinese azalea	4–6 ft Flowers (wide range of reds): May	Ditto; will thrive in limestone soils.	as above	
Azalea nudiflora— Pinxter bloom	5–6 ft Flowers (pink): Apr.–May	as above	as above	
Azalea poukhanensis— Korean azalea	3–4 ft Flowers (lavender): May	as above	as above	
Azalea arborescens— Sweet azalea	6–10 ft Flowers (white): June–July	Same as above but bushy and fragrant.	as above	
Azalea mucronulata— Manchurian azalea	5–6 ft Flowers (rosy purple): April	Same as above but upright and a very early bloomer.	as above	
Azalea rosea— Downy pinxterbloom	6–8 ft Flowers (pink): Apr.–May	Same as above but spreading.	as above	
Azalea schlippenbachi Royal azalea	5–6 ft Flowers (pale pink): May	Same as above, spreading and with large accented blooms.	as above	

Botanical and common name	Description	Conditions and habits of growth	Pruning and other remarks	Insects and diseases
Azalea viscosa—Swamp azalea	4–6 ft Flowers (white): June–July	Likes a wet soil and is thick and bushy. Latest azalea to bloom. Fragrant.	as above	
Benzoin aestivale—Spice bush	8–10 ft Flowers (pale yellow): March–Apr. Fruit (spicy red): Autumn	Likes moist ground in sun or ½ shade. Is upright and dense. Foliage yellow in fall.	No regular pruning necessary.	No serious pests or diseases.
Berberis thunbergi—Japanese barberry	4–6 ft Flowers (yellow): April Fruit (red): Sept.–Feb.	Likes full sun in good loam soil. Dense and bushy. Red autumn foliage.	Does not require regular pruning. Remove dead wood in old stock. Clipped hedges should be pruned 2 to 3 times a year. Top of hedges should be narrower than bottom to encourage dense growth.	Barberry aphid
Berberis Julianae—Wintergreen barberry	4–5 ft Flowers (yellow): Apr.–May Fruit (black): Sept.–Oct.	Likes full sun in good loam soil. Shiny, prickly foliage. Evergreen.	Does not require regular pruning.	
Berberis verruculosa—Warty barberry	2–3 ft Flowers (yellow): May–June Fruit (violet black): October	Likes full sun in protected places. Fruit fragrant. Evergreen.	as above	Asiatic garden beetle
Berberis sinensis—Chinese barberry	4–6 ft Flowers (yellow): May–June Fruit (purple): September	Likes full sun in good loam soil.	as above	Barberry worm

TABLE A.5
Characteristics of Shrubs (cont.)

Botanical and common name	Description	Conditions and habits of growth	Pruning and other remarks	Insects and diseases
Berberis wilsonae—Wilson barberry	2–3 ft Flowers (golden yellow): May Fruit (salmon red): Sept.	as above	as above	Red spiders Eight-spotted forester
Bignonia radicans—Trumpet creeper	30–40 ft Flowers (orange scarlet): July–Sept.	Likes sun in rich soil. Is a rapid grower and a self clinger.	Requires no specific pruning.	Has no serious pests or diseases
Buxus sempervirens—Common box	4–5 ft Flowers inconspicuous	Likes sun or ½ shade in rich loam soil. Dark green evergreen foliage.	No regular pruning is necessary. Formal hedge treatment requires shearing 2–4 times annually. Trim top of hedge narrower than bottom.	Boxwood leaf miner
Buxus japonica—Japanese box	4–5 ft Flowers inconspicuous	as above	as above	
Buxus sempervirens suffruticosa—True dwarf box	2 ft Flowers inconspicuous	Ditto; English box, slow growth.	as above	Oyster shell scale Spider mites Boxwood psyllid Giant hornet
Calycanthus floridus—Sweetshrub	3–6 ft Flowers (brown): June–July	Likes good, moist soil in shade. Thick and bushy with a remarkable fragrance.	No regular pruning is necessary.	Has no serious pests or diseases.
Celastrus scandens—American bittersweet	20–25 ft Flowers (greenish white): June Fruit (yellow and vermillion): Autumn	Likes good, average soil in sun or ½ shade. Has an irregular and tumbling growth.	Prune only to restrain plant. Makes a good ground cover for rocks and banks.	Two-marked tree-hopper Euonymous scale

Botanical and common name	Description	Conditions and habits of growth	Pruning and other remarks	Insects and diseases
Cercis canadensis American redbud	15–20 ft Flowers (rosy purple): Apr.	Likes sun or ½ shade in good woods soil. An early bloomer.	Shape plants when young, but prune as little as possible when plant is mature, removing only dead wood.	Two-marked tree-hopper
Cornus florida— Flowering dogwood	20–25 ft Flowers (white): Apr.–May Fruit (red): Aug.–Oct.	Likes sun or ½ shade in good, well-drained soil.	No regular pruning is necessary. Keep dead and diseased parts removed. Excellent fall foliage with red berries which are liked by birds.	Dogwood borer
Cornus florida rubra— Pink dogwood	12–15 ft Flowers (rosy pink): Apr.–May	as above	No regular pruning is necessary. Keep dead and diseased parts removed.	
Cornus alba— Tatarian dogwood	6–8 ft Flowers (cream-white): Apr.–May Fruit (blue-white): Aug. Oct.	Likes sun or shade in moist, good soil. Is upright and bushy with very red twigs and branches.	No regular pruning is necessary. Can be cut back severely without injury when overgrown, or can be cut to the ground in spring for bushy growth.	Dogwood scale Dogwood club-gall midge Flathead borer Leafhoppers
Cornus amomum— Silky dogwood	6–8 ft Flowers (white): May–June Fruit (blue): Aug.–Oct.	Likes sun or shade. Has an upright and bushy growth.	as above	Mulberry white fly Oyster shell scale
Cornus stolonifera— Red-osier dogwood	6–8 ft Flowers (white): May–June Fruit (white): Autumn	Likes sun or shade. Has a bushy, spreading growth with dark red branches.	as above	San Jose scale Cottony maple scale Dogwood bark-borer

TABLE A.5
Characteristics of Shrubs (cont.)

Botanical and common name	Description	Conditions and habits of growth	Pruning and other remarks	Insects and diseases
Cornus mas—Cornelian-cherry	10–12 ft Flowers (yellow): March Fruit (red): Fall	Likes sun or shade in moist, good soil. Has a dense upright growth and edible red fruit.	see above	
Cotoneaster horizonalis Rock cotoneaster	6–12 in Flowers (pink): May–June Fruit (bright red): Sept.	Likes full sun in a well-drained soil. Has a creeping habit of growth.	Does not require any specific pruning.	Lace bug Oyster shell scale San Jose scale
Cotoneaster rotundifolia Roundleaf cotoneaster	2–3 ft Flowers (white-pink): May–June Fruit (bright red): Sept.	see above	see above	
Cotoneaster divaricata—Spreading cotoneaster	5–6 ft Flowers (pink): May–June Fruit (bright red): Sept.	Likes full sun in well-drained soil. Has an upright habit of growth with spreading branches.	see above	
Crataegus cordata—Washington thorn	20–25 ft Flowers (white): May Fruit (scarlet): Sept.–Nov.	Likes sun in rich loam. Has abundant scarlet fruit.	Requires only minimum winter pruning to shape plant. Will make an excellent hedge.	Scurfy scale Eastern tent caterpillar
Crataegus oxyacantha—English hawthorn	15–20 ft Flowers (pink): May Fruit (red): Sept.–Nov.	see above	see above	Hawthorn lace bug Thorn-leaf aphid

Botanical and common name	Description	Conditions and habits of growth	Pruning and other remarks	Insects and diseases
Crataegus coccinea Thicket hawthorn	20–25 ft Flowers (white): Apr.–May Fruit (large, scarlet): Sept.–Nov.	See Crataegus cordata	See Crataegus cordata	Cottony maple scale San Jose scale Borers Spider mites Wooly aphids Thorn limb-borer
Chaenomeles Lagenaria— Flowering quince	6–8 ft Flowers (red, salmon pinkish, white): Mar.–Apr. Fruit (yellow): Oct.	Likes sun or ½ shade in a well-drained, good soil. Plant is spreading and bushy	Requires only minimum winter pruning to shape plant. If grown as a hedge, it may be cut back when the flowering period is over.	Scurfy scale
Chaenomeles Maulei Lesser— Flowering quince	3–4 ft Flowers (pink and white): Mar.	as above	as above	
Chaenomeles sinensis— Chinese quince	Up to 15 ft Flowers (light pink): May Fruit (dark yellow): Oct.	as above	as above	
Deutzia gracilis— Slender deutzia	3–5 ft Flowers (white): May	Likes sun in a well-drained, good soil, upright, round head.	Should be thinned out well once in 3 years by removing as much of the old wood as possible. The best time for this pruning is in early summer.	Leaf rollers
Deutzia lemoinei— Lemoine's deutzia	4–5 ft Flowers (white): May	as above but is spreading	as above showy large bloom	
Deutzia scabra— Fuzzy deutzia	6–8 ft Flowers (white): June–July	as above but upright	as above many upright branches	
Deutzia scabra candidissima White fuzzy deutzia	6–8 ft Flowers (double white): June	as above	as above	

TABLE A.5
Characteristics of Shrubs (cont.)

Botanical and common name	Description	Conditions and habits of growth	Pruning and other remarks	Insects and diseases
Deutzia scabra Pr. of Rochester Pink fuzzy deutzia	8–10 ft Flowers (double pale pink): June	"	"	
Eleagnus pungens— Bronze eleagnus	8–10 ft Flowers (bronze white): Oct.–Dec. Fruit (orange): Winter–Spring	Likes either sun or shade. Evergreen	Does not require regular pruning except to curb straggling habits of growth by shortening the longest shoots during summer. Green-leaved shoots that often appear among the variegated varieties should be removed.	No serious pests or diseases
Euonymus alatus— Winged euonymus	6–8 ft Flowers (yellow): May–June Fruit (purple pods): Sept.–Oct.	Likes sun in good, rich soil. Has a dense, spreading growth.	Does not require any specific pruning	Euonymus scale
Euonymus americanus Brook euonymus	6–8 ft Flowers (purplish green): June Fruit (orange and scarlet): Sept.–Oct.	Likes sun in good, rich soil. Has an upright growth.	as above	San Jose scale
Euonymus europaeus European burning bush	12–15 ft Flowers (yellow–green): May Fruit (scarlet): Sept–Oct.	as above	as above	Cottony maple scale Lilac leaf miner
Euonymus japonicus— Evergreen burning bush	8–15 ft Fruit (orange): Winter	as above Evergreen	Requires a little shaping when grown as a shrub.	

Botanical and common name	Description	Conditions and habits of growth	Pruning and other remarks	Insects and diseases
Euonymus patens—Spreading euonymus	5–6 ft Flowers (white): June–July Fruit (orange): Oct.–Nov.	as above Evergreen	Does not require any specific pruning	
Euonymus radicans—Wintercreeper	15–20 ft Flowers (greenish–white): June–July Fruit (pale greenish white): Oct.	Likes sun or ½ shade. A ground cover or vine.	When grown as a ground cover under trees or as a border for beds, it should be trimmed or cut over either in spring or summer	
Forsythia intermedia—Border forsythia	6–8 ft Flowers (yellow): Mar.–Apr.	Likes sun or ½ shade in good, rich soil. Has a slender, erect growth.	Special pruning is not necessary, except for thinning out every third year, or they may be clipped moderately each year as soon as the flowering period is over. When grown as a bush, the main branches should be allowed to grow 2–3 ft high and the secondary branches should be cut back to that height each year. This method stimulates the formation of long shoots during the summer which will be in full bloom from end to end the following spring.	No serious pests **or** diseases.
Forsythia intermedia spectabilis—Showy border forsythia	8–10 ft Flowers (yellow): Mar.–Apr.	Likes sun or ½ shade in good, rich soil. Has an upright. arching, and very showy growth.		

TABLE A.5
Characteristics of Shrubs (cont.)

Botanical and common name	Description	Conditions and habits of growth	Pruning and other remarks	Insects and Diseases
Forsythia suspensa—Weeping forsythia	6–8 ft Flowers (bright yellow): Apr.	Likes sun or ½ shade in good, rich soil. Has a pendulous growth.	as above	
Forsythia viridissima Greenstem forsythia	8–10 ft Flowers (bright yellow): Apr.	Likes sun or shade in good, rich soil. Has an erect growth with green stems.	as above	
Hamamelis virginiana—Common witch-hazel	10–15 ft Flowers (yellow): Oct.–Nov.	Likes sun or ½ shade in moist, open soil. Has an upright, bushy growth.	Prune only to shape the plants, particularly when they are young; older plants have no need of further formal pruning.	Witch hazel cone gall
Hedera helix—English ivy	60–80 ft Flowers (greenish): June Fruit (black): Sept.–Oct.	Likes sun in good rich soil. It is a dense, clinging evergreen vine, thriving on the north sides of buildings.	Ivy grown in the form of a bush may require a little shaping each year, merely removing a branch here and there. Old plants may be invigorated by cutting back in spring. If grown against walls, it should be cut back as close as possible to the walls in Feb. or March. At the same time, cut back the upper shoots well below the roof or gutters if the vine is grown on the side of a building. Also examine and cut the vine toward the beginning of July, removing long shoots that are protruding away from the wall.	Cabbage looper Soft scale Oleander scale Red spiders Aphids Long-tailed mealybug Leafhoppers Eight-spotted forester

Botanical and common name	Description	Conditions and habits of growth	Pruning and other remarks	Insects and diseases
Ilex cornuta—Chinese holly	6–8 ft Fruit (bright red): Sept.	Likes ½ shade. Has spreading branches, forming a broad, dense bush.	Do not clip back the shoots since they are naturally stiff and erect; instead, clean out some of the laterals of the shoots thus accentuating them. Holly hedges may be clipped back in the middle or end of summer.	Fall webworm
Ilex cornut burfordi—Burford holly	10–20 ft Fruit (large red): Oct.–Dec.	Likes ½ shade. Is a broad, dense tree with showy red berries in winter.	as above	Spider mites
Ilex crenata—Japanese holly	6–7 ft Flowers (white): June Fruit (black): Sept.–Apr.	Likes sun or ½ shade in good, peaty or acid soil.	Minimum pruning before spring growth to shape plant.	Holly scale
Ilex crenata convexa—Shell-leaf Jap. holly	4–6 ft Fruit (black): Sept.–Apr.	as above	Excellent for low compact hedge 1 to 2½ feet. Prune frequently to maintain hedge shape. Keep top of hedge narrower than bottom.	Citrus whitefly
Ilex crenata rotundifolia—Round-leaf Jap. holly	8–10 ft Fruit (black): Sept.–Apr.	as above	Good for medium compact hedge 3 to 4½ feet. Prune frequently to maintain hedge shape. Keep top of hedge narrower than bottom.	Holly leaf miner

TABLE A.5
Characteristics of Shrubs (cont.)

Botanical and common name	Description	Conditions and habits of growth	Pruning and other remarks	Insects and diseases
Ilex glabra—Inkberry	5–6 ft Flowers (white): July Fruit (black): Sept.	Likes a moist acid soil in ½ shade.	Minimum winter pruning only.	
Ilex verticillata—Black-alder	8–10 ft Fruit (bright red): Oct.–Dec.	Likes ½ shade. Has spreading branches.	as above	
Ilex vomitoria—Yaupon holly	5–15 ft Fruit (scarlet): Sept.–Apr.	Likes sun or shade. Can be used as a hedge.	as above	
Jasminum nudiflorum—Winter jasmine	3–4 ft Flowers (yellow): Feb.	Likes sun in rich loam soil. Has a slender pendulous habit of growth. Has green stems.	The bushy species require occasional thinning but no other formal treatment. They should have the flowering shoots cut back to within 2 buds of the base as soon as the flowers fade, but no further pruning should follow.	Has no serious pests or diseases
Jasminum primulium—Primrose jasmine	6–9 ft Flowers (yellow): Mar.–Apr.	Likes sun or ½ shade.	as above	
Juniperus chinensis pfitzeriana—Pfitzer juniper	3–5 ft	Likes sun in well-drained good soils. Has a spreading habit of growth. Has green stems.	Prune only when necessary to restrain plant.	Red-cedar bark beetle

Botanical and common name	Description	Conditions and habits of growth	Pruning and other remarks	Insects and diseases
Juniperus horizontalis—Creeping juniper	2–3 ft Light blue: Sept.	Likes sun in well-drained soils. Procumbent shrub with longitudinal trailing branches	No pruning necessary. Valued as ground cover for sandy and rocky soil.	Twig-blight Juniper webworm Bagworms Juniper scale Aphids Red spider Spruce spider mite
Kalmia latifolia—Mountain laurel	5–6 ft Flowers (white, pink): May–June	Likes partial shade, in a woodsy, loam soil. It is a broad-leaved evergreen.	The species have no need for formal pruning. Prune only to remove dead wood.	Mulberry white fly Leaf spot Leaf blight Lace bug Laurel psyllid
Kerria japonica—Kerria	4–6 ft Flowers (golden yellow): June–Sept.	Likes sun in good, rich soil. It is slender and broad and has very green branches.	Much of the older wood should be removed in order to encourage vigorous young wood. Prune as soon as the flowers fade; the previous year's wood should be slightly shortened after thinning out and the removal of old wood.	No serious pests and diseases

TABLE A.5
Characteristics of Shrubs (cont.)

Botanical and common name	Description	Conditions and habits of growth	Pruning and other remarks	Insects and diseases
Kerria japonica Flore-plena Double-flowering kerria	4–6 ft Flowers (golden yellow): June–Sept.	Ditto—Has double flowers	as above	as above
Kolkwitzia amabilis—Beauty-bush	6–8 ft Flowers (shell pink): May–June	Likes sun in good, rich soil. Has a tumbling dense growth and very abundant blooms.	Prune in winter to remove old and dead wood.	as above
Lagerstroemia indica—Crape myrtle	8–10 ft Flowers (white–pink): June–Aug.	Likes sun. Excellent flowering plant.	Minimum winter pruning to shape plant.	Crape myrtle aphid
Leucothoe catesbaei—Drooping leucothoe	2–3 ft Flowers (white): Apr.–May	Likes semi-shade in woodsy loam soil. Has a pendulous habit of growth, low branching with purple, bronze, and crimson fall foliage.	Plants treated as shrubs should have their older stems removed and the younger shoots shortened in late February before spring season starts. Shrubs grown for the color effect of their bright green barks should be cut close to the ground in March.	No serious pests or diseases
Lespedeza bicolor—Shrub bush clover	6–8 ft Flowers (purple): July–Oct.	Likes sun in good rich soil. It is slender and graceful with pea-shaped flowers.	To promote good bushy plants cut to the ground each year after they have bloomed.	as above

Botanical and common name	Description	Conditions and habits of growth	Pruning and other remarks	Insects and diseases
Ligustrum amurense—Amur privet	12–15 ft Flowers (white): June–July Fruit (black): Sept.–Oct.	Likes sun or ½ shade in average soil. It is a very hardy, upright shrub.	Does not require any formal pruning, except in hedge form.	Privet mite
Ligustrum ibota—Ibota privet	10–12 ft Flowers (white): June Fruit (black): Sept.–Oct.	Likes sun or ½ shade in average soil. Has spreading branches, upright, and with pale green foliage.	as above	Japanese scale Olive scale Twig blight
Ligustrum nepalense—Nepal privet	5–7 ft Flowers (white): May Fruit (black): Winter	Likes sun or shade in average soil.	as above	White peach scale
Ligustrum ovalifolium—California privet	12–15 ft Flowers (white): June Fruit (black): Oct.–Nov.	Ditto—Upright, half evergreen of rather stiff habit of growth.	as above	
Ligustrum sinensis—Chinese privet	7–10 ft Fruit (black): Sept.–Dec.	Likes sun in average soil.	Ditto—Good plant for inexpensive massing or hedge.	
Ligustrum lucidum—Glossy privet	6–8 ft Fruit (blue-black): Aug.–Oct.	Likes sun or ½ shade in average soil. A good evergreen shrub.	as above	Lilac leaf miner Lilac borer Red spider Citrus whitefly

TABLE A.5
Characteristics of Shrubs (cont.)

Botanical and common name	Description	Conditions and habits of growth	Pruning and other remarks	Insects and diseases
Lonicera fragrantissima Winter honeysuckle	6–8 ft Flowers (white): Mar.–Apr. Fruit (scarlet): May–July	Likes sun or shade in good rich soil. Has a spreading habit of growth and fragrant flowers.	The shrub species should be thinned out every 3–4 years and if overgrown the longer shoots should be cut back. Pruning is done best in summer, but do not prune every year. The climbing species require very little formal pruning if they have room to develop.	Long-tailed mealybug San Jose scale Fall webworm
Lonicera morrowi Morrow honeysuckle	6–8 ft Flowers (white): May Fruit (red): May–July	as above	as above	Oblique-banded leaf roller
Lonicera tatarica— Tatarian honeysuckle	8–10 ft Flowers (pink to white): May–June Fruit (red): May–July	Likes sun or shade in good rich soil. It is upright and dense with abundant red fruit.	as above	Oyster shell scale Honeysuckle sawfly Flea beetles
Malus floribunda— Japanese flowering crab	15–20 ft Flowers (rose–pink): Apr.–May Fruit (red): Fall	Likes sun in moist, rich soil. Has wide-spreading branches. Flowers change from pink to white.	Prune immediately after flowering to shape plant. Keep pruning at a minimum.	Subject to attack by insects and fungi on the common apple
Malus atrosanguinea Carmine crab	15–20 ft Flowers (carmine): Apr.–May Fruit (dark red): Fall.	"—Flowers do not fade to white.	as above	

Botanical and common name	Description	Conditions and habits of growth	Pruning and other remarks	Insects and diseases
Malus baccata—Siberian crab	20–40 ft Flowers (white): Apr.–May Fruit (red-yellow): Fall	Likes sun in moist rich soil. A large flowering tree with round head.	as above	
Malus sargenti—Sargent crab	8–10 ft Flowers (pure white): Apr.–May Fruit (dark red): Fall	Likes sun in moist rich soil. A low shrub or tree with horizontally spreading branches. Leaves change to orange and yellow in fall.	as above	
Malus scheideckeri—Scheidecker crab	15–20 ft Flowers (pale pink): May Fruit (yellow): Fall	Likes sun in moist, rich soil.	as above	
Myrica cerifera—Southern wax myrtle	15–25 ft Fruit (gray): Fall	Likes sun in dry good soil.	does not require formal pruning.	Has no serious pests or diseases.
Nandina domestica—Nandina	4–8 ft Flowers (white): May Fruit (red): Fall–Winter	Likes sun or shade in good soil.	Minimum pruning only to remove dead or old wood Plant for fruit effect.	as above
Philadelphus coronarius—Sweet mock-orange	8–10 ft Flowers (white): June	Likes sun in good rich soil. An upright grower with fragrant flowers.	Needs no formal pruning, and in fact is best if left untouched; perhaps thin out a little at intervals of a few years.	as above
Philadelphus lemoinei—Lemoine Mock orange	4–6 ft Flowers (white): June	Likes sun in good rich soil. a spreading grower with fragrant flowers.	as above	as above

TABLE A.5
Characteristics of Shrub (cont.)

Botanical and common name	Description	Conditions and habits of growth	Pruning and other remarks	Insects and diseases
Philadelphus virginalis—Virginal mock orange	6–8 ft Flowers (white): June	Likes sun in good rich soil. Upright grower with semi-double flowers.	as above	as above
Photinia glabra—Smooth photinia	5–10 ft Flowers (white): Feb. Fruit (red): Fall–Winter	Likes sun or shade in good soil. New growth is red.	Minimum pruning only to remove dead or old wood.	No serious pests or diseases
Pyracantha coccinea lalandi—Leland firethorn	8–10 ft Flowers (creamy white): April Fruit (orange): Aug.–Oct.	Likes sun or ½ shade in good soil. An upright grower with long shoots covered with orange berries in fall.	Prune in winter to shape plant. It is difficult to transplant, except for small plants.	Subject to scale insects
Pyracantha gibbsia yunnanensis—Yunnan firethorn	5–10 ft Flowers (white): May Fruit (coral-red): Fall–Winter	Ditto—except has red berries.	as above	
Rhamnus alnifolia—Alder buckthorn	2–3 ft Flowers (yellow-green): May–June Fruit (black): Sept.–Oct.	Likes sun. Low rather compact shrub with bright green foliage.	No special pruning is necessary.	No serious pests or diseases
Rhamnus caroliniana—Carolina buckthorn	15–25 ft Flowers (yellow): May–June Fruit (red to black): Sept.	Likes sun. Shrub with handsome leaves, changing to yellow in autumn.	as above	as above

Botanical and common name	Description	Conditions and habits of growth	Pruning and other remarks	Insects and diseases
Rhamnus cathartica—Common buckthorn	8–10 ft Flowers (green): June Fruit (shiny black): Sept.	Likes sun in well-drained soil. An open, upright grower.	as above	
Rhamnus frangula—Glossy buckthorn	10–12 ft Flowers (light yellow): July Fruit (red-black): Sept.	Like sun in well-drained soil. An open, upright grower with shiny foliage.	as above	
Rhododendron carolinianum—Carolina rhododendron	6–7 ft Flowers (pink): May	Like shade in woodsy loam. A broad-leaved evergreen. Requires acid soil conditions.	Needs no regular pruning except for the removal of the flower hands as soon as the flower fades. However, young plants should be clipped occasionally to induce a sturdy habit. Overgrown plants that are old may be cut back without serious injury but this should be done in March or April.	Lace bug Giant hornet
Rhododendron catawbiense—Catawba rhododendron	6–8 ft Flowers (red and purple): May	as above	as above	Pitted ambrosia beetle
Rhododendron maximum—Rosebay rhododendron	8–10 ft Flowers (blush): June–July	as above	as above	Rhododendron clear wing Azalea stem borer Broad-necked prionus

TABLE A.5
Characteristics of Shrubs (cont.)

Botanical and common name	Description	Conditions and habits of growth	Pruning and other remarks	Insects and diseases
Rhus copallina—Shining sumac	5–6 ft Flowers (greenish): July–Aug. Fruit (crimson): Sept.–Oct.	Likes dry, sunny locations. It has a spreading growth with shiny leaves. Planted for its lustrous foliage changing to reddish-purple in fall.	When grown for the large compound leaves and autumn coloration, the young shoots must be cut down to within a few inches of the ground in February or early March. If grown for shrubbery or mass effect, no special pruning, is required.	Has no serious pests or diseases
Rhus canadensis—Fragrant sumac	2–4 ft Flowers (yellow): Mar.–Apr. Fruit (red): Aug.	Likes dry, sunny locations. It is a low, spreading shrub, fragrant with leaves turning orange and scarlet in fall.	as above	
Rhus cotinus—Smoke tree	12–15 ft Flowers (smoky white): July–Aug. Fruit (red): Sept.–Oct.	Likes sun in well-drained soil. It is upright and graceful.	as above	
Rhus glabra—Smooth sumac	10–15 ft Flowers (greenish): July–Aug. Fruit (scarlet): Sept.–Oct.	Likes sun in well-drained soil. Has red autumn foliage and scarlet fruit.	as above	
Rhus typhina—Staghorn sumac	25–30 ft Flowers (greenish): June–July Fruit (crimson): Aug.–Sept.	Likes sun in well-drained soil. Has feathery foliage turning to brilliant scarlet and orange in autumn.	as above	

Botanical and common name	Description	Conditions and habits of growth	Pruning and other remarks	Insects and diseases
Rosa carolina— Pasture rose	3 ft Flowers (pink): July Fruit (red): Fall	Likes sun or semishade in heavy, rich loam. A low, bushy shrub, spreading by suckers. Well suited for borders of shrubberies.	Ramblers and climbers should have all the old flowering canes removed as soon as the flowers fade. Bush roses should have all the weak wood removed, and vigorous young canes from the root should be encouraged. This general pruning is best done in March.	Rose aphid Rose slugs
Rosa hugonis— Hugonis rose	5–6 ft Flowers (yellow): May Fruit (deep scarlet): July–Aug.	Likes sun or semishade in heavy, rich loam. An upright bushy shrub and very free-flowering.	as above	Eastern tent caterpillar
Rosa multiflora— Japanese rose	8–10 ft Flowers (white): June Fruit (red): Fall	Likes sun or semishade in heavy, rich loam. A tumbling or climbing grower with small, white flowers in numerous heads.	as above	San Jose scale
Rosa rugosa Rugosa rose	5–6 ft Flowers (white-pink): May–Sept. Fruit (brick red): Fall	Likes sun or semishade in heavy. rich loam. It is an upright bush with large red berries. Blooms all summer, foliage turning orange and scarlet in fall.	as above	Fuller's rose beetle Oblique-banded leaf roller
Rosa setigera— Prairie rose	5–6 ft Flowers (deep pink): June–July Fruit (red): Fall	Likes sun in heavy, rich loam. Has a pendulous growth.	as above	Rose midge

TABLE A.5
Characteristics of Shrubs (cont.)

Botanical and common name	Description	Conditions and habits of growth	Pruning and other remarks	Insects and diseases
Rosa blanda— Meadow rose	3–4 ft Flowers (pink): May Fruit (red): Sept.–Oct.	Likes sun in heavy rich loam.	as above	Black spot
Rosa wichuraiana— Wichuraiana rose	10–12 ft Flowers (white): June Fruit (red): Fall	Likes sun or semishade in heavy, rich loam. Has a trailing growth and is fragrant.	as above	Mildew
Rosa spinosissima— Scotch rose	4–5 ft Flowers (yellow-white): June Fruit (black): Sept.	Likes sun or semishade in heavy, rich loam. Has an open, spreading growth.	as above	Rose curculio Rose stem-girdler Black-banded leaf roller Flower thrips Rose chafer Rose leaf beetle Leaf hopper Red spider Rose scale Asiatic garden beetle Japanese beetle

Botanical and common name	Description	Conditions and habits of growth	Pruning and other remarks	Insects and diseases
Sambucus canadensis—American elder	6–8 ft Flowers (white): June–July Fruit (black): Aug.–Sept.	Likes shade in moist soil. It is a rapid and open grower.	If grown for colored foliage cut it to the ground in February; otherwise, no regular pruning is necessary.	Cloaked knotty horn
Sambucus nigra—European elder	25–30 ft Flowers (yellow-white): May–June Fruit (black): Aug.–Sept.	Large shrub or tree with deeply furrowed bark. It is a rapid and coarse grower. Likes shade in moist soil.	as above	
Sambucus racemosa—European red elder	10–12 ft Flowers (yellow-white): Apr.–May Fruit (scarlet): June–July	Likes shade in moist soil. A rapid grower with early red fruit.	as above	
Spiraea bumalda—Bumalda spirea	2–3 ft Flowers (pink): July	Likes partial shade and good soil. A low, flat bush.	Requires very little pruning, except to remove dead branches.	Cottony maple scale
Spiraea bumalda, Anthony Waterer—Anthony Waterer spirea	2–3 ft Flowers (crimson): June–July	Likes sun in any good soil. A dense and flat bush.	Remove old flower heads.	Spirea aphid
Spiraea prunifolia—Bridal wreath	8–10 ft Flowers (pure white): Apr.–May	Likes sun in any good soil.	as above	San Jose scale

TABLE A.5
Characteristics of Shrubs (cont.)

Botanical and common name	Description	Conditions and habits of growth	Pruning and other remarks	Insects and diseases
Spiraea thunbergi—Thunbergi spirea	4–5 ft Flowers (white): Apr.–May	Likes sun in any good soil. A low, pendulous shrub with feathery bright green foliage turning to orange and scarlet late in autumn.	as above	Oblique-banded leaf-roller Red spiders
Spiraea vanhouttei—Van Houtte spirea	5–6 ft Flowers (white): May–June	Likes sun in any good soil. Has arching, graceful branches with leaves a dark green above and pale bluish-green below.	as above	Oyster shell scale Spirea aphid
Symphoricarpus racemosus—Common snowberry	4–5 ft Flowers (pink): June Fruit (large snow white): Sept.–Nov.	Likes sun in any good soil. Has a pendulous growth.	Does not require any pruning.	Has no serious pests or diseases
Symphoricarpus vulgaris—Coral berry	3–4 ft Flowers (white): May–June Fruit (coral-pink): Oct.–Dec.	as above	as above	
Syringa chinensis—Chinese lilac	10–12 ft Flowers (purple-lilac): May–June	Likes sun in good rich soil. It is an upright, arching shrub, with loose panicles of bloom.	If the plants are flowering freely, no regular pruning is necessary. If the shrubs are not flowering well and growth is weak, thin out the branches removing some of the inside wood and the weak shoots in April. Inspect the shrubs again early in June and remove the weaker shoots. All suckers should be removed from the base of the plant at least once a year.	Lilac borer Giant hornet Lilac leaf-miner

Botanical and common name	Description	Conditions and habits of growth	Pruning and other remarks	Insects and diseases
Syringa persica—Persian lilac	8–10 ft Flowers (pale lilac): May–June	as above	as above	
Syringa vulgaris—Common lilac	12–15 ft Flowers (true lilac or white): May	as above	as above	Oblique-banded leaf roller Citrus whitefly Cottony maple scale Scurfy scale Euonymus scale White peach scale Promethea moth caterpillar Oyster shell scale Powdery mildew
Taxus baccata—English yew	30–40 ft Flowers (inconspicuous): Mar.–Apr. Fruit (olive-brown): Sept.–Oct.	Likes sun or partial shade in good, moist soil. A broad roundish head or shrubby. Leaves a lustrous dark green.	Prune only to shape or restrain plant.	Black vine weevil
Taxus brevifolia—Pacific yew	20–25 ft Flowers (inconspicuous): June Fruit (brown): Aug.–Oct.	Likes sun or partial shade in good moist soil. Usually with horizontally spreading branches. Leaves dark green, small and clustered.	as above	
Taxus cuspidata—Japanese yew	20–25 ft Flowers (inconspicuous): Mar.–Apr. Fruit (red): Oct.–Nov.	Likes sun or partial shade in good, moist soil. Has a rapid, spreading growth.	as above	Oleander scale Red spiders

TABLE A.5
Characteristics of Shrubs (cont.)

Botanical and common name	Description	Conditions and habits of growth	Pruning and other remarks	Insects and diseases
Viburnum rhytodiphyllum—Leather-leaf viburnum	8–10 ft Flowers (white): May Fruit (red to black): Sept.–Oct.	Likes partial shade in well drained soil. An evergreen with lustrous dark green foliage.	No special pruning is necessary.	
Viburnum acerifolium—Maple leaf viburnum	5–6 ft Flowers (yellow-white): May–June Fruit (black): Sept.	Likes shaded dry soil. Has a spreading growth. Good for woodland undergrowth.	as above	Aphids San Jose scale Oyster shell scale Cottony maple scale Red spiders
Viburnum carlesi—Fragrant viburnum	5–6 ft Flowers (pink-white): Apr.–May Fruit (blue-black): Sept.–Oct.	Shrub of broad round habit, very fragrant. Likes sun or partial shade in well-drained soil.	as above	Dogwood borer
Viburnum dentatum—Arrowwood	10–15 ft Flowers (white): May–June Fruit (blue-black): Oct.	Likes shade or sun in a good, moist soil. A tall and upright grower.	as above	
Viburnum Lentago—Nannyberry	15–20 ft Flowers (white): May–June Fruit (blue-black): Sept.–Oct.	Likes shade, plenty of moisture in good rich soil. A graceful treelike shrub.	as above	

Botanical and common name	Description	Conditions and habits of growth	Pruning and other remarks	Insects and diseases
Viburnum molle—Kentucky viburnum	8–10 ft Flowers (white): May Fruit (blue-black): Aug.–Sept.	Likes sun or partial shade in good soil. An upright and strong grower.	As above	
Viburnum prunifolium—Blackhaw	12–15 ft Flowers (white): May Fruit (blue-black): Sept.–Oct.	Likes sun or partial shade in good soil. A spreading round-headed shrub.	As above	
Viburnum tomentosum—Double file viburnum	8–10 ft Flowers (white): June Fruit (red to black): Aug.–Sept.	Likes sun or partial shade in good, rich soil. A spreading shrub with unusual flowers.	As above	

TABLE A.6
Characteristics of Evergreen Trees (cont.)

Botanical and common name	Description	Pruning and other remarks	Insects and diseases
Pinus strobus— White pine	90–150 ft; symmetrical, pyramidal head, in old age usually broad and very picturesque; Leaves slender, soft, serrulate, bluish-green; Fruit— narrow, cylindrical cones, 3–8 in. long, brown; Flower—none; Bark thick, deeply fissured into broad scaly ridges, purplish.	Likes a well-drained soil in sun. It is both an important timber tree and ornamental. Should never require pruning.	False pine webworm Pine pitch borer Pine needle scale Pine bark aphid Bark beetles Spittle bug
Pinus resinosa— Red pine	50–75 ft; a broad pyramidal head, with stout, spreading and sometimes pendulous branches; Leaves (2) flexible, long, coarse, dark green; Fruit—oval, symmetrical cones 1–2 in. long, nut-brown, fall the third year; Flower—none; Bark red-brown, shallowly fissured and scaly.	As above	Scotch pine scale insect Sawyer Ribbed pine borer Blue pine borer European pine-shoot moth
Pinus sylvestris— Scotch pine	50–75 ft; pyramidal when young, round-topped and irregular when old, spreading branches; Leaves (2) rigid, twisted, long, bluish-green; Fruit—short-stalked, conical-oblong cones, dull tawny-yellow, 1–2 in. long; Flower—none; Bark red or red-brown, rather thin and smooth on the upper trunk, darker below.	Likes a well drained soil in sun. Should never require pruning.	White pine weevil White pine blister rust
Pinus nigra— Austrian pine	80–100 ft; pyramidal with spreading branches, old age produces a flat-topped head; Leaves stiff, dark green, approx. 4–10 in. long; Fruit—ovoid cones, 2–3 in. long, yellow-brown; Flower—none; Bark usually light brown.	Likes a well-drained soil in sun. Does not require any pruning.	
Pinus palustris— Longleaf pine	80–100 ft; ascending branches, form an oblong head; Leaves (3), dark green, 8–18 in. long; Fruit—cylindrical dull brown cones, 5–8 in. long; Flower—none; Bark light orange-brown, separating into large, thin scales.	Likes a well-drained soil in sun. An important timber and resin tree. Does not require pruning.	

Botanical and common name	Description	Pruning and other remarks	Insects and diseases
Pinus taeda— Loblolly pine	80–120 ft; spreading branches, upper ones ascending, forming a compact, round-topped head; Leaves (3), slender but stiff, 4–6 in. long, bright green; Fruit—dull, pale reddish-brown cones; Flower—none; Bark bright red-brown, fissured into scaly ridges.	As above	
Pinus echinata— Shortleaf pine	100–120 ft; slender, often pendent branches in regular whorls, broad ovoid head; Leaves (2) slender, 3–6 in. long, dark bluish-green; Fruit—cones, 1–2 in. long, dull brown; Flower—none; Bark light cinnamon-red, broken into large scaly plates.	As above	
Pinus virginiana— Scrub pine	50–90 ft; bushy tree with slender horizontal or pendent branches; Leaves (2) rigid, usually twisted, dark green, 1–3 in. long; Fruit—reddish-brown cones, 1–2 in. long; Flower—none; Bark shallowly fissured into scaly plates, dark brown.	Likes a dry and barren soil in sun. Does not require pruning.	
Pinus rigida— Pitch pine	75–90 ft; open, irregular head with horizontal branches; Leaves (3) rigid, 3–6 in. long, spreading. dark green; Fruit—light brown cones 1–3 in. long; Flower—none; Bark red-brown, deeply fissured into broad, scaly rigdes.	Valuable for planting on dry and rocky soil.	
Tsuga canadensis Canada hemlock	60–90 ft; broad pyramidal head, long, slender, often pendulous branches; Leaves short and rounded, lustrous dark green, slightly grooved above, with white bands beneath; Fruit—oval, short-stalked cones 1 in. long; Flower—none; Bark yellow-brown.	Likes good, moist soil in either sun or partial shade. Good ornamental tree, also has some value for timber and tanning. Does not require any pruning unless used as a hedge.	Needle rusts Hemlock looper Spotted hemlock borer Red spider Hemlock spanworm Hemlock leaf-miner

TABLE A.6
Characteristics of Evergreen Trees (cont.)

Botanical and common name	Description	Pruning and other remarks	Insects and diseases
Tsuga caroliniana—Carolina hemlock	50–75 ft; compact, pyramidal head with often pendulous branches; Leaves short, lustrous dark green above with white bands beneath; Fruit—short-stalked cones, 1 in. long; Flower—none; Bark orange-red.	A more dense and compact tree than the Canada hemlock. An excellent ornamental. Likes good moist soil in either sun or partial shade. Does not require any pruning unless used as a hedge.	

TABLE A.7
Characteristics, Pruning, Insects, and Diseases of Deciduous Trees

Botanical and common name	Description	Pruning and other remarks	Insects and diseases
Acer platanoides—Norway maple	75–90 ft: Leaves bright green, 5-lobed, 4–6 in. across, slightly toothed with pointed teeth; Flower greenish yellow, April–May; Fruit—pendulous with nearly horizontal spreading wings, approx. 2 in. long, Sept.–October; Bark gray or grayish-brown.	Likes moisture in good soil. Round form with dense shade. An excellent shade tree. Leaves turn yellow in fall. Prune only to remove dead and dangerous branches and to shape tree. Prune in summer and early fall.	Norway maple aphid Leaf hoppers Cottony maple scale Terrapin scale Bladder gall mite Leopard moth Sugar maple borer Maple and oak twig pruner
Acer saccharum—Sugar maple	90–120 ft; Leaves light green, 3–5 lobed, 3–5½ in. across, sparingly, coarsely, toothed with narrow and deep depressions; Flower—greenish-yellow, April; Fruit—slightly divergent wings, nutlet approx. 1½ in. long, Sept.; Bark gray, furrowed.	Likes good, well-drained soil. Used as a street and shade tree. Dense regular habit with leaves turning yellow or orange and scarlet in fall. Yields syrup. Prune as above.	Forest tent caterpillar

Botanical and common name	Description	Pruning and other remarks	Insects and diseases
Acer rubrum—Red maple	90–120 ft; Leaves dark green and lustrous above, glaucous beneath, 3–5 lobed, 2–4 in. long, unequal rounded lobes; Flower red, rarely yellowish, March–April; Fruit—wings spread at a narrow angle, 2–4 in. long; nutlet approx. ¾ in. long, usually bright red when young, May–June; Bark gray.	Likes moisture in good soil. Conspicuous in early spring with red flowers and later its red fruit. Leaves turn bright scarlet and yellow in fall. Prune as above.	Bagworm Gypsy moth Brown-tail moth Green striped maple worm Green maple worm Elm span worm Oriental moth caterpillar
Acer saccharinum—Silver maple	90–120 ft; Leaves bright green above, silvery white beneath, deeply 5–lobed, 3–5 in. across; Flower greenish, Feb.–March; Fruit—wings divergent and hooked. 1–2 in. long, nutlet 1½ to 2½ in. long, May–June; Bark gray.	Likes moisture in good soil. A wide spreading tree with slender often pendulous branches. Leaves turn yellow in fall. Prune as above.	Box-elder bug Flat-headed borer Japanese beetle Pitted ambrosia beetle Alder blight aphid Carpenter worm Tussock moth White fly
Acer negundo—Box-elder	50–60 ft; Leaves bright green, lighter green below, pinnate, leaflets 3–5, 2–4 in. long coarsely toothed, terminal leaf 3–lobed; Flower yellowish, green before the leaves, March–April; Fruit—wings at acute angle and incurved, thick nutlet 1 to 1½ in. long, Sept.; Bark gray, branches glabrous.	Likes moisture in good soil. A hardy and drought-resisting maple. Rapid growth when young. Prune as in all other maples.	Maple trumpet Maple leaf-cutter Maple leaf-stem borer Maple nepticula Ocellate maple leaf-gall
Acer palmatum—Japanese maple	15–25 ft; Leaves bright green, deeply 5–9 lobed, 2–4 in. across; Flower purple, June; Fruit—wings spread at an obtuse angle, with nutlet approx. ½ in. long, Sept.; Bark gray, branchlets glabrous and slender.	Likes a rich soil. A shrub or small tree of several forms. Leaves turn bright red in fall. Prune as above.	Fusiform maple gall Bladder maple gall

TABLE A.7
Characteristics of Deciduous Trees (cont.)

Botanical and common name	Description	Pruning and other remarks	Insects and diseases
Acer ginnala—Amur maple	15–25 ft; Leaves dark green and lustrous above and light green beneath, 3–lobed, 1–3 in. long, 1 to 2½ in. wide; Flower fragrant, yellowish-white, May; Fruit—wings nearly parallel, with nutlet about 1 in. long, Sept.; Bark gray, branchlets glabrous and slender.	Likes a good loam soil. A graceful maple with fruit usually red in summer and the leaves turning bright red in fall. Prune as above.	Norway maple leaf-hopper
Acer pennsylvanicum—Striped maple	20–40 ft; Leaves large, bright green, 3–lobed, 5–7 in. long; Flower yellow, May–June; Fruit—wings spreading at a wide angle with nutlet about 1 in. long, Sept. Bark branches green, smooth, conspicuously striped with white lines.	A small tree with large bright green leaves turning clear yellow in autumn. The striped branches are conspicuous in winter. Prune as above.	Maple phenacoccus Gloomy scale Japanese scale insect Callous borer Ambrosia beetle Wilt Bleeding canker Leaf spots—purple eye spots Bull's-eye spot Tar spot Leaf blisters
Aesculus glabra—Ohio Buckeye	25–30 ft; Leaves—5 leaflets, finely toothed, 3–5 in. long. Flower pale greenish-yellow, May; Fruit prickly, 1–2 in. long.	A handsome small tree with leaves turning yellow in autumn. Likes moisture in good soil. Prune after blooming period. Keep inside of tree cleaned out.	Leaf blotch Bagworm Oyster shell scale English walnut scale Japanese beetle
Aesculus hippocastanus—Horsechestnut	60–75 ft; Leaves—5–7 leaflets, double toothed, 4–8 in. long, green beneath; Flower white, tinged with red, May–June; Fruit—prickly, about 2 in. across; Bark—smooth branches.	A showy flowering tree, used for shade and street tree plantings. Likes deep, good soil. Prune same as above.	Tussock moth Scurfy scale

Botanical and common name	Description	Pruning and other remarks	Insects and diseases
Betula lutea—Yellow birch	60–90 ft; Leaves ovate, 3–5 in. long, with long pale hairs on the veins above and below; Flower yellow, April; Fruit—short-stalked cones, approx. 1 in. long by ¾ in. thick; Bark yellowish or silvery-gray, separating into thin flakes, reddish-brown on old trunks, young bark aromatic and somewhat bitter.	Likes damp, good soil. An ornamental tree, attractive in spring with its long and slender pendulous catkins. Prune only to shape tree and to remove injured, diseased or dead branches. Prune in summer after the leaves have developed or in early autumn.	Leaf spots Leaf blisters Canker Die-back Case bearer Leaf miner Leaf skeletonizer Bronze birch borer
Betula nigra—River birch	60–90 ft; Leaves dark green above, whitish below, doubly toothed, 1–3 in. long; Flower yellow, April; Fruit—oblong cones, 1 to 1½ in. long, wing ½ or nearly as broad as nutlet; Bark reddish-brown or silvery-gray on younger branches, torn and ragged.	Likes a moist, sandy soil. A graceful tree with an oval head and slender branches. Has a torn and ragged bark. Prune as above.	
Betula papyrifera—Canoe birch	60–90 ft; Leaves smooth green, 1½ to 4 in. long, coarsely toothed; Flower yellow, April; Fruit—cylindrical cones, 1–2 in. long, pendulous; Bark white, torn and ragged.	Likes moisture in good soil. Has gleaming white paper bark. Prune as above.	
Carpinus betulus—European hornbeam	40–60 ft; Leaves double-toothed, rounded at base, dark green, approx. 4 in. long; Flower inconspicuous; Fruit—a ribbed nutlet hanging from a 3-lobed bract, fall; Bark gray, branches slender.	Likes good soil. It holds its leaves late into the winter. No pruning necessary.	No serious pests or diseases.
Carpinus caroliniana—American hornbeam	Ht.—30–40 ft; Flower—inconspicuous; Leaves sharply and doubly toothed, 2–4 in. long, dark green; Fruit—same as above; Bark gray, branches slightly pendulous.	A small bushy tree. Leaves turn scarlet and orange in fall. Likes good soil. No pruning necessary.	

TABLE A.7
Characteristics of Deciduous Trees (cont.)

Botanical and common name	Description	Pruning and other remarks	Insects and diseases
Celtis occidentalis—Hackberry	Ht.—50–75 ft; Leaves bright green, smooth and lustrous above, paler below, 2–4½ in. long; Flower—inconspicuous; Fruit—small, orange-red to dark purple, stone-pitted, fall; Bark gray, smooth.	Has a straight trunk and spreading, rigid or sometimes pendulous branches forming a round topped head. Bright green foliage turns light yellow in fall. Fruit interesting to birds. No pruning necessary.	Mourning cloak caterpillar Caterpillars Hackberry nipple gall Cottony maple scale Witches broom Bud gall
Cladrastis lutea—Yellow-wood	Ht.—30–40 ft; Leaves—7–9 bright green leaflets 2–4 in. long; Flower—white, fragrant, June; Fruit—pod, 2–3 in. long. Aug.–Sept.; Bark—smooth bark and yellow wood.	An ornamental tree with fragrant white flowers. Leaves turn yellow in fall. Woodsy loam soil. No pruning necessary.	No serious pests or diseases.
Fagus americana—American beech	Ht.—80–100 ft; Leaves dark bluish-green above and light green and smooth below, 2–5 in. long; Flower inconspicuous; Fruit—oval nuts in fall; Bark light gray.	Likes a well-drained soil. Has orange fall foliage. No pruning necessary except to remove dead or diseased branches.	Leaf mottle Beech blight aphid Woolly beech aphid Brown wood borer Leaf tier
Fagus sylvatica—European beech	Ht.—80–100 ft; Leaves lustrous, dark green above, light green beneath, 2–4 in. long; Flower inconspicuous; Fruit—nuts in clusters with upright prickles about 4 in. long; Bark dark gray.	Same as above.	Beech scale Two-lined chestnut borer Datana caterpillar Antlered maple caterpillars Gypsy moth
Fraxinus americana—White ash	Ht.—80–100 ft; Leaves dark green above and yellowish-green beneath, leaflets 5–9 usually 7, 2–6 in. long; Flower red, March; Fruit—1–2 in. long, cylindrical, 1-seeded nutlet; Bark dark green or brownish, smooth and shiny.	Likes good soil. A vigorous tree with the leaves turning deep purple or yellow in fall. No pruning necessary.	Leaf spots Sawfly Fall canker-worm Plant mite Ash timber beetle Ash borer

Botanical and common name	Description	Pruning and other remarks	Insects and diseases
Fraxinus excelsior—European ash	Ht.—80–100 ft; Leaves dark green above and lighter green beneath, 7–11 leaflets, 2–5 in. long; Flower inconspicuous; Fruit—1–2 in. long, narrow-oblong, 1 seeded nutlet; Bark—winter buds black, branches smooth.	Likes good soil. No pruning necessary except to remove dead or diseased branches.	Banded ash borer Lilac borer Carpenter borer Fall webworm Oyster shell scale Scurfy scale
Ginkgo biloba—Maidenhair tree	Ht.—80–100 ft; Leaves bright green, clusters of 3–5, 2–3 in. across, fan-shaped, golden-yellow in fall; Flower—inconspicuous; Fruit—an oval angular nut covered by a pulpy, ill-smelling, and acrid outer coat, about 1 in. long, yellow, kernel sweet, edible; Bark dark brown.	Likes a well-drained rich soil. Varies in shape from a tight pyramid to wide-spread irregularity. No pruning necessary.	No serious pests or diseases.
Gleditsia triacanthos—Honey-locust	Ht.—100–125 ft; Leaves bright green, 5½–8 in. long with 20–30 leaflets 1–1½ in. long; Flower—white, June; Fruit—pod, 12–18 in. long, Oct.–Dec.; Bark gray with spines 2–4 in. long on trunk and branches.	Used as an ornamental tree. The large, branched thorns make the tree conspicuous in winter. No pruning necessary except to keep diseased and dead branches removed.	Locust borer Locust leaf beetle Locust gall maker Bagworm Carpenter worm
Gleditsia triacanthos inermis—Thornless honey-locust	Same as above except thornless.	Prune as above.	
Juglans nigra—Black walnut	Ht.—100–150 ft; Leaves dark green, 15–23 leaflets, 2–4 in. long; Flower—inconspicuous; Fruit—nut broader than high, strongly and irregularly ridged, 1–1½ in. across and covered with an outer pulpy covering; Bark deeply furrowed and brown.	A tall tree with round head and dark green foliage. Nuts are edible. A valuable timber tree. No pruning necessary except to keep diseased and dead branches removed.	European canker Die-back Leaf spots Trunk decays Black walnut curculio Butternut curculio Codlin moth Walnut husk-maggot Walnut aphid Walnut datana Walnut scale

TABLE A.7
Characteristics of Deciduous Trees (cont.)

Botanical and common name	Description	Pruning and other remarks	Insects and diseases
Larix europaea—European larch	Ht.—80–100 ft; Leaves soft, bright green, approx. 1 in. long, deciduous; Flower—inconspicuous; Fruit—oval cones, 1–1½ in. long, violet-purple at maturity changing to grayish-brown; Bark dark grayish-brown, branches slender and yellowish.	Likes a moist, well-drained soil. Tree has a pyramidal, later irregular head. Looks like an evergreen but loses its leaves in fall. No pruning necessary.	
Larix leptolepis—Japanese larch	Ht.—60–80 ft; Leaves flattened, rather broad, light or bluish-green with white bands below, each with five rows of openings; Flower—inconspicuous; Fruit—same as above; Bark scales off in narrow strips leaving red scars; branches yellowish.	Likes a moist well-drained soil. Has short horizontal branches. A very rapid grower. No pruning necessary.	Leaf cast Larch case bearer Gypsy moth Sawfly Woolly larch aphid
Larix americana—American larch	Ht.—50–60 ft; Leaves light, bluish-green, 1–1½ in. long; Flower inconspicuous; Fruit—same as above but smaller; Bark reddish-brown; branches reddish-yellow.	Likes a moist, loamy soil in full sunlight. Has short horizontal branches forming a narrow pyramidal head. No pruning necessary.	
Liriodendron tulipifera—Tulip-tree	Ht.—120–150 ft; Leaves saddle-shaped, 3–5 in. long and about as wide, pale green; Flower tulip-shaped, 1½–2 in. long, greenish-white with a broad orange band near base, May–June; Fruit—cone-like, brown, 2½–3 in. long; Bark—brown.	A straight. pyramidal tree with smooth trunk. Leaves turn clear yellow in fall. Likes a moist, rich soil. Prune only to remove diseased and dead branches.	Tulip scale Promethea moth Tulip spot—gall Willow scurfy scale
Liquidambar styraciflua—Sweet gum	Ht.—100–125 ft; Leaves dark green and shiny above, paler beneath, 4–6 in. wide and long, 5–7 lobed; Flower inconspicuous; Fruit—lustrous, brown capsules about 1 in. long, surrounded at base by short scales, Oct., persisting during the winter; Bark red-brown, often with corky ridges or thick wings, deeply furrowed.	A pyramidal and symmetrical tree. Leaves turn deep crimson in fall. Likes a moist. rich soil. Prune only to remove diseased and dead branches.	Leaf tier Bagworm Fall webworm Forest tent caterpillar

Botanical and common name	Description	Pruning and other remarks	Insects and diseases
Magnolia acuminata—Cucumber tree	Ht.—70–90 ft; Leaves—4–9 in. long, light green beneath; Flower greenish-yellow, 2–3 in. high, May; Fruit conelike, red, 2–3 in. long, Aug.–Sept.; Bark—branches red-brown, shiny; trunk, soft silvery gray.	Likes a good, porous soil. A pyramidal tree with rather short branches, upright at first, later spreading. Prune as soon as flowers drop. Remove dead or diseased branches and clean out inside of tree.	Die-back Magnolia scale
Magnolia glauca—Sweet bay	Ht.—30–40 ft; Leaves shiny green, 3–5 in. long; Flower white, fragrant, June–July; Fruit conelike, dark red, 1½–2 in. long, Aug.–Sept.; Bark soft gray; branches slender smooth.	Likes a moist, rich soil. Almost evergreen in the South. Prune as above.	
Magnolia macrophylla—Bigleaf magnolia	Ht.—30–40 ft; Leaves large, 10–30 in. long, shiny dark green; Flower cup-shaped, approx. 10 in. across, fragrant, creamy-white, May–June; Fruit conelike, rose-colored, 2–3 in. long, Aug.–Sept.; Bark silvery gray.	A round headed tree with heavy branches. Likes a moist, rich soil. Prune as above.	
Magnolia tripetala—Umbrella magnolia	Ht. 30–40 ft; Leaves pale green beneath, 10–24 in. long; Flower white with a heavy odor, 7–10 in. across, May–June; Fruit conelike, rose-colored, 3–4 in. long, Aug.–Sept.; Bark silvery gray, smooth.	Tree with wide-spreading branches forming an open head. Likes a moist, rich soil. Prune as above.	
Magnolia soulangeana—Saucer magnolia	Ht.—20–25 ft; Leaves—shiny green, more or less hairy beneath; Flower purplish, nearly white, May; Fruit conelike, Aug.–Sept.; Bark gray, smooth.	Likes a moist, rich soil. Small tree or large shrub. Prune as above.	
Nyssa sylvatica—Sour gum	Ht.—80–100 ft; Leaves green. 2–4½ in. long, shiny above, turning bright scarlet in fall; Flower white, May–June; Fruit oval, blue-black, with thin acrid flesh, stone slightly ribbed; Bark gray.	Tree with slender spreading branches, forming a flat-topped cylindrical or sometimes broad head. Likes a moist rich soil. No pruning necessary.	No serious pests or diseases.

TABLE A.7
Characteristics of Deciduous Trees (cont.)

Botanical and common name	Description	Pruning and other remarks	Insects and diseases
Oxydendron arboreum—Sorrel tree	Ht.—50–60 ft; Leaves shining green, 3–8 in. long; Flower white, July–Aug.; Fruit—light gray tassels, Sept.–Oct.; Bark deeply fissured, gray.	A summer flowering tree with large shiny leaves, turning scarlet in fall, but remaining pale beneath. Likes a well-drained woodsy loam. Prune only to remove dead or diseased branches.	No serious pests or diseases.
Paulownia tomentosa—Empress tree	Ht.—40–60 ft; Leaves 10–20 in. long, 3-lobed, dark green; Flower pale violet, Apr.–May; Fruit—seeds, Sept.–Nov.; Bark gray.	A round-headed tree with heavy branches. Likes a light, deep loam. Very large leaves.	Has no serious pests or diseases.
Platanus occidentalis—American plane tree	Ht.—100–120 ft; Leaves 4–8 in. wide, 3-and sometimes 5-lobed; Flower inconspicuous; Fruit—heads smooth, consisting of several nutlets, about 1 in. across, Sept.–Oct. Bark almost creamy white, peeling in small plates, dark brown and fissured at base of older trunks.	A tall tree with round and oval head. Likes a moist rich soil. Often used for street trees. Prune during summer and fall. Remove diseased and dead branches and shape tree.	Lace bug Bagworm White fly Blight White-marked tussock moth Canker
Platanus orientalis—European plane tree	Ht.—80–100 ft; Leaves 4–8 in. wide, 5–7 lobed; Flower inconspicuous; Fruit—2–6 fruit heads, 1 in. thick and bristly; Bark peeling in large flakes, dull gray or greenish.	A broad, round head and short, thick trunk, often divided near base into several stems. Prune as above. Likes a well-drained average soil.	

Botanical and common name	Description	Pruning and other remarks	Insects and diseases
Populus alba—White poplar	Ht.—90–100 ft; Leaves 3–5 lobed, with triangular, coarsely-toothed lobes, 2–4 in. long, dark green above, white beneath; Flower pendulous catkins before leaves, approx. 2 in. long; Fruit oval, brown, 2–4 valved seeds, ripening before leaves are fully grown; Bark whitish-gray, smooth; rough at base of old trunks.	Large, irregular tree. Prune only to remove dead or diseased branches. Likes a moist, average soil.	Red-humped caterpillar Tent maker Poplar borer Willow leaf beetle Bronze birch borer Cottonwood borer Poplar sawfly
Populus tremuloides—Quaking aspen	Ht.—90–100 ft; Leaves—1½–2½ in. long, thin, smooth and shiny beneath; Flower—cottony catkins, April; Fruit—same as above except smaller; Bark smooth, reddish-brown.	Same as above. Leaves move in the slightest breeze.	Satin moth Forest tent caterpillar Spiny elm caterpillar
Populus nigra—Black poplar	Ht.—90–100 ft; Leaves light green beneath, rounded at base, smooth 2–3 in. long; Flower—catkins, approx. 2 in. long, April; Fruit—2-valved seeds on fruiting catkins 4–5 in. long; Bark deeply furrowed, often with large burs, branches smooth, orange, changing to ashy gray the second year.	A wide spreading tree. Prune only to remove dead and diseased branches.	Gypsy moth Cottonwood leaf beetle Oyster shell scale
Populus balsamifera—Cottonwood	Ht.—90–100 ft; Leaves smooth, bright green below, 3–4 in. long and as wide; Flower—catkins 3–4 in. long, April; Fruit—fruiting catkins 6–8 in. long, seeds 3–4 valved; Bark brown and smooth.	Upright spreading branches with an open broad head. Prune as above.	Poplar curculio Fall webworm Leaf blister Leaf spots
Quercus alba—White oak	Ht.—100–120 ft; Leaves 4–8 in. long, bright green above, narrow at base with 5–9 oblong entire lobes; Flower—greenish-yellow catkins, late spring; Fruit—brown acorn about 1 in long ¼ enclosed by a cup-shaped cap; Bark smooth, light reddish-brown.	Heavy, spreading branches, forming a broad, open head. Bright green foliage changing to deep red or violet purple in autumn. A	Datana caterpillar Saddle-backed caterpillar White blotch oak leaf miner

TABLE A.7
Characteristics of Deciduous Trees (cont.)

Botanical and common name	Description	Pruning and other remarks	Insects and diseases
quercus alba (cont.)		long-lived tree. Prune only to remove dead and diseased branches.	Obscure scale Lecanium scale Kermes scale Golden oak scale Two-lined chestnut borer Brown tail moth Orange striped oak worm Spiny oak worm Buck or maia moth
Quercus coccinea—Scarlet oak	Ht.—60–80 ft; Leaves bright green and smooth beneath, 3–6 in. long with 7 oblong lobes; Flower same as above; Fruit—oval acorn about ¾ in. long, ⅓ to ½ enclosed by a cup; Bark gray, with inner bark reddish; buds dark reddish brown.	Gradually spreading branches, forming a round-topped, rather open head. Bright green foliage turning brilliant scarlet in autumn. Likes a gravelly soil. Prune as above.	Forest tent-caterpillar California oak moth Hag moth caterpillar Saddle-backed caterpillar Oak mite Cecropia moth Carpenter worm
Quercus macrocarpa—Mossy-cup oak	Ht.—60–80 ft; Leaves dark green and shiny above, grayish or whitish beneath, 4–8 in. long; Flower same as above; Fruit—broad oval acorn about ¾–1½ in. long, ½ enclosed by a large cup,; Bark light brown, deeply furrowed and scaly.	A tall trunk and spreading branches, forming a broad head, pyramidal while young. Corky branches conspicuous in winter. Likes a rich soil. Prune as above.	Leopard moth Twig pruner Ribbed bud-gall Pacific oak twig girdler Flat-headed apple tree borer Ivory-dotted long horn Northern brenthian Twig blister Leaf blister

Botanical and common name	Description	Pruning and other remarks	Insects and diseases
Quercus palustris—Pin oak	Ht.—60–80 ft; Leaves bright green above, lighter green, shiny and smooth beneath, about 3–4½ in. long, with 5–7 oblong lobes; Flower same as above; Fruit—acorn ½–¾ in. across, ⅓ enclosed by a thin saucer-shaped cup; Bark—branches dark red-brown or orange, buds chestnut brown.	Slender branches, usually pendulous at the ends, forming a symmetrical pyramidal head while young, irregular and oblong in older trees. A rapid grower in rich soil. Prune as above.	Io moth Fall canker worm Spring canker worm Gypsy moth
Quercus phellos—Willow oak	Ht.—40–60 ft; Leaves light green, shiny above, 2–4 in. long; Flower same as above; Fruit—half round acorn about ½ in. high, enclosed only at base by a saucer shaped cup; Bark reddish-brown.	A conical round-topped head and willow-like leaves, turning pale yellow in autumn. Likes moist, clay soil. Prune as above.	
Quercus rubra—Red oak	Ht.—60–80 ft; Leaves dull green above, gray or white or sometimes pale yellow-green beneath, 4½–8½ in. long, with 7–11 lobes halfway to the middle; Flower same as above; Fruit—oval acorn, 1 in. high, ⅓ enclosed with half cup; Bark gray with branches becoming dark red.	Stout spreading branches form a broad round-topped head. Foliage turns dark red in autumn. Rapid grower in moist, rich soil. Prune as above.	
Quercus stellata—Post oak	Ht.—60–80 ft; Leaves dark green and rough above, grayish or brownish beneath, 4–8 in. long with 2–3 pairs of broad lobes; Flower same as above; Fruit—oval acorns ½–1 in. high, ⅓ or ½ enclosed by cup; Bark reddish-brown. deeply fissured and scaly.	A dense, round head with large dark green leaves. Prune as above.	

TABLE A.7
Characteristics of Deciduous Trees (cont.)

Botanical and common name	Description	Pruning and other remarks	Insects and diseases
Quercus velutina—Black oak	Ht.—80–100 ft; Leaves shiny dark green above, brown beneath, 4–8½ in. long with 7–9 broad lobes; Flower same as above; Fruit—oval acorn ½–⅜ in. high, ½ enclosed by cup; Bark dark brown, inner bark orange.	Large tree of rapid growth with slender branches and open narrow head. Foliage turns dull red or orange-brown in autumn. Will stand dry soil. Prune as above.	
Salix nigra—Black willow	Ht.—30–40 ft; Leaves 2–4 in. long, pale green, wedge-shaped, tapered to a point and finely toothed on the edge; Flower inconspicuous; Fruit—none; Bark dark brown, rough and scaly, branches yellowish.	Slender spreading branches, graceful. Likes a moist, rich soil. No regular pruning necessary.	Bagworm Carpenter worm Willow-leaf beetle Red-humped caterpillar
Salix babylonica—Weeping willow	Ht.—30–40 ft; Leaves 3–6 in. long, dark green above, grayish-green beneath, wedge-shaped, tapered to a point and finely toothed on the edge; Flower inconspicuous; Fruit—none; Bark smooth, brown.	Long, pendulous, swaying branches. Likes a moist, rich soil. No pruning is necessary.	Scurfy scale Cottonwood leaf beetle Yellow-spotted willow slug Elm sawfly
Salix discolor—Pussy willow	Ht.—15–20 ft; Leaves 2–4 in. long, dark green; Flower silver-gray, Mar.; Fruit—none; Bark smooth, gray.	Likes a moist, rich soil. Its bloom marks the beginning of spring. No regular pruning is necessary.	Spiny elm caterpillar Gypsy moth Satin moth Japanese beetle Fall webworm Powdery mildew Poplar borer Cone gall Willow shoot sawfly Willow scale

Botanical and common name	Description	Pruning and other remarks	Insects and diseases
Tilia americana—American linden	Ht.—80–100 ft; Leaves light green beneath, coarsely toothed with long pointed teeth, 4–8 in. long; Flower yellow, July; Fruit—nutlike, thick shelled without ribs; Bark smooth, green.	Likes a moist, rich soil, with fragrant rapid growth. No regular pruning is necessary.	Oyster shell scale Japanese beetle Leaf beetle Cecropia moth Linden borer
Tilia vulgaris—Common linden	Ht.—80–100 ft; Leaves dark green and smooth above, bright green beneath, 2–4 in. long, sharply toothed; Flower yellow-white, June; Fruit nutlike, thick-shelled, faintly ribbed; Bark smooth.	Likes a moist, rich soil, produces heavy shade and is much used as a street tree. No regular pruning is necessary.	Tussock moth Twig girdler Spring cankerworm Fall cankerworm Leaf blotch Leaf spot
Tilia cordata Littleleaf European linden	Ht.—60–80 ft; Leaves dark green, smooth, shiny above, 1½–2½ in. long, sometimes broader than long; Flower yellow-white, fragrant, July; Fruit nutlike, thin-shelled, slightly or not ribbed; Bark smooth or slightly hairy.	Likes a moist, rich soil. Has a fragrant dense foliage. No regular pruning is necessary.	
Tilia tomentosa—Silver linden	Ht.—60–80 ft; Leaves dark green above, whitish beneath, sharply and doubly toothed, 2–4 in. long; Flower yellow-white, June; Fruit nutlike, oval, minutely warty and slightly 5-angled; Bark hairy.	A broad, pyramidal tree, forming a dense shade, in moist rich soil. No regular pruning necessary.	
Ulmus americana—American elm	Ht.—100–120 ft; Leaves dark green, 3–6 in. long, unequal at base, doubly toothed, rough above and smooth beneath; Flower reddish-brown, April; Fruit—oval nut about ½ in. long, deeply notched at end, with short hairs; Bark light gray, scaly, and deeply fissured.	Likes moist, rich soil. A tall tree with limbs usually spreading outwards and forming a wide spreading head. A very graceful tree. Requires very little pruning.	Carpenter worm Fall webworm Leopard moth Scurfy scale Twig girdler Spring cankerworm Fall cankerworm Tussock moth Leaf beetle Spiny elm caterpillar Elm case bearer Cockscomb gall European elm scale Brown-tail moth

TABLE A.7
Characteristics of Deciduous Trees (cont.)

Botanical and common name	Description	Pruning and other remarks	Insects and diseases
Ulmus campestris—English elm	Ht.—120–150 ft; Leaves dark green and rough above, soft and downy below, 2–4 in. long, doubly toothed with about 12 pairs of veins; Flower inconspicuous; Fruit—small nut about ½ in. across, with a small closed notch at end; Bark light gray, deeply fissured.	Tall tree with straight stem and spreading or ascending branches. forming an oval or oblong head. Likes a moist, rich soil. Requires very little pruning.	Bagworm Japanese beetle Elm sawfly Elm leaf miner Elm leaf aphid Oyster shell scale Gypsy moth European bark beetle
Ulmus parvifolia—Chinese elm	Ht.—25–40 ft; Leaves 1–2 in. long, shiny green and smooth above; Flower inconspicuous; Fruit about ½ in. long, notched at end, seed in middle; Bark smooth.	A fast growing tree with slender and somewhat brittle branches, forming a broad round head with small leaves. Likes moist, rich soil. Requires very little pruning.	Elm borer Dutch elm disease Leaf spots
Ulmus fulva—Slippery Elm	Ht.—40–60 ft; Leaves dark green, very rough above, densely hairy beneath, 4–8 in. long; Flower pinkish, April; Fruit about ½ in. long, slightly notched; Bark red-brown, rough and downy.	Tree with spreading branches, usually forming a broad open head, with large foliage turning dull yellow in autumn.	

INDEX